Cliff Charpentier's

2001 FANTASY FOOTBALL DIGEST

by

Cliff Charpentier

Lerner Publications Company • Minneapolis

The author and publisher believe all information regarding NFL player transactions to be accurate up to May 2, 2001, when this book was set to go to press. For subsequent information, please consult the Fantasy Football Newsletter. An order form is provided on the color insert in this book.

Cover photo: © ALLSPORT USA/Elsa Hasch
Other photos: © ENDZONE

Composed in Times Ten and Helvetica
by Interface Graphics, Inc., Minneapolis, Minnesota

Manufactured in the United States of America

International Standard Book Number: 0-8225-0028-0
1 2 3 4 5 6 —   — 06 05 04 03 02 01

DEDICATIONS AND ACKNOWLEDGMENTS

Nearly two decades later, we're still fulfilling a fantasy that we started 18 years ago.

To keep something going for that length of time, I feel fortunate to have been surrounded by the support I have gotten.

To my wife Lori, why she still puts up with my obsession with sports I'm not sure but she's certainly keeps perspective on other things in my life.

To my children, Kelly, Cliff Jr. and Matthew who have become more involved giving me more hands-on support.

To my partner, Tom Kane Jr., we faced many battles together and continue to press on.

To my sister, Denise, without whom this fantasy would have run its course many years ago.

To Fred Livermore, whose presence in our company continues to expand and help us grow.

To Ben Fleischhacker, my nephew, who continues to be a valuable source for our company, serving in many ways.

To Julie Pedersen, who surely makes my life easier.

To Tom Nemo, a friend, always around when in need.

To Teri Scheirenbeck and Brenda Giesselmann, who continue to help support our project.

To the other significant contributors who continue with their hard work and dedication.

Jim Rubbelke	Bernie Fleischhacker
Terri Elizondo	Nicole Estby
Katie Engler	Natalie Kane
Pat McCusky	

To all you readers, thank you again for your years of support.

To all you fantasy football fans, good luck in 2001, I hope the digest helps bring you success.

CONTENTS

The Author's 2000 season 6

I. Initial Considerations 14

II. Helpful Facts from the 1999 Season 23
 Key Injuries, Trades, Holdouts and Other Events 24
 How the 2000 Rookies Fared 33

III. Free Agents and Other Player Moves 37

IV. Offseason Notes 43
 Key Player Movements and their Effects 43
 Significant Injury Updates 51
 New NFL Head Coaches 55

V. 2001 Rookie Class 59

VI. Rating the 2001 NFL Team Schedules 68

VII. A Team-by-Team 2000 Review/2001 Preview 71
 Arizona Cardinals 71
 Atlanta Falcons 73
 Baltimore Ravens 75
 Buffalo Bills 79
 Carolina Panthers 81
 Chicago Bears 83
 Cincinnati Bengals 87
 Cleveland Browns 89
 Dallas Cowboys 91
 Denver Broncos 93
 Detroit Lions 97
 Green Bay Packers 99
 Indianapolis Colts 101
 Jacksonville Jaguars 105
 Kansas City Chiefs 107
 Miami Dolphins 111
 Minnesota Vikings 113
 New England Patriots 117
 New Orleans Saints 119
 New York Giants 122
 New York Jets 124
 Oakland Raiders 127
 Philadelphia Eagles 129
 Pittsburgh Steelers 132
 St. Louis Rams 134
 San Diego Chargers 138
 San Francisco 49ers 140
 Seattle Seahawks 143
 Tampa Bay Buccaneers 145
 Tennessee Titans 148
 Washington Redskins 152

VIII. Rating the Players: Basic Scoring Method 155
 A Look at the Running Backs 158

A Look at the Wide Receivers.............................. 170
A Look at the Tight Ends.................................. 182
A Look at the Quarterbacks 189
A Look at the Kickers 196
Quick Picks – Mock Draft 203

IX. Rating the Players: Combined Basic/
Performance Scoring Method............................. 204
A Look at the Running Backs 206
A Look at the Wide Receivers.............................. 218
A Look at the Tight Ends.................................. 230
A Look at the Quarterbacks 237
A Look at the Kickers 244
Quick Picks – Mock Draft 245

X. Rating the Players: Distance Scoring Method.................... 246
A Look at the Running Backs 248
A Look at the Wide Receivers.............................. 259
A Look at the Tight Ends 271
A Look at the Quarterbacks 278
A Look at the Kickers 285
Quick Picks – Mock Draft 293

XI. Rating Opposing NFL Defenses............................. 294

XII. Drafting a Team Defense................................. 300

FANTASY FOOTBALL BASICS 302

I. Forming A Fantasy League 303

II. The League Commissioner 303

III. League Scheduling....................................... 304
Four-Team League 311
Six-Team League... 312
Eight-Team League....................................... 313
Ten-Team League 315
Twelve-Team League 316
Fourteen-Team League.................................... 319
Sixteen-Team League 321

IV. Playoffs & Payoffs 324

V. The Draft 326

VI. Roster Changes/Transactions 330

VII. Lineups 341

VIII. Selecting a Scoring Method 344

IX. Variations on Fantasy Football 369

X. 2001 NFL Schedule 378

To the Author... 382

Cliff Charpentier's 2000 All-Fantasy Team...................... 384

THE AUTHOR'S 2000 SEASON
TAKING A SMALLER BITE—MAY PROVE
TO BE EVEN MORE ENJOYABLE

After almost two decades of playing in a fantasy league of 16 franchises, situations begin to give. As each year's fantasy draft approached and it became more of a hassle to arrange a time and place for the draft, the will to cater to everyone had taken its toll on me. I knew I still enjoyed the game, knew there were a few that shared my passion, so I decided to make a change. I decided to let my large, 16 -team league fold and opted to participate in a more intimate 6-team league. Would this be as much fun? Would this be as fulfilling? The one thing I knew for sure it would be less frustrating. With that in mind I headed to my 2000, 6-team league draft.

THE DRAFT

Surely the draft for a smaller league is both more intimate and less formal. As the small group gathered, I started to realize perhaps this may be even more fun having a chance at more big, well-known stars.

The cards were shuffled and dealt and here's how I came out. In the first-round I would have the #2 overall pick. Lots of available selections here. As the draft got started, the team selecting #1 overall made Edgerrin James of the Indianapolis Colts their #1 pick. Now I'm up. Knowing the league was very small but I wouldn't pick again for ten selections, I opted to take quarterback, Kurt Warner of the St. Louis Rams coming off his "Cinderella' season of 1999. Warner, I believed was the best player available at the time, especially with James gone.

After picking second in the first-round, now I would pick fifth in the second round. With the likes of running backs, Edgerrin James, Stephen Davis, Marshall Faulk, Terrell Davis, and a few others already gone, I thought it best I get my hands on a running back that would likely produce consistently. I grabbed Emmitt Smith, who had rebounded to produce 45 touchdowns over the previous three years.

Following my first two round selections the rest of my draft went like this:

Round	Player	Position	Team
3rd	Antonio Freeman	WR	Green Bay Packers
4th	Curtis Martin	RB	New York Giants
5th	Tony Gonzalez	TE	Kansas City Chiefs
6th	Torry Holt	WR	St. Louis Rams
7th	Jeff Wilkins	K	St. Louis Rams
8th	Dorsey Levens	RB	Green Bay Packers
9th	Muhsin Muhammad	WR	Carolina Panthers
10th	Thomas Jones	RB	Arizona Cardinals
11th	Tim Brown	WR	Oakland Raiders
12th	Bubba Franks	TE	Green Bay Packers
13th	Germane Crowell	WR	Detroit Lions
14th	Charlie Garner	RB	San Francisco 49ers
15th	Al Del Greco	K	Tennessee Titans
16th	Vinny Testaverde	QB	New York Jets

I felt pretty good about my team but who wouldn't in a 6-team league. I felt good at running back, adding Curtis Martin, Dorsey Levens, Charlie Garner and rookie Thomas Jones to the mix. At wide receiver Antonio Freeman and Torry Holt looked like solid starters, especially with the 9-point hookup between Holt and Warner. I felt I had the best tight end in football with Tony Gonzalez. Certainly kickers Jeff Wilkins (Rams) and Al Del Greco (Titans) kicking for good teams would each be a force. Like I said, I felt good about my prospects.

REGULAR SEASON

For my regular season opener, my starting lineup looked like this.

QB	Kurt Warner	St. Louis Rams
RB	Curtis Martin	New York Jets
RB	Emmitt Smith	Dallas Cowboys
WR	Antonio Freeman	Green Bay Packers
WR	Torry Holt	St. Louis Rams
TE	Tony Gonzalez	Kansas City Chiefs
K	Jeff Wilkins	St. Louis Rams

WEEK No. 1

I got in trouble early in this season opener as my opponent, Astro Jump, having four players going to my one in the early games, jumped out with 24 points, 18 alone coming from quarterback, Daunte Culpepper, as he rushed for three touchdowns in his first start for the Vikings. (Only against me I thought.) Astro Jump also got a score from Marcus Robinson, while Cris Carter and Stephen Alexander got blanked. My lone early participant Tony Gonzalez went down without a score. In the late games, I closed the gap a little, as his kicker Sebastian Janikowski was held to one point, while I got two touchdowns out of Curtis Martin. However, Emmitt Smith and Antonio Freeman failed to score, so I trailed 25-12 going into Sunday Night. The only player going for him Sunday Night was running back Eddie George and of course he scored to push the score to 31-12. Having three St. Louis Rams to his Terrell Davis on Monday Night, I still had a chance. Davis did fail to score but I came up short, as Kurt Warner did throw for three scores but none to Torry Holt unfortunately and kicker Jeff Wilkins tacked on five, leaving me a touchdown short, losing 31-26.

WEEK No. 2

Having two players going in the early games, Antonio Freeman (Packers) and Tony Gonzalez (Chiefs), I was happy to have Freeman get me on the board by scoring twice, but Gonzalez failed to score. My opponent, SBA, had six of their players going early and got a touchdown by Randy Moss, two unlikely scores by tight end Jay Riesmersma (can you believe it?), and 11 points out of kicker Martin Gramatica. So heading into the late games, I was down 29-12 but had five players left to SBA's one. SBA's quarterback, Brad Johnson, threw for only one score, while my quarterback Kurt Warner matched that and my kicker Jeff Wilkins tallied 13 to make it 32-28 and I still had my two running backs left, Emmitt Smith on Sunday Night and Curtis Martin on Monday. My opponent gives me the "ok, you've got it locked, two players, blah, blah, blah, and you know what happened, and it could only happen to me, neither scored as I lose 32-28 and sit at 0-2.

WEEK No. 3

In desperate need of a win and facing a team that scored 43 points the week before, I thought I was in big trouble. My opponent, the Rabid Gerbils, went near dormant getting only a touchdown pass out of Steve Beuerlein and scores out of Robert Smith and Terry Glenn. Ironically, the two running backs I needed a score from last week to give me the win, Emmitt Smith and Curtis Martin, both score. Quarterback Kurt Warner chipped in two touchdown passes, while Jeff Wilkins tallied nine in a 27-15 win.

WEEK No. 4

In week 4, I was hoping to get to .500. My opponent, the Titans, had Rams' wide receiver Isaac Bruce while I had Rams' quarterback Kurt Warner, the other Rams' wide receivers Torry Holt and Az-Zahir Hakim and their kicker Jeff Wilkins. Well Bruce did score twice but so did Holt, which meant Warner threw for four touchdowns, Wilkins chipped in 11, which, coupled with Emmitt Smith's tally, gave me a 41-12 lead through the late games. I added nine more from Curtis Martin on a touchdown pass and run and a score from Tony Gonzalez to help wrap up a 56-36 win and push me to 2-2.

WEEK No. 5

Would the roll continue? Rams players Kurt Warner, Torry Holt and Jeff Wilkins again got me off to a fast start, as Warner threw for four more, Holt scored once and Wilkins tallied a whopping 19 points in the early games. My opponent, DX, fought back with their lone Ram, Marshall Faulk, who scored twice, Marvin Harrison who scored once, another unlikely tight end hit with Frank Wycheck scoring twice and kicker Mike Vanderjadt added four to put me up only 37-34 following the early games. I just kept thinking I'd hate to score this many points and lose this one. My opponent did get a score from Mike Alstott in the late games, but my insertion of Charlie Garner into the lineup paid immediate dividends. Garner scored twice and Tony Gonzalez added an insurance score on Monday Night to give me a 55-40 win and 3-2 record.

WEEK No. 6

Going into this week, I lost two potent weapons in Kurt Warner and Jeff Wilkins, both going down to injuries. Certainly I knew this would hurt. Replacement quarterback Vinny Testaverde's no points confirmed that, while replacement kicker, Al Del Greco did come through with 11 points, both playing in the early games. My other early game participants were Curtis Martin who failed to score but Antonio Freeman did get into the end zone. My opponent having only two early game players, countered with a single touchdown out of Eddie George, to give me a 17-6 early lead. In the late games, I got a score out of Charlie Garner but Muhsin Muhammad drew a blank, while my opponent's kicker Sebastian Janikowski tallied eight. This put me up 23-13 going into Sunday and Monday Night games, where

I had nobody left and Astro Jump had Qadry Ismail on Sunday and Daunte Culpepper and Cris Carter on Monday. I slid by Sunday Night without Ismail scoring but Culpepper's 12-point performance on Monday Night was a killer, as I lost a close one 26-23 to go 3-3.

WEEK No. 7

Having five players in the early games to my opponents two, I needed to get off to a good start. Quarterback Kurt Warner came through with three touchdown passes and two-point toss for ten points. Warner's receiver Torry Holt got blanked but I got touchdowns out of Az-Zahir Hakim and Tony Gonzalez, while my kicker Jeff Wilkins only produced one point. Meanwhile, my opponent, SBA, failed to get points out of both Jerome Bettis and Jay Riemersma, giving me a 23-0 lead early. In the late games, both Charlie Garner and Emmitt Smith came through with scores, but my opponent bounced back with Brian Griese throwing for three scores (9 points) and Terrell Owens scoring twice to put me up 35-21 going into Sunday Night. SBA had Randy Moss left on Sunday Night and Fred Taylor yet to go on Monday Night. Moss scored on Sunday Night to draw the score to 35-27, meaning the very capable Taylor had to score twice on Monday Night to beat me. Anxiety attacks up to and during the game were cured when Taylor failed to score as I pushed my record to 4-3.

WEEK No. 8

Well, at least this week I'd know early the likely outcome of my fantasy game. My opponent, the Rabid Gerbils, had all seven of their players going in the early games and I had six, with only Curtis Martin going Monday Night. The Gerbils tough backfield combination of quarterback Peyton Manning and running back Edgerrin James were exactly that, tough. Manning's three touchdown passes and James' two touchdowns gave the Gerbils a jump start. However, only kicker Jason Elam added more to the point total for 24 points. My team responded along the way with touchdowns out of Emmitt Smith, Torry Holt and Tony Gonzalez, but I was very disappointed with Kurt Warner only throwing one touchdown and kicker Al Del Greco scoring only two points, as I now trailed 24-23. Warner only one touchdown? Del Greco's missed field goal! How could I be down by one point? That's OK I still have a chance with Curtis Martin on Monday Night. As the Monday Night game proceeded and ended with Martin failing to score, I again asked myself: Warner only one touchdown? Del Greco's missed field goal. (I hate when that happens.) Losing 24-23 pushed me back to .500 at 4-4.

WEEK No. 9

Facing close friend Tom Nemo and the Titans is always fun, especially after beating him soundly the first time out 56-36. This time Tom vowed for revenge. Between the two teams, only one player was involved in the early games, as the Titans' Shannon Sharpe was blanked, which I of course, had to let him know, as if he didn't already. In the late games, scores came flying in as the lead seesawed. The Titans got nine points out of quarterback Mark Brunnell but fortunately none of his throws went to Jimmy Smith, who got blanked. The Titans did get a score from Ricky

Williams and five points from Mike Hollis. Meanwhile I got two touch-down passes out of Trent Green, a touchdown out of Charlie Garner and 10 points out of kicker Pete Stoyanovich, who had replaced injured Jeff Wilkins in St. Louis. This put me up 21-20 with my Tim Brown yet to go on Sunday Night and the Titans' Stephen Davis yet to go on Monday Night. Brown failed to give me an insurance score so it was up to my defense (what defense) to hold off Stephen Davis on Monday Night. Like I said what defense, as Davis does score and give the Titans their revenge with a 26-22 win. A tough loss for me which dropped me to 4-5.

WEEK No. 10

Hoping to get back to .500, I got a score out of Emmitt Smith, my lone player in the early games, to hopefully set the tone. My opponent, DX, who has five players in the early games responds with two touchdowns out of Keyshawn Johnson and four points out of kicker Mike Vanderjagt to go up 16-6. In the late games, with three players going I get only a touchdown out of Curtis Martin, while DX pushes their lead with 12 points out of quarterback, Rich Gannon to go up 28-12. This leaves four Rams' players in the Sunday Night game, three for me, Trent Green, Torry Holt and kicker Pete Stoyanovich, against DX's Marshall Faulk. Faulk amazingly gets shut out, but six points from Green and six from Stoyanovich aren't enough, as I lose 28-24 and now fall to 4-6.

WEEK No. 11

Hoping to get back on track, I'm a bit scared by the early games of this week. My lone participant Emmitt Smith does score, but opponent Astro Jump gets 15 points out of Daunte Culpepper, six out of Cris Carter and seven out of kicker Gary Anderson to go up 28-6 following the early games. Wow, a 4-7 record would really be a killer. I think my fantasy team heard my thought as in the late games, quarterback Trent Green produced 18 points, Torry Holt scored as I rebounded to take the lead 30-28 going into Sunday and Monday Night. Astro Jump had only Terrell Davis left on Monday Night while I had Curtis Martin Sunday Night and Tim Brown on Monday. Martin's Sunday Night score pushed my lead to 36-28 and with Terrell Davis and Tim Brown exchanging scores on Monday Night, I pull out a 42-34 win, pushing me back to a game under .500 at 5-6.

WEEK No. 12

At this point, the league had three 6-5 teams and three 5-6 teams. I needed to win desperately. SBA would again be tough as this, would be the rubber match, splitting the two earlier games. This week's early games provided plenty of fireworks as SBA got scores from all three of their participants with Randy Moss, Eric Moulds and Jay Reimersma all scoring. I fared well also as my three players put points on the board. Tim Brown scored once, Tony Gonzalez scored twice and kicker Al Del Greco tallied six as I took a 24-18 lead. Things settled down in the late games as SBA's Jamal Anderson failed to score and kicker Olindo Mare only tallied three for SBA. Both my running backs Emmitt Smith and Curtis Martin got blanked to close the score to 24-21. This left Monday Night with SBA having quarterback Brad Johnson and I having Trent Green and Torry Holt.

Johnson threw for three scores, Green threw for two and neither went to Holt to lock the score at 30-30. And with all of our four tie-breaker players not scoring that's the way the score stood, 30-30 and put me at 5-6-1.

WEEK No. 13

I still want and need to get back to .500 and a shot at one of the four playoffs spots. In one of the least exciting, offensively deficient games of the year, I got my wish. The Rabid Gerbils got off to a quick start with a Jimmy Smith touchdown on Thursday, while my single Thursday player, Emmitt Smith got blanked. Moving to Sunday's early games, the Gerbils got only two touchdown passes from Peyton Manning out of their four players, while Trent Green did the same to put me down 12-6. The Gerbils' Derrick Alexander failed to score in the late game, but Tony Gonzalez did and kicker, Al Del Greco tallied seven to put me up 19-12 going into Monday Night with the Gerbils kicker Ryan Longwell left. With 7-point lead and only a kicker left, it didn't look good. It was a long Monday Night but well worth the agony as Longwell produced only two extra points giving me a 19-14 win and a .500 record at 6-6-1.

WEEK No. 14

Up against my buddy but bitter rival Tom Nemo and the Titans, I knew I needed this win but so did he to lock in one of the four playoff spots. One win separated all six teams, each team had either six or seven wins. In the early games, I was in shock as Kurt Warner got shutout, which meant Torry Holt did as well. My only other early game participant was kicker Jeff Wilkins, who scored the Ram's lone point, a field goal, in a 16-3 loss to Carolina. That was the bad news. The good news was that the Titans' three early games participants all failed to score, which included running backs Stephen Davis, Tim Biakabatuka and wide receiver Isaac Bruce. In the late games, the Titans', Mark Brunell tallied nine points and kicker Mike Hollis tallied 12 but fortunately none of Brunell's touchdowns went to Jimmy Smith as he and tight end Anthony Becht failed to score for the Titans. For me, both my running backs came through with touchdowns, as I now trailed 21-15 going into Sunday Night. The Titans were done but I still had Antonio Freeman on Sunday Night and Tony Gonzalez on Monday Night. Because of our league's tie-breaking rules I would win if I got a touchdown out of either because I was home team and my first tie-breaker player, Al Del Greco, had kicked a field goal. The tie-breaking rules never had to be used, as both Freeman and Gonzalez scored to push me to 7-6-1 with one game to go. My 7-6-1 record put me in third place and already locked into a playoff spot as three teams were tied at 6-8 and couldn't oust me.

WEEK No. 15

With nothing really at stake, as I couldn't really change playoff positions, I paid little attention to the game. Good thing! Good thing there was nothing at stake and good thing I didn't pay close attention. Though the Rams were rolling up the score on the Vikings and I had three Rams, quarterback Kurt Warner, wide receiver Torry Holt and kicker Jeff Wilkins, it was all Marshall Faulk who scored four times and I just happened to be playing against him. Faulk's 24 points, helped in DX trouncing me 44-16. Not a pretty way to get into the playoffs but at least I was there. At 7-7-1 I was the third place finisher and would face the Rabid Gerbils next week in the first round of our playoffs.

PLAYOFFS
First Round

Disappointed with my .500 (7-7-1) season, I still felt good that I had made the playoffs and had a chance to win it all. Up against my nephew, the Rabid Gerbils, I was facing a team I had beaten twice during the regular season in rather low-scoring games. We would get started in this fantasy playoff game on Saturday as I had the lone player going in, Tim Brown. Brown's failure to score kept me from getting the jump that I so desperately felt I needed and wanted. On Sunday, the early games pitted my running back Curtis Martin and tight end Tony Gonzalez against his running back Robert Smith, wide receivers Ed McCaffrey and Derrick Alexander and kicker Ryan Longwell. Martin's touchdown posted early and all looked pretty good except Longwell was tallying some points. Despite shutting down Smith, McCaffrey and Alexander, Longwell's 15 points hurt immensely as the Gerbils went up 15-6 after the early games. In the late games, I had only Charlie Garner going, to face the Gerbils' Indianapolis Colts connection of Peyton Manning, Edgerrin James and Ken Dilger. Fortunately only Manning posted points getting nine but Garner's failure to score put me down 24-6 going into Monday Night. All was not totally lost I thought, as I still had potent Rams' players Kurt Warner, Torry Holt and Jeff Wilkins. Warner's two touchdown passes, one to Holt brought me close. With Jeff Wilkins sitting at five points, I only needed one more touchdown pass, one more touchdown, heck, I only needed one more anything. I was down 24-23 and one more extra point would give me a tie and a win, as I had the tie-breaker wrapped up. It was not to be, as I learned, whether you're in a 16-team or a 6-team league, losing a close game to get into the league Championship can leave you frustrated, upset and sleepless.

THIRD PLACE

Knowing the league Championship was no longer at stake, the Third Place game doesn't quite bear the same meaning. Regardless winning is winning and third is better than fourth place. It was close but led by touchdowns by Curtis Martin, Tim Brown and Tony Gonzalez, a touchdown pass from Kurt Warner and eight points from kicker Jeff Wilkins I prevailed 29-27 over SBA for a third place finish.

FINAL THOUGHTS

The big adjustment of going from a 16-team league to a 6-team league was not that significant. I found out fantasy football is fantasy football, regardless of league size. Watching my players each week was still exciting. I did, however, find out there seems to be more parity in a smaller league, where every team has great players playing each week. Luck seems to be the key as any team can truly beat any other team on a given week. As for my 7-7-1 record and third place finish was concerned, I was happy. Now that I know a little more about playing in a smaller league, I can try to maneuver my team to more wins in 2001.

I
INITIAL CONSIDERATIONS

PREPARING FOR YOUR 2001 FANTASY DRAFT
2000 Had Its Share of Key Injuries and Surprises,
2001 Will Unfold with New Stories and Heroes

A frequent mistake made by many Fantasy Football participants is to draft players for their fantasy teams based purely on the previous year's statistics and events. Here's a warning: Don't get caught in that mindset. Remember "That was then and this is now." Each and every year takes on its own characteristics. Because a player fares well or poorly one year doesn't mean he'll do the same the next. Injuries, contract holdouts, trades and poor play are all factors that contribute to a player doing well or poorly. These same factors may also affect another player's performance, which could also mislead you the next year when making your fantasy selections.

Free agency and offseason trades continue to play a significant role. Were you able to pick which players joined new teams would fare well? Did you feel James Stewart going to Detroit would be a significant fantasy factor or the same for Lamar Smith going to Miami to battle for the starting job? How about wide receiver Joe Horn who put up big numbers in moving to New Orleans from Kansas City?

How about the rookies of 2000? Did you jump on #5 overall pick, Jamal Lewis of Baltimore, who finished with 1,660 rushing-receiving yards but only six touchdowns. Though I'm sure you didn't draft him, did you jump on Mike Anderson of the Broncos following injuries to Terrell Davis and Olandis Gary. Anderson, a virtual unknown sixth-round pick, proved how good Denver's offensive line is by amassing 1,660 rushing-receiving yards and a whopping 15 touchdowns playing in just 14 games. There were others that put up decent numbers such as Travis Prentise the Browns' third-round pick who produced 703 total yards and eight touchdowns, wide receiver Peter Warrick, the #4 overall pick who grabbed a somewhat disappointing 51 receptions for 740 yards and seven touchdowns. Overall the 2000 rookies were a disappointment, especially the first-rounders.

Why is it that many of our preseason picks or predictions don't work out as well as we expected them to? Because of course, each and every season is unique. It took the injuries to Terrell Davis and Olandis Gary to give Mike Anderson his shot at fame. It took the injuries to Dorsey Levens to open the door for Ahman Green's breakout year, after coming over to Green Bay from Seattle in the offseason. Injuries to the likes of wide receivers Joey Galloway (Dallas), Carl Pickens (Tennessee) and running backs Duce Staley (Philadelphia) and Mike Alstott (Tampa Bay) cost them statistically. Others like Rob Moore (Arizona) and Corey Bradford (Green Bay) missed the entire season with injuries suffered in the preseason. When examining the previous year's statistics for next year's predictions, these players will not appear statistically where they normally would have had they been healthy or around all season. Certainly this would be misleading for someone drafting just from the previous year's statistics. How will the healthy return of these players in 2001 affect their statistics and those of the players who filled in for them?

Another thing you may want to consider when planning your 2001 fantasy draft is the direction that each NFL team is headed. Which teams are on the upswing and which teams may be on their way down. The Baltimore Ravens have taken a quick turn about and are at the top. The Philadelphia Eagles appear headed in the right direction behind their quarterback, Donovan McNabb, going 11-5 in 2000, after being 5-11 a year earlier. Teams like the Dallas Cowboys, San Francisco 49ers and Atlanta Falcons, all of whom realized some success in 1990s, are now headed in a downward direction from that success.

Many teams will again be active in making coaching changes this offseason. Buffalo turned away Wade Phillips to bring in Gregg Williams. Cleveland fired Chris Palmer, following a 5-27 tw year record, and have hired Butch Davis. Detroit has hired Marty Mornhinweg after dismissing Bobby Ross and Greg Moeller. Kansas City, hoping for another "Cinderella" year from Dick Vermeil, hired him to replace Gunther Cunningham. The Jets' Al Groh resigned and was replaced by Herman Edwards. In Washington, Marty Schottenheimer signed a 4-year deal following the departure of Norv Turner and Terry Robuskie.

How player's replacements do in implementing their new systems and changes will have an effect on how the players on their teams produce and fare in 2000. Also, while preparing for your 2001 fantasy season, be sure to keep a close eye on offseason happenings, such as progress of significant injuries and, of course, player moves. Free agency and offseason player moves continue to have a startling effect on the makeup of teams and the league. Big-money players changed teams last year and will again this year. In 2000, James Stewart jumped from Jacksonville to Detroit, Lamar Smith from New Orleans to Miami and Joe Horn from Kansas City to New Orleans. These are just a few of the players that changed teams in 2000, either via trades or free agency. Many more key transactions will have a big impact on the 2001 season. Such changes deserve your attention because they will affect the performance of the team the player is leaving as well as the one he's joining.

Which trends will carry over from 2000 to 2001? Which teams and, more specifically, which players will come to the forefront in 2001? The performance of a player or a team can change quickly and unexpectedly from year to year, especially with so many key players moving to new teams. To demonstrate how widely and significantly the statistical leaders can fluctuate from year to year, we're going to compare 1999's top 10 leaders with those of 2000. We'll be comparing the leaders and lists from each of the fantasy positions for both the Basic and Combine/Basic-Performance Scoring Methods. By doing this, you will gain a sense of the changes that have occurred among scoring and yardage leaders from year to year. (NOTE: A kicker's fantasy points are the same in both scoring methods so they're shown just once.)

BASIC SCORING METHOD — RUNNING BACKS
1999   2000

	NAME	TEAM	TDs	FANTASY POINTS		NAME	TEAM	TDs	FANTASY POINTS
1.	Davis	WASH	17	104	1.	Faulk	STL	26	160
2.	James	IND	17	102	2.	James	IND	18	110
3.	Smith	DALL	13	78	3.	L. Smith	MIA	16	96
4.	Stewart	JAC	13	78	4.	George	TENN	16	96
5.	George	TENN	13	78	5.	Anderson	DEN	15	92
6.	Faulk	STL	12	74	6.	Taylor	JAC	14	84
7.	Wheatley	OAK	11	66	7.	Green	GB	13	78
8.	Levens	GB	10	60	8.	Stewart	DET	11	72
9.	Hoard	MINN	10	60	9.	Martin	NYJ	11	69
10.	Bates	ARIZ	9	54	10.	Davis	WASH	11	66
	Kirby	CLE	9	54			CLE	9	54
	Allen	NE	9	54					
	Alstott	TB	9	54					

Here's a good example of seeing how things can change year to year. Only five players that landed in the top-ten in scoring in 1999 returned to that distinction in 2000.

Injuries to the likes of Dorsey Levens, Tyrone Wheatley and Mike Alstott played a big role in their inability to match their previous year's success. Others like Emmitt Smith just saw his performance drop off.

On the up side, Lamar Smith's move from New Orleans to Miami triggered resurgence in his career. The likes of rookie Mike Anderson in Denver and Ahman Green in Green Bay took advantage of injuries to Terrell Davis, Olandis Gary and Dorsey Levens to record breakout years. For Fred Taylor and Curtis Martin, staying healthy helped them push and rebound to significant scoring numbers.

Looking at the 2000 top-10 list we can already see, based on significant players returning from injury in 2001, this group will again change in a big way.

BASIC SCORING METHOD — WIDE RECEIVERS
1999   2000

	NAME	TEAM	TDs	FANTASY POINTS		NAME	TEAM	TDs	FANTASY POINTS
1.	Carter	MINN	13	78	1.	Moss	MINN	15	92
2.	Moss	MINN	12	75	2.	Harrison	IND	14	84
3.	Harrison	IND	12	74	3	Owens	SF	13	80
4.	Bruce	STL	12	74	4.	Tim Brown	OAK	11	66
5.	Jeffers	CAR	12	72	5.	Alexander	KC	10	60
6.	Mayes	SEAT	10	60	6.	McCaffrey	DEN	9	56
7.	Westbrook	WASH	9	56	7.	Rd Smith	DEN	9	54
8.	Dwight	ATL	9	54	8.	Freeman	GB	9	54
9.	Robinson	CHI	9	54	9.	Carter	MINN	9	54
10.	Hakim	STL	9	54	10.	Bruce	STL	9	54

In this group, only the top four finishers of 1999 again made the top-10 group for 2000. Chris Carter, Randy Moss, Marvin Harrison and Isaac Bruce made it both years.

For the likes of Patrick Jeffers, who suffered a season-ending injury in the preseason, and Marcus Robinson, Michael Westbrook and Tim Dwight, who all missed a significant part of the 2000 season due to injury, their success and possible return to the top-10 was halted. Meanwhile Az-Za-hir Hakim and Derrick Mayes dropped off in play and production.

For the newcomers, it was a series of veterans who regrouped and had very productive years. Tim Brown, Derrick Alexander, Ed McCaffrey, Rod Smith, Antonio Freeman, and Terrell Owens made up that group.

BASIC SCORING METHOD — TIGHT ENDS

1999   2000

	NAME	TEAM	TDs	FANTASY POINTS		NAME	TEAM	TDs	FANTASY POINTS
1.	Walls	CAR	12	72	1.	Gonzalez	KC	9	54
2.	Gonzalez	KC	11	66	2.	Harris	DALL	5	32
3.	Dudley	OAK	9	54	3.	Sharpe	BALT	5	30
4.	LaFluer	DALL	7	42	4.	Riemersma	BUF	5	30
5.	Williams	STL	6	36	5.	Thomason	PHIL	5	30
6.	Moore	GB	5	30	6.	Jones	SD	5	30
7.	Riemersma	BUF	4	24	7.	Wycheck	TENN	4	27
8.	Sloan	DET	4	24	8.	Glover	NO	4	24
9.	Pollard	IND	4	24	9.	Dudley	OAK	4	24
10.	Jones	JAC	4	24	10.	Pollard	IND	3	20
	Broughton	PHIL	4	24		Brady	JAC	3	20
						Williams	STL	3	20

About half of the players making the top-10 in this group in 1999, returned to that distinction in 2000. Tony Gonzalez, Ricky Dudley, Roland Williams, Jay Riemersma and Marcus Pollard are those returning.

For Wesley Walls, a knee injury forced him to miss half the season in 2000. For the likes of David LaFluer, Dave Moore, David Sloan, and Damon Jones, their production fell off.

On the up side, Jackie Harris went to Dallas in the offseason to become a scoring force for the Cowboys. The same was true for Shannon Sharpe, recovering from a knee injury the year before, going to Baltimore, and Andrew Glover going to New Orleans from Minnesota.

BASIC SCORING METHOD — QUARTERBACKS

1999   2000

	NAME	TEAM	PS TDs	RSH TDs	FANTASY POINTS		NAME	TEAM	PS TDs	RSH TDs	FANTASY POINTS
1.	Warner	STL	41	1	130	1.	Culpepper	MINN	33	7	143
2.	Beuerlein	CAR	36	2	120	2.	Garcia	SF	31	4	118
3.	Manning	IND	26	2	91	3.	Gannon	OAK	28	4	110
4.	Gannon	OAK	24	2	85	4.	Manning	IND	33	1	106
5.	McNair	TENN	12	8	85	5.	McNabb	PHIL	21	6	100
6.	Johnson	WASH	24	2	85	6.	Grbac	KC	28	1	90
7.	George	MINN	23	0	69	7.	King	TB	18	5	86
8.	Kitna	SEAT	23	0	69	8.	Stewart	PITT	11	5	75
9.	Favre	GB	22	0	67	9.	Brunell	JAC	20	2	73
10.	Grbac	KC	22	0	66	10.	Collins	NYG	22	1	72

Surprisingly, only three top-10 quarterbacks from 1999 again made that distinction in 2000. Peyton Manning, Rich Gannon and Elvis Grbac were those three.

The likes of Kurt Warner and Brad Johnson had their productions stalled by injuries. Jeff George lost his starting job in Minnesota and went to Washington, while the likes of Steve Beuerlein, Steve McNair, Jon Kitna and Brett Favre just saw their production fall off.

On the upswing were Daunte Culpepper, who surprised many by flourishing when taking over the Vikings starting job. Jeff Garcia got it together in San Francisco. Youngsters Donovan McNabb (Philadelphia) and Shawn King (Tampa Bay) started to come into their own, while veterans Kordell Stewart, Mark Brunell and Kerry Collins rebounded their year-end numbers in 2000.

BASIC AND COMBINED/BASIC SCORING METHOD — KICKERS
[identical for most scoring methods]

	1999				2000		
	NAME	TEAM	FANTASY POINTS		NAME	TEAM	FANTASY POINTS
1.	Vanderjadt	IND	145	1.	Stover	BALT	135
2.	Mare	MIA	144	2.	Longwell	GB	131
3.	Peterson	SEAT	134	3.	Nedney	CAR/DEN	126
4.	Hollis	JAC	130	4.	Gramatica	TB	126
5.	Wilkens	STL	124	5.	Vanderjadt	IND	121
6.	Stover	BALT	116	6.	Akers	PHIL	121
7.	Elam	DEN	116	7.	Del Greco	TENN	118
8.	Carney	SD	115	8.	Mare	MIA	117
9.	Conway	WASH	115	9.	Janikowski	OAK	112
10.	Longwell	GB	113	10.	Anderson	MINN	111

Of the kickers, four placed in the top-ten in both 1999 and 2000. Mike Vanderjadt, Olindo Mare, Matt Stover and Ryan Longwell made up that group.

Changes in team scoring because of more rapid player movement in recent years can be attributed to the varying of kicker results. However, injuries to Jeff Wilkins (St. Louis) and Jason Elam (Denver) are the biggest reason these two did not repeat as top-ten finishers.

COMBINED BASIC/PERFORMANCE POINT METHOD—
RUNNING BACKS

	1999						2000			
	NAME	TEAM	YARDS	TDs	FANTASY POINTS		NAME	TEAM	YARDS	TDs	FANTASY POINTS
1.	James	IND	2,139	17	304	1.	Faulk	STL	2,189	26	365
2.	Faulk	STL	2,429	12	301	2.	James	IND	2,303	18	325
3.	Davis	WASH	1,516	17	246	3.	George	TEN	1962	16	280
4.	George	TENN	1,762	13	241	4.	Anderson	DEN	1,669	15	248
5.	E. Smith	DALL	1,516	13	220	5.	Taylor	JAC	1,639	14	237
6.	Levens	GB	1,607	10	207	6.	Green	GB	1,734	13	236

7.	Garner	SF	1,764	6	198	7.	R. Smith	MINN	1,869	10	234
8.	Watters	SEAT	1,597	7	188	8.	Martin	NYJ	1,715	11	227
9.	Martin	NYJ	1,723	5	187	9.	Garner	SF	1,789	10	223
10.	Staley	PHIL	1,567	6	180	10.	Watters	SEAT	1,855	9	223

Here's a category that usually presents consistency year to year, unless injuries or player movement are factors. Six players, Edgerrin James, Marshall Faulk, Eddie George, Charlie Garner, Ricky Watters and Curtis Martin, were repeat top-10 finishers in 2000.

Injuries to Dorsey Levens and Duce Staley were the reasons they did not return to the top-10 in 2000, while Stephen Davis and Emmitt Smith each missed only one game but saw their performance drop off.

For Mike Anderson (Denver), injuries to Olandis Gary and Terrell Davis led to his remarkable rookie season. Ahman Green took advantage of the injury to Dorsey Levens in Green Bay. And veterans Robert Smith and Fred Taylor stayed healthy enough to rebound their numbers.

COMBINED BASIC/PERFORMANCE POINT METHOD—
WIDE RECEIVERS

1999

2000

	NAME	TEAM	YARDS	TDs	FANTASY POINTS		NAME	TEAM	YARDS	TDs	FANTASY POINTS
1.	Harrison	IND	1,667	12	233	1.	Moss	MINN	1,442	15	228
2.	Moss	MINN	1,456	12	214	2.	Owens	SF	1,462	13	218
3.	Carter	MINN	1,241	13	198	3.	Harrison	IND	1,413	14	217
4.	Smith	JAC	1,636	6	194	4.	Smith	DEN	1,701	9	216
5.	Robinson	CHI	1,400	9	188	5.	Alexander	KC	1,436	10	193
6.	Bruce	STL	1,197	12	186	6.	Bruce	STL	1,482	9	193
7.	Jeffers	CAR	1,098	12	177	7.	Holt	STL	1,642	6	193
8.	Crowell	DET	1,376	7	174	8.	McCaffrey	DEN	1,317	9	181
9.	Westbrook	WASH	1,226	9	170	9.	Horn	NO	1,358	8	175
10.	Muhammad	CAR	1,253	8	167	10.	Carter	MINN	1,274	9	173

Only 40 percent of the wide receiver, top-10 group of 1999 returned there in 2000. Marvin Harrison, Randy Moss, Chris Carter and Isaac Bruce are no surprises to show up both years.

Significant injuries to Marcus Robinson, Patrick Jeffers and Michael Westbrook forced them to miss big portions of or the entire 2000 season. Jimmy Smith missed a couple of games, while Germane Crowell and Muhsin Muhammad just saw their productions drop.

On the upswing, Terrell Owens, Rod Smith and Ed McCaffrey rebounded to solid numbers. Derrick Alexander finally put it together in Kansas City, as did Joe Horn in New Orleans, coming over from Kansas City in the offseason. Torry Holt continued to improve and his numbers reflect it.

COMBINED BASIC/PERFORMANCE POINT METHOD—
TIGHT ENDS

1999

NAME	TEAM	YARDS	TDs	FANTASY POINTS
1. Walls	CAR	822	12	146
2. Gonzalez	KC	849	11	145
3. Dudley	CAR	555	9	105
4. Sloan	DET	591	4	78
5. Wycheck	TENN	641	2	75
6. Jones	SD	670	2	72
7. LaFluer	DALL	322	7	69
8. Riemersma	BUF	496	4	67
9. Mitchell	NYG	520	3	65
10. Chamberlain	DEN	488	2	57

2000

NAME	TEAM	YARDS	TDs	FANTASY POINTS
1. Gonzalez	KC	1,203	9	167
2. Sharpe	BALT	810	5	105
3. Jones	SD	766	5	100
4. Brady	JAC	729	3	87
5. Lewis	PHIL	735	3	86
6. Wycheck	TENN	636	4	85
7. Dilger	IND	538	3	64
8. Riemersma	BUF	372	5	62
9. Carswell	DEN	495	3	61
10. Pollard	IND	439	3	58

Four tight ends found themselves in the top-10 in both 1999 and 2000, included were Tony Gonzalez, Frank Wycheck, Fred Jones and Jay Riemersma.

The most notable non-returner was Wesley Walls who missed nearly half the 2000 season with a knee injury. Others like Ricky Dudley, David Sloan, David LaFluer, Pete Mitchell and Byron Chamberlain saw their production fall off.

Shannon Sharpe took his services to Baltimore, after recovering from a 1999 knee injury, to return among the top tight ends in the league. Others like Chad Lewis, Dwayne Carswell and fellow Colt tight ends Ken Dilger and Marcus Pollard pushed their play and production in 2000.

COMBINED BASIC/PERFORMANCE SCORING METHOD—
QUARTERBACKS
1999

	NAME	TEAM	RSH YDS	PS YDS	RSH TDs	PS TDs	FANTASY POINTS
1.	Warner	STL	92	4,353	1	41	348
2.	Beuerlein	CAR	124	4,336	2	36	342
3.	Manning	IND	73	4,135	2	26	297
4.	Gannon	OAK	298	3,840	2	24	295
5.	Johnson	WASH	30	4,005	2	24	278
6.	Favre	GB	142	4,091	0	22	274
7.	Flutie	BUF	475	3,171	1	19	256
8.	Bledsoe	NE	101	3,985	0	19	254
9.	Kitna	SEAT	56	3,346	0	23	231
10.	Grbac	KC	15	3,389	0	22	228

COMBINED BASIC/PERFORMANCE SCORING METHOD—
QUARTERBACKS
2000

	NAME	TEAM	RSH YDS	PS YDS	RSH TDs	PS TDs	FANTASY POINTS
1.	Culpepper	MINN	470	3,937	7	33	370
2.	Garcia	SF	414	4,278	4	31	361
3.	Manning	IND	116	4,413	1	33	330
4.	Gannon	OAK	529	3,430	4	28	317
5.	McNabb	PHIL	629	3,365	6	21	314
6.	Grbac	KC	111	4,169	1	28	300
7.	Brunell	JAC	236	3,640	2	20	267
8.	Favre	GB	108	3,812	0	20	253
9.	Beuerlein	CAR	106	3,730	1	19	251
10.	Collins	NYG	72	3,610	1	22	249

Quarterback is usually a position that you usually see the same names year to year. This time around half the group returned to the top-10 in 2000 that appeared there in 1999. Steve Beuerlein, Peyton Manning, Rich Gannon, Brett Favre and Elvis Grbac made the top-10 distinction both years.

Injuries to Kurt Warner and Brad Johnson kept them from repeating, while Drew Bledsoe just dropped off in production and Doug Flutie and Jon Kitna lost their starting jobs at least for awhile.

On the upswing were Jeff Garcia, who came on strong for the 49ers, as did youngsters Daunte Culpepper (Vikings) and Donovan McNabb (Eagles), who came on for their respective teams. Veteran Mark Brunell stayed healthy to rebound his numbers.

Can this two-year comparison help you? It shows how radically top performers can change from year to year. This widespread change occurs for a variety of reasons: injuries, holdouts, trades and personnel movement. We can see that roughly 50 percent of the players from any one position who make the top-10 list one year make it back the next year. That's quite a change from one year to the next, and that's just the top-10 players.

Comparing these lists demonstrates how poorly we would have drafted in 2000 if we had based our decisions purely on statistics from the previous year. A review like this reminds us how many circumstances influence the success of a season. Again, overall in 2000 about half the players at fantasy positions who were top-10 finishers in 1999 returned to that list. This rate hold fairly true, year to year. Successful fantasy players realize that one great season (or a horrible one) does not necessarily indicate a trend. Injuries, holdouts, trades, suspensions and free-agent moves can all determine how a player does. To win consistently, a successful franchise owner will make forecasts for the upcoming season by examining helpful facts from the previous year, by keeping track of offseason player movement, by considering the general upward or downward movement of a player's team, and by combining these considerations with a general feel for the game.

Such successful fantasy owners probably had the foresight to gamble on Lamar Smith in 2000. Smith came to Miami to battle for the running back job, stepped in and had a remarkable year, recording 1,340 rushing-receiving yards and 16 touchdowns. Those fantasy owners who jumped on Mike Anderson lucked out when Olandis Gary and Terrell Davis went down hurt. Anderson, Denver's sixth-round pick, ran behind the Broncos' solid offensive line and produced 1,669 rushing-receiving yards and 15 touchdowns playing in just 14 games.

We have already found that free-agent signings, injuries, retirements, contract holdouts and suspensions can affect player's careers. Merely studying the 2000 statistics, although helpful, will not be enough to make you successful in 2001. That is why, in the following sections, we'll study many variables, such as the injuries, trades, contract holdouts, and other factors that may have influenced a player's statistics last year. We will also look at the effects these variables may have on the upcoming 2001 season. We'll look at offseason roster moves, such as free-agent moves, trades, acquisitions, and retirements. We'll take a close look at injury updates to see what effect they may have on the upcoming season. Then I hope you can combine all this information with your feel for both NFL football and fantasy football to make your 2001 season a huge success.

II
HELPFUL FACTS FROM THE 2000 SEASON

(Key injuries, trades, holdouts, and other events that affected
2000 performances and how the 2000 rookies fared)

Many fantasy franchise owners preparing for the draft make a big mistake by considering only the previous year's statistics. Many factors contribute to a player's success or failure, and all of them should be carefully examined.

In this section, we will review the 2000 season to learn some of the reasons for the statistical success or failure of certain players. We'll look at injuries, trades, contract holdouts, suspensions, and other events to see how each may have helped one player but hurt another. We'll also review the 2000 rookies' performances to see how they were affected by injuries and by other players' performances. (A rookie isn't always able to prove himself in his first year in the NFL.) We do this to evaluate the players' potential for 2000. We may be able to forecast a "sleeper" or predict which veterans may have comebacks.

Injuries, suspensions and holdouts to key players always play a significant role in season statistics. A knee injury to Olandis Gary along with ankle and leg injuries to Terrell Davis led to the emergence of Mike Anderson for Denver in 2000. Knee and ankle injuries to Dorsey Levens led to a breakout year for Ahman Green in Green Bay. Other veterans like Rob Moore (knee), Marcus Robinson (back), Bobby Engram (knee), Darnay Scott (broken leg), Tim Couch (thumb), Troy Aikman (concussions), Joey Galloway (knee), Rocket Ismail (knee), Brian Griese (shoulder), Olandis Gary (knee), Terrell Davis (ankle), Germane Crowell (foot), Dorsey Levens (knee), Fred Taylor (knee), O.J. McDuffie (toe), Jeff Blake (foot), Ricky Williams (ankle), Cam Cleeland (achilles), Jake Reed (leg), Duce Staley (foot), Plaxico Burress (wrist), Garrison Hearst (ankle), Kurt Warner (finger), Marshall Faulk (knee), Mike Alstott (knee), Yancey Thigpen, (hamstring), Brad Johnson (knee), and Michael Westbrook (knee) all missed either the entire 2000 season or a significant portion of it due to injury. Their 2000 numbers are certainly deceiving when trying to determine their 2001 potential.

These are circumstances from the previous year we should consider. Without acknowledging all the missed time due to injuries, holdouts, etc., we're likely to overlook a significant player this year. What follows is a team-by-team discussion of events that may have played a part in a certain player's success or failure in 2000 and what lingering effect those events may have going into 2001.

HERE'S THE KEY TO THIS BREAKDOWN:

IR — Injured and on injured reserve

PUPL — Physically unable to perform list

I — Injured but never on injured reserve

S — Suspended

TR — Traded

RT — Retired

RS — Re-signed

RL — Released

AC — Acquired

HO — Contract holdout

L — Leave of absence

AO — Absent for other reason

ARIZONA CARDINALS

IR—Rob Moore (Wide Receiver)

Moore suffered a season-ending knee injury in the 2000 preseason forcing him to miss the entire season. Moore led the Cardinals' wide receivers with five touchdown catches in 1999. His absence led to more exposure for second-year man, David Boston, who has likely worked his way into a permanent place on the roster.

I—Jake Plummer (Quarterback)

A rib injury forced Plummer to miss two games in 2000, helping in limiting him to 2,946 passing yards and only 13 touchdown passes.

ATLANTA FALCONS

I—Tim Dwight (Wide Receiver)

After recording nine touchdowns in a breakout 1999 season, Dwight scored only four times in 2000, missing five games, with a leg injury and an emergency appendectomy.

BALTIMORE RAVENS

I—Qadry Ismail (Wide Receiver)

Ismail, sidelined with a knee injury early in 2000, saw his numbers drop from 68 receptions for 1,105 yards and six touchdowns in 1999 to 49 receptions for 655 yards and five touchdowns in 2000.

BUFFALO BILLS

I—Rob Johnson (Quarterback)
Johnson, who won the starting job away from Doug Flutie, missed three games during the middle of the 2000 season with a shoulder injury and the season finale with a concussion. Missing the four games limited Johnson to 2,125 passing yards and 12 touchdowns.

I—Jay Riemersma (Tight End)
A knee injury kept Riemersma out of five games in 2000, even so he recorded 30 receptions and 5 touchdowns.

CAROLINA PANTHERS

IR—John Kasay (Kicker)
Kasay, one of the leagues most consistent kickers missed the entire 2000 season with a broken kneecap. In his absence, the Panthers first turned to Ritchie Cunningham and eventually to Joe Nedney to handle the kicking chores. Looking to 2000, Nedney is gone, so Kasay resumes his role.

IR—Wesley Walls (Tight End)
Walls, regarded as one of the top tight ends in the NFL, missed half the 2000 season with a knee injury, limiting him to only 31 receptions and two touchdowns. A year earlier Walls scored 12 times.

IR—Patrick Jeffers (Wide Receiver)
After recording 63 receptions for 1,082 yards and 12 touchdowns in 1999, Jeffers missed the entire 2000 season with a torn ACL suffered in the preseason.

I—Tim Biakabatuka (Running Back)
Bothered by a severe turf toe injury, Biakabatuka missed four games in 2000, resulting in 968 rushing-receiving yards and four touchdowns. Biakabatuka has suffered with injury through most of his career, which makes you wonder how long before Carolina looks elsewhere for a running game.

CHICAGO BEARS

IR—Marcus Robinson (Wide Receiver)
Robinson, who exploded for 84 receptions for 1,400 yards and nine touchdowns in 1999, was not so fortunate in 2000. Robinson missed one game early in the year with an ankle injury and wound up on the injured-reserve, missing four games with a bulging disk in his back. Robinson finished with 55 receptions for 738 yards and five touchdowns.

IR—Bobby Engram (Wide Receiver)
Engram, who led the Bears with 88 receptions in 1999, missed the entire 2000 season with a knee injury suffered in the preseason.

I—Cade McNown (Quarterback)
McNown missed six games midseason in 2000 with a shoulder injury.

CINCINNATI BENGALS

IR—Darnay Scott (Wide Receiver)
The Bengals lost their 1999 leading receiver for the entire 2000 season when Scott suffered a broken leg during the preseason. In 1999, Scott recorded 68 receptions for 1,022 yards and seven touchdowns.

CLEVELAND BROWNS

IR—Tim Couch (Quarterback)
Couch missed over half the 2000 season after suffering a fractured right thumb during a practice.

IR—Errict Rhett (Running Back)
Rhett missed the last 11 games of the 2000 season with a foot injury. Rhett's absence opened the door for rookie, Travis Prentise, who recorded 703 rushing-receiving yards and eight touchdowns.

I—Darrin Chiaverini (Wide Receiver)
Chiaverini, who recorded 44 receptions and four touchdowns as a rookie in 1999, missed almost the entire 2000 season with a knee injury, seeing action in only three games.

DALLAS COWBOYS

IR—Joey Galloway (Wide Receiver)
The speedster Galloway came over from Seattle in the offseason to help open up the Cowboys' passing attack. Galloway's presence was short-lived as he saw action in only the season opener in which he suffered a season-ending knee injury.

I—Troy Aikman (Quarterback)
When is it going to end for Troy Aikman? Soon we all hope. Aikman suffered another couple of concussions in 2000 and along with a lower back contusion was forced to miss five games. He says he's coming back for more.

I—Rocket Ismail (Wide Receiver)
After leading the Cowboys with 80 receptions for 1,097 yards and seven touchdowns in 1999, Ismail's numbers dropped in a big way in 2000. Ismail suffered a knee injury forcing him to miss the last eight games, which limited him to 25 receptions for 250 yards and two touchdowns.

DENVER BRONCOS

I—Olandis Gary (Running Back)
Gary, who had a superb rookie year in 1999 stepping in for the injured Terrell Davis, was not so fortunate in 2000. Gary, suffered a season-ending knee surgery in the 2000 season opener. A year earlier, Gary recorded 1,159 rushing yards and seven touchdowns. Gary's injury combined with that of Terrell Davis led to the emergence of Mike Anderson.

I—Terrell Davis (Running Back)
After battling back from a severe knee injury suffered in 1999, Davis again found the injury bug in 2000, missing 11 games with ankle and leg injuries. The absence of Davis and Gary led to the emergence of sixth-round pick Mike Anderson, who had an incredible year recording 1,669 rushing-receiving yards and 15 touchdowns.

I—Brian Griese (Quarterback)
A shoulder injury forced Griese to miss one game early in the 2000 season and five later on, which greatly limited his statistical success.

I—Jason Elam (Kicker)
Elam, who suffered two broken bones in his lower back in a game against Atlanta, was forced to miss three games in 2000.

DETROIT LIONS

I—Germane Crowell (Wide Receiver)
The Lions 1998 first-round pick had a breakout season in 1999, recording 81 receptions for 1,336 yards and seven touchdowns. Crowell was not so fortunate in 2000, missing seven games with a foot injury, dropping him to 34 catches for 430 yards and 3 touchdowns.

GREEN BAY PACKERS

IR—Corey Bradford (Wide Receiver)
Bradford missed the entire 2000 season with a broken leg suffered in the preseason. In 1999, Bradford had recorded 37 receptions for 637 yards and five touchdowns.

I—Dorsey Levens (Running Back)
Levens, who had rebounded from leg and ankle injuries from 1998, to record 1,034 rushing yards, along with 71 receptions for 573 yards while scoring ten times in 1999. Levens again fell victim to the injury bug in 2000, missing 11 games with knee and ankle injuries. Levens's absence led to the emergence of Ahman Green, who came from Seattle in the off-season. Green's performance of 1,734 rushing-receiving yards and 13 touchdowns, leaves Levens's future with the Packers a question mark.

INDIANAPOLIS COLTS

No Significant Injuries To Key Veterans

JACKSONVILLE JAGUARS

I—Fred Taylor (Running Back)
Taylor missed the first three games of 2000, recovering from a sprained knee. Remarkably, despite the three-game absence, Taylor still recorded 1,639 rushing-receiving yards and 14 touchdowns. What would he have done over a full 16 games?

I—Jimmy Smith (Wide Receiver)
A knee injury slowed Smith's production in 2000. Missing two games, Smith still recorded 91 receptions for 1,213 yards and eight touchdowns. A year earlier playing in 16 games, Smith recorded 116 receptions for 1,636 yards but only six touchdowns.

I—Mike Hollis (Kicker)
Hollis missed four games early in 2000, following back surgery.

KANSAS CITY CHIEFS

I—Donnell Bennett (Running Back)
Bennett, who is the off-and-on starter for the Chiefs at running back, was mostly off in 2000 missing ten games with foot and knee injuries.

MIAMI DOLPHINS

IR—Bert Emanuel (Wide Receiver)
Emanuel, who struggled when with Tampa Bay in 1998 and 1999, had the same problem in coming over to Miami in 2000. Emanuel missed over half the season with wrist and rib injuries. The rib injuries put him on the injured-reserved the last four weeks of the season.

PUPL—O.J. McDuffie (Wide Receiver)
The Dolphins #1 receiver missed most of the 2000 season nursing a toe injury. Seeing limited action in only six games, McDuffie recorded only 14 receptions and no touchdowns.

I—Jay Fiedler (Quarterback)
Fiedler, who took over the starting job at quarterback for Miami, missed two games midseason with a shoulder injury. Fiedler finished the year with 2,402 passing yards and 14 touchdowns.

I—Lamar Smith (Running Back)
Perhaps one of the biggest surprises of 2000 was Lamar Smith. Smith, who recorded 1,340 rushing-receiving yards and 16 touchdowns, would have pushed those numbers even further had he not missed one game with a hamstring injury.

I—Leslie Shepherd (Wide Receiver)
Another receiver the Dolphins were hoping would give their receiving corps a boost, Shepherd missed the last three games of 2000 with a knee injury. Shepherd finished with 35 receptions for 446 yards and four touchdowns.

I—Tony Martin (Wide Receiver)
A very disappointing year for Martin, another receiver the Dolphins were betting on to help. Martin missed seven games with a foot injury, resulting in only 26 catches and no touchdowns. Martin was released in the offseason.

MINNESOTA VIKINGS

No Significant Injuries To Key Veterans

NEW ENGLAND PATRIOTS

I—Robert Edwards (Running Back)
After bursting out for 1,115 rushing yards and 12 touchdowns as a rookie in 1998, Edwards has missed the entire 1999 and 2000 seasons. Edwards suffered a severe knee injury while playing in a sand football games affiliated with the NFL Pro Bowl following the '98 season. Edwards continues to try to work his way back.

NEW ORLEANS SAINTS

IR—Cam Cleeland (Tight End)
After recording an impressive 54 receptions for 684 yards and six touchdowns as a second-round pick in 1998, Cleeland has battled injuries since. Cleeland saw action in only 10 games in 1999 due to injury, but last season was more devastating as Cleeland suffered a ruptured achilles in the preseason, forcing him to miss the entire 2000 season.

I—Jeff Blake (Quarterback)
Blake, coming over from Cincinnati in the offseason, had the Saints on the right track in 2000, before suffering a season-ending broken foot forcing him to miss the last five games. Blake finished the year with 2,025 passing yards and 13 touchdown passes.

I—Ricky Williams (Running Back)
Well on his way to a terrific sophomore campaign, Williams suffered a regular season ending broken ankle, forcing him to miss the last six games. In the ten games he did play, Williams recorded 1,409 rushing-receiving yards and nine touchdowns. Just think of what he could have done over 16.

I—Jake Reed (Wide Receiver)
Brought over in the offseason along with Joe Horn to help boost the Saints passing game, Reed suffered a broken leg, forcing him to miss over half the 2000 season. Playing in just five games, Reed recorded only 16 receptions for 206 yards and no touchdowns. Following the season Reed headed back to Minnesota resigning with the Vikings.

NEW YORK GIANTS

I—Ike Hilliard (Wide Receiver)
Despite missing two games with a bruised sternum, Hilliard still managed to produce 55 receptions for 806 yards and eight touchdowns in 2000. A year earlier, Hilliard has recorded 72 receptions for 996 yards but only three scores.

I—Brad Daluiso (Kicker)
Daluiso missed two games early in the 2000 season with an ailing back.

NEW YORK JETS

No Significant Injuries To Key Veterans

OAKLAND RAIDERS

I — Tyrone Wheatley (Running Back)
Despite missing two games midseason with an ankle injury, Wheatley put up productive numbers for the second year in a row. Playing in 14 games, Wheatley recorded 1,046 rushing yards, 20 receptions for 156 more yards and 10 touchdowns in 2000.

I — Napoleum Kaufman (Running Back)
Kaufman's production has dropped off in the last couple seasons, but a knee injury forcing him to miss the last two games of 2000 might be worth noting. Kaufman finished 2000 with 626 yards and one touchdown.

PHILADELPHIA EAGLES

IR — Duce Staley (Running Back)
The mainstay of the Eagles ground attack, Staley was sorely missed as he missed the last 11 games of 2000 with a foot injury. The injury limited Staley to 344 rushing yards, 25 receptions for 201 yards and only one touchdown. A year earlier, Staley had rushed for 1,273 yards, caught 41 passes for another 294 yards and scored six times.

I — Torrence Small (Wide Receiver)
A hamstring injury forced Small to get off to a slow start in 2000, as he missed two games early in the year. Small finished the year with 40 receptions for 569 yards and three touchdowns. Small was released following the season.

PITTSBURGH STEELERS

I — Richard Huntley (Running Back)
Huntley looked to expand his 1999 stats in 2000 but was slowed by a hamstring injury and produced only 215 rushing yards, ten receptions for 91 yards and scored only three times playing in just 12 games. In 1999, Huntley had rushed for 567 yards, grabbed 27 receptions for 253 yards and scored eight times.

I — Troy Edwards (Wide Receiver)
After recording 61 receptions for 714 yards and scoring five times in 1999, Edwards showed much promise for 2000. A variety of hip and hamstring injuries limited Edwards to action in only ten games, where he produced only 18 receptions for 215 yards and no touchdowns.

ST. LOUIS RAMS

I — Kurt Warner (Quarterback)
Coming out of nowhere in 1999 and putting up unbelievable numbers, Warner faced huge expectations in 2000. A finger injury, however, kept Warner out of five games in 2000, resulting in Warner throwing for 3,429 yards and 21 touchdowns. A year earlier in 1999, Warner threw for a whopping 4,353 yards and 41 touchdowns.

I — Marshall Faulk (Running Back)
Amazing!! Despite missing two games midseason in 2000 with a knee in-

jury, Faulk still managed to produce 2,189 rushing-receiving yards and an NFL record 26 touchdowns.

I—Jeff Wilkins (Kicker)
Wilkins missed five games to a quad injury in 2000. His point total dropped from 124 a year before to 89.

SAN DIEGO CHARGERS

I—Curtis Conway (Wide Receiver)
Brought in over the 2000 offseason to help boost the Chargers' receiving corps. Conway did that, finishing with 53 receptions for 712 yards and five touchdowns. He could have pushed these numbers even further had he not missed a couple of games with a hamstring injury.

I—Ryan Leaf (Quarterback)
Since being the Chargers' first-round draft pick and the #2 overall pick in 1998, Leaf has battled all kinds of injuries and adversities. Leaf reclaimed the starting job in 2000, but a wrist injury forced him to miss five games midseason. Leaf finished the year with 1,883 passing yards and 11 touchdowns. Leaf departed to Tampa Bay in the offseason.

I—Jeff Graham (Wide Receiver)
For two straight seasons, Jeff Graham has missed two games to injury and for two straight years he has fallen just short of 1,000 yards. Playing in 14 games in 1999, Graham recorded 57 receptions for 968 yards and two touchdowns. Missing two games to hamstring and back injuries in 2000, Graham finished with 55 catches for 907 yards and four touchdowns.

I—Robert Chancey (Running Back)
Brought over from Dallas to compete for the starting running back job in 2000, Chancey had won the job. However, a neck injury ended his season after just three games as he recorded 141 rushing yards and two touchdowns in those games.

SAN FRANCISCO 49ERS

PUPL—Garrison Hearst (Running Back)
Hearst continues to battle back from the severe ankle injury he received over two years ago. Though missing the entire 2000 season, Hearst was put on the active roster late in the year.

SUSP,I—Terrell Owens (Wide Receiver)
Missing one game to a suspension for an unexceptable touchdown celebration and one game to a toe injury limited Owen's year end numbers. Despite the two game absence Owen's still produced 97 receptions for 1,451 yards and 13 touchdowns in 2000.

SEATTLE SEAHAWKS

I—Derrick Mayes (Wide Receiver)
After having somewhat of a breakout season in 1999, coming over from Green Bay, Mayes struggled through injury and poor play in 2000. In

1999, Mayes recorded 62 receptions for 829 yards and 10 touchdowns. In 2000, playing in only 11 games recorded only 29 receptions for 264 yards and one touchdown.

TAMPA BAY BUCCANEERS

I—Mike Alstott (Running Back)
A sprained knee kept Alstott out of three games in 2000. The result was only 558 rushing-receiving yards and five touchdowns. A year earlier in 1999, Alstott recorded 1,188 rushing-receiving yards and nine touchdowns.

TENNESSEE TITANS

I—Carl Pickens (Wide Receiver)
Coming over from Cincinnati in the offseason, Pickens faced big expectations from the Titans. Sidelined with a hamstring injury most of the season, Pickens finished 2000 with only 10 receptions for 242 yards and no touchdowns playing in five games.

I—Yancey Thigpen (Wide Receiver)
Battling injuries since joining the Titans, 2000 was no different for Thigpen. Thigpen missed time early in the year with a hamstring injury and late in the year with an ankle injury. On the season, limited to just nine games, Thigpen finished with only 15 receptions for 289 yards and two touchdowns.

I—Derrick Mason (Wide Receiver)
Mason, who eventually led the Titan receivers with 63 receptions for 95 yards and six touchdowns, missed the first two games of the year with a thigh injury. Mason's emergence may have the Titans thinking about life without Yancey Thigpen and Carl Pickens.

IR—Kevin Dyson (Wide Receiver)
After playing in just one game, Dyson unfortunately suffered a season-ending knee injury in practice. On his way to a good season, Dyson had already logged six catches for 104 yards and one touchdown.

WASHINGTON REDSKINS

IR—Michael Westbrook (Wide Receiver)
After finally staying healthy in 1999 and realizing some of the potential many had expected for years, Westbrook again fell victim to injury in 2000. A knee injury sidelined Westbrook the last 14 games of 2000. A year earlier in 1999, Westbrook produced 65 receptions for 1,191 yards and nine touchdowns.

I—Brad Johnson (Quarterback)
A knee injury had Johnson in and out of the lineup in 2000, forcing him to miss four games. The absence contributed to the drop to 2,505 passing yards and 11 touchdowns, compared to 4,005 passing yards and 24 touchdowns a year earlier.

HOW THE 2000 ROOKIES FARED

A rookie doesn't always have an opportunity to prove himself in his first year of NFL action, so it's a good idea to look back and see what events — such as injuries or contract holdouts — may have affected his season. Keep in mind that many prize rookie prospects, especially contract holdouts, may have missed some action not because of injury but because they had trouble learning their team's strategies and systems. Still, these are prime, blue-chip players who somehow impressed the scouts while they were in college. Chances are that they still have potential, even if it wasn't fully realized in their first season.

Here's a look at how the rookies of 2000 performed. First, we'll take a look at the players from the first two rounds — the NFL scouts' blue-chippers — and then we'll look at potential standouts who were picked in later rounds of the draft.

ROUND 1

POSITION IN DRAFT	NAME	POS	TEAM DRAFTED BY
4	Peter Warrick	WR	Cincinnati

Sometimes talent and year-end results don't always come out the way you'd think. Warrick, the Bengals first-round pick, fared about as well as he could with the inept Cincinnati passing game. Warrick finished his rookie season with 51 receptions for 592 yards and seven touchdowns. Expect his future numbers to climb only if his team's quarterback does.

5	Jamal Lewis	RB	Baltimore

This rookie had quite an impressive rookie campaign. Lewis rushed for 1,364 yards, caught 27 passes for 296 more yards and scored six times in helping the Ravens to their Super Bowl run.

7	Thomas Jones	RB	Arizona

Jones had a disappointing inaugural year. Jones, who missed a game with pleurisy, eventually lost his starting job to Michael Pittman. To improve his rookie numbers of 373 rushing yards, 32 receptions for 208 yards and two touchdowns, he'll have to improve dramatically and beat out Pittman for work.

8	Plaxico Burress	WR	Pittsburgh

The rookie season for Burress was very disappointing, both in terms of production and injury. Burress missed the last six games of 2000 on the injured-reserve, with broken bones and ligament damage in his wrist. Prior to the injury, Burress had recorded only 22 receptions for 273 yards and no touchdowns in ten games. Before Burress can improve his numbers in 2001, the Steelers must improve their passing game.

10	Travis Taylor	WR	Baltimore

Taylor missed the last seven games of his rookie season with a broken collarbone. Prior to the injury, Taylor was far from impressive, suffering from frequent dropped passes, recording only 28 receptions for 276 yards and three touchdowns in the nine games he did play.

11   Ron Dayne   RB   NY Giants
As a rookie in 2000, Dayne had a less-than-impressive performance as he recorded 770 rushing yards, caught only three passes for 11 yards and scored five times

14   Bubba Franks   TE   Green Bay
The Packers hoped Franks would step in for the departed Mark Chmura and make an impact. Franks struggled through his inaugural year and finished with 34 catches for 363 yards and only one touchdown.

17   Sebastian Janikowski K   Oakland
Janikowski got off to a slow start as a rookie, hitting only 8 of his first 17 field goal attempts. Janikowski finished the year hitting a disappointing 22 of 32 (.688) attempts. However the Raiders are confident the strong-legged rookie will rebound in his sophomore season.

18   Chad Pennington   QB   NY Jets
Not expected to play much as a rookie, with veteran Vinny Testaverde around, Pennington remains a long-term project for the Jets.

19   Shaun Alexander   RB   Seattle
Alexander was expected to push Ricky Watters for work, but the veteran remained the mainstay of the Seahawks' ground attack. Watters recorded 1,855 rushing-receiving yards and nine touchdowns, while Alexander produced a disappointing 354 rushing-receiving yards and two touchdowns. Alexander is still expected to push Watters out of work in the near future, likey this year if Watters is dealt elsewhere.

21   Sylvester Morris   WR   Kansas City
A bit short of what the Chiefs were hoping for, Morris produced 48 receptions for 678 yards and three touchdowns as a rookie.

29   R. Jay Soward   WR   Jacksonville
Soward was expected to help stretch defenses as a #3 receiver but recorded only 14 receptions, playing in nine games before being placed on the reserve non-football list late in the year with an unspecified illness.

31   Trung Canidate   RB   St. Louis
Ankle, foot and wrist injuries allowed Canidate to see action in only two games as a rookie in 2000.

ROUND 2

32   Dennis Northcutt   WR   Cleveland
Though having trouble hanging onto many accurate passes, Northcutt still managed 39 receptions for 422 yards but no touchdowns as a rookie in 2000. He'll have to improve his consistency to be a fantasy factor in the future.

38   Todd Pinkston   WR   Philadelphia

Pinkston didn't get much of a shot as a rookie, producing only ten receptions all year.

47   Jerry Porter   WR   Oakland

Porter never really got a shot to show much in 2000 as a rookie, suffering a season-ending hamstring injury early on, forcing him to miss the last 15 games. The Raiders still believe he'll contend and push James Jett and Andre Rison for the #2 wide receiver spot.

ROUND 3

63   Travis Prentice   RB   Cleveland

Prentice got steady playing time pretty much all year, recording 512 rushing yards, 37 receptions for another 191 yards and scored eight times.

76   J. R. Redmond   RB   New England

Redmond did not acclimate himself to the NFL as quickly as the Patriots had hoped but he did manage to produce 532 rushing-receiving yards and three touchdowns. Kevin Faulk, however, got the bulk of the work.

78   Laveranues Coles   WR   NY Jets

At one point, Coles showed promise, recording 15 receptions in a three-game span, but late in the year he was a casualty to a knee injury. His future has some bright prospects.

79   JaJuan Dawson   WR   Cleveland

Dawson had an impressive training camp and nine receptions, including a touchdown in the first two regular season games. A season-ending broken collarbone forced him to miss the last 14 games of his rookie season. If healthy, he has a big future ahead.

ROUND 4

115   Frank Moreau   RB   Kansas City

Thrown occasionally into the Chiefs's running back by committee scenario, Moreau produced 179 rushing yards and four touchdowns in 2000.

ROUND 5

156   Sammy Morris   RB   Buffalo

Morris worked himself in and out of the featured back spot with Buffalo, battling Antowain Smith and Shawn Bryson. On the year, Morris recorded 341 rushing yards, along with 37 receptions for 268 yards and six touchdowns. Certainly Morris deserves fantasy attention in the future.

ROUND 6

169   Neil Rackers   K   Cincinnati

Rackers had a less than impressive rookie campaign hitting only 12 of 21 (.571) of his field goal tries. Of those nine misses, all nine were from less than 50 yards, and four were from less than 40 yards. Rackers may be looking for a new line of work unless he gets himself on track.

174   Paul Edinger   K   Chicago

Having a decent rookie season, Edinger hit 21 of 27 (.778) field goal attempts, including two 50-plus yarders in the season finale.

189   Mike Anderson   RB   Denver

A perfect example of how injuries to one player (or two) provide opportunity for another player. As a sixth-round pick on the depth chart behind Terrell Davis and Olandis Gary, Anderson was very unlikely to see action. Injuries to both Davis and Gary led to opportunity and the emergence of Anderson who made the most of it, rushing for 1,500 yards, grabbing 23 passes for 169 yards and scored 15 times. What happens when they are all healthy in 2001 is a huge question.

III
FREE AGENTS
AND OTHER PLAYER MOVES
FREE AGENCY AGAIN
SHAKES UP TEAM ROSTERS

As the 2001 offseason gets into gear, the free-agent signings have begun again. Teams are trying to balance signing competitive talent and meeting the salary cap requirements. In 1995, each team had to meet a $36.5 million salary cap. In 1996, the cap rose to $40.7 million, in 1997, the cap went to $41.45 million, and in 1998 the salary cap jumped to $51.5 million, helped by the NFL's new TV contract. In 1999 the salary cap went to $57.288 million and grew to $62.172 million in 2000. This offseason the cap grew to $67.4 million. Salary cap problems continue to linger for many teams. Teams like San Francisco, who maneuvered the salary cap to help in their success in the 90's, are now caught up in the results of those moves. These questions certainly provide for an interesting offseason.

Will teams aggressively chase players in the 2001 offseason the way they did in 2000 and the years prior? A couple of the key moves were Joe Horn (Chiefs) to the Saints and James Stewart (Jaguars) to Detroit. If this year's early signing of Brad Johnson with Tampa Bay along with the release of Elvis Grbac by Kansas City and his being signed by Baltimore is any indication, we're off and running with lots of player movement again this offseason.

Keep as current as you can. Let's start this section with a review of some of the terms and dates associated with free agency in the NFL.

- **Unrestricted Free Agents**
  Unrestricted free agents are players who have completed four or more seasons in the NFL and whose contracts have expired. On July 22, 2001, their exclusive rights revert to their original NFL clubs, assuming that the clubs have made a June 1 tender to them. Players with fewer than four years of experience also become unrestricted free agents if they have not received a qualifying offer or minimum tender offer from their current teams.

- **Restricted Free Agents**
  Restricted free agents are defined as players who have completed at least three, but fewer than four, seasons in the NFL, and whose contracts have expired. These players were given qualifying offers from their original NFL teams and were free to negotiate with any club until April 16. At that time, if a restricted free agent had not accepted an offer from another team, his original team had the right to match the offer and retain the player. If the original team chooses not to match the offer, it may receive draft-pick compensation. The value of the compensation depends on the amount of the qualifying offer made to the restricted free agent.

- **Franchise Players:** An NFL team may designate one player as its "Franchise" player. There are two types of "franchise" players.

First Option: Exclusive—A team commits to an exclusive franchise player by committing to a minimum offer of the average salary of the top-five players at the player's position.

The Second Option: If a new team submits an offer sheet to a franchise player, it must offer compensation of two number-one draft choices to that player's team. Offer sheets to these players must be submitted by 4:00 PM (EST) on July 15. Once a franchise player is so designated, his team must offer him either 120 percent of his previous year's salary, or the average salary of the top-five players in the league (whichever is greater) at his position, whichever is greater.

- **Transition Players**
An NFL team may also designate a player as a "transition" player. This gives the team the right of first refusal and the right to match any offer given to the player by another team, but not the right to draft-pick compensation. The minimum offer to a transition player must be either 120 percent of his previous year's salary, or the average salary of the top-10 players in the league at his position, whichever is greater.

2001 DATES TO KEEP IN MIND

February 1: Contracts of veteran players expire.

February 8: Teams must designate franchise and/or transitional players by this date.

February 22–26: NFL scouting combine (Indianapolis, Indiana).

March 1: Clubs must submit qualifying offers to their restricted free-agents (those for whom they wish to retain the right of first refusal). Clubs must submit minimum salary offers to players with less than three years of experience (those for whom they wish to retain exclusive negotiating rights).

March 2: NFL trading begins. Veteran free-agent signings begin.

April 16: Offer sheets must be submitted to restricted free agents by this date.

April 21–22: NFL college draft.

April 21–22: Original teams must exercise their right of first refusal on restricted free agents by this date.

June 1: Teams must make offers to their own unrestricted free agents by this date, if they wish to retain rights to those players. This gives teams exclusive negotiating rights to these players for the rest of the season, if the players are not signed by another team by July 15.

Teams must send tender to unsigned restricted free agents or extend qualifying offer to retain exclusive negotiating rights.

July 22:	Exclusive rights to unrestricted veteran free agents revert to original clubs on this date, provided that those clubs have tendered an offer by June 1.
September 9:	NFL regular season begins.

Once again this year, teams will try to find ways to avoid losing their highly coveted players who have become free agents. The Cincinnati Bengals early on tagged star running back Corey Dillon as their "franchise" player to protect their best offensive weapon. Despite moves like this, many good players will again jump ship in 2001. In 2000, Joe Horn's jump to New Orleans from Kansas City helped the Saints passing game immensely. Horn joined another offseason acquisition, quarterback Jeff Blake (Bengals), who at least until he got hurt, helped to push the Saints passing attack. Horn finished 2000 with a surprising 94 receptions, for 1,340 yards and eight touchdowns. Tight end Shannon Sharpe's jump from the Denver Broncos to Baltimore provided leadership to help lead the Ravens to the Super Bowl. Sharpe finished with 67 receptions for 810 yards and five touchdowns. Lamar Smith's arrival in Miami helped legitimize the Dolphins running game. Smith rushed for 1,139 yards, caught 31 passes for 201 yards and scored 16 times, surprising the fantasy football world.

On the flip side, Joey Galloway going to Dallas from Seattle was a bust only because of a season-ending injury early on. Other busts would include Jake Reed (Saints) from Minnesota and Errict Rhett (Browns) both also suffering serious injuries.

Another group to keep in mind is this year's crop of rookie draft picks. Each of these first-year players must sign a contract before appearing in training camp. Missed time in training camp sets any player back physically and mentally, but for a rookie it is especially harmful because it delays his number one job—learning his new team's system so he can play as soon as possible. Long holdouts by rookies have lessened; since the NFL is forcing them to sign early in August or sit out the season.

In summary, it's important to keep an eye on both veteran free agents and on early-round draft choices. As the veterans are signed, we need to evaluate their effects on both the teams they are leaving and the teams they are joining. What vacancies are these teams filling? How must they manipulate their salary structure to sign the new player and stay under the salary cap? The biggest concern with rookies is to get them signed early and into training camp. It is a great advantage to keep up with possible holdouts or free agents who may have signed with a new team in 2001. As the season approaches and these players begin missing preseason conditioning and games, tracking their progress becomes even more important. Following are lists of the various free agents whose contracts have expired, along with their 2001 signing status. Also, a list of key players who are not free agents but who have either been released or have switched teams via another means, follows.

NOTE: This list of free-agent signings, along with incoming rookies signings, will be updated in our first Fantasy Sports, Inc. preseason newsletter, available in early August—a must if you want to prepare properly for your fantasy draft.

2001 FREE AGENTS

Free-Agent Types	Status Key	
U—Unrestricted	**S w/**=Signed with	**TR**=Traded
R—Restricted	**RS**=Resigned with Current Team	**NCO**=No Contract Offer
T—Transitional	**RT**=Retired	**Blank**=No Status Update Yet
F—Franchise	**RL**=Released	

RUNNING BACKS

NAME	TEAM	TYPE	STATUS	NAME	TEAM	TYPE	STATUS
Michael Pittman	ARIZ	R		Antonio Carter	NE	U	
Ron Rivers	ATL	U		Harold Shaw	NE	R	
Charles Evans	BALT	U		Terry Allen	NO	U	
Sam Gash	BALT	U		Fred McAfee	NO	R	
Priest Holmes	BALT	U	S w/KC	Brian Milne	NO	R	
Jonathan Linton	BUF	R		Jerald Moore	NO	R	
James Allen	CHI	R		Tiki Barber	NYG	U	RS
Curtis Enis	CHI	R	S w/CLE	Greg Comella	NYG	R	
Corey Dillon	CIN	F		Leon Johnson	NYJ	U	
Steve Bush	CIN	U		Zack Crockett	OAK	U	
Marc Edwards	CLE	U	S w/NE	Terry Kirby	OAK	U	RS
Robert Thomas	DALL	R		Chris Warren	PHIL	U	
Howard Griffith	DEN	U	RS	Jerome Bettis	PITT	U	RS
Mario Bates	DET	U		Chris Fuamatu-Ma'afala	PITT	R	S w/NE
Cory Schlesinger	DET	U		Kenny Bynum	SD	U	
Brock Olivo	DET	R	RS	Fred Beasley	SF	R	
Ahman Green	GB	R		Charlie Garner	SF	U	S w/OAK
Anthony Johnson	JAC	U		Rahih Abdullah	TB	R	RS
Daimon Shelton	JAC	U		Skip Hicks	WASH	R	
Jermaine Williams	JAC	R		Adrian Murrell	WASH	U	
				Mike Sellers	WASH	R	

OTHER KEY RUNNING BACK MOVES (NOT INVOLVING FREE AGENTS)

NAME	TEAM	STATUS
Kimble Anders	KC	RL
Donnell Bennett	KC	RL
Robert Chancey	SD	RL
Curtis Enis	CHI	RL then S w/CLE then RT
Napoleum Kaufman	OAK	RT
Robert Smith	MINN	RT
Thurman Thomas	BUF	RT

WIDE RECEIVERS

NAME	TEAM	TYPE	STATUS	NAME	TEAM	TYPE	STATUS
Tim Dwight	ATL	R		Willie Jackson	NO	U	RS
Jammi German	ATL	R	RS	Jake Reed	NO	U	S w/MINN
Patrick Johnson	BALT	R		Joe Jurevicius	NYG	R	
Marcus Nash	BALT	R		Dwight Stone	NYJ	U	
Eric Moulds	BUF	U	RS	Dedric Ward	NYJ	U	
Michael Bates	CAR	U		David Dunn	OAK	U	
Isaac Byrd	CAR	U		Yatil Green	OAK	U	
Donald Hayes	CAR	R		James Jett	OAK	U	RS
Eric Metcalf	CAR	U	S w/OAK	Terry Mickens	OAK	U	
Jim Turner	CAR	R		Andre Rison	OAK	U	
Iheanyi Uwaezuoke	CAR	U		Will Blackwell	PITT	U	
Macey Brooks	CHI	U		Courtney Hawkins	PITT	U	
Eddie Kennison	CHI	U	S w/DEN	Bobby Shaw	PITT	R	
David Patten	CLE	U	S w/NE	Hines Ward	PITT	R	
James McKnight	DALL	U	S w/MIA	Reggie Jones	SD	R	RS
Desmond Howard	DET	U	RS	Kevin Williams	SF	U	
Brian Stablein	DET	U		Az-Zahir Hakim	STL	R	
Corey Bradford	GB	R		Tony Horne	STL	R	
E.G. Green	IND	R	RS	Chris Thomas	STL	U	
Kevin Lockett	KC	U	S w/WASH	Fabien Bownes	SEAT	U	
Bert Emanuel	MIA	U	S w/NE	Sean Dawkins	SEAT	U	
Jeff Ogden	MIA	R		Derrick Mason	TENN	U	RS
Leslie Shepherd	MIA	U		Albert Connell	WASH	U	S w/NO
Lamar Thomas	MIA	U		Andre Reed	WASH	U	
Matt Hatchette	MINN	U	S w/NYJ	Kenny Shedd	WASH	U	
Nate Jacquet	MINN	U		James Thrash	WASH	U	S w/PHIL
Chris Walsh	MINN	U					

OTHER KEY WIDE RECEIVER MOVES (NOT INVOLVING FREE AGENTS)

NAME	TEAM	STATUS
Sean Dawkins	SEAT	RL
Irving Fryar	WASH	RL
Charles Johnson	PHIL	RL
Tony Martin	MIA	RL
Derrick Mayes	SEAT	RL
Carl Pickens	TENN	RL then S w/DALL
Torrance Small	PHIL	RL
Yancey Thigpen	TENN	RL

TIGHT ENDS

NAME	TEAM	TYPE	STATUS	NAME	TEAM	TYPE	STATUS
Chris Gedney	ARIZ	U		Alonzo Mayes	MIA	R	
Terry Hardy	ARIZ	R		Ed Perry	MIA	U	
Brian Kozlowski	ATL	U	RS	John Davis	MINN	U	RS
Ben Coates	BALT	U		Andrew Jordan	MINN	U	RS
Frank Wainwright	BALT	U		Johnnie McWilliams	MINN	U	
Kris Mangam	CAR	R		Eric Bjornson	NE	U	S w/OAK
John Allred	CHI	U		Cam Cleeland	NO	R	
Kaseem Sinceno	CHI	R	RS	Pete Mitchell	NYG	U	S w/DET
O.J. Santiago	CLE	U	RS	Bradford Banta	NYJ	U	
Byron Chamberlain	DEN	U	S w/MINN	Rickey Dudley	OAK	U	S w/CLE
Walter Rasby	DET	U	S w/WASH	Luther Broughton	PHIL	U	
Tyrone Davis	GB	U	RS	Jeff Thomason	PHIL	U	
Ryan Wetnight	GB	U		Roland Williams	STL	R	
Marcus Pollard	IND	F		Itula Mills	SEAT	R	
Jason Dunn	KC	U	RS	Patrick Hape	TB	U	S w/DEN
Troy Drayton	KC	U		Blake Spence	TB	R	
				James Jenkins	WASH	U	

NAME	TEAM	STATUS
Fred Baxter	Free Agent	S w/CHI

QUARTERBACKS

NAME	TEAM	TYPE	STATUS	NAME	TEAM	TYPE	STATUS
Danny Kanell	ATL	U		Todd Bouman	MINN	R	
Trent Dilfer	BALT	U		Bubby Brister	MINN	U	
Alex Van Pelt	BUF	U		John Friesz	NE	U	RL
Shane Matthews	CHI	U	RS	Billy Joe Tolliver	NO	U	
Randall Cunningham	DALL	U		Ray Lucas	NYJ	R	S w/MIA
Stoney Case	DET	U		Jim Harbaugh	SD	U	S w/DET
Scott Mitchell	CIN	U		Moses Moreno	SD	R	
Tony Graziani	CLE	U		Rick Mirer	SF	U	
Brian Griese	DEN	R	RS	Jon Kitna	SEAT	U	S w/CIN
Gus Frerotte	DEN	U	RS	Brad Johnson	WASH	U	S w/TB
Danny Wuerffel	GB	U					
Billy Joe Hobert	IND	U					
Mike Quinn	MIA	U					

OTHER KEY QUARTERBACKS MOVES (NOT INVOLVING FREE AGENTS)

NAME	TEAM	STATUS
Troy Aikman	DALL	RT
Tony Banks	BALT	RL then S w/DALL
Steve Beuerlein	CAR	RL
Doug Flutie	BUF	RL then S w/SD
Elvis Grbac	KC	RL then S w/BALT
Matt Hasslebeck	GB	TR to SEAT
Damon Huard	MIA	RL then S w/NE
Ryan Leaf	SD	RL then S w/TB
Mike Tomczak	DET	RL
Eric Zeier	TB	TR to ATL

KICKERS

NAME	TEAM	TYPE	STATUS	NAME	TEAM	TYPE	STATUS
Morten Andersen	ATL	U		Brett Conway	NYJ	U	S w/WASH
Steve Christie	BUF	U	RS	John Carney	SD	U	
Joe Nedney	CAR	U	S w/TENN	Wade Richey	SF	R	S w/SD
Ryan Longwell	GB	U	RS	Jeff Wilkins	STL	U	RS
Olindo Mare	MIA	U	RS	Eddie Murray	WASH	U	
Brad Daluiso	NYG	U					

OTHER KEY KICKERS MOVES (NOT INVOLVING FREE AGENTS)

NAME	TEAM	STATUS
Doug Brien	NO	RL
Ritchie Cunningham	FA	S w/CIN
Aaron Elling	FA	S w/MIA
Jay Feely	FA	S w/ATL
Al Del Greco	TENN	RL
Chad Holliman	FA	S w/ATL
Danny Kight	FA	S w/IND
Andy Kohl	FA	S w/PITT
John Matich	FA	S w/MINN
Brian Natkin	FA	S w/DET
Jamie Rheem	FA	S w/SF
Derek Schorels	FA	S w/CLE
Matt Simonton	FA	S w/NYG
Justin Skinner	FA	S w/PHIL
Brett Sterba	FA	S w/GB
Jay Taylor	FA	S w/BUF
Lawrence Tynes	FA	S w/KC

IV
OFFSEASON NOTES
Key Player Movements and Their Effects
Significant Injury Updates, New NFL Head Coaches

Troy Aikman (Quarterback)
Retired from: Dallas Cowboys
A household name for over a decade, Troy Aikman opted to retire this offseason following the suffering of countless concussions. Aikman, who had been the part of three Super Bowl teams, is headed for TV, landing a job with FOX.

Kimble Anders (Running Back)
Released by: Kansas City Chiefs
Under new head coach Dick Vermeil, the Chiefs are looking to abandon their running-back-by-committee approach and released Kimble Anders in the offseason. Anders rushed for 76 yards and scored twice in 2000.

Tony Banks (Quarterback)
Released by: Baltimore Ravens
Signed by: Dallas Cowboys
Banks had a strong finish in 1999, when he threw for 2,136 yards and 17 touchdowns playing in just 11 games. Many thought 2000 would be a big year for him. He got off to a pretty good start but then struggled badly losing his starting job to Trent Dilfer. Banks was released following the season as the Ravens signed free-agent Elvis Grbac (Kansas City). Later, Banks was signed by the Dallas Cowboys, who were looking for someone to step in for the departed Troy Aikman, who was released following the season. The Cowboys feel Banks at 27 is young enough and experienced enough in the NFL to be developed into a solid, consistent quarterback. Of course, they also love his strong arm, especially with speedsters Joey Galloway and Rocket Ismail.

Donnell Bennett (Running Back)
Released by: Kansas City Chiefs
Bennett, an off-and-on starter for the Chiefs, was released in the offseason. Bennett struggled late in 2000 with a knee injury requiring arthoscopic surgery, finishing with only 41 rushing-receiving yards and two touchdowns.

Steve Beuerlein (Quarterback)
Released by: Carolina Panthers
In a move to both save money and turn to its youth, the Panthers released veteran Steve Beuerlein in the offseason. Beuerlein, had posted career numbers in 1999, throwing for 4,436 yards and 36 touchdowns but dropped to 3,730 yards and only 19 touchdowns in 2000. With Beuerlein gone, the Panthers will likely turn to Jeff Lewis, who's been waiting in the wings since coming to Carolina three years ago. Lewis, once the heir apparent to John Elway in Denver, came to Carolina looking for a starting job. Many believe he's full of potential.

Eric Bjornson (Tight End)
Free agent with: New England Patriots
Signed by: Oakland Raiders
After spending just one year with the Patriots coming over from Dallas, Bjornson takes his services to Oakland for 2001. With Ricky Dudley off to Cleveland, Bjornson provides some veteran stability. In 2000, with New England, Bjornson recorded 20 receptions for 152 yards and scored twice.

Doug Brien (Kicker)
Released by: New Orleans Saints
With Brien's accuracy on field goal tries on a downward trend, the Saints released him following the season. After hitting an impressive 20 of 22 (.909) attempts in 1998, Brien hit 24 of 29 (.828) in 1999 and 23 of 29 (.793) last season. The Saints are on the lookout for a replacement.

Larry Centers (Running Back)
Released by: Washington Redskins
Regarded as one of the league's best receiving backs, Centers was released following the 2000 season. In 2000, Centers recorded only 103 rushing yards but grabbed 80 receptions for 600 yards, while scoring three times.

Byron Chamberlain (Tight End)
Free agent with: Denver Broncos
Signed with: Minnesota Vikings
Chamberlain, who grabbed 22 receptions for 283 yards and caught one touchdown with Denver in 2000, comes to Minnesota in 2001. With the Vikings, Chamberlain could quickly see plenty of playing time, which could result in 40 plus receptions and an opportunity for many yards and scores as the Vikings likely will pass more with Robert Smith now gone.

Robert Chancey (Running Back)
Released by: San Diego Chargers
Chancey, brought in by the Chargers from Dallas prior to the 2000 season to challenge for the starting job, was released after a very disappointing season. Chancey had rushed for 141 yards and scored twice in three games before missing the remainder of the season with a neck injury.

Albert Connell (Wide Receiver)
Free agent with: Washington Redskins
Signed with: New Orleans Saints
The Saints, looking for someone to tandem with Joe Horn, have signed Albert Connell. Connell, who had a breakout year in 1999 with Washington, recording 62 receptions, for 1,132 yards and seven touchdowns, dropped to 39 receptions for 762 yards and three touchdowns in 2000, missing a few games to a knee injury.

Brett Conway (Kicker)
Free agent with: New York Jets
Signed with: Washington Redskins
Conway kicked in four total games in 2000, spending time with Oakland, Washington and the New York Jets. He signed with Washington for the upcoming 2001 season. Conway, who hit all six of his field goal tries, likely steps in for veteran Eddie Murray, who finished out the 2000 season as the Redskins' kicker.

Ritchie Cunningham (Kicker)
Free agent signed with: Cincinnati Bengals
The Bengals, not happy with the performance of Neil Rackers, their sixth-round pick of a year ago, have signed veteran Ritchie Cunningham, who has spent a couple of stints in the NFL. Rackers hit a woeful 12 of 21 (.571) field goal tries in 2000.

Sean Dawkins (Wide Receiver)
Released by: Seattle Seahawks
Looking to save money and turn to their younger players, the Seahawks released Sean Dawkins and Derrick Mayes in the offseason. Dawkins led Seattle with 63 receptions for 731 yards and one touchdown in 2000.

Al Del Greco (Kicker)
Released by: Tennessee Titans
Though the veteran Del Greco hit a respectable 27 of 33 (.818) field goals in 2000, he had a part in three of the Titans' losses, leading to his release following the season. With Del Greco let go, Tennessee signed veteran Joe Nedney. Nedney is coming off a strong season, where in relief of Jason Elam in Denver and John Kasay in Carolina, he hit an impressive 34 of 38 (.895) field goal tries in 2000.

Ricky Dudley (Tight End)
Free agent with: Oakland Raiders
Signed with: Cleveland Browns
After dropping from 39 receptions for 555 yards and nine touchdowns in 1999, to 29 receptions for 350 yards and four touchdowns in 2000, Dudley fell out of favor in Oakland and has signed with Cleveland for the upcoming 2001 season. The Browns are likely to be more conservative on offense than the Raiders, so don't expect huge numbers for Dudley in 2001.

Tim Dwight (Wide Receiver)
Traded from: Atlanta Falcons
Acquired by: San Diego Chargers
Part of the deal that landed Michael Vick in Atlanta, Tim Dwight heads to San Diego. The speedy Dwight missed half the 2000 season with a leg injury and an emergency appendectomy. Healthy a year earlier, Dwight recorded nine touchdowns on just 32 receptions. Dwight is also an excellent kick returner.

Bert Emanuel (Wide Receiver)
Free agent with: Miami Dolphins
Signed with: New England Patriots
Emanuel, who came to Miami from Tampa Bay last season and who saw action in only six games in 2000 because of wrist and rib injuries, joins the New England Patriots for the 2001 season. Emanuel, who has struggled through injuries fairly consistently in recent years, recorded only seven receptions for 132 yards and one touchdown in 2000. Emanuel hasn't done much since producing 65 receptions for 991 yards and nine touchdowns for Atlanta in 1997. I don't expect very much from him in 2001, battling for playing time behind Terry Glenn with Troy Brown and another offseason acquisition, David Patten coming over from Cleveland.

Curtis Enis (Running Back)
Released by: Chicago Bears
Signed with: Cleveland Browns
The Bears released their former #1 draft pick, following another disappointing season in 2000, a season where he managed only 152 rushing-receiving yards and one touchdown. Heading to Cleveland, a team looking to head in new direction, I can't see Enis being much of a help here either, though he'll get a shot to push for work.

Jay Feely (Kicker)
Free agent with: Atlanta Falcons
Feely joins practice squad player Jake Arians, who was brought in to battle veteran Morten Andersen for the Falcons' kicking job in 2001.

Doug Flutie (Quarterback)
Free agent with: Buffalo Bills
Signed with: San Diego Chargers
Following the 2000 season, with former Chargers' first-round draft pick Ryan Leaf finally officially a bust, San Diego signed aging veteran Doug Flutie. Flutie departs Buffalo, where, though he produced success, was always being pushed aside in favor of Rob Johnson. Flutie threw for 1,700 yards and eight touchdowns, seeing spot duty in 11 games in 2000. In San Diego, the Chargers welcome a chance in 2001 to try and quickly turn around or at least get on the right track, following a 1-15 season in 2000.

Irving Fryar (Wide Receiver)
Released by: Washington Redskins
With a number of receivers nursing injuries in 2000, the Redskins called on the aging Fryar to help out. Fryar did produce 41 receptions for 548 yards and five touchdowns but was released following the season.

Charlie Garner (Running Back)
Free agent with: San Francisco 49ers
Signed with Oakland Raiders
Garner, coming off his best season ever, has jumped ship, going from the San Francisco 49ers to the Oakland Raiders. In Oakland, Garner will push Tyrone Wheatley for work. Wheatley has had back to back productive years and is the suspected #1 back for now. Garner produced 1,789 rushing-receiving yards and scored ten times in 2000 with the 49ers.

Elvis Grbac (Quarterback)
Released by: Kansas City Chiefs
Signed by: Baltimore Ravens
Despite coming off a career year in 2000, Elvis Grbac was released by the Kansas City Chiefs following the season. The Chiefs, under new head coach Dick Vermeil, didn't want to ante up to retain Grbac. Grbac, who threw for an impressive 4,169 yards and 28 touchdowns for the Chiefs in 2000, comes to Baltimore to help give their offense a boost and he will. Certainly the Ravens already possess a great defense and with Grbac now aboard on offense, they're looking to make another run at the Super Bowl. Along the way, Grbac should put up good numbers and help his receivers do the same, surely to the delight of fantasy fans.

Trent Green (Quarterback)
Traded from: St. Louis Rams
Acquired by: Kansas City Chiefs
Following the release of Elvis Grbac, the Chiefs and new head coach Dick Vermeil were on the prowl for a replacement as the starting quarterback. The Chiefs landed Trent Green. He was actually the starter for St. Louis back in 1999, before a knee injury gave way to Kurt Warner's "Cinderella" season. As the starter for the Washington Redskins back in 1998, Green threw for 3,441 yards and 23 touchdowns.

Jim Harbaugh (Quarterback)
Free agent with: San Diego Chargers
Signed with: Detroit Lions
Harbaugh, the off-and-on starter for the Chargers the last couple of seasons, takes his services to Detroit to serve as backup to Charlie Batch.

Matt Hasselbeck (Quarterback)
Traded from: Green Bay Packers
Acquired by: Seattle Seahawks
Believing Jon Kitna was no longer the short or long term answer at quarterback, the Seahawks opted to head in a new direction. With Jon Kitna off to Cincinnati via free agency, the Seahawks signed Green Bay backup Matt Hasselbeck. Hasselbeck, many feel, who hit 10 of 19 passes for 104 yards and one touchdown in 2000 serving as backup to Brett Favre in Green Bay, has huge upside potential. For Mike Holmgren, it's another chance to groom a quarterback to take him back to the promised land.

Matthew Hatchette (Wide Receiver)
Free agent with: Minnesota Vikings
Signed with: New York Jets
With Jake Reed off to New Orleans in 2000, Matthew Hatchette was expected to step in to the #3 receiver role and put up decent numbers. Hatchette's 16 receptions for 190 yards and two touchdowns were very disappointing as Randy Moss and Cris Carter stole more of the show than was expected. Hatchette now takes his services to New York, where with the Jets he'll have a chance to step in and do much more statistically in 2001.

Damon Huard (Quarterback)
Released by: Miami Dolphins
With Dan Marino retired, Huard lost the battle of the starting job to Jay Fiedler in 2000 and became expendable heading in to 2001. The Dolphins signed Ray Lucas (Jets) in the offseason.

Brad Johnson (Quarterback)
Free agent with: Washington Redskins
Signed with: Tampa Bay Buccaneers
The Buccaneers may have found their missing piece in signing Brad Johnson in the offseason. Johnson, who put up big numbers in his first year with the Redskins in 1999, recording 4,005 passing yards and 24 touchdowns, struggled in 2000. A knee injury limited Johnson to 2,605 passing yards and only 11 touchdowns playing in 12 games. Healthy in 2001, Johnson should bring healthy numbers to the Bucs' offense.

Charles Johnson (Wide Receiver)
Released by: Philadelphia Eagles
After acquiring free agent James Thrash (Washington) and drafting Freddie Mitchell out of UCLA, the Eagles released Charles Johnson. Johnson brought to Philadelphia two years ago, has been disappointing as the team's #1 wide receiver.

Napoleon Kaufman (Running Back)
Retired from: Oakland Raiders
Kaufman, who had been pushed to take a backseat behind Tyrone Wheatley the last two seasons, has opted to retire. Kaufman rushed for 499 yards, caught 13 passes for 127 yards and scored once in 2000.

Eddie Kennison (Wide Receiver)
Free agent: Chicago Bears
Signed with: Denver Broncos
Speedy Eddie Kennison makes his third move in three years. From St. Louis, to New Orleans, to Chicago and now to Denver where he'll likely step in as the #3 receiver behind Rod Smith and Ed McCaffrey. Kennison led the Bears in 2000 with 55 receptions for 549 yards and two touchdowns.

Jon Kitna (Quarterback)
Free agent with: Seattle Seahawks
Signed with: Cincinnati Bengals
The Seahawks and Mike Holmgren gave Jon Kitna virtually two years to lock onto the starting role but Kitna's inconsistency led to Seattle opting to try to develop young Matt Hasselbeck, coming over from Green Bay this recent offseason. Kitna departs to Cincinnati, where he'll challenge young Akili Smith for the starting job. In 2000, Kitna threw for 2,658 yards and 18 touchdowns playing in 15 games.

Ryan Leaf (Quarterback)
Released by: San Diego Chargers
Signed with: Tampa Bay Buccaneers
After three tortuous years, the Chargers finally let their 1998 first-round draft pick Ryan Leaf go following the 2000 season. The Chargers gave him another shot in 2000, but he couldn't answer their hopes, throwing for 1,883 yards and 11 touchdowns playing in 11 games. Following his release, Leaf signed with Tampa Bay, where he thought he'd have a chance to battle Shawn King for the starting job. To his surprise, the Bucs also signed Brad Johnson a short time later, which leaves Leaf likely looking for another team.

Kevin Lockett (Wide Receiver)
Unrestricted free agent with: Kansas City Chiefs
Signed with: Washington Redskins
With the offseason free agent losses of James Thrash (Eagles) and Albert Connell (Saints), the Redskins were in need of help at wide receiver. The Redskins signed Kevin Lockett, who'll battle for work. In 2000, Lockett grabbed 33 receptions for 422 yards and scored twice for Kansas City.

Ray Lucas (Quarterback)
Free agent with: New York Jets
Signed with: Miami Dolphins
The Miami Dolphins released Damon Huard in the offseason and have brought in Ray Lucas to battle Jay Fiedler for the starting job in 2001. Lucas, who threw for 1,678 yards and 14 touchdowns playing in nine games when Vinny Testaverde was out hurt in 1999, threw for only 206 yards and no touchdowns, seeing action in five games in 2000.

Tony Martin (Wide Receiver)
Released by: Miami Dolphins
The Dolphins released Martin, following a disappointing season where he produced only 26 receptions for 393 yards and no touchdowns, missing seven games with a foot injury in 2000. The Dolphins, looking to rebolster their receiving crew, have brought in James McKnight from Dallas and Dedric Ward from the New York Jets in the offseason.

Derrick Mayes (Wide Receiver)
Released by: Seattle Seahawks
One year after coming to Seattle from Green Bay and leading the Seahawks with 62 receptions for 829 yards and scoring ten times in 1999, Derrick Mayes was released. He was released following a season where he struggled through injuries and lost his starting job, recording only 29 receptions for 264 yards and one touchdown.

James McKnight (Wide Receiver)
Free agent with: Dallas Cowboys
Signed with: Miami Dolphins
In 2000 James McKnight stepped up, with Joey Galloway and Rocket Ismail hurt, to lead the Dallas Cowboys with 52 receptions for 926 yards and two touchdowns. With Galloway and Ismail expected back healthy in 2001, McKnight saw the writing on the wall and took his services to Miami for 2001. McKnight should get a good shot at playing time, with Tony Martin released in the offseason, with O.J. McDuffie and Leslie Shepherd coming off injuries and with Bert Emanuel off to New England.

Pete Mitchell (Tight End)
Free agent with: New York Giants
Signed with: Detroit Lions
Mitchell, a nice pass-catching tight end, takes his services to Detroit in 2001. He'll join David Sloan to give the Lions a solid pair of tight ends. Mitchell, who caught only 25 passes in 2000 because of a knee injury, caught 58 in 1999, along with six touchdowns.

Joe Nedney (Kicker)
Free agent with: Carolina Panthers
Signed with: Tennessee Titans
Nedney did a fantastic job in 2000, first filling in for the injured Jason Elam in Denver and then the bulk of the year filling in for the injured John Kasay in Carolina. Along the way, Nedney hit a remarkable 34 of 38 (.895) field goals and all 24 of his extra point attempts. With Kasay expected back healthy in 2001, Nedney moved on, signing with Tennessee, replacing Al Del Greco, who was released following the 2000 season. Nedney, kicking for the potent Titans, should put up strong 2001 fantasy numbers.

David Patten (Wide Receiver)
Free agent with : Cleveland Browns
Signed with: New England Patriots
Patten, who recorded 38 receptions for 546 yards and one touchdown with Cleveland in 2000, comes to New England to battle another offseason acquisition, Bert Emanuel (Miami) for work behind starter Terry Glenn.

Carl Pickens (Wide Receiver)
Released by: Tennessee Titans
Signed with: Dallas Cowboys
Once among the league's elite receivers, Pickens has quickly fallen. The disgruntled Pickens got his wish to leave Cincinnati in 2000 but in coming to Tennessee managed only ten receptions for 242 yards and failed to score, as he was bothered by a hamstring injury most of the year. Pickens was released following the season by Tennessee and later signed with Dallas. The Cowboys are looking for insurance with both Joey Galloway and Rocket Ismail returning from injuries.

Jake Reed (Wide Receiver)
Free agent with: New Orleans Saints
Signed with: Minnesota Vikings
Just a year after going to New Orleans to help bolster the Saints' passing attack, Reed returns to Minnesota. Reed missed over half the 2000 season with a broken leg, finishing with only 16 receptions for 206 yards and two touchdowns, playing in just five games. Reed returns to Minnesota to likely reassume his #3 receiver role now that Matthew Hatchette moved on in the offseason joining the New York Jets.

Wade Richey (Kicker)
Free agent with: San Francisco 49ers
Signed with: San Diego Chargers
The San Diego Chargers have lured veteran kicker Wade Richey from the San Francisco 49ers to handle their kicking chores. Richey's signing marks the end of John Carney's long reign in San Diego. This comes a year after Richey had a surprisingly poor year hitting only 15 of 22 (.682) field goal tries in 2000. The year previous, Richey hit a very impressive 21 of 23 (.913) attempts. In San Francisco, this left only Jamie Rheem, a free agent kicker signed at press time, to battle for the job.

Matt Simonton (Kicker)
Free agent signed with: New York Giants
The Giants signed free agent Matt Simonton in the offseason to push veteran Brad Daluiso, who hit 17 of 23 (.739) field goals in 2000.

Torrence Small (Wide Receiver)
Released by: Philadelphia Eagles
The Eagles brought Small in two years ago from Indianapolis to help bolster their receiving crew, but he has been less than impressive. Small, missing two games to a hamstring injury in 2000, finished with 40 receptions for 569 yards and scored three times. He was released following the season. Looking to 2001, the Eagles have already brought in and signed James Thrash from Washington.

Robert Smith (Running Back)
Retired from: Minnesota Vikings
Smith, coming off his best year ever, elected to retire following the season. Smith rushed for 1,521 yards, caught 36 passes for 348 yards and scored ten times in 2000. This leaves a huge hole to fill for the Vikings, who have Moe Williams and Doug Chapman in place for now to battle for the vacancy, though their eyes are open for other options.

Yancey Thigpen (Wide Receiver)
Released by: Tennessee Titans
Thigpen, an expensive free agent brought to Tennessee two years ago, struggled with injuries since joining the Titans and was released following the 2000 season. Thigpen, seeing action in only nine games due to hamstring and ankle injuries, finished with only 15 receptions for 289 yards and two touchdowns in 2000.

Thurman Thomas (Running Back)
Retired from: Buffalo bills
Though he spent the 2000 season with the Miami Dolphins, Thomas returned to Buffalo to retire in a Bills' uniform, which he had worn for many years while tearing up the league.

James Thrash (Wide Receiver)
Free agent with: Washington Redskins
Signed with: Philadelphia Eagles
Thrash, who stepped up and stepped in for the injured Michael Westbrook in 2000, heads to Philadelphia. Thrash, who caught only three passes in 1999, jumped to 50 receptions in 2000, going for 653 yards while scoring twice. He'll be a welcome addition to the Eagles' receiving crew.

Dedric Ward (Wide Receiver)
Unrestricted free agent with: New York Jets
Signed with: Miami Dolphins
The Dolphins, whose receiving crew struggled through numerous injuries in 2000, have brought in both Dedric Ward and James McKnight to battle for jobs in 2001. Ward caught 54 passes for 801 yards and scored three times with the Jets in 2000.

Eric Zeier (Quarterback)
Traded from: Tampa Bay Buccaneers
Acquired by: Atlanta Falcons
Zeier heads to Atlanta to battle Chris Chandler for the starting job after serving as backup in Tampa Bay in 2000. Zeier, whose had some experience as an NFL starter, may be the move to youth the Falcons are looking for.

SIGNIFICANT INJURY UPDATES

What follows is a list of significant fantasy players who are recovering from injuries. When possible I have also included statements on their status by their teams. These status reports were from April 1 and May. Be sure to track further progress in our preseason Fantasy Football Newsletters.

RUNNING BACKS

Mike Anderson (Denver Broncos)
Anderson, who was a huge surprise in 2000, rushing for 1,500 yards and scoring 15 times, had surgery for cartilage damage to his knee following the season. The Broncos say he's doing well and in good shape for the upcoming 2001 season.

Jerome Bettis (Pittsburgh Steelers)
Bettis, who had surgery early in February to clear up scar tissue in his knee, signed a 6-year, $35 million deal in the offseason, leading me to believe the Steelers believe he'll be ready for 2001.

Trung Canidate (St. Louis Rams)
The Rams first-round pick of a year ago did not see action the last six weeks of the 2000 season because of a broken wrist. The Rams report he's in good shape and ready for the upcoming season.

Terrell Davis (Denver Broncos)
Davis, who missed the last six weeks of the 2000 season with a leg injury, was said to be progressing very well when contacting the Broncos in the spring.

Robert Edwards (New England Patriots)
It's been over two years since Edwards hurt his knee severely in a sand football game affiliated with the Pro Bowl. The Patriots #1 draft pick of 1998 remains with the team but still with a very uncertain future ahead of him. Edwards rushed for 1,115 yards, caught 35 passes for 331 yards and scored 12 times as a rookie in '98.

Olandis Gary (Denver Broncos)
Gary missed virtually all the 2000 season, suffering a knee injury in the season opener. There was still uncertainty when contacting the Broncos in the spring as to how soon Gary would be back. We'll keep an eye on this and provide an update in our preseason newsletters.

Garrison Hearst (San Francisco 49ers)
Hearst, who has been out over two years with complications from a leg injury, still remains a huge question mark for the 49ers. This is certainly an injury we'll track closely, as training camp nears in our preseason newsletter.

Dorsey Levens (Green Bay Packers)
Levens missed the last 11 games of 2000 with a knee injury. The Packers said he was still experiencing swelling in the knee and hoped to provide more optimistic updates as training camp nears. This is another injury we'll update in our preseason newsletters. Levens, even if healthy, has a tough task ahead of him: winning his starting job back from Ahman Green, who played so well in his absence in 2000.

Errict Rhett (Cleveland Browns)
Rhett, brought to Cleveland from Baltimore in 2000 to help boost the Browns' running attack, lasted only five games suffering a season-ending foot injury. The Browns said in early spring he is ready to go and expect him ready to battle for the starting running back job.

Duce Staley (Philadelphia Eagles)
After two straight 1,000-yard seasons, Staley fell well short in 2000, suf-

fering a season-ending foot injury that forced him to miss the last 11 games. It may have been too early to tell when asked this spring, but the Eagles stated they were counting on him to be ready for 2001.

Ricky Williams (New Orleans Saints)
Williams was on his way to a big sophomore season in 2000, until a broken ankle forced him to miss the last six games. The Saints say Williams is in good shape and ready for the 2001 campaign. In the ten games he did play, Williams rushed for 1,000 yards, caught 44 passes for 409 yards and scored nine times.

WIDE RECEIVERS

Corey Bradford (Green Bay Packers)
Bradford missed the entire 2000 season with a broken leg suffered in the preseason. The Packers reported in the spring he was in good shape and was expected to be ready to go in 2001. In 1999, Bradford recorded 37 receptions for 637 yards and scored five times.

Plaxico Burress (Pittsburgh Steelers)
Plaxico Burress missed the last six weeks of the 2000 season with a broken wrist. He is on schedule with his recovery and should be ready for minicamp the Steelers reported in spring.

Darren Chiaverini (Cleveland Browns)
Chiaverini, who showed some real promise as a rookie in 1999, wasn't so fortunate in his sophomore season, missing the last 14 weeks of the year to a knee injury. The Browns told us in spring that he's ready to go for 2001. In 1999, Chiaverini recorded 44 receptions for 487 yards and five touchdowns.

JuJuan Dawson (Cleveland Browns)
Dawson, a rookie who had an impressive preseason and was off to a solid start in 2000, lasted only two games before suffering a broken collarbone that ended his season. The Browns said in spring Dawson was in good shape heading into the 2001 season. In the two games he did play, Dawson recorded nine receptions and one touchdown in 2000.

Kevin Dyson (Tennessee Titans)
Dyson injured a knee during a practice in 2000, ending his season after just three games. Speaking to the Titans in the spring, Dyson was in rehab, and at that time they expected him to be ready for the upcoming 2001 season. With Carl Pickens and Yancey Thigpen gone, theTitans hope Dyson can step in alongside Derrick Mason and have an impact.

Bobby Engram (Chicago Bears)
Another Bears' receiver coming off a solid 1999 season, Engram had produced 88 receptions for 947 yards and four touchdowns in 1999. In 2000 he wasn't so fortunate, suffering a season-ending knee injury prior to the regular season. When speaking to the Bears in the spring, they stated Engram was coming along very well and was expected to be ready for the upcoming season.

Joey Galloway (Dallas Cowboys)
In 2000, $42 million over seven years lured Galloway to Dallas, but

unfortunately he lasted only one game before suffering a season-ending knee injury. The Cowboys expect the speedster, who was going through rehab in the spring, to be ready for the 2001 season.

Rocket Ismail (Dallas Cowboys)
Ismail suffered a season-ending knee injury in 2000 about midway through the year. This followed a breakout year in 1999, when he produced 80 receptions for 1,097 yards and seven touchdowns. The Cowboys still had reservations in the spring of when Ismail would be ready to return. Certainly it's an injury we'll update in our preseason newsletters.

Patrick Jeffers (Carolina Panthers)
Jeffers, who missed the entire 2000 season with a torn ACL, was still in rehab when contacting the Panthers in the spring. We'll further update Jeffers injury in our preseason newsletter. In 1999, Jeffers recorded 63 receptions for 1,082 yards and 12 touchdowns.

Rob Moore (Arizona Cardinals)
Moore missed the entire 2000 season with a knee injury. When contacting the Cardinals in the spring, they stated Moore was progressing well, practicing daily and was expected to be ready for the 2001 season.

Jerry Porter (Oakland Riaders)
Porter, the Raiders' second-round pick of a year ago, missed all but one game in 2000 with a hamstring injury. The Raiders say he's ready to go for 2001.

Marcus Robinson (Chicago Bears)
Coming off a breakout year when he produced a whopping 84 receptions for 1,400 yards and nine touchdowns, Robinson faced huge expectations heading into 2000. Robinson, however, suffering from a bulging disc in his back, missed the last five games of the year, resulting in a drop to 55 receptions for 738 yards and five touchdowns. The Bears say he's ready to go for the 2001 season.

Darnay Scott (Cincinnati Bengals)
With Carl Pickens off to Tennessee in 2000, Scott was expected to step in as the Bengal's #1 receiver and help bring along rookie Peter Warrick. Scott never got the chance, suffering two broken bones in his leg during the preseason. The Bengals do expect Scott ready for the 2001 season and to help the Bengals' passing attack in a big way.

Leslie Shepherd (Miami Dolphins)
Shepherd missed the last four games of 2000 with a knee injury. The Dolphins contacted in the spring said he was in good shape and was ready to play, though he's an unrestricted free-agent and they weren't sure if he would be brought back in 2001.

Travis Taylor (Baltimore Ravens)
Taylor missed the last seven games of his rookie season of 2000 with a broken collarbone. Prior to the injury, Taylor had recorded 28 receptions for 276 yards and three touchdowns. The Ravens report he is in good shape and expect him 100 percent ready for 2001.

Michael Westbrook (Washington Redskins)
Westbrook missed the last 14 games of the 2000 season with a knee injury.

When contacting the Redskins in the spring, they reported Westbrook was working out daily and in good shape.

TIGHT ENDS

Wesley Walls (Carolina Panthers)
Walls, regarded as one of the league's best tight ends, missed virtually half the 2000 season with a knee injury. In contacting the Panthers in the spring, they said Walls was in rehab but were uncertain at the time of his healthy return. We'll surely keep an eye on his progress over the offseason. Healthy in 1999, Walls produced 63 receptions for 822 yards and scored 12 times.

Tony McGee (Cincinnati Bengals)
McGee missed the last two weeks of the 2000 season with a fractured ankle. The Bengals expect him ready for training camp and the 2001 season.

Cam Cleeland (New Orleans Saints)
Cleeland suffered a ruptured achilles in the 2000 preseason, forcing him to miss the entire season. Cleeland was expected to be ready for the Saints' second minicamp in June.

QUARTERBACKS

Tim Couch (Cleveland Browns
Couch missed over half the 2000 season with a fractured thumb on his throwing hand. The Browns report he is in good shape and expected to be ready to go in the upcoming 2001 season.

Jeff Blake (New Orleans Saints)
Blake, who came to New Orleans in 2000 to take over as the starting quarterback, did and was faring well until suffering a broken foot forcing him to miss the last five games of the season. The Saints say they expect he'll be at full strength by training camp. Returning to be the starter, however, may not be that easy, as Aaron Brooks stepped up as his replacement and will provide a challenge in 2001.

KICKERS

John Kasay (Carolina Panthers)
Kasay, one of the league's most consistent kickers, missed the entire 2000 season with a dislocated knee cap. When talking to the Panthers this spring, there remained some uncertainty of his return as he continued through rehab. We'll keep a close eye on Kasay's status in our preseason newsletters.

NEW NFL HEAD COACHES

Arizona Cardinals
In: Dave McGinnis
Out: Vince Tobin
Following a 4-12 season in 1997, the Cardinals went 9-7 in 1998 and the future looked bright under head coach Vince Tobin. However, the Cardinals took an about-face in 1999 finishing at 6-10. The Cardinals' 2000 season went even worse. Head coach Tobin was told to take a walk after the team started out 3-11. Defensive coordinator Dave McGinnis then

stepped in with two games to go. The Cardinals lost those last two games, finishing at 3-13. McGinnis was kept on as the team's new head coach. He's taking over a team that has some talent but just hasn't ever put it together for any duration. Last year's first-round pick, Thomas Jones, was disappointing as a rookie running back and will continue to be pushed by Michael Pittman. The big push for McGinnis will be to get quarterback Jake Plummer to return to the form he displayed back in 1998, when this team looked to be on the right track. McGinnis may push this team to more than the three wins of a year ago, but I don't see a big turnaround any time soon.

Buffalo Bills
In: Gregg Williams
Out: Wade Phillips
Wade Phillips was presented the head coaching job of the Bills heading into the 1998 season, coming off a year when they had gone 6-10 under retiring coach Marv Levy. Phillips quickly helped turn the team around, first going 10-6 in 1998 and then 11-5 in 1999. The progress stopped in 2000, as the elements of some of the Bills' successful team had aged to the point of being ineffective. Quarterback Jim Kelly was two years removed, and settling on a quarterback between Rob Johnson and Doug Flutie remained a controversy. Running back Thurman Thomas was far beyond his productive years. Antowain Smith, a former #1 pick, had tried but failed to fill the void. With the team in transition, the Bills fell to 8-8, and Phillips was gone following the 2000 season. Replacing Phillips is Gregg Williams, who comes over after being the Tennessee Titans' defensive coordinator in 2000. Williams is known to be an excellent people person and one of the league's better defensive minds, helping the Titans to the top of the defensive ranking in 2000. Williams is looking to install a version of the West Coast offense, which will not involve having a quarterback controversy. Doug Flutie is off to quarterback the San Diego Chargers, leaving Rob Johnson the job. Johnson and wide receiver Eric Moulds will benefit statistically. But what about on the ground? Willimas has to find an every-down back, something that has been difficult for the Bills since Thurman's heyday ended.

Cleveland Browns
In: Butch Davis
Out: Chris Palmer
Given the task of bringing along a new franchise into the NFL can be a tough task, which is exactly what Chris Palmer found out. Palmer, brought in to coach the "new" Cleveland Browns, didn't expect immediate great success but was expected to fare better than he did. In Palmer's two-year run, the Browns went 2-14 in 1999 and 3-13 a year later. Palmer was replaced following the 2000 season with Butch Davis. Davis, at 49, brings new energy to a franchise that needs it in a hurry. Davis had just spent six years reviving the University of Miami program. He takes over a team that is young—as a franchise and in talent. In Tim Couch, he does have a young quarterback with talent to build around. Couch is returning, after missing over half the last season with a fractured thumb on his throwing hand. He has a couple of talented young receivers in Kevin Johnson and Dennis Northcutt, but the running game is still in question. Rookie Travis

Prentise stepped in for the injured Errict Rhett in 2000, but there remains questions here. Though this is a team with possible future potential, Butch Davis has his work ahead of him in 2001 and beyond.

Detroit Lions
In: Marty Mornhinweg
Out: Gary Moeller
The Lions wanted to build on their 8-8 finish of 1998, following their disappointing 5-11 1997 season. In 2000, trying to push from mediocrity, the Lions changed gears after a 5-4 start, turning the team over to Gary Moeller with Bobby Ross being escorted out of the picture. Moeller finished out the season as the Lions wound up 9-7. Looking to get the team to push as a contender in 2001, the Lions hired Marty Mornhinweg, who had spent the last four seasons as the San Francisco 49ers offensive coordinator. Mornhinweg brings with him the West Coast offense philosophy. This bodes well for quarterback Charlie Batch and his receivers. Mornhinweg, had a hand in the quick success Jeff Garcia had with the 49ers in 2000. Mornhinweg's first task is to find a way to keep Charlie Batch healthy and injury free and helping to get him stronger. Running back James Stewart should also benefit, as the Lions will be more open on offense. This could be a great fit for a team with a young quarterback looking to push mediocrity in the future.

Houston Texans
In: Dom Capers
In losing their team, the Oilers, to Tennessee three years ago, Houston has been waiting anxiously to again be involved as an NFL franchise. Their wish comes true in 2002, as the Houston Texans will take the field. Looking for a head coach to take on a task of starting up a franchise the Texans, I believe, made a solid choice in picking Dom Capers. Capers was also the man the Carolina Panthers chose to start up as coach of their franchise when they began. Capers found a way to put together a nice blend of talent to help the Panthers produce a competitive team even in their young years. With Houston, Capers signs a $9.5 million deal over five years, as the Texans hope to get the franchise off on the right foot.

Kansas City Chiefs
In: Dick Vermeil
Out: Gunther Cunningham
When head coach Marty Schottenheimer walked away following a 7-9, 1998 season, the Kansas City Chiefs turned to their defensive coordinator Gunther Cunningham. Cunningham spent two seasons as head coach of the Chiefs, going 9-7 in 1999 and dropping to 7-9 in 2000. Looking for a quick fix, the Chiefs are turning to 64-year-old Dick Vermeil, who just two years ago caused quite a stir at the other end of the state when in St. Louis. Has Vermeil got any magic left? He certainly doesn't have the weapons in place that he did when with the Rams. There is certainly no Marshall Faulk in the Chiefs' running game, and there is not a Kurt Warner at the helm of the offense either. The Chiefs apparently believe Vermeil can get it done, signing him to a 3-year deal. Surely Vermeil has some holes to fill as far as offensive weapons go. It may not be immediately in 2001, but a year or two down the road, Vermeil's magic may be back.

New York Jets
In: Herman Edwards
Out: Al Groh
Being the replacement for Bill Parcells as head coach of the New York Jets would not be an easy "Bill" to fill. The Jets turned to their linebacker coach, Al Groh, heading into the 2000 season, following an 8-8 season under Parcells in 1999, when Vinny Testaverde was hurt most of the year. Groh guided the Jets to a 9-7 mark in 2000 and looked to have the team headed in the right direction. Surprisingly Groh resigned following the 2000 season, choosing to grab the coaching job at his alma matter, the University of Virginia instead. The Jets elected to bring in Herman Edwards as Groh's replacement. Edwards, who was assistant head coach in Tampa Bay in 2000, has spent nine years as an assistant coach. Edwards steps in to a team that has aging talent in quarterback Vinny Testaverde and running back Curtis Martin, their two best offensive players. Can Edwards push this team into the playoffs? He'll have to find a way to keep his stars healthy and he'll have to do it soon, as the Jets are likely to find themselves in a rebuilding mode in the near future.

Washington Redskins
In: Marty Schottenheimer
Out: Norv Turner/Terry Robiskie
After a 6-10 finish in 1998, the Redskins under Norv Turner got things turned around in 1999, finishing 10-6. Offensively, quarterback Brad Johnson and running back Stephen Davis were the catalysts to help supply consistency on offense. Heading into 2000, the Redskins were looking for more of the same success but after a 9-7 loss to the Giants and a 7-6 start, Turner was fired and replaced by Terry Robiskie as interim coach for the last three games. Following the Redskins' 8-8 finish, the Redskins opted to bring in Marty Schottenheimer. Schottenheimer was given the title of head coach and director of football operations. Having previous NFL head-coaching experience and success in doing so, Schottenheimer, the Redskins believed, was the best choice. Schottenheimer pretty much wiped out the existing Redskins' coaching staff and brought in his own staff. Having quarterback Jeff George and running back Stephen Davis to build the offense around, he has the weapons that will help give him a chance to see success with some immediacy.

V

2001 ROOKIE CLASS
Falcons Believe They Can Fly behind Vick
Chargers Hope Future Is a 'Brees'
Vikings Hope to 'Bennett'Fit without Smith
Wide Receivers Again Deep in Draft

Many observers believed last year's draft, which included the likes of blue-chippers Peter Warrick (Cincinnati), Plaxico Burress (Pittsburgh), Travis Taylor (Baltimore), Sylvester Morris (Kansas City) and a number of others, was deep at the wide receiver position. The same is being said about this year's rookie crop. The 2001 first-rounders—David Terrell (Chicago), Koren Robinson (Seattle), Rod Gardner (Washington), Santana Moss (Miami), Freddie Mitchell (Philadelphia) and Reggie Wayne (Indianapolis)—all have a chance to start or are headed to teams where they could make an impact with significant playing time as rookies.

Other than the wide receivers, quarterbacks Michael Vick (Atlanta) and Drew Brees (San Diego) got plenty of hype. Vick, a tremendous athlete, was the first player chosen in the draft. He's going to Atlanta, following a trade the Falcons made with San Diego to acquire the #1 pick a day before the draft. Though being the #1 overall pick, Vick is unlikely to be the starter on opening day and may see very little playing time in 2001. He'll be playing and learning behind veteran Chris Chandler. Brees, who was the next quarterback taken, lasted all the way to the second round and went to San Diego. The Chargers have to be happy getting Brees at that point, remembering just three years earlier they took Ryan Leaf, who became a major bust as the #2 overall pick in the draft.

At running back, the Chargers filled an immediate need, taking LaDainian Tomlinson out of TCU as the #5 overall pick. The Vikings, looking for a replacement for retired Robert Smith, grabbed Wisconsin's Michael Bennett later in the first-round at #27. Other teams, with not such an immediate need, grabbed some talented backs in the second round but surprisingly San Francisco, who lost Charlie Garner to Oakland, waited until the third round to select Kevan Barlow out of Pittsburgh.

Only two teams selected tight ends in the first two rounds. Baltimore, which already has Shannon Sharpe on hand, grabbed Todd Heap out of Arizona State as the last pick of the first round. And Atlanta, having Reggie Kelly as their current starter, couldn't pass on the talented Alge Crumpler out of North Carolina in the second round.

How will this year's rookie crop pan out? Who will actually stand out and make an impact? Who will make an immediate impact as a rookie and who will be groomed for future success? Remember, success stories don't always come from the first and second rounds. In 2000, sixth-round pick Michael Anderson came out of nowhere to produce 1,500 rushing yards and 15 touchdowns, filling in for the injured Terrell Davis and Olandis Gary in Denver. This has happened to the Broncos before, as Terrell

Davis is a former sixth-round pick himself in 1995 and Olandis Gary was a fourth-round pick in 1999. This shows us that even pro scouts, who watch and evaluate these players all year long, very often misjudge a player's potential for a number of reasons. So who will really become a standout from this year's draft? It's not an easy prediction. In this section, I will evaluate the 2001 rookies to try to determine who will make waves immediately and who will be groomed for future stardom. The rookies who will make a difference right away in 2001 are those who are going to teams with immediate needs. The players whose success will come later are those who are headed for teams that are planning for the future.

When evaluating this year's rookies, we'll first take a look at last year's draftees from the first couple of rounds — "Blue Chippers." Analyzing both successful and unsuccessful seasons by these players helps us see how this year's rookies may fare. After a quick look at last year's draft choices, I will list this year's draft choices from fantasy-positions only quarterbacks, running backs, wide receivers, tight ends and kickers. Finally, I will give key player-by-player evaluations of this year's rookie crop. For a more extensive review of the 2000 rookies, see Section II, How the 2000 Rookies Fared.

2000 BLUE-CHIPPERS

ROUND #1

OVERALL PICK	NAME	POS	COLLEGE	NFL TEAM
4	Peter Warrick	WR	Florida State	Cincinnati
5	Jamal Lewis	RB	Tennessee	Baltimore
7	Thomas Jones	RB	Virginia	Arizona
8	Plaxico Burress	WR	Michigan State	Pittsburgh
10	Travis Taylor	WR	Florida	Baltimore
11	Ron Dayne	RB	Wisconsin	NY Giants
14	Bubba Franks	TE	Miami	Green Bay
17	Sebastian Janikowski	K	Florida State	Oakland
18	Chad Pennington	QB	Marshall	NY Jets
19	Shaun Alexander	RB	Alabama	Seattle
21	Sylvester Morris	WR	Jackson State	Kansas City
27	Anthony Becht	TE	West Virginia	NY Jets
29	R. Jay Soward	WR	USC	Jacksonville
31	Trung Canidate	RB	Arizona	St. Louis

ROUND #2

32	Dennis Northcutt	WR	Arizona	Cleveland
36	Rodd Pinkston	WR	Southern Mississippi	Philadelphia
47	Jerry Porter	WR	West Virginia	Oakland

Looking at last year's first-round picks, no players set the league on fire. The #4 overall pick, Peter Warrick (Cincinnati), produced only 51 receptions for 592 yards and scored seven times. The #5 overall pick, running back Jamal Lewis (Baltimore), was the most rewarding first-round pick to his team. Lewis produced 1,660 rushing-receiving yards and scored six times during the regular season, before helping the Ravens on their Super Bowl run. The other first-round running backs, Thomas Jones (Arizona), Ron Dayne (NY Giants), Shaun Alexander (Seattle) and Trung Canidate (St. Louis), had less than impressive rookie seasons. The same could be said for wide receivers Plaxico Burress (Pittsburgh), Travis Taylor (Baltimore) and R. Jay Soward (Jacksonville), who missed significant playing time to injury. Kansas City's Sylvester Morris put up decent numbers, recording 48 receptions for 678 yards but scored only three times. Tight ends Bubba Franks (Green Bay) and Anthony Becht (NY Jets) were disappointing, and strong-legged kicker Sebastian Janikowki (Oakland) also struggled.

Of the second-round picks—of which there were only three fantasy-positioned players, all wide receivers—none had standout years. This included Dennis Northcutt (Cleveland), Todd Pinkstron (Philadelphia) and Jerry Porter (Oakland). This doesn't mean, however, these first and second-round blue-chippers won't have impacts as second-year players in 2001.

Remember this, however, when considering a rookie on your fantasy draft, does this rookie have a chance to make an immediate impact? Does his team need help at a particular position? These are moves that could help make or break your fantasy team.

2001 ROOKIE CLASS BY ROUND

ROUND #1

OVERALL PICK	NAME	POS	COLLEGE	NFL TEAM
1	Michael Vick	QB	Virginia Tech	Atlanta
5	LaDainian Tomlinson	RB	TCU	San Diego
8	David Terrell	WR	Michigan	Chicago
9	Koren Robinson	WR	North Carolina State	Seattle
15	Rod Gardner	WR	Clemson	Washington
16	Santana Moss	WR	Miami	NY Jets
25	Freddie Mitchell	WR	UCLA	Philadelphia
27	Michael Bennett	RB	Wisconsin	Minnesota
30	Reggie Wayne	WR	Miami	Indianapolis
31	Todd Heap	TE	Arizona State	Baltimore

ROUND #2

32	Drew Brees	QB	Purdue	San Diego
33	Quincy Morgan	WR	Kansas State	Cleveland
35	Alge Crumpler	TE	North Carolina	Atlanta
36	Chad Johnson	WR	Oregon State	Cincinnati
38	Anthony Thomas	RB	Michigan	Chicago
41	Robert Ferguson	WR	Texas A&M	Green Bay
49	LaMont Jordan	RB	Maryland	NY Jets
52	Chris Chambers	WR	Wisconsin	Miami
53	Quincy Carter	QB	Georgia	Dallas
58	Travis Henry	RB	Tennessee	Buffalo
59	Marques Tuiasosopo	QB	Washington	Oakland

ROUND #3

65	James Jackson	RB	Miami	Cleveland
66	Sean Brewer	TE	San Jose State	Cincinnati
74	Steve Smith	WR	Utah	Carolina
77	Marvin Minnis	WR	Florida State	Kansas City
80	Kevan Barlow	RB	Pittsburgh	San Francisco
82	Heath Evans	RB	Auburn	Seattle
85	Travis Minor	RB	Florida State	Miami
90	Shad Meier	TE	Kansas City	Tennessee

ROUND #4

98	Bill Gramatica	K	South Florida	Arizona
100	Rudi Johnson	RB	Auburn	Cincinnati
106	Chris Weinke	QB	Florida State	Carolina
108	George Wayne	RB	Texas Christian	Kansas City
109	Sage Rosenfels	QB	Iowa State	Washington
115	Moran Norris	RB	Kansas	New Orleans
116	Milton Wynn	WR	Washington State	St. Louis
119	Jabari Holloway	TE	Notre Dame	New England
121	Correll Buckhalter	RB	Nebraska	Philadelphia
124	Justin McCareins	WR	Northern Illinois	Tennessee
125	Jesse Palmer	QB	Florida	NY Giants
129	Brandon Manumaleuna	TE	Arizona	St. Louis
131	Cedric James	WR	Texas Christian	Minnesota

ROUND #5

136	Vinny Sutherland	WR	Purdue	Atlanta
140	Alex Bannister	WR	Eastern Kentucky	Seattle
141	Billy Baber	TE	Virginia	Kansas City
147	Tony Stewart	TE	Penn State	Philadelphia
148	Scotty Anderson	WR	Grambling	Detroit
149	Mike McMahon	QB	Rutgers	Detroit
150	Derrick Blaylock	RB	Stephen F. Austin	Kansas City
153	Onomo Ojo	WR	California-Davis	New Orleans
154	Darnerian McCants	WR	Delaware State	Washington
155	A. J. Feely	QB	Oregon	Philadelphia
159	Eddie Berlin	WR	Northern Iowa	Tennessee
160	Jon Markam	K	Vanderbilt	NY Giants
161	Chris Barnes	RB	New Mexico State	Baltimore
162	Jonathan Carter	WR	Troy State	NY Giants

ROUND #6

166	Bobby Newcombe	WR	Nebraska	Arizona
169	Cedrick Wilson	WR	Tennessee	San Francisco
172	Josh Booty	QB	Louisiana State	Seattle
174	Jameel Cook	RB	Illinois	Tampa Bay
173	Dedrian Brown	RB	Syracuse	Carolina
177	Josh Heupel	QB	Oklahoma	Miami
180	Arthur Love	TE	South Carolina State	New England
190	Kevin Kasper	WR	Iowa	Denver
195	Dan O'Leary	TE	Notre Dame	Buffalo
197	Francis St. Paul	WR	Northern Arizona	St. Louis
198	David Martin	WR	Tennessee	Green Bay

ROUND #7

204	T.J. Houshmandzadeh	WR	Oregon State	Cincinnati
205	Dauntae Finger	TE	North Carolina	Tampa Bay
208	John Capel	WR	Florida	Chicago
214	Reggie Germany	WR	Ohio State	Buffalo
216	Owen Pochman	K	Brigham Young	New England
218	Chris Tayler	WR	Texas A&M	Pittsburgh
224	Eric Johnson	TE	Yale	San Francisco
227	Mike Roberg	TE	Idaho	Carolina
228	Derek Combs	RB	Ohio State	Oakland
229	Ken-Yon Rambo	WR	Ohio State	Oakland
235	Richmond Flowers	WR	Chattanooga	Jacksonville
236	Quentin McCord	WR	Kentucky	Atlanta
245	Andre King	WR	Miami (Fla)	Cleveland
246	Tevita Ofahengaue	TE	Brigham Young	Arizona

GOOD ROOKIE PROSPECTS
FROM THE 2001 DRAFT

How many good fantasy players will come from this year's draft? Or, more accurately and perhaps importantly, which players have a shot at making an immediate impact, and which ones are being groomed for the future? Let's take a look at some of these prospects.

RUNNING BACKS

LaDainian Tomlinson *(1st Round, San Diego Chargers/College: TCU)*
The Chargers are thrilled to have landed Tomlinson as the #5 overall pick. By draft day, the Chargers wanted and likely needed Tomlinson with more immediacy than Vick. Tomlinson, who led the nation with 2,158 rushing yards in 2000 with TCU, is someone the Chargers believe can be an immediate impact player. Fantasy fans take note of a player who can step in and put up decent numbers right away as a rookie.

Deuce McAllister *(1st Round, New Orleans/College: Mississippi)*
Two years after giving up all their draft picks to draft Ricky Williams, the Saints made Deuce McAllister their #1 draft pick. At 6'1", 220, McAllister has good size and speed but has a question of durability, suffering shoulder and ankle injuries in college. He's an interesting pick for the Saints, who are making some kind of statement to Ricky Williams.

Michael Bennett *(1st Round, Minnesota Vikings/College: Wisconsin)*
What do the Vikings do now that Robert Smith is retired? Apparently they weren't as sold on Moe Williams and Doug Chapman as they wanted people to believe and made Michael Bennett their first-round draft pick. He's not very big at 5'9", 207 pounds, but he is explosive and fast. And much like Robert Smith, he's a threat to break one at anytime. He's certainly a rookie who can have an impact as a fantasy player right away in 2001.

Anthony Thomas *(2nd Round, Chicago Bears/College: Michigan)*
Thomas is a threat to push James Allen in a hurry. Thomas lacks great speed but is a hard running, solid back, who rushed for 1,551 yards in 2000 for Michigan. He's certainly more durable than Allen, at 6'1", 225 pounds. Like I said, he could push for work early as a rookie in 2001.

Kevan Barlow *(3rd Round, San Francisco 49ers/College: Pittsburgh)*
It was surprising that the 49ers, who lost Charlie Garner to Oakland in the offseason, waited so long to go after a running back. The 49ers grabbed Barlow in the third-round and have uncertainty on their hands looking to 2001. Barlow rushed for 1,053 yards and caught only 13 passes for 134 yards while scoring eight times. The 49ers felt Barlow had second-round potential and were heppy to get him in the third round, believing his all around skills fit their West Coast offense.

LaMont Jordan *(2nd Round, New York Jets/College: Maryland)*
With Curtis Martin still in the fold, Jordan is more of a long-term than a short-term answer. At 5'9", 230 pounds, he's a strong runner, who has decent size and good speed. For now it looks like his role is to back up

Curtis Martin. Down the line he could become a help to the Jets.

Travis Henry *(2nd Round, Buffalo Bills/College: Tennessee)*
At only 5'9", 225 pounds, Henry is a low-center-of-gravity runner, who will work hard for his yards. Thrown into the Bills' backfield mix of Antowain Smith, Shawn Bryson, Jonathan Linton and Sammy Morris, it's a crapshoot as to when Henry would see action.

Travis Minor *(3rd Round, Miami Dolphins/College: Florida State)*
At 5'10", 195 pounds, Minor is more of a third-down threat who can catch the ball well and will likely battle for that role with the Dolphins.

Heath Evans *(3rd Round, Seattle Seahawks/College: Auburn)*
A strong, powerful fullback type, Evans will be exactly that, having a better chance to produce occasional short-yardage scores rather than rack up many yards.

WIDE RECEIVERS

David Terrell *(1st Round, Chicago Bears/College: Michigan)*
For a team that has its deficiencies and uncertainties at quarterback, the Chicago Bears certainly like to have talented wide receivers. At 6'3", about 215 pounds, Terrell is big, strong and fast and has great big-play ability. In 2000, Terrell grabbed 63 passes and scored 13 times. He should make a nice fit alongside Marcus Robinson for the Bears. The only question is how often the Bears' quarterbacks will get him the ball.

Koren Robinson *(1st Round, Seattle Seahawks/College: North Carolina State)*
Head coach Mike Holmgren got his quarterback to build his offense around when acquiring Matt Hasselbeck in the offseason from Green Bay. Now he's finding targets for Hasselbeck. In Robinson, the Seahawks have a great athlete with good speed and excellent hands. He's a player with unlimited potential, if he decides to work hard but he may need some guidance in doing so. Robinson has huge upside potential as a fantasy pick if he and Hasselbeck click early on.

Rod Gardner *(1st Round, Washington Redskins/College: Clemson)*
At 6'2", just under 220 pounds, Gardner is a nice size target. He is more of a possession receiver who occasionally can get deep. With James Thrash (Eagles) and Albert Connell (Saints) departed, the Redskins have a prime candidate to start opposite Michael Westbrook, though offseason acquisition, Kevin Lockett (Chiefs) will challenge.

Freddie Mitchell *(1st Round, Philadelphia Eagles/College UCLA)*
Headed to a team in need at wide receiver, Mitchell has a chance to make an impact as a rookie if he works at it. At 5'11", about 190 pounds, Mitchell is known to be a guy who wants to make "the" play. He possesses great hands and body control and should become a nice target for Donovan McNabb. Mitchell has the potential to be the Eagles #1 receiver, which should push his fantasy stock.

Santana Moss *(1st Round, New York Jets/College: Miami (Fla)*
Moss is a potential game breaker as both a receiver and a kick returner. At 5'9", 185 pounds, Moss has great speed and quickness, which should

give him potential as a rookie to have an impact, depending how often the Jets use him.

Reggie Wayne *(1st Round, Indianapolis Colts/College: Miami (Fla)*
Continually looking for a consistent receiving mate for Marvin Harrison, the Colts nabbed Reggie Wayne late in first round. Wayne is not much of a deep threat but will be a consistent, sure-handed possession receiver who can take a hit over the middle. He's a receiver coming to training camp with a spot open for him to make an impact if he works hard.

Quincy Morgan *(2nd Round, Cleveland Browns/College: Kansas State)*
At 6'1", 210 pounds, Morgan comes to the Browns with good size and speed. He has the potential to make big plays but can be inconsistent. On a team that needs to mature, Morgan will get his shot but as a fantasy factor I don't see big potential as a rookie.

Chad Johnson *(2nd Round, Cincinnati Bengals/College: Oregon State)*
The Bengals drafted Peter Warrick in the first round a year ago and have veteran Darnay Scott returning healthy from an injury from a year ago, so the drafting of Johnson was a bit of a surprise. He has some potential, possessing good size (6'1", 190 pounds) and hands but may need some time to develop, which he'll get behind Warrick and Scott.

Robert Ferguson *(2nd Round, Green Bay Packers/College: Texas A&M)*
The Packers got a receiver they believe has long-term potential but at least for now needs some work on the finer parts of the game. At 6'1", 205 pounds, Ferguson, can get deep on occasion, having the ability to make the big play. Coming to Green Bay and working with Brett Favre may bring him along quicker than expected.

Chris Chambers *(2nd Round, Miami Dolphins/College: Wisconsin)*
The Dolphins, who have not had good luck with the wide receiver position in recent years, bring another questionable player into the fold. Chambers does have exceptional speed, and can jump for tough catches but has yet to become a consistent receiver. He needs to further work on the finer points of the game, though he's a nice red-zone option for the Dolphins even as a rookie.

Stevonne Smith *(3rd Round, Carolina Panthers/College: Utah)*
At 5'8", 177 pounds, Smith will be used more in a kick-returner role.

Marvin Minnis *(3rd Round, Kansas City/College: Florida State)*
At 6'0" and 175 pounds, Minnis has great receiving skills, but his slender frame may make things tough coming off the line. He's likely to be an occasional slot receiver.

TIGHT ENDS

Todd Heap *(1st Round, Baltimore/College: Arizona State)*
No hurry here, as the Ravens make Todd Heap their first-round pick to come in and learn from aging standout Shannon Sharpe. At 6'4", 250 plus pounds, Heap possesses good hands and the desire to want the ball in go-to situations. He's a nice player to develop behind Sharpe, though the Ravens are going to use the two in two tight end sets.

Alge Crumpler *(2nd Round, Atlanta Falcons/College: North Carolina)*
At 6'2", 265 pounds, Alge Crumpler is a little undersized by most NFL tight end standards. However, he has a huge upside in being a hard working, strong athlete, who could become a solid player for the Falcons if he works at it.

Sean Brewer *(3rd Round, Cincinnati Bengals/College: San Jose State)*
Brewer brings a 6'4", 255 frame with him into the NFL. His good size and good speed will help, but he has a ways to go to become a factor in the NFL, especially playing behind Tony McGee and Marco Battaglio in Cincinnati.

Shad Meier *(3rd Round, Tennessee Titans/College: Kansas State)*
With good hands and good size at 6'4" and 255 pounds, Meier is unlikely to unseat veteran Frank Wycheck any time soon.

QUARTERBACKS

Michael Vick *(1st Round, Atlanta Falcons/College: Virginia Tech)*
Truly the best athlete of the draft, Vick was born to compete and win. Though he's only 6'0", 215 pounds, he has the ability to be a dominant player because of his skills. He can throw long and short passes accurately, he can run and run well, he can improvise. He simply scares opposing defenses. However, Vick, because he's played only two years of college football, is not likely ready to be part of the "big show" yet. He may be "a" player or "the" player in a year or two but for now will likely serve his time learning from veteran Chris Chandler.

Drew Brees *(2nd Round, San Diego Chargers/College: Purdue)*
The Chargers are still getting over their blunder on Ryan Leaf, whom they made the #2 overall pick three years ago. Brees, who doesn't possess the "great" arm, does possess the intangibles that make great quarterbacks. Leadership, respect and mental toughness will likely make him a success in the future but for now he'll likely learn from veteran Doug Flutie, an offseason acquisition by the Chargers.

Chris Weinke *(4th Round, Carolina Panthers/College: Florida State)*
Older or let's say more mature at 28, Weinke may see his age play in his favor. With veteran Steve Beuerlein gone from the Panthers, Weinke can push unproven Jeff Lewis. Weinke may have a shot at seeing playing time as a rookie in 2001. He has the tools to do something short term.

Quincy Carter *(1st Round, Dallas Cowboys/College: Georgia)*
The Cowboys have resolved their immediate quarterback needs, following Troy Aikman's departure to retirement, by signing Tony Banks in the offseason. Looking long-term, however, the Cowboys chose Quincy Carter in the second round of this year's draft. At 6'2", 220 pounds, Carter has good size and a strong arm and can run but is a project for the Cowboys with success expected down the road.

Marque Tuiasosopo *(2nd Round, Oakland Raiders/College: Washington)*
When Rich Gannon's career is over, which is unlikely in the near future, the Raiders have their hopes likely set on Tuiasosopo.

KICKERS

Bill Gramatica *(4th Round, Arizona Cardinals/College: South Florida)*
After Cary Blanchard hit only 16 of 23 (.696) field goal tries in 2000, the Arizona Cardinals surveyed their kicking options for 2001. In Gramatica, the Cardinals get the brother of Tampa Bay kicker, Martin Gramatica. This Gramatica has a very strong leg, is excellent on kickoffs but has struggled with accuracy, hitting 16 of 24 (.667) field goals in 2000 but did hit a 63 yarder.

Jon Markam *(5th Round, New York Giants/College: Vanderbilt)*
Markam comes in to challenge veteran Brad Daluiso, who hit 17 of 23 (.739) field goals in 2000, and free-agent Matt Simonton, a free agent signed in the offseason.

Owen Pochman, *(7th Round, New England Patriots/College: Brigham Young)*
Pochman, who has a strong leg, comes in to battle veteran Adam Vinatieri for the Patriots kicking chores. Pochman hit 18 of 27 (.667) field goals in 2000.

VI
RATING THE 2001 NFL TEAM SCHEDULES

Which players from which teams should you pick in your fantasy draft? Who's going to fare well in 2001? One thing to consider when selecting your fantasy team for 2001 is the strength or weakness of the teams your players will face during the 2001 NFL season. Obviously, a player playing an easy schedule has a good chance of having a statistically successful year.

First, we'll look at last year's standings and see how each team did. Then we'll look at each team's 2001 schedule and rate that schedule according to how the current year's opposition performed in 2000.

This is not a foolproof method of selecting players, but it is an important factor to consider when choosing between two players whom you have rated almost equal.

The following pages show the final 2000 NFL standings, followed by rankings for each team's 2001 schedule.

2000 AMERICAN CONFERENCE STANDINGS						
Eastern Division						
TEAM	**W**	**L**	**T**	**PCT.**	**PTS.**	**OPP.**
Miami	11	5	0	.688	323	226
Indianapolis	10	6	0	.625	429	326
New York Jets	9	7	0	.563	321	321
Buffalo	8	8	0	.500	315	350
New England	5	11	0	.313	276	338
Central Division						
TEAM	**W**	**L**	**T**	**PCT.**	**PTS.**	**OPP.**
Tennessee	13	3	0	.813	346	191
Baltimore	12	4	0	.750	333	165
Pittsburgh	9	7	0	.563	321	255
Jacksonville	7	9	0	.438	367	327
Cincinnati	4	12	0	.250	185	359
Cleveland	3	13	0	.188	161	419
Western Division						
TEAM	**W**	**L**	**T**	**PCT.**	**PTS.**	**OPP.**
Oakland	12	4	0	.750	479	299
Denver	11	5	0	.688	485	369
Kansas City	7	9	0	438	355	354
Seattle	6	10	0	.375	320	405
San Diego	1	15	0	.063	269	440

2000 NATIONAL CONFERENCE STANDINGS						

Eastern Division

TEAM	W	L	T	PCT.	PTS.	OPP.
New York Giants	12	4	0	.750	328	246
Philadelphia	11	5	0	.688	351	245
Washington	8	8	0	.500	281	269
Dallas	5	11	0	.313	294	361
Arizona	3	13	0	.188	210	443

Central Division

TEAM	W	L	T	PCT.	PTS.	OPP.
Minnesota	11	5	0	.688	397	371
Tampa Bay	10	6	0	.625	388	269
Detroit	9	7	0	.563	307	307
Green Bay	9	7	0	.563	353	323
Chicago	5	11	0	.313	216	355

Western Division

TEAM	W	L	T	PCT.	PTS.	OPP.
New Orleans	10	6	0	.625	354	305
St. Louis	10	6	0	.625	540	471
Carolina	7	9	0	.438	310	310
San Francisco	6	10	0	.375	388	422
Atlanta	4	12	0	.250	252	413

How can this ranking of schedules help you? I recommend that when you're deciding on a fantasy draft pick, you lean toward players on teams that face the easier schedules. The flip side is, obviously that you should shy away from players on teams that face tough schedules because you recognize that they will have a harder time coming up with productive season. The exceptions to this are the great players from good teams. Players like Marshall Faulk, Randy Moss and Edgerrin James will produce for you no matter what kind of schedules they face. For the most part, however, it is worth the look to grab players from teams facing weaker foes.

What are some of the tentative conclusions we can draw from this year's schedule difficulty rankings? Look out for players from the Washington Redskins and the Denver Broncos, who share the spot for the league's easiest schedule. If healthy, the likes of Stephen Davis, Terrell Davis, Olandis Gary or Mike Anderson may be headed for big numbers. Besides facing the lowly Arizona Cardinals twice within the division, the Redskins face Chicago (5-11) and San Diego (1-15) outside the division. The Broncos have the Chargers (1-15) twice within the division and face Dallas (5-11) and Arizona (3-13) outside the division.

From whom do we possibly shy away? The Minnesota Vikings face the league's toughest schedule. They face Tampa Bay (10-6) and Green Bay (9-7), twice each within the division. And outside the division face a very tough schedule including the Giants (12-4), Tennessee (13-3), Baltimore (12-4), Philadelphia (11-5), New Orleans (10-6) and Pittsburgh (9-7). However, this will hardly keep me or you from picking Randy Moss. Also facing tough schedules are Tampa Bay, Indianapolis and Green Bay, all of whom possess quality offensive players, making your choices tough.

This schedule ranking is not a precise way to pick players, especially considering the amount of player movement that takes place during the off-season in recent years, but the ranking should give you a sense of what kind of opposition your fantasy players will face in 2001.

Here, then, are the 2001 schedule rankings. They are based on the win-loss records of opponents during the 2000 season. Rankings go from the easiest schedule, at the top, to the most difficult at the bottom.

	2000 DIFFICULTY RANKINGS OF TEAM SCHEDULES (2001 Opponents' Combined 2000 Records)			
	EASIEST SCHEDULE TO TOUGHEST			
	TEAM	**WON**	**LOST**	**TIE**	**PCT.**
1.	Washington	118	138	0	.461
2.	Denver	118	138	0	.461
3.	Philadelphia	119	137	0	.465
4.	San Diego	119	137	0	.465
5.	Buffalo	120	136	0	.469
6.	Detroit	122	134	0	.477
7.	Atlanta	122	134	0	.477
8.	Chicago	123	133	0	.480
9.	Carolina	124	132	0	.484
10.	Oakland	124	132	0	.484
11.	Cleveland	125	131	0	.488
12.	New England	126	130	0	.492
13.	Dallas	127	129	0	.496
14.	New Orleans	127	129	0	.496
15.	Cincinnati	127	129	0	.496
16.	Seattle	127	129	0	.496
17.	Arizona	128	128	0	.500
18.	Baltimore	128	128	0	.500
19.	Jacksonville	128	128	0	.500
20.	Kansas City	129	127	0	.504
21.	San Francisco	130	126	0	.508
22.	New York Giants	130	126	0	.508
23.	St. Louis	131	125	0	.512
24.	Pittsburgh	132	124	0	.516
25.	Tennessee	132	124	0	.516
26.	Miami	133	123	0	.520
27.	New York Jets	133	123	0	.520
28.	Green Bay	135	121	0	.527
29.	Indianapolis	138	118	0	.539
30.	Tampa Bay	142	114	0	.555
31.	Minnesota	147	109	0	.574

VII
A TEAM-BY-TEAM
2000 REVIEW/2001 PREVIEW

Here is a team-by-team review/preview, with teams listed alphabetically. I first evaluate each team by fantasy position, then give an overall estimation of the team's offensive potential, and, finally, list all the players the team has either gained or lost as of May 1, 2001.

RB = Running Back, **WR** = Wide Receiver, **TE** = Tight End, **QB** = Quarterback, and **K** = Kicker

ARIZONA CARDINALS

Home Stadium: Sun Devil Stadium
Playing Surface: Grass
Head Coach: Dave McGinnis
2000 Record: 3-13

*Plummer, Working with fewer Tools without Moore,
Hopes to Unclog Problems in 2001*

RB: Hoping to resolve their never-ending need to produce a consistent running attack, the Cardinals made Thomas Jones out of Virginia their #1 draft pick of 2000. The Cardinals had given up on Adrian Murrell, who had been acquired two years earlier from the New York Jets. He, like most other Cardinals' running back options in recent years, had become a disappointment. Jones was a new chance of a breath of fresh air, a draft pick the Cardinals hoped to develop in a hurry. Jones was given his shot but after producing 70 yards on 23 carries the second week of the 2000 season, never again neared that level. Eventually Jones lost his starting job to Michael Pittman, who certainly provided a more consistent attack. On the season, Jones finished with a disappointing 373 rushing yards, added 208 more yards on 32 receptions but scored only twice. Pittman, meanwhile, was much more formidable rushing for 719 yards, added a whopping 73 receptions for 579 yards, and as a significant weapon out of the backfield scored six times. Despite Pittman's decent showing, the Cardinals have to be extremely disappointed in how their running game turned out in 2000. Obviously hoping to have drafted a 1,000-yard rusher in Thomas Jones, that just didn't happen at least not as a rookie. The key to the Cardinals' future success, including in 2001, is the ability to move the ball on the ground. Michael Pittman provides a solid attack on the ground and an added dimension of being a very good receiver. But it's a consistent 1,000-yard man that the Cardinals needs and the jury remains out whether Jones can be that man.

WR: Coming into the 2000 season, the Cardinals' biggest problem looked to be at wide receiver. Who would be the two starters among veterans Frank Sanders and Rob Moore and second-year man David Boston, their first-round draft pick of 1999? Their three-receiver problem was solved early as Rob Moore was lost for the season. Moore tore his ACL in pre-season, which allowed to David Boston a much bigger role. Boston, who grabbed 40 receptions as a rookie in '99, was going to expand his role regardless, as he had played well enough as a rookie to earn more. With Moore out of the picture, however, the opening was there for Boston to do even more. Boston took advantage by leading the team with 71 receptions for 1,156 yards and scoring seven times. Along the way, Boston recorded four 100-yard games and twice going over 90 yards. For Frank Sanders, his production continued to drop. Sanders, who recorded 89 receptions in 1998 and 79 in 1999, dropped to 54 in 2000 and went for 749 yards and six touchdowns. These numbers represent a disappointing trend for Sanders. In addition to Boston and Sanders, the Cardinals got 17 receptions for 219 yards and one touchdown out of Mar Tay Jenkins and similar numbers out of Mac Cody, who also produced 17 receptions, going for 212 yards but no touchdowns. Looking to 2001, Rob Moore looks to be ready to return healthy and push to return as the team's #1 receiver, though David Boston has become the Cardinals' and Jake Plummer's go-to guy and will push Frank Sanders for the #2 spot. Boston will look to expand his numbers of 2000. Meanwhile, Frank Sanders will hope to rebound his negative trend. First and foremost, the Cardinals have to find a way to protect quarterback Jake Plummer, whose task getting the ball to his receivers hasn't been easy.

TE: Not much of a fantasy factor is the Cardinal's tight end position and that didn't change much in 2000. Terry Hardy who led the Cardinals' tight ends with 30 receptions but no touchdowns in 1999, again led the group in 2000, this time recording 27 receptions for 160 yards and one touchdown. Chris Gedney, returning from colon surgery, chipped in ten receptions. Again, far from a coveted fantasy group, the Cardinal tight end position, which will again likely see Terry Hardy as its main cog, is unlikely to produce numbers worthy of fantasy consideration in 2001.

QB: In the aftermath of the 1998 season, when Jake Plummer threw for 3,737 yards and 17 touchdowns, helping the Cardinals to a 9-7 record, Plummer signed a four-year contract extension worth $29.7 million, including a $14 million signing bonus. Things haven't gone as expected since. Plummer struggled in both 1999 and 2000. Plummer did miss two games in 2000 with a rib injury but his 2,946 passing yards and 13 touchdowns were far from impressive for a guy making nearly $30 million over six years. Plummer actually started out alright, throwing for nine touchdowns through the first six games but was far from impressive the rest of the way. Plummer is the key for the Cardinals, who are trying to put together a better offensive line to protect him. He certainly has the weapons, now it's up to him and the Cardinals' offensive line to help reestablish his confidence.

K: The Cardinal kicking job is like a revolving door, with players going in and out all the time. In 2000 Cary Blanchard took over for Chris Jacke, who kicked for Arizona in 1999. Blanchard's 16 of 23 (.696) field goal performance likely led to the Cardinals drafting Bill Gramatica out of South Florida as their fourth-round draft pick. Gramatica, the brother of Tampa Bay's Martin Gramatica, also possesses a strong leg but has some questions with his accuracy. Gramatica will battle Blanchard for the job but drafting a kicker this early usually means the team has an idea he'll be around during the season.

Overall: The Cardinals, who went 6-10 in 1999, continued to spiral downward under head coach Vince Tobin in 2000 to finish 3-13, including losing their last seven games. Tobin was obviously fired, in fact prior to the end of the season, following the Cardinals' 3-11 start, after which defensive coordinator, Dave McGinnis was given the job. McGinnis has the tough task of trying to convince a team that has some talent that they can win. Quarterback Jake Plummer will be asked to step up his game after struggling the last two seasons. Plummer's targets of David Boston, Frank Sanders and Rob Moore are capable if Plummer can get them the ball. The running game questions are still not adequately answered, as last year's first-round draft pick Thomas Jones is a bust thus far. Michael Pittman seems to have a lock on the starting job unless Jones improves his game over the offseason.

Offseason Fantasy-Position Moves

	Arriving	From:	Departing	To:
RB	Clarence Williams	Free Agent		
WR	Bryan Gilmore	Free Agent		
QB	Sean Keenan	Free Agent		

ATLANTA FALCONS

Home Stadium: Georgia Dome
Playing Surface: Grass
Head Coach: Dan Reeves
2000 Record: 4-12

Jamal, Like Always, Is the Key
That Makes the Falcons Fly

RB: How would running back Jamal Anderson fare returning from major knee surgery? This was a huge question for the Atlanta Falcons and fantasy fans going into the 2000 season. Anderson, after having a career year in 1998 when he recorded 1,846 rushing yards, caught 27 passes for another 319 yards and scored 16 times, saw action only into week 2 of the 1999 season before suffering the season-ending injury. Anderson's return in 2000 went somewhat as expected. No, he certainly wasn't back to his 1998 form when he produced 12, 100-yard games. In 2000, Anderson did hit the 1,000-yard mark, rushing for 1,024 yards, grabbed 42 receptions for 382 yards and scored six times. Anderson rushed for over 100 yards in a game only once. Not bad for most backs but not quite the Jamal Anderson of old but then again he was coming off major knee surgery. Other than Anderson, the Falcons got little other help with their running game. Maurice Smith was the second leading rusher with 69 yards and fullback Bob Christian rushed for only 19 yards but did grab 44 passes for 315 yards. Looking to 2001, the story will be the same. The Falcons will go, especially on the ground, if Jamal goes. The knee has had more time to rest this offseason so Falcon fans and fantasy fans wait anxiously for the preseason where it can again be tested. If Anderson is not 100 percent many feel Maurice Smith is ready to step in and make an impact.

WR: The Falcons, looking to give their passing attack a boost, brought aboard speedy Shawn Jefferson in 2000, luring him away from the New England Patriots. Jefferson, the Falcons hoped, would take some pressure off of Terance Mathis. Jefferson did provide some spark but not enough. Jefferson in fact led the team with 60 receptions, going for 822 yards but scored only twice. Mathis, who led the team with 81 catches for 1,016 yards and six touchdowns in 1999 dropped off significantly finishing with 57 receptions for 579 yards and six touchdowns. Tim Dwight, who had finished off 1999 so strong and had scored nine on just 32 receptions that year, fell victim to a leg injury and an emergency appendectomy. Playing in eight games, Dwight recorded only 26 receptions for 406 yards and four touchdowns, one coming on a punt return. Certainly Dwight's speed and production were missed. Part of the problem for the Falcon receivers was quarterback Chris Chandler's struggles. Chandler threw for only 2,236 yards and ten touchdowns playing in 14 games in 2000. Far from what the Falcon's passing game needs or expects out of him. Looking to 2001, Chandler is the key. Shawn Jefferson should again be a big factor and push his 2000 numbers. Can the aging Terance Mathis get back on track? I believe so. The talent is there, and he especially needs Chris Chandler to rebound. Speedy Tim Dwight won't be back, departing to San Diego in the trade to bring Michael Vick to Atlanta. This may hurt the passing game. With Dwight not around to stretch defenses, Mathis and Jefferson may be easier to cover, though Jefferson was brought aboard to do exactly that a year ago.

TE: The Falcons, comfortable enough with their second-round pick of 1999, Reginald Kelly, let O.J. Santiago step away prior to the 2000 season. Kelly, who produced only eight receptions as a rookie in 1999, stepped up to grab 31 receptions for 340 yards and scored twice in 2000. The Falcons also got Brian Koslowski to chip in 15 receptions for 151 yards, and he also scored twice. Looking to 2001, the Falcons, though somewhat pleased with Reginald Kelly, looked to take another step in upgrading the job by making talented Alge Crumpler out of North Carolina their second-round draft pick. Crumpler will push Kelly for the starting job and work in 2001.

QB: In the Falcon's Super Bowl run of 1998, Chris Chandler put up very good numbers, 3,154 passing yards and 25 touchdowns despite missing two games to injury. It has been all downhill since. Chandler struggled through injury and just struggled in 1999, partially because of the loss of Jamal Anderson to the running game. This placed more pressure on the passing game. In 2000, Chandler's struggles continued despite Anderson's return. Chandler, in and out of the lineup with a concussion and losing his starting job at times, finished with a disappointing 2,236 passing yards and ten touchdowns. The Falcons turned to backup veteran Danny Kanell and undrafted free agent Bob Johnson. The Falcons' quarterback situation took a big turn in the offseason. The Falcons traded up to get the #1 overall pick of this year's draft and with it landed highly coveted Michael Vick out of Virginia Tech. Vick, an incredibly talented athelete, will for now serve as backup to veteran Chris Chandler, but the Falcons believe they've got themselves a franchise player for down the road.

K: Veteran Morten Anderson struggled early in 2000, missing six field goals in a 17 field goal attempt span but after that hit his last nine in a row to finish with 25 of 31 (.806) attempts. Is this the year the Falcons let Anderson go and turn to Jake Arians, who spent the 2000 season on the practice squad? We'll keep a close eye as the preseason progresses. The Falcons have also signed a number of free agents to battle for the job, including Jay feely and Chad Holliman.

Overall: The slide continues for Atlanta, which went 5-11 (1999) and 4-12 (2000) since their Super Bowl run in 1998. Damaged goods, Jamal Anderson worked his way back from a severe knee injury but he is not the dominant player he was three years ago. Anderson is the key for Atlanta, who need him to again be a force on the ground. Through the air, aging quarterback Chris Chandler has to reprove he can still get it done after struggling the last two seasons. The receiving corps of Shawn Jefferson, and Terrance Mathis is formidable. The question is can the Falcons get it going again in the right direction? All this makes for a tough job for head coach Dan Reeves, though the future looks brighter with Michael Vick now aboard.

Offseason Fantasy-Position Moves

	Arriving	From:		Departing	To:
RB	Travis Jervey	Free Agent	WR	Tim Dwight	SD
RB	Ronnie Robinson	Free Agent			
RB	Rodney Thomas	Free Agent			
WR	Corey Brown	Free Agent			
WR	Shawn Mills	Free Agent			
WR	Moreno Philyan	Free Agent			
QB	Eric Zeier	TB			
K	Jay Feely	Free Agent			
K	Chad Hollimar	Free Agent			

BALTIMORE RAVENS
Home Stadium: PSI Net Stadium
Playing Surface: Grass
Head Coach: Brian Billick
2000 Record: 12-4

Billick, Rookie Jamal Lewis Lead Ravens to Super Season

RB: Leading up to the 2000 season, the Ravens looked to improve their running attack after letting their leading rusher of 1999 get away to Cleveland. Errict Rhett, who led the Ravens with 852 yards a year earlier, departed to join the Browns. This left Priest Holmes, a 1,000-yard rusher in 1998 but injured most of 1999, to battle inbound rookie Jamal Lewis, the Raven's first-round draft pick and #5 overall pick of the 2000 draft. The Ravens had high hopes for Lewis, hoping he could become a factor early in the season if he progressed well. Holmes got the start to open the season, and his 119 yard performance in the season opener kept Lewis a background factor. Holmes quickly slowed, and soon Lewis was sharing the backfield duties with Holmes. By game #4 Lewis was becoming more of a factor, rushing for 116 yards on 25 carries. The two continued to share the load, but the swing to Lewis quickly took place. Lewis followed with four more 100-yard games and three games of 90-plus yards. On the season Lewis finished with 1,364 rushing yards, 296 more receiving yards on 27 receptions and six touchdowns. Holmes finished the year with 588 rushing yards, 221 receiving yards on 32 receptions and one touchdown. Obafemi Ayanbadejo chipped in only 37 rushing yards but more significantly caught 23 passes for 168 yards before missing the second half of the year injured. Lewis's work didn't stop in the regular season, as the Ravens' run-first, low-mistake offense dictated a heavy work load for Lewis again in the playoffs. Lewis helped plow the Ravens into the Super Bowl and capped things off with a 102-yard performance in the Super Bowl to help get the victory. Looking to 2001, Lewis can be expected to build on his rookie numbers of 2000. Topping the 1,500-yard mark and ten touchdowns are well within reach. Meanwhile, Priest Holmes will likely be shopping his talents elsewhere.

WR: Coming off a career year in 1999, Qadry Ismail looked to have another stellar year in 2000. Ismail's 68 receptions for 1,105 yards and six touchdowns led the team. The year 2000, however, was not going to give Ismail the same result. A sprained knee ligament kept Ismail out two games early in the year, and his year-end numbers reflect that. For the year, Ismail finished with 49 receptions for 655 yards and five touchdowns. Numbers, however, that still led the team's wide receivers. Injuries plagued other Ravens' wide receivers as well. Patrick Johnson suffered a broken collarbone in training camp, never really got on track and finished with only 12 catches for 156 yards and two touchdowns playing in six games. Jermaine Lewis became more of a factor returning kicks, returning two punts for touchdowns but managed only 19 catches for 161 yards and one touchdown reception. Rookie, first-round pick Travis Taylor did a nice job until suffering a season-ending broken clavicle about mid-season. Taylor produced 28 receptions for 276 yards and three touchdowns in the nine games he did play. Brandon Stokley became a factor down the stretch, replacing Patrick Johnson as the starter and caught 11 passes and two touchdowns late in the year. Looking to 2001, the Ravens need to keep their receivers healthy. Ismail and Taylor are likely to start and put up decent numbers, with Stokley and Patrick Johnson battling for the #3 job. Most importantly remember that Brian Billick and the Ravens, who liked to run the football and were fairly conservative on offense in 2000, will likely open things up more in 2001 now that Elvis Grbac is aboard at quarterback.

TE: Coming off a season where the team's top tight end had only 13 receptions, the Ravens knew they had to make a move. They did! A huge One! The Ravens lured perennial all-Pro Shannon Sharpe from the Broncos. Sharpe, despite his known talent, had some questions because he was working his way back from a broken collarbone suffered in 1999. Sharpe answered all the questions. The vocal Sharpe became a team leader and rebounded his own numbers by producing 67 receptions for 810 yards and five touchdowns. Sharpe remains one of the league's most consistent and best tight ends. The Ravens also made a move looking to the future, making Todd Heap out of Arizona State their first-round draft pick. Heap can learn from one of the best in Shannon Sharpe and can provide stability for years to come at tight end for Baltimore. Expect to see the two in two tight end sets at times.

QB: The Ravens rewarded quarterback Tony Bank for his strong finish in 1999 by signing him to a 4-year deal worth about $18 million. Banks, over the last 11 games of 1999, had thrown for 2,136 yards and 17 touchdowns. Banks started out the 2000 season by throwing for eight touchdowns in the first three weeks, including a five-touchdown performance against Jacksonville on week #2. From there on, he became very erratic and never threw another touchdown pass. On week #8, head coach Brian Billick replaced Banks with Trent Dilfer. Dilfer took over, gained more and more confidence and led the Ravens on their Super Bowl run, though the Ravens took on a more conservative offensive approach. On the year, playing in 11 games, Banks threw for 1,578 yards and eight touchdowns. Dilfer, playing in nine games threw for 1,502 yards and 12 touchdowns. Looking to 2001, despite Dilfer's 11-1 record as the starter, including the Super Bowl victory, the Ravens went looking for help elsewhere. Dilfer's lack of success or kick consistency previously in his career made them leery. The Ravens signed Elvis Grbac following his release from Kansas City to a 5-year, $30 million deal. Grbac, who threw for 4,169 yards and 28 touchdowns with Kansas City in 2000, will allow the Ravens to open up their offense. If for some reason Grbac struggles, the Ravens may also explore the use of last year's third-round pick Chris Redman. Many feel Redman, who has looked impressive in practice, could be ready to be given a shot. Meanwhile, Tony Banks was released but later signed with the Dallas Cowboys.

K: Another very solid season for Matt Stover, who hit a remarkable 35 of his 39 (.897) field goal attempts in 2000. I think the Ravens have little reason to look elsewhere.

Overall: Wow, what a run! In just two short seasons, Brian Billick brought the Ravens the gold at the end of the rainbow. The great defense and nucleus is there to make another run. The Ravens have to feel charmed in having Jamal Lewis, who looks to be an elite back for years to come. Not having to rely too much on the passing game, Billick stayed conservative with Trent Dilfer in 2000 and it worked. This time out, however, the Ravens will have more offensive potential in 2001, bringing in Elvis Grbac at quarterback. The move will certainly give the Ravens' receivers a shot at better numbers. It should be another great year in Baltimore.

Offseason Fantasy-Position Moves

Arriving		From:		Departing		To:
QB	Elvis Grbac	KC		WR	Billy Davis	Released
				QB	Tony Banks	DALL

Eric Moulds/Buffalo Bills

BUFFALO BILLS

Home Stadium: Ralph Wilson Stadium
Playing Surface: Astro Turf
Head Coach: Gregg Williams
2000 Record: 8-8

Buffalo May Have Trouble Paying the Bills
Re-sign Mould for $40 Million over Six Years

RB: Since topping the 1,000-yard mark in 1998, Antowain Smith has come no where near reaching that kind of performance level. The Bills, like they did in 1999 when Jonathan Linton pushed Smith for work, gave other backs opportunity to do the same in 2000. Smith, who rushed for only 42 yards on 17 carries in the 2000 season opener, was quickly challenged by Shawn Bryson and eventually by fifth-round draft pick Sammy Morris. Morris and Bryson both got a chance to be the feature back but somewhat ironically Smith got his shot again in the season finale and rushed for 147 yards on just 17 carries and scored three times. On the year, Bryson ended up leading the team with 591 rushing yards, while grabbing 32 receptions for 271 yards but scored only twice. Smith was next with 354 rushing yards, caught only three passes for 20 yards and scored four times. The rookie Morris rushed for 341 yards, caught 37 passes for 268 yards and scored six times. Morris fell off in the second half due to a high ankle sprain. Jonathan Linton, so much a factor in 1999, rushed for only 112 yards, caught three passes for eight yards and scored only once. How does this all bode for the upcoming 2001 season? Despite Antowain's Smith rebound finale in the 2000 season, his inconsistency over the past two seasons has likely cost him the starting job. I expect Shawn Bryson and Sammy Morris to battle for the every-down spot. Both seem to provide fairly consistent ground gains and the ability to catch the ball out of the backfield, both essential items the Bills need on offense. Another player to throw into the mix is rookie second-round draft pick Travis Henry out of Tennessee, who'll also push for work. It's also possible to see more of what we saw in 2000—running back by committee if no one steps up consistently. This is surely a situation we'll keep an eye on as the preseason rolls around and the regular season nears.

WR: Following a breakout year in 1998, when Eric Moulds produced 67 receptions for 1,398 yards and seven touchdowns, Moulds struggled some in 1999, as his numbers fell to 65 catches for 994 yards and only seven scores. Moulds got back on track and then some in 2000, busting out with a 94 reception, 1,326 yard, five touchdown season. Along the way Moulds produced seven 100-yard games. Certainly he made a leap into the league's elite receivers. Besides Moulds, the Bills need to find a solid #2 receiver to compliment him. Peerless Price, the Bills second-round pick of 1999 did step up to record 52 receptions for 762 yards and three touchdowns, including an eight-reception, 132-yard, one-touchdown performance in the season finale. Jeremy McDaniel did a nice job in chipping 43 receptions for 697 yards while scoring twice. The 2001 season should be more of the same as Eric Moulds will be high on many fantasy charts, especially in yardage leagues and especially with new head coach Gregg Williams implementing a version of the West Coast offense. The Bills standout receiver inked a 6-year, $40 million deal, including a $12.5 signing bonus in the offseason. The #2 receiver still may be in question but Peerless Price may be the answer. The Bills will continue to use Jeremy McDaniel and may take a closer look at Avion Black, last year's fourth-round pick who didn't get much of a shot in 2000.

TE: Coming off a season where he showed a lot of potential in recording 37 receptions for 496 yards and four touchdowns in 1999, Jay Riemersma was rewarded with a 4-year, $12 million deal. Riemersma got off a strong start in 2000, scoring twice in the first three weeks, before suffering a knee injury that kept him out four weeks. In returning, Riemersma ended the season recording 31 receptions for 372 yards and scored five times. Hoping to stay healthy in 2001, Riemersma should put up much more significant numbers to please both Bill's and fantasy fans.

QB: Flutie or Johnson, Johnson or Flutie—the quarterback controversy continued in Buffalo. Despite good success under Flutie in the past, Rob Johnson was given the reins late in the 1999 season and opened the 2000 season. Johnson fared OK until suffering a shoulder injury about mid-season. Doug Flutie came in for four games and helped the Bills win three of them. When Johnson returned, he got his starting job back but in struggling, gave way again to Flutie. The team finished 8-8 and perhaps much had to do with the quarterback controversy. On the season, Johnson finished with 2,125 passing yards and 12 touchdowns, while Flutie finished with 1,700 yards and eight touchdowns. Looking to 2001, the controversy had to stop because neither would have flourished when always having to look over their shoulder. The Bills, despite the worry of Johnson's proneness to injury, released Doug Flutie, who went on to sign with San Diego, leaving Johnson room to breath and hopefully produce in 2001.

K: Hitting 26 of 35 (.743) field goal attempts is a decent year at best for Steve Christie, who struggled to hit 25 of 34 (.735) the year before. The real concern is how Christie ended the 2000 season, missing his last three of four attempts. Are the Bills concerned enough to look elsewhere? They did re-sign him in the offseason but also signed free-agent Jay Taylor to push for the job.

Overall: Following a drop from 11-5 in 1999 to 8-8 in 2000, the Bills opted to fire head coach Wade Phillips. His replacement Gregg Williams has some talent to work with but has his work cut out for him. Can he find an every-down back in the lot of Sammy Morris, Shawn Bryson, Antowain Smith, Jonathan Linton or even second-round draft pick Travis Henry? Can quarterback Rob Johnson stay healthy now that he has the starting job and Doug Flutie is gone? All-pro Eric Moulds is re-signed and will again be a huge weapon, but who'll be the #2 receiver to take some pressure off. These are a lot of questions for a new head coach to answer.

Offseason Fantasy-Position Moves

	Arriving	From:		Departing	To:
RB	Phillip Crosby	Free Agent	RB	Thurman Thomas	Retired
WR	Stephen Campbell	Free Agent	QB	Doug Flutie	SD
WR	Matt Davison	Free Agent			
WR	Teddy Johnson	Free Agent			
WR	Jonathan Pittman	Free Agent			
QB	Pete Gonzalez	Free Agent			
QB	Tim Hasselbeck	Free Agent			
K	Jay Taylor	Free Agent			

CAROLINA PANTHERS

Home Stadium: Ericsson Stadium
Playing Surface: Grass
Head Coach: George Seifert
2000 Record: 7-9

Panthers Need "Walls" to Stay Up and Healthy

RB: Looking for backup insurance because of Tim Biakabatuka's prone-ness to injury, the Panthers signed Natrone Means following his release by San Diego prior to the 2000 season. The move didn't pay off, however, as Means became a bust and was released early on. The Panthers then again turned to Biakabatuka. Biakabatuka was faring pretty well until a painful turf toe injury forced him to miss five games. To that point he had rushed for 609 yards, had grabbed 33 receptions for 329 yards and has scored four times playing in ten games. With Biakabatuka out, the Panthers turned the bulk of the rushing load over to Brad Hoover. Hoover produced one 100-yard game in his four starts and finished the year with 290 rushing yards, grabbed 15 receptions for 112 yards and scored once. Biakabatuka returned very late in the year but was far from being a factor, rushing six times for 18 yards over the last two games. Biakabakuta finished the year with 627 rushing yards, 34 receptions for 341 yards and scored the four touchdowns. The Panthers also got a little help from Chris Hetherington, who tallied only 65 rushing yards, caught 14 passes for 116 yards but did score three times. William Floyd, who missed the last six games of the year with a knee injury, tallied 33 rushing yards, caught 17 passes for 114 yards and scored twice before the injury. Looking to 2001, the Panthers are unlikely to stick with the injury-prone Biakabatuka as their #1 option at running back, possibly looking elsewhere for another source to provide their ground attack. Meanwhile, William Floyd was released following the season.

WR: With Patrick Jeffers having a breakout year in 1999 and Muhsin Muhammad stepping his game up a couple of notches, the Panthers' receiving corps looked again to do big damage in 2000. Jeffers, the speedy wideout, was coming off a season where he produced an impressive 63 receptions for 1,082 yards while scoring 12 times. Muhammad jumped from 68 receptions in 1998 to a whopping 96 receptions for 1,253 yards and eight touchdowns in 1999. Again, both looked to put up big numbers again in 2000. Didn't happen! Jeffers suffered a season-ending knee injury in the preseason, tearing his ACL, which was a devastating blow to the Panthers' passing game. Who would step in? Donald Hayes, who caught only 11 passes in 1999 and expected to become the team's #3 receiver, made the jump to starter. Hayes turned into a very solid replacement, recording 66 receptions for 926 yards and scoring three times. Was Muhammad's production hurt? Not in the least. Muhammad topped his phenomenal 1999 numbers by posting 102 receptions for 1,188 yards and six touchdowns. An incredible season. In addition to Muhammad and Hayes, Isaac Byrd chipped in 22 receptions for 241 yards and two touchdowns, stepping in as the #3 receiver. Looking to 2001, the Panthers, if Jeffers is healthy, have found a wealth of receiving talent. Muhammad has stepped up to be among the league's elite receivers and should again put up big numbers. The healthy return of Patrick Jeffers should be closely watched, as his return will determine the #2 receiving role for Carolina, though regardless, Donald Hayes has earned additional playing time whether as the #2 or #3 receiver. The Panthers will also throw third-round draft pick Stevonne Smith out of Utah into the mix. Another big question will be how the receivers will fare with Steve Beuerlein gone. Beuerlein was released in the offseason, likely turning the starting job over to backup Jeff Lewis.

TE: Certainly one of the league's top tight ends, Wesley Walls always figures to be a solid fantasy pick. This was especially true going into the 2000 season coming off a 1999 season where he produced 63 receptions for 822 yards and a whopping 12 touchdowns. Through the first eight games of 2000, Walls got off to a solid start, recording 31 receptions for 422 yards and scored twice, but his season quickly ended as he suffered a severe knee injury that would keep him out of the rest of the season. In his absence, the Panthers turned to Kris Mangum, who filled in admirably but obviously was no Wesley Walls. Magnum finished the year with 19 receptions for 215 yards and one touchdown. Looking to 2001, it's Wesley Walls that Panthers' and fantasy fans hope to see return 100 percent. When he's healthy, Walls is always capable of topping 750 yards and the ten-touchdown plateau—a huge accomplishment for a tight end.

QB: It's hard to repeat a career-year performance. This is what Steve Beuerlein found out in 2000, especially with a wounded running game and missing one of the leagues top receiving tight ends for half the season. Beuerlein was coming off a 4,436 yard, 36 touchdown performance heading into the 2000 season. Beuerlein did get off to a solid first half, recording three 300-yard games and ten touchdowns over the first seven games but did not push those numbers very well in the second half as he never hit the 300-yard mark again. On the season, he finished with 3,730 passing yards and 19 touchdowns, quite a far drop from the year before. Part of the reason was the Panthers' offensive line, which allowed 69 sacks—certainly something the Panthers have to remedy in 2001, if they expect things to improve. Looking to 2001, Beuerlein won't be back, being released in the offseason. Instead the Panthers will likely turn to Jeff Lewis. Lewis, who came to the Panthers prior to the 1999 season believing he could battle for the starting job, doesn't have much actual experience. Prior to coming to Carolina, Lewis was backup to John Elway in Denver and believed to be heir to the quarterback job there when Elway retired. Lewis, however, jumped ship and will finally get his shot to start. Lewis will be challenged by fourth-round draft pick Chris Weinke out of Florida State. Weinke, who gave baseball a try before returning to college to give football a shot, is 28. This may bode well in having a very mature rookie. Weinke will be anxiously awaiting if Lewis struggles.

K: John Kasay, one of the league's more consistent kickers, missed the entire 2000 season after also missing the last three games of 1999 with a torn ACL. With Kasay out, the Panthers turned to NFL veteran Ritchie Cunningham. Cunningham's 5 of 7 (.714) field goal performance, with the two misses being inside 30 yards cost him the job after just five games. The Panthers then turned to another NFL veteran Joe Nedney. Nedney was impressive. Nedney finished out the year for Carolina by hitting 24 of 26 (.923) field goals while in a Panther uniform. He had earlier kicked for Denver and finished 34 of 38 (.895) on the year. The Panthers may have been in a dilemma, but Kasay's knee looks to be healthy, so Nedney took his services to Tennessee, signing with the Titans in the offseason.

Overall: Where is this team headed? It went from 8-8 in 1999 to 7-9 in 2000. Surely injuries to Wesley Walls, Patrick Jeffers and Tim Biakabatuka hurt significantly and played a huge role in the Panthers lack of success. Then there's the 69 sacks allowed. Where does George Siefert start? There has to be improvement on the offensive line. Perhaps a replacement for the injury-prone Tim Biakabatuka is in order. Through the air, aging Steve Beuerlein was let go in the offseason, likely turning the offense over to unproven Jeff Lewis. Having a healthy Patrick Jeffers back won't hurt, and Muhsin Muhammad's climb to elite status will help any passing game. Though again, much will depend on the performance of unproven Jeff Lewis.

Offseason Fantasy-Position Moves

	Arriving	From:		Departing	To:
RB	R. J. Bowers	Free Agent	RB	William Floyd	Released
RB	Thadd Buttone	Free Agent	TE	Brian Kinchen	Released
RB	Chad Dukes	Free Agent	QB	Steve Beuerlein	Released
RB	Nick Goings	Free Agent	K	Joe Nedney	TENN
WR	Kevin Coffey	Free Agent			
WR	Jermale Kelly	Free Agent			
WR	Kofi Shuck	Free Agent			

CHICAGO BEARS

Home Stadium: Soldier Field
Playing Surface: Grass
Head Coach: Dick Jauron
2000 Record: 5-11

Even under Dick Jauron Things Continue to Be Un"Bear"able

RB: After three years of trying to build something around their #1 draft pick of 1998, Curtis Enis, the Chicago Bears opted to take a different approach. Enis, who suffered a severe knee injury midway through his rookie season, hasn't ever seemed to fully recover from the injury. In 2000 the Bears decided to give James Allen a shot at carrying the bulk of the rushing load. Allen responded with fairly impressive numbers, rushing for 1,120 yards, catching 39 passes for another 291 yards and scoring three times. Along the way, however, he manufactured only one 100-yard game. Enis, seeing spot duty and missing a number of games with a shoulder injury, finished with only 84 yards rushing, while catching eight passes for 68 yards and scored only once. Looking to 2001, it would seem that James Allen would be the mainstay of the running game. Curtis Enis's days with the Bears are over as he was released in the offseason, later signing with Cleveland. Looking to 2001, the Bears were not apparently satisfied to just sit on having James Allen be their only option at running back. The Bears made Anthony Thomas out of Michigan their second-round draft pick, and Thomas comes in to challenge Allen for the job.

WR: Coming off a breakout season in 1999, there were plenty of expectations in 2000 for Marcus Robinson. Robinson was coming off a season where he produced 84 receptions for a staggering 1,400 yards and nine touchdowns, as he quickly became one of the league's most feared deep-threat receivers. The Bears also had a nice tandem receiver to go with Robinson in Bobby Engram, who also was coming off a strong year. Engram actually led the team in 1999, with 88 receptions, going for 947 yards while scoring four times. However, as we all know year to year, things happen to change or alter our expectations. Robinson got off to a good start recording 25 receptions for 418 and four touchdowns over the first five games, until an ankle injury kept him from a game and slowed him for awhile. He returned but only to suffer from a bulging disk in his back, which sidelined him the last four games of the year. On the year, playing in 11 games, Robinson finished with a disappointing 55 receptions for 738 yards and five touchdowns. Bobby Engram wasn't even that fortunate, suffering a season-ending knee injury in the third game of the season after recording only 16 receptions in the span. With Engram out, offseason acquisition Eddie Kennison from New Orleans expanded his role and recorded 55 receptions for 549 yards and two touchdowns. Marty Booker also got to expand his role and numbers, recording 47 receptions for 490 yards and two touchdowns. The Bear also received help from Macey Brooks, who produced 26 receptions for 216 yards but failed to score. Looking to 2001, the health of the Bears' passing game seems to be accountable to the health of their receivers. I again expect a rebound to big things for Marcus Robinson if he can stay healthy. The Bears also upgraded their receiving crew by making David Terrell out of Michigan their first-round draft pick. Terrell, a big, fast receiver, should become a factor right away with Robinson and Terrell likely starters. Terrell has excellent big-play ability. Engram, if healthy, will push for work at the #3 spot along with Marty Booker. Meanwhile Eddie Kennison departed in the offseason to join the Denver Broncos.

TE: At tight end, former first-round pick John Allred continues to struggle. In 2000, knee and ankle injuries forced him to miss the last 11 games of the season. The Bears did get some help from 2000 offseason acquisition Kaseem Sinceno (Eagles). Sinceno led the Bears' tight ends with 23 receptions going for 206 yards but failed to score. Allred finished with nine receptions and the only touchdown from a Bear tight end—that coming in the season opener. Looking to 2001, Sinceno seems to have earned himself a spot battling Allred for work but regardless neither seems to be much of a big fantasy candidate.

QB: The Bears have been playing musical quarterbacks. In 1999 the Bears tried to bring along their #1 draft pick, Cade McNown, out of UCLA. Though he didn't begin the season as a starter, he got his shots along with Shane Matthews and Jim Miller. Heading into 2000, the Bears thought McNown, who had now had the chance to develop more, would be the team starter at the season's outset. McNown started the first eight games with mixed reviews until a shoulder injury sidelined him for six weeks. Upon his return, he saw action the Bear last two games but was far from impressive. On the season, playing in ten games, McNown recorded 1,646 passing yards and eight touchdowns. Shane Matthews, who saw action in six games, recorded 964 passing yards and three touchdowns. Jim Miller, seeing action in three games, recorded 382 passing yards and one touchdown. Looking to 2001, Cade McNown will unlikely be given the starting job without a challenge from Matthews, who was re-signed in the offseason, and Miller. Head coach Dick Jauron is leaving the spot open for competition — a competition we'll have to monitor as the preseason nears.

K: Hoping to solidify their kicking game, the Bears made Paul Edinger out of Michigan State their sixth-round draft pick. Edinger struggled early in the season missing two of his first four kicks but came on as the season progressed including hitting two 50-plus yarders in the season finale. On the year, Edinger hit 21 of 27 (.778) field goal tries and has likely locked up the Bear's kicking chores for awhile.

Overall: The last three seasons, the Bear have gone 4-12, 6-10 and 5-11. There seems to be little room for optimism that things are about to improve soon. New offensive coordinator John Shoop has to figure out a way to improve both the Bears' running game and passing game. Can James Allen continue to carry the load by himself? The Bears' choosing of Anthony Thomas shows their uncertainty, and Thomas will push Allen hard for the job. Curtis Enis, the Bears' #1 draft pick of 1998, has been a bust and was released in the offseason. Though blessed with a talented receiving corps of Marcus Robinson, rookie David Terrell, Bobby Engram and company, will any Chicago quarterback step up with consistency? There are more questions than answers for a team whose best fantasy prospects remain their receivers.

Offseason Fantasy-Position Moves

	Arriving	From:		Departing	To:
WR	Fred Coleman	Free Agent	RB	Curtis Enis	CLE
TE	Fred Baxter	Free Agent	WR	Eddie Kennison	DEN

Corey Dillon/Cincinnati Bengals

CINCINNATI BENGALS

Home Stadium: Cinergy Field
Playing Surface: Astro Turf
Head Coach: Bruce Coslet
2000 Record: 5-11

Dillon Really the Lone Bright Spot

RB: For his fourth straight NFL season Corey Dillon has lit it up for over 1,000 yards on the ground. Dillon is the Bengal's offense. The futile Cincinnati offense finished 29th in the league overall but don't blame that on Dillon. Dillon rushed for 1,435 yards, caught 18 passes for 158 yards and scored seven times in 2000. During the year, Dillon recorded three 100-yard games, two 200-yard games including a 278 yard performance against Denver that broke the NFL single-game mark. These are incredible numbers especially for a player on such a poor team. Other than Dillon, the Bengals got 324 rushing yards, 19 catches for 168 yards and three touchdowns out of Brandon Bennett. There were few other significant contributions. Nick Williams, Curtis Keaton and Clif Groce combined for 72 yards rushing, 18 receptions for 129 yards and no touchdowns between them. Looking to 2001, will Corey Dillon still be around? Dillon has expressed desire to leave in the past. He turned down an initial offer of $60 million over eight years including a $12 million signing bonus. Now given the "franchise" designation, Dillon may have trouble escaping to play elsewhere. Regardless of where he ends up playing, Corey Dillon will again leave a big mark in 2001.

WR: During the 2000 offseason, knowing Carl Pickens would be gone and no longer part of the picture, the Bengals made a move to replace him and find a tandem mate for Darnay Scott. The Bengals made Peter Warrick out of Florida State their #1 draft pick. This, the Bengals thought, would be a solid duo to also help bring along young quarterback, Akili Smith. This great plan never came about, as Darnay Scott suffered two broken bones in his right leg during the preseason and was lost for the year. This left Warrick to step up to be the team's #1 receiver—quite a load to put on a rookie, especially with a team carrying uncertainty at the quarterback position. Warrick stepped up and did his best under the circumstances. On the year, despite not recording one 100-yard game, Warrick finished with 51 receptions for 592 yards and seven touchdowns. Interestingly enough, only four of his touchdowns came on receptions, two came on runs and one on an 82 yard punt return. Again, he did well under tough circumstances. With Scott out, finding a replacement became tough. Craig Yeast, Danny Farmer and Ron Dugans all got their chance to step in, with none coming close to helping fill Scott's shoes. Yeast led the way with only 24 receptions for 301 yards and no touchdowns. Danny Farmer, who was a starter at season's end, was next with 19 receptions for 268 yards and he too did not score. Ten of his receptions, however, did come in the last two games, one game of which he had five receptions for 102 yards. Ron Dugans chipped in 14 receptions for 125 yards and the only other touchdown by a wide receiver, other than that scored by Peter Warrick. Looking to 2001, the Bengals obviously hope Scott returns healthy. His return to team with Warrick would give the Bengals the talented tandem they were hoping for when they drafted Warrick a year ago. The Bengals also added another possible dimension to the receiving equation by making Chad Johnson out of Oregon State their second-round draft pick. Johnson will likely battle for work behind Scott and Warrick and also provides insurance in the event Scott isn't fully recovered from his leg injury.

TE: Tony McGee, who once produced 58 receptions six years ago, has seen his production decline ever since. Respectively over that period McGee has recorded 58, 38, 34 and 22 receptions. In 2000, McGee finished with 26 receptions, a slight but insignificant jump, as he accumulated 309 yards and only one touchdown. Besides McGee, the Bengals got 13 receptions for 105 yards and no touchdowns out of Marco Battaglia and three receptions out of Steve Bush. Looking to 2001, McGee and Battaglia will have another challenger in third-round pick Sean Brewer out of San Jose State. Regardless I don't expect any significant numbers for any fantasy team owner, as even McGee is unlikely to boost his production in 2001 in any significant way.

QB: The Bengals, hoping their first-round pick of 1999 had gained the experience to step up in his second year, gave Akili Smith the starting nod in 2000. Smith's play was erratic at best. As the season wore on, the Bengals went back and forth between Smith and veteran Scott Mitchell, with Mitchell finishing the year as the starter over the last four games. Neither's stats were impressive as Smith, seeing action in 11 games, recorded only 1,253 yards and three touchdowns. Mitchell, appearing in eight games threw, for 966 yards and only three touchdowns. Miserable numbers and performances that had the Bengals looking for a challenger for Akili Smith heading into the 2001 season. They found that person in Jon Kitna, who came over from Seattle in the offseason, signing a 4-year, $10 million deal. Kitna, who had struggled as the Seahawk's starter in 2000 with Seattle, hopes to get it going with a fresh start and should make the battle with Akili Smith for the #1 quarterback job interesting as the preseason roles around.

K: Unimpressed with Doug Pelfrey's performances, the Bengals made Neil Rackers out of Illinois their sixth-round draft pick in 2000. Rackers struggled pretty much all year, missing his first three attempts and five of his first eight. On the year, Rackers finished by hitting 12 of 21 (.571) attempts, with all of his nine misses coming inside 50 yards. The Bengals have since brought in Ritchie Cunningham, who has previous NFL experience with a number of clubs, to challenge for the job.

Overall: The Bengals racked up a 3-13 record in 1998 and two straight 4-12 seasons in 1999 and 2000. The Bengals' strides to turn things around haven't worked. Quarterback Akili Smith, their #1 draft choice of 1999, has been a bust so far. The Bengals may be looking for someone to step in and challenge Smith and have brought in Jon Kitna from Seattle. Until the quarterbacking situation improves, talented receivers Peter Warrick and Darnay Scott will not put up the production their capable of, though new offensive coordinator Bob Bratkowski will go to a more wide-open offense. Do the Bengals have their ace in the hole, Corey Dillon, or do they?

Dillon, by far the team's best and most consistent offensive weapon, is a free agent, but the Bengals hung the "franchise" tag on him to protect their star. If he's around, he'll again put up big numbers for the Bengals.

Offseason Fantasy-Position Moves

	Arriving	From:	Departing	To:
RB	Kalani Sitake	Free Agent		
WR	Romondo North	Free Agent		
WR	Chris Roster	Free Agent		
QB	Jon Kitna	SEAT		
K	Ritchie Cunningham	Free Agent		

CLEVELAND BROWNS

Home Stadium: Cleveland Brown Stadium
Playing Surface: Grass
Head Coach: Butch Davis
2000 Record: 3-13

Injuries Stood in Way of Brown Progress in 2000

RB: With a struggling running game to say the least coming out of the 1999 season, the Browns knew they had to make a move coming into the 2000 season. The Browns signed free agent Errict Rhett away from the Baltimore Ravens. Rhett, the Browns hoped, would provide a chance at a consistent running game. It started out that way, as Rhett rushed for 257 yards through the first four games, while grabbing 14 receptions for 78 yards but failed to score. In week #5, however, Rhett fell victim to a season-ending foot injury, putting the Browns back into the predicament they were in prior to the season. The Browns turned to third-round draft pick Travis Prentise for the most part and Jamel White somewhat. Prentise did an adequate job, recording 512 rushing yards, 37 receptions for 191 more yards while scoring eight times. White finished the year with only 145 rushing yards, caught 13 passes for 100 yards but did not score. Fullback Marc Edwards did little on the ground, rushing twice for nine yards but did catch 16 passes for 128 yards and scored twice. Looking to 2001, the Browns hope to have Rhett back healthy so they can move Prentise into more of a third-down role, which they feel he's better suited for. Rhett is very capable of not only helping the Browns' running attack, if he returns healthy, but also of being a decent second running back for fantasy teams, especially in yardage leagues as the 1,000-yard plateau is within reach. In the event Rhett is not 100 percent or struggles, the Browns have another option in their third-round draft choice, James Jackson out of Miami (FLA), who'll also be battling for work. The Browns also expect to run more under new head coach, Butch Davis, which should help boost rushing numbers for someone. In the offseason, fullback Marc Edwards departed via free agency to New England.

WR: Coming off a rookie season of 66 receptions for 986 yards and eight touchdowns, Kevin Johnson looked to be a fantasy player worthy of attention heading into the 2000 season. Darrin Chiaverini also seemed to be worthy of attention as he finished the 1999 season, recording 37 receptions for 415 yards and five touchdowns over the last seven games. Johnson did again lead the team in receptions in 2000 but his 57 receptions for 669 yards and no touchdowns were disappointing and may be attributed to the loss of quarterback Tim Couch for over half the season. Chiaverini caught eight passes and one touchdown over the first four weeks and then was lost for the year with a knee injury. Rookie second-round pick Danny Northcutt got his chances but came along slowly and finished with 39 receptions for 422 yards and no touchdowns. Offseason acquisition David Patten (Giants) stepped in to record 38 receptions for 546 yards and one touchdown—a nice surprise. Rookie third-round pick JaJuan Dawson, who had an impressive training camp and was off to a solid start, and was likely going to make a big impact, caught nine passes including one touchdown over the first two games but suffered a season-ending broken collarbone. Looking to 2001, Kevin Johnson will again be the Browns #1 receiver. If healthy, JaJuan Dawson will push Darrin Chiaverini and second-round pick Quincy Morgan out of Kansas State for the #2 spot, with Danny Northcutt getting more time to develop. David Patten, however, is no longer part of the equation, signing as a free-agent with New England in the offseason. All of the receivers hope to have a healthy Tim Couch around for a full season at quarterback, which should help everyone's numbers.

TE: With veteran Irv Smith coming off a disappointing 24 reception performance in 1999, the Browns turned their attention to a younger look. Mark Campbell, returning from a nine-reception campaign in '99, was to battle speedy fourth-round pick Aaron Shea out of Michigan for work. Shea became a nice surprise, recording 30 receptions for 302 yards and two touchdowns. Campbell caught only 12 passes all year and one touchdown. Looking to 2001, the Browns have tried to upgrade at tight end, signing Ricky Dudley away from the Oakland Raiders. Dudley, who caught 29 passes for 350 yards and scored four times with Oakland in 2000, has the potential to push those numbers with Cleveland in 2001.

QB: Tim Couch, the Brown's first-round pick and #1 overall pick of the 1999 draft, showed some good signs as a rookie in winning the job from veteran Ty Detmer. Couch started off the year helping the Browns to two wins in their first three games, throwing for 735 yards and five touchdowns over that span. His performance and the Browns' performance slipped from there as he was part of four straight losses and then his season ended with a fractured right thumb suffered in a practice. The Browns turned to sixth-round draft pick Spergon Wyman and veteran Doug Pedersen. The Browns continued their downward spiral and won only one game of their last nine. Pedersen threw for 1,047 yards and only two touchdowns and played in ten games. Wynn threw for 167 yards and one touchdown in seven appearances. The Browns, looking to 2001, hope to have Tim Couch, their "franchise" player, back. Couch still remains the Browns' hope for future success. Doug Pedersen was released in the offseason.

K: Not much of a fantasy factor, as Phil Dawson was given only 17 field goal attempts in 2000. His 14 of 17 (.824) performance was decent, but he finished with only 59 total points for the year as the Browns struggled offensively.

Overall: The Browns, in existence for two seasons, have gone 2-14 in 1999 and 3-13 in 2000. There is certainly plenty of room for improvement. Injuries to quarterback Tim Couch and running back Errict Rhett hurt their chances to improve in 2000. Having both back in 2001 should help get the Browns back on track. Rhett should provide a consistent ability to run the football, while Couch's return should provide the passing attack. Receivers Kevin Johnson, JaJuan Dawson, Darrin Chiaverini and rookie second-round pick Quincy Morgan have a chance to improve their numbers.

Offseason Fantasy-Position Moves

	Arriving	From:		Departing	To:
RB	Curtis Enis	CHI	RB	Marc Edwards	NE
WR	Daymon Carroll	Free Agent	RB	Madre Hill	Released
TE	Ricky Dudley	OAK	WR	David Patten	NE
QB	Kelly Holcomb	IND	QB	Doug Pederson	Released
K	Derek Schorels	Free Agent			

DALLAS COWBOYS

Home Stadium: Texas Stadium
Playing Surface: Texas Turf
Head Coach: Dave Campo
2000 Record: 5-11

Troy "Aik"man Wants To Return For More
But Is Denied

RB: The beat goes on for running back Emmitt Smith, who has rekindled his career over the past three seasons following a subpar 1997 season. Smith, who rushed for 1,397 yards, caught 27 passes for 119 more yards and scored 13 times in 1999, didn't quite match those numbers in 2000 but did put up decent year-end numbers. On the season, Smith rushed for 1,209 yards, caught 11 passes for 79 yards and scored nine times. Along the way Smith recorded six 100-yard games, including a stint when he topped the 100-yard mark three consecutive weeks. Not bad for a back on the downside of a sterling career. The Cowboys again saw Chris Warren work as Smith's backup, that is until late in the year when he was released and eventually was signed by the Philadelphia Eagles. While with the Cowboys, Warren rushed for 264 yards, caught 31 passes for 302 yards and scored three times, playing in 11 games. The Cowboys also got 88 yards rushing, 14 receptions for 72 yards and one touchdown from Michael Wiley, and six rushes for 28 yards from Troy Hambrich. Looking to 2001, Emmitt says he wants to do it again. Sometimes you wonder why a player who has had so much success and such a distinguished career wants to continue. You'd think his production would drop off, but Smith just keeps getting it done. With Warren gone, the Cowboys may give Troy Hambrich a shot at Smith's backup job, with Michael Riley handling more of a third-down role and Robert Thomas slated in at fullback. Regardless, Emmitt is the only one fantasy fans will wonder how far he can push his numbers in 2001.

WR: When Michael Irvin did not come back, due to a spinal injury, the

Cowboys made a big offseason move leading up to the 2000 season by signing speedy wide receiver Joey Galloway away from Seattle. Galloway signed a seven-year deal worth a reported $42 million. With Galloway aboard and Rocket Ismail coming off a season where he recorded 80 receptions for 1,097 yards and seven touchdowns in his first year with Dallas, the Cowboys believed they had a tandem that could inspire fear into many opposing defenses. That belief was very short-lived, however, as Galloway suffered a season-ending knee injury in the season opener, after catching just four passes, one of which went for a touchdown. With Galloway out, Ismail and James McKnight tried to pick up the slack. Ismail, to the Cowboy's disbelief, was also lost for the year. Ismail suffered a season-ending knee injury, forcing him to miss the last eight games of the year. Ismail finished the year with only 25 receptions for 350 yards and one touchdown. McKnight was now joined by Wane McGarity to help pick up the pieces. Neither receiver had potential of a Galloway or Ismail and, the Cowboys passing game struggled. McKnight did finish with a respectable 52 receptions for 926 yards and only two touchdowns. McGarity finished with 25 receptions for 250 yards and three touchdowns. Jason Tucker chipped in with 15 receptions for 141 yards and one touchdown. Looking to 2001, the Cowboys hopes are high for both Galloway and Ismail to return healthy to wreak havoc on defenses like they were suppose to do a year earlier. If completely healthy, both players have 1,000-yard seasons in reach, depending on the quarterback situation. Meanwhile, James McKnight has moved on, signing as a free-agent with the Miami Dolphins. In turn, the Cowboys signed Carl Pickens following his release from the Tennessee Titans. Pickens, once considered one of the league's premier receivers, has struggled the last couple seasons and was bothered with a hamstring injury in 2000. He is, however, very capable of helping the Cowboy aerial attack in 2001.

TE: The Cowboys saw their former first-round draft pick of 1997, David LaFluer step up to grab 35 receptions for 332 yards and score seven times in 1999. In addition, the Cowboys opted to sign veteran Jackie Harris away from Tennessee. The two would form a nice 1-2 tight end tandem punch for Dallas. Despite his success in 1999, LaFluer took a backseat to Harris, who produced right from the outset. LaFluer was slowed by a pelvic area pain and later had knee surgery following the season. Harris began the year scoring four times in the first four games. On the season, he recorded 38 receptions for 306 yards while scoring five times. With Harris stealing most of the show, LaFluer became less of a factor overall and as a scoring force. LaFluer finished the year with only 12 catches for 109 yards and one touchdown—a far cry from his seven scores from a year earlier. Looking to 2001, the Cowboys look like they like the ability of Harris to get downfield so I expect he'll again fare well. The questions for LaFluer, at 6'7", will the Cowboys return to using him as a scoring force in the "red zone" and will he be healthy? All of this is too uncertain as LaFluer's fantasy stock takes a big tumble.

QB: Remarkable as it may seem Troy Aikman has thrown for over 20 touchdowns only once in his career, which can be most attributed to injuries. The 2000 season was no different, as Aikman finished the season throwing for only seven touchdowns and 1,632 yards, as he missed five games due to injury. Aikman's age may also have something to do with his declining production, but two concussions and a lower back contusion kept him out of those five games. Why does he go on? He's certainly had his share of success. So here we are in 2001 and he says he wants to do it again, after almost countless concussions. It was just too painful at times to watch, and even Cowboys' owner Jerry Jones must have agreed letting Aikman go following the season, though Aikman had said he wanted to continue. This leaves a big void to fill. In the offseason, the Cowboys signed Tony Banks, following his release from Baltimore. Banks, who has seen time as a starter in both St. Louis and Baltimore, has the tools but has been known to be inconsistant. Young at 27, Banks, the Cowboys feel, has time to develop, and his strong arm will benefit speedsters Joey Galloway and Rocket Ismail. Looking long term, the Cowboys made Quincy Carter out of Georgia their second-round draft pick.

K: Tim Seder beat out a cast of free agents to lock onto the Cowboys' kicking chores heading into the 2000 season. His 25 of 33 (.758) performance is likely keep him around again in 2001.

Overall: Not much left here of the dynamic team that saw such great success in the 90s. From 10-6 in 1998 to 8-8 in 1999 to 5-11 a year ago, the rapid decline is just too apparent. Emmitt Smith still seems to have enough to at least fuel a decent running attack and be a solid fantasy football pick. At quarterback, the Cowboys will have a new look with Tony Banks, as Troy Aikman was let go and eventually retired following the season despite wanting another shot. Aikman moves on to join the Fox TV crew, where he'll be much safer. His replacement will be blessed with a solid core of receivers, if Joey Galloway and Rocket Ismail return healthy from the injuries of 2000. Newly acquired Carl Pickens along with tight end Jackie Harris are also a force.

Offseason Fantasy-Position Moves

	Arriving	From:		Departing	To:
RB	John Avery	Free Agent	WR	James McKnight	MIA
WR	Carl Pickens	TENN	QB	Troy Aikman	Retired
QB	Tony Banks	BALT			

DENVER BRONCOS

Home Stadium: Invesco Field
Playing Surface: Grass
Head Coach: Mike Shanahan
2000 Record: 11-5

With Davis and Gary out, Anderson Helps Broncos Run

RB: Coming into the 2000 season the biggest question for Denver was what do we do with Olandis Gary now that Terrell Davis was apparently back healthy? Gary had stepped in for the injured Davis to the tune of 1,159 yards rushing, 159 more receiving on 21 receptions and seven touchdowns and this over the last 12 games of 1999. With Davis returning from a knee injury, the Broncos still turned to Gary, who after rushing for 80 yards on 13 carries in the season opener, suffered a season-ending knee injury himself. Davis, ironically stepped in for Gary, but he too went down but with a less severe ankle injury that would sideline him for a short while. In week #2, in stepped unknown, unheralded, sixth-round draft pick Mike Anderson. Mike who? We all know Mike who now. Anderson jumped right in and grabbed the spotlight. He rushed for 131 yards on 31 carries and two touchdowns in his debut against Atlanta. The next week against Oakland he rushed for 187 yards on 32 carries. He hit the 100-yard mark one more time before Terrell Davis returned midseason to reclaim his starting job. Davis lasted just two games before suffering a season-ending leg injury. In comes Anderson again, producing three more 100-yard games, including a 195 yard, two touchdown performance against Seattle and a week later, a whopping 251-yard, four-touchdown performance against New Orleans. On the season, playing in 14 games, Anderson finished with 1,500 rushing yards, 23 receptions for 169 more yards and 15 touchdowns—a shock and surprise to the league and fantasy fans. Looking to 2001, what do the Broncos do with all this talent? Davis and Gary are expected back. With Anderson's unbelievable rookie showing, somebody is bound to go, as other teams drool over the prospects. We'll have to keep a close eye on this situation, though there's speculation at this point that Gary or Anderson will be moved to fullback with Howard Griffith now gone.

WR: Having two receivers that recorded over 70 receptions each in 1999, Denver and fantasy fans had every reason to believe similar numbers were in store again in 2000 from Rod Smith and Ed McCaffrey. Nobody likely saw the coming of the huge jump for both, however. Ed McCaffrey, who recorded 71 receptions for 1,018 yards and seven touchdowns in 1999, jumped to a whopping 101 receptions, for 1,317 yards and nine touchdowns in 2000. Rod Smith, who recorded 79 receptions, for 1,020 yards and four touchdowns in 1999 jumped to a very impressive 100 receptions for 1,602 yards and eight touchdowns. And this on a team known for their runners. There was little else from the Broncos' wide receivers but how could there be? Robert Brooks was the next best with three, that's right, three receptions. Looking to 2001, I don't think both Smith and McCaffrey will again hit the 100-reception mark. However, both are again capable of 80-plus receptions, 1,200-1,500 yards and of scoring 7-10 times each. Meanwhile, in the offseason, the Broncos strengthened their receiving crew by adding speedy Eddie Kennison, who comes over from Chicago. Kennison caught 55 passes for 549 yards and scored twice for Chicago in 2000.

TE: With Shannon Sharpe out of the picture in departing to Baltimore as a free agent, the Broncos looked for answers at the tight end position. In 1999, when Sharpe was lost for the last 12 games of the season with a broken collarbone, the Broncos had turned mostly to Byron Chamberlain, who recorded 32 receptions for 488 yards and scored twice and Dwayne Carswell, who recorded 24 receptions for 201 yards and scored twice. The Broncos made no move to upgrade the position heading into 2000, so it was Carswell, Chamberlain and Desmond Clark, who had recorded only one reception in 1999 to battle for work. Carswell stepped up in a big way, recording 49 receptions for 495 yards while scoring three times. Desmond Clark was next with 27 receptions for 339 yards and three scores, while

Byron Chamberlain finished with 22 catches for 283 yards and one score. Certainly there is no Shannon Sharpe in the group. In the offseason, Chamberlain left via free agency to join the Minnesota Vikings. So this leaves Carswell and Clark to pretty much split the work. I'm not too excited about either for the 2001 season, though Carswell could push the 500 yard, five touchdown plateau.

QB: The Broncos, with John Elway's retirement in 1999, elected to give young Brian Griese a shot at being not only their quarterback of the future but also the present. Griese's inaugural season of 1999 had its ups and downs, as he finished the year throwing for 3,032 yards and 14 touchdowns playing in 14 games. The Broncos stuck with Griese heading into the 2000 season. Griese started out well, helping the Broncos to two wins in their first three games before suffering a shoulder injury. He returned after missing only one game, played seven more games until his separated shoulder sidelined him five more weeks, and returning for a brief appearance in the season final. Griese finished the year throwing for an impressive 2,688 yards and 19 touchdowns playing in ten games, really more like nine games as he threw only two passes in the season finale. Gus Frerotte, who guided the team to five wins in the last six games, also fared well. Seeing action in nine games, Frerotte threw for 1,776 yards and nine touchdowns. Looking to 2001, the Broncos are waiting to see how Griese looks following surgery though their signing him to a 6-year, $39 million deal in the offseason must tell us something. They expect he'll again be there. If healthy all year, big fantasy numbers should be in store.

K: A mediocre performance from one of the league's better kickers, Jason Elam hit only 18 of 24 (.750) field goal attempts in 2000. A year earlier, Elam had a much better 29 of 36 (.806) performance, much more characteristic of what can be expected in 2001.

Overall: A quick turn for the better for the Broncos, who went 6-10 in 1999 and jumped to 11-5 in 2000. The Broncos turned things around in a hurry in the aftermath of John Elway retiring just two years ago. Young Brian Griese seems to be developing in a hurry, though a shoulder injury kept him out of five games in 2000 and he's still working his way back from shoulder surgery. Veteran Gus Frerotte stepped in and kept the ship running in his absence. Receivers Rod Smith and Ed McCaffrey keep getting it done and then some, with both topping the 100-receptions mark in 2000. On the ground, the Broncos had another remarkable year. In 1999, Terrell Davis suffered a knee injury and fourth-round draft pick Olandis Gary stepped in to have a surprisingly big year. In 2000, with Gary and Davis both out hurt, unknown sixth-round draft pick Mike Anderson picked up the slack to the tune of 1,500 yards and 15 touchdowns. The question is what do they do with all three healthy backs in 2000?

Offseason Fantasy-Position Moves

	Arriving	From:		Departing	To:
RB	Mike Stack	Free Agent	TE	Byron Chamberlain	MINN
WR	Eddie Kennison	CHI			
WR	Ryan Thelwell	Free Agent			
TE	Patrick Hape	TB			
QB	Steve Stenstrom	Free Agent			

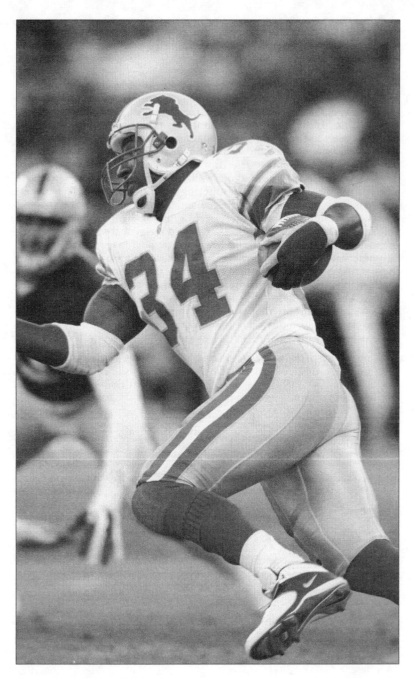

James Stewart/Detroit Lions

DETROIT LIONS

Home Stadium: Pontiac Silverdome
Playing Surface: Astro Turf
Head Coach: Marty Mornhinweg
2000 Record: 9-7

New Head Coach Mornhinweg Hoping Lions Will Roar a Little
Louder in 2001 but Have a "Batch" of Things to Work on

RB: After trying musical running backs in 1999—utilizing Greg Hill, Sedrick Irvin and Ron Rivers to try and fill the vacancy left by the retired Barry Saunders—the Lions opted for a new plan heading into the 2000 season. The Lions lured James Stewart away from the Jacksonville Jaguars, signing him to a 5-year deal worth $25 million, including a $7.5 million signing bonus. Stewart was as good as the Lions had hoped. Stewart was a consistent ground force and on the season rushed for 1,184 yards, caught 32 passes for another 287 yards while scoring 11 times. Along the way, he produced only three 100-yard games but he consistently pounded out 50 to 80 yards, though he did rush for 164 yards against the Jets the second to last game of the year. The Lions had again found a legitimate ground game. Besides Stewart, the Lions looked for and got very little help elsewhere. Mario Bates 127 rushing yards on 31 carries was next best. He also grabbed 15 passes for 109 yards but failed to score. Cory Schlesinger tallied only three rushing yards while catching 12 passes for 73 yards while he too failed to score. This shows what a workhorse Stewart was for the Lions, something they will expect again from him in 2001. As a fantasy participant, Stewart again is expected to push the 1,200-1,400 total yard level and score 10-14 times, certainly making him a very sought after commodity.

WR: Herman Moore, once rated among the league's most elite receivers, has suffered injuries and age has seen slow production. Heading into the 2000 season, Moore was coming off a year in which he missed the first ten games of the season with a knee injury. In returning healthy, Moore had found he would have to battle the younger Johnnie Morton and Germane Crowell for work. In fact, a shoulder injury kept him out of the season opener so he wouldn't see any action until week #2. As basically the teams #3 receiver, Moore finished the 2000 season recording 40 receptions for 434 yards and three touchdowns. This is a far cry from his heyday. His numbers were this limited, despite seeing additional action during a seven-game stretch when Germane Crowell was out with a foot injury. For the two receivers, Germane Crowell and Johnnie Morton, whom many thought would carry decent fantasy value into the 2000 season, both had good 1999 seasons. Crowell, the Lions 1998 second-round draft pick, was coming off a year where he produced 81 receptions for 1,338 yards and seven touchdowns. Crowell had recorded 27 receptions for 308 yards and three touchdowns into the sixth game of the season in 2000 but then suffered a foot injury that sidelined him for five weeks. He returned later in the year to finish with 34 receptions for 430 yards and the three touchdowns. Johnnie Morton, who caught at least one pass in each game, saw his production drop to 61 receptions for 788 yards and three touchdowns. Besides these primary three wideouts, the Lions got Larry Foster to chip in 17 catches for 75 yards and one touchdown. No Lions' wide receiver had a 100-yard game: all season, which is remarkable. This could be attributed to three things, quarterback Charlie Batch's inconsistency, having three receivers to split up the load and production and the fact that now having James Stewart allows the Lions to rely on the run more. Looking to 2001, I believe the Lions will continue to run more with James Stewart, but the aging Herman Moore will be less of a factor, if a factor at all, being asked to take a pay cut to stay. I believe that Germane Crowell and Johnnie Morton's numbers will rebound but are unlikely to reach the levels they reached in 1999.

TE: David Sloan, who had battled injuries most of his early career, finally stayed healthy a full season and showed some of the potential the Lions had always believed was there. Sloan's 47 receptions for 591 yards and four touchdowns were what many thought might be just a glimpse of what might come in 2000. Such was not the case, as Sloan, much like the Lions' wide receivers, saw his production drop. Again likely attributed to the Lions running more with James Stewart now aboard. Sloan's numbers dropped to 32 receptions for 379 yards and two touchdowns. A disappointing result for fantasy fans who thought Sloan had more fantasy value than that. Besides Sloan the Lions got ten receptions and one touchdown out of Walter Rasby and three receptions out of Alfred Pupunu. David Sloan will again be a factor in the Lions' offense in 2001, though he'll have to make room for Pete Mitchell coming over via free agency from the New York Giants. Mitchell, a good pass-catching tight end, should steal some of the show.

QB: The Lions were hoping young Charlie Batch could build on his 1999 performance coming into the 2000 season. Batch, who became the Lions started in 1999, had missed five games with a sprained thumb. In the 11 games he did play, Batch had thrown for 1,957 yards and 13 touchdowns. Batch missed the 2000 season opener nursing a knee injury and was replaced by Stoney Case, as backup Mike Tomczak had broken his leg in preseason. Case helped the Lions to a 14-10 win over New Orleans, but Batch returned as the starter the following week. Batch continued as the starter, even through a stretch after suffering broken ribs against the New York Giants on week #12. Not playing at 100 percent, Batch dropped off down the stretch, throwing only two touchdowns over the last five games. For the year, Batch finished with 2,489 passing yards and 13 touchdowns playing in 15 games, a disappointing year. Looking to 2001, Batch will again return as the starter, hoping to stay healthy. Overall, however, I don't see big statistical numbers because Lions will want to run James Stewart often. For insurance, the Lions signed veteran Jim Harbaugh (Chargers) to be his backup and meanwhile Mike Tomczak was released.

K: Jason Hanson has hit over 80 percent of his field goal attempts for three straight seasons. Despite struggling early on in 2000, missing six of his first 16 attempts, Hanson finished by hitting 24 of 30 (.800) for the year. This consistency makes him a valued fantasy factor every year.

Overall: Improving by one game in 2000 to 9-7 from 8-8 in 1999 was a plus. The Lions did this despite quarterback Charlie Batch being hurt much of the year and his receiving crew having a mediocre year at best. Both Germane Crowell and Johnnie Morton's numbers dropped significantly. That's the bad news! The good news is the addition of running back James Stewart, who provided a consistent running game, helped in the overall improvement. I look for another solid year for Stewart again in 2001, giving their offense a balance they desperately need.

Offseason Fantasy-Position Moves

	Arriving	From:		Departing	To:
RB	DeWayne Miles	Free Agent	TE	Walter Rasby	WASH
RB	Stephen Trejo	Free Agent	QB	Mike Tomczak	Released
RB	Lamont Warren	Free Agent			
WR	Versie Gaddis	Free Agent			
WR	Sly Johnson	Free Agent			
TE	Bradford Banta	NYJ			
TE	Pete Mitchell	NYG			
TE	Brian Natrin	Free Agent			
TE	Kawasek Penn	Free Agent			
TE	Leonard Stephens	Free Agent			
TE	John Warrig	Free Agent			
QB	Neo Aaga	Free Agent			
QB	Jim Harbaugh	SD			
K	Brad Bohn	Free Agent			

GREEN BAY PACKERS
Home Stadium: Lambeau Field
Playing Surface: Grass
Head Coach: Mike Sherman
2000 Record: 9-7

Despite Loss of Levens, Packers Running Game Gets "Green" Light

RB: With Dorsey Levens seeming to become more injury prone the last few seasons, the Packers opted to acquire Ahman Green from Seattle as insurance for the 2000 offseason. Levens had missed extensive action in 1998 with leg and knee injuries. In 1999 Levens missed two games with cracked ribs. Despite missing the two games, Levens finished the '99 season rushing for 1,034 yards, caught 71 passes for 573 yards and scored ten times. Levens was forced to sit out the first two games of the 2000 season nursing a knee injury. With Levens out, Ahman Green stepped in to handle the rushing load, doing an adequate job but not turning heads rushing for 87 yards in the two games Levens missed. Levens returned to the starting lineup but again was sidelined a couple games later and eventually was lost for the season with a knee injury forcing him to miss the last eight games of the year. Each time Levens was hurt, Green stepped in, but it wasn't until the last nine games that Green really took off after becoming more familiar with the offense. Taking over when Levens got hurt in game #8 of 2000, Green rushed for 863 yards, caught 48 passes for 313 yards and scored ten times over those last eight and a half games. For the season, Green finished with 1,175 rushing yards, caught 73 passes for 559 yards and scored 13 times. Levens playing in just five games finished with only 224 rushing yards, caught 16 passes for 146 yards ands scored three times. Has Leven's recent proneness to injury the last few seasons lost him the starting job to Green? Green's performance of a year ago make that likely especially with how the Packers finished winning their last four games. If Green continues to improve playing in the Packers' offense, he could push 1,500-1,800 total yards and 15 touchdowns in 2001. Levens, who resigned a 3-year deal in the offseason, will be back to challenge Green in 2001 for his spot.

WR: In 1998 Antonio Freeman had become a very coveted fantasy pick when producing 84 receptions for 1,424 yards and scoring 14 times. These were numbers Freeman slipped from when posting 71 receptions for 1,074 and six touchdowns in 1999. Would he rebound in 2000? No, Freeman came nowhere near those levels, struggling both on and off the field. His play and attitude took a step backward. Freeman was kept out of the season finale after missing a team meeting prior to the game. For the season, Freeman dropped to 62 receptions for 912 yards and nine touchdowns. These numbers showed Freeman was headed in the wrong direction. Bill Schroeder, who had a solid 1999 season when he recorded 71 receptions for 1,051 yards and five touchdowns, had another decent year in 2000. Schroeder finished with 65 receptions for 999 yards and four touchdowns. Corey Bradford, who had recorded five touchdowns on just 37 receptions in 1999, missed the entire 2000 season with leg and knee injuries. The Packers did get 21 receptions for 322 yards and one touchdown out of Donald Driver and ten receptions for 134 yards out of Charles Lee, a seventh-round draft pick. Looking to 2001, many questions surface because of how the Packers felt about Antonio Freeman at season's end in 2000. With Freeman's play and attitude on the decline, will he be around? Regardless Bill Schroeder will again be a factor, and we'll have to keep an eye on the progress of Corey Bradford's healthy return. There is speculation that Charles Lee will get much more of a shot in 2001. There is also rookie second-round pick Robert Ferguson out of Texas A & M, who has some raw talent but will work himself into a role. He's a player who will need some work playing at this high of a level, having played only one year at the Division I Level in College.

TE: With Mark Chmura facing possible charges for sexual assault prior to the 2000 season, the Packers made a move to cover his likely absence. The Packers made Bubba Franks out of Miami their first-round draft pick, hoping he could step right in and make an impact. Franks would team with veteran Tyrone Davis to handle the tight end work, at least initially. Franks never really came on and finished up being a disappointment and with disappointing numbers. He finished his rookie year with 34 receptions for 363 yards and only one touchdown. Tyrone Davis who had been a scoring force in 1998, scoring seven times on 18 receptions, finished with 19 receptions for 177 yards and only two scores. Looking to 2001, the Packers hope Franks can be brought along. In doing so, fantasy fans will reap the benefit statistically of Franks being Brett Favre's #1 tight end.

QB: After five straight seasons of 30-plus touchdown passes, Brett Favre fell to 22 touchdown passes in 1999 but still threw for over 4,000 (4,091) yards. Coming into 2000, many thought Favre, recovered from the thumb injury that plagued him in '99, would rebound statistically. He recorded 1,779 passing yards and ten touchdowns over the first seven games of

2,000, numbers that still weren't really up to his standards. Even down the stretch, Favre's numbers were not impressive as the Packers turned more to the run with Ahman Green doing the work. On the season, Favre finished with 3,812 passing yards and 20 touchdowns, surely a far cry from his numbers in his big five-year statistical run. Perhaps it's the Packers' change in philosophy, which seems to have them running more, or perhaps his talent and production are just on the decline. Either way, there's no way to deny he's not the fantasy player he was even three years ago. Rebounding to the 30 touchdown plateau seems less and less likely. In the offseason, the Packers showed their desire to keep Favre around for a long time, signing him to a 10-year deal. Meanwhile, his backup, Matt Hasselbeck, who showed some real promise, gets his chance to start in Seattle being traded to the Seahawks in the offseason.

K: Ryan Longwell keeps getting it done for the Packers. The 2000 season marked his fourth straight solid season in Green Bay as he hit 33 of 38 (.868) field goals, with two of his misses coming outside 50 yards. Becoming a free agent in the offseason, the Packers quickly got him to re-sign to stay on in Green Bay.

Overall: Despite the injuries to Dorsey Levens, who continued to battle injuries in the last few seasons, the Packers' running game did well in 2000. Offseason acquisition Ahman Green did a great job of filling in and perhaps winning the permanent role. Through the air, Brett Favre saw his numbers continue to drop, as do his wide receivers. Antonio Freeman became a problem both on and off the field, which hurt the team in numerous ways. The good sign for the Pack was winning their last four games. Funny, however, for the first time in a half a dozen years the primary fantasy prospect from Green Bay may not be Brett Favre. It may be Ahman Green heading into 2001.

Offseason Fantasy-Position Moves

	Arriving	From:		Departing	To:
RB	Chris Gall	Free Agent	QB	Matt Hasselbeck	SEAT
WR	Jason Franklin	Free Agent			
WR	Mike Horacek	JAC			
WR	Rodney Williams	Free Agent			
QB	Jonathan Beasley	Free Agent			
QB	Henry Burris	Free Agent			
QB	Cleo Lemon	Free Agent			
K	Brett Sterba	Free Agent			

INDIANAPOLIS COLTS
Home Stadium: RCA Dome
Playing Surface: Astro Turf
Head Coach: Jim Mora
2000 Record: 10-6

Despite Slight Dropoff — Indianapolis Still Peyton's Place

RB: Prior to the 1999 season, there was plenty of debate about which running back should and would be taken first — Heisman Trophy Winner and more highly touted Ricky Williams or perhaps a more well-rounded back in Edgerrin James. The Colts took James with the #4 overall pick, one pick prior to New Orleans taking Williams at #5. The move or selection has paid off in a huge way. James seems to be a perfect fit for the Colts' offense. James' ability to catch the football, as well as run, is the dimension the Colts were looking for. As a rookie in 1999, Edgerrin James led the NFL with 1,553 rushing yards. Along the way, he also recorded 62 receptions for another 586 yards while scoring 13 times. Coming into 2000, some may have wondered if James was indeed that good. There is no more wondering now. The numbers grew even bigger. For the second straight season, James led the NFL in rushing, this time with 1,709 yards. He maintained his ability as a great receiver out of the backfield as well, recording 63 receptions for 594 yards and 18 touchdowns, 13 on the ground and five more through the air. Along the way, James recorded nine 100-yard games including, one 200-yard performance against Seattle when he rushed for 219 yards and three touchdowns. It's hard to argue with any of those numbers that the Colts didn't make the right choice when selecting James over Ricky Williams. For precaution the Colts acquired Fred Lane from Carolina prior to the 2000 season, but Lane was found shot to death shortly thereafter. A backup was hardly needed as Lenny Gordon's 13 yards on four rushes was next best to James' numbers. James has proven to be a great runner, to be a great receiver and to have great durability. I'll take him in 2001, if I can get him.

WR: The Colts' talent doesn't stop at Edgerrin James. Marvin Harrison also has quickly taken the league by storm over the past two seasons. After recording 59 receptions for 776 yards and seven touchdowns, playing in 12 games in 1998 (missed four games with a separated shoulder), Harrison has seen his numbers erupt. In 1999, Harrison busted out grabbing a phenomenal 115 receptions for 1,663 yards and 12 touchdowns, along the way producing nine, 100-yard games. Could he top or near those levels in 2000 or was 1999 a fluke? No fluke! In 2000, Harrison recorded 102 receptions for 1,413 yards and scored 14 times. Along the way, Harrison recorded eight, 100-yard games, with seven of them coming in the first eight games. His yardage numbers dropped in the second half of the season but his touchdown production was consistent all year. The seemingly yearly problem is to find a #2 receiver to go with Harrison. Jerome Pathon, who had missed the last seven games of the 1999 season with a shoulder injury, stepped up to record 50 receptions for 646 yards and scored three times. Terrence Wilkins, who missed the first two games of the year because of a concussion suffered in preseason, recorded 43 catches for 569 yards and three touchdowns. E. G. Green, who continues to battle the yearly injury bug, recorded 18 catches for 201 yards and one score. Looking to 2001, Harrison will again be a highly sought after fantasy pick. His chemistry with quarterback Peyton Manning continues to evolve. I look for another 1,300-1,500 yard, 12-15 touchdown season. In addition the Colts tried to upgrade their #2 spot by drafting Reggie Wayne out of Miami (FLA) in the first round of this year's draft. Wayne will battle Jerome Pathon and Terrence Wilkins for work and production, which should take some of the pressure off of Marvin Harrison.

TE: The Colts' talented of tight ends, Ken Dilger and Marcus Pollard, continue to share the load and the resulting statistics. In 1999, Dilger had 40 receptions, scoring twice, and Pollard recorded 34 receptions, scoring four times. In 2000, Dilger again led the way, recording 47 receptions for 538 yards while scoring three times. Pollard ended up with 30 receptions for 439 yards, while scoring three times. Pollard became a free agent after the season but the Colts, not wanting to lose him, tagged him as their franchise player. With both being talented receivers, the only problem for fantasy fans is that the two will again share the statistical success in 2001?

QB: Being the #1 pick of the 1998 draft, Peyton Manning came into the league with many expectations. He's pretty much lived up to all of them thus far. As a rookie in '98, Manning threw for 3,739 yards and 26 scores. In 1999, Manning upped his yardage numbers to 4,135 yards while again throwing for 26 touchdowns. Could he continue to press upward? He did. In 2000, Manning pushed his numbers to 4,413 yards and 33 touchdowns. The 33 touchdown passes tied him for the league lead with Daunte Culpepper. Along the way, Manning recorded four, 300-yard games and one, 400-yard game. He threw for three touchdowns in a game five times and twice threw for four touchdowns. If he stays healthy he's pushing a path toward Canton. The question for 2001? Can he continue to push his numbers? I'd love to draft him on my fantasy team and find out.

K: Two straight superb years for Mike Vanderjagt. After hitting 34 of 38 (.895) field goal tries in 1999, Vanderjagt followed up that performance by hitting 25 of 27 (.926) tries in 2000 and all 46 point after attempts. The Colts are fortunate with having another consistent weapon in their kicker, Mike Vanderjagt.

Overall: The Colts quick turnaround from 3-13 in 1998 to 13-3 in 1999 took a slight dip in 2000 as they finished at 10-6 but again lost their first playoff game. Quarterback Peyton Manning and wide receiver Marvin Harrison makes up one of the league's most feared passing tandems. The Colts, however, must still push to find a true #2 receiver to take some of the pressure off Harrison. The tight ends Ken Dilger and Marcus Pollard add to the passing game. Another weapon through the air in Edgerrin James. James who is also one of the league's best ground gainers, throws a challenge to Marshall Faulk as the league's best all-around back. For fantasy production you can't go wrong with James, Manning or Harrison.

Offseason Fantasy-Position Moves

	Arriving	From:		Departing	To:
RB	Kevin Brown	Free Agent	QB	Kelly Holcomb	CLE
RB	Dewayne Hogan	Free Agent			
RB	Brett Millican	Free Agent			
RB	Wes Ours	Free Agent			
RB	Dominic Rhodes	Free Agent			
WR	Troy Albea	Free Agent			
WR	Jason Franklin	Free Agent			
WR	Aaron Jones	Free Agent			
WR	Marcus Williams	Free Agent			
WR	Dwayne Wilmot	Free Agent			
TE	Josh Kew	Free Agent			
TE	Justin Snow	Free Agent			
QB	Dave Meyer	Free Agent			
K	Danny Kight	Free Agent			

Fred Taylor/Jacksonville Jaguars

JACKSONVILLE JAGUARS
Home Stadium: ALLTELL Stadium
Playing Surface: Grass
Head Coach: Tom Coughlin
2000 Record: 7-9

"Taylor-Made" Offense Perfect for Jaguars

RB: Fred Taylor made a huge splash as a rookie in 1998, when stepping in for the injured James Stewart, recording 1,223 rushing yards, adding 421 more on 44 receptions and scoring 17 times. In his sophomore season of 1999, he was not so fortunate, as he missed six games to injury, finished with only 815 rushing-receiving yards and six touchdowns. Ironically, while Taylor was out hurt, James Stewart took over the backfield load. Coming into the 2000 season, Stewart figured his starting role was lost departed via free agency to Detroit. The Jaguars, because of Stewart's departure, were faced with a problem at the 2000 season outset. Fred Taylor could not open the year at running back, as he was nursing a knee injury. The Jaguars turned to Stacy Mack and Chris Howard. Mack rushed for 145 yards and one touchdown during the three-game span that Taylor was out, and Howard rushed for 52 yards and one touchdown. Taylor returned on week #4 and got off to a slow start. By week #7, however, his fourth week back, Taylor rushed for 112 yards against Tennessee, his first of nine consecutive 100-yard games, including a 234 yard, three touchdown performance against Pittsburgh. On the year, playing in 13 games, Taylor finished with 1,399 rushing yards, 36 receptions for 240 yards and scored 14 times. Again, that was after missing the first three games and a slow start. Other than Taylor, the Jaguars got 145 yards rushing, no receptions and one touchdown out of Mack. Anthony Johnson rushed for 112 yards, caught 12 passes for 153 yards and scored once for the only other notable performances. Looking to 2001, Jaguar and fantasy fans are hoping to keep Taylor healthy. If he does escape injury, a 2,000 rushing-receiving year and 15-touchdown performance is attainable for this talented back.

WR: One of the most respected receiving tandems in the league remains Jimmy Smith and Keenan McCardell of Jacksonville. Of the two, however, Smith had really picked up his statistical numbers, especially in receptions and yardage, in the last couple of seasons, making him a very attractive fantasy value. In 1998, Smith recorded 78 receptions for 1,182 yards while scoring six times. That same year, McCardell recorded 64 receptions for 892 yards and also six touchdowns. A year later in 1999, Smith jumped his totals to a whopping 116 receptions for 1,636 yards while again scoring six times. McCardell finished the year at 78 receptions for 891 yards and five touchdowns. How would the two fare coming into the 2000 season? Certainly Smith was the hotter fantasy commodity. The Jaguars also had added a new weapon to the fold coming into the 2000 season, by making speedy R. Jay Soward out of USC, their #1 draft pick. Both Smith and McCardell got off to fast starts, especially Smith who had a 15 reception, 291 yard, three touchdown performance against Baltimore on week #2. The numbers kept growing for both receivers all year long, though a knee injury kept Smith out of action a couple of games. Playing in 14 games, Smith still led the team with 94 receptions that went for 1,207 yards while scoring five times. McCardell, this time wasn't far behind. McCardell recorded 91 receptions, actually had more yards with 1,231 and more touchdowns with eight. The rookie R. Jay Soward was a big disappointment, recording only 14 receptions for 154 yards and one touchdown. Alvis Whitted chipped in 13 catches for 137 yards and three scores. Looking to 2001, Smith will again be a highly coveted fantasy pick and will again push big yardage numbers but his touchdown production always seems limited. McCardell proved in 2000 he can push his numbers which should draw expanded fantasy attention. The Jaguars still feel R. Jay Soward has a chance to develop though he was a bust as a rookie.

TE: In bringing Kyle Brady to Jacksonville from New York in 1999, the Jaguars felt the Jet's former first-round pick had potential. In his first year with the Jaguars, Brady finished with a disappointing 32 receptions for 346 yards and one touchdown. That same year Damian Jones was much more effective in the red zone, scoring four times on just 19 receptions. Brady worked to become a bigger part of the offense in 2000 and he was. Brady pushed his numbers to 64 receptions for 729 yards and scored three times. Jones, meanwhile, nursing a knee injury, caught one pass all year. Looking to 2001, Brady will again realize success in yardage numbers for sure but needs to pick up his scoring to become more of a fantasy attraction.

QB: Injuries more than anything seem to stand in the way of Mark Brunell putting up significant fantasy numbers. In 1998, Brunell finished the season throwing for 2,601 yards and 20 touchdowns, missing four games to an ankle injury. In 1999, slowed by a knee injury, Brunell threw for 3,060 yards and only 14 touchdowns. Would he and could he stay healthy in 2000 to up those numbers? Brunell, for a change, stayed healthy for all 16 games, threw for 3,640 yards but still a disappointing 20 touchdowns. He also rushed for 236 yards and two rushing touchdowns. The lack of or low touchdown pass totals may just be attributed to Fred Taylor's ability to score on the ground. Looking to 2001, we'll see if a healthy Brunell is capable of throwing for 3,500 plus yards. The 20-25 touchdown range is likely again his limit because the Jaguars score so often on the ground.

K: Coming off a year when he hit 31 of 38 (.816) field goal tries, Mike Hollis looked again to be a solid fantasy pick in 2000. Hollis fared well again. Despite missing four games with a back problem, Hollis hit 24 of 26 (.923) field goal tries and tallied 105 points. With Hollis out, Steve Lindsey stepped in to hit 5 of 7 (.714) attempts in his four-game stretch. With Hollis healthy again, I expect another exceptional year in 2001.

Overall: The drop to 7-9 in 2000 was a big disappointment for a team believed to be headed in the right direction. Offensively on the ground, the Jaguars are set if Fred Taylor stays healthy. Taylor is very capable of being among the leagues top yardage and touchdown producers among running backs if healthy all year. Through the air, quarterback Mark Brunell is another one who seems to attract injuries though he stayed healthy throughout 2000. With a receiving crew that consists of Jimmy Smith, Keenan McCardell and tight end Kyle Brady, the Jaguars can expect big yardage numbers in 2001. However, the problem of not getting into the end zone through the air still looms over each player involved in the Jaguars' passing game.

Offseason Fantasy-Position Moves

	Arriving	From:		Departing	To:
RB	Elvis Joseph	Free Agent	RB	Kevin Clements	Released
RB	Dustin McClintock	Free Agent	WR	Reggie Barlow	Released
RB	Patrick Washington	Free Agent	WR	Mike Horacek	GB
RB	Jerry Westbrooks	Free Agent	TE	Rich Griffith	Released
WR	Marcellus Harris	Free Agent	QB	Jamie Martin	Released
WR	Antonio Stanley	Free Agent			
WR	Randel Williams	Free Agent			
TE	Nick Franklin	Free Agent			
TE	Ryan Prince	Free Agent			
QB	Jimmy Blanchard	Free Agent			

KANSAS CITY CHIEFS

Home Stadium: Arrowhead Stadium
Playing Surface: Grass
Head Coach: Dick Vermeil
2000 Record: 7-9

Vermeil, "Ram"med Home Winner in St. Louis, Could Be "Chief" Reason Brought to Kansas City

RB: It seems for virtually a decade, the scenario has been the same for the Kansas City's running attack. The running-back-by-committee approach surely plays havoc on fantasy owners as they shy away, not knowing who will step up any given year or whether the production will be spread out so much it won't even matter. Coming into the 2000 season, there were certainly questions coming off the 1999 season. In '99, Donnell Bennett led the Chiefs with 627 rushing yards, caught ten passes for 41 yards and scored eight times playing in 13 games. The rest of the statistical pie was pretty much split up by four players. Bam Morris produced 414 rushing yards. Tony Richardson was next with 387 rushing yards but he added 141 more on 24 receptions and scores once. Kimble Anders, who began the year as the starter, rushed for 181 yards and two touchdowns before suffering a season-ending achilles injury. Mike Cloud also chipped in 128 yards. Not much was different in 2000, except the production order. This time Tony Richardson led the team, as he rushed for 697 yards, added 58 receptions for 468 yards while scoring six times. Kimble Anders, who worked himself in and out of the lineup, rushed for 331 yards, caught 15 passes for 76 yards and scored twice. Rookie Frank Moreau chipped in 179 yards on the ground and scored four times. Mike Cloud contributed only 84 rushing yards and a score while Donnell Bennett, who battled foot and knee injuries, finished with only 24 rushing yards all year. The Chiefs, knowing their limits on the ground, tried to open up the aerial attack behind Elvis Grbac in 2000, which also contributed to the lower rushing numbers. That, however, was under now fired coach Gunther Cunningham. Looking to 2001, under new head coach Dick Vermeil, the philosophy may change. Likely Vermeil will look for one candidate to be an every-down back. Originally it looked like Tony Richardson may be that guy, but the offseason signing of Priest Holmes (Ravens) changed that. Holmes, a 1,000-yard rusher in 1998, was injured much of 1999 and lost his starting role to rookie Jamal Lewis. In 2000 Holmes should give the Ravens' running attack a boost. Holmes rushed for 588 yards in 2000, while grabbing 32 receptions for 221 yards but scored only once. He could easily double these numbers in 2001 with Kansas City. Meanwhile, in the offseason, the Chiefs released Kimble Anders and Donnell Bennett.

WR: Coming into the 2000 season, the Chiefs wanted to open up their passing game more behind quarterback, Elvis Grbac. This was interesting coming off a year when the team's leading receiver Derrick Alexander produced 54 receptions for 832 yards and five touchdowns; a year when Andre Rison dropped to 21 receptions and was being let go; a year when Joe Horn, who showed great promise in tallying 35 receptions for 586 yards and six touchdowns in 1999, was departing via free agency to New Orleans; a year when Kevin Lockett, someone the Chiefs had hoped would blossom, recorded 34 receptions for 426 yards and two touchdowns. The Chiefs obviously had confidence that Derrick Alexander would step up his game and felt their first-round selection, Sylvester Morris out of Jackson State, would make an immediate impact. Of course, the Chiefs also knew they had the best tight end in the league in Tony Gonzalez. Alexander did step up, recording 78 receptions for 1,391 yards while scoring ten times, along the way producing six 100-yard games. The rookie Morris did produce, especially early on, when he produced a six-reception, 112-yard, three-touchdown performance against San Diego, the third game of the year. However, Morris never scored again the rest of the year. For the season, Morris finished with 48 catches for 678 yards and three touchdowns. Besides Alexander and Morris, the Chiefs also got 33 receptions for 422 yards and two touchdowns out of Kevin Lockett. Looking to 2001, much of the possible success of the Chiefs' receivers will be in the hands of new head coach Dick Vermeil. Will he continue to go for a more wide-open aerial assault? He sure liked it when in St. Louis, which should push the numbers of Alexander and Morris. Third-round pick Marvin Minnis out of Florida State should see some action, especially now that Kevin Lockett has moved on via free agency, signing with the Washington Redskins in the offseason.

TE: All-pro tight end Tony Gonzalez was coming off a strong year in 1999. Gonzalez had recorded 76 receptions going for 849 yards while scoring 11 times in 1999. He headed into the 2000 season with Kansas City looking to throw more. Gonzalez moved to another level among tight ends. He finished the 2000 season recording 93 receptions for 1,203 yards while recording nine touchdowns. Along the way, he recorded six 100-yard games, and in fact, had four 100-yard games in a row at one point—an incredible year, especially for a tight end. Other than Gonzalez, the Chiefs received ten total receptions between Troy Dayton (8) and Jason Dunn (2). Gonzalez has fantasy fans drooling for what lies ahead in 2001.

QB: The Chiefs under Gunther Cunningham in 2000 opted to turn the passing game loose. The result for quarterback Elvis Grbac was obvious.

His numbers went up. Grbac, who threw for 3,389 yards and 22 touchdowns a year earlier in 1999, jumped to 4,169 passing yards and 28 touchdowns in 2000. Along the way, Grbac topped the 300-yard mark five times including a 504 yard performance against Oakland midseason. Grbac threw for three or more touchdowns three times including a five-touchdown performance against San Diego the third week of the season. Certainly nice fantasy numbers for those fantasy owners who had him. But how about in 2001? Elvis Grbac was released in the offseason and later signed with Baltimore. This left a huge void to fill for new head coach Dick Vermeil. Vermeil turned to his old team, the St. Louis Rams, and acquired Trent Green. Green had come to the Rams two years ago from Washington as the starter but lost his job to a knee injury which led to Kurt Warner's "Cinderella" season. Green is more than capable. In 1998, his last year with the Redskins, Green threw for 3,441 yards and 23 touchdowns. The big question will be if Vermeil will allow the Chiefs and Trent Green to continue to push the pass in their offensive scheme as he did when he was with the Rams.

K: Aging kicker Pete Stoyanovich saw his numbers drop from his usual accuracy to hitting 21 of 28 (.750) field goal attempts in 1999. Despite the drop off, the Chiefs stuck with him heading into the 2000 season. After Stoyanovich missed one of his first three attempts through five games, the Chiefs turned to ex-Seahawk Todd Peterson. Peterson came in to hit 15 of 20 (.750) field goal tries over the last 11 games. Likely this is a solid enough performance to keep him around in 2001, though free agent Lawrence Tynes was signed in the offseason.

Overall: After going 9-7 in 1999, the Chiefs fell to 7-9 in 2000. The Chiefs continued their running-back-by-committee approach in 2000 under head coach Gunther Cunningham. Under new head coach Dick Vermeil, a feature back seems likely, and offseason acquisition Priest Holmes should fit the bill. Through the air, quarterback Elvis Grbac pushed his numbers to new heights in 2000, as the Chiefs again under Gunther Cunningham elected to become more of a passing team. Grbac, however, is gone being replaced in the offseason. Will Dick Vermeil continue this philosophy? This will have a huge bearing on not only the Chiefs' new quarterback Trent Green's numbers but on his receivers Derrick Alexander, Sylvester Morris and Tony Gonzalez as well.

Offseason Fantasy-Position Moves

	Arriving	From:		Departing	To:
WR	Tony Horne	STL	RB	Kimber Anders	Released
WR	Dave Klemic	Free Agent	RB	Donnell Bennett	Released
WR	J. J. Moses	Free Agent	WR	Kevin Lockett	WASH
QB	Bubby Brister	MINN	QB	Elvis Grbac	BALT
QB	Trent Green	STL			
QB	Ryan Helming	Free Agent			
K	Lawrence Tynes	Free Agent			

Lamar Smith/Miami Dolphins

MIAMI DOLPHINS

Home Stadium: Pro Player Stadium
Playing Surface: Grass
Head Coach: Dave Wannstedt
2000 Record: 11-5

Lamar Finally Gives Dolphins Much Needed Ground Game

RB: Coming into the 2000 season, the Miami Dolphins hadn't had a 1,000-yard rusher since 1996, when Karim Abdul-Jabbar had rushed for 1,116 yards as a rookie. It wasn't like they hadn't tried via draft picks, trades, free-agent pickups. It just wasn't to be. Despite making John Avery their #1 draft pick in 1998 and then signing a former #1 pick in Lawrence Phillips, neither move blossomed. And then in 1999, the Dolphins drafted two second-round running backs in J.J. Johnson (Mississippi State) and Rob Konrad (Syracuse), while also drafting highly regarded Cecil Collins out of McNeese State in the fifth-round. But there was still no 1,000-yard rusher. Moving toward the 2000 season, the Dolphins elected to pick up two veteran running backs who had been released by their teams. Lamar Smith had been released by New Orleans, and Thurman Thomas had been released by Buffalo. Smith would get a crack at the starting tailback spot, and Thomas was to be used as a third-down threat. Smith, who had reasonable success both in New Orleans and Seattle, was given the starting spot from the outset. In the season opener, he rushed for 145 yards and one touchdown against Seattle and never looked back. Three more 100-yard games came, but his consistency along the way was hugely welcomed by the Dolphins. He missed only one game with a hamstring injury. Smith topped all expectations by rushing for 1,139 yards, grabbing 31 receptions for another 201 yards and scored 16 times. There was little other production to speak of. J.J. Johnson chipped in 168 yards on the ground, caught ten passes for 61 yards and scored once. Thurman Thomas ran for 136 yards, grabbed 16 receptions for 117 yards and scored once. He was released following the season so he could retire as a Buffalo Bill. Autry Denson tallied 108 rushing yards, caught 14 passes for 105 yards but failed to score. Rob Konrad rumbled for only 39 yards while catching 14 passes for 83 yards and he too failed to score. Lamar Smith was the big story—one that's likely to continue in 2001 as he continues to produce as the Dolphins' featured back. The Dolphins did, however, add rookie third-round pick Travis Minor out of Florida State to the fold. Minor, a quick, change-of-direction-type runner, could provide a nice change of pace from Lamar Smith for the Dolphins. He'll likely be a third-down player for now but will look to fill the every-down role eventually.

WR: Coming into the 2000 season, many felt and hoped O.J. McDuffie would rebound to the performance he had in 1998, when he led the NFL with 90 receptions. In 1999, he had missed four games to injury, which limited him to 43 receptions for 516 yards and two touchdowns. It wasn't to happen, as McDuffie missed the first seven games of the year with a toe injury and was placed on the Physically Unable to Perform list. McDuffie finished the year playing in only six games and caught only 14 passes.

McDuffie wasn't the only Dolphin' receiver with injury problems. Tony Martin, who had led the club in 1999 with 67 catches for 1,037 yards and five touchdowns, missed seven games in 2000 with also a toe injury. He finished the year with only 26 receptions for 393 yards and no touchdowns. Bert Emanuel struggled through wrist and knee injuries to record only seven receptions. Leslie Shepherd, an offseason acquisition, played in only 12 games, suffering a knee injury at season's end, and finished with 35 receptions for 446 yards and four touchdowns. The only receiver who stayed healthy all year was Oronde Gadsden, who, of course, led the way with 56 receptions for 786 yards and six touchdowns. What happens coming into 2001? Tony Martin, who would have cost the Dolphins about $3 million against the salary cap, was released following the season as he opted not to restructure his contract. O.J. McDuffie was re-signed, but there's some uncertainty there. The Dolphins did sign free agent James McKnight away from Dallas. McKnight, who led the Cowboys with 52 receptions in 2000, should be a help, as should Dedric Ward, who comes over from the Jets. The Dolphins also have rookie second-round pick Chris Chambers out of Wisconsin to throw into the mix. Chambers has the size and ability to leep, which will make him an excellent red-zone target. Oronde Gadsden seems to be the only sure bet to put up decent fantasy numbers as we await the fate and injury update to Leslie Shepherd, though Shepherd was unlikely to be re-signed. Meanwhile, Bert Emanuel moved on, signing as a free agent with New England for 2001.

TE: With he release in 2000 of Troy Drayton, who led the Dolphin tight ends with 32 receptions and only one touchdown in 1999, no move was made to upgrade the position. This left Hunter Goodwin, who had recorded eight receptions in 1999, to battle Jed Weaver for the job. The results from a fantasy standpoint were very ugly as Weaver topped the duo's output with ten receptions for 179 yards and no touchdowns, while Weaver recorded six receptions for 36 yards and one touchdown. Neither actually did much until the season finale, when Weaver got a little more involved in the offseason, grabbing five receptions for 63 yards, while Weaver had only two receptions but one went for a touchdown. Looking to 2001, again not much to get excited about from a fantasy standpoint, unless the Dolphins make a move to get their tight ends more involved in the offense and upgrade the position.

QB: Facing a season when they would be without Dan Marino for the first time since 1984, the Dolphins had some tough decisions to make on his replacement. His heir apparent had looked to be Damon Huard, who had stepped in when Marino was hurt in 1999. The Dolphins had other ideas as well. The Dolphins acquired free-agent Jay Fiedler from the Jaguars. Fiedler had been Mark Brunell's backup in Jacksonville. The battle for the starting job was eventually won by Fiedler. In leading the Dolphins to an 11-5 record (10-4 under him), Fiedler did not put up big numbers. He missed two games to a shoulder injury but in the 14 games he did play, Fiedler threw for only 2,404 and 14 touchdowns. Looking to 2001, Fiedler will again likely be at the helm and should expand on his numbers but not too considerably, as the Dolphins like to run often behind Lamar Smith. I do believe, however, nearing 3,000 passing yards and 15-20 touchdowns is possible. There is a good chance, however, Fiedler will be pushed by Ray Lucas, who came over from the New York Jets in the offseason. Meanwhile, Damon Huard was released and later signed with New England.

K: Heading into the season finale in 2000, Olindo Mare had missed only one field goal attempt all year, hitting an incredible 26 of 27 (.962) attempts. Despite missing two of four field goals that day, he finished with an impressive 28 of 31 (.903) for the year. Certainly this production will keep him in Miami in 2001 and will again grab plenty of fantasy attention, as Mare signed a 6-year, $12 million deal in the offseason.

Overall: Only one year after future Hall of Famer Dan Marino retired, the Dolphins finished at 11-5, after going 9-7 in 1999. Their success came from having a solid defense and from finally finding a legitimate running game behind Lamar Smith. Smith's 1,340 rushing-receiving yards (1,139 on the ground) and 16 touchdowns provided a solid offensive attack all year. Through the air, Jay Fiedler, the free-agent acquisition from Jacksonville, did what he had to do to win, without putting up significant passing numbers. Other than Oronde Gadsden, Fiedler's receiving crew, which included O.J. McDuffie, Tony Martin, Leslie Shepherd and Bert Emanuel, fought injuries all year. The mix for continued success is there under head coach Dave Wannstedt, who inked a one-year contract extension in the offseason. If your looking for fantasy players with value from this team, stick with Lamar Smith.

Offseason Fantasy-Position Moves

Arriving		From:	Departing		To:
RB	Eric Johnson	Free Agent	RB	Bernie Parmalee	Released
RB	Matt Kalapinski	Free Agent	RB	Thurman Thomas	Released
WR	Ronnie Anderson	Free Agent	WR	Bert Emanuel	NE
WR	Robert Baker	Free Agent	WR	Tony Martin	Released
WR	David Foye	Free Agent	TE	Hunter Goodwin	Released
WR	James McKnight	DALL	QB	Damon Huard	NE
WR	Dedric Ward	NYJ			
QB	Ray Lucas	NYJ			
K	Aaron Elling	Free Agent			

MINNESOTA VIKINGS

Home Stadium: Hubert H. Humphrey Metrodome
Playing Surface: Astro Turf
Head Coach: Denny Green
2000 Record: 11-5

Vikings' Voyage Will Be Tougher without Smith

RB: As a fantasy football participant, we've all wondered what kind of numbers Robert Smith could put up if he stayed healthy all season. Heading into the 2000 season, Smith had yet to play an entire 16-game schedule without missing time due to injury. Despite knowing this, the Vikings had let go Leroy Hoard, who had filled in so well in recent years when Smith was injured. This was a pretty risky maneuver, with Moe Williams, having little NFL experience, as his backup. Smith hit the season with a vengeance, rushing for 109 yards in the season opener against Chicago and just kept pounding away. He played virtually every down even in third-down situations and to everyone's amazement he played all 16 games despite a knee problem at times. On the season, Smith easily reached a career high of 1,521 rushing yards, caught 36 passes for another 348 yards while scoring ten times. Along the way, Smith topped the 100-yard mark eight times, including a stretch of five straight games. He had finally shown Viking and fantasy fans what he could do if healthy an entire season. The Vikings got little production elsewhere, but they didn't need it. Moe Williams rushed for 67 yards, while catching four passes. Fullback Jim Kleinsasser rushed for 43 yards and caught ten passes for 98 yards. Neither one scored. Smith was the story during the season and after the season. In completing a career year, Smith gave somewhat of a surprise announcement in retiring. Perhaps he thought he could never repeat his 2000 performance. He retired after eight years, 6,813 rushing yards, 178 receptions for 1,292 yards and 37 total receptions. He retired without a Super Bowl ring but he retired fairly healthy, though his knee still needed attention. What does this leave the Vikings for 2001? Initially it left the inexperienced Moe Williams and Doug Chapman, but the Vikings made Michael Bennett out of Wisconsin their first-round draft pick. Bennett has great speed and, like his predecessor Robert Smith, should be able to keep defenses off guard and occasionally break for long scores. Bennett will be an excellent fantasy prospect for a rookie, likely skipping right into a starting role.

WR: Arguably the Vikings have the best receiver in football in Randy Moss. Throw in aging but still very productive veteran Cris Carter and you may have the most feared receiving duo in football. Leading into only his third season in 2000, Moss had already made a big name for himself. As a rookie in 1998, Moss recorded 69 receptions for 1,313 yards while scoring 17 times. As a sophomore in 1999, Moss jumped to 80 receptions for 1,413 yards, while scoring 12 times. Would defenses be able to shut him down in 2000 knowing his talent? They tried but Moss again proved just how good he was, though, surprisingly, he recorded only 77 receptions finished with a whopping 1,437 yards and scored 15 times. Moss just continues to make big plays consistently. He produced 100-yard games eight times. How about his receiving mate Cris Carter? You'd think Moss's arrival would have slowed his numbers. Coming off a 1999 season when he produced 90 receptions for 1,241 yards and 13 touchdowns, how far would Carter's production drop? It wouldn't! Carter finished 2000, recording 96 catches for 1,274 yards but his touchdown level did drop to nine. The Vikings didn't ask for much help elsewhere. Chris Walsh chipped in 18 catches for 191 yards and no touchdowns, and Matthew Hatchette, who many thought would step in for the departed Jake Reed (New Orleans) in the #3 role to make a significant contribution, finished with only 16 receptions for 190 yards while scoring twice. Looking to 2001, Moss will be back to again cause havoc for opposing defenders but so will Carter, who held a press conference at season's end to announce his return for another year. For Moss, 1,500 yards and 15 touchdowns are likely within reach, for Carter 1,200 yard range and 10-12 touchdowns. And as far as the #3 receiver, Matthew Hatchette departed to the New York Jets, and Jake Reed finds himself back with the Vikings after his one-year stint with the New Orleans Saints and likely resumes his #3 receiver role.

TE: With Andrew Glover, their leading receiving tight end, being released in the 2000 offseason (later signed with New Orleans), the Vikings had a hole to fill. Their prospects were Andrew Jordan, John Davis and free-agent acquisition Johnny McWilliams coming over from Arizona. All three saw action, with no significant production from any one player until late in the year when McWilliams produced ten receptions over the last three games, two went for touchdowns. On the year, McWilliams led the group with 22 receptions for 180 yards while scoring three times. John Davis was next recording 17 catches for 202 yards and scored once. Andrew Jordan chipped in eight catches for 63 yards. Certainly not big fantasy numbers. In the offseason, the Vikings, unsure if McWilliams would re-sign, signed Byron Chamberlain away from Denver. Chamberlain, who grabbed 22 receptions for 283 yards and scored once for the Broncos in 2000, may give a boost to the Viking's tight end position.

QB: How could he turn his high-powered, pass-happy offense over to a young, unproven quarterback in Daunte Culpepper? Green stuck with his convictions and gave Culpepper the reins to start the year. Certainly the physical ability was there. Culpepper, built more like a linebacker, has a strong arm and could run, but did he have what it takes to get it done in the NFL, let alone on a team that loves to pass like the Vikings do? In the season opener against Chicago, he began a little sluggish but his three touchdown runs helped the Vikings to a 30-27 win. He just kept getting better from there. On the season, Culpepper finished with 3,937 passing yards and an impressive 33 touchdown passes, tying him for the league lead with Peyton Manning. He also rushed for 470 yards and scored seven times on the ground. Daunte Culpepper was as good as Green had expected and perhaps even better. Look for another big year in 2001 for Culpepper.

K: Remember back to 1998 when Gary Anderson didn't miss a regular season kick, hitting all 35 attempts. After a miserable 1999 campaign when he struggled to hit only 19 of 30 (.633) attempts, Anderson neared his '98 perfection in 2000, hitting 22 of 23 (.957) attempts. Kicking for the Vikings again makes him an attractive fantasy pick in 2001.

Overall: Despite electing to go with a young, unproven quarterback in 2000, the Vikings improved by one game, finishing at 11-5. The young quarterback Daunte Culpepper proved himself in a hurry and all year long, finishing the year tied with the most touchdown passes. Culpepper had the luxury of working with one of the best receiving tandems in the league—Randy Moss and Chris Carter—both of whom again had big years. Looking to 2001, big numbers can be expected from the three, especially if the running game doesn't get a boost. Robert Smith, coming off the best year of his career, retired following the 2000 season. The Vikings selection of Wisconsin's Michael Bennett in the first round of this year's draft should fill that void nicely.

Offseason Fantasy-Position Moves

	Arriving	From:		Departing	To:
RB	James Wofford	Free Agent	WR	Matthew Hatchette	NYJ
WR	Kenny Clark	Free Agent	QB	Todd Bouman	Released
WR	Billy Cockerham	Free Agent	QB	Bubby Brister	KC
WR	Jake Reed	NO			
TE	Byron Chamberlain	DEN			
TE	Jeff Kostrewa	Free Agent			
K	John Matich	Free Agent			

Drew Bledsoe/New England patriots

NEW ENGLAND PATRIOTS

Home Stadium: Foxboro Stadium
Playing Surface: Grass
Head Coach: Bill Belichick
2000 Record: 5-11

Bledsoe Needs More Support on the Run

RB: Still hurting from the loss of their #1 draft pick, Robert Edwards, who suffered a severe knee injury following a solid rookie campaign of 1997, the Patriots were trying to pick up the pieces. Heading into the 2000 season, the Patriots were looking at a number of options to try and secure some semblance of a running attack. They had 5'8" Kevin Faulk, their #1 draft pick of 1999, who failed to prove he was an every-down answer as a rookie. The Patriots also signed veteran Raymont Harris in the offseason. Harris was trying to return to the NFL, after sitting out the 1999 season nursing a knee injury. And then there was third-round draft pick J.R. Redmond. Harris was gone before the season started, so it was the undersized Faulk who got the call. As the season wore on, Faulk began sharing the rushing load duties with Redmond and, late in the year, with seventh-rounder Patrick Pass a bit. At season's end, none of the players had really stepped up, as the Patriots failed to have a back reach the 100-yard mark in any game all season. Faulk led the team with only 570 yards on the ground but did end up catching an impressive 51 receptions for 465 yards and scored five times. Redmond, who looked at times like he could become the team's feature back, finished with 406 rushing yards, caught 20 passes for 126 yards and scored three times. Fullback Tony Carter chipped in 90 rushing yards and nine catches for 73 yards while scoring twice. Pass finished with 58 rushing yards and four receptions. The Patriots finished the season pretty much how it had begun looking for an every-down back. Looking to 2001, the question still looms. Kevin Faulk is undersized and should be returning kicks and being used in third-down situations rather than as an every-down back. The question is can J.R. Redmond step into the every-down role? He showed some shortcomings as a rookie. If the Patriots don't feel Redmond can develop quickly enough, they may be again looking to fill that role this offseason, though there is some optimism that Robert Edwards may be ready to return, though I wouldn't hold my breath.

WR: In losing speedy Shawn Jefferson to Atlanta in the 2000 offseason, the Patriots knew they had to find a #2 receiver to start opposite Terry Glenn. Tony Simmons, who had big-play capability, would likely challenge Troy Brown for the job. Brown was coming off a season where he had recorded 36 receptions for 471 yards and one touchdown, missing four games to an ankle injury. Chris Calloway, an offseason free-agent signee from Atlanta, would also be thrown into the battle. Brown was given his shot at season's outset. He took it and never looked back. Brown posted career numbers of 83 receptions for 944 yards and five touchdowns, one of which came on a punt return. Brown produced four 100-yard games along the way. Terry Glenn, the team's supposed #1 receiver, finished the year recording 79 receptions for 963 yards and six touchdowns, perhaps a bit disappointing for

Patriots' and fantasy fans. Other than Brown and Glenn, the Patriots got only 14 receptions out of Tony Simmons and 12 total receptions out of Chris Calloway, Curtis Jackson and Shock Davis. Looking to 2001, Glenn will be one of the starters but the Patriots signed veteran Bert Emanuel, who has struggled with injuries in recent years, coming over from the Miami Dolphins, and David Patten, who comes over from Cleveland, where he caught 38 passes in 2000. The #2 job may be up in the air, despite Brown's 83 receptions a year ago. The Patriots, however, need better production from Brown and Glenn, as their running game remains suspect. I look for 1,000-1,200 from either or both in 2001 and 8-12 touchdowns.

TE: With Ben Coates released in the 2000 offseason, the Patriots knew they had a vacancy to fill. Coates, once considered one of the league's top tight ends, had seen his production drop to 32 receptions and two touchdowns in 1999 from 68 receptions and six touchdowns in 1998. The Patriots elected to bring aboard Eric Bjornson to challenge Rod Rutledge, their second-round pick of 1998. Neither was coming off a very good season. Bjornson, with the Cowboys in 1999, had recorded only ten receptions for 13 yards and one touchdown, while Rutledge had tallied only seven receptions for 66 yards and had failed to score. Bjornson was the better receiver and from a fantasy standpoint had more potential. Bjornson did get the call to start the season. Grabbing most of the work through the first eight games, Bjornson recorded 20 receptions for 150 yards and scored twice. Bjornson gave way in the second half to Rutledge and by season's end to Jeremy Wiggins who had come over from the Jets midseason. Wiggins came on strong at season's end, grabbing 16 receptions for 203 yards and scored once over the last four games. Rutledge finished the year recording only 15 catches for 103 yards and one score. Looking to 2001, the only reason to keep an eye out here is because of the strong finish by Wiggins. If the Patriots try to help him build on his performance, he could become a fantasy factor. Meanwhile, Bjornson took his services to Oakland for 2001 via free agency.

QB: Sometimes a player is limited in what he can do statistically because of the talent or lack thereof he's surrounded with. Once, a high-touted college prospect, having Hall Of Fame potential, Bledsoe now dabbles in statistical mediocrity. He peaked in 1996 and 1997, with 27 and 28 touchdowns, while also topping the 4,000 (4,086) yard mark in 1996. Since that time, a lack of the Patriots finding a consistent ground game and an unimpressive offensive line have contributed to Bledsoe's lack of good numbers. Bledsoe had thrown for fairly good yardage numbers—3,985 in 1999—but only had 19 touchdowns. In 2000, with the Patriots not improving their ground attack, Bledsoe did as much as he could but again was limited to throwing for 3,291 yards and on 17 touchdowns. Looking to 2001, I believe little will change unless the Patriots surround Bledsoe with better support, though his receivers Terry Glenn and Troy Brown have stepped up. The Patriots did show their confidence in Bledsoe in the offseason, signing him to a 10-year, $103 million deal.

K: There was some speculation coming into the 2000 season that the Patriots may be looking for a challenger to Adam Vinatieri for their kicking chores. Vinatieri, coming off a season where he hit 26 of 33 (.788) field goals in 1999, did hold onto his job. Vinatieri opened the 2000 season by missing four of his first ten field goal attempts. He recovered to only miss two the rest of the year, finishing hitting 27 of 33 (.818) attempts, which I believe will keep him around in 2001, though the Patriots did make Owen Pochman out of Brigham Young their seventh-round draft pick to battle for the job.

Overall: Despite getting a new head coach in Bill Belichick, the Patriots finished 5-11 in 2000, three games worse than the year before. They continue to try to address their biggest need, which is to provide a solid running game to help keep the pressure off quarterback Drew Bledsoe. Since the injury to 1998 first-round pick Robert Edwards, the Patriots have done little on the ground. Kevin Faulk and 2000 third-round pick J.R. Redmond didn't get it done in 2000 and likely won't in 2001. This again puts the big burden on Drew Bledsoe and the passing game. His targets of Terry Glenn and Troy Brown are good and should get support from offseason acquisitions Bert Emanuel and David Patten but, without the offensive line support and the support of a better ground game, Bledsoe will be pressed too hard again in 2001.

Offseason Fantasy-Position Moves

	Arriving	From:		Departing	To:
RB	Larry Bowie	Free Agent	RB	Harold Shaw	Released
RB	Marc Edwards	CLE	TE	Eric Bjornson	OAK
WR	Ronny Daniels	Free Agent	QB	John Friesz	Released
WR	Bert Emanuel	MIA			
WR	Scott McCready	Free Agent			
WR	David Patten	CLE			
WR	Walter Williams	Free Agent			
QB	Damon Huard	MIA			
QB	Ben Leard	Free Agent			

NEW ORLEANS SAINTS

Home Stadium: Louisiana Superdome
Playing Surface: Astro Turf
Head Coach: Jim Haslett
2000 Record: 10-6

Williams, Horn Provide More Heavenly Performance

RB: Sometimes accolades and expectations come too soon for players. In 1999, Ricky Williams, the college Heisman Trophy Winner, came into the NFL with all kinds of accolades from his college days and all kinds of expectations of him in the NFL. As the #5 overall pick in the '99 draft, many felt, especially head coach at the time, Mike Ditka, that Williams could and would step in and carry to respectability a team that was coming off a 6-10 season. Expectations far exceeded what became reality. As a rookie in 1999, Williams struggled through injuries, especially turf toe, that sidelined him four weeks. The end result was 884 rushing yards, 28 receptions for 172 yards and only two touchdowns. A disappointing set of numbers for Saints' and fantasy fans from the Heisman Trophy Winner. How would Williams fare in his sophomore season became a huge question for fantasy fans, with many shying away at fantasy drafts. Williams set out to prove to everyone he was worth all the hype he received as a rookie. He got off to only a fair start but by week #3 recorded the first of five consecutive 100-yard games. Williams pounded opposing defenses for ten games until he suffered a season-ending broken ankle. Too bad because he was on the way to significant numbers. In the ten games he did play, Williams rushed for exactly 1,000 yards, caught 44 passes for another 489 yards and scored nine times. Expand that pace of numbers over 16 games, and he was well on his way to nearing 2,000 rushing-receiving yards and 15 touchdowns. With Williams out, the Saints turned to a number of backs including Jerald Moore, Chad Morton, Terrell Smith and at year's end veteran Terry Allen. Allen's 179 rushing yards and two touchdowns led the way, while Jerald Moore rushed for 156 yards, Chad Morton 136 yards but also caught 30 passes for 213 yards and Terrell Smith rushed for 131 yards, caught 12 passes for 65 yards. Really all the numbers are insignificant expect for Williams, who gave us a taste of what he's capable of. He returned in the playoffs but wasn't 100 percent. He will be, however, at the 2001 season outset, and I'm sure he'll attract much more fantasy attention this time around, though the Saints made an interesting first-round selection in this year's draft. The Saints chose Deuce McAllister out of Mississippi. McAllister comes aboard to push Williams or send a message. Either way the Saints running attack looks to be in great shape for years to come.

WR: New head coach Jim Haslett knew he wanted to step up his passing game heading into the 2000 season. He decided to make a few moves that he believed would help. He traded away the Saints' leading receiver of 1999, Eddie Kennison (61 catches, 834 yards, four touchdowns) to Chicago. Andrew Hastings, who caught 40 passes in 1999 wouldn't be part of the equation. Haslett and the Saints then signed free agents Joe Horn (Chiefs) and Jake Reed (Vikings). Horn was coming off a year in Kansas City when he caught only 35 passes and six touchdowns but showed some real potential, and Reed was coming over from the Vikings where he had some great seasons. The moves paid off at least in the case of Joe Horn. Horn had a breakout year, recording a surprising 94 receptions for 1,340 yards and eight touchdowns. Reed was in and out of the lineup with an ankle injury and eventually a broken leg, finishing the year with only 16 receptions. Veteran Willie Jackson, a Cincinnati Bengal castoff, stepped in to make an impact, recording 37 receptions for 523 yards and six touchdowns, with all six of the touchdowns coming over the last eight games. Keith Poole, who had recorded 42 receptions in 1999, became less of a factor, recorded only 21 catches for 293 yards and one touchdown. Robert Wilson chipped in 11 catches. Looking to 2001, the future looks much better than it did entering the 2000 season. Joe Horn gives the Saints a legitimate threat all the time and Willie Jackson has shown what he can do. The Saints also signed free-agent Albert Connell away from the Redskins. Connell, who caught 39 receptions for 762 yards and scored three times in 1999, signed a 5-year, $14 million deal, which included a $2.5 million signing bonus. I look for big numbers again from Joe Horn and perhaps Albert Connell in 2001. Meanwhile, Jake Reed has departed, heading back to the Minnesota Vikings.

TE: As a rookie in 1998, Cam Cleeland quickly made a name for himself by tallying 54 receptions for 684 yards and four touchdowns. Exposing himself as a fantasy factor to contend with, Cleeland was among the top-rated tight ends going into the '99 season. Ankle, knee and hamstring injuries, however, limited him to action in just ten games as he finished with 26 receptions for 325 yards while scoring once. Presumed to be back healthy in 2000, Cleeland again was given distinction among the league's top tight ends. Saints' and fantasy fans were quickly disappointed as Cleeland suffered an achilles injury in the preseason, ending his 2000 season. With Cleeland out, the Saints turned to offseason acquisition Andrew Glover (Vikings). Glover stepped in to record 21 receptions for 281 yards and four touchdowns. Lamont Hall also chipped in, recording five catches for 33 yards and one score. Looking to 2001, Saints' fans are hoping Cleeland returns healthy, while fantasy fans are likely to be cautious. A healthy Cleeland could push good numbers in an offense becoming more open to the passing game.

QB: The Saints, looking to upgrade their quarterback position from the musical signal-callers of 1999, elected to lure Jeff Blake away from the Cincinnati Bengals in the 2000 offseason. A year earlier Billy Joe Hobert, Danny Wuerffel and Jay Delhomme had all been given a shot. With Blake, the Saints knew they had an athletic signal-caller with a strong arm. Blake stepped in to put up decent numbers in leading the Saints to seven wins in their first ten games before suffering a season-ending broken foot in week #11. Through those ten games, Blake had registered 2,205 passing yards and 13 touchdowns. With Blake out, free-agent pickup, unheard of, underrated Aaron Brooks stepped in. Brooks quickly made a name for himself, throwing for 1,514 yards and nine touchdowns playing in just eight games. Looking to 2001, Blake looks to return healthy but there will be open competition for the job with Brooks. Either has the potential to reach 3,000 yards and the 20 touchdown range.

K: Doug Brien was one successful field goal away from equaling his previous years numbers. Brien hit 23 of 29 (.793) field goals in 2000, after hitting 24 of 29 (.828) attempts a year earlier. Accuracy numbers that were not enough to keep Brien in a Saint uniform, as he was released following the season, leaving the Saints looking for a replacement.

Overall: Under new head coach Jim Haslett, the Saints experienced a quick and huge turnaround from 3-13 in 1999 under Mike Ditka to 10-6 in 2000. Ricky Williams shook off his poor rookie showing to put together solid numbers through ten games, until suffering a broken ankle that forced him to miss the last six games. Williams, however, proved he will be a force in the NFL and a big fantasy factor as well. Though rookie, first-round pick Deuce McAllister may also be heard from. At quarterback, Jeff Blake suffered an injury that gave Aaron Brooks a chance in 2000, and Brooks took advantage to the point that the two will be battling for the starting job in training camp. Whichever quarterback wins the job will have Joe Horn and offseason acquisition Albert Connell (Redskins) to throw to. Horn who had a breakout season after jumping over from the Chiefs in 2000, should again put up big numbers in 2001. The Saints also hope Cam Cleeland returns healthy from his achilles injury.

Arriving		From:		Departing		To:
WR	Albert Connell	WASH		WR	Jake Reed	MINN
				K	Doug Brien	Released

NEW YORK GIANTS

Home Stadium: Giants Stadium
Playing Surface: Astro Turf
Head Coach: Jim Fassel
2000 Record: 12-4

Giants Take "Super" Giant Step Forward

RB: Heading into the 2000 season, the Giants were looking for new life at running back. A year earlier in 1999, injuries to offseason acquisition Gary Brown and to second-round draft pick Joe Montgomery and mediocre play from their other backs led to the Giants making Ron Dayne out of Wisconsin their #1 draft pick. Dayne, a big powerful back, would hopefully supply the Giants an every-down answer, while Tiki Barber would resume his third-down duties. As the 2000 season started, Dayne was getting the bulk of the carries, but Barber was carrying the show. In the season opener, Dayne carried the ball 23 times, rushing for 78 yards and scored once. Barber rushed only 13 times but tallied 144 yards and scored twice. From there the rushing load throughout the year was split, favoring one or the other in any given game. However, by season's end, Barber was getting the bulk of the carrying, while retaining his receiving duties. For the season, Barber reached the 1,000-yard mark, rushing for 1,006 yards, caught 70 passes for another 719 yards and scored nine times. Dayne finished the year rushing for 770 yards, caught only three passes for 11 yards and scored five times. Greg Comella didn't do much on the ground, rushing for only 45 yards but did catch 36 passes for 274 yards and did not score. By season's end and in the playoffs, Ron Dayne's role had sunk to virtually nothing as Tiki Barber became the focus of the Giant attack. Is this the direction the Giants are again headed in 2001? Will the Giants turn more of their offense over to Barber? They did reward him with a 6-year, $24 million contract in the offseason. I don't think he can take the punishment for an entire season without someone to share the load. I look for Dayne to again be utilized to punish defenses, but I believe it's Tiki Barber who'll show the explosiveness to again make him an effective back and fantasy pick in 2001.

WR: After going quite a few years trying to find or resolve deficiencies at the wide receiver position, the Giants finally had not only one 1,000-yard receiver but surprisingly almost two in 1999. Amani Toomer, a former second-round pick, stepped up to record 79 receptions for 1,183 yards and score six times. Ike Hilliard, a former first-round pick, jumped his numbers to 72 receptions for 996 yards and scored three times. Both players had not come close to this kind of production previously. Heading into the 2000 season, expectations for the two had taken on new meaning. Both players again fared well. Toomer again led the team in receptions, this time with 78 for 1,094 yards, while scoring seven times. Hilliard dropped back to 55 receptions for 787 yards, but did score eight times, missing two games with a bruised sternum. Other than Toomer and Hilliard, the Giants also got 25 receptions for 271 yards and one touchdown, six receptions for 92 yards and one touchdown out of Ron Dixon. Looking to 2001, the Giants' receivers have fantasy value and will be well sought after. Amani Toomer, who signed a 4-year extension in the offseason, and Ike Hilliard are both capable of 1,000-yard seasons and of scoring 7-10 times in 2001.

TE: In looking to upgrade the tight end position, the Giants made a move in 1999 to lure Pete Mitchell from Jacksonville. The three previous years, the Giants' top receiving tight end had been Howard Cross with 13 receptions. With Mitchell aboard, the Giants brought the tight end position more into the game plan, resulting in 58 receptions for 520 yards and six touchdowns in 1999. A quick contrast to previous years for the Giants. Heading into 2000, Mitchell's fantasy value had picked up. However, a nagging knee injury requiring arthoscopic surgery slowed Mitchell's play, in fact forcing him to miss the first two games of the year. His overall production dropped to 25 receptions for 245 yards and one touchdown. A very disappointing year for Mitchell. Other than Mitchell, the Giants got eight receptions and a surprising three touchdowns out of Dan Campbell and only four receptions out of Howard Cross. Looking to 2001, the Giants will be without Mitchell, who left via free agency to join the Detroit Lions. This likely gives Dan Campbell a great shot to expand his numbers.

QB: Despite offering Kerry Collins $16.9 million over four years, including a $4.8 signing bonus, the Giants opened the 1999 season with Kent Graham at quarterback. Collins did finally take over in the second half as the team's starter and finished the year with 1,697 passing yards and eight touchdowns playing in ten games. Coming into the 2000 season, Collins was given the starting nod from the outset, as Kent Graham was released prior to the season, not accepting a pay cut. Collins steadily improved, as did his numbers, throughout the year. Collins over the last eight games threw for over 300 yards, three times and for three touchdowns twice. For the season, Collins finished with 3,610 passing yards and 22 touchdowns. Impressive numbers for a New York Giants' quarterback. Looking to 2001, Collins has entrenched himself not only as the Giants' starter but as a player that will be putting up significant numbers, certainly making him a significant fantasy consideration.

K: For two straight seasons, Brad Daluiso has missed time due to injury. In 1999 he missed a large portion of the season with a knee injury, while in 2000 Daluiso missed less significant time, two games with an ailing back. Daluiso returned to action after missing those games to finish by hitting 17 of 23 (.739) field goal attempts, including three of his last four attempts. Will his struggles dictate the Giants bringing in a challenger? The Giants did sign free agent Matt Simonton in the offseason and made Jon Markam out of Vanderbilt their fifth-round draft choice, though many feel Markam will be hard pressed to win the job.

Overall: From 7-9 in 1999 to 12-4 in 2000 and a nice playoff run, the Giants under head coach Jim Fassel were headed in the right direction. The Giants rewarded Fassel with a new four-year deal following the season. First-round draft pick running back Ron Dayne showed some glimpses of steady play but was really outshined by the fleet-footed Tiki Barber who got it done for the Giants on the ground and through the air. At quarterback, the much traveled Kerry Collins seems to have found a home in New York, after years of disgruntlement. Receivers like Amani Toomer and Ike Hilliard have really picked up their game. As a whole, this used to be a team many fantasy owners shied away from because of the lack of offensive numbers. That's no longer the case as the Giants have stepped up their game and in doing so the players have stepped up their numbers.

Offseason Fantasy-Position Moves

	Arriving	From:		Departing	To:
RB	Anthony Green	Free Agent	TE	Pete Mitchell	DET
RB	Mark Kacmarynski	Free Agent			
RB	Adam Wright	Free Agent			
WR	Pat Woodcock	Free Agent			
TE	Marcelius Rivers	Free Agent			
K	Matt Simonton	Free Agent			

NEW YORK JETS

Home Stadium: Giant's Stadium
Playing Surface: Astro Turf
Head Coach: Herman Edwards
2000 Record: 9-7

Jets Fast Start Ultimately Crashes

RB: Curtis Martin, coming off a 1999 season where he produced 1,464 rushing yards, 45 receptions for 259 yards and five touchdowns was a highly regarded fantasy pick heading into the 2000 season with fantasy owners wishing he'd just boost his touchdown production. Martin got off to a fast start in 2000, rushing for 110 yards, grabbing six receptions and scoring twice in the season opener against Green Bay. He remained pretty steady all year and had two exceptional games. Martin rushed for 143 yards and scored three times against New England and later rushed for 203 yards and scored once against Indianapolis. On the year, Martin finished with 1,207 rushing yards, caught a whopping 70 passes for another 508 yards and scored 11 times, nine on the ground and two via receptions. He was the most consistent, reliable offensive weapon the Jets have had since joining the Jets three years ago. Other than Martin, the Jets got only 63 rushing yards out of Ritchie Anderson but his 88 receptions for 853 yards while scoring twice were huge contributions to the Jets' offense. Bernie Parmalee chipped in 87 rushing yards while grabbing nine receptions for 66 yards and scored twice, however, he was released following the season. What can we expect looking to 2001? He's been so consistent that believing Curtis Martin will again be in the 1,500-1,800 rushing-receiving yard range is likely. It's the touchdown range that has uncertainty, which could be anywhere from 6-12 scores. However, anybody seeing the ball as often as Martin does is hard to shy away from. And don't forget Ritchie Anderson in yardage leagues, as Anderson should again put up good reception and yardage numbers, which could increase, if Martin ever spends time nursing any kind of injury. Another option, if Martin gets hurt, will now be second-round draft pick La Mont Jordan out of Maryland. Jordan is the heir apparent to Martin's job when he's done, but the Jets will likely find a way to let him contribute now as well.

WR: In losing a dominant player like a Keyshawn Johnson, you'd think a team would make a quick move to fill that vacancy with another talented player of near or like ability. The Jets, losing Keyshawn to Tampa Bay prior to the 2000 season, opted to not make such a move but instead promoted Wayne Chrebet to be their #1 receiver. Chrebet, who had missed the first five games on the 1999 season with a foot injury, finished that year recording 48 receptions for 631 yards and only three touchdowns in the 11 games he did play. A year earlier, healthy all year, Chrebet had recorded 75 receptions for 1,083 yards and eight touchdowns. Remember, however, those were numbers he'd posted as the #2 receiver alongside Keyshawn. Next question, who would now become the #2 receiver opposite Chrebet? Dedric Ward, who had recorded 22 receptions in 1999, would battle speedy rookie third-round pick Laveranues Coles out of Florida State. As the season began, it was Ward who got off to a fast start, recording 100-yard performances in each of the first two games but quickly dropped off from there, not recording another 100-yard game until the season finale. Chrebet, meanwhile, wasn't putting up big numbers but was making big catches. On the year, Chrebet finished with 69 receptions for 937 yards and eight touchdowns. Ward finished with 54 catches for 801 yards and three touchdowns. Coles, who struggled through problems late in the year, finished with 22 receptions for 370 yards and one score. Windrell Hayes chipped in six receptions for 126 yards. Looking to 2001, Chrebet returns to be the #1 receiver. Ward was released following the season. This opens the door for rookie first-round pick Santana Moss and offseason acquisition Mathew Hatchette, who comes over from Minnesota, where he had a disappointing season in 2000 as the Viking's #3 receiver. The two will battle Laveraunes Coles and Windell Hayes for work in the #2, #3 and #4 roles for the Jets. At only 5'9", the rookie Moss is a bit undersized but has game-breaking ability.

TE: Heading into the 2000 season, the Jets knew they had to make a move to step up their tight end position. In 1999, the trio of Eric Green, Fred Baxter and Blake Spence had tallied 18 receptions between them. This poor output led to the Jets selecting Anthony Becht out of West Virginia as their #1 draft pick. Becht a nice size target at 6'5" possessing good hands was expected to step in and help quickly. It didn't happen that way, as the Jets really didn't get the tight ends involved much in their offense early on. Becht, who finished the year with only 16 receptions for 144 yards and two touchdowns, caught 12 of those 16 passes over the last eight games. The only other tight end to catch a pass was Fred Baxter, who caught two, both, however, went for touchdowns. Looking to 2001, if the Jets don't get Becht more involved in the offense, it seems a waste they made him a first-round draft choice. I look for his numbers to take a significant climb, especially his touchdown production, as the Jets start to use his big frame in the red zone.

QB: Could Vinny Testaverde, returning after missing virtually the entire 1999 season with an achilles injury, return to the form of 1998, when he recorded 3,256 passing yards but more importantly 29 touchdown passes playing in just 14 games? Though his yardage numbers weren't strong to start the year, Testaverde threw for seven touchdowns in the first four games. He cooled off some but sporadically had big games. On week #8 he threw for 378 yards and four touchdowns in a 40-37 win over Miami and in the season finale threw for 481 yards and two touchdowns against Baltimore in a 34-20 loss. Losing wide receiver Keyshawn Johnson to Tampa Bay surely didn't help. Looking to 2001, Testaverde will be back but without a #1 receiver like Keyshawn. If the Jets sometime want to turn the team over to their #1 draft pick of a year ago, Chad Pennington, Testaverde's stock will likely take a tumble.

K: Coming off a season where he hit a very solid 27 of 33 (.818) field goal attempts in 1999, John Hall struggled in 2000, hitting only 21 of 32 (.656) attempts. Of his 11 misses, only one was from beyond 50 yards and four beyond 40 yards. Though Hall is signed for two more years, the Jets turned to Brett Conway for the season finale. Do the Jets seem alarmed enough to look elsewhere in 2001? Meanwhile, Conway signed with the Washington Redskins in the offseason.

Overall: Despite improving one game from 8-8 in 1999 to 9-7 in 2000, the Jets finish in 2000 is a concern. They lost their last three games and six of their last nine. Are the big-name stars of this team beyond their years? Quarterback Vinny Testaverde saw his numbers drop in 2000, after returning from nearly missing an entire season with an achilles injury. The loss of Keyshawn Johnson to Tampa Bay hurt more than the Jets thought offensively as they asked Wayne Chrebet to pick up more of the slack. Finding a #2 receiver to go with Chrebet remains a concern, though rookie Santana Moss or offseason acquisition Matthew Hatchette, coming over from the Vikings, may help. On the ground, Curtis Martin is still there, but is he showing signs of carrying too much of the load, producing only three 100-yard games in 2000? This may be why the Jets made LaMont Jordan their second-round draft pick. This may quickly become a team of transition, moving in some new players looking to the future. New head coach Herman Edwards has some tough decisions to make, though he does hope to help the offense by going to a more West Coast approach.

Offseason Fantasy-Position Moves

	Arriving	From:		Departing	To:
RB	Matt Cornella	Free Agent	WR	Dedric Ward	MIA
RB	Jamie Reader	Free Agent	TE	Bradford Banta	DET
RB	Reggie White	Free Agent	QB	Ray Lucas	MIA
WR	Matt Farmer	Free Agent	K	Brett Conway	WASH
WR	Matthew Hatchette	MINN			
WR	Phil McGroghan	Free Agent			
TE	Scott Slutzker	Free Agent			
TE	Daniel Wilcox	Free Agent			
QB	Tory Woodbury	Free Agent			

OAKLAND RAIDERS

Home Stadium: Network Associates Coliseum
Playing Surface: Grass
Head Coach: Jon Gruden
2000 Record: 12-4

Wheatley Continues to Lead Raiders' Rush, Though Garner Will Push in 2001

RB: Amazing really, to think a player can get chances with two teams, is plagued by injuries during those stints, pretty much is given up on but finds success on a new team. That's Tyrone Wheatley's story. Wheatley, a first-round pick of the New York Giants back in 1995, struggled through injuries there and was virtually a bust. Following his release, he hooked up with Miami, but there too he was a bust. One more time, one more chance for Wheatley, when he was signed by Oakland prior to the 1999 season. Wheatley showed what many always thought he could do. Sharing the load but more stealing the show from Napoleon Kaufman, Wheatley rushed for 931 yards, caught 21 passes for 196 yards but most importantly scored 11 times to the delight of fantasy fans. Could he keep the ball rolling and stay healthy in 2000? He did miss two games midseason with an ankle injury but for the most part stayed healthy, this time cracking the 1,000 yard mark, rushing for 1,046 yards, caught 20 passes for 156 yards and scored ten times. Less impressive and getting less work was Napoleon Kaufman. Kaufman, who had produced 894 rushing-receiving yards and scored three times in 1999, dropped to 626 rushing-receiving yards and only one touchdown. The Raiders also got 213 rushing yards, 27 receptions for 299 yards and four touchdowns out of Randy Jordan. Zack Crockett chipped in 130 rushing yards and caught ten passes for 62 yards while failing to score. And John Ritchie who didn't rush a down did contribute 26 receptions for 173 yards and he too failed to score. For Raider and fantasy fans, the story here is Tyrone Wheatley. Wheatley has pushed past his injuries to become an effective back and continues to push his numbers. Heading to 2001, things will look quite different for the Raiders. First, Napoleon Kaufman retired, then the Raiders signed free agent Charlie Garner away from the San Francisco 49ers. The Raiders now have Garner and Wheatley to utilize in their backfield. Garner is coming off a year where he rushed for 1,142 yards, caught 68 passes for 647 yards and scored ten times. It'll be interesting to see how the Raiders use Garner and Wheatley, though early on it was believed Garner would serve as backup to Wheatley. However, Garner brings too much to the table to not get his share of the action.

WR: There was some concern when Rich Gannon came to Oakland in 1999 that the numbers for at least Tim Brown would drop significantly. During Brown's 1997 season, when Jeff George was in Oakland, Brown produced a whopping 104 receptions for 1,408 yards but only scored five times. In 1999, Brown, now working with Gannon, produced a solid 90 receptions for 1,344 yards and six touchdowns. With this continuing success, Brown's fantasy value regained some momentum heading into 2000. Brown rewarded those fantasy owners who grabbed him with 11 touchdowns on 76 receptions while tallying 1,128 receiver yards. Other than Brown, the Raiders had been looking for a #2 receiver, as James Jett's production had dropped the last couple seasons. The Raiders made a couple of moves, by first making Jerry Porter out of West Virginia their #2 pick and then by signing aging free agent Andrew Rison. Rison, who had struggled in Kansas City the year before, became a pleasant surprise, stepping in to record 41 receptions for 606 yards while scoring six times. James Jett was again a disappointment, recording only 20 catches for 356 yards and two touchdowns, while David Dunn chipped in four receptions and the rookie Porter caught only one pass, struggling with a hamstring injury. Looking to 2001, Tim Brown again is a sure thing, but Andre Rison could be gone. The Raiders did re-sign James Jett in the offseason, still liking his speed, but ultimately would like Jerry Porter to step up and produce good numbers.

TE: Despite showing at times the ability to score from anywhere, Ricky Dudley frustrated Raiders' and fantasy fans with his inconsistency. In 1999 he recorded only 39 receptions for 555 yards but scored nine times. The nine touchdowns of course had fantasy owners excited going into the 2000 season. Dudley again showed his inconsistency when producing only 29 receptions for 350 yards and disappointingly scoring only four times. In fact, the four touchdowns came in just two games as he scored twice in each of those games. Other than Dudley, the Raiders got 13 receptions for 107 yards out of Jerry Brigham while scoring twice. Looking to 2001, Dudley is gone, signing with the Cleveland Browns. With Dudley gone, the Raiders signed Eric Bjornson via free agency from New England. Bjornson produced one touchdown on 20 receptions with the Patriots in 2000. Bjornson will battle Jerry Brigham, Mondriel Fulcher and another offseason acquisition Roland Williams (Rams) for the tight end duties.

QB: Coming to the Raiders in 1999, Rich Gannon was coming off a year when he produced only 2,305 passing yards and ten touchdowns in 1998 playing with Kansas City. Gannon's 3,840 passing yards and 24 touchdowns passes came pretty much as a surprise to fantasy owners. How would he follow up his first year with the Raiders? Would he again be an effective quarterback and more importantly put up significant fantasy numbers? Gannon got off to a very slow start, throwing for only 721 yards and three touchdowns through the first four games. In three of those games, he didn't even reach the 200-yard mark. He turned it around from there, however. Following the Raiders' bye week on week #5, Gannon threw for 310 yards and two touchdowns in a 34-28 win over San Francisco. He rolled pretty well from there. Though he threw for over 300 yards once more, he threw for two or more touchdowns in eight of the last twelve games, including a three, four and even five touchdown performance, which came in the season finale against Carolina in, a 52-9 win, Gannon finished the year throwing for 3,430 yards and 28 touchdowns. Looking to 2001, there remains little question that Gannon not only is the leader of the Raider offense but that he can also put up significant numbers in the process. Meanwhile, looking down the road, the Raiders made Marques Tuiasosopo out of Washington their second-round draft pick.

K: In 1999, the Raiders first gave Michael Hustad the kicking chores as he hit 20 of 31 (.645) field goals over the first 13 games and then turned to Joe Nedney [5 of 7 (.714)] to finish the year. Looking to start fresh and have someone to hopefully stick with, the Raiders made strong-legged Sebastian Janikowski out of Florida State their #1 draft pick. Janikowski got off to a slow start missing three of his first five kicks. He continued to struggle but improved late in the year following his return after missing two games with a bacterial infection. The Raiders have invested too much to turn away from Janikowski now despite his disappointing 22 of 32 (.688) field goal performance as a rookie.

Overall: From 8-8 in 1999 to 12-4 in 2000, the Raiders under Jon Gruden are on the right track. Running back Tyrone Wheatley has found a home in Oakland and provides the Raiders with a consistent ground game. After years of searching for a steady back and years of struggling from injury, the Raiders and Wheatley are a perfect match. However, in 2001, the Raiders are taking it a step further bringing in Charlie Garner from San Francisco to push Wheatley and the Raiders' running game to bigger levels. Through the air, Rich Gannon has become a leader and has put up better numbers than many expected. The biggest benefactor of Gannon's play is Tim Brown, who continues to unravel opposing defenses for consistent yards and scores. The Raiders, meanwhile, continue to search for a permanent #2 receiver to play opposite Brown and hope last year's #2 draft pick Jerry Porter eventually becomes the answer.

Offseason Fantasy-Position Moves

	Arriving	From:		Departing	To:
RB	Charlie Garner	SF	RB	Napoleon Kaufman	Retired
TE	Eric Bjornson	NE	TE	Ricky Dudley	CLE
TE	Roland Williams	STL			

PHILADELPHIA EAGLES
Home Stadium: Veterans Stadium
Playing Surface: Astro Turf
Head Coach: Andy Reid
2000 Record: 11-5

McNabb Spreads His Wings to Help Eagles Fly

RB: Following Ricky Watters departure in 1998, Duce Staley had put to rest the view that the Philadelphia ground game would not suffer much. In '98, despite competing with Charlie Garner for the starting spot, Staley still rushed for 1,065 yards, caught 57 receptions for 432 yards and scored six times. In 1999, Staley now having the starting job outright, rushed for 1,273 yards, grabbed 41 receptions for another 294 yards and scored six times again. Heading into the 2000 season, Staley had obviously begun to attract more fantasy attention especially in yardage leagues. Staley began the year strong, rushing for 101 yards, caught four passes for 61 yards and scored once in the season opener against Dallas. His numbers dropped some the next few weeks, and he was never able to rebound, as he suffered a season-ending foot injury in game five, forcing him to miss the last 11 games. A big loss for Eagles' and fantasy fans. With Staley out, the bulk of the load was turned over to Darnell Autry. Autry, along with Stanley Pritchett, Cecil Martin, Brian Mitchell and eventually Chris Warren, who was signed following his release from Dallas, filled in. Autry, playing in ten games produced 334 rushing yards, caught 24 passes for 275 yards and scored four times. Pritchett gained 225 yards on the ground, grabbed 25 receptions for 193 yards and scored once. Martin tallied 77 rushing yards, caught 31 passes for 219 yards and failed to score. Mitchell rushed for 187 yards, caught 13 passes for 89 yards and scored five times, two on kick returns. Warren played in only the season finale, in which he rushed for 42 yards, but stayed on to be the Eagles main back in the playoffs. Looking to 2001, there's still huge concern about Duce Staley's foot, though the Eagles were somewhat optimistic in the spring. Yet they have their eyes and ears open, their looking for a solid backup that might have to step in and make an impact. They may also turn to their draft choices. Fourth-round Correll Buckholter out of Nebraska and fifth-rounder Tony Stewart out of Penn State will both be given a look.

WR: The Eagles were looking to upgrade their wide receiver position heading into the 1999 season, and brought aboard two free agents in Charles Johnson (Steelers) and Torrence Small (Colts). Their results in their first year with Philadelphia were very disappointing. Johnson grabbed 34 receptions for 414 yards and one touchdown in the season's first nine games before suffering a season-ending knee injury. Small wasn't much better, grabbing 49 receptions for 655 yards and four touchdowns, missing two games with a rib injury. The Eagles stuck with the two heading into 2000, though they made Todd Pinkston out of Southern Mississippi their second-round draft pick. Johnson, pretty much stayed healthy this time around and finished the year recording 56 receptions for 642 yards and scored seven times, but never recorded a 100-yard game. Small, who again missed two games, this time with a hamstring injury early in the year, recorded 40 receptions for 569 yards and scored three times. Other than Johnson and Small, the Eagles got ten receptions for 181 yards and no touchdowns out of Todd Pinkston and nine receptions for 80 yards and one touchdown out of Na Brown. Looking to 2001, the Eagles let go of both Charles Johnson and Torrence Small, who would have cost the Eagles over $2 million toward the salary cap. This opened the door for the Eagles to sign James Thrash (Redskins) via free agency to a 5-year deal. Thrash will be thrown in to battle rookie first-round pick Freddie Mitchell out of UCLA, Todd Pinkston and Na Brown for spots, now that Johnson and Small are gone. At this point, Thresh and the rookie Mitchell would be projected starters, with Mitchell talented enough to become the team's #1 receiver.

TE: Heading into the 2000 season, fantasy fans weren't expecting much out of the Eagles' tight end position, as Luther Broughton looked to battle Chad Lewis and Jeff Thomason for work. Lewis, however, became a pleasant surprise for the Eagles, stepping to the forefront to put up pro-bowl numbers, recording 69 receptions for 735 yards but scoring a disappointing three times. Jeff Thomason was actually a more effective red zone target, scoring five times on just ten receptions, while Broughton caught only 12 passes and no touchdowns all year. Lewis's performance surely won't go unnoticed by fantasy fans, who'll push up his fantasy values among tight ends. The question for Lewis is can he step up his touchdown production?

QB: It was only a matter of time before Donovan McNabb, the Eagles's first-round pick of 1999, would get his chance. McNabb got his chance about mid-season as a rookie and showed some promising signs. Overall he saw action in 11 games in which he recorded 948 passing yards, eight passing touchdowns, while rushing for 313 yards. Working hard in the offseason, by the 2000 season, McNabb had become the Eagles' starter of the present as well as the future. How long would he take to develop? Was he ready? As a double-threat quarterback, McNabb passed and ran the Eagles to 11 wins despite having a mediocre receiving crew. On the year, McNabb's numbers were surprising. He had thrown for 3,365 yards and 21 touchdowns, again with a suspect receiving corps. Then there was what he did on the ground, where he rushed for a whopping 629 yards, while scoring six times. McNabb had become a leader, a double-threat signal-caller that kept opposing defenses off guard. Looking to 2001, he's only going to get better and his passing numbers should improve as his receivers step up, but he's always got his rushing numbers to carry him as a fantasy factor.

K: Coming into the 2000 season, the Eagles had elected to turn their kicking chores over to David Akers, who had been their kickoff specialist the year before, as veteran Norm Johnson handled the field goal duties. Akers responded in a very accurate way, hitting 29 of 33 (.879) field goal attempts on his way to 122 points. With the Eagles again expected to fare well in 2001, Akers fantasy value will climb.

Overall: The Eagles went 5-11 in 1999 and then turned it around to go 11-5 in 2000. They accomplished this despite the loss of their workhorse running back Duce Staley, who was lost early in the year to a foot injury. There's concern that Staley may not be fully ready at the outset of the 2001 season, so alternatives are being looked at. The biggest reason for the turnaround was the play of second-year quarterback and 1999 first-round pick Donovan McNabb. McNabb moved the Eagles to 11 wins based on his passing and running ability and looks to push those numbers in 2001. His receivers remain a concern, however, though tight end Chad Lewis has become a find and Charles Johnson and Torrence Small haven't and were released in the offseason, leaving free agent James Thrash, who should help, as should rookie first-round pick Freddie Mitchell.

Offseason Fantasy-Position Moves

	Arriving	From:		Departing	To:
RB	Anthony Gray	Free Agent	WR	Charles Johnson	Released
RB	Brennan Oats	Free Agent	WR	Torrence Small	Released
WR	Scott Keys	Free Agent			
WR	Eric McCready	Free Agent			
WR	Kenny Mitchell	Free Agent			
WR	Sean Scott	Free Agent			
WR	James Thrash	WASH			
WR	Elijah Thurman	Free Agent			
TE	Carlos Nuno	Free Agent			
K	Justin Skinner	Free Agent			

PITTSBURGH STEELERS
Home Stadium: Three Rivers Stadium
Playing Surface: Astro Turf
Head Coach: Bill Cowher
2000 Record: 9-7

The "Bus" Still Hasn't Run Out of Gas

RB: Coming off a season where his load had been lessened, Jerome "the Bus" Bettis became a tough fantasy value to figure out. In 1999, a leg injury had slowed Bettis but also the play of Richard Huntley also helped lead to Bettis's numbers dropping. Huntley, who had rushed for 567 yards, had caught 27 receptions for 253 yards and most importantly had scored eight times in 1999, was a concern. Bettis had put up decent numbers in '99, rushing for 1,091 yards, adding 110 more on 21 receptions and scoring seven times. But were we seeing the demise of his production and playing? Bettis got off to a very rough start rushing for only eight yards on nine carries in the season-opening loss to Baltimore. Huntley didn't fare well either, recording 31 yards on seven carries. Following the Steelers' bye week on week #2, Bettis took off from there. On week #3, he rushed for 22 yards and a touchdown against Cleveland and followed that up with six more 100-yard games, and two games of 90-plus yards. For the year, Bettis finished with 1,341 rushing yards, caught 14 passes for 108 yards and scored eight times. Huntley, nursing a hamstring injury part of the year, recorded only 215 rushing yards and ten receptions for 91 yards and scored three times. Chris Fuamatu-Ma'afala, who replaced Jon Witman at fullback, when he was lost for the season, rushed for 149 yards and grabbed 11 receptions for 107 yards while scoring once. Fuamatu-Ma'afala also fell victim to injury, forcing Dan Kreider to step in. Kreider rushed for only 24 yards and grabbed five receptions for 42 yards while failing to score. Looking to 2001, with the Steelers' offense so centered around running the football, I expect "the Bus" to again be a major ground force, which will again dictate plenty of yards but his scoring remains a concern for fantasy fans, though 8-10 touchdowns is likely. The Steelers showed their confidence by inking him to a 6-year deal in the offseason worth around $35 million. There's still the possibility that Richard Huntley will again get more involved in the offense. That more than anything would hurt Bettis's scoring numbers in 2001. Meanwhile, Jon Witman was released, likely moving

Don Kreider in as the starting fullback spot.

WR: For the past decade it seems, the Steelers have tried to upgrade their receiving crew either by draft picks or by free agency. Despite two receivers grabbing 61 receptions a piece in 1999, the Steelers continued to try to upgrade the position. Troy Edwards and Hines Ward had tied for the team lead in '99, each recording 61 receptions with Edwards going for 714 yards and five touchdowns, while Ward's went for 638 yards and five scores. Still not happy with mediocre success, the Steelers made Plaxico Burress, out of Michigan State, their #1 draft pick heading into the 2000 season. Burress at 6'6", possessed good speed and the big-play potential the Steelers were looking for. At the season's outset, Burress grabbed four receptions for 77 yards in the season opener against Baltimore. He never from that point matched those numbers, recording only 22 receptions for 273 yards and no touchdowns through ten games, before suffering bone and ligament damage to his wrist that ended his season—quite a disappointment for Steelers' and fantasy fans. The rest of the Steelers' receiving crew was unimpressive as well. Hines Ward was their leader with 48 catches for 672 yards and four touchdowns. Bobby Shaw was a bit of a surprise with 40 receptions for 672 yards and four touchdowns as well. Veteran Courtney Hawkins was a minor factor with 19 receptions for 238 yards and a score. Troy Edwards, who missed time with hamstring and hip injuries, finished with 18 receptions for 215 yards and failed to score, playing in ten games. Will Blackwell, barely used in the mix, recorded only two receptions. Looking to 2001, the Steelers expect and need Burress and Troy Edwards to step up, while Courtney Hawkins and Will Blackwell are likely gone. Unless they prove they can throw consistently, this is a team I'd shy away from when looking for fantasy receivers in 2001.

TE: Despite being a #1 draft pick back in 1996, Mark Bruener has made more of an impact as a blocker than receiver. In 1999, his 19 receptions (two for touchdowns) were unimpressive but his blocking was impressive enough to the Steelers for them to ink him to a 4-year deal worth just over $10 million. Again in 2000, his numbers weren't very impressive, 17 receptions for 192 yards and three touchdowns but his blocking for Jerome Bettis was. A highly paid tight end that I'd stay away from in picking my fantasy team as he's unlikely to put up significant numbers in 2001.

QB: Kordell Stewart's rocky performances the last few seasons have had the Steelers looking for another direction to go at quarterback. Mike Tomazak had actually ended the 1999 season as the team's starter, but he had departed in the 2000 offseason to Detroit. This left Stewart to battle new incoming free-agent Kent Graham, coming over from the New York Giants. At the 2000 season outset, the Giants turned to Graham to open the season. Graham was the starter into week #5 when he injured his hip against Jacksonville. Stewart stepped in and helped the Steelers comeback and win. Stewart guided the Steelers to another win (15-0 over Cincinnati the following week), but Graham recaptured his job when he returned on week #7. When Graham was struggling, Stewart soon got another chance and remained the starter through season's end, helping the Steelers to four victories in their last five games. Starting 11 games, Stewart finished the year throwing for 1,860 yards and 11 touchdowns, while rushing for 436 yards and seven scores. He had thrown for eight touchdowns and ran for six over the last six games—play more reminiscent of when he first took over as quarterback in Pittsburgh. Stewart looks to have regained the starting job and the confidence to go with it. He may be a nice fantasy sleeper pick, as most fantasy owners may still elect to shy away.

K: In his first year with the Steelers, Kris Brown, their seventh-round pick of 1999, hit an impressive 25 of 29 (.862) field goal tries. His second year was not far off that pace as he hit 25 of 30 (.833) attempts. Now if the Steelers could just get him more scoring chances, he'll become more of a fantasy factor.

Overall: Going from 6-10 in 1999 to 9-7 in 2000 was impressive, but it was winning four of the last five games that had Steelers' fans excited. Quarterback Kordell Stewart seemed to regain his confidence and helped direct the Steelers' run. His ability to run as well as pass kept opposing defenses off-guard. I believe he's actually a better running quarterback than passing, which may keep his receivers from any kind of big output. Regardless, Plaxico Burress, the Steelers' #1 pick of a year ago, hopes to return from his wrist injury to make an impact. He and Troy Edwards need to step up their game. On the ground, Jerome Bettis returned to form in 2000 and again was the Steelers' most consistent offensive weapon. If the "Bus" doesn't burn out of fuel, he'll likely do it again in 2001, especially if the Steelers have things turned around.

Offseason Fantasy-Position Moves

	Arriving	From:		Departing	To:
RB	Eddie Faulkner	Free Agent	RB	Jon Witman	Released
RB	Rod Frazier	Free Agent			
RB	Cedric Washington	Free Agent			
WR	Tim Baker	Free Agent			
WR	Joey Getherall	Free Agent			
WR	Vaness Provitt	Free Agent			
K	Andy Kohl	Free Agent			

ST. LOUIS RAMS

Home Stadium: Trans World Dome
Playing Surface: Astro Turf
Head Coach: Mike Martz
2000 Record: 10-6

The Rams Tumble Some but Faulk Still Amazes

RB: How do you top or come near a season that produced 1,000 rushing yards and 1,000 receiving yards? That's what Marshall Faulk and fantasy fans faced heading into the 2000 season. Faulk, in his first year with the Rams in 1999, coming over from Indianapolis, produced 1,381 rushing yards, caught 87 passes for another 1,048 yards while scoring 12 times in helping St. Louis on their quest to the Super Bowl. Some, but not many, wondered if Faulk could repeat that kind of performance. Faulk got off to a good start in 2000 and just kept coming. Though he produced only four 100-yard rushing games, he also produced two 100-yard receiving games. Only three times in the 14 games he played did he not combine for over 100 yards rushing and receiving, and two out of those three games, he topped the 90-yard mark. Faulk had seven multiple touchdown games, three four-touchdowns games and one three-touchdown performance. When all was said and done, he finished the year with 1,359 rushing yards, caught 81 passes for another 830 yards and set an NFL record by scoring 26 touchdowns. And remember, he did this playing in just 14 games, missing two games midseason with a knee injury. Other than Faulk, there wasn't much else to speak of. Justin Watson filled in when Faulk was out and produced 249 rushing yards, ten receptions for 56 yards and four touchdowns. Robert Holcombe chipped in 70 rushing yards, grabbed eight receptions for 90 yards and scored four times. And rookie first-round pick Trung Canidate, who was supposed to take some of the load off Faulk battled ankle, foot and wrist injuries to be a bust. Looking to 2001, Faulk will again be a top-rated fantasy pick and well he should be. If healthy all year, 2,000 rushing-receiving yards and 20 touchdowns are reachable. Other than Faulk the Rams hope their #1 pick of a year, Trung Canidate can do a better job taking some of the load off of Faulk.

WR: After a couple of down years in 1997 and 1998, Isaac Bruce rebounded to show some of his old form. Regarded as one of the league's premier receivers, Bruce had averaged over 100 receptions back in 1995 and 1996. Fantasy fans were waiting for a rebound and got it in 1999 when Bruce stayed healthy enough to produce 77 receptions for 1,165 yards and scored 12 times. Could he do it again in 2000? Bruce again stayed healthy all season, this time recording 87 receptions for a whopping 1,471 yards but his touchdown production dropped to nine. Not far behind was the Rams' 1999 first-round pick Torry Holt. Holt, who had produced 52 receptions for 788 and six touchdowns as a rookie in 1999, jumped his numbers considerable in 2000. Holt finished with 82 receptions for an unbelievable 1,635 yards but only six touchdowns. The Rams talented receiving corps doesn't stop there. Az-Zahir Hakim finished with 53 receptions for 734 yards and scored five times, once on a punt return. Ricky Proehl, who missed four games with a hamstring pull, recorded 31 receptions for 441 yards and four touchdowns. Looking to 2001, Isaac Bruce and Torry Holt will again he heavily weighted on most fantasy charts, especially for fantasy teams and league's involving yardage. Reaching or nearing 1,500 is possible for both. The 10-15 touchdown range is also possible but more difficult to predict.

TE: Despite being a very pass-oriented team, the Rams didn't see their tight end position produce much statistically the last couple seasons. Ernie Conwell, who had grabbed 38 receptions and four touchdowns back in 1997, had been nursing a knee injury from midway through the 1998 season and all through the 1999 season. Filling in for Conwell in 1999 was Roland Williams, who recorded 25 receptions for 233 yards and six touchdowns. With Conwell presumed to be returning healthy in 2000, fans were curious as to how the Rams would use the two receivers and how much they would be used in the offense. With the uncertainty of what would happen, most smart fantasy fans shied away heading into 2000 and good thing. The Rams kept the tight ends pretty much out of the flow. Roland Williams led the way with only 11 receptions, though three went for touchdowns. Conwell and Jerry Robinson combined for ten receptions total and no scores. Surely a Rams' situation I'd shy away from in 2001.

QB: How do you follow up a "Cinderella" season like Kurt Warner had in 1999? A virtual unknown, Warner got his chance when Trent Green went down. Green had been lured to St. Louis, following a 3,441 yard, 23 touchdown performance with Washington in 1998. Green suffered a season-ending knee injury prior to the 1999 season, so Warner got the call. What followed was a fairy-tale season. Warner tore apart the league, throwing for 4,353 yards and 41 touchdown passes enroute to leading the Rams to a Super Bowl win. Could he and would he do it again in 2000? He started out like he would, throwing for 2,260 yards and 16 touchdowns in the season's first six games. He threw for over 300 yards in each of those games, including one for over 400 yards. In game #7, however, Warner injured a finger on his throwing hand, which sidelined him for five weeks. In his absence, Trent Green stepped in and put up some very impressive numbers as well. When Warner returned he wasn't quite as sharp. He finished the year throwing for 3,429 yards and 21 touchdowns playing in 11 games. Add Trent Green's 2,063 passing yards and 16 touchdowns and you get a feel for what may have been if Warner had stayed healthy all year. Heading into 2001, Warner will and should be a top fantasy prospect. If healthy all year, big numbers will again be in store. Meanwhile, Trent Green, shopping his services, has departed to Kansas City, where he'll start for former coach Dick Vermeil.

K: Jeff Wilkins missed four of his last seven field goal tries in 1999, but the Rams stuck with him. Good move, as Wilkins hit all 17 of his field goal tries in 2000. He missed five games with a pulled quad muscle or would have been among the league's scoring leaders. During his absence, Jeff Hall and Pete Stoyanovich filled in. Wilkins returned and will be back and around for a long time, signing a five-year, $6.5 million deal in the offseason.

Overall: The Rams dropped a few notches in 2000. From a 13-3 record and Super Bowl win in 1999 to 10-6 a year ago. Despite the three fewer wins, the Rams continued their offensive fireworks. Marshall Faulk, despite missing two games to a knee injury, proved he's still the elite of the elite, producing 2,189 rushing-receiving yards and scored an NFL record 26 touchdowns playing in just 14 games. Quarterback Kurt Warner nursed a finger injury part of the 2000 season but when healthy continued his assault on the league throwing to the likes of Isaac Bruce, Torry Holt and Az-Zahir Hakim. I don't see this unit slowing down much in 2001. If healthy, all will again put together fantasy numbers that'll keep fantasy owners again very healthy and happy.

Offseason Fantasy-Position Moves

Arriving		From:		Departing		To:
RB	Avelon Carson	Free Agent	WR	Tony Horne	KC
WR	Lavel Bailey	Free Agent	TE	Roland Williams	OAK
WR	Tony Miles	Free Agent	QB	Trent Green	KC
TE	Byron Black	Free Agent			
QB	Paul Justin	Free Agent			

Terrell Fletcher/San Diego Chargers

SAN DIEGO CHARGERS

Home Stadium: Qualcomm Stadium
Playing Surface: Grass
Head Coach: Mike Riley
2000 Record: 1-15

Chargers Shake Loose a Leaf—Get Flutie to Lead New Charge

RB: Coming off a season when their best running back, Natrone Means, was hurt most of the year nursing a knee injury and their most productive back rushed for only 365 yards, the Chargers looked for new options heading into the 2000 season. Means was let go and in doing so, the Chargers had to find alternate plans. Big Jermaine Fazande, who had finished strong in 1999 and was the team's leading rusher with 365 yards, would be one option. Another option or challenge for Fazande would be another bigger power back, Robert Chancey, coming over from Dallas in the offseason to battle for the job. The two shared or battles for most of the work, while Terrell Fletcher likely continued with his third-down duties. Chancey pushed his way into the starting role at the 2000 season's outset and rushed for 141 yards and two touchdowns through the first three games. But weight problems and ineffectiveness led the Chargers to turn to Fazande and eventually to Terrell Fletcher to handle the main back chores. On the year, the Chargers ground game was unimpressive and surely hurt the overall offense. It was Fletcher's 384 rushing yards that led the team. He also grabbed 48 receptions for 355 yards and scored four times. Fazande, who nursed an ankle injury early in the year, was next, rushing for 368 yards, caught 16 passes for 104 yards and scored twice. Chancey had the 141 rushing yards and caught only one pass for six yards. Kenny Bynum chipped in 26 rushing yards and two receptions for 13 yards while failing to score. Looking to 2001, you'd think the only direction for the Chargers' running game to go is up but that's what they thought heading into the 2000 season. Chancey was released early in the offseason. This pushed the Chargers to make a move in this year's draft, landing La Dainian Tomlinson out of Texas Christian in the first round. Tomlinson is expected to step in and have an immediate impact and should be an interesting fantasy prospect for 2001.

WR: Another area that the Chargers have been trying to improve is at wide receiver. Despite making moves in the early rounds on draft picks and picking up free agents, there hasn't been much in the way of consistent good play. Mikhael Ricks, the Chargers second-round pick of 1998, was the latest in a number of early round picks that San Diego had hoped to develop. Others included Bryan Still, a former second-round pick as well, and former fourth rounder, Charlie Jones, but none moved to the forefront. With their young receivers not working out, the Chargers brought in veteran free agent Jeff Graham from Philadelphia in 1999, and he responded by leading the receiving corps by grabbing 57 receptions for 968 yards but only two touchdowns. Seeing a formula work fairly well, the Chargers brought in veteran Curtis Conway from Chicago heading into the 2000 season. The two struggled some with injury but for the most part were pretty productive. Graham again led the way, grabbing 55 receptions this time for 907 yards while scoring four times, despite missing three games to hamstring and back injuries. Conway missed a couple of games also with hamstring problems but finished with 53 receptions for 712 yards while scoring five times. Other than Graham and Conway, the Chargers got 17 receptions for 186 yards out of Reggie Jones, 13 receptions for 182 yards and one touchdown out of Trevor Gaylor and only three receptions out of Mikhael Ricks before releasing him. Looking to 2001, the Chargers are likely to stay with the mix that has brought them some decent success. Veterans Jeff Graham and Curtis Conway will likely to be counted on again to produce in the passing game. Offseason acquisition Tim Dwight, coming over from Atlanta, should be able to use his speed to help open up defenses, and having veteran Doug Flutie at quarterback should also help.

TE: Despite the problems the Chargers have had at the wide receiver position the last few years, tight end has been a bright spot. Freddie Jones continues to improve. Since coming to the Chargers as their second-round pick of 1997, Jones had recorded 41, 57 and 56 receptions, 505, 602 and 670 yards and 2, 3 and 2 touchdowns respectively his first three seasons. Heading into the 2000 season, Jones continued his successful ways, this time jumping his numbers to 71 receptions for 766 yards and five touchdowns. Other than Jones, the Chargers received six receptions and one touchdown out of Eric Heiden and one reception out of Reginald Davis. Looking to 2001, Freddie Jones will again be a receiving force for the Chargers and will again draw fantasy attention as a tight end capable of 700 plus yards and six plus touchdowns.

QB: You want to believe when you make someone your first-round draft pick and #2 pick overall in the draft that the player is going to help you both now and in the future. The San Diego Chargers had that hope and belief when selecting Ryan Leaf #2 overall back in 1998. It's been pretty much a nightmare ever since. Let's just say the path taken by Peyton Manning, who was selected one pick ahead of Leaf, and Leaf's path with the Chargers have been a little different. Manning has developed and developed quickly for the Indianapolis Colts. Leaf has struggled through injuries, poor play problems with the team, you name it. The Chargers turned to veterans Jim Harbaugh and Erik Kramer along with Moses Moreno during Leaf's brief stint, and were going to turn the reins back over to Leaf heading into the 2000 season. Leaf had recovered from shoulder surgery and had looked decent in the preseason. Though the Chargers weren't winning, they stuck with Leaf until he suffered a wrist injury on week #4. The Chargers again turned to Jim Harbaugh and Moses Moreno but when Leaf returned healthy he returned to the starting job. At season's end, Leaf had tallied 1,883 yards and 11 touchdowns playing in 11 games, leading the Chargers to only one victory. Ryan was given his release following the season and later signed with Tampa Bay. The Chargers looked for a new starter and brought in veteran Doug Flutie via free agency from Buffalo. Flutie has been the Bills' off-and-on starter for the last couple seasons. In San Diego, as long as he's healthy he'll likely be given an opportunity to start. The Chargers, having the #1 overall pick in the draft, had the chance to land Michael Vick but instead opted to trade the pick and landed Purdue's Drew Brees in the second-round, who they'll develop for the future. Meanwhile, Jim Harbaugh moved on to sign with

Detroit in the offseason, where he'll back up Charlie Batch.

K: Amazing what a year can do. John Carney went from putting up fairly significant numbers, hitting 31 of 36 (.861) field goals in 1999 to hitting 18 of 25 (.720) tries in 2000 as the Chargers won only one game. Looking to 2001, Carney's long tenure with the Chargers is over, as San Diego signed Wade Richey via free agency from San Francisco in the offseason. Richey, whose 15 of 22 (.682) in 2000 was a concern, is now on a team that went 1-15 a year ago, which may really limit his potential success in 2001.

Overall: From 8-8 in 1999 to a dismal 1-15 finish in 2000, the Chargers and head coach Mike Riley have to be wondering what to do next. The running game continues to be a problem. Every move the Chargers make to upgrade turns to disaster. The Chargers weren't looking for a 1,000-yard back, they were looking for a 500-yard back. Terrell Fletcher, a third-down prototype, was called on too often in 2000 to fill the every-down role. That was the Chargers' first order of business in the offseason, and drafting La Dainian Tomlinson should be a huge help to their running game. At quarterback, there's also desperate need. Ryan Leaf, their prized first-round pick of 1998, has been a bust, and he was released following the season. The Chargers are turning to veteran Doug Flutie, who comes in from Buffalo. And looking to the future, they made Drew Brees out of Purdue their second-round draft pick. At wide receiver are two veterans, Jeff Graham and Curtis Conway, who put in respectable performances in 2000. Can they continue? One big addition is speedster Tim Dwight, who came over in the Michael Vick deal. Freddie Jones at tight end remains the Chargers' best and most consistent weapon.

Offseason Fantasy-Position Moves

	Arriving	From:		Departing	To:
RB	Mukala Sikyala	Free Agent	RB	Robert Chancey	Released
RB	Ed Wilder	Free Agent	QB	Jim Harbaugh	DET
RB	Terry Witherspoon	Free Agent	QB	Ryan Leaf	TB
WR	Tim Dwight	ATL			
WR	Dondre Gilliam	Free Agent			
WR	DeRonnie Pitts	Free Agent			
WR	Nate Turner	Free Agent			
TE	Robert Ellis	Free Agent			
TE	Marty Mauer	Free Agent			
QB	Dave Dickerson	Free Agent			
QB	Doug Flutie	BUF			
K	Wade Richey	SF			

SAN FRANCISCO 49ERS

Home Stadium: 3 Com Park
Playing Surface: Grass
Head Coach: Steve Mariucci
2000 Record: 6-10

Rice (or roni)—No Longer a San Francisco Treat

RB: A devastating loss for the 49ers came when running back Garrison Hearst suffered a severe leg injury in the playoffs following the 1998 season. How do you replace a player that had just produced over 2,000 rushing-receiving yards and nine touchdowns? The 49ers examined a couple of options, including signing Lawrence Phillips, who had had a rough time since coming into the NFL, and also signing Charlie Garner, who had shown flashes when with Philadelphia but had a history of injuries. Phillips never worked out, and Garner became the mainstay of the 49ers' ground game. Garner rushed for 1,229 yards, caught 56 passes for another 535 yards but scored only six times. Garner's 1999 performance, especially because he had proven he could stay healthy, boosted his fantasy stock heading into the 2000 season. Garner had a very steady first half but seemed to sort of run out of gas as the season finished. He produced only three games of over 100-yards rushing, once topping the 200-yard mark (201) against Dallas early in the year. He also had one game of 100-yards receiving. For the season, Garner finished with 1,142 rushing yards and seven rushing touchdowns along with 647 receiving yards on 68 receptions while grabbing three receiving touchdowns. Other than Garner, fullback Fred Beasley rushed for only 147 yards, caught 31 passes for another 233 yards and scored six times. Paul Smith chipped in 72 rushing yards and caught two passes for another 55 yards, and Terrell Jackson combined for only 54 total yards while scoring once. If it wasn't Charlie Garner, the 49ers weren't doing much on the ground. Looking to 2001, things are likely to be a lot different. Garner, an unrestricted free agent, took his services to Oakland, signing with the Raiders in the offseason. This leaves the 49ers with a huge void. Garrison Hearst is said to be progressing from his leg injury of two years ago but can't be counted on. The 49ers waited until the third round of the draft to land a running back, selecting Kevan Barlow out of Pittsburgh. Barlow, who rushed for 1,053 yards in 2000 while in college, is no sure thing but the 49ers projected him as a second-round pick and are happy to have landed him in the third round. He should get a shot to start. He has good all-round skills and should fit well in the 49ers' West Coast offense. Meanwhile at fullback, last year's second-round pick Paul Smith has the 49ers excited. Smith may see more duty than what's been projected thus far.

WR: Heading into the 2000 season, there was concern among fantasy fans about the potential of the 49ers' receiving crew. The numbers for the likes of Terrell Owens, Jerry Rice and J.J. Stokes had tumbled with the absence and later retirement of Steve Young. Owens, for example, went from 67 catches for 1,097 yards and 14 touchdowns with a healthy Steve Young in 1998 to 60 receptions for 754 yards and four touchdowns with him missing most of the '99 season and Jeff Garcia at the helm. Rice went from 82 receptions for 1,15 yards and nine touchdowns to 67 catches for 830 yards and five touchdowns. And now heading into 2000, Garcia would have the reins from the outset. So for those who shied away from the 49ers' receivers, especially Terrell Owens, Garcia proved to everyone it was their loss. Garcia surprised many having a big statistical year, which of course benefited his receivers. For those that gambled on Owens, they were rewarded with 97 receptions for 1,451 yards and 13 touchdowns. He did this despite missing two games, one to a toe injury and one to suspension for an unacceptable touchdown celebration. The aging Rice surprisingly came up with decent numbers, recording 75 receptions for 805 yards and seven touchdowns. Stokes, however, did not make a good impression, dropping to 30 catches for 524 yards and three scores, while Tai Streets, a receiver the 49ers believe can do some damage in the future, recorded 19 receptions for 287 yards but failed to score. Looking to 2001, Owens can again be expected to be a major fantasy factor. Rice, who for so many years displayed his phenomenal talent in a 49er uniform moves on, so J.J. Stokes and Tai Streets can now battle for the #2 position.

TE: Greg Clark was coming off a season in which a rib injury slowed him nearly half the season. Clark managed to produce only 34 receptions for 347 yards and did not score a touchdown. The bright spot was that 23 of his receptions came in the second half when he was healthy. Clark's fantasy value was uncertain looking to the 2000 season, especially because of the 49ers' uncertain quarterback situation. Clark managed to stay healthy throughout 2000, played steady all year and put up unimpressive numbers. He finished the year with 38 receptions for 342 yards and two touchdowns—numbers that don't have fantasy owners over excited at his 2000 potential.

QB: The likelihood of Steve Young retiring following a season when he suffered yet another concussion became a reality prior to the 2000 season. Young being sidelined for most of 1999 was a huge disappointment to fantasy owners who had just seen him record 4,170 passing yards, 36 touchdown passes, 454 rushing yards and six touchdowns a year earlier in 1998. With Young sidelined part way into 2000, the 49ers turned to backups Jeff Garcia and Steve Senstrom. Neither lit the world on fire, so it's no wonder that Garcia got little fantasy respect heading into 2000. Garcia, however, became one of the surprises of the year. Despite the 49ers' struggle to finish 6-10, Garcia put up big numbers. Garcia threw for 4,278 yards and 31 touchdowns. Along the way he threw for over 300 yards, six times, including a 402-yard performance against Chicago late in the year. He produced ten multiple-touchdown pass games, two games of three touchdowns and three games of four touchdown passes. Surely some may have predicted statistical improvement but not to the degree that Garcia jumped. Looking to 2001, Garcia has shown he's very capable of putting up significant fantasy numbers, so it's unlikely he'll be overlooked as a fantasy prospect this time out.

K: This is the second time in three years that Wade Richey has struggled with his accuracy. In 1998, Richey's 18 of 27 (.667) field goal tries had the 49ers concerned. He recovered to 21 of 23 (.913) attempts in 1999 but his 15 of 22 (.682) performance in 2000 was a concern. But no more, as Richey signed as a free agent with San Diego in the offseason, which leaves the 49ers looking for a replacement in 2001. The 49ers had only signed free agent Jamie Rheem at press time.

Overall: From 4-12 in 1999 to 6-10 in 2000, not much of an improvement. Despite the poor record, the 49ers' passing game got a boost in 2000 as Jeff Garcia, in his first full year as a starter, threw for over 4,000 yards and 31 touchdowns. His statistical success trickled down to his receivers, which I believe will continue in 2001, especially for Terrell Owens. Jerry Rice has likely seen his last days as a 49er, so youngsters J.J. Stokes and Tai Streets will see their fantasy stock take a jump. On the ground, Charlie Garner got it done in a big way again in 2000 but he's gone via free agency. His replacement, which may be third-round pick Kevan Barlow or last year's second-round pick Paul Smith, will be a big key to the 49ers' offense and will likely reap big statistical success.

Offseason Fantasy-Position Moves

	Arriving	From:		Departing	To:
RB	Tommy Banks	Free Agent	RB	Travis Jervey	Released
RB	Jason Isom	Free Agent	K	Wade Richey	SD
RB	Jared McGram	Free Agent			
RB	J. T. Thatcher	Free Agent			
WR	Hilton Alexander	Free Agent			
WR	Dwight Carter	Free Agent			
WR	Antonio Chatman	Free Agent			
WR	James Farris	Free Agent			
WR	Grant Heard	Free Agent			
WR	Steve Jackson	Free Agent			
WR	James Johnson	Free Agent			
TE	Neil Johnson	Free Agent			
TE	Ben Steele	Free Agent			
QB	Kevin Nawracaj	Free Agent			
K	Jamie Rheem	Free Agent			

SEATTLE SEAHAWKS

Home Stadium: Kingdome
Playing Surface: Astro Turf
Head Coach: Mike Holmgren
2000 Record: 6-10

Holmgren's New Pupil—Green Bay's Hasselbeck

RB: Heading into his tenth NFL season, Ricky Watters still knew he could produce but the Seattle Seahawks must have had their uncertainties. Despite a 1999 season in which Ricky Watters had produced 1,210 rushing yards, 40 receptions for another 387 yards and scored seven times, the Seahawks either had their doubts or were looking to the future. The Seahawks made powerful Shaun Alexander out of Alabama their first-round draft pick. This was after dealing Ahman Green, Watters's previous backup, to Green Bay. Speculation was that Alexander would be sharing the load with Watters but by midseason would likely be handling the bulk of the duties. Alexander did share some of the load right from the start but Watters's steady play kept him as the main back all season. When all was said and done, Watters recorded 1,242 rushing yards, impressively caught 63 passes for another 613 yards and scored nine times, seven on the ground and two through the air. He only produced two games of 100-yards rushing and one game of 100-yards receiving but he was steady all year. Alexander, meanwhile, finished the year with 313 rushing yards, caught only five passes for 41 yards and scored only twice. Other than Watters and Alexander the only other significant contribution was Mack Strong, who caught 22 receptions for 136 yards and scored once, while rushing for only nine yards. How about in 2001? Ricky Watters, despite his strong 2000 showing, is likely gone as the Seahawks look to the future. The veteran Watters can help a good number of teams who'll be after his services. This gives Shaun Alexander a great chance to step in and show what he can do. His talent I believe will get him in the 1,500 rushing-receiving yard range and near the double-digit touchdown mark.

WR: Heading into the 2000 season, the Seahawks had become accustomed to life without Joey Galloway, so his being dealt to Dallas prior to the season didn't have much effect. Galloway was a long holdout in 1999 and when he finally returned produced only 22 receptions for 335 yards and scored one touchdown playing the season's last eight games. The Seahawks, in need of a wide receiver, turned to head coach Mike Holmgren's old team the Packers and acquired Derrick Mayes. Mayes, coming off a year with injuries in 1999, stepped up once putting on the Seahawks' uniform and finished the 1999 season, leading the club with 62 receptions for 829 yards, while scoring ten times. So heading into 2000, with Galloway off to Dallas, Mayes seemed like the most logical Seahawks receiver to put up good fantasy numbers. Other than Mayes, the other receiver to keep an eye on was Sean Dawkins, who had come over from New Orleans in 1999 to record 58 receptions for 992 yards and seven touchdowns. Well, things don't always turn out as they're planned. Mayes arrived out of shape, fought ankle and finger injuries, lost his starting job to third-round pick Darrell Jackson and finished 2000 with only 29 receptions for 264 yards and one touchdown. Sean Dawkins, however, fared OK, producing 63 receptions for 731 yards and five touchdowns but the best surprise was the rookie Jackson, who recorded 53 receptions for 713 yards and scored six times. Looking to 2001, I look for Jackson, who improved in 2000, to improve his numbers in a big way in 2001. He'll have to as the Seahawks released both Mayes and Dawkins in the offseason and looking for a #2 receiver heading into 2001. The Seahawks made Koren Robinson out of North Carolina State their first round draft choice. Robinson, a very talented receiver with good size and speed, is expected to step in and contribute right away for the Seahawks.

TE: Christian Fauria, struggled through injuries early in his career but even when healthy has not put up big-time fantasy numbers to draw much attention. The year 2000 wasn't much different for Fauria, who got off to a rough start with a hamstring injury that forced him to miss the first two games of the year. He returned and stayed healthy the rest of the year, finishing with 28 receptions for 237 yards and two touchdowns. Fauria wasn't the only tight end seeing frequent action in 2000. Itula Mili equaled Fauria's reception level with 28, while recording 288 yards and three touchdowns. With Mili now sharing the tight end load with Fauria, neither will be given much fantasy attention in 2001.

QB: Jon Kitna came off the 1999 season, having produced 3,346 yards and 23 touchdowns, in his first year as the Seahawks' starter. There seemed to be good hope for his improvement in 2000, especially under the tutorship of Mike Holmgren. It didn't happen! Kitna struggled early and never really rebounded in confidence as the season progressed. The Seahawks and Mike Holmgren turned to Brock Huard at times. Kitna regained the starting job but continued to struggle. On the year, Kitna finished with 2,658 yards and 18 touchdowns, seeing action in 15 games. Huard threw for 540 yards and three touchdowns appearing in five games. It didn't take long for Mike Holmgren and the Seahawks to make a quarterback decision following the season. The Seahawks acquired Matt Hasselbeck from the Green Bay Packers. Hasselbeck, Brett Favre's backup, will come in to be developed into the immediate starter. This time Holmgren made his own choice in picking someone to develop, rather than be presented with someone as he was with Kitna. Hasselbeck threw for only 104 yards and one touchdown in the four games he played with Green Bay in 2000. He has huge potential. Kitna, meanwhile, has moved on via free-agency to Cincinnati, where he'll battle Akili Smith for the Bengal's starting job.

K: After losing Todd Peterson to Kansas City in the offseason, the Seahawks settled on Kris Heppner in 2000. Heppner's 7 of 10 (.700) field goal attempts kept him around only four games. The Seahawks then turned to young Rian Lindell, whose 15 of 17 (.882) should keep him in a Seahawks uniform.

Overall: Head coach Mike Holmgren has some decisions to make heading into the 2000 season. From 9-7 in 1999 to 6-10 in 2000, the Seahawks need to get things headed in the right direction. Despite Watters's 1,855 rushing-receiving yards, and nine touchdowns in 2000, he's unlikely part of the Seahawks' ground game plans in 2000, as they will get a better look at their #1 draft pick of a year ago, Shaun Alexander, who has been waiting in the wings. Jon Kitna's reign at quarterback is over, as his struggles in 2000 cost him the starting job. The Seahawks and Mike Holmgren are instead turning to big Matt Hasselbeck, Brett Favre's backup in Green Bay, who was brought over in the offseason. Hasselbeck, many believe, will quickly develop under Holmgren. His receivers are a bit of a concern, with second-year man Darrell Jackson and rookie first-round pick Koren Robinson the likely starters.

Offseason Fantasy-Position Moves

	Arriving	From:		Departing	To:
RB	Lyold Garden	Free Agent	WR	Sean Dawkins	Released
RB	Jay Graham	Free Agent	WR	Derrick Mayes	Released
WR	Kerwin Cook	Free Agent	QB	Jon Kitna	CIN
WR	Jerry Dorsey	Free Agent			
WR	Corey Nelson	Free Agent			
TE	Russell Stewart	Free Agent			
QB	Matt Hasselbeck	GB			

TAMPA BAY BUCCANEERS
Home Stadium: Raymond James Stadium
Playing Surface: Grass
Head Coach: Tony Dungy
2000 Record: 10-6

Buccaneers Looking for Warrick to Get It "Dunn" More Often in 2001

RB: Back in 1997, when Warrick Dunn was made the Tampa Bay Buccaner first-round draft pick, the thought was that the Bucs would have a great 1-2 punch in Dunn sharing the backfield load with big, powerful Mike Alstott. That year, the combination seemed to work well, as Dunn ran for 978 yards, caught 39 passes for another 462 yards and scored seven times. That year Alstott rushed for 665 yards, caught 23 passes for 178 yards and scored ten times. The next year, Dunn cracked the 1,000-yard mark, rushing for 1,026 yards, caught 34 passes for 344 yards but scored only twice. Alstott, meanwhile, rushed for 846 yards, caught 22 passes for 152 yards and scored nine times. In 1999, the roles changed somewhat, though Alstott continued being more of the scoring force. Alstott this time carried more of the rushing load, running for 949 yards while catching 27 passes for 239 yards and scoring nine times. Dunn became more of a receiving factor. He did rush for 616 yards but upped his reception level to 64 going for 589 yards and scored twice. Heading into 2000, fantasy owners had labeled Alstott the consistent scorer and Dunn a backup fantasy back in perhaps a yardage league. Would their roles hold? The year certainly began that way, as Alstott rushed for 299 yards and scored five times in the season's first five games. Over that same period, Dunn rushed for 196 yards, caught 11 passes for 105 yards and scored only once. As the season progressed, however, the offense began to evolve more around Warrick Dunn, with Dunn getting more of the rushing load, which expanded even more when Alstott missed three games late in the year with a knee injury. Dunn took full advantage, rushing for 210 yards and scoring twice against Dallas and rushing for 145 yards and scoring three times against St. Louis, both late in the year. On the season, Dunn finished with 1,133 rushing yards, caught 44 passes for 422 yards and scored a surprising nine times. Alstott, missing the three games to injury, finished with 465 rushing yards, caught 13 passes for 93 yards and scored five times. Because of Dunn's finish in 2000, the Bucs plan on making him the feature back heading into 2001. This should grow his yardage numbers and give him a chance to hit double-digit scoring. Meanwhile, for Alstott the roles have somewhat reversed as he'll likely see more third-down duties but likely still get his share of short-yardage touchdowns.

WR: The Buccaneers have been trying to upgrade their receiving corps for years both via the draft and free agency. In 1997, the Buccaneers made Reidel Anthony out of Florida their #1 draft pick. Anthony did lead the Buccaneers receivers as a rookie in 1998, but his 35 receptions for 448 yards and four touchdowns were far below expectations. Heading into 1998, the Buccaneers made another move to upgrade, this time through free agency, signing Bert Emanuel (Falcons) to a four-year, $16 million deal. He was another disappointment, missing five games to injury and finished with only 41 receptions. Anthony again led the team with 51 receptions, this time going for 708 yards while scoring seven times. Again, a disappointing set of numbers from the Bucs' and fantasy perspectives. Little changed in 1999 as the Buccaneers receiving corps was again disappointing, so heading into 2000, another move was certainly in order as Emanuel and Anthony had played as the Bucs had hoped. This time Tampa Bay went after and landed Keyshawn Johnson (Jets). The Bucs inked him to an eight-year, $56 million deal, including a $13 million signing bonus. Would Keyshawn be the Bucs answer? He was coming off a year in which he produced 89 receptions for 1,109 yards and scored eight times with New York. He put together a solid year for the Bucs, through disappointing according to his standards, as he grabbed 71 receptions for 874 yards and eight touchdowns. Besides Keyshawn, the Bucs got 51 receptions for 772 yards and one touchdown out of Jaquez Green and 15 catches for 232 yards and four touchdowns out of Anthony. Looking to 2001, the Bucs look like they've finally found a tandem they can live and work with in Keyshawn Johnson and Jacquez Green, both of whom could likely build on their numbers, especially Keyshawn now that the Buccaneers have a new quarterback in veteran Brad Johnson.

TE: Dave Moore is a steady performer both as a player and a fantasy performer. Coming off a season in 1999 when he produced 23 receptions for 276 yards but a rather impressive five touchdowns, more of the same was expected heading into 2000. That's about what fantasy fans got, as Moore produced 29 receptions for 288 yards but only three touchdowns. Other than Moore, the Bucs got seven total receptions for 40 yards between Patrick Hape and Todd Yoder. Looking to 2001, Moore again can be expected to see minimal yardage numbers but has a shot at 4-6 touchdowns. Hape, meanwhile, signed with Denver in the offseason.

QB: Back in 1995, the Buccaneers made Trent Dilfer their #1 draft pick, believing they had somebody to build their offense around. Dilfer struggled miserably early in his career. It got to the point where he was asked to stay away from mistakes offensively so the Bucs could let their strong defenses win games. In 1997 and 1998, he did throw for 21 touchdowns each season. In 1999, he helped guide the team to a 6-4 record before suffering a season-ending broken collarbone. The Bucs turned to their second-round pick Shaun King out of Tulane. King played well enough, avoiding mistakes, and learning quickly, to maintain the starting job at season's end and would have it at the outset of 2000, which led to the release of Dilfer, who later signed with Baltimore. King's 2000 season, though not very spectacular, still helped the Bucs to a 10-6 record, though the wins came more from defense than anything. On the year, King finished with 2,769 yards and 18 touchdowns. He had played well enough during the year to provide ten wins but didn't provide the necessary things to get the Bucs to the promised land. Following the season, the Bucs felt they were still had a missing piece—a quarterback who could lead their offense and compliment their strong defense. Initially the Bucs signed former Charger first-round draft pick Ryan Leaf. Then the Bucs made a much bolder move. The Bucs sought out and won the battle with a number of teams signing Brad Johnson. Johnson was coming off a year where he had struggled with a knee injury, throwing for only 2,505 yards and 11 touchdowns with the Redskins in 2000. A year earlier, healthy all year, Johnson had recorded 4,005 passing yards and 24 touchdowns. Johnson has had success both in Washington and Minnesota, and the Bucs hope he can do the same here.

K: Martin Gramatica, the Bucs third-round pick of 1999, put in his second straight solid season in 2000 hitting 28 of 34 (.824) field goals, producing 126 points. I look for another good year in 2001, with his point total climbing with Brad Johnson now at quarterback.

Overall: A good defense wins games but does not always win you the games that get you to the Super Bowl. The Buccaneers have learned this the hard way but are ready to get more offensive about it. In the offseason, the Bucs signed Brad Johnson via free agency from Washington. Johnson, the Bucs hope, is the missing link to their quest to get to the Super Bowl. This Johnson should help the other Johnson (Keyshawn) and Jaquez Green put up better numbers in 2001. On the ground, there is a bit of a different look, as Warrick Dunn's strong finish in 2000 now has him in a feature role that should balloon his year-end numbers, while Mike Alstott becomes more of a third-down option. Bringing Brad Johnson to the fold gives head coach Tony Dungy and the Bucs the one added dimension they feel they were missing. It should be an interesting year to watch the Bucs, even on offense.

Offseason Fantasy-Position Moves

	Arriving	From:		Departing	To:
WR	Margin Hoors	Free Agent	TE	Patrick Hape	DEN
WR	Khorl Ivy	Free Agent	QB	Eric Zeier	ATL
WR	Robert Kilow	Free Agent			
WR	Jacquay Nunnally	Free Agent			
WR	Frank Rice	Free Agent			
WR	Alex Willis	Free Agent			
QB	Brad Johnson	WASH			
QB	Ryan Leaf	SD			

TENNESSEE TITANS
Home Stadium: Adelphia Stadium
Playing Surface: Grass
Head Coach: Jeff Fisher
2000 Record: 13-3

Eddie Continues to Get It Done "By George"

RB: The first three seasons Eddie George was in the NFL, he frustrated many fantasy fans by producing good yardage numbers but not putting up big scoring numbers. As a rookie in 1996, George rushed for 1,368 yards but scored only eight times. In 1997, George rushed for 1,399 yards and scored seven times. In 1998, George not only ran for 1,294 yards but grabbed 37 receptions for 310 yards but scored only six times. Things began to change in 1999. George again was in the 1,300-yard rushing range, tallying 1,304 rushing yards, he added 458 more yards on 47 receptions but this time out produced 13 touchdowns. His fantasy stock for Basic Scoring leagues immediately grew heading into 2000. Many felt he had finally become the scorer he should have been but the Titans just didn't give him much scoring opportunity. In 2000, George started out strong with three 100-yard games in the first six contests and scoring five times. There was a little lull, but George finished with three more 100-yard games over the last six and scored eleven times over that span. He also had one 100-yard receiving game in those last six games. For the season, George pushed his numbers to new heights. He rushed for 1,509 yards, caught 50 passes for 453 yards and scored 16 touchdowns, 14 on the ground and two through the air. He had surely become a complete fantasy player. Other than George, only Rodney Thomas's 175 rushing yards and eight receptions for 35 yards and one touchdown are worth mentioning. Thomas was given his release following the season. As for Eddie George in 2001, he'll again be among the top of everyone's fantasy charts both in Performance/Yardage leagues and in Basic/Scoring leagues. I look for George as the Titans' best and most consistent offensive weapon to wreak havoc on opposing defenses to the tune of 1,800-2,000 rushing-receiving yards and the 15 touchdown range again in 2001.

WR: The Titans have spent some big money in recent years to try and give their receiving corps a boost. In 1998, Tennessee lured Yancey Thigpen aboard from Pittsburgh to the tune of a 5-year, $21 million deal. The offer was made following a year when Thigpen caught 79 receptions for 1,398 yards and caught seven touchdowns with Pittsburgh in 1997. However, injuries plagued Thigpen's play in 1998 and 1999, and he recorded only 38 receptions while recording seven touchdowns over that span. He missed 11 games in 1998 to a knee injury and five games to ankle injury in 1999. One nice surprise the Titans did get in 1999 was the play of their 1998 first-round pick Kevin Dyson. Dyson, who had a poor showing as a rookie in '98, jumped to 54 receptions for 658 yards and four touchdowns in 1999. Heading into 2000, the Titans were still not happy with the production of their receiving corps and signed Carl Pickens, who came over from Cincinnati. Pickens, once regarded as one of the league's top receivers, was disgruntled as a Bengal and was happy to jump ship. In a strange 2000 season, Thigpen, Pickens and Dyson all missed significant time due to injury. Thigpen missed seven games with ankle and hamstring injuries, wasn't that impressive when he did play and finished with only 15 receptions for 289 yards and two touchdowns. Pickens missed about nine games with a hamstring injury but by season's end had played himself out of the mix and finished with only 10 receptions for 242 yards and no touchdowns. Dyson suffered a knee injury in practice early in the year, saw action in only one game in which he recorded six receptions for 104 yards and one touchdown. With those three out, surprisingly Derrick Mason stepped up. Mason jumped in to record 63 receptions for 895 yards and five touchdowns. Chris Sanders chipped in 33 receptions for 536 yards but no scores. Looking to 2001, the high-priced Thigpen and Pickens were released following the season, though Pickens later signed with Dallas. The Titans then elected to reward Derrick Mason by signing him to a five-year, $23.45 million deal. Mason will again be called on in a big way, with Chris Sanders battling Kevin Dyson, if Dyson's knee is OK, and Chris Coleman, an undrafted rookie from 2000, for 2001 playing time.

TE: Frank Wycheck had another solid year in 2000. After a few mediocre years to open his career, Wycheck has produced 70, 69 and now 70 receptions respectively the last three seasons. In that same span, he had tallied 768, 641 and 636 yards, along with 2, 2 and 4 touchdowns. It's the low touchdown total that's the only thing that holds him back as a huge fantasy prospect for the 2001 season. The Titans did give themselves another option or more of a long-term answer at tight end in making Shad Meier out of Kansas State their third-round draft pick.

QB: Steve McNair is known to have the ability to score both by throwing for yards and touchdowns and by rushing for yards and scores. Perhaps, however, it's been his rushing portion that has kept him as an interesting fantasy prospect each year, as his passing numbers have been less than impressive. Back in 1997, McNair threw for only 2,665 yards and 14 touchdowns. Meanwhile, on the ground, he rushed for 674 yards and scored eight times. In 1998, he expanded his passing yards to 3,228 yards but again was limited on touchdown passes, recording only 15. On the ground, however, McNair rushed for 570 yards but dropped to four touchdowns. Heading into 1999, fantasy interest was wavering. He still lacked any consistency of throwing for big yards or scores and his rushing numbers were dropping as running back, Eddie George's were climbing. In 1999, McNair missed five games to back surgery and finished with 2,179 yards passing and only 12 touchdowns. Again on the ground it was a different story as he ran for 337 yards and scored a whopping eight times. As a fantasy prospect for 2000, only his running ability seemed attractive. McNair again put up poor passing numbers, recording only 2,847 passing yards and 15 touchdowns. This time, however, his rushing numbers were not as good as hoped. H did rush for 404 yards but failed to score a rushing touchdown. Looking to 2001, McNair has become a scary fantasy prospect especially in touchdown or Basic Scoring leagues.

K: Veteran Al Del Greco has been cruising along as one of the league's most reliable kickers but in 2000 that changed. Despite his hitting 27 of 33 (.818) field goals, he had a hand in three of the team's losses. Del Greco was released following the season, which had the Titans in search for a replacement. The Titans landed Joe Nedney, who had an impressive year in 2000, filling in first in Denver, with Jason Elam hurt and later in Carolina, with John Kasay hurt. Nedney hit 34 of 38 (.895) field goals in 2000, which obviously caught the Titans attention.

Overall: Two straight 13-3 seasons shows the Titans have been on the right course to consistent winning. On the ground, Eddie George continues to improve and so do his numbers. Having George provide a reliable ground game has been a huge reason for the Titans' success. Along the way, George has become one of the league's most sought-after fantasy players, especially now that his scoring has improved. Through the air, Steve McNair seems to do just what is needed to win but having a receiving crew that was banged up and unproductive in 2000 didn't help his numbers either. Following the season, both Carl Pickens and Yancey Thigpen were released turning the work over to youngsters Derrick Mason, Chris Sanders and Kevin Dyson if Dyson's recovered from his knee injury in 2001.

Offseason Fantasy-Position Moves

	Arriving	From:		Departing	To:
RB	Rashad Bartholomew	Free Agent	RB	Lorenzo Neal	Released
RB	Mike Green	Free Agent	RB	Rodney Thomas	Released
WR	Andrew Bennett	Free Agent	WR	Carl Pickens	DALL
WR	Tyson Henshaw	Free Agent	WR	Yancey Thigpen	Released
WR	Steve Neal	Free Agent	TE	Michael Roan	Released
WR	Jimmy Redmond	Free Agent	K	Al Del Greco	Released
WR	Michael Snowden	Free Agent			
WR	Marshaun Tucker	Free Agent			
TE	Robby Snelling	Free Agent			
QB	Chris Sanders	Free Agent			
K	Joe Nedney	CAR			

Jeff George/Washington Redskins

WASHINGTON REDSKINS

Home Stadium: FED EX Field
Playing Surface: Grass
Head Coach: Marty Schottenheimer
2000 Record: 8-8

Redskins "Turner" over to Schottenheimer to Get It Turned Around

RB: Heading into the 1999 season, there would be a battle for the starting running back job between Stephen Davis and Skip Hicks. Hicks looked like the leading candidate, since he had been the Redskins first choice to replace the ailing Terry Allen at the end of the '98 season. Davis surprised some by outdueling Hicks and winning the starting job at the outset of the '99 season. He got off to a terrific start and never looked back from there. On the season, Davis rushed for a very surprising 1,405 yards, grabbed 23 receptions for 111 yards and scored 17 times and did it playing in only 14 games, missing the last two with an ankle injury. His performance was very much to the delight of the fantasy owners who had drafted him. Hicks was not much of a factor, recording only 329 rushing-receiving yards and three touchdowns. Davis's performance made him a very sought after fantasy pick heading into 2000. Could he repeat those numbers? Davis, who missed one game with an injured arm, finished the year down from his explosive 1999 year, as he recorded 1,318 rushing yards, caught 33 passes for another 313 yards and scored 11 times. Certainly these numbers disappointed many fantasy fans. Besides Davis, the Redskins may have only gotten 103 rushing yards out of Larry Centers, but his 80 receptions for 600 yards were significant, though he only scored three times. Skip Hicks again put up rather insignificant numbers, rushing for 78 yards, while grabbing five receptions for 43 yards and scoring only once. Adrian Murrell, a former 1,000-yard rusher with Arizona, was an offseason acquisition brought aboard for more insurance. He managed only 50 yards rushing while catching 16 passes for 93 yards and failing to score. Looking to 2001, it's again Stephen Davis who will excite fantasy fans as their fantasy drafts approach. Remember this is a new year, a year that pushing his numbers back up in the 1,800-2,000 rushing-receiving yard range and 12-15 touchdown range is again possible. Meanwhile, in the offseason, Larry Centers was released.

WR: Coming into the 1999 season it was difficult to figure the Washington Redskins' receivers. Michael Westbrook continued to struggle through injuries in 1998, though he still led the club with 44 receptions for 736 yards and scored six times playing in 11 games, showing potential when he was healthy. Leslie Shepherd, who had caught 43 passes in 1998, was off to Cleveland, which left Albert Connell as the Redskins' other receiver. The two would be working with quarterback Brad Johnson, who had been signed in the offseason from Minnesota. The results were amazing. The Redskins opened up their offense, and both Westbrook and Connell became 1,000-yard receivers. Westbrook finished the year with 65 receptions for 1,191 yards and scored nine times. Connell was the big surprise, with 62 receptions for 1,132 yards and seven scores. Could they do it again in 2000, was the question asked prior to fantasy drafts. Westbrook survived only into the second game before a knee injury sidelined him for the season after just nine catches. Connell was erratic and he too suffered a knee injury but not as severe. Playing in 14 games, he recorded a disappointing 39 catches for 762 yards and three touchdowns. Stepping in to make an impression was James Thrash, who recorded 50 receptions for 653 yards but only two touchdowns. Veteran Irving Fryar was called on, and he responded with 41 receptions for 548 yards and five touchdowns. Andre Reed didn't help as much as expected and chipped in only ten receptions. Heading into 2001, both Albert Connell, whose poor attitude won't be missed, was released and later signed with New Orleans. Irving Fryar was also released. James Thrash, who was the Redskins' top receiver in 2000, is also gone, departing via free agency to Philadelphia. The word is still not certain on Michael Westbrook, who is recovering from his knee injury. This left the Redskins looking for help at wide receiver. There was talk of bringing along Derrius Thompson, who has bounced between the practice squad and active roster the last couple seasons but the Redskins resolved their wide receiver dilemma by first signing free-agent Kevin Lockett (Chiefs) and by making Rod Gardner out of Clemson their first-round draft pick. Both will battle for work alongside Michael Westbrook. With hard-throwing Jeff George now at the helm, look for some decent numbers from the Redskins' receivers if they can stay healthy.

TE: The Redskin's second-round draft pick of 1998, Stephen Alexander, was a productive tight end waiting to happen. In his rookie season, Alexander initially was watching veteran Jamie Asher as the team starter but a season-ending knee injury to Asher gave Alexander a better shot. He finished his rookie campaign recording 37 receptions for 383 yards and scored four times, looking to build his numbers in 1999. Despite the acquisition of quarterback Brad Johnson, Alexander's numbers dropped as Johnson looked to his wide receivers often. Alexander finished 1999 with a disappointing 29 catches for 324 yards and only three touchdowns. There was still hope he'd get more involved in the offense in 2000. He did, to the tune of 47 receptions for 510 yards but only two touchdowns. These numbers don't have fantasy fans over zealous for 2001, though Jeff George helped Ricky Dudley to very productive numbers when in Oakland. What might happen here?

QB: With Trent Green coming off a 3,441 yard, 23 touchdown performance in 1998 but headed to St. Louis, the Redskins were in search of a quarterback. The Redskins landed Brad Johnson, who was coming off a year in which an ankle injury had lost him the starting job in Minnesota to Randall Cunningham. Johnson came aboard and helped open up the Redskins' passing game and put up fairly impressive numbers, recording 4,005 passing yards and 24 touchdowns—numbers that had Redskins' and fantasy fans excited heading into 2000. Johnson, however, wasn't quite as sharp in 2000, and losing Michael Westbrook early in the year didn't help. Johnson had thrown for 2,139 yards and ten touchdowns through nine games before a knee injury put him on the sidelines. He returned after being out about a month, but by then Jeff George, his replacement, was getting a long look. Johnson did get the call for the season finale but knew he was about to move on again. Johnson was courted by a number of teams in the offseason and elected to sign with Tampa Bay where he'll become the Bucs' starter. Meanwhile, for the Redskins, strong-armed Jeff George gets the starting job. George threw for 1,389 yards and seven touchdowns playing in six games with the Redskins in 2000. The Redskins hope he can retrigger the Washington passing game, which should help the Redskins' receivers to bigger numbers in 2001.

K: A brutal year for Redskins' kickers, as players were shuffled in and out like a revolving door. Brett Conway started the year, kicked in two games, hit 3 of 3 field goals, was bothered by a quad injury and was waived. Next was Michael Husted, who lasted four games, hitting only 4 of 8 field goal attempts. Then there was Kris Hepper, who also lasted four games, hitting 4 of 6 attempts. Veteran Eddie Murray came in to finish out the year, kicking in six games, hitting 8 of 12 attempts. The Redskins are in search for a more reliable answer to their kicking woes in 2001 and did sign veteran Brett Conway in the offseason. Conway has plenty of NFL experience kicking for a number of teams.

Overall: A slide in offensive production and a record drop from 10-6 in 1999 to 8-8 in 2000 led to the dismissal of head coach Norv Turner. The Redskins are turning things over to Marty Schottenheimer. Schottenheimer takes over a team that has plenty of potential. When running the football, the Redskins are in good shape with Stephen Davis. Davis, whose numbers took a dip in 2000 from his breakout year in 1999, were still good. Davis will again be a huge factor for the Redskins' offense and fantasy teams. Through the air, there's a changing of the guard. Brad Johnson, who had come over to have a big year in 1999 but struggled some in 2000, has departed to Tampa Bay. The Redskins are still in good shape with veteran Jeff George taking over. George has the arm to make the offense go. The questions surrounding the receiving crew—with Albert Connell gone to New Orleans, James Thrash to Philadelphia and Michael Westbrook recovering from a knee injury—have been resolved by the acquisition of Kevin Lockett and drafting of Rod Gardner.

Offseason Fantasy-Position Moves

	Arriving	From:		Departing	To:
RB	Mike Cerimele	Free Agent	RB	Larry Centers	Released
RB	Jamaal Dinkins	Free Agent	WR	Albert Connell	NO
RB	Stanley Stephens	Free Agent	WR	Irving Fryar	Released
RB	Kenny Watson	Free Agent	WR	James Thrash	PHIL
WR	Latof Grim	Free Agent	QB	Brad Johnson	TB
WR	Kevin Lockett	KC			
WR	Justin Skaggs	Free Agent			
TE	Ivan Mercer	Free Agent			
TE	Walter Rasby	DET			
TE	John Sigmund	Free Agent			
K	Brett Conway	NYJ			

VIII
RATING THE PLAYERS:
BASIC SCORING METHOD

In the Basic Scoring Method, points are awarded to the players who actually score or throw touchdowns (or kick field goals or extra points, in the case of kickers), with no consideration for the yardage a player may accumulate or the distance covered by a touchdown play.

The Basic Scoring Method is the simplest scoring method, but it may be the hardest to draft for. This method probably involves more luck than skill in predicting who will score touchdowns. When most sports enthusiasts sit down at their first fantasy football draft, they feel they are pretty much up on the game. Their tendency is to draft well-known, established names; but during the season, they may get a rude awakening. Their highly paid scatback rushes up and down the field week after week, but when it's time for the two-yard touchdown plunge, the ball is given to the big fullback. Such had been the case in Detroit in recent years, as Barry Sanders ran and received up and down the field and gave the ball up to Derrick Moore when the team got near the goal line. This limited Sanders to seven and three touchdowns, respectively, in 1993 and 1994. But with Moore gone in 1995, Sanders's touchdown total climbed to 11, and in 1997 hit the 14 mark. In 1995 Edgar Bennett rushed and received for 1,715 yards but scored only seven times. Bam Morris rushed for only 559 yards but scored nine times. In 1996, Garrison Hearst led the Bengals with 847 rushing yards but never scored a rushing touchdown. Ki-Jana Carter became the designated scorer, rushing for only 264 yards but scoring eight rushing touchdowns. In 1997 Karim Abdul-Jabbar running for Miami, rushed for only 892 yards but scored 16 times. Marcus Allen rushed for only 505 yards but scored 11 times. In 1998, Leroy Hoard of the Vikings rushed for only 479 yards but scored 10 times. Robert Smith was the team's main rusher with 1,187 yards but he scored only eight times. In recent years, more teams have left their scatback players in near the goal line to reap some scoring rewards after laboring to pick up all that yardage. Nevertheless, don't think that a roster of million-dollar players guarantees a successful fantasy football team.

In the following pages, I'm going to help you plan your basic drafting strategy. I'll follow that with some things to keep in mind when choosing players from each position. Next, I'll offer a look at the players' 2000 statistical results. And, finally, I'll rate the players for 2001. No rookies are included in my player ratings. It's too early to size up how rookies will fit into each team's scheme, so I rate them separately, in Section V of this chapter.

DRAFTING STRATEGY BY ROUNDS
(A Guide for the Beginner)

1   The draft consists of 12 rounds.

2. Of the 12 players, seven are starters and five are reserves.

3. The starting seven comprise:

1 Quarterback		1 Quarterback
2 Running Backs	OR	2 Running Backs
2 Wide Receivers	FLEX OPTION	3 Receivers
1 Tight End		1 Kicker
1 Kicker		

4. The five reserves can be from any position.

5. Any player from any starting position can be drafted in any round.

What are the keys to drafting a successful fantasy football team? Why are some franchises consistent winners, year after year? In studying the successful franchises of the leagues I participate in, I have found a number of factors. One of these is preparation: successful franchise owners are always ready for the unexpected. If a player they were hoping to get is grabbed just before their turn, they have an alternate choice. These owners also make sure they review the previous season to learn about significant injuries that might have drastically reduced the year-end stats of prime players. They won't overlook these players as candidates for their drafts. (In Section II: "Helpful Facts from the 2000 Season," I note which players sustained significant injuries last season. Take a look at it before you head into your 2001 draft.) Following is a system that will give you the best chances for a successful draft.

ROUND 1: For the first round, I recommend grabbing the best six-point player available. In the past, this would almost automatically have been a running back, but in recent years, wide receivers such as Marvin Harrison, Randy Moss and Terrell Owens have also turned into consistent scorers. Quarterbacks may throw a lot of touchdown passes, but they are awarded only three points for each, as opposed to the six awarded to the player who actually scores the touchdown. However, a quarterback like Steve Young may throw for 25 to 30 touchdowns and run for five more (when he's healthy), so he merits first-round consideration, as does Brett Favre, who may again throw 30 to 40 touchdowns. Kickers, especially in recent years, are scoring a lot of points; but I still recommend taking a six-point player first. Though a kicker may occasionally top 140 points, you can still get a good 100-point kicker in later rounds, whereas the six-point players will be picked up early.

ROUND 2: In this round, choose the best player available, perhaps with six-point players—running backs, wide receivers, and tight ends. There is another possibility: If you have an inkling that a particular quarterback may be on his way to an outstanding year (30-plus touchdowns), you may elect to grab him in this round if none of the six-point players really excites you. (Some owners get panicky in the early rounds if they think they might get stuck with a mediocre player at a key position. If you pick a quarterback in this round, you might just set off a chain reaction of quarterback picking by other owners. This works to your advantage if it happens, because it leaves you more six-point players to choose from in the third round.

ROUND 3: Now it's time to consider a three-point player, either a quarterback or a kicker if you haven't already chosen one. I find that a trend usually develops in the third round. If the first two or three choices are quarterbacks, the rest of the franchises will panic and choose a quarterback. If the first few picks are kickers, the rest will follow that lead. Kickers and quarterbacks play important roles on your fantasy football team. I've seen kickers carry a fantasy team for two or three weeks. A quarterback who throws 30 touchdowns in a year gives you (on the average) six points weekly from that position. (If you have already selected your quarterback by this round, it's a good idea to again pick the best six-point player available.)

ROUNDS 4 and 5: It's time to pick up at least one of your wide receivers. By now the best ones are gone, but how about taking a stab at somebody? In 2000 those who grabbed less heralded Derrich Alexander or Ed McCaffrey in the middle rounds were all rewarded with 10 and 9 touchdowns respectively.

ROUNDS 6, 7, and 8: By the end of the eighth round, you should have your seven starting positions filled.

ROUNDS 9 through 12: This is the time to pick your reserves and take some long shots on rookies. Those who picked rookie Jamal Lewis in 2000 are certainly glad they did. Make sure that you have at least one backup at quarterback, running back, and wide receiver, since these seem to be the most injury-prone positions.

NOTE: If you draft a receiver who is a favorite target of your quarterback, you get a nine-point play every time there is a touchdown completion between the two (three points for the pass and six points for the touchdown). This can make a difference, especially if you have a tandem like Brett Favre and Antonio Freeman. Now let's take a look at what to consider in choosing players at the various positions

A LOOK AT THE RUNNING BACKS
(A Guide for the Beginner)

Considerations in Choosing a RUNNING BACK

Choosing a good running back is usually crucial to putting together a competitive team. Here, listed in order of usefulness, are some considerations for choosing your running backs. After this review are the 1999 statistics, followed by my 2000 player ratings.

1. First, review players' previous performances, especially from last season. Injuries, player movement, holdouts and the like should be noted. Players like Dorsey Levens, Ricky Williams and Terrell Davis had significant injuries.

2. Look for running backs that both play for good teams and who are the primary back for their team. And most importantly, make sure this back is used in goal-line situations. You don't want a back who is removed when his team gets inside the ten-yard line.

3. Next, review backs that are used as designated scorers, such as Marcus Allen, who in 1993 rushed for only 764 yards but scored 15 times. In 1995 Bam Morris rushed for only 559 yards but scored nine times. In 1996 Ki-Jana Carter of Cincinnati rushed for only 264 yards but scored eight times. In 1997 Marcus Allen again rushed for only 505 yards but scored 11 times. In 1998, Leroy Hoard rushed for only 479 yards but scored 10 times.

4. Look at the situations where a rookie can step in and make an impact. In 1998, both Fred Taylor in Jacksonville (17 TDs) and Robert Edwards in New England (12 TDs) found themselves in positions as rookies to have big years. In 2000 Travis Prentice in Cleveland scored eight times.

In looking at the 2000 statistics, you'll find the players ranked by their fantasy-point totals. Remember that in the Basic Scoring Method, fantasy points are calculated by scoring six points for every touchdown rushed or caught and three points for every touchdown pass thrown.

(RUNNING BACKS — BASIC SCORING METHOD)

NAME	TEAM	GP	RSH	RUSH YARDS	REC	REC YARDS	TOTAL YARDS	RUSH TDs	REC TDs	TOTAL TDs	CONV PTS	FAN-TASY PTS
1. M. Faulk	STL	14	253	1,359	81	830	2,189	18	8	26	4	160
1999		16	253	1,381	87	1,048	2,429	7	5	12	2	74
1998 w/IND		16	324	1,319	86	908	2,227	6	4	10	0	60
3 Yr - TOTALS		46	830	4,059	254	2,786	6,845	31	17	48	6	294
2. James	IND	16	387	1,709	63	594	2,303	13	5	18	2	110
1999		16	369	1,553	62	586	2,139	13	4	17	0	102
1998		-	-	-	-	-	-	-	-	-	-	-
3 Yr - TOTALS		32	756	3,262	125	1,180	4,442	26	9	35	2	212
3. L. Smith	MIA	15	309	1,139	31	201	1,340	14	2	16	0	96
1999 (w/NO)		13	60	205	20	151	356	0	1	1	0	6
1998 (w/NO)		14	138	457	24	249	706	1	2	3	0	21
3 Yr - TOTALS		42	507	1,801	75	601	2,402	15	5	20	0	123
4. George	TEN	16	403	1,509	50	453	1,962	14	2	16	0	96
1999		16	320	1,304	47	458	1,762	9	4	13	0	78
1998		16	348	1,294	37	310	1,604	5	1	6	2	38
3 Yr - TOTALS		48	1071	4,107	134	1,221	5,328	28	7	35	2	212
5. M. Anderson +	DEN	14	297	1,500	23	169	1,669	15	0	15	2	92
1999		-	-	-	-	-	-	-	-	-	-	-
1998		-	-	-	-	-	-	-	-	-	-	-
3 Yr - TOTALS		14	297	1,500	23	169	1,669	15	0	15	2	92
6. Taylor	JAC	13	292	1,399	36	240	1,639	12	2	14	0	84
1999		10	159	732	10	83	815	6	0	6	0	36
1998		15	264	1,223	44	421	1,644	14	3	17	0	102
3 Yr - TOTALS		38	715	3,354	90	744	4,098	32	5	37	0	222
7. Green	GB	16	263	1,175	73	559	1,734	10	3	13	0	78
1999 (w/SEA)		8	26	120	0	0	120	0	0	0	0	0
1998 (w/SEA)		9	35	209	3	2	211	1	0	1	0	6
3 Yr - TOTALS		33	324	1,504	76	561	2,065	11	3	14	0	84
8. Stewart	DET	16	339	1,184	32	287	1,471	10	1	11	6	72
1999 (w/JAC)		14	249	931	21	108	1,039	13	0	13	0	78
1998 (w/JAC)		3	53	217	6	42	259	2	1	3	0	18
3 Yr - TOTALS		33	641	2,332	59	437	2,769	25	2	27	6	168
9. Cu. Martin	NYJ	16	317	1,207	70	508	1,715	9	2	11	0	69
1999		16	367	1,464	45	259	1,723	5	0	5	0	30
1998		15	369	1,287	43	365	1,652	8	1	9	0	54
3 Yr - TOTALS		47	1053	3,958	158	1,132	5,090	22	3	25	0	153
10. S. Davis	WAS	15	332	1,318	33	313	1,631	11	0	11	0	66
1999		14	290	1,405	23	111	1,516	17	0	17	2	104
1998		13	34	109	21	263	372	0	2	2	0	12
3 Yr - TOTALS		42	656	2,832	77	687	3,519	28	2	30	2	182
11. R. Smith	MIN	16	295	1,521	36	348	1,869	7	3	10	0	60
1999		13	221	1,015	24	166	1,181	2	0	2	0	12
1998		14	249	1,187	28	291	1,478	6	2	8	0	48
3 Yr - TOTALS		43	765	3,723	88	805	4,528	15	5	20	0	120
12. Wheatley	OAK	14	232	1,046	20	156	1,202	9	1	10	0	60
1999		16	242	936	21	196	1,132	8	3	11	0	66
1998 (w/NYG)		4	14	52	0	0	52	0	0	0	0	0
3 Yr - TOTALS		34	488	2,034	41	352	2,386	17	4	21	0	126
13. Garner	SF	16	258	1,142	68	647	1,789	7	3	10	0	60
1999		16	241	1,229	56	535	1,764	4	2	6	0	36
1998 (w/PHI)		10	96	381	19	110	491	4	0	4	0	24
3 Yr - TOTALS		42	595	2,752	143	1,292	4,044	15	5	20	0	120
14. E. Smith	DAL	16	294	1,203	11	79	1,282	9	0	9	0	54
1999		15	329	1,397	27	119	1,516	11	2	13	0	78
1998		16	319	1,332	27	175	1,507	13	2	15	0	90
3 Yr - TOTALS		47	942	3,932	65	373	4,305	33	4	37	0	222
15. R. Williams	NO	10	248	1,000	44	409	1,409	8	1	9	0	54
1999		12	253	884	28	172	1,056	2	0	2	0	12
1998		-	-	-	-	-	-	-	-	-	-	-
3 Yr - TOTALS		22	501	1,884	72	581	2,465	10	1	11	0	66

2000 STATISTICAL RESULTS
(RUNNING BACKS — BASIC SCORING METHOD)

NAME	TEAM	GP	RSH	RUSH YARDS	REC	REC YARDS	TOTAL YARDS	RUSH TDs	REC TDs	TOTAL TDs	CONV PTS	FAN-TASY PTS
16. Barber	NYG	16	213	1,006	70	719	1,725	8	1	9	0	54
1999		15	62	258	66	609	867	0	2	3	0	18
1998		16	52	166	42	348	514	0	3	3	0	18
3 Yr - TOTALS		47	327	1,430	178	1,676	3,106	8	6	15	0	90
17. Watters	SEA	16	278	1,242	63	613	1,855	7	2	9	0	54
1999		16	325	1,210	40	387	1,597	5	2	7	0	42
1998		16	319	1,239	52	373	1,612	9	0	9	2	59
3 Yr - TOTALS		48	922	3,691	155	1,373	5,064	21	4	25	2	155
18. Dunn	TB	16	248	1,133	44	422	1,555	8	1	9	0	54
1999		15	195	616	64	589	1,205	0	2	2	0	12
1998		16	245	1,026	44	344	1,370	2	0	2	0	12
3 Yr - TOTALS		47	688	2,775	152	1,355	4,130	10	3	13	0	78
19. Prentice +	CLE	15	173	512	37	191	703	7	1	8	0	48
1999		-	-	-	-	-	-	-	-	-	-	-
1998		-	-	-	-	-	-	-	-	-	-	-
3 Yr - TOTALS		15	173	512	37	191	703	7	1	8	0	48
20. Bettis	PIT	16	355	1,341	14	108	1,449	8	0	8	0	48
1999		16	299	1,091	21	110	1,201	7	0	7	0	45
1998		15	316	1,185	16	90	1,275	3	0	3	0	18
3 Yr - TOTALS		47	970	3,617	51	308	3,925	18	0	18	0	111
21. Dillon	CIN	16	315	1,435	18	158	1,593	7	0	7	0	42
1999		15	263	1,200	31	290	1,490	5	1	6	0	36
1998		15	262	1,130	28	178	1,308	4	1	5	0	30
3 Yr - TOTALS		46	840	3,765	77	626	4,391	16	2	18	0	108
22. Crockett	OAK	11	43	130	10	62	192	7	0	7	0	42
1999		11	45	91	8	56	147	4	1	5	0	30
1998 w/JAC		3	2	5	2	5	10	0	0	0	0	0
3 Yr - TOTALS		25	90	226	20	123	349	11	1	12	0	72
23. J. Anderson	ATL	16	282	1,024	42	382	1,406	6	0	6	2	38
1999		2	19	59	2	34	93	0	0	0	0	0
1998		16	410	1,846	27	319	2,165	14	2	16	2	98
3 Yr - TOTALS		34	711	2,929	71	735	3,664	20	2	22	4	136
24. Ja. Lewis +	BAL	16	309	1,364	27	296	1,660	6	0	6	2	38
1999		-	-	-	-	-	-	-	-	-	-	-
1998		-	-	-	-	-	-	-	-	-	-	-
3 Yr - TOTALS		16	309	1,364	27	296	1,660	6	0	6	2	38
25. Pittman	ARI	16	184	719	73	579	1,298	4	2	6	0	36
1999		10	64	289	16	196	485	2	0	2	0	12
1998		6	29	91	0	0	91	0	0	0	0	0
3 Yr - TOTALS		32	277	1,099	89	775	1,874	6	2	8	0	48
26. Morris +	BUF	12	93	341	37	268	609	5	1	6	0	36
1999 (w/KC)		-	-	-	-	-	-	-	-	-	-	-
1998 (w/KC)		-	-	-	-	-	-	-	-	-	-	-
3 Yr - TOTALS		12	93	341	37	268	609	5	1	6	0	36
27. Richardson	KC	16	147	697	58	468	1,165	3	3	6	0	36
1999		16	84	387	24	141	528	1	0	1	0	6
1998		10	20	45	2	13	58	2	0	2	0	12
3 Yr - TOTALS		42	251	1,129	84	622	1,751	6	3	9	0	54
28. Beasley	SF	15	50	147	31	233	380	3	3	6	0	36
1999		13	58	276	32	282	558	4	0	4	0	24
1998		1	0	0	1	11	11	0	0	0	0	0
3 Yr - TOTALS		29	108	423	64	526	949	7	3	10	0	60
29. K. Faulk	NE	15	164	570	51	465	1,035	4	1	5	2	32
1999		11	67	227	12	98	325	1	1	2	0	12
1998		-	-	-	-	-	-	-	-	-	-	-
3 Yr - TOTALS		26	231	797	63	563	1,360	5	2	7	2	44
30. Dayne +	NYG	16	228	770	3	11	781	5	0	5	0	30
1999		-	-	-	-	-	-	-	-	-	-	-
1998		-	-	-	-	-	-	-	-	-	-	-
3 Yr - TOTALS		16	228	770	3	11	781	5	0	5	0	30

NAME	TEAM	GP	RSH	RUSH YARDS	REC	REC YARDS	TOTAL YARDS	RUSH TDs	REC TDs	TOTAL TDs	CONV PTS	FAN-TASY PTS
31. Br. Mitchell *	PHI	14	25	187	13	89	276	2	1	5	0	30
1999 (w/WAS)		16	40	220	31	305	525	1	0	1	0	6
1998 (w/WAS)		16	39	208	44	306	514	2	0	3	0	18
3 Yr - TOTALS		46	104	615	88	700	1,315	5	1	9	0	54
32. Alstott	TB	13	131	465	13	93	558	5	0	5	0	30
1999		16	242	949	27	239	1,188	7	2	9	0	54
1998		16	215	846	22	152	998	8	1	9	0	54
3 Yr - TOTALS		45	588	2,260	62	484	2,744	20	3	23	0	138
33. A. Smith	BUF	10	101	354	3	20	374	4	0	4	0	24
34. Biakabutuka	CAR	12	173	627	34	341	968	2	2	4	0	24
35. Moreau +	KC	10	67	179	0	0	179	4	0	4	0	24
36. Jordan	OAK	13	46	213	27	299	512	3	1	4	0	24
37. Autry	PHI	10	112	334	24	275	609	3	1	4	0	24
38. Fletcher	SD	15	116	384	48	355	739	3	1	4	0	24
39. Holcombe	STL	13	21	70	8	90	160	3	1	4	0	24
40. Watson	STL	9	54	249	10	56	305	4	0	4	0	24
41. Huntley	PIT	12	46	215	10	91	306	3	0	3	2	20
42. Hetherington	CAR	10	23	65	14	116	181	2	1	3	0	18
43. J. Allen	CHI	16	290	1,120	39	291	1,411	2	1	3	0	18
44. B. Bennett	CIN	15	90	324	19	168	492	3	0	3	0	18
45. Levens	GB	5	77	224	16	146	370	3	0	3	0	18
46. Redmond +	NE	11	125	406	20	126	532	1	2	3	0	18
47. Warren **	PHI	12	74	296	32	303	599	2	1	3	0	18
48. Centers	WAS	15	20	103	80	600	703	0	3	3	0	18
49. Bryson	BUF	16	161	591	32	271	862	0	2	2	2	14
50. T. Allen	NO	4	46	179	1	7	186	2	0	2	2	14
51. Jackson	SF	7	5	6	5	48	54	1	1	2	2	14
52. Jones +	ARI	14	112	373	32	208	581	2	0	2	0	12
53. Ayanbadejo	BAL	8	15	37	23	168	205	1	1	2	0	12
54. Holmes	BAL	16	137	588	32	221	809	2	0	2	0	12
55. W. Floyd	CAR	10	16	33	17	114	147	1	1	2	0	12
56. Edwards	CLE	12	2	9	16	128	137	0	2	2	0	12
57. Rb. Thomas	DAL	12	15	51	23	117	168	0	2	2	0	12
58. T. Davis	DEN	5	78	282	2	4	286	2	0	2	0	12
59. Griffith	DEN	12	5	4	16	101	105	0	2	2	0	12
60. Ma. Bates	DET	12	31	127	15	109	236	2	0	2	0	12
61. Anders	KC	10	76	331	15	76	407	2	0	2	0	12
62. Carter	NE	15	37	90	9	73	163	2	0	2	0	12
63. R. Anderson	NYJ	16	27	63	88	853	916	0	2	2	0	12
64. Parmalee	NYJ	4	27	87	9	66	153	2	0	2	0	12
65. Chancey	SD	3	42	141	1	6	147	2	0	2	0	12
66. Fazande	SD	11	119	368	16	104	472	2	0	2	0	12
67. McCrary	SD	13	7	8	18	141	149	0	2	2	0	12
68. Alexander +	SEA	16	64	313	5	41	354	2	0	2	0	12
69. Neal	TEN	7	1	-2	9	31	29	0	2	2	0	12
70. Sellers	WAS	7	1	2	8	78	80	0	2	2	0	12
71. Gash	BAL	5	2	2	6	30	32	0	1	1	0	6
72. Linton	BUF	6	38	112	3	8	120	0	1	1	0	6
73. Mi. Bates *	CAR	5	5	13	5	38	51	0	1	1	0	6
74. Hoover	CAR	11	89	290	15	112	402	1	0	1	0	6
75. Enis	CHI	10	36	84	8	68	152	1	0	1	0	6
76. Wiley +	DAL	8	24	88	14	72	160	0	1	1	0	6
77. Coleman	DEN	7	54	183	1	5	188	1	0	1	0	6
78. D. Smith	DEN	1	0	0	1	1	1	0	1	1	0	6
79. Henderson	GB	14	2	16	35	234	250	0	1	1	0	6
80. Finn	IND	5	1	1	4	13	14	0	1	1	0	6
81. Howard	JAC	2	21	52	3	26	78	1	0	1	0	6
82. A. Johnson	JAC	10	28	112	12	153	265	1	0	1	0	6
83. Mack	JAC	3	54	145	0	0	145	1	0	1	0	6
84. Stith +	JAC	7	20	55	0	0	55	1	0	1	0	6
85. D. Bennett	KC	6	27	24	2	17	41	1	0	1	0	6

2000 STATISTICAL RESULTS
(RUNNING BACKS — BASIC SCORING METHOD)

NAME	TEAM	GP	RSH	RUSH YARDS	REC	REC YARDS	TOTAL YARDS	RUSH TDs	REC TDs	TOTAL TDs	CONV PTS	FAN-TASY PTS
86. Cloud	KC	6	30	84	2	16	100	1	0	1	0	6
87. J. Johnson	MIA	8	50	168	10	61	229	1	0	1	0	6
88. T. Thomas	MIA	9	28	136	16	117	253	0	1	1	0	6
89. Milne	NO	3	2	1	5	33	34	0	1	1	0	6
90. Moore	NO	5	37	156	0	0	156	1	0	1	0	6
91. Montgomery	NYG	1	1	4	0	0	4	1	0	1	0	6
92. Kaufman	OAK	14	93	499	13	127	626	0	1	1	0	6
93. Pritchett	PHI	13	58	225	25	193	418	1	0	1	0	6
94. Staley	PHI	5	79	344	25	201	545	1	0	1	0	6
95. Fuamatu-Ma'afala	PIT	6	21	149	11	107	256	1	0	1	0	6
96. Jenkins *	SD	5	8	6	1	1	7	0	0	1	0	6
97. Rogers *	SEA	0	0	0	0	0	0	0	0	1	0	6
98. Strong	SEA	13	3	9	22	136	145	0	1	1	0	6
99. Rd. Thomas	TEN	12	61	175	8	35	210	0	1	1	0	6
100. Hicks	WAS	6	29	78	5	43	121	1	0	1	0	6
101. M. Williams	MIN	11	23	67	4	31	98	0	0	0	2	2
102. Makovicka	ARI	6	3	8	6	18	26	0	0	0	0	0
103. McKinley	ARI	2	0	0	2	13	13	0	0	0	0	0
104. Christian	ATL	16	9	19	44	315	334	0	0	0	0	0
105. Rivers	ATL	2	8	27	0	0	27	0	0	0	0	0
106. M. Smith	ATL	5	19	69	1	5	74	0	0	0	0	0
107. Barnes	CHI	6	15	81	1	7	88	0	0	0	0	0
108. Groce	CIN	6	4	-2	11	45	43	0	0	0	0	0
109. Keaton +	CIN	3	6	24	0	0	24	0	0	0	0	0
110. N. Williams	CIN	9	10	54	7	84	138	0	0	0	0	0
111. Rhett	CLE	5	71	258	14	78	336	0	0	0	0	0
112. Saleh	CLE	1	0	0	1	22	22	0	0	0	0	0
113. White	CLE	10	47	145	13	100	245	0	0	0	0	0
114. Hambrick	DAL	1	6	28	0	0	28	0	0	0	0	0
115. Gary	DEN	1	13	80	3	10	90	0	0	0	0	0
116. Irvin	DET	5	9	49	8	90	139	0	0	0	0	0
117. Olivo	DET	3	0	0	3	50	50	0	0	0	0	0
118. Schlesinger	DET	11	1	3	12	73	76	0	0	0	0	0
119. Goodman	GB	3	3	-2	1	0	-2	0	0	0	0	0
120. Ba. Mitchell	GB	1	2	8	0	0	8	0	0	0	0	0
121. Parker	GB	8	18	85	9	50	135	0	0	0	0	0
122. Abdul-Jabbar	IND	1	1	-2	0	0	-2	0	0	0	0	0
123. Gordon	IND	2	4	13	0	0	13	0	0	0	0	0
124. Dukes	JAC	1	2	2	0	0	2	0	0	0	0	0
125. Shelton	JAC	6	2	3	4	48	51	0	0	0	0	0
126. J. Williams	JAC	1	2	8	0	0	8	0	0	0	0	0
127. Denson	MIA	9	31	108	14	105	213	0	0	0	0	0
128. Dyer +	MIA	1	0	0	2	14	14	0	0	0	0	0
129. Konrad	MIA	9	15	39	14	83	122	0	0	0	0	0
130. Kleinsasser	MIN	11	12	43	10	98	141	0	0	0	0	0
131. Morrow	MIN	1	0	0	1	2	2	0	0	0	0	0
132. Palmer	MIN	1	0	0	1	-2	-2	0	0	0	0	0
133. C. Floyd	NE	2	2	-1	1	21	20	0	0	0	0	0
134. Harris	NE	3	13	36	4	20	56	0	0	0	0	0
135. Pass +	NE	4	18	58	4	17	75	0	0	0	0	0
136. Shaw	NE	4	9	12	2	11	23	0	0	0	0	0
137. McAfee	NO	2	2	37	0	0	37	0	0	0	0	0
138. Morton +	NO	14	36	136	30	213	349	0	0	0	0	0
139. T. Smith +	NO	12	29	131	12	65	196	0	0	0	0	0
140. Comella	NYG	15	10	45	36	274	319	0	0	0	0	0
141. Sowell	NYJ	6	2	0	6	84	84	0	0	0	0	0
142. Kirby	OAK	1	11	51	3	19	70	0	0	0	0	0
143. Ritchie	OAK	11	0	0	26	173	173	0	0	0	0	0
144. Lee	PHI	2	1	2	1	20	22	0	0	0	0	0
145. Ce. Martin	PHI	14	13	77	31	219	296	0	0	0	0	0
146. Kreider	PIT	5	2	24	5	42	66	0	0	0	0	0

2000 STATISTICAL RESULTS
(RUNNING BACKS — BASIC SCORING METHOD)

NAME		TEAM	GP	RSH	RUSH YARDS	REC	REC YARDS	TOTAL YARDS	RUSH TDs	REC TDs	TOTAL TDs	CONV PTS	FAN-TASY PTS
147. Witman		PIT	3	3	5	5	33	38	0	0	0	0	0
148. Zereoue		PIT	2	6	14	0	0	14	0	0	0	0	0
149. Bynum		SD	2	7	26	2	13	39	0	0	0	0	0
150. Brown		SEA	2	3	6	2	9	15	0	0	0	0	0
151. Jervey		SF	1	1	0	0	0	0	0	0	0	0	0
152. Jo. Lewis		SF	1	1	6	0	0	6	0	0	0	0	0
153. P. Smith	+	SF	8	18	72	2	55	127	0	0	0	0	0
154. Canidate	+	STL	2	3	6	1	4	10	0	0	0	0	0
155. Hodgins		STL	3	1	3	2	5	8	0	0	0	0	0
156. Abdullah		TB	4	16	70	2	14	84	0	0	0	0	0
157. Stecker		TB	5	12	31	1	15	46	0	0	0	0	0
158. Roan		TEN	1	0	0	3	12	12	0	0	0	0	0
159. Murrell		WAS	9	20	50	16	93	143	0	0	0	0	0

+   DENOTES COLLEGE DRAFT PICKS
*   Br. Mitchell   (PHI)   Scored TD's on a 89 yard kickoff return and a 72 yard punt return.
*   Mi. Bates   (CAR)   Scored TD on a 92 yard kickoff return.
*   Jenkins   (SD)   Scored TD on a 93 yard kickoff return.
*   Rogers   (SEA)   Scored TD on a 81 yard kickoff return.
**   Warren   (PHI)   Played in 11 games with Dallas.
**   Harris   (NE)   Played in 2 games with Denver.

RATING THE PLAYERS FOR 2001
(Running Backs — Basic Scoring Method)
GRAB ONE IF YOU CAN

☐ **1. Marshall Faulk (St. Louis Rams)**

A change of scenery certainly hasn't hurt Marshall Faulk's scoring numbers. Faulk scored ten times when playing with the Colts in 1998. In 1999, coming to the Rams, he expanded that to 12 touchdowns and, last year, playing in only 14 games, set the NFL record with 26 touchdowns. How can you shy away from that kind of production in grabbing a fantasy pick?

☐ **2. Edgerrin James (Indianapolis Colts)**

James followed up his impressive rookie campaign of scoring 18 touchdowns in 1999 by scoring 17 times in 2000. Another 15 to 20 touchdowns is in store in 2001 for this talented back.

☐ **3. Fred Taylor (Jacksonville Jaguars)**

Taylor produced an impressive 17 touchdowns as a rookie in 1998, playing in 15 games. Injuries have slowed him since, as he scored only six times in 1999 but rebounded to 14 a year ago. If he can stay healthy, I expect nearing or topping the 15-touchdown mark is in order in 2001.

☐ **4. Stephen Davis (Washington Redskins)**

Davis had a breakout year in 1999, as he scored 17 times playing in 14 games. Last year Davis missed only one game but dropped to 11 scores. I look for a rebound in 2001 and a possible 13-15 scores as the Redskins face the league's easiest schedule.

☐ **5. Eddie George (Tennessee Titans)**

George struggled early in his career scoring consistently but has exploded for 13 and 16 touchdowns respectively the last two seasons. Being the main focus of the Titan offense will again get him big scoring numbers in 2001.

BEST OF THE REST

☐ **6. Terrell Davis (Denver Broncos)**

The potential is there. Looking back to 1998, when Davis scored 23 times, we know what he can do. If he can stay healthy, which has been a problem the last two years, Davis can use the Broncos' offensive line to help him rebound to big scoring numbers again.

☐ **7. Ricky Williams (New Orleans Saints)**

As a rookie in 1999, Williams struggled miserably and recorded only two touchdowns. He was on the way to much bigger things in 2000, until a broken ankle sidelined him the last six games. His nine touchdowns, however, in the ten games he did play shows us he's on course to be a big-time fantasy factor as a scorer. The selection of Deuce McAllister in the first round by the Saints raises some questions.

☐ **8. Ahman Green (Green Bay Packers)**

One man's misery is another man's gain. Knee and ankle injuries to Dorsey Levens opened the door for Ahman Green in 2000. Green took full advantage to the tune of 13 touchdowns. The only question for 2001 is, will he retain the starting role over a healthy Levens? We'll have to watch as the regular season nears, but his 2000 performance was just too good to ignore.

☐ **9. Lamar Smith (Miami Dolphins)**
Prior to coming to Miami in 2000, Lamar Smith had mediocre success when with Seattle and New Orleans. Smith, however, became a nice fit for the Dolphins, and his 16 touchdowns surprised and delighted fantasy fans. I expect at least another 12-plus touchdowns in 2001.

☐ **10. James Stewart (Detroit Lions)**
Stewart scored 13 times subbing for the injured Fred Taylor when with Jacksonville in 1999. Coming to Detroit to be the main ball carrier for the Lions in 2000, Stewart scored 11 times. Maintaining his feature role for the Lions in 2001, another 10-14 scores are in order.

STRONG LONG SHOTS

☐ **11. Curtis Martin (New York Jets)**
Curtis Martin's scoring numbers seem to bounce all over the board, as he has scored 9, 5 and 11 touchdowns respectively the last three seasons. As the most consistent offensive weapon the Jets have, I expect another double-digit touchdown performance in 2001.

☐ **12. Tyrone Wheatley (Oakland Raiders)**
A bust prior to coming to the Raiders two years ago, Tyrone Wheatley has found a home and has become a scoring force. Wheatley produced 11 touchdowns in 1999 and 10 a year ago playing in only 14 games. Another 10-13 are in store for 2001, though offseason acquisition Charlie Garner may cut into those totals.

☐ **13. Jamal Anderson (Atlanta Falcons)**
Anderson scored 16 times when healthy back in 1998, but a knee injury allowed him to see action in only two games in 1999. Recovered in 2000, Anderson rebounded but scored only six times. I believe with more time to build on his recovery, he'll return to double-digit scoring in 2001.

☐ **14. Jamal Lewis (Baltimore Ravens)**
Lewis scored only six times as a rookie in 2000, but he demonstrated there's plenty more to come.

☐ **15. Ricky Watters (Seattle Seahawks)**
For Watters, who has scored 9, 7 and 9 touchdowns the last three seasons respectively, his role will dictate his scoring success in 2001. He may be on his way out of Seattle, as young Shawn Alexander gets his shot. Regardless, Watters proved in 2000 he can still get it done, no matter what team he ends up with.

☐ **16. Emmitt Smith (Dallas Cowboys)**
Smith is seeing his touchdown production on a decline as the Cowboys have struggled as a team through injuries. He has scored 15, 13 and 9 touchdowns respectively the last three seasons. I believe he'll still near or top the ten-touchdown mark in 2001.

☐ **17. Warrick Dunn (Tampa Bay Buccaneers)**
Dunn expanded his role and his scoring in 2000 and scored nine times. The Bucs look to feature Dunn even more in 2001, making for the likelihood of even more scoring.

☐ **18. Jerome Bettis (Pittsburgh Steelers)**
Many thought Richard Huntley would cut heavily into the numbers of
Jerome Bettis in 2000, but Bettis pushed hard, played well and scored
eight times. The Steelers rewarded Bettis with a six-year deal in the
offseason, showing their confidence that Bettis will continue to be a
scoring force for some time.

☐ **19. Corey Dillon (Cincinnati Bengals)**
Dillon is regarded as one of the league's better backs based on his
yardage numbers. the Bengals need to find a way to get him more scoring chances in 2001. Dillon has steadily improved, scoring 5, 6 and 7
times the last three seasons.

☐ **20. Tiki Barber (New York Giants)**
Barber outshined Giants' first-round draft pick Ron Dayne in 2000, resulting in nine touchdowns. He'll again get plenty of opportunity in
2001.

HAVE THE POTENTIAL

☐ **21. Duce Staley (Philadelphia Eagles)**
Staley had been a major force for the Eagles on the ground for two
seasons, until a foot injury sidelined him over half the 2000 season. If
healthy, he'll return to again be the mainstay of the Eagles' ground attack, but there's concern his foot may not be ready.

☐ **22. Michael Pittman (Arizona Cardinals)**
Pittman outduelled rookie first-round pick Thomas Jones in 2000, and
if he maintains the starting position, his touchdown production should
fall in the 7-10 range.

☐ **23. Errict Rhett (Cleveland Browns)**
Rhett, brought in from Baltimore to lead the Browns' running attack
in 2000, missed over half the season with a foot injury. The Browns
hope he can return to health and produce plenty of scores in 2001,
though Travis Prentise may stand in the way.

☐ **24. Charlie Garner (Oakland Raiders)**
Garner scored ten times as the 49ers' feature back in 2000, but now he
goes to Oakland where he'll push Tyrone Wheatley for work.

☐ **25. Priest Holmes (Kansas City Chiefs)**
Holmes, a former 1,000-yard rusher, has been banged up much of the last
two seasons. He comes to Kansas City to push for the every-down job.

SOLID SLEEPERS

☐ **26. Tim Biakabatuka (Carolina Panthers)**
Injuries always seem to stand in the way of Biakabatuka's success.
However, when he's healthy he can be a scoring force.

☐ **27. Shaun Alexander (Seattle Seahawks))**
The Seahawks' first-round draft pick of a year ago, will see his fantasy
stock take a quick climb if he takes over the feature back position from
Ricky Watters sooner than later.

☐ **28. James Allen (Chicago Bears)**
He had 1,411 rushing-receiving yards in 2000 but only four touchdowns.
Allen will face the challenge of rookie second-round pick Anthony

Thomas in 2001.

□ **29. Travis Prentise (Cleveland Browns)**
Prentise, the Browns' third-round pick of a year ago, got his chance when Errict Rhett fell victim to injury. Prentise scored eight times in 2000 but his 2001 statistical success will depend on his role, with Rhett returning healthy.

□ **30. Antowain Smith (Buffalo Bills)**
Smith's 147 yard, three-touchdown performance in the 2000 season finale put him back in the Bills' running back derby in 2001.

KEEP AN EYE ON

□ **31. J. R. Redmond (New England Patriots)**
The Patriots' third-round pick of a year ago was a disappointment and scored only three times as a rookie. The Patriots still believe there's future potential.

□ **32. Olandis Gary (Denver Broncos)**
Gary returns from a knee injury that kept him out virtually all of 2000. A year earlier, he showed his potential. His role and potential to score will likely depend on the health of Terrell Davis.

□ **33. Garrison Hearst (San Francisco 49ers)**
Hearst has missed the last two seasons with complications from a leg injury. Keep an eye on his progress, which seems to be going better.

□ **34. Sammy Morris (Buffalo Bills)**
Antowain Smith, Shawn Bryson and Jonathan Linton all battling for playing time with the Bills and scores in 2001.

□ **35. Mike Alstott (Tampa Bay Buccaneers)**
After scoring 10, 9 and 9 times the three previous seasons, Alstott scored only five times in 2000, missing three games to injury. He's slated for a reduced role behind Warrick Dunn in 2001, which will likely continue to limit his scoring success.

□ **36. Dorsey Levens (Green Bay Packers)**
Knee and ankle injuries plagued Levens in 2000, opening the door for Ahman Green. Green's success puts Levens's future scoring success in jeopardy.

□ **37. Mike Anderson (Denver Broncos)**
A sixth-round pick of a year ago, Anderson made the most of his chance in 2000, scoring 15 times subbing for the injured Terrell Davis and Olandis Gary. His role in 2001, however, is in question with the other two returning healthy.

□ **38. Ron Dayne (New York Giants)**
Dayne, the Giants' first-found pick of 2000, was out-performed in 2000 by veteran Tiki Barber, which may happen again in 2001.

□ **39. Thomas Jones (Arizona Cardinals)**
The Cardinals' first-round pick of a year ago was a disappointment as a rookie in 2000 and must fight off the challenge of Michael Pittman to put up significant scoring numbers in 2001.

□ **40. Tony Richardson (Kansas City Chiefs)**
The running-back-by-committee approach will likely end under new

head coach Dick Vermeil. Richardson may push offseason acquisition Priest Holmes for the role in 2001.

PRIME PROSPECTS

☐ **41. Terrell Fletcher (San Diego Chargers)**
With first-round pick La Dainian Tomlinson now aboard, Fletcher likely will resume his third-down role.

☐ **42. Richard Huntley (Pittsburgh Steelers)**
After scoring eight times in 1999, Huntley scored only three times in 2000. The potential is still there for six-plus scores.

☐ **43. Kevin Faulk (New England Patriots)**
Faulk will likely continue to battle J. R. Redmond for playing time and scores, unless the Patriots find a quick way to resolve their running woes, though Redmond is the projected starter.

☐ **44. Shawn Bryson (Buffalo Bills)**
He had 862 rushing-receiving yards but only two touchdowns in 2000. Bryson is another Bills back in the battle for playing time and statistical success in 2001.

☐ **45. Chris Warren (Philadelphia Eagles)**
Warren's role and production rests on the healthy return of Duce Staley.

☐ **46. Zack Crockett (Oakland Raiders)**
Crockett's seven touchdowns in 2000 kept defenses off-guard in the red zone when trying to stop Tyrone Wheatley.

☐ **47. Frank Moreau (Kansas City Chiefs)**
Moreau is another choice new head coach Dick Vermeil may look to in 2001. Moreau scored four times in 2000.

☐ **48. Fred Beasley (San Francisco 49ers)**
The 49ers' fullback expanded his touchdown production from four in 1999 to six in 2000.

☐ **49. Paul Davis (San Francisco 49ers)**
The 49ers' second-round pick of a year ago may find a much-expanded workload in 2001.

☐ **50. Jonathan Linton (Buffalo Bills)**
Another of the Bills' backs battling for work.

NOTE: *51–75* and *Rookie Prospects* on the next page.

DON'T BE SURPRISED

51. Autry (PHIL)
52. Hoover (CAR)
53. Fuamatu-Ma'afala (PITT)
54. Cloud (KC)
55. Canidate (STL)
56. M. Williams (MINN)
57. R. Anderson (NYJ)
58. Edwards (NE)
59. Montgomery (NYG)
60. Hambrich (DALL)

YOU NEVER KNOW

61. J. J. Johnson (MIA)
62. Henderson (GB)
63. Pritchett (PHIL)
64. Murrell (WASH)
65. Denson (MIA)
66. Br. Bennett (CIN)
67. Wiley (DALL)
68. Hicks (WASH)
69. Watson (STL)
70. Edwards (NE)

WORTH MENTIONING

71. Chapman (MINN)
72. Strong (SEAT)
73. Irvin (DET)
74. Parker (GB)
75. Christian (ATL)

ROOKIE PROSPECTS

NAME	TEAM	COMMENT
☐ 1. Michael Bennett	MINN	Answer to Robert Smith's departure.
☐ 2. La Dainian Tomlinson	SD	The Chargers have found themselves talented back to carry the load.
☐ 3. Anthony Thomas	CHI	Will be pushing James Allen.
☐ 4. Kevan Barlow	SF	Nice, all-round back to push for 49ers starting job.
☐ 5. Travis Henry	BUF	Too many players battling for job.
☐ 6. Deuce McAllister	NO	What is Ricky Williams—chopped liver?
☐ 7. Lamont Jordan	NYJ	Future for Jets behind Curtis Martin.
☐ 8. Heath Evans	SEAT	Strong, fullback type.
☐ 9. James Jackson	CLE	Will battle for work with Browns.
☐10. Correll Buckhalter	PHIL	If Duce Staley isn't ready, has a shot.

A LOOK AT THE WIDE RECEIVERS
(A Guide for the Beginner)

Considerations in Choosing a Wide Receiver

If you have played fantasy football and used the Basic Scoring Method, you know that wide receivers were unpredictable scorers until Jerry Rice came along. Rice, in turn, led the way for the likes of Randy Moss and Antonio Freeman, who are developing into consistent scorers when they are healthy. It is still a challenge, however, to guess how most receivers will perform in this method. Let's take a look at some positive and negative characteristics to look for when you're drafting wide receivers.

1. First, look at players' previous performances. Injuries, player movement, holdouts, and suspensions should be noted. Players like Marcus Robinson, Qadry Ismail and Joey Galloway all had their seasons marred in 2000.

2. Look for receivers from pass-oriented teams like the 49ers or Packers and more recently the Vikings, who have become pass-happy. Obviously, these players are more likely to have productive years.

3. Look for receivers who are favorites of a particular quarterback. Many quarterbacks single out a receiver whom they go to in clutch touchdown situations, such as Randy Moss, who is a favorite target of Daunte Culpepper.

4. Look for quarterback changes to have varying effects on wide receivers. When a quarterback and wide receiver have played together for years, the performance of the receiver may drop off if his regular quarterback leaves. On the other hand, a new quarterback may come to a team and open up the offense, giving receivers more opportunities. Warren Moon did this for Cris Carter in 1994, as did Jeff Blake for Carl Pickens in both 1994 and 1995. Jeff George's arrival in Oakland in 1997 helped boost James Jett to 12 scores. In 1998, Randall Cunningham's emergence helped rookie Randy Moss to huge numbers.

5. Keep an eye on rookie wide receivers, especially from teams looking for a starter at that position. Rookies don't usually draw much coverage, because they are unproven receivers. In 1995 Chris Sanders surprised many with a nine-touchdown season for Houston. Rookies Keyshawn Johnson (NY Jets) and Marvin Harrison (Indianapolis) both turned in productive rookie campaigns in 1996. In 1998 Randy Moss quickly became the talk of the league.

In the 2000 statistics, players are ranked by their fantasy-point totals. Remember that in the Basic Scoring Method, fantasy points are calculated by awarding six points for every touchdown rushed or caught and three points for every touchdown pass thrown.

NAME	TEAM	GP	RSH	RUSH YARDS	REC	REC YARDS	TOTAL YARDS	RUSH TDs	REC TDs	TOTAL TDs	CONV PTS	FAN-TASY PTS
1. Moss	MIN	16	3	5	77	1,437	1,442	0	15	15	2	92
1999		16	4	43	80	1,413	1,456	0	11	12	0	75
1998		16	1	4	69	1,313	1,317	0	17	17	4	106
3 Yr - TOTALS		48	8	52	226	4,163	4,215	0	43	44	6	273
2. Harrison	IND	16	0	0	102	1,413	1,413	0	14	14	0	84
1999		16	1	4	115	1,663	1,667	0	12	12	2	74
1998		12	0	0	59	776	776	0	7	7	2	44
3 Yr - TOTALS		44	1	4	276	3,852	3,856	0	33	33	4	202
3. Owens	SF	14	3	11	97	1,451	1,462	0	13	13	2	80
1999		14	0	0	60	754	754	0	4	4	0	24
1998		16	4	53	67	1,097	1,150	1	14	15	2	92
3 Yr - TOTALS		44	7	64	224	3,302	3,366	1	31	32	4	196
4. Tm. Brown	OAK	16	3	12	76	1,128	1,140	0	11	11	0	66
1999		16	1	4	90	1,344	1,348	0	6	6	0	36
1998		16	1	-7	81	1,012	1,005	0	9	9	0	54
3 Yr - TOTALS		48	5	9	247	3,484	3,493	0	26	26	0	156
5. Alexander	KC	16	3	45	78	1,391	1,436	0	10	10	0	60
1999		15	2	82	54	832	914	1	2	3	0	18
1998		14	0	0	54	992	992	0	4	4	0	24
3 Yr - TOTALS		45	5	127	186	3,215	3,342	1	16	17	0	102
6. McCaffrey	DEN	16	0	0	101	1,317	1,317	0	9	9	2	56
1999		15	0	0	71	1,018	1,018	0	7	7	0	42
1998		15	0	0	64	1,053	1,053	0	10	10	2	62
3 Yr - TOTALS		46	0	0	236	3,388	3,388	0	26	26	4	160
7. R. Smith	DEN	16	6	99	100	1,602	1,701	1	8	9	0	54
1999		14	0	0	79	1,020	1,020	0	4	4	0	24
1998		16	6	63	86	1,222	1,285	1	6	7	0	42
3 Yr - TOTALS		46	12	162	265	3,844	4,006	2	18	20	0	120
8. Freeman	GB	15	2	5	62	912	917	0	9	9	0	54
1999		15	1	-2	74	1,074	1,072	0	6	6	0	36
1998		15	3	5	84	1,424	1,429	0	14	14	2	86
3 Yr - TOTALS		45	6	8	220	3,410	3,418	0	29	29	2	176
9. Carter	MIN	16	0	0	96	1,274	1,274	0	9	9	0	54
1999		15	0	0	90	1,241	1,241	0	13	13	0	78
1998		15	1	-1	78	1,011	1,010	0	12	12	0	72
3 Yr - TOTALS		46	1	-1	264	3,526	3,525	0	34	34	0	204
10. Bruce	STL	16	1	11	87	1,471	1,482	0	9	9	0	54
1999		15	5	32	77	1,165	1,197	0	12	12	2	74
1998		4	1	30	32	457	487	0	1	1	0	6
3 Yr - TOTALS		35	7	73	196	3,093	3,166	0	22	22	2	134
11. J. Smith	JAC	14	0	0	91	1,213	1,213	0	8	8	0	48
1999		16	0	0	116	1,636	1,636	0	6	6	2	38
1998		16	0	0	78	1,182	1,182	0	8	8	0	48
3 Yr - TOTALS		46	0	0	285	4,031	4,031	0	22	22	2	134
12. Horn	NO	16	6	18	94	1,340	1,358	0	8	8	0	48
1999 (w/KC)		15	2	15	35	586	601	0	6	6	0	36
1998 (w/KC)		10	1	-8	14	198	190	0	1	1	0	6
3 Yr - TOTALS		41	9	25	143	2,124	2,149	0	15	15	0	90
13. Hilliard	NYG	14	3	19	55	787	806	0	8	8	0	48
1999		16	3	16	72	996	1,012	0	3	3	0	18
1998		16	1	4	51	713	717	0	2	2	0	12
3 Yr - TOTALS		46	7	39	178	2,496	2,535	0	13	13	0	78
14. Toomer	NYG	16	5	91	78	1,094	1,185	1	7	8	0	48
1999		16	1	4	79	1,183	1,187	0	6	6	0	36
1998		13	0	0	27	360	360	0	5	5	0	30
3 Yr - TOTALS		45	6	95	184	2,637	2,732	1	18	19	0	114
15. Chrebet	NYJ	16	3	-3	69	937	934	0	8	8	0	48
1999		11	0	0	48	631	631	0	3	3	0	18
1998		16	0	0	75	1,083	1,083	0	8	8	0	48
3 Yr - TOTALS		43	3	-3	192	2,651	2,648	0	19	19	0	114

NAME	TEAM	GP	RSH	RUSH YARDS	REC	REC YARDS	TOTAL YARDS	RUSH TDs	REC TDs	TOTAL TDs	CONV PTS	FAN-TASY PTS
16. Ks. Johnson	TB	16	2	5	71	874	879	0	8	8	0	48
1999 (w/NYJ)		16	5	6	89	1,170	1,176	0	8	8	0	48
1998 (w/NYJ)		16	2	60	83	1,131	1,191	1	10	11	0	66
3 Yr - TOTALS		48	9	71	243	3,175	3,246	1	26	27	0	162
17. Boston	ARI	16	3	4	71	1,156	1,160	0	7	7	0	42
1999		14	5	0	40	473	473	0	2	2	0	12
1998		-	-	-	-	-	-	-	-	-	-	-
3 Yr - TOTALS		30	8	4	111	1,629	1,633	0	9	9	0	54
18. Warrick + *	CIN	16	16	148	51	592	740	2	4	7	0	42
1999		-	-	-	-	-	-	-	-	-	-	-
1998		-	-	-	-	-	-	-	-	-	-	-
3 Yr - TOTALS		16	16	148	51	592	740	2	4	7	0	42
19. C. Johnson	PHI	15	5	18	56	642	660	0	7	7	0	42
1999		9	0	0	34	414	414	0	1	1	0	6
1998 (w/PIT)		16	1	4	65	815	819	0	7	7	4	46
3 Yr - TOTALS		40	6	22	155	1,871	1,893	0	15	15	4	94
20. Rice	SF	16	1	-2	75	805	803	0	7	7	0	42
1999		16	2	13	67	830	843	0	5	5	0	30
1998		16	0	0	82	1,157	1,157	0	9	9	4	58
3 Yr - TOTALS		48	3	11	224	2,792	2,803	0	21	21	4	130
21. F. Sanders	ARI	16	0	0	54	749	749	0	6	6	0	36
1999		15	0	0	79	954	954	0	1	1	0	6
1998		16	4	0	89	1,145	1,145	0	3	3	0	18
3 Yr - TOTALS		47	4	0	222	2,848	2,848	0	10	10	0	60
22. Muhammad	CAR	16	2	12	102	1,183	1,195	0	6	6	0	36
1999		15	0	0	96	1,253	1,253	0	8	8	0	48
1998		15	0	0	68	941	941	0	6	6	2	38
3 Yr - TOTALS		46	2	12	266	3,377	3,389	0	20	20	2	122
23. Gadsden	MIA	16	0	0	56	786	786	0	6	6	0	36
1999		14	0	0	48	803	803	0	6	6	0	36
1998		15	0	0	48	713	713	0	7	7	0	42
3 Yr - TOTALS		45	0	0	152	2,302	2,302	0	19	19	0	114
24. Glenn	NE	16	4	39	79	963	1,002	0	6	6	0	36
1999		13	0	0	69	1,147	1,147	0	4	4	0	24
1998		10	2	-1	50	792	791	0	3	3	0	18
3 Yr - TOTALS		39	6	38	198	2,902	2,940	0	13	13	0	78
25. W. Jackson +	NO	14	0	0	37	523	523	0	6	6	0	36
1999		-	-	-	-	-	-	-	-	-	-	-
1998		-	-	-	-	-	-	-	-	-	-	-
3 Yr - TOTALS		14	0	0	37	523	523	0	6	6	0	36
26. Rison	OAK	14	0	0	41	606	606	0	6	6	0	36
1999 (w/KC)		12	0	0	21	218	218	0	0	0	0	0
1998 (w/KC)		13	2	12	40	542	554	0	5	5	0	30
3 Yr - TOTALS		39	2	12	102	1,366	1,378	0	11	11	0	66
27. D. Jackson +	SEA	16	1	-1	53	713	712	0	6	6	0	36
1999		-	-	-	-	-	-	-	-	-	-	-
1998		-	-	-	-	-	-	-	-	-	-	-
3 Yr - TOTALS		16	1	-1	53	713	712	0	6	6	0	36
28. Holt	STL	16	2	7	82	1,635	1,642	0	6	6	0	36
1999		15	3	25	52	788	813	0	6	6	0	36
1998		-	-	-	-	-	-	-	-	-	-	-
3 Yr - TOTALS		31	5	32	134	2,423	2,455	0	12	12	0	72
29. Mason *	TEN	14	1	1	63	895	896	0	5	6	0	36
1999		5	0	0	8	89	89	0	0	1	0	6
1998		14	0	0	25	333	333	0	3	3	0	18
3 Yr - TOTALS		33	1	1	96	1,317	1,318	0	8	10	0	60
30. Mathis	ATL	15	1	-5	57	679	674	0	5	5	0	30
1999		16	1	0	81	1,016	1,016	0	6	6	0	36
1998		16	1	-6	64	1,136	1,130	0	11	11	0	66
3 Yr - TOTALS		47	3	-11	202	2,831	2,820	0	22	22	0	132

2000 STATISTICAL RESULTS
(WIDE RECEIVERS - BASIC SCORING METHOD)

NAME	TEAM	GP	RSH	RUSH YARDS	REC	REC YARDS	TOTAL YARDS	RUSH TDs	REC TDs	TOTAL TDs	CONV PTS	FAN-TASY PTS
31. Q. Ismail	BAL	13	0	0	49	655	655	0	5	5	0	30
1999		16	1	4	68	1,105	1,109	0	6	6	0	36
1998		-	-	-	-	-	-	-	-	-	-	-
3 Yr - TOTALS		29	1	4	117	1,760	1,764	0	11	11	0	66
32. Moulds	BUF	16	2	24	94	1,326	1,350	0	5	5	0	30
1999		14	1	1	65	994	995	0	7	7	0	42
1998		16	0	0	67	1,368	1,368	0	9	9	0	54
3 Yr - TOTALS		46	3	25	226	3,688	3,713	0	21	21	0	126
33. Robinson	CHI	11	1	9	55	738	747	0	5	5	0	30
1999		16	0	0	84	1,400	1,400	0	9	9	0	54
1998		3	0	0	4	44	44	0	1	1	0	6
3 Yr - TOTALS		30	1	9	143	2,182	2,191	0	15	15	0	90
34. McCardell	JAC	16	0	0	94	1,207	1,207	0	5	5	0	30
1999		16	0	0	78	891	891	0	5	5	2	32
1998		14	0	0	64	892	892	0	6	6	2	38
3 Yr - TOTALS		46	0	0	236	2,990	2,990	0	16	16	4	100
35. Tr. Brown *	NE	16	6	46	83	944	990	0	4	5	0	30
1999		12	0	0	36	471	471	0	1	1	0	6
1998		7	0	0	23	346	346	0	1	1	0	6
3 Yr - TOTALS		35	6	46	142	1,761	1,807	0	6	7	0	42
36. Conway	SD	14	3	31	53	712	743	0	5	5	0	30
1999 (w/CHI)		9	1	-2	44	426	424	0	4	4	0	24
1998 (w/CHI)		14	5	48	54	733	781	0	3	3	0	18
3 Yr - TOTALS		37	9	77	151	1,871	1,948	0	12	12	0	72
37. Dawkins	SEA	15	0	0	63	731	731	0	5	5	0	30
1999		16	0	0	58	992	992	0	7	7	0	42
1998 (w/NO)		15	0	0	53	823	823	0	1	1	0	6
3 Yr - TOTALS		46	0	0	174	2,546	2,546	0	13	13	0	78
38. Hakim *	STL	15	5	19	53	734	753	0	4	5	0	30
1999		14	4	44	36	677	721	0	8	9	0	54
1998		7	2	30	20	247	277	1	1	2	0	12
3 Yr - TOTALS		36	11	93	109	1,658	1,751	1	13	16	0	96
39. Fryar	WAS	14	2	16	41	548	564	0	5	5	0	30
1999		12	0	0	26	254	254	0	2	2	0	12
1998 (w/PHI)		15	3	46	48	556	602	0	2	2	0	12
3 Yr - TOTALS		41	5	62	115	1,358	1,420	0	9	9	0	54
40. Dwight *	ATL	11	5	8	26	406	414	0	3	4	0	24
41. Schroeder	GB	15	2	11	65	999	1,010	0	4	4	0	24
42. Shepherd	MIA	12	4	3	35	446	449	0	4	4	0	24
43. Shaw	PIT	14	0	0	40	672	672	0	4	4	0	24
44. H. Ward	PIT	16	4	53	48	672	725	0	4	4	0	24
45. Graham	SD	13	0	0	55	907	907	0	4	4	0	24
46. Proehl	STL	12	0	0	31	441	441	0	4	4	0	24
47. Anthony	TB	10	0	0	15	232	232	0	4	4	0	24
48. Morton	DET	16	4	25	61	788	813	0	3	3	2	20
49. Small	PHI	14	1	1	40	569	570	0	3	3	2	20
50. Stokes	SF	14	1	6	30	524	530	0	3	3	2	20
51. Lewis *	BAL	8	3	38	19	161	199	0	1	3	0	18
52. Taylor +	BAL	9	3	11	28	276	287	0	3	3	0	18
53. Price	BUF	16	2	32	52	762	794	0	3	3	0	18
54. D. Hayes	CAR	15	0	0	66	926	926	0	3	3	0	18
55. McGarity *	DAL	11	6	49	25	250	299	1	0	3	0	18
56. Crowell	DET	9	1	12	34	430	442	0	3	3	0	18
57. Moore	DET	14	0	0	40	434	434	0	3	3	0	18
58. Pathon	IND	15	1	3	50	646	649	0	3	3	0	18
59. Wilkins	IND	12	3	8	43	569	577	0	3	3	0	18
60. Whitted	JAC	6	0	0	13	137	137	0	3	3	0	18
61. Morris +	KC	15	0	0	48	678	678	0	3	3	0	18
62. D. Ward	NYJ	16	4	23	54	801	824	0	3	3	0	18
63. Horne *	STL	4	2	6	4	32	38	0	2	3	0	18
64. Connell	WAS	13	0	0	39	762	762	0	3	3	0	18

2000 STATISTICAL RESULTS
(WIDE RECEIVERS - BASIC SCORING METHOD)

NAME	TEAM	GP	RSH	RUSH YARDS	REC	REC YARDS	TOTAL YARDS	RUSH TDs	REC TDs	TOTAL TDs	CONV PTS	FAN-TASY PTS
65. Jefferson	ATL	14	1	1	60	822	823	0	2	2	0	12
66. P. Johnson	BAL	6	2	21	12	156	177	0	2	2	0	12
67. Stokley	BAL	6	1	6	11	184	190	0	2	2	0	12
68. McDaniel	BUF	16	0	0	43	697	697	0	2	2	0	12
69. Byrd	CAR	8	0	0	22	241	241	0	2	2	0	12
70. Booker	CHI	14	2	-1	47	490	489	0	2	2	0	12
71. Kennison	CHI	16	3	72	55	549	621	0	2	2	0	12
72. McKnight	DAL	15	0	0	52	926	926	0	2	2	0	12
73. Lockett	KC	13	0	0	33	422	422	0	2	2	0	12
74. Hatchette	MIN	11	0	0	16	190	190	0	2	2	0	12
75. Jett	OAK	11	0	0	20	356	356	0	2	2	0	12
76. Thigpen	TEN	9	0	0	15	289	289	0	2	2	0	12
77. Thrash	WAS	14	10	82	50	653	735	0	2	2	0	12
78. R. Ismail	DAL	8	8	73	25	350	423	0	1	1	2	8
79. Driver	GB	12	1	4	21	322	326	0	1	1	2	8
80. Coles +	NYJ	8	2	15	22	370	385	0	1	1	2	8
81. Jenkins *	ARI	13	1	-4	17	219	215	0	0	1	0	6
82. Uwaezuoke *	CAR	4	0	0	4	46	46	0	0	1	0	6
83. White +	CHI	7	0	0	10	87	87	0	1	1	0	6
84. Dugans +	CIN	7	0	0	14	125	125	0	1	1	0	6
85. Chiaverini	CLE	3	0	0	8	68	68	0	1	1	0	6
86. Dawson +	CLE	2	0	0	9	97	97	0	1	1	0	6
87. Patten	CLE	11	0	0	38	546	546	0	1	1	0	6
88. Galloway	DAL	1	0	0	4	62	62	0	1	1	0	6
89. Tucker	DAL	10	4	42	15	141	183	1	0	1	0	6
90. McGriff	DEN	2	0	0	2	51	51	0	1	1	0	6
91. Foster	DET	7	2	31	17	175	206	0	1	1	0	6
92. Howard *	DET	3	0	0	2	14	14	0	0	1	0	6
93. E. G. Green	IND	5	0	0	18	201	201	0	1	1	0	6
94. Soward +	JAC	9	3	28	14	154	182	0	1	1	0	6
95. Emanuel	MIA	6	3	-2	7	132	130	0	1	1	0	6
96. Ogden *	MIA	3	0	0	2	24	24	0	0	1	0	6
97. Simmons	NE	10	0	0	14	231	231	0	1	1	0	6
98. Poole	NO	10	0	0	21	293	293	0	1	1	0	6
99. Dixon +	NYG	7	2	13	6	92	105	0	1	1	0	6
100. Jurevicius	NYG	10	0	0	25	271	271	0	1	1	0	6
101. Dunn *	OAK	4	0	0	4	33	33	0	0	1	0	6
102. N. Brown	PHI	9	0	0	9	80	80	0	1	1	0	6
103. Blackwell *	PIT	1	0	0	2	23	23	0	0	1	0	6
104. Hawkins	PIT	8	0	0	19	238	238	0	1	1	0	6
105. Gaylor +	SD	6	0	0	13	182	182	0	1	1	0	6
106. Bailey	SEA	4	0	0	6	62	62	0	1	1	0	6
107. Mayes	SEA	11	0	0	29	264	264	0	1	1	0	6
108. J. Green	TB	15	5	13	51	773	786	0	1	1	0	6
109. K. Williams *	TB	3	0	0	2	35	35	0	0	1	0	6
110. Dyson	TEN	1	0	0	6	104	104	0	1	1	0	6
111. A. Reed	WAS	6	0	0	10	103	103	0	1	1	0	6
112. Cody	ARI	10	0	0	17	212	212	0	0	0	0	0
113. Mitchell	ARI	3	0	0	5	80	80	0	0	0	0	0
114. C. Williams	ARI	1	0	0	1	5	5	0	0	0	0	0
115. Finneran	ATL	4	0	0	7	60	60	0	0	0	0	0
116. German	ATL	1	0	0	1	10	10	0	0	0	0	0
117. B. Davis	BAL	2	0	0	3	62	62	0	0	0	0	0
118. Cavil	BUF	3	0	0	4	66	66	0	0	0	0	0
119. Hankton	CAR	3	0	0	4	38	38	0	0	0	0	0
120. Bates	CHI	4	1	-2	4	42	40	0	0	0	0	0
121. M. Brooks	CHI	11	0	0	26	216	216	0	0	0	0	0
122. Engram	CHI	3	1	1	16	109	110	0	0	0	0	0
123. Milburn	CHI	2	1	6	1	8	14	0	0	0	0	0
124. Farmer	CIN	7	0	0	19	268	268	0	0	0	0	0
125. Griffin	CIN	2	0	0	2	25	25	0	0	0	0	0

NAME	TEAM	GP	RSH	RUSH YARDS	REC	REC YARDS	TOTAL YARDS	RUSH TDs	REC TDs	TOTAL TDs	CONV PTS	FAN-TASY PTS
126. Yeast	CIN	12	1	15	24	301	316	0	0	0	0	0
127. B. Brown	CLE	2	0	0	2	14	14	0	0	0	0	0
128. L. Jackson	CLE	1	0	0	1	5	5	0	0	0	0	0
129. Kv. Johnson	CLE	16	0	0	57	669	669	0	0	0	0	0
130. Northcutt +	CLE	14	9	33	39	422	455	0	0	0	0	0
131. Brazzell	DAL	2	0	0	2	12	12	0	0	0	0	0
132. Hodge	DAL	2	0	0	4	60	60	0	0	0	0	0
133. R. Brooks	DEN	2	0	0	3	51	51	0	0	0	0	0
134. Miller	DEN	1	0	0	1	7	7	0	0	0	0	0
135. Montgomery	DEN	1	0	0	1	10	10	0	0	0	0	0
136. Stablein	DET	7	0	0	8	53	53	0	0	0	0	0
137. Lee +	GB	6	0	0	10	134	134	0	0	0	0	0
138. Barlow	JAC	1	0	0	1	28	28	0	0	0	0	0
139. Parker	KC	3	1	-7	3	41	34	0	0	0	0	0
140. Martin	MIA	9	0	0	26	393	393	0	0	0	0	0
141. McDuffie	MIA	6	1	-3	14	143	140	0	0	0	0	0
142. Walsh	MIN	11	0	0	18	191	191	0	0	0	0	0
143. Walters +	MIN	2	1	3	1	5	8	0	0	0	0	0
144. Calloway	NE	5	0	0	5	95	95	0	0	0	0	0
145. S. Davis	NE	1	0	0	2	12	12	0	0	0	0	0
146. C. Jackson	NE	2	0	0	5	44	44	0	0	0	0	0
147. J. Reed	NO	5	0	0	16	206	206	0	0	0	0	0
148. Wilson	NO	4	0	0	11	154	154	0	0	0	0	0
149. T. Davis	NYG	2	0	0	2	40	40	0	0	0	0	0
150. Brisby	NYJ	3	0	0	4	60	60	0	0	0	0	0
151. W. Hayes +	NYJ	4	1	2	6	126	128	0	0	0	0	0
152. Stone	NYJ	3	3	3	0	0	3	0	0	0	0	0
153. Porter +	OAK	1	0	0	1	6	6	0	0	0	0	0
154. Douglas	PHI	1	0	0	1	9	9	0	0	0	0	0
155. Pinkston +	PHI	7	0	0	10	181	181	0	0	0	0	0
156. Van Dyke	PHI	1	0	0	1	8	8	0	0	0	0	0
157. Burress +	PIT	10	0	0	22	273	273	0	0	0	0	0
158. Edwards	PIT	10	3	4	18	215	219	0	0	0	0	0
159. Jacquet	SD	1	0	0	1	25	25	0	0	0	0	0
160. Jones	SD	6	0	0	17	186	186	0	0	0	0	0
161. Ricks	SD	2	0	0	3	35	35	0	0	0	0	0
162. J. Williams +	SEA	5	1	-5	8	99	94	0	0	0	0	0
163. Streets	SF	11	1	0	19	287	287	0	0	0	0	0
164. Pickens	TEN	5	0	0	10	242	242	0	0	0	0	0
165. C. Sanders	TEN	15	0	0	33	536	536	0	0	0	0	0
166. Westbrook	WAS	2	0	0	9	103	103	0	0	0	0	0

+	DENOTE COLLEGE DRAFT PICKS		
*	Warrick	(CIN)	Scored TD on a 82 yard punt return.
*	Mason	(TEN)	Scored TD on a 69 yard punt return.
*	Tr. Brown	(NE)	Scored TD on a 66 yard punt return.
*	Hakim	(STL)	Scored TD on a 86 yard punt return.
*	Dwight	(ATL)	Scored TD on a 70 yard punt return.
*	Lewis	(BAL)	Scored TD's on 89 and 54 yard punt returns.
*	McGarity	(DAL)	Scored TD's on 64 and 59 yard punt returns.
*	Horne	(STL)	Scored TD on a 103 yard kickoff return.
*	Jenkins	(ARI)	Scored TD on a 98 yard kickoff return.
*	Uwaezucke	(CAR)	Scored TD on a 64 yard punt return.
*	Howard	(DET)	Scored TD on a 95 yard punt return.
*	Ogden	(MIA)	Scored TD on a 81 yard punt return.
*	Dunn	(OAK)	Scored TD on a 88 yard kickoff return.
*	Blackwell	(PIT)	Scored TD on a 98 yard kickoff return.
*	K. Williams	(TB)	Scored TD on a 73 yard punt return.

RATING THE PLAYERS FOR 2001
(Wide Receivers—Basic Scoring Method)
GRAB ONE IF YOU CAN

☐ **1. Randy Moss (Minnesota Vikings)**
Three years in the league and Moss has tallied 17, 12 and 15 touchdowns respectively. There were questions coming into 2000 about his production now that Daunte Culpepper would be at quarterback. Moss and Culpepper answered those questions.

☐ **2. Terrell Owens (San Francisco 49ers)**
How would Owens fare with Jeff Garcia being the full-time starter in 2000? Thirteen touchdowns playing in 14 games put to rest any questions, and 2001 should be even better as they continue to work together.

☐ **3. Marvin Harrison (Indianapolis Colts)**
Harrison has scored 12 and 14 times respectively the last two seasons. As the favorite target of Peyton Manning, he should continue to push the 15-touchdown mark in 2001.

☐ **4. Isaac Bruce (St. Louis Rams)**
After scoring 12 times in 1999, Bruce dropped to nine scores in 2000, as Marshall Faulk stole most of the Rams' scoring glory with 26 touchdowns. I look for Bruce to potentially reach or surpass the dozen touchdown mark in 2001.

☐ **5. Cris Carter (Minnesota Vikings)**
There was some concern Carter would retire following the 2000 season, but he'll be back. His scoring 12, 13 and 9 touchdowns the last three seasons maintains him as a solid fantasy consideration again in 2001.

BEST OF THE REST

☐ **6. Ed McCaffrey (Denver Broncos)**
Always around the double-digit scoring mark, McCaffrey has scored 10, 7 and 9 touchdowns respectively the last three seasons.

☐ **7. Antonio Freeman (Green Bay Packers)**
Freeman, who scored 14 times in 1998, struggled to six touchdowns in 1999 and then rebounded somewhat to nine scores in 2000. As the likely go-to guy for Brett Favre again in 2001, there's the potential to again top double-digit scoring.

☐ **8. Tim Brown (Oakland Raiders)**
Always among the leading yardage players, Brown has become more of a touchdown scorer as well, producing 9, 6 and 11 touchdowns respectively the last three years. I expect another double-digit scoring in 2001 as he continues to work with Rich Gannon.

☐ **9. Derrick Alexander (Kansas City Chiefs)**
A breakout year for Alexander in 2000 as he grabbed 78 receptions for 1,391 yards and scored ten times. With Dick Vermeil now in as head coach, I can't imagine his scoring numbers dropping in 2001, despite Elvis Grbac's exit.

☐ **10. Jimmy Smith (Jacksonville Jaguars)**
Smith has recorded 116 and 91 receptions over the last two seasons but

only 6 and 8 touchdowns over that period. His ten touchdown season or better is just waiting to happen.

STRONG LONG SHOTS

☐ **11. Rob Smith (Denver Broncos)**
He had 100 receptions for over 1,600 yards and nine touchdowns in 2000. I expect Smith to again near or top the ten-touchdown mark in 2001.

☐ **12. Marcus Robinson (Chicago Bears)**
Robinson recorded nine touchdowns on 84 receptions in his breakout year of 1999. He dropped to only five touchdowns on 55 receptions in 2000, as he missed five games to first an ankle injury and later in the year a bulging disc in his back. If healthy all of 2001, I see a rebound to the ten-touchdown range.

☐ **13. Keyshawn Johnson (Tampa Bay Buccaneers)**
Bringing in Brad Johnson at quarterback should boost Keyshawn's scoring chances in 2001. Johnson scored eight times on 71 receptions in 2000, his first year with the Bucs.

☐ **14. Joe Horn (New Orleans Saints)**
The move for Horn from Kansas City to New Orleans in 2000 was perfect for Horn, who scored eight times on 94 receptions. As the Saints #1 go-to receiver, he'll again be a good bet to score in the ten-touchdown range.

☐ **15. Joey Galloway (Dallas Cowboys)**
After signing Galloway, the Cowboys expected big things of him in 2000. But a knee injury ended his season after just one game. Healthy in 2001, I expect Galloway to near or reach double-digit scoring.

☐ **16. Muhsin Muhammad (Carolina Panthers)**
Muhammad has recorded 96 and 102 receptions respectively the last two seasons but surprisingly only eight and six touchdowns. Anybody seeing the ball that often, however, is always a threat to reach double-digit scoring.

☐ **17. Eric Moulds (Buffalo Bills)**
Though his reception level jumped in a huge way to 94 catches in 2000, Moulds scored only five times. In 1998, on just 67 receptions, Moulds scored nine times, an area I believe he'll again reach in 2001 as the Bill's #1 receiver.

☐ **18. Wayne Chrebet (New York Jets)**
Chrebet's new role as the Jets #1 receiver in 2000 got him eight touchdowns on 69 receptions in 2000. He'll again be called often to score in 2001 leading to another shot at 8-12 scores.

☐ **19. Amani Toomer (New York Giants)**
Toomer has started to bust out as a receiver the last two years, recording 79 and 78 receptions and 6 and 8 touchdowns. I expect he'll continue to climb his touchdown numbers in 2001.

☐ **20. Michael Westbrook (Washington Redskins)**
Westbrook has battled injuries most of his career. Finally staying healthy in 1999, he produced nine touchdowns on 65 receptions. In 2000, it was back to being injured as he missed the last 14 games of the

year with a knee injury. If he can return and stay healthy in 2001, I see a return to nearing the ten-touchdown mark.

HAVE THE POTENTIAL

☐ **21. David Boston (Arizona Cardinals)**
He went from 40 receptions and only two touchdowns as a rookie in 1999 to 71 receptions and seven touchdowns in 2000. A quick climb that should continue in 2001, though Cardinals' veteran receiver Rob Moore is expected back healthy, following a knee injury that caused him to miss the entire 2000 season.

☐ **22. Torry Holt (St. Louis Rams)**
Holt jumped from 52 receptions as a rookie in 1999 to 82 receptions in 2000, but both years scored only six times. He has the potential to score more but has a talented cast of Rams to battle with for touchdown production.

☐ **23. J. J. Stokes (San Francisco 49ers)**
With Jerry Rice out of the picture, Stokes's playing time should grow and so should his scoring numbers in 2001.

☐ **24. Darrell Jackson (Seattle Seahawks)**
As a rookie in 2000, Jackson stepped up to become the Seahawks' #1 receiver, recording 53 receptions and scoring six times. He'll easily push these numbers in 2001.

☐ **25. Terry Glenn (New England Patriots)**
Glenn's numbers continue to climb. He has recorded 50, 69 and 79 receptions the last three seasons respectively and 3, 4 and 6 touchdowns along the way.

SOLID SLEEPERS

☐ **26. Peter Warrick (Cincinnati Bengals)**
He scored seven times as a rookie in 2000, including two times on punt returns. The Bengals' quarterback situation raises questions as does the healthy return of Darnay Scott, who'll want to steal some of the show.

☐ **27. Terrence Mathis (Atlanta Falcons)**
After recording 11 and 6 touchdowns on 64 and 81 receptions in 1998 and 1999, at his dropped to only five touchdowns on 57 receptions in 2000. The entire Falcon passing game has been struggling and must turn it around for Mathis to get back on track.

☐ **28. Ike Hilliard (New York Giants)**
Hilliard scored only three times on 72 receptions in 1999 but scored eight times on 55 catches in 2000, missing two games to a bruised sternum. The Giants are welcoming more aerial scores under Jim Fassel.

☐ **29. Derrick Mason (Tennessee Titans)**
Mason out-performed both high-priced free-agent acquisitions Yancey Thigpen and Carl Pickens in 2000. His 63 receptions and six touchdowns are just a spring board for what he could do in 2001.

☐ **30. Germane Crowell (Detroit Lions)**
After recording 81 receptions and seven touchdowns in 1999, Crowell dropped to 34 receptions and only three touchdowns in 2000, missing

six games to a foot injury. Healthy in 2001, he should push his scoring numbers though the Lions seem content to run more now that James Stewart is aboard.

KEEP AN EYE ON

☐ **31. Oronde Gadsden (Miami Dolphins)**
He has scored 7, 6 and 6 touchdowns the last three seasons.

☐ **32. Darnay Scott (Cincinnati Bengals)**
Scott missed the entire 2000 season with two broken bones in his leg. Hoping to return healthy, he'll also hope the Bengals' quarterback situation improves to better his scoring chances.

☐ **33. Patrick Jeffers (Carolina Panthers)**
He scored 12 times on 63 receptions in 1999 but missed the entire 2000 season with a torn ACL. Keep an eye on the progress of his healthy return.

☐ **34. Qadry Ismail (Baltimore Ravens)**
Scored six times on 68 receptions in 1999 and five times on 49 receptions in 2000, missing three games to injury. Elvis Grbac's arrival should help.

☐ **35. Troy Brown (New England Patriots)**
Brown had a breakout year in 2000, as he recorded 83 receptions but scored only five touchdowns.

☐ **36. Keenan McCardell (Jacksonville Jaguars)**
It's surprising he doesn't score more. McCardell has produced 85, 64, 78 and 94 receptions the last four seasons and 5, 6, 5 and 5 touchdowns over that period.

☐ **37. Rocket Ismail (Dallas Cowboys)**
Ismail produced seven touchdowns on 80 receptions in 1999 but missed almost half the 2000 season with a knee injury. An uncertain healthy return and the Cowboy quarterback situation raises questions.

☐ **38. Rob Moore (Arizona Cardinals)**
The Cardinals expect to have their veteran receiver back healthy, after missing the entire 2000 season with a knee injury.

☐ **39. Kevin Johnson (Cleveland Browns)**
He had 66 receptions and eight touchdowns as a rookie in 1999, to no touchdowns on 57 receptions in 2000. Johnson really missed quarterback Tim Couch, who missed over half the season with a broken thumb.

☐ **40. Johnnie Morton (Detroit Lions)**
Morton scored five times while tallying 80 receptions in 1999, but dropped to only three touchdowns on 61 catches in 2000. The arrival of James Stewart and a more effective running game is likely why the Lions' passing numbers have dropped.

PRIME PROSPECTS

☐ **41. James Thrash (Philadelphia Eagles)**
With Charles Johnson and Torrence Small released, newcomer James Thrash battles rookie Freddie Mitchell to be #1 receiver for Philadelphia.

☐ **42. Bill Schroeder (Green Bay Packers)**
Schroeder has produced 74 and 65 receptions the last two seasons but

has only scored five and four touchdowns respectively.

☐ **43. Bobby Engram (Chicago Bears)**
After recording a surprising 88 receptions but only four touchdowns in 1999, Engram missed the 2000 season with a knee injury. A healthy return should spawn big reception numbers again, giving him plenty of chances to score, though he'll likely battle rookie first-round pick David Terrell for work in 2001.

☐ **44. Curtis Conway (San Diego Chargers)**
Despite missing a couple of games to a hamstring injury in 2000, Conway scored five times on just 53 receptions—numbers I believe he'll push in 2001 with Doug Flutie in town.

☐ **45. Shawn Jefferson (Atlanta Falcons)**
Jefferson came to Atlanta in 2000 hoping to give their passing game a boost and he did in recording 60 receptions but only two touchdowns. Touchdown production he could easily push in 2001.

☐ **46. Sylvester Morris (Kansas City Chiefs)**
The Chiefs first-round draft pick of 2000 produced 48 receptions and three touchdowns last year. He'll work to improve these numbers in his sophomore year.

☐ **47. Jeff Graham (San Diego Chargers)**
Graham is looking to push his 55 reception, four touchdown totals of a year ago, now that the Chargers' quarterbacking position has more stability with Doug Flutie aboard.

☐ **48. Az-Zahir Hakim (St. Louis Rams)**
Another of the Rams' fleet-footed receivers, Hakim can score both by reception or on kick returns. Hakim has scored 9 and 5 touchdowns in the last two seasons.

☐ **49. Plaxico Burress (Pittsburgh Steelers)**
Burress had a very disappointing rookie year for the Steeler's #1 draft pick of 2000 as he recorded only 22 receptions in ten games before missing the last six games with a wrist injury. The Steelers are still counting on him to step up in 2001.

☐ **50. O. J. McDuffie (Miami Dolphins)**
Since leading the NFL with 90 receptions in 1998, while scoring seven times, McDuffie has battled numerous injuries. If he's healthy in 2001, he'll be a fantasy factor.

NOTE: *51–90* and *Rookie Ratings* on the next page.

DON'T BE SURPRISED

51. J. Green (TB)
52. H. Ward (PITT)
53. Dyson (TENN)
54. Price (BUF)
55. Dawson (CLE)
56. Dwight (SD)
57. Rison (OAK)
58. Sanders (ARIZ)
59. Connell (NO)
60. Bradford (GB)

YOU NEVER KNOW

61. Jett (OAK)
62. Kennison (DEN)
63. McKnight (MIA)
64. Taylor (BALT)
65. Lockett (WASH)
66. Pathon (IND)
67. Emanuel (NE)
68. Hayes (CAR)
69. Wilkins (IND)
70. Patten (NE)

DON'T COUNT THEM OUT

71. Porter (OAK)
72. Chiaverini (CLE)
73. Shaw (PITT)
74. Anthony (TB)
75. Moore (DET)

76. Pickens (DALL)
77. Simmons (NE)
78. Jackson (NO)
79. Hatchette (NYJ)
80. J. Reed (MINN)

WORTH MENTIONING

81. Soward (JAC)
82. Proehl (STL)
83. N. Brown (PHIL)
84. Thigpen (????)
85. Rice (????)

86. D. Ward (MIA)
87. Thompson (WASH)
88. McDaniel (BUF)
89. Booker (CHI)
90. Jurevicuis (NYG)

ROOKIE PROSPECTS

NAME	TEAM	COMMENT
☐ 1. Rod Gardner	WASH	Redskins have found another big target for strong-armed George.
☐ 2. David Terrell	CHI	Talented receiver to tandem with Marcus Robinson.
☐ 3. Koren Robinson	SEAT	His success will rest on arm of unproven Hasslebeck.
☐ 4. Freddie Mitchell	PHIL	Could become Eagles' #1 receiver with Charles Johnson released.
☐ 5. Santana Moss	NYJ	Could help answer some of Jets' receiving problems.
☐ 6. Robert Ferguson	GB	Favre needs help at wide receiver.
☐ 7. Reggie Wayne	IND	Is he the #2 answer opposite Marvin Harrison?
☐ 8. Chris Chambers	MIA	Could help Dolphins in red zone.
☐ 9. Quincy Morgan	CLE	How good is the Brown passing game?
☐10. Chad Johnson	CIN	Did the Bengals need another wide receiver?

A LOOK AT THE TIGHT ENDS
(A Guide for the Beginner)

Considerations in Choosing a Tight End

1. First, look at players' previous performances. Injuries, player movement, holdouts, and the like should be noted. Cam Cleeland has his 2000 year-end totals hurt by injury.

2. If a team has one or two good wide receivers, opponents are forced to double-cover them, leaving the tight end open more often, especially in close situations. Tony Gonzalez is certainly fortunate to play alongside Derrick Alexander.

3. Tight ends from pass-oriented offenses like the 49ers or Packers have a better chance for a productive year than those from running teams.

4. Look for tight ends who seem to be favorite receivers of a particular quarterback. Shannon Sharpe, for example, has become a favorite target of both Tony Banks and Trent Dilfer. Although tight ends are less likely to be receivers than some other players, scoring receptions by tight ends are more common than before, as tight ends have grown more important in many teams' offensive schemes. The likes of Tony Gonzalez and Shannon Sharpe have brought all tight ends more attention.

5. Look for quarterback changes to have an adverse effect on a tight end's productivity. When a quarterback and tight end have played together for years, the performance of the tight end may drop off if his regular quarterback leaves.

In the 2000 statistics, players are ranked by their fantasy-point totals. Remember that in the Basic Scoring Method, fantasy points are calculated by awarding six points for every touchdown rushed or caught and three points for every touchdown pass thrown.

2000 STATISTICAL RESULTS
(TIGHT ENDS — BASIC SCORING METHOD)

	NAME	TEAM	GP	REC	REC YARDS	RSH TDs	REC TDs	TOTAL TDs	CONV PTS	FANTASY PTS
1.	Gonzalez	KC	15	93	1,203	0	9	9	0	54
	1999		15	76	849	0	11	11	0	66
	1998		16	59	621	0	2	2	0	12
	3 Yr - TOTALS		46	228	2,673	0	22	22	0	132
2.	Harris	DAL	16	39	306	0	5	5	2	32
	1999 (w/TEN)		8	26	297	0	1	1	2	8
	1998 (w/TEN)		14	43	412	0	2	2	0	12
	3 Yr - TOTALS		38	108	1,015	0	8	8	4	52
3.	Sharpe	BAL	15	67	810	0	5	5	0	30
	1999 (w/DEN)		4	23	224	0	0	0	0	0
	1998 (w/DEN)		16	64	768	0	10	10	0	60
	3 Yr - TOTALS		35	154	1,802	0	15	15	0	90
4.	Riemersma	BUF	11	31	372	0	5	5	0	30
	1999		13	37	496	0	4	4	0	24
	1998		13	25	288	0	6	6	0	36
	3 Yr - TOTALS		37	93	1,156	0	15	15	0	90
5.	Thomason	PHI	7	10	46	0	5	5	0	30
	1999 (w/GB)		7	14	140	0	2	2	0	12
	1998 (w/GB)		6	9	89	0	0	0	0	0
	3 Yr - TOTALS		20	33	275	0	7	7	0	42
6.	F. Jones	SD	15	71	766	0	5	5	0	30
	1999		16	56	670	0	2	2	0	12
	1998		16	57	602	0	3	3	2	20
	3 Yr - TOTALS		47	184	2,038	0	10	10	2	62
7.	Wycheck	TEN	16	70	636	0	4	4	0	27
	1999		16	69	641	0	2	2	0	15
	1998		16	70	768	0	2	2	0	12
	3 Yr - TOTALS		48	209	2,045	0	8	8	0	54
8.	Glover	NO	10	21	281	0	4	4	0	24
	1999 (w/MIN)		14	28	327	0	1	1	0	6
	1998 (w/MIN)		15	35	522	0	5	5	0	30
	3 Yr - TOTALS		39	84	1,130	0	10	10	0	60
9.	Dudley	OAK	14	29	350	0	4	4	0	24
	1999		13	39	555	0	9	9	0	54
	1998		15	36	549	0	5	5	2	32
	3 Yr - TOTALS		42	104	1,454	0	18	18	2	110
10.	Pollard	IND	13	30	439	0	3	3	2	20
	1999		14	34	374	0	4	4	0	24
	1998		10	24	309	0	4	4	4	28
	3 Yr - TOTALS		37	88	1,122	0	11	11	6	72
11.	Brady	JAC	16	64	729	0	3	3	2	20
	1999		13	32	346	0	1	1	2	8
	1998 (w/NYJ)		12	30	315	0	5	5	0	30
	3 Yr - TOTALS		41	126	1,390	0	9	9	4	58
12.	Williams	STL	8	11	102	0	3	3	2	20
	1999		13	25	233	0	6	6	0	36
	1998		8	15	144	0	1	1	0	6
	3 Yr - TOTALS		29	51	479	0	10	10	2	62
13.	Carswell	DEN	15	49	495	0	3	3	0	18
	1999		11	24	201	0	2	2	0	12
	1998		4	4	51	0	0	0	0	0
	3 Yr - TOTALS		30	77	747	0	5	5	0	30
14.	D. Clark	DEN	12	27	339	0	3	3	0	18
	1999		1	1	5	0	0	0	0	0
	1998		-	-	-	-	-	-	-	-
	3 Yr - TOTALS		13	28	344	0	3	3	0	18
15.	Dilger	IND	15	47	538	0	3	3	0	18
	1999		14	40	479	0	2	2	0	12
	1998		13	31	303	0	1	1	2	8
	3 Yr - TOTALS		42	118	1,320	0	6	6	2	38

2000 STATISTICAL RESULTS
(TIGHT ENDS — BASIC SCORING METHOD)

	NAME	TEAM	GP	REC	REC YARDS	RSH TDs	REC TDs	TOTAL TDs	CONV PTS	FANTASY PTS
16.	McWilliams	MIN	8	22	180	0	3	3	0	18
	1999 (w/ARI)		9	11	71	0	1	1	0	6
	1998 (w/ARI)		13	26	284	0	4	4	0	24
	3 Yr - TOTALS		30	59	535	0	8	8	0	48
17.	Da. Campbell +	NYG	8	8	46	0	3	3	0	18
	1999		-	-	-	-	-	-	-	-
	1998		-	-	-	-	-	-	-	-
	3 Yr - TOTALS		8	8	46	0	3	3	0	18
18.	Lewis	PHI	15	69	735	0	3	3	0	18
	1999		6	8	88	0	3	1	0	18
	1998		-	-	-	-	-	-	-	-
	3 Yr - TOTALS		21	77	823	0	6	4	0	36
19.	Bruener	PIT	13	17	192	0	3	3	0	18
	1999		10	18	176	0	0	0	0	0
	1998		9	19	157	0	2	2	0	12
	3 Yr - TOTALS		32	54	525	0	5	5	0	30
20.	Mili	SEA	12	28	288	0	3	3	0	18
	1999		5	5	28	0	1	1	0	6
	1998		1	1	20	0	0	0	0	0
	3 Yr - TOTALS		18	34	336	0	4	4	0	24
21.	Moore	TB	13	29	288	0	3	3	0	18
	1999		13	23	276	0	5	5	0	30
	1998		13	24	255	0	4	4	0	24
	3 Yr - TOTALS		39	76	819	0	12	12	0	72
22.	T. Davis	GB	9	19	177	0	2	2	2	14
	1999		11	20	204	0	2	2	0	12
	1998		10	18	250	0	7	7	0	42
	3 Yr - TOTALS		30	57	631	0	11	11	2	68
23.	Kelly	ATL	12	31	340	0	2	2	0	12
24.	Kozlowski	ATL	10	15	151	0	2	2	0	12
25.	Walls	CAR	8	31	422	0	2	2	0	12
26.	Shea +	CLE	13	30	302	0	2	2	0	12
27.	Sloan	DET	13	32	379	0	2	2	0	12
28.	Drayton	KC	7	8	70	0	2	2	0	12
29.	Bjornson	NE	8	20	152	0	2	2	0	12
30.	Wiggins **	NE	6	18	207	0	2	2	0	12
31.	Baxter	NYJ	3	4	22	0	2	2	0	12
32.	Becht +	NYJ	9	16	144	0	2	2	0	12
33.	Brigham	OAK	9	13	107	0	2	2	0	12
34.	Fauria	SEA	13	28	237	0	2	2	0	12
35.	G. Clark	SF	14	38	342	0	2	2	0	12
36.	Alexander	WAS	16	47	510	0	2	2	0	12
37.	Hardy	ARI	14	27	160	0	1	1	0	6
38.	Jackson	BUF	4	5	36	0	1	1	0	6
39.	Crawford	CAR	4	4	47	0	1	1	0	6
40.	Mangum	CAR	11	19	215	0	1	1	0	6
41.	Allred	CHI	5	9	109	0	1	1	0	6
42.	McGee	CIN	12	26	309	0	1	1	0	6
43.	M. Campbell	CLE	7	12	80	0	1	1	0	6
44.	LaFleur	DAL	7	12	109	0	1	1	0	6
45.	Chamberlain	DEN	9	22	283	0	1	1	0	6
46.	Rasby	DET	7	10	78	0	1	1	0	6
47.	Franks +	GB	14	34	363	0	1	1	0	6
48.	Goodwin	MIA	4	6	36	0	1	1	0	6
49.	J. Davis	MIN	9	17	202	0	1	1	0	6
50.	Rutledge	NE	6	15	103	0	1	1	0	6
51.	Hall	NO	4	5	33	0	1	1	0	6
52.	Mitchell	NYG	12	25	245	0	1	1	0	6
53.	Heiden	SD	5	6	32	0	1	1	0	6
54.	Kinney +	TEN	10	19	197	0	1	1	0	6

	NAME	TEAM	GP	REC	REC YARDS	RSH TDs	REC TDs	TOTAL TDs	CONV PTS	FANTASY PTS
55.	Coates	BAL	7	9	84	0	0	0	2	2
56.	Gedney	ARI	8	10	75	0	0	0	0	0
57.	Tant +	ARI	1	1	4	0	0	0	0	0
58.	Collins	BUF	4	6	72	0	0	0	0	0
59.	Kinchen	CAR	1	1	7	0	0	0	0	0
60.	Dragos	CHI	3	4	28	0	0	0	0	0
61.	Lyman +	CHI	1	1	4	0	0	0	0	0
62.	Mayes	CHI	3	4	40	0	0	0	0	0
63.	Sinceno	CHI	10	23	206	0	0	0	0	0
64.	Battaglia	CIN	10	13	105	0	0	0	0	0
65.	Bush	CIN	2	3	39	0	0	0	0	0
66.	Pupunu	DET	2	3	32	0	0	0	0	0
67.	Wetnight	GB	3	3	20	0	0	0	0	0
68.	D. Jones	JAC	1	1	12	0	0	0	0	0
69.	Dunn	KC	2	2	26	0	0	0	0	0
70.	Weaver	MIA	6	10	179	0	0	0	0	0
71.	Jordan	MIN	5	8	63	0	0	0	0	0
72.	Cross	NYG	4	4	30	0	0	0	0	0
73.	Broughton	PHI	7	12	104	0	0	0	0	0
74.	Cushing	PIT	3	4	17	0	0	0	0	0
75.	Geason	PIT	3	3	66	0	0	0	0	0
76.	R. Davis	SD	1	1	8	0	0	0	0	0
77.	Swift	SF	1	1	8	0	0	0	0	0
78.	Conwell	STL	6	5	40	0	0	0	0	0
79.	Robinson	STL	4	5	52	0	0	0	0	0
80.	Hape	TB	5	6	39	0	0	0	0	0
81.	Yoder	TB	1	1	1	0	0	0	0	0
82.	Flemister	WAS	1	1	8	0	0	0	0	0

+ DENOTES COLLEGE DRAFT PICKS
** Wiggins (NE) Played in 2 games with the New York Jets.

RATING THE PLAYERS FOR 2001
(Tight Ends—Basic Scoring Method)
GRAB ONE IF YOU CAN

☐ **1. Tony Gonzalez (Kansas City Chiefs)**
After scoring only two times on 59 receptions in 1998, Gonzalez has jumped to scoring 11 and 9 touchdowns the last two seasons, while grabbing 76 and 93 receptions respectively. Certainly approaching double-digit scoring is in order again in 2001.

☐ **2. Wesley Walls (Carolina Panthers)**
Walls had many fantasy fans excited heading into 2000, coming off a year when he scored 12 touchdowns on 63 receptions. He got off to a slow start scoring only twice in eight games before suffering a season-ending knee injury. The Panthers look forward to having him back as a scoring force again in 2001.

☐ **3. Shannon Sharpe (Baltimore Ravens)**
After scoring ten times in 1998, Sharpe failed to score in 1999 missing most of the year with a broken collarbone. Sharpe changed teams in 2000, coming to Baltimore, where, despite grabbing 67 receptions, he scored only five times. With the Ravens looking to pass more with Elvis Grbac aboard in 2001, look for Sharpe's touchdown numbers to rebound.

☐ **4. Jay Riesmersma (Buffalo Bills)**
A steady performer for Buffalo the last three seasons, Riemersma has recorded 25, 37 and 31 receptions respectively while tallying 6, 4 and 5 touchdowns. The five touchdowns in 2000 came despite missing five games to a knee injury. I look for 6-8 scores in 2001.

☐ **5. Fred Jones (San Diego Chargers)**
Perhaps the Chargers' most steady offensive performer the last three seasons, Jones has recorded 57, 56 and 71 receptions respectively. After scoring only three touchdowns in 1998 and two in 1999, Jones jumped to five scores in 2000. This number should grow in 2001 with the Chargers quarterbacking situation more in order.

BEST OF THE REST

☐ **6. Jackie Harris (Dallas Cowboys)**
The Cowboys brought Harris to Dallas in 2000 to help David LaFluer handle the tight end duties. Harris outplayed LaFluer in grabbing 39 receptions and five touchdowns and is looking for more in 2001.

☐ **7. Frank Wycheck (Tennessee Titans)**
Despite grabbing 63, 70, 69 and 70 receptions the last four seasons respectively, Wycheck has only scored 4, 2, 4 and 4 touchdowns over that same period. Anybody seeing the ball that often is always a threat to score a half a dozen times.

☐ **8. Cam Cleeland (New Orleans Saints)**
After busting into the NFL and scoring six times as a rookie in 1998, Cleeland has had injuries get the best of him. This included 2000 when a ruptured achilles cost him the entire season. The Saints hope to have him back pushing the 5–8 touchdown range in 2001, which he easily could with the Saints taking to the pass more.

☐ **9. Chad Lewis (Philadelphia Eagles)**
From eight receptions in 1999 to 69 receptions and three touchdowns in 2000, Lewis has stepped up his production and fantasy value in a hurry.

☐ **10. Kyle Brady (Jacksonville Jaguars)**
Brady had a disappointing first year with the Jaguars, as he recorded only one touchdown on 32 receptions in 1999. In 2000, Brady jumped to 64 receptions but scored only three times. We can see him being more involved in the offense, which should eventually turn into more scores.

STRONG LONG SHOTS

☐ **11. Dwayne Carswell (Denver Broncos)**
Carswell stepped up from 24 receptions and two touchdowns in 1999, to 49 receptions and three touchdowns in 2000. He should push these numbers in 2001, especially with Bryon Chamberlain out of the picture, departing to Minnesota in the offseason.

☐ **12. Greg Clark (San Francisco 49ers)**
His 38 receptions but only two touchdowns in 2000, I believe will go up in 2001, as Jeff Garcia continues to become more and more comfortable at the helm of the 49ers' offense.

☐ **13. Stephen Alexander (Washington Redskins)**
After scoring four times as a rookie in 1998 on 37 receptions, he dropped to only 29 receptions in 1999, scoring three times. In 2000, Alexander rebounded to 47 receptions but scored only twice. Looking to 2001, I look for increased touchdowns with Jeff George at quarterback. George helped boost Ricky Dudley's numbers when in Oakland.

☐ **14. Dave Moore (Tampa Bay Buccaneers)**
Over the last five seasons, Moore has recorded 27, 19, 24, 23 and 29 receptions respectively while scoring 3, 4, 4, 5 and 3 touchdowns. Numbers he could push now that Brad Johnson is aboard at quarterback.

☐ **15. Bubba Franks (Green Bay Packers)**
His 34 receptions but only one touchdown were disappointing numbers for the Packers' first-round draft pick of 2000. The Packers believe he'll push these numbers in his sophomore season.

HAVE THE POTENTIAL

☐ **16. Marcus Pollard (Indianapolis Colts)**
Sharing tight end duties with Ken Dilger, Pollard has recorded 24, 34 and 30 receptions and 4, 4 and 3 touchdowns respectively the last three seasons. A consistency to bear in mind for 2001.

☐ **17. Byron Chamberlain (Minnesota Vikings)**
Chamberlain caught 49 passes for 495 yards, while scoring three times for Denver in 2000. He brings his talent to the pass-happy Vikings in 2001.

☐ **18. David Sloan (Detroit Lions)**
Hampered by injuries most of his career, Sloan finally stayed healthy enough in 1999 to record 47 receptions and four touchdowns. In 2000, his numbers dropped off to 32 receptions and two scores. As long as he stays healthy, 4-6 touchdowns is possible.

☐ **19. Ken Dilger (Indianapolis Colts)**
Despite splitting tight end duties with Marcus Pollard the last three seasons, Dilger has grown his numbers steadily. Over that period, he has recorded 31, 40 and 44 receptions and scored 1, 2 and 3 touchdowns—a trend that should continue in 2001.

☐ **20. Ricky Dudley (Cleveland Browns)**
From nine touchdowns on 39 receptions in 1999, to four touchdowns on 29 receptions in 2000, Dudley saw his numbers take a quick tumble a year ago. Though he still looks attractive as a fantasy pick, he is no longer a Raider in 2001, he's a Cleveland Brown.

DON'T BE SURPRISED

21. Mitchell (DET)
22. Becht (NYJ)
23. Fauria (SEAT)
24. T. Davis (GB)
25. McGee (CIN)
26. Bruener (PITT)
27. D. Clark (DEN)
28. Shea (CLE)
29. Mili (SEAT)
30. Wiggins (NE)

YOU NEVER KNOW

31. Hardy (ARIZ)
32. Bjornson (OAK)
33. Kelly (ATL)
34. LaFluer (DALL)
35. Williams (OAK)
36. McWilliams (MINN)
37. Sinceno (CHI)
38. Brigham (OAK)
39. Glover (NO)
40. D. Campbell (NYG)

WORTH MENTIONING

41. Allred (CHI)
42. M. Campbell (CLE)
43. D. Jones (JAC)
44. Conwell (STL)
45. Thomason (PHIL)

ROOKIE PROSPECTS

NAME	TEAM	COMMENT
☐ 1. Todd Heap	BALT	Talented but will play behind Shannon Sharpe for now.
☐ 2. Alge Crumpler	ATL	Will push Reggie Kelly for work.

A LOOK AT THE QUARTERBACKS
(A Guide for the Beginner)
Considerations in Choosing a Quarterback

1. First, look at players' previous performances. Injuries, player movement, holdouts, and the like should be noted. Year-end performances by Kurt Warner, Brian Griese and Jeff Blake were all affected in 2000 by injury.

2. Quarterbacks who play for passing teams have the edge. Look for a quarterback with a high number of pass attempts, one who will assure you of at least 25 to 30 touchdown passes for the year. Jeff Garcia and Brett Favre are good prospects.

3. Look for a quarterback who doesn't mind running the ball, especially near the goal line. Because six points are awarded for a touchdown run and only three points for a touchdown pass, quarterbacks who like to rush for touchdowns are a plus. And if your quarterback is like Daunte Culpepper of the Vikings, who throws a lot of touchdowns and runs for several more, you've got yourself a great fantasy candidate.

4. Avoid situations in which the starting quarterback may change from week to week. Some teams use one quarterback one week, then switch the following week, depending on the player's performance. It would obviously hurt you if you didn't know whether your quarterback was going to play. That was the situation in Chicago and Cincinnati during 2000.

In the 2000 statistics, players are ranked by their fantasy-point totals. Remember that in the Basic Scoring Method, fantasy points are calculated by awarding six points for every rushing touchdown and three points for every touchdown pass thrown. No yardage statistics are included, because the Basic Scoring Method awards no points for yardage gained. It is not important how a player's team did, or how he ranks in any category except fantasy points. A player may have a poor passing percentage and may not throw for many yards, but if he ranks high in throwing and rushing touchdowns, he will help you win.

2000 STATISTICAL RESULTS
(QUARTERBACKS — BASIC SCORING METHOD)

NAME	TEAM	GP	RUSHES	PASS COMP	PASS ATTS	PASS PCT	RUSH TDs	TD PASS	CONV PTS	FANTASY POINTS
1. Culpepper	MIN	16	89	297	474	62.7	7	33	2	143
1999		1	3	0	0	0.0	0	0	0	0
1998		-	-	-	-	-	-	-	-	-
3-Yr Totals		17	92	297	474	62.7	7	33	2	143
2. Garcia	SF	16	72	355	561	63.3	4	31	1	118
1999		13	46	225	375	60.0	2	11	1	46
1998		-	-	-	-	-	-	-	-	-
3-Yr Totals		29	118	580	936	62.0	6	42	2	164
3. Gannon	OAK	16	89	284	473	60.0	4	28	2	110
1999		16	46	304	515	59.0	2	24	1	85
1998		12	44	206	354	58.2	3	10	0	48
3-Yr Totals		44	179	794	1,342	59.2	9	62	3	243
4. Manning	IND	16	37	357	571	62.5	1	33	1	106
1999		16	35	331	533	62.1	2	26	1	91
1998		16	15	326	575	56.7	0	26	3	81
3-Yr Totals		48	87	1014	1,679	60.4	3	85	5	278
5. McNabb	PHI	16	86	330	569	58.0	6	21	1	100
1999		11	47	106	216	49.1	0	8	3	27
1998		-	-	-	-	-	-	-	-	-
3-Yr Totals		27	133	436	785	55.5	6	29	4	127
6. Grbac	KC	15	30	326	547	59.6	1	28	0	90
1999		16	19	294	499	58.9	0	22	0	66
1998		8	7	98	188	52.1	0	5	0	15
3-Yr Totals		39	56	718	1,234	58.2	1	55	0	171
7. King	TB	16	73	233	428	54.4	5	18	2	86
1999		6	18	89	146	61.0	0	7	0	21
1998		-	-	-	-	-	-	-	-	-
3-Yr Totals		22	91	322	574	56.1	5	25	2	107
8. Stewart	PIT	15	78	151	289	52.2	7	11	0	75
1999		14	55	160	275	58.2	2	6	0	36
1998		16	81	252	458	55.0	2	11	1	46
3-Yr Totals		45	214	563	1,022	55.1	11	28	1	157
9. Brunell	JAC	16	48	311	512	60.7	2	20	1	73
1999		15	47	259	441	58.7	1	14	4	52
1998		13	49	208	354	58.8	0	20	1	61
3-Yr Totals		44	144	778	1,307	59.5	3	54	6	186
10. K. Collins	NYG	16	40	311	529	58.8	1	22	0	72
1999		10	19	191	332	57.5	2	8	2	38
1998		11	30	170	353	48.2	1	12	2	44
3-Yr Totals		37	89	672	1,214	55.4	4	42	4	154
11. Beuerlein	CAR	16	44	324	533	60.8	1	19	2	65
1999		16	27	343	571	60.1	2	36	0	120
1998		12	22	216	343	63.0	0	17	1	52
3-Yr Totals		44	93	883	1,447	61.0	3	72	3	237
12. Testaverde	NYJ	16	25	328	590	55.6	0	21	2	65
1999		1	0	10	15	66.7	0	1	0	3
1998		14	24	259	421	61.5	1	29	0	93
3-Yr Totals		31	49	597	1,026	58.2	1	51	2	161
13. Griese	DEN	10	28	216	336	64.3	1	19	1	64
1999		14	46	261	452	57.7	2	14	0	54
1998		1	4	1	3	33.3	0	0	0	0
3-Yr Totals		25	78	478	791	60.4	3	33	1	118
14. Warner	STL	11	18	235	347	67.7	0	21	1	64
1999		16	23	325	499	65.1	1	41	1	130
1998		1	0	4	11	36.4	0	0	0	0
3-Yr Totals		28	41	564	857	65.8	1	62	2	194
15. Bledsoe	NE	16	47	312	531	58.8	2	17	0	63
1999		16	42	305	539	56.6	0	19	0	57
1998		14	28	263	481	54.7	0	20	0	60
3-Yr Totals		46	117	880	1,551	56.7	2	56	0	180

2000 STATISTICAL RESULTS
(QUARTERBACKS — BASIC SCORING METHOD)

NAME	TEAM	GP	RUSHES	PASS COMP	PASS ATTS	PASS PCT	RUSH TDs	TD PASS	CONV PTS	FANTASY POINTS
16. Favre	GB	16	27	338	580	58.3	0	20	2	62
1999		16	28	341	595	57.3	0	22	1	67
1998		16	40	347	551	63.0	1	31	1	100
3-Yr Totals		48	95	1026	1,726	59.4	1	73	4	229
17. Kitna	SEA	15	47	259	418	62.0	1	18	0	60
1999		15	35	270	495	54.5	0	23	0	69
1998		6	20	98	172	57.0	1	7	0	27
3-Yr Totals		36	102	627	1,085	57.8	2	48	0	156
18. Green	STL	8	20	145	240	60.4	1	16	0	54
1999		-	-	-	-	-	-	-	-	-
1998 (w/WAS)		15	42	278	509	54.6	2	23	1	82
3-Yr Totals		23	62	423	749	56.5	3	39	1	136
19. Batch	DET	15	44	221	412	53.6	2	13	0	51
1999		11	29	151	270	55.9	2	13	1	52
1998		12	41	173	303	57.1	1	11	0	39
3-Yr Totals		38	114	545	985	55.3	5	37	1	142
20. Fiedler	MIA	14	54	204	357	57.1	1	14	0	48
1999 (w/JAC)		7	13	61	94	64.9	0	2	1	7
1998 (w/MIN)		5	4	3	7	42.9	0	0	0	0
3-Yr Totals		26	71	268	458	58.5	1	16	1	55
21. Blake	NO	11	57	184	302	60.9	1	13	0	45
1999 (w/CIN)		14	63	215	389	55.3	2	16	2	62
1998 (w/CIN)		8	15	51	93	54.8	0	3	0	9
3-Yr Totals		33	135	450	784	57.4	3	32	2	116
22. McNair	TEN	16	71	248	396	62.6	0	15	0	45
1999		11	72	187	331	56.5	8	12	1	85
1998		16	76	289	493	58.6	4	15	0	69
3-Yr Totals		43	219	724	1,220	59.3	12	42	1	199
23. R. Johnson	BUF	12	43	175	306	57.2	1	12	0	42
1999		2	8	25	34	73.5	0	2	0	6
1998		6	23	67	107	62.6	1	8	0	30
3-Yr Totals		20	74	267	447	59.7	2	22	0	78
24. McNown	CHI	10	50	154	280	55.0	3	8	0	42
1999		15	32	127	235	54.0	0	8	2	26
1998		-	-	-	-	-	-	-	-	-
3-Yr Totals		25	82	281	515	54.6	3	16	2	68
25. Plummer	ARI	14	37	270	475	56.8	0	13	0	39
1999		12	39	201	381	52.8	2	9	0	39
1998		16	51	324	547	59.2	4	17	0	75
3-Yr Totals		42	127	795	1,403	56.7	6	39	0	153
26. Brooks	NO	8	41	113	194	58.2	2	9	0	39
1999		-	-	-	-	-	-	-	-	-
1998		-	-	-	-	-	-	-	-	-
3-Yr Totals		8	41	113	194	58.2	2	9	0	39
27. B. Johnson	WAS	12	22	227	364	62.4	1	11	0	39
1999		16	27	316	519	60.9	2	24	1	85
1998 (w/MIN)		4	12	65	101	64.4	0	7	0	21
3-Yr Totals		32	61	608	984	61.8	3	42	1	145
28. Dilfer	BAL	9	20	134	226	59.3	0	12	0	36
29. Frerotte	DEN	9	22	138	232	59.5	1	9	0	33
30. Leaf	SD	11	28	161	322	50.0	0	11	0	33
31. Chandler	ATL	14	21	192	331	58.0	0	10	0	30
32. Flutie	BUF	11	36	132	231	57.1	1	8	0	30
33. Banks	BAL	11	19	150	274	54.7	0	8	1	25
34. Cunningham	DAL	6	23	74	125	59.2	1	6	1	25
35. Harbaugh	SD	7	16	123	202	60.9	0	8	0	24
36. Aikman	DAL	11	10	156	262	59.5	0	7	1	22
37. Couch	CLE	7	12	137	215	63.7	0	7	0	21
38. George	WAS	6	7	113	194	58.2	0	7	0	21
39. Mitchell	CIN	8	10	89	187	47.6	1	3	0	15

NAME	TEAM	GP	RUSHES	PASS COMP	PASS ATTS	PASS PCT	RUSH TDs	TD PASS	CONV PTS	FANTASY POINTS
40. Case	DET	5	16	56	91	61.5	1	1	1	10
41. Matthews	CHI	6	10	102	178	57.3	0	3	0	9
42. Smith	CIN	11	41	118	267	44.2	0	3	0	9
43. B. Huard	SEA	5	5	49	89	55.1	0	3	0	9
44. D. Brown	ARI	4	1	40	69	58.0	0	2	0	6
45. D. Johnson	ATL	4	3	36	67	53.7	0	2	0	6
46. Kanell	ATL	5	1	57	116	49.1	0	2	0	6
47. Pederson	CLE	10	18	117	210	55.7	0	2	0	6
48. Martin	JAC	5	7	22	33	66.7	0	2	0	6
49. O'Donnell	TEN	6	9	36	64	56.3	0	2	0	6
50. Mirer	SF	1	2	10	20	50.0	0	1	1	4
51. Greisen	ARI	2	1	6	10	60.0	0	1	0	3
52. Miller	CHI	3	7	47	82	57.3	0	1	0	3
53. Stoerner	DAL	1	0	4	6	66.7	0	1	0	3
54. Hasselbeck	GB	4	6	10	19	52.6	0	1	0	3
55. Moon	KC	2	2	15	34	44.1	0	1	0	3
56. D. Huard	MIA	3	0	39	63	61.9	0	1	0	3
57. Bishop	NE	7	6	3	9	33.3	0	1	0	3
58. Pennington +	NYJ	1	1	2	5	40.0	0	1	0	3
59. Graham	PIT	8	8	68	149	45.6	0	1	0	3
60. Redman	BAL	1	1	2	3	66.7	0	0	0	0
61. Van Pelt	BUF	1	0	4	8	50.0	0	0	0	0
62. Craig	CAR	4	2	0	0	0.0	0	0	0	0
63. Lewis	CAR	5	8	16	32	50.0	0	0	0	0
64. Hartsell	CHI	1	0	0	1	0.0	0	0	0	0
65. Thompson	CLE	1	1	1	1 1	0.0	0	0	0	0
66. Wynn +	CLE	7	3	22	54	40.7	0	0	0	0
67. Wright	DAL	4	12	22	53	41.5	0	0	0	0
68. Jackson +	DEN	2	1	0	1	0.0	0	0	0	0
69. Quinn	JAC	1	2	0	0	0.0	0	0	0	0
70. Brister	MIN	2	5	10	20	50.0	0	0	0	0
71. Brady +	NE	1	0	1	3	33.3	0	0	0	0
72. Friesz	NE	1	0	11	21	52.4	0	0	0	0
73. Garrett	NYG	2	4	0	0	0.0	0	0	0	0
74. Lucas	NYJ	5	6	21	41	51.2	0	0	0	0
75. Hoying	OAK	1	2	0	2	0.0	0	0	0	0
76. Detmer	PHI	2	1	0	1	0.0	0	0	0	0
77. Moreno	SD	6	5	27	53	50.9	0	0	0	0
78. T. Brown	SEA	1	0	0	1	0.0	0	0	0	0
79. Rattay +	SF	1	2	1	1 1	0.0	0	0	0	0
80. Hamilton +	TB	1	1	0	0	0.0	0	0	0	0
81. Zeier	TB	3	2	3	3 1	0.0	0	0	0	0
82. Husak +	WAS	1	1	2	2 1	0.0	0	0	0	0

+ DENOTES COLLEGE DRAFT PICKS

RATING THE PLAYERS FOR 2001
(Quarterbacks — Basic Scoring Method)
GRAB ONE IF YOU CAN

☐ **1. Daunte Culpepper (Minnesota Vikings)**
Many questioned head coach Denny Green when he elected to go with the young Culpepper in 2000. Thirty three touchdown passes and seven rushing touchdowns later there are far fewer questions.

☐ **2. Kurt Warner (St. Louis Rams)**
Warner likely wouldn't have equaled his 41 touchdown mark of 1999 but still would have likely thrown for 30 touchdowns had he not missed action with a finger injury. Warner threw for 21 touchdowns, missing five games in 2000 but should rebound in a big way in 2001.

☐ **3. Jeff Garcia (San Francisco 49ers)**
Garcia struggled on his relief role, filling in for the injured Steve Young in 1999 but came on in 2000 as the full-time starter to record 31 touchdown passes and four rushing scores. I look for another productive year offensively from Garcia and the 49ers' offense in 2001.

☐ **4. Peyton Manning (Indianapolis Colts)**
Three years in the league and his play and numbers continue to improve. Manning threw for 26 touchdowns in each of his first two seasons and climbed to 33 touchdown passes in 2000. He's not going to slow down.

☐ **5. Brian Griese (Denver Broncos)**
Had a shoulder injury not sidelined Griese six games in 2000, his 19 touchdown passes would have ballooned to 25-30. I believe he'll reach these numbers in 2001.

BEST OF THE REST

☐ **6. Brett Favre (Green Bay Packers)**
After recording five straight 30 plus touchdown seasons, Favre has recorded 22 and 20 touchdowns the last two seasons. I wouldn't, however, dismiss the possibility of him going over 25 touchdowns in 2001.

☐ **7. Rich Gannon (Oakland Raiders)**
Gannon has found himself a home in Oakland, and his 28 touchdown passes and four running scores are evidence that he's in command of the Raiders' offense. I look for another 25 plus touchdown passes and a number of running scores in 2001.

☐ **8. Donovan McNabb (Philadelphia Eagles)**
McNabb is coming on quickly. McNabb, taking over the full-time quarterbacking job in 2000, recorded 21 passing touchdowns and six rushing scores. He'll push these numbers in 2001 as he continues to improve.

☐ **9. Elvis Grbac (Baltimore Ravens)**
Grbac takes the 28 touchdown passes he threw a year ago for the Kansas City Chiefs to Baltimore to help open up the Ravens' offense in 2001.

☐ **10. Mark Brunell (Jacksonville Jaguars)**
Brunell finally stayed healthy an entire season in 2000 and recorded 20

touchdown passes and two more on the ground. Having talented receivers, perhaps this is the year Brunell pushes the 25 touchdown mark.

STRONG LONG SHOTS

☐ **11. Kerry Collins (New York Giants)**
With Kerry Collins at the helm, the Giants are no longer a run-first team. Collins threw for 22 touchdowns in 2000, and, with Amani Toomer and Ike Hilliard to look to again in 2001, continued solid touchdown numbers should follow.

☐ **12. Brad Johnson (Tampa Bay Buccaneers)**
Johnson comes to Tampa Bay to provide leadership and an ability to move the ball consistently through the air. This should make the Bucs' receiving crew, especially Keyshawn Johnson, very happy.

☐ **13. Jeff George (Washington Redskins)**
With Brad Johnson off to Tampa Bay, George takes over full-time in 2001. Though the Redskins like to run Stephen Davis often, George should put up decent touchdown numbers though there are questions in the Redskins' receivers corps.

☐ **14. Vinny Testaverde (New York Jets)**
With Keyshawn Johnson departed in 2000, Testaverde still managed 21 touchdown passes. Statistically Testaverde will continue to miss Keyshawn, but another 20-25 touchdowns is possible in 2001.

☐ **15. Drew Bledsoe (New England Patriots)**
From 28 touchdown passes in 1997, Bledsoe has seen his numbers steadily decline as he has recorded 20, 19 and 17 touchdowns the last three seasons. The Patriots, however, aren't too concerned, signing him to a 10-year, $103 million deal in the offseason which may trigger a rebound in 2001.

HAVE THE POTENTIAL

☐ **16. Trent Green (Kansas City Chiefs)**
Elvis Grbac threw 28 touchdowns for the Chiefs in 2000, and Trent Green will step in and fare well also, especially with Dick Vermeil running the ship.

☐ **17. Jeff Blake/Aaron Brooks (New Orleans Saints)**
A broken foot to Jeff Blake led to the emergence of Aaron Brooks in 2000, which leads to an interesting battle for 2001. Regardless of who is at the helm the Saints are no longer a run-only offense.

☐ **18. Rob Johnson (Buffalo Bills)**
With Doug Flutie off to San Diego and no longer hanging over his shoulder, Johnson should expand his numbers in 2001.

☐ **19. Kordell Stewart (Pittsburgh Steelers)**
Stewart showed signs of rebounding in 2000. Though he threw for only 11 touchdowns, he ran for seven, giving Steelers' and fantasy fans hope for 2001.

☐ **20. Chris Chandler (Atlanta Falcons)**
After throwing for 25 touchdowns in 1998, Chandler and the entire Falcons' offense has struggled. Looking to 2001, the Falcons have a fairly easy schedule and, a rebound could be in store.

KEEP AN EYE ON

☐ **21. Tony Banks (Dallas Cowboys)**
Troy Aikman is gone and Banks is the likely replacement. He has been known to be inconsistent, though he gets Joey Galloway and Rocket Ismail as targets.

☐ **22. Jeff Lewis (Carolina Panthers)**
Steve Beuerlein is gone, and Jeff Lewis is likely in as the starter. There are many questions that surround Lewis, but his receiving crew has plenty of possibilities.

☐ **23. Charlie Batch (Detroit Lions)**
The Lions seem more content to run more now that James Stewart is aboard.

☐ **24. Steve McNair (Tennessee Titans)**
Eddie George steals too much scoring glory.

☐ **25. Jake Plummer (Arizona Cardinals)**
Plenty of talent at wide receiver for the Cardinals, but Plummer continues to be a fantasy disappointment.

☐ **26. Doug Flutie (San Diego Chargers)**
Can anybody help this passing attack?

☐ **27. Matt Hasselbeck (Seattle Seahawks)**
The former Packers' backup gets his shot to start.

☐ **28. Jay Fiedler/Ray Lucas (Miami Dolphins)**
Fiedler threw only 14 touchdowns playing in 14 games in 2000, as the Dolphins enjoyed running Lamar Smith often. Fiedler may also face challenge of offseason acquisition Ray Lucas.

☐ **29. Tim Couch (Cleveland Browns)**
Couch threw seven touchdown passes in seven games prior to suffering a season-ending fractured right thumb in 2000. He threw for 15 touchdowns playing in 15 games as a rookie in 1999.

☐ **30. Cade McNown/Jim Miller/Shane Matthews (Chicago Bears)**
The Bears' wide receivers have trouble staying healthy, and McNown has thrown only eight touchdowns in each of his first two seasons. McNown also has Miller and Matthews always waiting in the event he struggles.

☐ **31. Jon Kitna/Akili Smith (Cincinnati Bengals)**
Good receiving talent but will either emerge?

ROOKIE PROSPECTS

NAME	TEAM	COMMENT
☐ 1. Michael Vick	ATL	Has bright future but will learn from Chris Chandler for now.
☐ 2. Drew Brees	SD	Will learn from veteran Doug Flutie for now.
☐ 3. Chris Weinke	CAR	At 28 Weinke has maturity to push Jeff Lewis for work.
☐ 4. Quincy Carter	DALL	Future hope for Dallas, it's Tony Banks for now.

A LOOK AT THE KICKERS

(A Guide for the Beginner)

Considerations in Choosing a Kicker

1. First, look at players' previous performances. Injuries, player movement, holdouts, and the like should be noted.

2. A kicker can't accumulate points without opportunities to score, so one of your main concerns is the team he's playing for. You're in good shape with a kicker from a strong offensive team that will get close enough for a lot of field-goal attempts. Even a good defensive team will provide its kicker with plenty of scoring opportunities. Mike Hollis continues to see his numbers climb as the Jaguars give him more and more scoring chances.

3. Consider a team's coaching philosophy. In Indianapolis, there's a tendency for the offense to move into field-goal range and let their kickers do their thing. Thus, they get more three-point attempts than a lot of other kickers.

4. A kicker who has played for the same team for a few years is a good bet. Kickers are treated as if they were a dime a dozen, so if one has been with a team for a few years, there must be some confidence that he will be consistent year after year.

5. Consider the opposition a kicker will face in 2001. Favor kickers who will face easy schedules, since this should result in more scoring opportunities. (See Section VI, "Rating the 2001 NFL Team Schedules.")

In the 2000 statistics that follow, players are ranked by their fantasy-point totals. Remember that in the Basic Scoring Method, the Performance Point Method, and the Combined Basic/Performance Scoring Method, fantasy points are calculated by awarding three points for each field goal and one point for each extra point.

2000 STATISTICAL RESULTS
(KICKERS — BASIC, & COMBINED
BASIC/PERFORMANCE SCORING METHODS)

	NAME	TEAM	GP	EXTRA POINTS	EXTRA PT ATT	ACC RATE	FG	FG ATT	ACC RATE	FANTASY POINTS
1.	Stover	BAL	16	30	30	1.000	35	39	.897	135
	1999		16	32	32	1.000	28	33	.848	116
	1998		16	24	24	1.000	21	28	.750	87
	3 Yr-TOTALS		48	86	86	1.000	84	100	1.190	338
2.	Longwell	GB	16	32	32	1.000	33	38	.868	131
	1999		16	38	38	1.000	25	30	.833	113
	1998		16	41	43	.953	29	33	.879	128
	3 Yr-TOTALS		48	111	113	.982	87	101	1.161	372
3.	Nedney **	CAR	15	24	24	1.000	34	38	.895	126
	1999 (w/OAK)		3	13	13	1.000	5	7	.714	28
	1998 (w/ARI)		12	30	30	1.000	13	19	.684	69
	3 Yr-TOTALS		30	67	67	1.000	52	64	1.231	223
4.	Gramatica	TB	16	42	42	1.000	28	34	.824	126
	1999		15	25	25	1.000	27	32	.844	106
	1998		-	-	-	-	-	-	-	-
	3 Yr-TOTALS		31	67	67	1.000	55	66	1.200	232
5.	Vanderjagt	IND	16	46	46	1.000	25	27	.926	121
	1999		16	43	43	1.000	34	38	.895	145
	1998		14	23	23	1.000	27	31	.871	104
	3 Yr-TOTALS		46	112	112	1.000	86	96	1.116	370
6.	Akers	PHI	16	34	36	.944	29	33	.879	121
	1999		5	2	2	1.000	3	5	.600	11
	1998 (w/WAS)		1	2	2	1.000	0	2	.000	2
	3 Yr-TOTALS		22	38	40	.950	32	40	1.250	134
7.	Del Greco	TEN	16	37	38	.974	27	33	.818	118
	1999		16	43	43	1.000	21	25	.840	106
	1998		16	28	28	1.000	36	39	.923	136
	3 Yr-TOTALS		48	108	109	.991	84	97	1.155	360
8.	Mare	MIA	16	33	34	.971	28	31	.903	117
	1999		16	27	27	1.000	39	46	.848	144
	1998		16	33	34	.971	22	27	.815	99
	3 Yr-TOTALS		48	93	95	.979	89	104	1.169	360
9.	Janikowski +	OAK	14	46	46	1.000	22	32	.688	112
	1999		-	-	-	-	-	-	-	-
	1998		-	-	-	-	-	-	-	-
	3 Yr-TOTALS		14	46	46	1.000	22	32	1.455	112
10.	G. Anderson	MIN	16	45	45	1.000	22	23	.957	111
	1999		16	46	46	1.000	19	30	.633	103
	1998		16	59	59	1.000	35	35	1.000	164
	3 Yr-TOTALS		48	150	150	1.000	76	88	1.158	378
11.	Christie	BUF	16	31	31	1.000	26	35	.743	109
	1999		16	33	33	1.000	25	34	.735	108
	1998		16	41	41	1.000	33	41	.805	140
	3 Yr-TOTALS		48	105	105	1.000	84	110	1.310	357
12.	Seder *	DAL	15	27	27	1.000	25	33	.758	108
	1999		-	-	-	-	-	-	-	-
	1998		-	-	-	-	-	-	-	-
	3 Yr-TOTALS		15	27	27	1.000	25	33	1.320	108
13.	Brown	PIT	16	32	33	.970	25	30	.833	107
	1999		16	30	31	.968	25	29	.862	105
	1998		-	-	-	-	-	-	-	-
	3 Yr-TOTALS		32	62	64	.969	50	59	1.180	212
14.	Vinatieri	NE	16	25	25	1.000	27	33	.818	106
	1999		16	29	30	.967	26	33	.788	107
	1998		16	32	32	1.000	31	39	.795	127
	3 Yr-TOTALS		48	86	87	.989	84	105	1.250	340
15.	Brien	NO	16	37	37	1.000	23	29	.793	106
	1999		15	20	21	.952	24	29	.828	92
	1998		15	31	31	1.000	20	22	.909	91
	3 Yr-TOTALS		46	88	89	.989	67	80	1.194	289

2000 STATISTICAL RESULTS
(KICKERS — BASIC, & COMBINED
BASIC/PERFORMANCE SCORING METHODS)

	NAME	TEAM	GP	EXTRA POINTS	EXTRA PT ATT	ACC RATE	FG	FG ATT	ACC RATE	FANTASY POINTS
16.	Hollis	JAC	12	33	33	1.000	24	26	.923	105
	1999		16	37	37	1.000	31	38	.816	130
	1998		16	45	45	1.000	21	26	.808	108
	3 Yr-TOTALS		44	115	115	1.000	76	90	1.184	343
17.	Elam	DEN	13	49	49	1.000	18	24	.750	103
	1999		16	29	29	1.000	29	36	.806	116
	1998		16	58	58	1.000	23	27	.852	127
	3 Yr-TOTALS		45	136	136	1.000	70	87	1.243	346
18.	Hanson	DET	15	29	29	1.000	24	30	.800	101
	1999		16	28	29	.966	26	32	.813	106
	1998		16	27	29	.931	29	33	.879	114
	3 Yr-TOTALS		47	84	87	.966	79	95	1.203	321
19.	Andersen	ATL	16	23	23	1.000	25	31	.806	98
	1999		16	34	34	1.000	15	21	.714	79
	1998		16	51	52	.981	23	28	.821	120
	3 Yr-TOTALS		48	108	109	.991	63	80	1.270	297
20.	Hall	NYJ	15	30	30	1.000	21	32	.656	93
	1999		16	27	29	.931	27	33	.818	108
	1998		16	45	46	.978	25	35	.714	120
	3 Yr-TOTALS		47	102	105	.971	73	100	1.370	321
21.	Wilkins	STL	11	38	38	1.000	17	17	1.000	89
	1999		16	64	64	1.000	20	28	.714	124
	1998		15	25	26	.962	20	26	.769	85
	3 Yr-TOTALS		42	127	128	.992	57	71	1.246	298
22.	Richey	SF	16	43	45	.956	15	22	.682	88
	1999		16	30	31	.968	21	23	.913	93
	1998		16	49	51	.961	18	27	.667	103
	3 Yr-TOTALS		48	122	127	.961	54	72	1.333	284
23.	Daluiso	NYG	13	34	34	1.000	17	23	.739	85
	1999		6	9	9	1.000	7	9	.778	30
	1998		16	32	32	1.000	21	27	.778	95
	3 Yr-TOTALS		35	75	75	1.000	45	59	1.311	210
24.	Edinger +	CHI	15	21	21	1.000	21	27	.778	84
	1999		-	-	-	-	-	-	-	-
	1998		-	-	-	-	-	-	-	-
	3 Yr-TOTALS		15	21	21	1.000	21	27	1.286	84
25.	Carney	SD	15	27	27	1.000	18	25	.720	81
	1999		15	22	23	.957	31	36	.861	115
	1998		15	19	19	1.000	26	30	.867	97
	3 Yr-TOTALS		45	68	69	.986	75	91	1.213	293
26.	Peterson	KC	11	25	25	1.000	15	20	.750	70
27.	Lindell	SEA	12	25	25	1.000	15	17	.882	70
28.	Blanchard	ARI	16	18	19	.947	16	23	.696	66
29.	Dawson	CLE	13	17	17	1.000	14	17	.824	59
30.	Rackers +	CIN	15	21	21	1.000	12	21	.571	57
31.	Heppner **	WAS	8	17	17	1.000	10	15	.667	47
32.	Stoyanovich	STL	8	26	26	1.000	5	8	.625	41
33.	Murray	WAS	6	7	8	.875	8	12	.667	31
34.	Conway **	NYJ	4	8	8	1.000	6	6	1.000	26
35.	Cunningham	CAR	4	9	9	1.000	5	7	.714	24
36.	Hall	STL	3	9	9	1.000	4	5	.800	21
37.	Lindsey	JAC	4	5	5	1.000	5	7	.714	20
38.	Husted	WAS	4	8	9	.889	4	8	.500	20
39.	Holmes	NYG	2	3	3	1.000	2	2	1.000	9
40.	Lechler	OAK	1	7	7	1.000	0	1	.000	7
41.	Bentley	WAS	1	0	0	.000	1	1	1.000	3

+	DENOTES COLLEGE DRAFT PICKS		
*	Seder	(DAL)	Scored TD on a 1 yard run.
**	Nedney	(CAR)	Played in 3 games with Denver and 2 games with Oakland.
**	Heppner	(WAS)	Played in 4 games with Seattle.
**	Conway	(NYJ)	Played in 1 game with Oakland and 2 games with Washington.

RATING THE PLAYERS FOR 2001
(Kickers — Basic and Combined Basic/Performance Scoring Methods)

GRAB ONE IF YOU CAN

☐ **1. Ryan Longwell (Green Bay Packers)**
The Packers stalled a bit more often in the red zone in 2000, which meant eight more field goal tries in 2000 for Longwell. His 33 of 38 (.868) field goal performance shows that, if the Packers get him there, he'll come through.

☐ **2. Mike Vanderjadt (Indianapolis Colts)**
Vanderjadt dropped over 20 points overall in 2000 but still hit a very accurate 25 of 27 (.926) field goal tries. The talented Colts just have to keep getting him more scoring chances.

☐ **3. Martin Gramatica (Tampa Bay Buccaneers)**
The Buccaneers' offense and defense improved to give Gramatica 17 more extra point attempts and two more field goal tries in 2000 over the previous year. With Brad Johnson now at quarterback, the scoring chances should be even better in 2001.

☐ **4. Jeff Wilkins (St. Louis Rams)**
Wilkins missed five games to a pulled quad muscle in 2000. He did hit all 17 field goal tries in the 11 games he did play. Healthy in 2001, he should put up good numbers, kicking for the high-powered Rams.

☐ **5. Matt Stover (Baltimore Ravens)**
Stover hit 35 of 39 (.897) field goal tries in 2000, as he led the league in scoring. In 2001, with Elvis Grbac aboard, I believe his field goal chances will go down and his extra point chances will climb as the Ravens will become more efficient in the red zone.

BEST OF THE REST

☐ **6. Jason Elam (Denver Broncos)**
Elam hit 18 of 24 (.750) field goal attempts in 2000, missing three games to a back injury. Healthy in 2001, I see Elam climb back to healthier numbers.

☐ **7. Joe Nedney (Tennessee Titans)**
Nedney, who kicked for both Denver and Carolina in 2000 as a replacement for Jason Elam and John Kasay, hit an impressive 34 of 38 (.895) field goal tries. Now he gets his chance in Tennessee, which is sure to provide him plenty of scoring chances in 2001.

☐ **8. David Akers (Philadelphia Eagles)**
The Eagles settled on David Akers in 2000, and he didn't disappoint them, hitting 29 of 33 (.879) field goal attempts. With the Eagles facing the second easiest schedule in 2001, Akers should have another productive fantasy season.

☐ **9. Sebastian Janikowski (Oakland Raiders)**
As the Raiders' first-round draft choice of 2000, Janikowski struggled, hitting only 22 of 32 (.688) field goal attempts and missing two games with a bacterial infection in his foot. His 2001 season should be better.

☐ **10. Gary Anderson (Minnesota Vikings)**
After struggling in 1999, hitting only 19 of 30 (.633) field goals, Anderson returned to his accurate ways in 2000, hitting 22 of 23 (.957) attempts. My biggest concern, however, is that Anderson and the Vikings face the league's toughest schedule in 2001.

STRONG LONG SHOTS

☐ **11. John Kasay (Carolina Panthers)**
Kasay returns after missing the last three games of 1999 and the entire 2000 season with a severe knee injury. The Panthers just hope Kasay, always one of the league's most consistent kickers, is the same player he was prior to the injury.

☐ **12. Olindo Mare (Miami Dolphins)**
His accuracy improved to an impressive 28 of 31 (.903) field goal tries in 2000, but Mare had 15 fewer field goal tries. The Dolphins face the sixth most difficult schedule in 2001, so I'm not sure his overall numbers can improve, although I expect he'll still fare well.

☐ **13. Mike Hollis (Jacksonville Jaguars)**
Hollis improved his accuracy over the last three seasons, including 24 of 26 (.923) on his field goal tries of 2000. The Jaguars just need to get him scoring chances as they did in 1999, when he hit 31 of 38 (.816) attempts.

☐ **14. Steve Christie (Buffalo Bills)**
Christie has not had impressive accuracy numbers in the last two seasons, including hitting only 26 of 35 (.743) field goals in 2000, but his 34 of 35 extra point attempts seem to be enough to keep his overall scoring numbers in the 110 point range.

☐ **15. Jason Hanson (Detroit Lions)**
For four straight seasons, Hanson has hit over 80 percent of his field goal attempts, but his scoring numbers have progressively gone down, as he has recorded 117, 114, 106, and 101 points over that period.

HAVE THE POTENTIAL

☐ **16. Adam Vinatieri/Owen Pochman (New England Patriots)**
Vinatieri has scored a consistent 107 and 106 points the last two seasons, while hitting also a very consistent 26 of 33 (.788) and 27 of 33 (.818) field goal tries. Similar numbers are expected in 2001, though Vinatieri faces the challenge of rookie Owen Pochman.

☐ **17. Kris Brown (Pittsburgh Steelers)**
Brown is another kicker who has recorded consistent numbers over the last two seasons, hitting 25 of 29 (.862) for 105 points in 1999 and 25 of 30 (.833) field goal attempts for 107 points in 2000.

☐ **18. Brett Conway (Washington Redskins)**
Conway should get a good shot at decent numbers as the Redskins face the league's easiest schedule.

☐ **19. ????? (New Orleans Saints)**
Doug Brien is gone but whoever steps in here to kick for the improved Saints will get their share of scoring chances.

☐ **20. ????? (San Francisco 49ers)**
Wade Richey—and his woeful 15 of 22 (.682) on field goal tries in 2000—is gone. New 49ers' kickers should get their chances. At press time, only free agent Jamie Rheem had been signed.

KEEP AN EYE ON

☐ **21. Morten Andersen/Jake Arians (Atlanta Falcons)**
The last two seasons Morten Andersen has scored 79 and 98 points as the Falcons' offense struggled. Are the Falcons any better in 2001?

☐ **22. Tim Seder (Dallas Cowboys)**
How bad will life be without Troy Aikman? The Cowboys still have plenty of weapons on offense.

☐ **23. Todd Peterson (Kansas City Chiefs)**
How will the Chiefs do without Elvis Grbac?

☐ **24. Brad Daluiso/Jon Markam (New York Giants)**
Missing three games to an ailing back in 2000, Daluiso hit 17 of 23 (.739) field goals on his way to 85 points. He faces a challenge from rookie Jon Markam and a fairly tough schedule in 2001, which will make pushing good numbers difficult.

☐ **25. Cary Blanchard/Bill Gramatica (Arizona Cardinals)**
For a kicker, scoring 66 points over a 16-game schedule is scary, which is what Blanchard did in 2000. Rookie Bill Gramatica to challenge in 2001.

☐ **26. Jeff Hall/Brett Conway (New York Jets)**
A miserable 21 of 32 (.656) on field goal tries in 2000 and a difficult schedule in 2001 makes me leery of Hall. Will Brett Conway step in as he did late in 2000?

☐ **27. Wade Richey (San Diego Chargers)**
Can Doug Flutie help this offense?

☐ **28. Rian Lindell (Seattle Seahawks)**
A team in transition with a new, young, inexperienced quarterback.

☐ **29. Phil Dawson (Cleveland Browns)**
This team is still finding its way.

☐ **30. Paul Edinger (Chicago Bears)**
The Bears continue to struggle as do their scoring chances.

☐ **31. Neil Rackers/Ritchie Cunningham (Cincinnati Bengals)**
Have the Bengals got anything figured out other than Corey Dillon? Rackers's 12 of 21 (.571) on field goal attempts in 2000 is also a concern, which is why Ritchie Cunningham was brought in over the off-season.

A 2001 QUICK PICKS—MOCK DRAFT

(My Top "30" Overall Picks for the Basic Scoring method)

NAME	TEAM	POS	COMMENTS
1. Faulk	STL	RB	NFL record 26 TDs playing in just 14 games in 2000.
2. James	IND	RB	Has scored 17 & 18 times in first two NFL seasons.
3. Culpepper	MINN	QB	Can put up scoring numbers through the air and on the ground.
4. Warner	STL	QB	Injury slowed numbers in 2000 after posting 41 TDs in 1999.
5. Taylor	JAC	RB	If healthy all season, likely to top 15 touchdowns.
6. S. Davis	WASH	RB	Dropped to 11 TDs in 2000, after scoring 17 in 1999, looking for rebound.
7. George	TENN	RB	Has scored 13 and 16 times last two seasons.
8. Garcia	SF	QB	Quickly improved numbers as 49ers' full-time starter in 2000.
9. Manning	IND	QB	Tied for NFL lead with 33 TDs in 2000.
10. T. Davis	DEN	TB	If can stay healthy big TD numbers will return.
11. Moss	MINN	WR	Always capable of 15 touchdown range.
12. Williams	NO	RB	Scored nine times in just ten games before injury in 2000.
13. Owens	SF	WR	QB improving as should Owens's TD numbers.
14. Green	GB	RB	Stole show and likely job from Levens in 2000 with 13 TDs.
15. Griese	DEN	QB	19 TDs playing in just ten games before inury in 2000.
16. Harrison	IND	WR	As Manning's favorite target, plenty TDs to come.
17. Smith	MIA	RB	Surprised many with 16 TD performance in 2000.
18. Favre	GB	QB	Looking to rebound touchdown numbers in 2000.
19. Bruce	STL	WR	When stays healthy is among league's best.
20. Stewart	DET	RB	Steady performer as Lions' "main" back.
21. Carter	MINN	WR	Still can get it done, especially as scorer.
22. Gannon	OAK	QB	Has found fit with Raiders.
23. McNabb	PHIL	QB	Quickly has become one of league's best double-threat QBs.
24. Martin	NYJ	RB	Very capable of solid TD numbers as Jets' most consistent weapon.
25. Wheatley	OAK	RB	???s now that Garner has been brought aboard.
26. Freeman	GB	WR	Very capable of 12-touchdown range.
27. Anderson	ATL	RB	Will continue to improve from injured knee.
28. Lewis	BALT	RB	Showed huge potential to score as rookie in 2000.
29. Watters	SEAT	RB	Scored 9, 7 and 9 times last three seasons.
30. Grbac	BALT	QB	28 TDs as Chief's signal caller in 2000.

This Mock Draft is expanded and updated in *Cliff's Quick Picks: Fantasy Football Draft at a Glance*—a huge 8-panel cheatsheet that examines the top-100 overall picks for the Basic and Combined Basic/Performance methods. Potential fantasy draft picks are also broken down by fantasy position, including the *top-50* running backs and wide receivers, and the *top-25* tight ends, quarterbacks and kickers. *Cliff's Quick Picks* will be available in mid-August and updated weekly, right around your fantasy draft time. Be sure to order! Details and order form, along with a toll-free phone number, and website address appear on the hard insert in the middle of this book.

IX
RATING THE PLAYERS: COMBINED BASIC/PERFORMANCE SCORING METHOD

As the game of fantasy football progressed, leagues began incorporating more player statistics into their scoring. A popular way of doing this was to combine the Basic Scoring and Performance Point methods. I decided to add such a combined method to my book. In several sections, I will evaluate and rate players' performances based on a combination of these two scoring methods. This means that a player will be awarded points both for scoring touchdowns and for the yardage he earns.

Combining the two methods may seem simple when you think of running backs like Edgerrin James, Marshall Faulk or Jamal Anderson, who score with frequency and also accumulate a lot of yardage. But how about someone like Marcus Allen, who rushed for only 764 yards in 1993 but scored 15 times? Where does a player like this fit in? How about Curtis Duncan? Duncan had 954 receiving yards in 1992, on 82 receptions, but scored only once. Or how about Ki-Jana Carter, who rushed for only 264 yards in 1996 but scored nine times? And Karim Abdul-Jabbar who rushed for only 892 yards in 1997 but scored 16 times, or Leroy Hoard, who rushed for only 479 yards in 1998 but scored 10 times. Combining the two methods really adds a twist to the game.

In the following pages, I'm going to help you plan your basic drafting strategy. Then I'll follow with some things to keep in mind when choosing players from each position. Next, I'll offer a look at the players' 2000 statistical results. And, finally, I'll rate the players for the 2001 season. No rookies are included in my player ratings. It's too early to size up how rookies will fit into each team's scheme, so I rate them separately, in Section V of this chapter. I will, however, incorporate the rookies in my Quick Picks/Fantasy Draft At a Glance Cheatsheet which comes out in mid-August. This is a more appropriate time to assess how rookies are fitting into their NFL offenses.

Combined Basic/Performance Scoring Method
DRAFTING STRATEGY BY ROUNDS
(A Guide for the Beginner)

1. The draft consists of 12 rounds.

2. Of the 12 players, seven are starters and five are reserves.

3. The starting seven comprise:

1 Quarterback		1 Quarterback
2 Running Backs	OR	2 Running Backs
2 Wide Receivers	FLEX OPTION	3 Receivers
1 Tight End		1 Kicker
1 Kicker		

4. The five reserves can be from any position.

5. Any player from any starting position can be drafted in any round.

ROUND 1: This method makes drafting very interesting, especially in the early rounds. In 1992 Steve Young's 3,465 passing yards, 25 passing touchdowns, 540 rushing yards, and four rushing touchdowns led all scorers, totaling 314 points. In 1993 Young easily did it again, this time totaling 327 points. In fact, both Young and John Elway outscored the closest non-quarterback, Jerry Rice. The gap was even bigger in 1994, when three quarterbacks—Steve Young (366 points), Brett Favre (314 points), and Dan Marino (314 points)—outscored the first non-quarterback, Emmitt Smith (303 points). In 1995 it was a bit closer, as quarterback Brett Favre produced 357 points but running back Emmitt Smith was right behind with 351. In 1996 the quarterbacks again were dominant with six signal-callers outscoring Emmitt Smith, the top running back. In 1997 only Kordell Stewart (314 points) and Brett Favre (311 points) outdistanced running back Barry Sanders's 306 points. In 1998, Steve Young's 391 points was just ahead of Terrell Davis's 344. In 2000, quarterback Daunte Culpepper edged out running back Marshall Faulk with 370 points to Faulk's 365, but Faulk missed two games.

ROUND 2: By the end of the second round, especially if your league has 12 or more franchises, you should try to have both a quarterback with high scoring potential and either a good rushing-receiving back or a very good wide receiver.

ROUND 3: If, for some reason, you decide not to choose a quarterback and running back in the first two rounds, it's almost essential to have both by the end of this round. If you already do have one of each, it's probably time to grab the best non-quarterback available. That means running backs or wide receivers who will be in the 1,000-yard range and who have the potential to score 10 or more times.

ROUNDS 4 and 5: These rounds should be used to fill out your backfield. You should have a quarterback, two running backs, and hopefully both wide receivers by now.

ROUNDS 6 through 9: Up to this point in the draft, because of their low point totals, tight ends and kickers have not been a priority. To fill out your starting lineup, you can select these players in the next four rounds.

ROUNDS 10 through 12: Don't think these final rounds aren't important. You need to draft high-quality backups in case your starters get injured. Also, take a stab at a rookie or two. One might turn out to be a big fantasy player.

A LOOK AT THE RUNNING BACKS

(A Guide for the Beginner)

Considerations in Choosing a Running Back

1. First, look at players' previous performances. Don't overlook players who may have missed portions of the previous year because of injuries, holdouts, and the like. Dorsey Levens, Ricky Williams and Terrell Davis all missed significant time in 2000 because of injuries.

2. Find the running backs who consistently gain 1,500 to 2,000 rushing yards in a season, and who have the potential to cross the goal line 15 times. Edgerrin James should top your list, along with Marshall Faulk.

3. Since players tend to earn more points from their yardage (performance points) than from their touchdowns (basic points), choose running backs who carry the ball often and accumulate a lot of yards.

4. Running backs who score lots of short-yardage touchdowns but who don't rush for many yards are *not* good early round picks.

In the 2000 statistics that follow, you'll find the players ranked by their fantasy-point totals. Remember that in the Combined Basic/Performance Scoring Method, fantasy points are calculated by adding up the following: six points for every touchdown scored, three points for every touchdown thrown, one point for every 10 yards rushing, one point for every 10 yards receiving, and one point for every 20 yards passing.

2000 STATISTICAL RESULTS
(RUNNING BACKS — COMBINED BASIC/PERFORMANCE SCORING METHOD)

NAME	TEAM	GP	RSH TDs	REC TDs	TOTAL TDs	BASIC PTS	RSH YARDS	REC YARDS	TOTAL YARDS	PERF PTS	CONV PTS	FAN-TASY PTS
1. M. Faulk	STL	14	18	8	26	160	1,359	830	2,189	205	4	365
1999		16	7	5	12	74	1,381	1,048	2,429	227	2	301
1998		16	6	4	10	60	1,319	908	2,227	208	0	268
3 Yr - TOTALS		46	31	17	48	294	4,059	2786	6,845	640	6	934
2. James	IND	16	13	5	18	110	1,709	594	2,303	215	2	325
1999		16	13	4	17	102	1,553	586	2,139	202	0	304
1998		-	-	-	-	-	-	-	-	-	-	-
3 Yr - TOTALS		32	26	9	35	212	3,262	1180	4,442	417	2	629
3. George	TEN	16	14	2	16	96	1,509	453	1,962	184	0	280
1999		16	9	4	13	78	1,304	458	1,762	163	0	241
1998		16	5	1	6	38	1,294	310	1,604	148	2	186
3 Yr - TOTALS		48	28	7	35	212	4,107	1221	5,328	495	2	707
4. M. Anderson +	DEN	14	15	0	15	92	1,500	169	1,669	156	2	248
1999		-	-	-	-	-	-	-	-	-	-	-
1998		-	-	-	-	-	-	-	-	-	-	-
3 Yr - TOTALS		14	15	0	15	92	1,500	169	1,669	156	2	248
5. Taylor	JAC	13	12	2	14	84	1,399	240	1,639	153	0	237
1999		10	6	0	6	36	732	83	815	75	0	111
1998		15	14	3	17	102	1,223	421	1,644	153	0	255
3 Yr - TOTALS		38	32	5	37	222	3,354	744	4,098	381	0	603
6. Green	GB	16	10	3	13	78	1,175	559	1,734	158	0	236
1999 (w/SEA)		8	0	0	0	0	120	0	120	10	0	10
1998 (w/SEA)		9	1	0	1	6	209	2	211	19	0	25
3 Yr - TOTALS		33	11	3	14	84	1,504	561	2,065	187	0	271
7. R. Smith	MIN	16	7	3	10	60	1,521	348	1,869	174	0	234
1999		13	2	0	2	12	1,015	166	1,181	106	0	118
1998		14	6	2	8	48	1,187	291	1,478	135	0	183
3 Yr - TOTALS		43	15	5	20	120	3,723	805	4,528	415	0	535
8. Cu. Martin	NYJ	16	9	2	11	66	1,207	508	1,715	161	0	227
1999		16	5	0	5	30	1,464	259	1,723	157	0	187
1998		15	8	1	9	54	1,287	365	1,652	153	0	207
3 Yr - TOTALS		47	22	3	25	150	3,958	1132	5,090	471	0	621
9. Garner	SF	16	7	3	10	60	1,142	647	1,789	163	0	223
1999		16	4	2	6	36	1,229	535	1,764	162	0	198
1998 (w/PHI)		10	4	0	4	24	381	110	491	41	0	65
3 Yr - TOTALS		42	15	5	20	120	2,752	1292	4,044	366	0	486
10. Watters	SEA	16	7	2	9	54	1,242	613	1,855	169	0	223
1999		16	5	2	7	42	1,210	387	1,597	146	0	188
1998		16	9	0	9	56	1,239	373	1,612	148	2	204
3 Yr - TOTALS		48	21	4	25	152	3,691	1373	5,064	463	2	615
11. S. Davis	WAS	15	11	0	11	66	1,318	313	1,631	151	0	217
1999		14	17	0	17	104	1,405	111	1,516	142	2	246
1998		13	0	2	2	12	109	263	372	31	0	43
3 Yr - TOTALS		42	28	2	30	182	2,832	687	3,519	324	2	506
12. L. Smith	MIA	15	14	2	16	96	1,139	201	1,340	121	0	217
1999 (w/NO)		13	0	1	1	6	205	151	356	27	0	33
1998 (w/NO)		14	1	2	3	18	457	249	706	66	0	84
3 Yr - TOTALS		42	15	5	20	120	1,801	601	2,402	214	0	334
13. Barber	NYG	16	8	1	9	54	1,006	719	1,725	160	0	214
1999		15	0	2	3	18	258	609	867	75	0	93
1998		16	0	3	3	18	166	348	514	42	0	60
3 Yr - TOTALS		47	8	6	15	90	1,430	1676	3,106	277	0	367
14. Stewart	DET	16	10	1	11	72	1,184	287	1,471	136	6	208
1999 (w/JAC)		14	13	0	13	78	931	108	1,039	95	0	173
1998 (w/JAC)		3	2	1	3	18	217	42	259	25	0	43
3 Yr - TOTALS		33	25	2	27	168	2,332	437	2,769	256	6	424
15. Dunn	TB	16	8	1	9	54	1,133	422	1,555	142	0	196
1999		15	0	2	2	12	616	589	1,205	107	0	119
1998		16	2	0	2	12	1,026	344	1,370	123	0	135
3 Yr - TOTALS		47	10	3	13	78	2,775	1355	4,130	372	0	450

2000 STATISTICAL RESULTS
(RUNNING BACKS — COMBINED BASIC/PERFORMANCE SCORING METHOD)

NAME	TEAM	GP	RSH TDs	REC TDs	TOTAL TDs	BASIC PTS	RSH YARDS	REC YARDS	TOTAL YARDS	PERF PTS	CONV PTS	FAN-TASY PTS
16. Ja. Lewis +	BAL	16	6	0	6	38	1,364	296	1,660	153	2	191
1999		-	-	-	-	-	-	-	-	-	-	-
1998		-	-	-	-	-	-	-	-	-	-	-
3 Yr - TOTALS		16	6	0	6	38	1,364	296	1,660	153	2	191
17. Dillon	CIN	16	7	0	7	42	1,435	158	1,593	145	0	187
1999		15	5	1	6	36	1,200	290	1,490	138	0	174
1998		15	4	1	5	30	1,130	178	1,308	118	0	148
3 Yr - TOTALS		46	16	2	18	108	3,765	626	4,391	401	0	509
18. R. Williams	NO	10	8	1	9	54	1,000	409	1,409	132	0	186
1999		12	2	0	2	12	884	172	1,056	98	0	110
1998		-	-	-	-	-	-	-	-	-	-	-
3 Yr - TOTALS		22	10	1	11	66	1,884	581	2,465	230	0	296
19. Bettis	PIT	16	8	0	8	48	1,341	108	1,449	135	0	183
1999		16	7	0	7	42	1,091	110	1,201	111	0	153
1998		15	3	0	3	18	1,185	90	1,275	116	0	134
3 Yr - TOTALS		47	18	0	18	108	3,617	308	3,925	362	0	470
20. E. Smith	DAL	16	9	0	9	54	1,203	79	1,282	120	0	174
1999		15	11	2	13	78	1,397	119	1,516	142	0	220
1998		16	13	2	15	90	1,332	175	1,507	139	0	229
3 Yr - TOTALS		47	33	4	37	222	3,932	373	4,305	401	0	623
21. Wheatley	OAK	14	9	1	10	60	1,046	156	1,202	109	0	169
1999		16	8	3	11	66	936	196	1,132	102	0	168
1998 (w/NYG)		4	0	0	0	0	52	0	52	3	0	3
3 Yr - TOTALS		34	17	4	21	126	2,034	352	2,386	214	0	340
22. J. Anderson	ATL	16	6	0	6	38	1,024	382	1,406	126	2	164
1999		2	0	0	0	0	59	34	93	8	0	8
1998		16	14	2	16	98	1,846	319	2,165	201	2	299
3 Yr - TOTALS		34	20	2	22	136	2,929	735	3,664	335	4	471
23. Pittman	ARI	16	4	2	6	36	719	579	1,298	117	0	153
1999		10	2	0	2	12	289	196	485	43	0	55
1998		6	0	0	0	0	91	0	91	6	0	6
3 Yr - TOTALS		32	6	2	8	48	1,099	775	1,874	166	0	214
24. J. Allen	CHI	16	2	1	3	18	1,120	291	1,411	128	0	146
1999		8	0	0	0	0	119	91	210	18	0	18
1998		5	1	1	2	12	270	77	347	32	0	44
3 Yr - TOTALS		29	3	2	5	30	1,509	459	1,968	178	0	208
25. Richardson	KC	16	3	3	6	36	697	468	1,165	104	0	140
1999		16	1	0	1	6	387	141	528	40	0	46
1998		10	2	0	2	12	45	13	58	3	0	15
3 Yr - TOTALS		42	6	3	9	54	1,129	622	1,751	147	0	201
26. K. Faulk	NE	15	4	1	5	32	570	465	1,035	94	2	126
1999		11	1	1	2	12	227	98	325	25	0	37
1998		-	-	-	-	-	-	-	-	-	-	-
3 Yr - TOTALS		26	5	2	7	44	797	563	1,360	119	2	163
27. Biakabutuka	CAR	12	2	2	4	24	627	341	968	88	0	112
1999		11	6	0	6	36	718	189	907	83	0	119
1998		7	3	1	4	24	427	138	565	52	0	76
3 Yr - TOTALS		30	11	3	14	84	1,772	668	2,440	223	0	307
28. Prentice +	CLE	15	7	1	8	48	512	191	703	57	0	105
1999		-	-	-	-	-	-	-	-	-	-	-
1998		-	-	-	-	-	-	-	-	-	-	-
3 Yr - TOTALS		15	7	1	8	48	512	191	703	57	0	105
29. Dayne +	NYG	16	5	0	5	30	770	11	781	71	0	101
1999		-	-	-	-	-	-	-	-	-	-	-
1998		-	-	-	-	-	-	-	-	-	-	-
3 Yr - TOTALS		16	5	0	5	30	770	11	781	71	0	101
30. R. Anderson	NYJ	16	0	2	2	12	63	853	916	80	0	92
1999		16	0	3	3	18	84	302	386	27	0	45
1998		4	0	0	0	0	2	12	14	0	0	0
3 Yr - TOTALS		36	0	5	5	30	149	1167	1,316	107	0	137

2000 STATISTICAL RESULTS
(RUNNING BACKS — COMBINED BASIC/PERFORMANCE SCORING METHOD)

	NAME	TEAM	GP	RSH TDs	REC TDs	TOTAL TDs	BASIC PTS	RSH YARDS	REC YARDS	TOTAL YARDS	PERF PTS	CONV PTS	FAN-TASY PTS
31.	Bryson	BUF	16	0	2	2	14	591	271	862	77	2	91
32.	Fletcher	SD	15	3	1	4	24	384	355	739	63	0	87
33.	Morris +	BUF	12	5	1	6	36	341	268	609	51	0	87
34.	Holmes	BAL	16	2	0	2	12	588	221	809	70	0	82
35.	Centers	WAS	15	0	3	3	18	103	600	703	62	0	80
36.	Alstott	TB	13	5	0	5	30	465	93	558	47	0	77
37.	Autry	PHI	10	3	1	4	24	334	275	609	53	0	77
38.	Jordan	OAK	13	3	1	4	24	213	299	512	43	0	67
39.	Warren **	PHI	12	2	1	3	18	296	303	599	49	0	67
40.	Redmond +	NE	11	1	2	3	18	406	126	532	45	0	63
41.	Beasley	SF	15	3	3	6	36	147	233	380	26	0	62
42.	Jones +	ARI	14	2	0	2	12	373	208	581	47	0	59
43.	Kaufman	OAK	14	0	1	1	6	499	127	626	51	0	57
44.	Staley	PHI	5	1	0	1	6	344	201	545	51	0	57
45.	B. Bennett	CIN	15	3	0	3	18	324	168	492	38	0	56
46.	Crockett	OAK	11	7	0	7	42	130	62	192	14	0	56
47.	A. Smith	BUF	10	4	0	4	24	354	20	374	31	0	55
48.	Br. Mitchell *	PHI	14	2	1	5	30	187	89	276	21	0	51
49.	Levens	GB	5	3	0	3	18	224	146	370	32	0	50
50.	Watson	STL	9	4	0	4	24	249	56	305	26	0	50
51.	Fazande	SD	11	2	0	2	12	368	104	472	37	0	49
52.	Anders	KC	12	2	0	2	12	331	76	407	35	0	47
53.	Huntley	PIT	12	3	0	3	20	215	91	306	26	2	46
54.	Alexander +	SEA	16	2	0	2	12	313	41	354	28	0	40
55.	Hoover	CAR	11	1	0	1	6	290	112	402	33	0	39
56.	Pritchett	PHI	13	1	0	1	6	225	193	418	33	0	39
57.	T. Davis	DEN	5	2	0	2	12	282	4	286	26	0	38
58.	Moreau +	KC	10	4	0	4	24	179	0	179	12	0	36
59.	Holcombe	STL	13	3	1	4	24	70	90	160	10	0	34
60.	T. Allen	NO	4	2	0	2	14	179	7	186	17	2	31
61.	Rhett	CLE	5	0	0	0	0	258	78	336	31	0	31
62.	Hetherington	CAR	10	2	1	3	18	65	116	181	12	0	30
63.	Ma. Bates	DET	12	2	0	2	12	127	109	236	17	0	29
64.	Fuamatu-Ma'afala	PIT	6	1	0	1	6	149	107	256	22	0	28
65.	Morton +	NO	14	0	0	0	0	136	213	349	28	0	28
66.	Ayanbadejo	BAL	8	1	1	2	12	37	168	205	14	0	26
67.	Henderson	GB	14	0	1	1	6	16	234	250	20	0	26
68.	Christian	ATL	16	0	0	0	0	19	315	334	25	0	25
69.	Comella	NYG	15	0	0	0	0	45	274	319	25	0	25
70.	J. Johnson	MIA	8	1	0	1	6	168	61	229	19	0	25
71.	T. Thomas	MIA	9	0	1	1	6	136	117	253	19	0	25
72.	Chancey	SD	3	2	0	2	12	141	6	147	12	0	24
73.	Parmalee	NYJ	4	2	0	2	12	87	66	153	12	0	24
74.	A. Johnson	JAC	10	1	0	1	6	112	153	265	17	0	23
75.	Carter	NE	15	2	0	2	12	90	73	163	10	0	22
76.	Coleman	DEN	7	1	0	1	6	183	5	188	16	0	22
77.	W. Floyd	CAR	10	1	1	2	12	33	114	147	10	0	22
78.	Ce. Martin	PHI	14	0	0	0	0	77	219	296	22	0	22
79.	Rb. Thomas	DAL	12	0	2	2	12	51	117	168	9	0	21
80.	McCrary	SD	13	0	2	2	12	8	141	149	8	0	20
81.	Moore	NO	5	1	0	1	6	156	0	156	14	0	20
82.	Rd. Thomas	TEN	12	0	1	1	6	175	35	210	14	0	20
83.	Edwards	CLE	12	0	2	2	12	9	128	137	7	0	19
84.	Mack	JAC	13	1	0	1	6	145	0	145	13	0	19
85.	White	CLE	10	0	0	0	0	145	100	245	19	0	19
86.	Jackson	SF	7	1	1	2	14	6	48	54	4	2	18
87.	Wiley +	DAL	8	0	1	1	6	88	72	160	12	0	18
88.	Denson	MIA	9	0	0	0	0	108	105	213	17	0	17
89.	Enis	CHI	10	1	0	1	6	84	68	152	11	0	17
90.	Griffith	DEN	12	0	2	2	12	4	101	105	5	0	17

2000 STATISTICAL RESULTS
(RUNNING BACKS — COMBINED BASIC/PERFORMANCE SCORING METHOD)

	NAME	TEAM	GP	RSH TDs	REC TDs	TOTAL TDs	BASIC PTS	RSH YARDS	REC YARDS	TOTAL YARDS	PERF PTS	CONV PTS	FAN-TASY PTS
91.	Sellers	WAS	7	0	2	2	12	2	78	80	5	0	17
92.	Linton	BUF	6	0	1	1	6	112	8	120	9	0	15
93.	Hicks	WAS	6	1	0	1	6	78	43	121	8	0	14
94.	Ritchie	OAK	11	0	0	0	0	0	173	173	14	0	14
95.	T. Smith +	NO	12	0	0	0	0	131	65	196	14	0	14
96.	Strong	SEA	13	0	1	1	6	9	136	145	8	0	14
97.	Cloud	KC	6	1	0	1	6	84	16	100	7	0	13
98.	Howard	JAC	2	1	0	1	6	52	26	78	6	0	12
99.	Neal	TEN	7	0	2	2	12	-2	31	29	0	0	12
100.	Murrell	WAS	9	0	0	0	0	50	93	143	11	0	11
101.	Irvin	DET	5	0	0	0	0	49	90	139	10	0	10
102.	Mi. Bates *	CAR	5	0	0	1	6	13	38	51	3	0	9
104.	Parker	GB	8	0	0	0	0	85	50	135	9	0	9
105.	P. Smith	SF	8	0	0	0	0	72	55	127	9	0	9
106.	Stith +	JAC	7	1	0	1	6	55	0	55	3	0	9
107.	D. Bennett	KC	6	1	0	1	6	24	17	41	2	0	8
108.	Kleinsasser	MIN	11	0	0	0	0	43	98	141	8	0	8
109.	Milne	NO	3	0	1	1	6	1	33	34	2	0	8
110.	Sowell	NYJ	6	0	0	0	0	0	84	84	8	0	8
111.	M. Williams	MIN	11	0	0	0	2	67	31	98	6	2	8
112.	N. Williams	CIN	9	0	0	0	0	54	84	138	8	0	8
113.	Barnes	CHI	6	0	0	0	0	81	7	88	7	0	7
114.	Gash	BAL	5	0	1	1	6	2	30	32	1	0	7
115.	Konrad	MIA	9	0	0	0	0	39	83	122	7	0	7
116.	Abdullah	TB	4	0	0	0	0	70	14	84	6	0	6
117.	Finn	IND	5	0	1	1	6	1	13	14	0	0	6
118.	Jenkins *	SD	5	0	0	1	6	6	1	7	0	0	6
119.	Kirby	OAK	1	0	0	0	0	51	19	70	6	0	6
120.	Montgomery	NYG	1	1	0	1	6	4	0	4	0	0	6
121.	Rogers *	SEA	5	0	0	1	6	0	0	0	0	0	6
122.	T. Smith	DEN	1	0	1	1	6	0	1	1	0	0	6
123.	M. Smith	ATL	5	0	0	0	0	69	5	74	6	0	6
124.	Kreider	PIT	5	0	0	0	0	24	42	66	5	0	5
125.	Harris **	NE	3	0	0	0	0	36	20	56	4	0	4
126.	McAfee	NO	2	0	0	0	0	37	0	37	4	0	4
127.	Pass +	NE	4	0	0	0	0	58	17	75	4	0	4
128.	Groce	CIN	6	0	0	0	0	-2	45	43	3	0	3
129.	Olivo	DET	3	0	0	0	0	0	50	50	3	0	3
130.	Shelton	JAC	6	0	0	0	0	3	48	51	3	0	3
131.	Stecker	TB	5	0	0	0	0	31	15	46	3	0	3
132.	Bynum	SD	2	0	0	0	0	26	13	39	2	0	2
133.	C. Floyd	NE	2	0	0	0	0	-1	21	20	2	0	2
134.	Hambrick	DAL	1	0	0	0	0	28	0	28	2	0	2
135.	Lee	PHI	2	0	0	0	0	2	20	22	2	0	2
136.	Rivers	ATL	2	0	0	0	0	27	0	27	2	0	2
137.	Saleh	CLE	1	0	0	0	0	0	22	22	2	0	2
138.	Schlesinger	DET	11	0	0	0	0	3	73	76	2	0	2
139.	Witman	PIT	3	0	0	0	0	5	33	38	2	0	2
140.	Dyer +	MIA	1	0	0	0	0	0	14	14	1	0	1
141.	Gordon	IND	2	0	0	0	0	13	0	13	1	0	1
142.	Keaton +	CIN	3	0	0	0	0	24	0	24	1	0	1
143.	Roan	TEN	1	0	0	0	0	0	12	12	1	0	1
144.	Shaw	NE	4	0	0	0	0	12	11	23	1	0	1
145.	Abdul-Jabbar	IND	1	0	0	0	0	-2	0	-2	0	0	0
146.	Brown	SEA	2	0	0	0	0	6	9	15	0	0	0
147.	Canidate +	STL	2	0	0	0	0	6	4	10	0	0	0
148.	Dukes	JAC	1	0	0	0	0	2	0	2	0	0	0
149.	Goodman	GB	3	0	0	0	0	-2	0	-2	0	0	0
150.	Hodgins	STL	3	0	0	0	0	3	5	8	0	0	0

2000 STATISTICAL RESULTS
(RUNNING BACKS — COMBINED BASIC/PERFORMANCE
SCORING METHOD)

	NAME	TEAM	GP	RSH TDs	REC TDs	TOTAL TDs	BASIC PTS	RSH YARDS	REC YARDS	TOTAL YARDS	PERF PTS	CONV PTS	FAN-TASY PTS
151.	Jo. Lewis +	SF	1	0	0	0	0	6	0	6	0	0	0
152.	Makovicka	ARI	6	0	0	0	0	8	18	26	0	0	0
153.	McKinley	ARI	2	0	0	0	0	0	13	13	0	0	0
154.	Ba. Mitchell	GB	1	0	0	0	0	8	0	8	0	0	0
155.	Morrow	MIN	1	0	0	0	0	0	2	2	0	0	0
156.	Palmer	MIN	1	0	0	0	0	0	-2	-2	0	0	0
157.	J. Williams	JAC	1	0	0	0	0	8	0	8	0	0	0
158.	Zereoue	PIT	2	0	0	0	0	14	0	14	0	0	0

+   DENOTES COLLEGE DRAFT PICKS

*	Br. Mitchell	(PHI)	Scored TD's on a 89 yard kickoff return and a 72 yard punt return.
*	Mi. Bates	(CAR)	Scored TD on a 92 yard kickoff return.
*	Jenkins	(SD)	Scored TD on a 93 yard kickoff return.
*	Rogers	(SEA)	Scored TD on a 81 yard kickoff return.
**	Warren	(PHI)	Played in 11 games with Dallas.
**	Harris	(NE)	Played in 2 games with Denver.

RATING THE PLAYERS FOR 2001
(Running Backs — Combined Basic/Performance Scoring Method)
GRAB ONE IF YOU CAN

☐ **1. Edgerrin James (Indianapolis Colts)**
Just two years in the league but already among the elite, James has topped the 2,000-yard mark in both of his seasons and scored 17 and 18 touchdowns respectively. As a primary weapon for the Colts on the ground and through the air, I see another 2,000 plus yards and 15-20 touchdowns in 2001.

☐ **2. Marshall Faulk (St. Louis Rams)**
Faulk left the Indianapolis Colts in 1998, after recording 2,227 rushing-receiving yards and ten touchdowns. He's continued his success since joining the Rams, including an impressive 2,189 rushing-receiving yards and an NFL record 26 touchdowns despite missing two games in 2000. His impressive production will continue in 2001.

☐ **3. Eddie George (Tennessee Titans)**
Always posting strong yardage numbers, George has posted strong scoring numbers as well the last two seasons. Over the last two years, George recorded 1,762 and 1,962 rushing-receiving yards respectively, while scoring 13 and 16 times. These are surely numbers he'll again push in 2001.

☐ **4. Fred Taylor (Jacksonville Jaguars)**
As a rookie in 1998, Taylor recorded 1,744 rushing-receiving yards and 17 touchdowns. He's been battling injuries since, though he finished with 1,639 yards and 13 touchdowns despite missing three games to injury in 2000. If he can stay healthy, big yardage and scoring numbers are in store again in 2001.

☐ **5. Stephen Davis (Washington Redskins)**
After recording 1,516 rushing-receiving yards and 17 touchdowns in a breakout year in 1999, Davis saw his production drop in 2000. His 1,631 yards and 11 touchdowns were still good, but I believe he'll push his production in 2001 under new head coach Marty Schottenheimer.

BEST OF THE REST

☐ **6. Terrell Davis (Denver Broncos)**
A string of knee, ankle and leg injuries have kept Davis out of the spotlight the last two seasons. Looking back to 1998 when he recorded an astounding 2,008 rushing yards, 25 receptions for 217 yards and 23 touchdowns, we get a feel for what he can do when healthy. He is expected to be 100 percent in 2001, though Olandis Gary and Mike Anderson will be as well.

☐ **7. Ricky Williams (New Orleans Saints)**
Out to prove himself after struggling through injuries as a rookie, Ricky Williams was well on his way to doing so, until an ankle injury ended his season after ten games in 2000. His 1,409 rushing-receiving yards and nine touchdowns in those ten games give us an idea of where he could go over 16 games in 2001, though rookie first-round pick Deuce McAllister may become a factor.

☐ **8. Ahman Green (Green Bay Packers)**
Green stepped in for the injured Dorsey Levens in 2000 to become a huge surprise, recording 1,734 rushing-receiving yards and 13 touchdowns. This performance has fantasy fans excited for his 2001 potential, though Dorsey Levens's healthy return may stand in the way.

☐ **9. Curtis Martin (New York Jets)**
Always a consistent yardage producer, Martin finally topped the double-digit scoring mark in 2000, scoring 11 times. I look for another 1,600-1,800 yard, ten plus touchdown season in 2001, for the Jets' most consistent offensive weapon.

☐ **10. James Stewart (Detroit Lions)**
Coming to Detroit from Jacksonville in 2000, Stewart did just what the Lions had hoped in recording 1,471 rushing-receiving yards and scoring 11 times. As the Lions feature back, Stewart can likely approach or top the 1,500 yard mark and 10-14 touchdown range in 2001.

STRONG LONG SHOTS

☐ **11. Lamar Smith (Miami Dolphins)**
Smith was a nice surprise for the Dolphins, who have had trouble in finding a consistent ground game in recent years. Smith recorded 1,340 rushing-receiving yards and 16 touchdowns in 2000. The Dolphins will continue to make good use of Smith's ability in 2001, nearing the 1,500 yard, 12-15 touchdown range.

☐ **12. Corey Dillon (Cincinnati Bengals)**
One of the league's most consistent runners, Dillon has rushed and received for 1,308, 1,490 and 1,593 yards over the past three seasons respectively, during which time his touchdown production has steadily grown, recording 5, 6 and 7 scores over that same period.

☐ **13. Jamal Lewis (Baltimore Ravens)**
Lewis recorded an impressive 1,660 rushing-receiving yards as a rookie in 2000 but produced only six touchdowns. I look for both his yardage and touchdown numbers to grow in 2001.

☐ **14. Tyrone Wheatley (Oakland Raiders)**
Coming to the Raiders in 1999, Wheatley surprised many by recording 1,132 rushing-receiving yards and 11 touchdowns. Missing two games to injury in 2000, Wheatley recorded 1,202 yards and ten touchdowns. If healthy all year, Wheatley should top the 1,000-yard, 12-touchdown mark in 2001, though new acquisition Charlie Garner may have something to say about that.

☐ **15. Jamal Anderson (Atlanta Falcons)**
After missing most of the 1999 season with a knee injury, Anderson returned to record 1,406 rushing-receiving yards and six touchdowns in 2000. He's not quite back to the form that produced 2,165 rushing-receiving yards and 16 touchdowns in 1998 before the injury but he's working at it.

☐ **16. Emmitt Smith (Dallas Cowboys)**
Smith's 1,449 rushing-receiving yards and nine touchdowns were down from his two previous years but the talent and determination are still there to hold his fantasy value in 2001.

☐ **17. Warrick Dunn (Tampa Bay Buccaneers)**
Becoming more of the focus of the offense in 2000, Dunn recorded 1,555 rushing-receiving yards and scored nine times. He is set to continue to take on more of the load in 2001, but Mike Alstott is still likely to steal some of the scoring glory.

☐ **18. Jerome Bettis (Pittsburgh Steelers)**
Bettis jumped from 1,201 rushing-receiving yards in 1999 to 1,449 in 2000 and scored eight times as compared to seven the year before. The Steelers rewarded Bettis with a 6-year deal in the offseason, leading me to believe he'll push those numbers in 2001.

☐ **19. Tiki Barber (New York Giants)**
It wasn't rookie first-round pick Ron Dayne who excited Giants' and fantasy fans in 2000, it was Tiki Barber. Barber recorded 1,725 rushing-receiving yards and nine touchdowns, numbers he's never neared in the past and I don't believe he'll match in the future, because I think durability will become an issue.

☐ **20. Ricky Watters (Seattle Seahawks)**
Despite the Seahawks making Shawn Alexander their #1 draft pick in 2000, Ricky Watters remained the feature back to the tune of 1,855 rushing-receiving yards and nine touchdowns. Looking to 2001, however, Alexander is expected to step up, which means Watters may be playing elsewhere.

HAVE THE POTENTIAL

☐ **21. Priest Holmes (Kansas City Chiefs)**
Hurt much of the last two seasons, Holmes got his chance at a starting spot in Kansas City.

☐ **22. Duce Staley (Philadelphia Eagles)**
A year after producing 1,273 rushing yards, 41 receptions for 294 more yards and six touchdowns in 1999, Staley missed the majority of the 2000 season with a foot injury. The Eagles are uncertain about how healthy Staley will be come the 2001 season.

☐ **23. James Allen (Chicago Bears)**
After struggling for three seasons to make a success out of 1998 first-round draft pick, Curtis Enis, the Bears have finally given James Allen his chance. Allen's 1,411 rushing-receiving yards and three touchdowns in 2000 are just a glimpse of what may lie ahead in 2001, though he faces a challenge from rookie second-round pick Anthony Thomas.

☐ **24. Tim Biakabatuka (Carolina Panthers)**
He certainly has plenty of potential for yards and scores, but injuries seem to always stand in the way. In 2000, Biakabatuka missed four games to turf toe, which limited him to 968 rushing-receiving yards and four touchdowns. A year earlier, he missed five games to injury and recorded 907 rushing-receiving yards and six touchdowns.

☐ **25. Michael Pittman (Arizona Cardinals)**
Thomas Jones was the Cardinals' first-round draft pick in 2000, but Michael Pittman hung on as the team's feature back most of the year. Pittman's 1,298 rushing-receiving yards and six touchdowns of 2000 are

numbers he could surpass in 2001, if he holds off the challenge from Jones.

SOLID SLEEPERS

☐ **26. Charlie Garner (Oakland Raiders)**
Garner, for the second straight season since coming to the 49ers, topped the 1,700 rushing-receiving yard mark in 2000 and upped his touchdown production from 6 in 1999 to 10 in 2000. Now with Oakland, he'll be competing with Tyrone Wheatley for work.

☐ **27. Errict Rhett (Cleveland Browns)**
Coming over from Baltimore in 2000, Rhett was expected to be the mainstay of the Browns' running attack. A foot injury ended Rhett's season after just five games, as rookie third-round pick Travis Prentise stepped in. How Rhett and Prentise will be used by the Browns is the key to their statistical success in 2001.

☐ **28. J. R. Redmond (New England Patriots)**
The Patriots hope their third-round pick of a year ago can be more of a factor in 2001 and push harder to keep the starting job.

☐ **29. Sammy Morris (Buffalo Bills)**
Until the Bills figure out their running back derby it's hard to rate anyone very high. Morris, who produced 609 rushing-receiving yards and six touchdowns as a rookie in 2000 is certainly one of the candidates, which also include Antowain Smith, Shawn Bryson and Jonathan Linton.

☐ **30. Travis Prentise (Cleveland Browns)**
He had 703 rushing-receiving yards and eight touchdowns as a rookie in 2000, but a healthy return of Errict Rhett leaves uncertainty.

KEEP AN EYE ON

☐ **31. Shaun Alexander (Seattle Seahawks)**
The Seahawks' first-round draft choice of a year ago took a backseat to veteran Ricky Watters in 2000, but if Watters departs and Alexander becomes the feature back in 2001, his fantasy stock will climb quickly.

☐ **32. Antowain Smith (Buffalo Bills)**
Though he's struggled in recent years, Smith had a 147-yard, three-touchdown performance to close out the 2000 season, which has him back in the hunt.

☐ **33. Thomas Jones (Arizona Cardinals)**
Jones, the Cardinals' first-round pick of a year ago, was pretty much a bust as a rookie and must unseat Michael Pittman to gain any fantasy attention in 2001.

☐ **34. Dorsey Levens (Green Bay Packers)**
Knee and ankle injuries sidelined Levens most of 2000. In his absence, Ahman Green stepped in to have a big year, which may cost Levens in the future trying to win back his starting job.

☐ **35. Garrison Hearst (San Francisco 49ers)**
Hearst has missed the last two seasons recovering from a leg injury. There is a chance he'll return in 2001, and if he does and he's healthy his fantasy stock will take a huge jump.

☐ **36. Kevin Faulk (New England Patriots)**
Not really thought to be an every-down back, Faulk is filling the role the best he can, recording 1,035 rushing-receiving yards and five touchdowns in 2000. Last year's third-round pick, J.R. Redmond, is expected to push Faulk in 2001.

☐ **37. Shawn Bryson (Buffalo Bills)**
Another Bills' back looking for more work. Bryson recorded 862 rushing-receiving yards and two touchdowns in 2000.

☐ **38. Olandis Gary (Denver Broncos)**
Gary returns after missing virtually the entire 2000 season with a knee injury. His 2001 success will depend on the health of Terrell Davis.

☐ **39. Mike Anderson (Denver Broncos)**
Despite 1,669 rushing-receiving yards and 15 touchdowns in 2000, Anderson faces the healthy returns of Terrell Davis and Olandis Gary.

☐ **40. Terrell Fletcher (San Diego Chargers)**
Fletcher likely resumes his third-down role now that rookie La Dainian Tomlinson is aboard.

PRIME PROSPECTS

☐ **41. Darnell Autry (Philadelphia Eagles)**
Autry's potential and production will depend on the health of Duce Staley.

☐ **42. Mike Alstott (Tampa Bay Buccaneers)**
Warrick Dunn is taking over more of the backfield load, which is certain to cost Alstott statistically.

☐ **43. Paul Davis (San Francisco 49ers)**
May become more of a factor in his second year.

☐ **44. Richard Huntley (Pittsburgh Steelers)**
Huntley showed some potential in 1999, producing 820 rushing-receiving yards and eight touchdowns, but didn't show much in 2000. His 2001 potential likely depends on Jerome Bettis's health.

☐ **45. Chris Warren (Philadelphia Eagles)**
His production will depend on healthy return of Duce Staley.

☐ **46. Tony Richardson (Kansas City Chiefs)**
Richardson will be pushed for work by offseason acquisition Priest Holmes.

☐ **47. Jonathan Linton (Buffalo Bills)**
One of a cluster of Bills' running backs pushing for work.

☐ **48. Zack Crockett (Oakland Raiders)**
Crockett didn't have many yards, but he did score seven times in 2000.

☐ **49. Frank Moreau (Kansas City Chiefs)**
Another back new head coach Dick Vermeil will look at in 2001.

☐ **50. Fred Beasley (San Francisco 49ers)**
The 49ers' fullback is not likely to produce big yardage numbers but 6-8 touchdowns are possible, though Paul Davis may push for work.

DON'T BE SURPRISED

51. Autry (PHIL)
52. Hoover (CAR)
53. Fuamatu-Ma'afala (PITT)
54. Cloud (KC)
55. Canidate (STL)
56. M. Williams (MINN)
57. R. Anderson (NYJ)
58. Edwards (NE)
59. Montgomery (NYG)
60. Hambrich (DALL)

YOU NEVER KNOW

61. J. J. Johnson (MIA)
62. Henderson (GB)
63. Pritchett (PHIL)
64. Murrell (WASH)
65. Denson (MIA)
66. Br. Bennett (CIN)
67. Wiley (DALL)
68. Hicks (WASH)
69. Watson (STL)
70. Edwards (NE)

WORTH MENTIONING

71. Chapman (MINN)
72. Strong (SEAT)
73. Irvin (DET)
74. Parker (GB)
75. Christian (ATL)

ROOKIE PROSPECTS

NAME	TEAM	COMMENT
☐ 1. Michael Bennett	MINN	Answer to Robert Smith's departure.
☐ 2. La Dainian Tomlinson	SD	The Chargers have found themselves talented back to carry the load.
☐ 3. Anthony Thomas	CHI	Will be pushing James Allen.
☐ 4. Kevan Barlow	SF	Nice, all-round back to push for 49ers starting job.
☐ 5. Travis Henry	BUF	Too many players battling for job.
☐ 6. Deuce McAllister	NO	What is Ricky Williams—chopped liver?
☐ 7. Lamont Jordan	NYJ	Future for Jets behind Curtis Martin.
☐ 8. Heath Evans	SEAT	Strong, fullback type.
☐ 9. James Jackson	CLE	Will battle for work with Browns.
☐10. Correll Buckhalter	PHIL	If Duce Staley isn't ready, has a shot.

A LOOK AT THE WIDE RECEIVERS

(A Guide for the Beginner)

Considerations in Choosing a Wide Receiver

1. First, look at players' previous performances. Don't overlook players who may have missed portions of the previous year because of injuries, holdouts, and the like. Injuries hurt the year-end numbers of Marcus Robinson, Qadry Ismail and Joey Galloway in 2000.

2. Grab the wideouts who are both consistent yardage gainers and consistent scorers. You want wide receivers who get you around 1,500 receiving yards and 12 to 15 touchdowns. Randy Moss could top your list, followed by Marvin Harrison and Terrell Owens.

3. Favor wide receivers who consistently top the 1,000-yard mark, even if their touchdown totals tend to be fairly low. Tim Brown is a good example.

4. If you're in search of a wideout in the later rounds, take a yardage man first. Jimmy Smith of Jacksonville is not a consistent scorer but is a very consistent 1,100–1,300 yard man.

In the 2000 statistics that follow, players are ranked by their fantasy point totals. Remember that the Combined Basic/Performance Scoring Method awards six points for every touchdown scored, three points for every touchdown pass thrown, one point for every 10 yards rushing, one point for every 10 yards receiving, and one point for every 20 yards passing.

2000 STATISTICAL RESULTS
(WIDE RECEIVERS — COMBINED BASIC/PERFORMANCE SCORING METHOD)

	NAME	TEAM	GP	RSH TDs	REC TDs	TOTAL TDs	BASIC PTS	RSH YARDS	REC YARDS	TOTAL YARDS	PERF PTS	CONV PTS	FAN-TASY PTS
1.	Moss	MIN	16	0	15	15	92	5	1,437	1,442	136	2	228
	1999		16	0	11	12	72	43	1,413	1,456	142	0	214
	1998		16	0	17	17	106	4	1,313	1,317	124	4	230
	3 Yr-TOTALS		48	0	43	44	270	52	4,163	4,215	402	6	672
2.	Owens	SF	14	0	13	13	80	11	1,451	1,462	138	2	218
	1999		14	0	4	4	24	0	754	754	70	0	94
	1998		16	1	14	15	92	53	1,097	1,150	108	2	200
	3 Yr-TOTALS		44	1	31	32	196	64	3,302	3,366	316	4	512
3.	Harrison	IND	16	0	14	14	84	0	1,413	1,413	133	0	217
	1999		16	0	12	12	74	4	1,663	1,667	159	2	233
	1998		12	0	7	7	44	0	776	776	71	2	115
	3 Yr-TOTALS		44	0	33	33	202	4	3,852	3,856	363	4	565
4.	R. Smith	DEN	16	1	8	9	54	99	1,602	1,701	162	0	216
	1999		14	0	4	4	24	0	1,020	1,020	96	0	120
	1998		16	1	6	7	42	63	1,222	1,285	119	0	161
	3 Yr-TOTALS		46	2	18	20	120	162	3,844	4,006	377	0	497
5.	Alexander	KC	16	0	10	10	60	45	1,391	1,436	133	0	193
	1999		15	1	2	3	18	82	832	914	85	0	103
	1998		14	0	4	4	24	0	992	992	93	0	117
	3 Yr-TOTALS		45	1	16	17	102	127	3,215	3,342	311	0	413
6.	Bruce	STL	16	0	9	9	54	11	1,471	1,482	139	0	193
	1999		15	0	12	12	74	32	1,165	1,197	112	2	186
	1998		4	0	1	1	6	30	457	487	48	0	54
	3 Yr-TOTALS		35	0	22	22	134	73	3,093	3,166	299	2	433
7.	Holt	STL	16	0	6	6	36	7	1,635	1,642	157	0	193
	1999		15	0	6	6	36	25	788	813	73	0	109
	1998		-	-	-	-	-	-	-	-	-	-	-
	3 Yr-TOTALS		31	0	12	12	72	32	2,423	2,455	230	0	302
8.	McCaffrey	DEN	16	0	9	9	56	0	1,317	1,317	125	2	181
	1999		15	0	7	7	42	0	1,018	1,018	95	0	137
	1998		15	0	10	10	62	0	1,053	1,053	99	2	161
	3 Yr-TOTALS		46	0	26	26	160	0	3,388	3,388	319	4	479
9.	Horn	NO	16	0	8	8	48	18	1,340	1,358	127	0	175
	1999 (w/KC)		15	0	6	6	36	15	586	601	54	0	90
	1998 (w/KC)		10	0	1	1	6	-8	198	190	15	0	21
	3 Yr-TOTALS		41	0	15	15	90	25	2,124	2,149	196	0	286
10.	Carter	MIN	16	0	9	9	54	0	1,274	1,274	119	0	173
	1999		15	0	13	13	78	0	1,241	1,241	120	0	198
	1998		15	0	12	12	72	-1	1,011	1,010	93	0	165
	3 Yr-TOTALS		46	0	34	34	204	-1	3,526	3,525	332	0	536
11.	Tm. Brown	OAK	16	0	11	11	66	12	1,128	1,140	104	0	170
	1999		16	0	6	6	36	4	1,344	1,348	128	0	164
	1998		16	0	9	9	54	-7	1,012	1,005	93	0	147
	3 Yr-TOTALS		48	0	26	26	156	9	3,484	3,493	325	0	481
12.	J. Smith	JAC	14	0	8	8	48	0	1,213	1,213	115	0	163
	1999		16	0	6	6	38	0	1,636	1,636	156	2	194
	1998		16	0	8	8	48	0	1,182	1,182	114	0	162
	3 Yr-TOTALS		46	0	22	22	134	0	4,031	4,031	385	2	519
13.	Moulds	BUF	16	0	5	5	30	24	1,326	1,350	128	0	158
	1999		14	0	7	7	42	1	994	995	94	0	136
	1998		16	0	9	9	54	0	1,368	1,368	128	0	182
	3 Yr-TOTALS		46	0	21	21	126	25	3,688	3,713	350	0	476
14.	Toomer	NYG	16	1	7	8	48	91	1,094	1,185	109	0	157
	1999		16	0	6	6	36	4	1,183	1,187	110	0	146
	1998		13	0	5	5	30	0	360	360	30	0	60
	3 Yr-TOTALS		45	1	18	19	114	95	2,637	2,732	249	0	363
15.	Boston	ARI	16	0	7	7	42	4	1,156	1,160	111	0	153
	1999		14	0	2	2	12	0	473	473	42	0	54
	1998		-	-	-	-	-	-	-	-	-	-	-
	3 Yr-TOTALS		30	0	9	9	54	4	1,629	1,633	153	0	207

2000 STATISTICAL RESULTS
(WIDE RECEIVERS — COMBINED BASIC/PERFORMANCE
SCORING METHOD)

	NAME	TEAM	GP	RSH TDs	REC TDs	TOTAL TDs	BASIC PTS	RSH YARDS	REC YARDS	TOTAL YARDS	PERF PTS	CONV PTS	FAN-TASY PTS
16.	**Muhammad**	**CAR**	**16**	**0**	**6**	**6**	**36**	**12**	**1,183**	**1,195**	**110**	**0**	**146**
	1999		15	0	8	8	48	0	1,253	1,253	119	0	167
	1998		15	0	6	6	38	0	941	941	88	2	126
	3 Yr-TOTALS		46	0	20	20	122	12	3,377	3,389	317	2	439
17.	**McCardell**	**JAC**	**16**	**0**	**5**	**5**	**30**	**0**	**1,207**	**1,207**	**113**	**0**	**143**
	1999		16	0	5	5	32	0	891	891	82	2	114
	1998		14	0	6	6	38	0	892	892	82	2	120
	3 Yr-TOTALS		46	0	16	16	100	0	2,990	2,990	277	4	377
18.	**Freeman**	**GB**	**15**	**0**	**9**	**9**	**54**	**5**	**912**	**917**	**85**	**0**	**139**
	1999		15	0	6	6	36	-2	1,074	1,072	102	0	138
	1998		15	0	14	14	86	5	1,424	1,429	137	2	223
	3 Yr-TOTALS		45	0	29	29	176	8	3,410	3,418	324	2	500
19.	**Chrebet**	**NYJ**	**16**	**0**	**8**	**8**	**48**	**-3**	**937**	**934**	**87**	**0**	**135**
	1999		11	0	3	3	18	0	631	631	58	0	76
	1998		16	0	8	8	48	0	1,083	1,083	101	0	149
	3 Yr-TOTALS		43	0	19	19	114	-3	2,651	2,648	246	0	360
20.	**Glenn**	**NE**	**16**	**0**	**6**	**6**	**36**	**39**	**963**	**1,002**	**93**	**0**	**129**
	1999		13	0	4	4	24	0	1,147	1,147	108	0	132
	1998		10	0	3	3	18	-1	792	791	75	0	93
	3 Yr-TOTALS		39	0	13	13	78	38	2,902	2,940	276	0	354
21.	**Ks. Johnson**	**TB**	**16**	**0**	**8**	**8**	**48**	**5**	**874**	**879**	**81**	**0**	**129**
	1999 (w/NYJ)		16	0	8	8	48	6	1,170	1,176	110	0	158
	1998 (w/NYJ)		16	1	10	11	66	60	1,131	1,191	110	0	176
	3 Yr-TOTALS		48	1	26	27	162	71	3,175	3,246	301	0	463
22.	**Tr. Brown ***	**NE**	**16**	**0**	**4**	**5**	**30**	**46**	**944**	**990**	**92**	**0**	**122**
	1999		12	0	1	1	6	0	471	471	43	0	49
	1998		7	0	1	1	6	0	346	346	32	0	38
	3 Yr-TOTALS		35	0	6	7	42	46	1,761	1,807	167	0	209
23.	**Hilliard**	**NYG**	**14**	**0**	**8**	**8**	**48**	**19**	**787**	**806**	**74**	**0**	**122**
	1999		16	0	3	3	18	16	996	1,012	95	0	113
	1998		16	0	2	2	12	4	713	717	65	0	77
	3 Yr-TOTALS		46	0	13	13	78	39	2,496	2,535	234	0	312
24.	**Mason ***	**TEN**	**14**	**0**	**5**	**6**	**36**	**1**	**895**	**896**	**84**	**0**	**120**
	1999		5	0	0	1	6	0	89	89	6	0	12
	1998		14	0	3	3	18	0	333	333	26	0	44
	3 Yr-TOTALS		33	0	8	10	60	1	1,317	1,318	116	0	176
25.	**Schroeder**	**GB**	**15**	**0**	**4**	**4**	**24**	**11**	**999**	**1,010**	**93**	**0**	**117**
	1999		16	0	5	5	30	0	1,051	1,051	98	0	128
	1998		9	0	1	1	6	0	452	452	41	0	47
	3 Yr-TOTALS		40	0	10	10	60	11	2,502	2,513	232	0	292
26.	**Rice**	**SF**	**16**	**0**	**7**	**7**	**42**	**-2**	**805**	**803**	**74**	**0**	**116**
	1999		16	0	5	5	30	13	830	843	76	0	106
	1998		16	0	9	9	58	0	1,157	1,157	107	4	165
	3 Yr-TOTALS		48	0	21	21	130	11	2,792	2,803	257	4	387
27.	**Gadsden**	**MIA**	**16**	**0**	**6**	**6**	**36**	**0**	**786**	**786**	**75**	**0**	**111**
	1999		14	0	6	6	36	0	803	803	74	0	110
	1998		15	0	7	7	42	0	713	713	65	0	107
	3 Yr-TOTALS		45	0	19	19	114	0	2,302	2,302	214	0	328
28.	**Graham**	**SD**	**13**	**0**	**4**	**4**	**24**	**0**	**907**	**907**	**85**	**0**	**109**
	1999		14	0	2	2	12	0	968	968	91	0	103
	1998 (w/PHI)		15	0	2	2	12	0	600	600	54	0	66
	3 Yr-TOTALS		42	0	8	8	48	0	2,475	2,475	230	0	278
29.	**Warrick + ***	**CIN**	**16**	**2**	**4**	**7**	**42**	**148**	**592**	**740**	**65**	**0**	**107**
	1999		-	-	-	-	-	-	-	-	-	-	-
	1998		-	-	-	-	-	-	-	-	-	-	-
	3 Yr-TOTALS		16	2	4	7	42	148	592	740	65	0	107
30.	**Hayes**	**CAR**	**15**	**0**	**3**	**3**	**18**	**0**	**926**	**926**	**86**	**0**	**104**
	1999		6	0	2	2	12	0	270	270	25	0	37
	1998		3	0	0	0	0	0	62	62	5	0	5
	3 Yr-TOTALS		24	0	5	5	30	0	1,258	1,258	116	0	146

2000 STATISTICAL RESULTS
(WIDE RECEIVERS — COMBINED BASIC/PERFORMANCE SCORING METHOD)

	NAME	TEAM	GP	RSH TDs	REC TDs	TOTAL TDs	BASIC PTS	RSH YARDS	REC YARDS	TOTAL YARDS	PERF PTS	CONV PTS	FAN-TASY PTS
31.	F. Sanders	ARI	16	0	6	6	36	0	749	749	68	0	104
	1999		15	0	1	1	6	0	954	954	88	0	94
	1998		16	0	3	3	18	0	1,145	1,145	109	0	127
	3 Yr-TOTALS		47	0	10	10	60	0	2,848	2,848	265	0	325
32.	D. Jackson +	SEA	16	0	6	6	36	-1	713	712	63	0	99
33.	C. Johnson	PHI	15	0	7	7	42	18	642	660	57	0	99
34.	Robinson	CHI	11	0	5	5	30	9	738	747	69	0	99
35.	McKnight	DAL	15	0	2	2	12	0	926	926	86	0	98
36.	Dawkins	SEA	15	0	5	5	30	0	731	731	67	0	97
37.	Conway	SD	14	0	5	5	30	31	712	743	66	0	96
38.	Hakim *	STL	15	0	4	5	30	19	734	753	66	0	96
39.	D. Ward	NYJ	16	0	3	3	18	23	801	824	77	0	95
40.	Morton	DET	16	0	3	3	20	25	788	813	74	2	94
41.	Mathis	ATL	15	0	5	5	30	-5	679	674	62	0	92
42.	Q. Ismail	BAL	13	0	5	5	30	0	655	655	60	0	90
43.	Price	BUF	16	0	3	3	18	32	762	794	72	0	90
44.	Connell	WAS	13	0	3	3	18	0	762	762	71	0	89
45.	Rison	OAK	14	0	6	6	36	0	606	606	53	0	89
46.	H. Ward	PIT	16	0	4	4	24	53	672	725	65	0	89
47.	Jefferson	ATL	14	0	2	2	12	1	822	823	75	0	87
48.	Shaw	PIT	14	0	4	4	24	0	672	672	61	0	85
49.	W. Jackson	NO	14	0	6	6	36	0	523	523	45	0	81
50.	Thrash	WAS	14	0	2	2	12	82	653	735	68	0	80
51.	Fryar	WAS	14	0	5	5	30	16	548	564	49	0	79
52.	Morris +	KC	15	0	3	3	18	0	678	678	61	0	79
53.	J. Green	TB	15	0	1	1	6	13	773	786	72	0	78
54.	Pathon	IND	15	0	3	3	18	3	646	649	57	0	75
55.	McDaniel	BUF	16	0	2	2	12	0	697	697	61	0	73
56.	Small	PHI	14	0	3	3	20	1	569	570	51	2	71
57.	Wilkins	IND	12	0	3	3	18	8	569	577	52	0	70
58.	Kennison	CHI	16	0	2	2	12	72	549	621	56	0	68
59.	Stokes	SF	14	0	3	3	20	6	524	530	47	2	67
60.	Shepherd	MIA	12	0	4	4	24	3	446	449	41	0	65
61.	Proehl	STL	12	0	4	4	24	0	441	441	39	0	63
62.	Dwight *	ATL	11	0	3	4	24	8	406	414	36	0	60
63.	Kv. Johnson	CLE	16	0	0	0	0	0	669	669	60	0	60
64.	Crowell	DET	9	0	3	3	18	12	430	442	40	0	58
65.	Moore	DET	14	0	3	3	18	0	434	434	38	0	56
66.	Patten	CLE	11	0	1	1	6	0	546	546	49	0	55
67.	Booker	CHI	14	0	2	2	12	-1	490	489	42	0	54
68.	C. Sanders	TEN	15	0	0	0	0	0	536	536	48	0	48
69.	Lockett	KC	13	0	2	2	12	0	422	422	35	0	47
70.	R. Ismail	DAL	8	0	1	1	8	73	350	423	37	2	45
71.	McGarity *	DAL	11	1	0	3	18	49	250	299	26	0	44
72.	Taylor +	BAL	9	0	3	3	18	11	276	287	26	0	44
73.	Coles +	NYJ	8	0	1	1	8	15	370	385	34	2	42
74.	Jett	OAK	11	0	2	2	12	0	356	356	30	0	42
75.	Anthony	TB	10	0	4	4	24	0	232	232	17	0	41
76.	Northcutt	CLE	14	0	0	0	0	33	422	455	41	0	41
77.	Thigpen	TEN	9	0	2	2	12	0	289	289	24	0	36
78.	Driver	GB	12	0	1	1	8	4	322	326	27	2	35
79.	Martin	MIA	9	0	0	0	0	0	393	393	35	0	35
80.	Lewis *	BAL	8	0	1	3	18	38	161	199	15	0	33
81.	Byrd	CAR	8	0	2	2	12	0	241	241	20	0	32
82.	Poole	NO	10	0	1	1	6	0	293	293	25	0	31
83.	Jurevicius	NYG	10	0	1	1	6	0	271	271	24	0	30
84.	Whitted	JAC	6	0	3	3	18	0	137	137	11	0	29
85.	Stokley	BAL	6	0	2	2	12	6	184	190	16	0	28
86.	Mayes	SEA	11	0	1	1	6	0	264	264	21	0	27
87.	Hatchette	MIN	11	0	2	2	12	0	190	190	14	0	26

2000 STATISTICAL RESULTS
(WIDE RECEIVERS — COMBINED BASIC/PERFORMANCE SCORING METHOD)

	NAME	TEAM	GP	RSH TDs	REC TDs	TOTAL TDs	BASIC PTS	RSH YARDS	REC YARDS	TOTAL YARDS	PERF PTS	CONV PTS	FAN-TASY PTS
88.	Hawkins	PIT	8	0	1	1	6	0	238	238	20	0	26
89.	P. Johnson	BAL	6	0	2	2	12	21	156	177	14	0	26
90.	Simmons	NE	10	0	1	1	6	0	231	231	19	0	25
91.	E. G. Green	IND	5	0	1	1	6	0	201	201	18	0	24
92.	Yeast	CIN	12	0	0	0	0	15	301	316	24	0	24
93.	Burress +	PIT	10	0	0	0	0	0	273	273	23	0	23
94.	Farmer	CIN	7	0	0	0	0	0	268	268	23	0	23
95.	Foster	DET	7	0	1	1	6	31	175	206	17	0	23
96.	Jenkins *	ARI	13	0	0	1	6	-4	219	215	17	0	23
97.	Pickens	TEN	5	0	0	0	0	0	242	242	22	0	22
98.	Streets	SF	11	0	0	0	0	0	287	287	22	0	22
99.	Gaylor +	SD	6	0	1	1	6	0	182	182	15	0	21
100.	Soward +	JAC	9	0	1	1	6	28	154	182	15	0	21
101.	Horne *	STL	4	0	2	3	18	6	32	38	1	0	19
102.	Tucker	DAL	10	1	0	1	6	42	141	183	13	0	19
103.	Edwards	PIT	10	0	0	0	0	4	215	219	18	0	18
104.	J. Reed	NO	5	0	0	0	0	0	206	206	18	0	18
105.	Cody	ARI	10	0	0	0	0	0	212	212	17	0	17
106.	Jones	SD	6	0	0	0	0	0	186	186	17	0	17
107.	Dyson	TEN	1	0	1	1	6	0	104	104	10	0	16
108.	Dawson +	CLE	2	0	1	1	6	0	97	97	9	0	15
109.	Emanuel	MIA	6	0	1	1	6	-2	132	130	9	0	15
110.	Pinkston +	PHI	7	0	0	0	0	0	181	181	15	0	15
111.	M. Brooks	CHI	11	0	0	0	0	0	216	216	14	0	14
112.	Dugans +	CIN	7	0	1	1	6	0	125	125	8	0	14
113.	Walsh	MIN	11	0	0	0	0	0	191	191	14	0	14
114.	Wilson	NO	4	0	0	0	0	0	154	154	14	0	14
115.	Dixon +	NYG	7	0	1	1	6	13	92	105	7	0	13
116.	A. Reed	WAS	6	0	1	1	6	0	103	103	7	0	13
117.	White +	CHI	7	0	1	1	6	0	87	87	7	0	13
118.	Galloway	DAL	1	0	1	1	6	0	62	62	6	0	12
119.	W. Hayes +	NYJ	4	0	0	0	0	2	126	128	12	0	12
120.	Lee +	GB	6	0	0	0	0	0	134	134	12	0	12
121.	Bailey	SEA	4	0	1	1	6	0	62	62	5	0	11
122.	Chiaverini	CLE	3	0	1	1	6	0	68	68	5	0	11
123.	McDuffie	MIA	6	0	0	0	0	-3	143	140	11	0	11
124.	Engram	CHI	3	0	0	0	0	1	109	110	10	0	10
125.	McGriff	DEN	2	0	1	1	6	0	51	51	4	0	10
126.	Westbrook	WAS	2	0	0	0	0	0	103	103	10	0	10
127.	Uwaezuoke *	CAR	4	0	0	1	6	0	46	46	3	0	9
128.	Blackwell *	PIT	1	0	0	1	6	0	23	23	2	0	8
129.	N. Brown	PHI	9	0	1	1	6	0	80	80	2	0	8
130.	Dunn *	OAK	4	0	0	1	6	0	33	33	2	0	8
131.	Ogden *	MIA	3	0	0	1	6	0	24	24	2	0	8
132.	Ja. Williams +	SEA	5	0	0	0	0	-5	99	94	8	0	8
133.	Ka. Williams *	TB	3	0	0	1	6	0	35	35	2	0	8
134.	Calloway	NE	5	0	0	0	0	0	95	95	7	0	7
135.	Howard *	DET	3	0	0	1	6	0	14	14	1	0	7
136.	Mitchell	ARI	3	0	0	0	0	0	80	80	6	0	6
137.	Cavil	BUF	3	0	0	0	0	0	66	66	5	0	5
138.	B. Davis	BAL	2	0	0	0	0	0	62	62	5	0	5
139.	Hodge	DAL	2	0	0	0	0	0	60	60	5	0	5
140.	Brisby	NYJ	3	0	0	0	0	0	60	60	4	0	4
141.	R. Brooks	DEN	2	0	0	0	0	0	51	51	4	0	4
142.	Finneran	ATL	4	0	0	0	0	0	60	60	4	0	4
143.	T. Davis	NYG	2	0	0	0	0	0	40	40	3	0	3
144.	Hankton	CAR	3	0	0	0	0	0	38	38	3	0	3
145.	C. Jackson	NE	2	0	0	0	0	0	44	44	3	0	3
146.	Parker	KC	3	0	0	0	0	-7	41	34	3	0	3
147.	Barlow	JAC	1	0	0	0	0	0	28	28	2	0	2

2000 STATISTICAL RESULTS
(WIDE RECEIVERS — COMBINED BASIC/PERFORMANCE SCORING METHOD)

	NAME	TEAM	GP	RSH TDs	REC TDs	TOTAL TDs	BASIC PTS	RSH YARDS	REC YARDS	TOTAL YARDS	PERF PTS	CONV PTS	FAN-TASY PTS
148.	Bates	CHI	4	0	0	0	0	-2	42	40	2	0	2
149.	Jacquet	SD	1	0	0	0	0	0	25	25	2	0	2
150.	Ricks	SD	2	0	0	0	0	0	35	35	2	0	2
151.	Stablein	DET	7	0	0	0	0	0	53	53	2	0	2
152.	Brazzell	DAL	2	0	0	0	0	0	12	12	1	0	1
153.	S. Davis	NE	1	0	0	0	0	0	12	12	1	0	1
154.	German	ATL	1	0	0	0	0	0	10	10	1	0	1
155.	Griffin	CIN	2	0	0	0	0	0	25	25	1	0	1
156.	Montgomery	DEN	1	0	0	0	0	0	10	10	1	0	1
157.	B. Brown	CLE	2	0	0	0	0	0	14	14	0	0	0
158.	Douglas	PHI	1	0	0	0	0	0	9	9	0	0	0
159.	L. Jackson	CLE	1	0	0	0	0	0	5	5	0	0	0
160.	Milburn	CHI	2	0	0	0	0	6	8	14	0	0	0
161.	Miller	DEN	1	0	0	0	0	0	7	7	0	0	0
162.	Porter +	OAK	1	0	0	0	0	0	6	6	0	0	0
163.	Stone	NYJ	3	0	0	0	0	3	0	3	0	0	0
164.	Van Dyke	PHI	1	0	0	0	0	0	8	8	0	0	0
165.	Walters +	MIN	2	0	0	0	0	3	5	8	0	0	0
166.	C. Williams	ARI	1	0	0	0	0	0	5	5	0	0	0

+	DENOTES COLLEGE DRAFT PICKS		
*	Warrick	(CIN)	Scored TD on a 82 yard punt return.
*	Mason	(TEN)	Scored TD on a 69 yard punt return.
*	Tr. Brown	(NE)	Scored TD on a 66 yard punt return.
*	Hakim	(STL)	Scored TD on a 86 yard punt return.
*	Dwight	(ATL)	Scored TD on a 70 yard punt return.
*	Lewis	(BAL)	Scored TD's on 89 and 54 yard punt returns.
*	McGarity	(DAL)	Scored TD's on 64 and 59 yard punt returns.
*	Horne	(STL)	Scored TD on a 103 yard kickoff return.
*	Jenkins	(ARI)	Scored TD on a 98 yard kickoff return.
*	Uwaezucke	(CAR)	Scored TD on a 64 yard punt return.
*	Howard	(DET)	Scored TD on a 95 yard punt return.
*	Ogden	(MIA)	Scored TD on a 81 yard punt return.
*	Dunn	(OAK)	Scored TD on a 88 yard kickoff return.
*	Blackwell	(PIT)	Scored TD on a 98 yard kickoff return.
*	Ka. Williams	(TB)	Scored TD on a 73 yard punt return.

RATING THE PLAYERS FOR 2001
(Wide Receivers—Combined Basic/Performance Scoring Method)

GRAB ONE IF YOU CAN

☐ **1. Randy Moss (Minnesota Vikings)**
Three years in the league and Moss has been very consistent, producing 1,313, 1,413 and 1,437 receiving yards, along with 17, 12 and 15 touchdowns. Another 1,300-1,500 yards and around 15 touchdowns can be expected.

☐ **2. Marvin Harrison (Indianapolis Colts)**
Being Peyton Manning's favorite target has resulted in big numbers the last two seasons. Harrison's 1,663 and 1,413 yards, along with 12 and 14 touchdowns he's produced the last two years, are numbers he'll near again in 2001.

☐ **3. Isaac Bruce (St. Louis Rams)**
Bruce struggled through injuries in 1997 and 1998 but has stayed healthy the last two seasons to produce excellent numbers. Bruce produced 1,165 receiving yards and 12 touchdowns in 1999 and 1,471 yards and nine touchdowns in 2000. If he stays healthy in 2001, big numbers again lie ahead.

☐ **4. Terrell Owens (San Francisco 49ers)**
After producing 1,097 yards and 15 touchdowns in 1998, Owens saw his numbers suffer miserably when Steve Young went down to injury in 1999. Jeff Garcia stepped up his play in 2000, and Owens benefited, recording 1,451 receiving yards and 13 touchdowns, playing in 14 games. 2001 should be another big year for Owens.

☐ **5. Tim Brown (Jacksonville Jaguars)**
Brown consistently puts up strong yardage numbers, and his touchdowns production usually hovers around ten. In the last three seasons, Brown has recorded 1,012, 1,344 and 1,128 receiving yards, while scoring 9, 6 and 11 touchdowns respectively.

BEST OF THE REST

☐ **6. Rod Smith (Denver Broncos)**
As Smith works more with young quarterback Brian Griese, his numbers will grow. Smith jumped to 100 receptions for an impressive 1,602 yards and scored nine times in 2000.

☐ **7. Torry Holt (St. Louis Rams)**
In just his second season, Holt jumped from 788 receiving yards in 1999 to a whopping 1,635 in 2000, while scoring six times for the second straight year. As a major cog in the Rams' passing machine, Holt should have big yardage numbers and perhaps improved scoring numbers in 2001.

☐ **8. Joe Horn (New Orleans Saints)**
The Saints got their money's worth in luring Joe Horn from Kansas City in 2000, as Horn recorded a surprising 94 receptions for 1,340 yards and eight touchdowns. As the Saints #1 receiver, Horn should see another 1,200-1,500 yard and 8-10 scores in 2001.

☐ **9. Jimmy Smith (Jacksonville Jaguars)**
Smith's yardage numbers are always impressive but his touchdown numbers aren't. Over the past five seasons, Smith has recorded 1,244, 1,324, 1,182, 1,636 and 1,213 yards but only 7, 4, 8, 6 and 8 touchdowns. His yardage numbers, however, are enough to carry him in this scoring method.

☐ **10. Derrick Alexander (Kansas City Chiefs)**
After recording 54 receptions and less than 1,000 yards in each of the first two seasons with the Chiefs, Alexander jumped to 78 receptions for 1,391 yards and ten touchdowns in 2000. I don't see his numbers falling off much with Dick Vermeil coming in as head coach.

STRONG LONG SHOTS

☐ **11. Cris Carter (Minnesota Vikings)**
The aging Carter just keeps getting it done. The last three seasons he has recorded 78, 90 and 96 receptions for 1,010, 1,241 and 1,274 yards while scoring 12, 13 and nine times. No wonder why he opted to not retire following the 2000 season.

☐ **12. Eric Moulds (Buffalo Bills)**
An impressive 67-reception, 1,368-yard, nine-touchdown performance in 1998 was followed by a disappointing 65-catch, 994-yard, seven-touchdown performance in 1999. Moulds rebounded in 2000 in a big way to grab 94 receptions for 1,326 yards but scored only five times. He'll try to maintain these numbers in 2001, though I believe he'll easily improve his touchdown numbers.

☐ **13. Marcus Robinson (Chicago Bears)**
Following a breakout year in 1999, when he recorded 84 receptions for a whopping 1,400 yards and nine touchdowns, Robinson missing four games to injury in 2000, dropped to 55 receptions for 738 yards and five touchdowns. Healthy in 2001, we should see a return to much better set of numbers.

☐ **14. Antonio Freeman (Green Bay Packers)**
From 84 receptions for 1,424 yards and 14 touchdowns in 1998, Freeman saw his numbers drop. In 2000, Freeman recorded only 62 receptions for 912 yards but did score nine times. He has to get refocused in 2001. If he does, his numbers should rebound to the 1,200-1,400 yard range and double-digit scoring.

☐ **15. Muhsin Muhammad (Carolina Panthers)**
From 96 receptions for 1,253 yards and eight touchdowns in 1999 to 102 receptions for 1,183 yards and six touchdowns in 2000, Muhammad has proven he's a player to reckon with again in 2001.

☐ **16. Keyshawn Johnson (Tampa Bay Buccaneers)**
In his last two season with the Jets, Keyshawn recorded 83 and 89 receptions for 1,131 and 1,170 yards, while scoring 11 and 8 times. Coming to Tampa Bay in 2000, Johnson dropped to 71 receptions for 874 yards and eight touchdowns. He should easily improve these numbers in 2001 with Brad Johnson now aboard at quarterback.

☐ **17. Ed McCaffrey (Denver Broncos)**
Though battling Rod Smith for receiving numbers, McCaffrey remains very consistent. McCaffrey has scored 10, 7 and 9 touchdowns over the

last three seasons respectively, while recording 1,053, 1,018 and 1,317 yards. He's too consistent to overlook in 2001.

☐ **18. Keenan McCardell (Jacksonville Jaguars)**
McCardell saw his receptions and yardage numbers jump in 2000, but his touchdown numbers remain a fantasy concern. From 78 receptions for 891 yards and five touchdowns in 1999 to 94 receptions for 1,207 yards and another five touchdowns in 2000, McCardell has good enough yardage numbers to make him a solid fantasy pick in this scoring method again in 2001.

☐ **19. Amani Toomer (New York Giants)**
Two straight 1,000-yard seasons (1,183 and 1,094), while scoring six times in 1999 and eight times in 2000, makes Toomer an attractive fantasy pick in 2001.

☐ **20. Joey Galloway (Dallas Cowboys)**
The Cowboys put up $42 million over seven years to bring Galloway to Dallas in 2000 and were extremely disappointed when he suffered a season-ending knee injury in the season opener. The Cowboys expect him back healthy and putting up healthy numbers in 2001.

HAVE THE POTENTIAL

☐ **21. David Boston (Arizona Cardinals)**
From 40 receptions for 473 yards and two touchdowns as a rookie in 1999 to 71 receptions for 1,156 yards and seven touchdowns in 2000, Boston has quickly stepped into recognition, though veteran Rob Moore's healthy return may have some affect.

☐ **22. Wayne Chrebet (New York Jets)**
With Keyshawn gone in 2000, Chrebet was cast into the Jet's #1 receiver role. His 69 receptions for 937 yards and eight touchdowns were a bit disappointing, though he looks to retain that role in 2001.

☐ **23. Terry Glenn (New England Patriots)**
Glenn has been fairly consistent the last two seasons, recording 69 receptions for 1,147 yards and four touchdowns in 1999 to 79 receptions for 963 yards and six touchdowns in 2000.

☐ **24. Michael Westbrook (Washington Redskins)**
Staying healthy in 1999, Westbrook finally had the kind of year the Redskins were waiting for, recording 65 receptions for 1,191 yards and nine touchdowns. The injury bug returned in 2000, as he missed 14 games to a knee injury. The Redskins hope to have him back healthy in 2001, putting up numbers similar to 1999.

☐ **25. Derrick Mason (Tennessee Titans)**
Despite the presence of high-priced free agents Yancey Thigpen and Carl Pickens, the Titans turned to Derrick Mason more and more in 2000, resulting in 63 receptions for 895 yards and six touchdowns. He'll easily boost these numbers in 2001 with Thigpen and Pickens now gone.

SOLID SLEEPERS

☐ **26. Troy Brown (New England Patriots)**
Glenn grabbed 79 receptions in 2000 but averaged only 14.7 yards on six touchdowns. Troy Brown seems more of the deep-threat for the Patriots.

☐ **27. Germane Crowell (Detroit Lions)**
He went from 81 receptions for 1,338 yards and seven touchdowns in 1999 to 34 receptions for 430 yards and two touchdowns in 2000, as he missed six games with a foot injury. Regardless, I believe he won't reach his 1999 levels again, as the Lions rely on the run more, with James Stewart now aboard.

☐ **28. J.J. Stokes (San Francisco 49ers)**
Stokes should get a better chance to shine in 2001 with Jerry Rice no longer involved.

☐ **29. Qadry Ismail (Baltimore Ravens)**
From a career year in 1999, recording 68 receptions for 1,105 yards and six touchdowns, to a very disappointing 2000 campaign personally (the team obviously did well), Ismail missed three games to injury as the Ravens became more run oriented. With Elvis Grbac aboard for 2001, I look for Ismail's numbers to rebound.

☐ **30. Terrence Mathis (Atlanta Falcons)**
Mathis produced 64 receptions for 1,136 yards and 11 touchdowns in 1998 and 81 receptions for 1,016 yards and six touchdowns in 1999, but he fell on hard times along with the Falcons' passing game in 2000. His 57 receptions for 679 yards and five touchdowns in 2000 are a bit scary unless the Falcons' passing game regroups.

KEEP AN EYE ON

☐ **31. Darren Jackson (Seattle Seahawks)**
Jackson looks to push his rookie numbers of 713 receiving yards and six touchdowns, especially with Derrick Mayes and Sean Dawkins released.

☐ **32. Darnay Scott (Cincinnati Bengals)**
Scott missed the entire 2000 season after suffering two broken bones in his leg during the preseason. The Bengals hope to have him healthy to team with Peter Warrick in 2001 and boost the Cincinnati passing game.

☐ **33. Patrick Jeffers (Carolina Panthers)**
He had 63 receptions for 1,082 yards and 12 touchdowns in 1999 but missed the entire 2000 season with a torn ACL. The Panthers and fantasy fans hope for a healthy return in 2001.

☐ **34. Ike Hilliard (New York Giants)**
As the Giants' passing game has picked up the last two seasons, so have Hilliard's numbers. In 1999, Hilliard recorded 72 receptions for 996 yards but scored only three times. In 2000, missing two games to a bruised sternum, Hilliard still recorded 55 receptions for 787 yards and this time scored eight times. If he can stay healthy all of 2001, he'll deserve of a good fantasy look.

☐ **35. Bill Schroeder (Green Bay Packers)**
He had 1,051 and 999 yards, along with 5 and 4 touchdowns, the last two seasons.

☐ **36. Jeff Graham (San Diego Chargers)**
Since coming to San Diego two years ago, Graham has fallen just short of 1,000 yards both years, recording 968 and 907 yards, while scoring 2 and 4 touchdowns.

☐ **37. Johnny Morton (Detroit Lions)**
The Lions run more with James Stewart now aboard, and this is costing Morton statistically.

☐ **38. Shawn Jefferson (Atlanta Falcons)**
He had 822 yards on 60 receptions but only two touchdowns in his first year with the Falcons in 2000.

☐ **39. Peter Warrick (Cincinnati Bengals)**
If Darnay Scott returns healthy and the Bengals can improve at quarterback, Warrick may be able to show more in 2001.

☐ **40. Rocket Ismail (Dallas Cowboys)**
A knee injury kept Ismail out of half the 2000 season. His healthy return and the Cowboys' quarterbacking job leave concerns.

PRIME PROSPECTS

☐ **41. Kevin Johnson (Cleveland Browns)**
From 66 receptions for 986 yards and eight touchdowns as a rookie in 1999 to 57 receptions for 669 yards in 2000, Johnson missed quarterback Tim Couch who was out injured much of the year.

☐ **42. James Thrash (Philadelphia Eagles)**
Newcomer to Eagles, Thrash will battle rookie Freddie Mitchell for #1 receiver job with Charles Johnson and Torrence Small released.

☐ **43. Oronde Gadsden (Miami Dolphins)**
Gadsden has recorded 48, 48 and 53 receptions for 713, 803 and 786 yards and 7, 6 and 6 touchdowns over the last three seasons.

☐ **44. Rob Moore (Arizona Cardinals)**
The Cardinal's #1 wideout is expected back healthy in 2001 after missing the entire 2000 season with a knee injury.

☐ **45. Curtis Conway (San Diego Chargers)**
Despite missing a couple of games to injury in 2000, Conway recorded 53 receptions for 712 yards and scored five times in his first year in a Chargers' uniform.

☐ **46. Plaxico Burress (Pittsburgh Steelers)**
The Steelers' first-round draft pick of 2000 had a disappointing rookie year, grabbing only 22 receptions and missing almost half the year with a broken wrist. 2001 should be better.

☐ **47. Bobby Engram (Chicago Bears)**
A knee injury sidelined Engram all of 2000. In 1999, though, he recorded 88 receptions for 947 yards and scored four times. In 2001 he'll face a stiff challenge from first-round draft pick David Terrell.

☐ **48. Sylvester Morris (Kansas City Chiefs)**
He had 48 receptions for 678 yards and three touchdowns as a rookie in 2000.

☐ **49. Az-Zahir Hakim (St. Louis Rams)**
He had 734 yards on 53 receptions and scored five times in 2000. Always a threat on kick returns as well, Hakim scored nine times in 1999.

☐ **50. O. J. McDuffie (Miami Dolphins)**
McDuffie led the NFL with 90 receptions in 1998 but has struggled with injuries since. If he can stay healthy in 2001 . . .

DON'T BE SURPRISED

51. J. Green (TB)
52. H. Ward (PITT)
53. Dyson (TENN)
54. Price (BUF)
55. Dawson (CLE)
56. Dwight (SD)
57. Rison (OAK)
58. Sanders (ARIZ)
59. Connell (NO)
60. Bradford (GB)

YOU NEVER KNOW

61. Jett (OAK)
62. Kennison (DEN)
63. McKnight (MIA)
64. Taylor (BALT)
65. Lockett (WASH)
66. Pathon (IND)
67. Emanuel (NE)
68. Hayes (CAR)
69. Wilkins (IND)
70. Patten (NE)

DON'T COUNT THEM OUT

71. Porter (OAK)
72. Chiaverini (CLE)
73. Shaw (PITT)
74. Anthony (TB)
75. Moore (DET)

76. Pickens (DALL)
77. Simmons (NE)
78. Jackson (NO)
79. Hatchette (NYJ)
80. J. Reed (MINN)

WORTH MENTIONING

81. Soward (JAC)
82. Proehl (STL)
83. N. Brown (PHIL)
84. Thigpen (???)
85. Rice (????)

86. D. Ward (MIA)
87. Thompson (WASH)
88. McDaniel (BUF)
89. Booker (CHI)
90. Jurevicuis (NYG)

ROOKIE PROSPECTS

NAME	TEAM	COMMENT
☐ 1. Rod Gardner	WASH	Redskins have found another big target for strong-armed George.
☐ 2. David Terrell	CHI	Talented receiver to tandem with Marcus Robinson.
☐ 3. Koren Robinson	SEAT	His success will rest on arm of unproven Hasslebeck.
☐ 4. Freddie Mitchell	PHIL	Could become Eagles' #1 receiver with Charles Johnson released.
☐ 5. Santana Moss	NYJ	Could help answer some of Jets' receiving problems.
☐ 6. Robert Ferguson	GB	Favre needs help at wide receiver.
☐ 7. Reggie Wayne	IND	Is he the #2 answer opposite Marvin Harrison?
☐ 8. Chris Chambers	MIA	Could help Dolphins in red zone.
☐ 9. Quincy Morgan	CLE	How good is the Brown passing game?
☐10. Chad Johnson	CIN	Did the Bengals need another wide receiver?

A LOOK AT THE TIGHT ENDS

(A Guide for the Beginner)

Considerations in Choosing a Tight End

1. First, look at players' previous performances. Don't overlook players who may have missed portions of the previous year because of injuries, holdouts, and the like. In 2000 Cam Cleeland missed the season do to injuries.

2. Look for a tight end who will get 750 or more receiving yards and who has a shot at seven or more touchdowns. Tony Gonzalez has done well in recent years, as has Shannon Sharpe.

3. Find a tight end who is a certain quarterback's favorite receiver, such as Tony Gonzalez, who is a favorite target for Elvis Grbac.

4. Pick a tight end from a predominantly passing team.

In the 2000 statistics that follow, players are ranked by their fantasy-point totals. Remember that the Combined Basic/Performance Scoring Method awards six points for every touchdown scored, three points for every touchdown pass thrown, one point for every 10 yards rushing, one point for every 10 yards receiving, and one point for every 20 yards passing.

2000 STATISTICAL RESULTS
(TIGHT ENDS — COMBINED BASIC/PERFORMANCE SCORING METHOD)

	NAME	TEAM	GP	RSH TDs	REC TDs	TOTAL TDs	BASIC PTS	RSH YARDS	REC YARDS	TOTAL YARDS	PERF PTS	CONV PTS	FAN-TASY PTS
1.	Gonzalez	KC	15	0	9	9	54	0	1,203	1,203	113	0	167
	1999		15	0	11	11	66	0	849	849	79	0	145
	1998		16	0	2	2	12	0	621	621	54	0	66
	3 Yr - TOTALS		46	0	22	22	132	0	2,673	2,673	246	0	378
2.	Sharpe	BAL	15	0	5	5	30	0	810	810	75	0	105
	1999 (w/DEN)		4	0	0	0	0	0	224	224	20	0	20
	1998 (w/DEN)		16	0	10	10	60	0	768	768	70	0	130
	3 Yr - TOTALS		35	0	15	15	90	0	1,802	1,802	165	0	255
3.	F. Jones	SD	15	0	5	5	30	0	766	766	70	0	100
	1999		16	0	2	2	12	0	670	670	60	0	72
	1998		16	0	3	3	20	0	602	602	53	2	73
	3 Yr - TOTALS		47	0	10	10	62	0	2,038	2,038	183	2	245
4.	Brady	JAC	16	0	3	3	20	0	729	729	67	2	87
	1999		13	0	1	1	8	0	346	346	31	2	39
	1998 (w/NYJ)		12	0	5	5	30	0	315	315	26	0	56
	3 Yr - TOTALS		41	0	9	9	58	0	1,390	1,390	124	4	182
5.	Lewis	PHI	15	0	3	3	18	0	735	735	68	0	86
	1999		6	0	1	1	18	0	77	77	5	0	23
	1998		-	-	-	-	-	-	-	-	-	-	-
	3 Yr - TOTALS		21	0	4	4	36	0	812	812	73	0	109
6.	Wycheck	TEN	16	0	4	4	24	0	636	636	61	0	85
	1999		16	0	2	2	12	0	641	641	63	0	75
	1998		16	0	2	2	12	0	768	768	72	0	84
	3 Yr - TOTALS		48	0	8	8	48	0	2,045	2,045	196	0	244
7.	Dilger	IND	15	0	3	3	18	0	538	538	46	0	64
	1999		14	0	2	2	12	0	479	479	42	0	54
	1998		13	0	1	1	8	0	303	303	24	2	32
	3 Yr - TOTALS		42	0	6	6	38	0	1,320	1,320	112	2	150
8.	Riemersma	BUF	11	0	5	5	30	0	372	372	32	0	62
	1999		13	0	4	4	24	0	496	496	43	0	67
	1998		13	0	6	6	36	0	288	288	23	0	59
	3 Yr - TOTALS		37	0	15	15	90	0	1,156	1,156	98	0	188
9.	Carswell	DEN	15	0	3	3	18	0	495	495	43	0	61
	1999		11	0	2	2	12	0	201	201	14	0	26
	1998		4	0	0	0	0	0	51	51	3	0	3
	3 Yr - TOTALS		30	0	5	5	30	0	747	747	60	0	90
10.	Pollard	IND	13	0	3	3	20	0	439	439	38	2	58
	1999		14	0	4	4	24	0	374	374	32	0	56
	1998		10	0	4	4	28	0	309	309	26	4	54
	3 Yr - TOTALS		37	0	11	11	72	0	1,122	1,122	96	6	168
11.	Harris	DAL	16	0	5	5	32	0	306	306	24	2	56
	1999 (w/TEN)		8	0	1	1	8	0	297	297	27	2	35
	1998 (w/TEN)		14	0	2	2	12	0	412	412	32	0	44
	3 Yr - TOTALS		38	0	8	8	52	0	1,015	1,015	83	4	135
12.	Alexander	WAS	16	0	2	2	12	0	510	510	41	0	53
	1999		14	0	3	3	18	0	324	324	25	0	43
	1998		11	0	4	4	24	0	383	383	34	0	58
	3 Yr - TOTALS		41	0	9	9	54	0	1,217	1,217	100	0	154
13.	Dudley	OAK	14	0	4	4	24	-7	350	343	29	0	53
	1999		13	0	9	9	54	0	555	555	51	0	105
	1998		15	0	5	5	52	-2	549	547	26	2	78
	3 Yr - TOTALS		42	0	18	18	130	-9	1,454	1,445	106	2	236
14.	Walls	CAR	8	0	2	2	12	0	422	422	38	0	50
	1999		16	0	12	12	72	0	822	822	74	0	146
	1998		14	0	5	5	30	0	506	506	44	0	74
	3 Yr - TOTALS		38	0	19	19	114	0	1,750	1,750	156	0	270
15.	D. Clark	DEN	12	0	3	3	18	0	339	339	28	0	46
	1999		1	0	0	0	0	0	5	5	0	0	0
	1998		-	-	-	-	-	-	-	-	-	-	-
	3 Yr - TOTALS		13	0	3	3	18	0	344	344	28	0	46

2000 STATISTICAL RESULTS
(TIGHT ENDS — COMBINED BASIC/PERFORMANCE
SCORING METHOD)

	NAME	TEAM	GP	RSH TDs	REC TDs	TOTAL TDs	BASIC PTS	RSH YARDS	REC YARDS	TOTAL YARDS	PERF PTS	CONV PTS	FAN-TASY PTS
16.	Glover	NO	10	0	4	4	24	0	281	281	22	0	46
	1999 (w/MIN)		14	0	1	1	6	0	327	327	27	0	33
	1998 (w/MIN)		15	0	5	5	30	0	522	522	46	0	76
	3 Yr - TOTALS		39	0	10	10	60	0	1,130	1,130	95	0	155
17.	Sloan	DET	13	0	2	2	12	0	379	379	33	0	45
	1999		15	0	4	4	24	0	591	591	54	0	78
	1998		7	0	1	1	6	0	146	146	12	0	18
	3 Yr - TOTALS		35	0	7	7	42	0	1,116	1,116	99	0	141
18.	Mili	SEA	12	0	3	3	18	0	288	288	26	0	44
	1999		5	0	1	1	6	0	28	28	0	0	6
	1998		1	0	0	0	0	0	20	20	2	0	2
	3 Yr - TOTALS		18	0	4	4	24	0	336	336	28	0	52
19.	G. Clark	SF	14	0	2	2	12	0	342	342	29	0	41
	1999		11	0	0	0	0	0	347	347	29	0	29
	1998		10	0	1	1	8	0	124	124	7	2	15
	3 Yr - TOTALS		35	0	3	3	20	0	813	813	65	2	85
20.	Kelly	ATL	12	0	2	2	12	0	340	340	29	0	41
	1999		5	0	0	0	0	0	146	146	12	0	12
	1998		-	-	-	-	-	-	-	-	-	-	-
	3 Yr - TOTALS		17	0	2	2	12	0	486	486	41	0	53
21.	Moore	TB	13	0	3	3	18	0	288	288	23	0	41
	1999		13	0	5	5	30	0	276	276	22	0	52
	1998		13	0	4	4	24	0	255	255	18	0	42
	3 Yr - TOTALS		39	0	12	12	72	0	819	819	63	0	135
22.	Franks +	GB	14	0	1	1	6	0	363	363	32	0	38
	1999		-	-	-	-	-	-	-	-	-	-	-
	1998		-	-	-	-	-	-	-	-	-	-	-
	3 Yr - TOTALS		14	0	1	1	6	0	363	363	32	0	38
23.	Shea +	CLE	13	0	2	2	12	0	302	302	24	0	36
	1999		-	-	-	-	-	-	-	-	-	-	-
	1998		-	-	-	-	-	-	-	-	-	-	-
	3 Yr - TOTALS		13	0	2	2	12	0	302	302	24	0	36
24.	Bruener	PIT	13	0	3	3	18	0	192	192	14	0	32
	1999		10	0	0	0	0	0	176	176	14	0	14
	1998		9	0	2	2	12	0	157	157	10	0	22
	3 Yr - TOTALS		32	0	5	5	30	0	525	525	38	0	68
25.	McGee	CIN	12	0	1	1	6	0	309	309	26	0	32
	1999		13	0	2	2	12	0	344	344	27	0	39
	1998		11	0	1	1	6	0	363	363	30	0	36
	3 Yr - TOTALS		36	0	4	4	24	0	1,016	1,016	83	0	107
26.	McWilliams	MIN	8	0	3	3	18	0	180	180	14	0	32
	1999 (w/ARI)		9	0	1	1	6	0	71	71	3	0	9
	1998 (w/ARI)		13	0	4	4	24	0	284	284	21	0	45
	3 Yr - TOTALS		30	0	8	8	48	0	535	535	38	0	86
27.	Thomason	PHI	7	0	5	5	30	0	46	46	2	0	32
	1999 (w/GB)		7	0	2	2	12	0	140	140	12	0	24
	1998 (w/GB)		6	0	0	0	0	0	89	89	6	0	6
	3 Yr - TOTALS		20	0	7	7	42	0	275	275	20	0	62
28.	Wiggins **	NE	6	0	2	2	12	0	207	207	19	0	31
29.	Chamberlain	DEN	9	0	1	1	6	0	283	283	23	0	29
30.	T. Davis	GB	9	0	2	2	14	0	177	177	15	2	29
31.	Fauria	SEA	13	0	2	2	12	0	237	237	17	0	29
32.	Williams	STL	8	0	3	3	20	0	102	102	7	2	27
33.	Mitchell	NYG	12	0	1	1	6	0	245	245	20	0	26
34.	Bjornson	NE	8	0	2	2	12	0	152	152	12	0	24
35.	Mangum	CAR	11	0	1	1	6	0	215	215	18	0	24
36.	J. Davis	MIN	9	0	1	1	6	0	202	202	17	0	23
37.	Becht +	NYJ	9	0	2	2	12	0	144	144	10	0	22
38.	Kozlowski	ATL	10	0	2	2	12	0	151	151	10	0	22
39.	D. Campbell	NYG	8	0	3	3	18	0	46	46	3	0	21

2000 STATISTICAL RESULTS
(TIGHT ENDS — COMBINED BASIC/PERFORMANCE SCORING METHOD)

	NAME	TEAM	GP	RSH TDs	REC TDs	TOTAL TDs	BASIC PTS	RSH YARDS	REC YARDS	TOTAL YARDS	PERF PTS	CONV PTS	FAN-TASY PTS
40.	Kinney +	TEN	10	0	1	1	6	0	197	197	15	0	21
41.	Brigham	OAK	9	0	2	2	12	0	107	107	6	0	18
42.	Drayton	KC	7	0	2	2	12	0	70	70	6	0	18
43.	Hardy	ARI	14	0	1	1	6	0	160	160	11	0	17
44.	Sinceno	CHI	10	0	0	0	0	0	206	206	16	0	16
45.	Weaver	MIA	6	0	0	0	0	0	179	179	16	0	16
46.	Allred	CHI	5	0	1	1	6	0	109	109	8	0	14
47.	LaFleur	DAL	7	0	1	1	6	0	109	109	8	0	14
48.	Rutledge	NE	6	0	1	1	6	0	103	103	8	0	14
49.	Baxter	NYJ	3	0	2	2	12	0	22	22	1	0	13
50.	M. Campbell	CLE	7	0	1	1	6	0	80	80	5	0	11
51.	Rasby	DET	7	0	1	1	6	0	78	78	4	0	10
52.	Crawford	CAR	4	0	1	1	6	0	47	47	3	0	9
53.	Broughton	PHI	7	0	0	0	0	0	104	104	8	0	8
54.	Goodwin	MIA	4	0	1	1	6	0	36	36	2	0	8
55.	Hall	NO	4	0	1	1	6	0	33	33	2	0	8
56.	Jackson	BUF	4	0	1	1	6	0	36	36	2	0	8
57.	Coates	BAL	7	0	0	0	2	0	84	84	5	2	7
58.	Heiden	SD	5	0	1	1	6	0	32	32	1	0	7
59.	Collins	BUF	4	0	0	0	0	0	72	72	6	0	6
60.	Battaglia	CIN	10	0	0	0	0	0	105	105	5	0	5
61.	Geason	PIT	3	0	0	0	0	0	66	66	5	0	5
62.	Gedney	ARI	8	0	0	0	0	0	75	75	4	0	4
63.	Bush	CIN	2	0	0	0	0	0	39	39	3	0	3
64.	Conwell	STL	6	0	0	0	0	23	40	63	3	0	3
65.	Jordan	MIN	5	0	0	0	0	0	63	63	3	0	3
66.	Robinson	STL	4	0	0	0	0	0	52	52	3	0	3
67.	Dragos	CHI	3	0	0	0	0	0	28	28	2	0	2
68.	Dunn	KC	2	0	0	0	0	0	26	26	2	0	2
69.	Hape	TB	5	0	0	0	0	0	39	39	2	0	2
70.	Mayes	CHI	3	0	0	0	0	0	40	40	2	0	2
71.	Pupunu	DET	2	0	0	0	0	0	32	32	2	0	2
72.	Cross	NYG	4	0	0	0	0	0	30	30	1	0	1
73.	D. Jones	JAC	1	0	0	0	0	0	12	12	1	0	1
74.	Cushing	PIT	3	0	0	0	0	0	17	17	0	0	0
75.	R. Davis	SD	1	0	0	0	0	0	8	8	0	0	0
76.	Flemister	WAS	1	0	0	0	0	0	8	8	0	0	0
77.	Kinchen	CAR	1	0	0	0	0	0	7	7	0	0	0
78.	Lyman +	CHI	1	0	0	0	0	0	4	4	0	0	0
79.	Swift	SF	1	0	0	0	0	0	8	8	0	0	0
80.	Tant +	ARI	1	0	0	0	0	0	4	4	0	0	0
81.	Wetnight	GB	3	0	0	0	0	0	20	20	0	0	0
82.	Yoder	TB	1	0	0	0	0	0	1	1	0	0	0

+   DENOTES COLLEGE DRAFT PICKS
**   Wiggins   (NE)   -Played in 2 games with the New York Jets.

RATING THE PLAYERS FOR 2001
(Tight Ends—Combined Basic and Performance Point Scoring Method)
GRAB ONE IF YOU CAN

☐ **1. Tony Gonzalez (Kansas City Chiefs)**
A tight end recording over 1,000 yards in a season is quite a feat. Gonzalez's 93 receptions for 1,203 yards and nine touchdowns in 2000 separate him from the rest of the league's tight ends.

☐ **2. Shannon Sharpe (Baltimore Ravens)**
A broken collarbone sidelined Sharpe much of the 1999 season. When he returned healthy for 2000, jumped ship to join the Baltimore Ravens. Sharpe's 67 receptions for 810 yards and five touchdowns show he can produce regardless of who he plays for. In fact, I believe his numbers can grow in 2001 with Elvis Grbac aboard in Baltimore.

☐ **3. Wesley Walls (Carolina Panthers)**
After recording 822 receiving yards on 63 receptions, while scoring 12 times in 1999, Walls was a hot fantasy prospect heading into 2000. A knee injury forced him to miss half the season, however, as he finished with only 31 receptions for 422 yards and two touchdowns. He'll turn around these numbers if healthy all year in 2001.

☐ **4. Fred Jones (San Diego Chargers)**
A very steady performer, Jones has recorded 41, 57, 56 and 71 receptions since coming into the league, which went for 505, 602, 670 and 766 yards, while he has scored 2, 3, 2 and 5 times. The trend is going upward, which should continue in 2001, as he continues being the Chargers most consistent offensive weapon.

☐ **5. Frank Wycheck (Tennessee Titans)**
Wycheck has recorded 53, 63, 70, 69 and 70 receptions over the past five seasons, while tallying 511, 748, 768, 641 and 636 yards and scored 6, 4, 2, 2 and 4 touchdowns. He's too consistent to overlook.

BEST OF THE REST

☐ **6. Kyle Brady (Jacksonville Jaguars)**
Brady ballooned his numbers to 64 receptions for 724 yards and three touchdowns in his second year with the Jaguars in 2000. Numbers he'll continue to push these numbers in 2001.

☐ **7. Chad Lewis (Philadelphia Eagles)**
Lewis jumped from obscurity in 2000, to record 69 receptions for 735 yards but scored only three times. Being no longer obscure, Lewis will be chased by many fantasy owners in 2001.

☐ **8. Jackie Harris (Dallas Cowboys)**
The aging veteran came to the Cowboys in 2000 proving he's still got plenty left, recording 39 receptions for 306 yards while scoring five times in 2000.

☐ **9. Jay Riesmersma (Buffalo Bills)**
Riesmersma's string of 288, 496 and 372 yards and 6, 4 and 5 touchdowns over the last three seasons shows how much of a part of the Bills' offense he's become.

10. Cam Cleeland (New Orleans Saints)

Injuries have plagued Cleeland since his rookie campaign of 1998, when he recorded 54 receptions for 684 yards and six touchdowns. In 2000, Cleeland missed the entire season with a ruptured achilles. Hoping to be back healthy and stay that way, Cleeland has the potential to rebound to or surpass his rookie numbers in 2001 because the Saints like to throw more now.

STRONG LONG SHOTS

11. Ken Dilger (Indianapolis Colts)

Dilger has had a steady climb over the last three seasons, as he has tallied 303, 479 and 538 yards while recording 1, 2 and 3 touchdowns.

12. Stephen Alexander (Washington Redskins)

Though Alexander dropped from scoring three touchdowns in 1999 to only two in 2000, his yardage jumped to 510 yards on 47 catches. As he continues to get more involved in the offense, his numbers will continue to grow.

13. Dwayne Carswell (Denver Broncos)

Carswell jumped from 24 receptions in 1999 to 49 in 2000, while also jumping to 495 yards and three touchdowns. He'll likely grow these numbers in 2001 with Byron Chamberlain off to Minnesota.

14. Greg Clark (San Francisco 49ers)

The potential for bigger numbers is there, especially seeing how quickly quarterback Jeff Garcia has come on. Clark's 38 receptions for 342 yards and two touchdowns of 2000 can easily be pushed in 2001.

15. Bubba Franks (Green Bay Packers)

The Packers were hoping Franks, their #1 draft pick of a year ago, would do better than the 34 receptions for 363 yards and one touchdown he produced as a rookie in 2000. They still believe there is plenty of future potential here.

HAVE THE POTENTIAL

16. Marcus Pollard (Indianapolis Colts)

Steady as he goes, Pollard recorded 24, 34 and 30 receptions the last three seasons and, has steadily climbed in yardage with 309, 374 and 439 yards, while scoring 4, 4 and 3 times. You shouldn't overlook his consistency heading into 2001.

17. David Sloan (Detroit Lions)

In 1999, Sloan finally stayed healthy enough to record 47 receptions for 591 yards and four touchdowns. His numbers slipped some in 2000, recording 34 receptions for 379 yards and two touchdowns, as the Lions seem to be content to run more with James Stewart aboard.

18. Dave Moore (Tampa Bay Buccaneers)

Moore has produced 237, 217, 255, 276 and 288 yards and 3, 4, 4, 5 and 3 touchdowns over the last five seasons.

19. Ricky Dudley (Cleveland Browns)

He had 555 receiving yards and nine touchdowns on 39 receptions in 1999 and 350 yards and four touchdowns on 29 receptions in 2000. However, Dudley won't be back in Oakland in 2001, signing with Cleveland in the offseason.

☐ **20. Byron Chamberlain (Minnesota Vikings)**
Chamberlain, who caught 49 passes but scored only three times in 2000, looks to push those scoring numbers in 2001.

DON'T BE SURPRISED	YOU NEVER KNOW
21. Mitchell (DET)	31. Hardy (ARIZ)
22. Becht (NYJ)	32. Bjornson (OAK)
23. Fauria (SEAT)	33. Kelly (ATL)
24. T. Davis (GB)	34. LaFluer (DALL)
25. McGee (CIN)	35. Williams (OAK)
26. Bruener (PITT)	36. McWilliams (MINN)
27. D. Clark (DEN)	37. Sinceno (CHI)
28. Shea (CLE)	38. Brigham (OAK)
29. Mili (SEAT)	39. Glover (NO)
30. Wiggins (NE)	40. D. Campbell (NYG)

WORTH MENTIONING

41. Allred (CHI)
42. M. Campbell (CLE)
43. D. Jones (JAC)
44. Conwell (STL)
45. Thomason (PHIL)

ROOKIE PROSPECTS

NAME	TEAM	COMMENT
☐ 1. Todd Heap	BALT	Talented but will play behind Shannon Sharpe for now.
☐ 2. Alge Crumpler	ATL	Will push Reggie Kelly for work.

A LOOK AT THE QUARTERBACKS

(A Guide for the Beginner)

Considerations in Choosing a Quarterback

1. First, look at players' previous performances. Don't overlook players who may have missed portions of the previous year because of injuries, holdouts, and the like. Kurt Warner, Brian Griese and Jeff Blake were all affected in 2000 by injuries.

2. Look for quarterbacks who will give you decent rushing yardage on top of significant passing numbers. They'll occasionally provide a valuable rushing touchdown, as well. Daunte Culpepper is always a good consideration when talking of a quarterback who can opt to run but so is Donovan McNabb of Philadelphia.

3. Look for a quarterback who plays for a predominantly passing team—one who has a chance to throw for over 4,000 yards and close to 30 touchdowns. Kurt Warner quickly comes to mind.

4. Stay away from quarterbacks who are not guaranteed a starting assignment week after week. Some teams use one quarterback one week and then switch to another the following week, depending on the players' performances. Such was the case in Chicago in 2000. Quarterbacks in that situation are risky draft choices in fantasy football.

5. Stay away from teams that like to grind it out on the ground. These teams' quarterbacks have little chance of putting together big statistical seasons.

In the 2000 statistics that follow, players are ranked by their fantasy-point totals. Remember that the Combined Basic/Performance Scoring Method awards six points for every touchdown scored, three points for every touchdown pass thrown, one point for every 10 yards rushing, one point for every 10 yards receiving, and one point for every 20 yards passing.

2000 STATISTICAL RESULTS
(QUARTERBACKS — COMBINED BASIC/PERFORMANCE SCORING METHOD)

	NAME	TEAM	GP	RSH TDs	PASS TDs	BASIC PTS	RSH YARDS	PS YARDS	PERF PTS	CONV PTS	FANTASY POINTS
1.	Culpepper	MIN	16	7	33	143	470	3,937	227	2	370
	1999		1	0	0	0	6	0	0	0	0
	1998		-	-	-	-	-	-	-	-	-
	3 Yr - TOTALS		17	7	33	143	476	3,937	227	2	370
2.	Garcia	SF	16	4	31	118	414	4,278	243	1	361
	1999		13	2	11	46	221	2,544	137	1	183
	1998		-	-	-	-	-	-	-	-	-
	3 Yr - TOTALS		29	6	42	164	635	6,822	380	2	544
3.	Manning	IND	16	1	33	106	116	4,413	224	1	330
	1999		16	2	26	91	73	4,135	206	1	297
	1998		16	0	26	81	62	3,739	182	3	263
	3 Yr - TOTALS		48	3	85	278	251	12,287	612	5	890
4.	Gannon	OAK	16	4	28	110	529	3,430	207	2	317
	1999		16	2	24	85	298	3,840	210	1	295
	1998 (w/KC)		12	3	10	48	168	2,305	124	0	172
	3 Yr - TOTALS		44	9	62	243	995	9,575	541	3	784
5.	McNabb	PHI	16	6	21	100	629	3,365	214	1	314
	1999		11	0	8	27	313	948	69	3	96
	1998		-	-	-	-	-	-	-	-	-
	3 Yr - TOTALS		27	6	29	127	942	4,313	283	4	410
6.	Grbac	KC	15	1	28	90	111	4,169	210	0	300
	1999		16	0	22	66	15	3,389	162	0	228
	1998		8	0	5	15	27	1,142	56	0	71
	3 Yr - TOTALS		39	1	55	171	153	8,700	428	0	599
7.	Brunell	JAC	16	2	20	73	236	3,640	194	1	267
	1999		15	1	14	52	208	3,060	160	4	212
	1998		13	0	20	61	192	2,601	139	1	200
	3 Yr - TOTALS		44	3	54	186	636	9,301	493	6	679
8.	Favre	GB	16	0	20	62	108	3,812	191	2	253
	1999		16	0	22	67	142	4,091	207	1	274
	1998		16	1	31	100	133	4,212	211	1	311
	3 Yr - TOTALS		48	1	73	229	383	12,115	609	4	838
9.	Beuerlein	CAR	16	1	19	65	106	3,730	186	2	251
	1999		16	2	36	120	124	4,436	222	0	342
	1998		12	0	17	52	26	2,613	127	1	179
	3 Yr - TOTALS		44	3	72	237	256	10,779	535	3	772
10.	Collins	NYG	16	1	22	72	71	3,610	177	0	249
	1999		10	2	8	38	36	2,316	115	2	153
	1998 (w/NO)		11	1	12	44	153	2,213	118	2	162
	3 Yr - TOTALS		37	4	42	154	260	8,139	410	4	564
11.	Testaverde	NYJ	16	0	21	65	32	3,732	181	2	246
	1999		1	0	1	3	0	96	4	0	7
	1998		14	1	29	93	104	3,256	163	0	256
	3 Yr - TOTALS		31	1	51	161	136	7,084	348	2	509
12.	King	TB	16	5	18	86	353	2,769	159	2	245
	1999		6	0	7	21	38	875	42	0	63
	1998		-	-	-	-	-	-	-	-	-
	3 Yr - TOTALS		22	5	25	107	391	3,644	201	2	308
13.	Bledsoe	NE	16	2	17	63	158	3,291	168	0	231
	1999		16	0	19	57	101	3,985	197	0	254
	1998		14	0	20	60	44	3,633	177	0	237
	3 Yr - TOTALS		46	2	56	180	303	10,909	542	0	722
14.	Warner	STL	11	0	21	64	17	3,429	167	1	231
	1999		16	1	41	130	92	4,353	218	1	348
	1998		1	0	0	0	0	39	1	0	1
	3 Yr - TOTALS		28	1	62	194	109	7,821	386	2	580
15.	McNair	TEN	16	0	15	45	404	2,847	168	0	213
	1999		11	8	12	85	337	2,179	133	1	218
	1998		16	4	15	69	570	3,228	203	0	272
	3 Yr - TOTALS		43	12	42	199	1311	8,254	504	1	703

2000 STATISTICAL RESULTS
(QUARTERBACKS — COMBINED BASIC/PERFORMANCE SCORING METHOD)

	NAME	TEAM	GP	RSH TDs	PASS TDs	BASIC PTS	RSH YARDS	PS YARDS	PERF PTS	CONV PTS	FANTASY POINTS
16.	**Griese**	**DEN**	**10**	**1**	**19**	**64**	**104**	**2,688**	**137**	**1**	**201**
	1999		14	2	14	54	138	3,032	156	0	210
	1998		1	0	0	0	-4	2	0	0	0
	3 Yr - TOTALS		25	3	33	118	238	5,722	293	1	411
17.	**Stewart**	**PIT**	**15**	**7**	**11**	**75**	**436**	**1,860**	**124**	**0**	**199**
	1999		14	2	6	30	256	1,464	105	0	135
	1998		16	2	11	46	406	2,560	154	1	200
	3 Yr - TOTALS		45	11	28	151	1098	5,884	383	1	534
18.	**Plummer**	**ARI**	**14**	**0**	**13**	**39**	**183**	**2,946**	**154**	**0**	**193**
	1999		12	2	9	39	121	2,111	106	0	145
	1998		16	4	17	75	217	3,737	193	0	268
	3 Yr - TOTALS		42	6	39	153	521	8,794	453	0	606
19.	**Kitna**	**SEA**	**15**	**1**	**18**	**60**	**130**	**2,658**	**133**	**0**	**193**
	1999		15	0	23	69	56	3,346	162	0	231
	1998		6	1	7	27	67	1,177	60	0	87
	3 Yr - TOTALS		36	2	48	156	253	7,181	355	0	511
20.	**Batch**	**DET**	**15**	**2**	**13**	**51**	**199**	**2,489**	**131**	**0**	**182**
	1999		11	2	13	52	90	1,957	98	1	150
	1998		12	1	11	39	229	2,178	118	0	157
	3 Yr - TOTALS		38	5	37	142	518	6,624	347	1	489
21.	**Fiedler**	**MIA**	**14**	**1**	**14**	**48**	**267**	**2,402**	**133**	**0**	**181**
	1999 (w/JAC)		7	0	2	7	26	656	32	1	39
	1998 (w/MIN)		5	0	0	0	-6	41	1	0	1
	3 Yr - TOTALS		26	1	16	55	287	3,099	166	1	221
22.	**R. Johnson**	**BUF**	**12**	**1**	**12**	**42**	**306**	**2,125**	**127**	**0**	**169**
	1999		2	0	2	6	61	298	19	0	25
	1998		6	1	8	30	137	910	54	0	84
	3 Yr - TOTALS		20	2	22	78	504	3,333	200	0	278
23.	**B. Johnson**	**WAS**	**12**	**1**	**11**	**39**	**58**	**2,505**	**125**	**0**	**164**
	1999		16	2	24	85	30	4,005	193	1	278
	1998		4	0	7	21	15	747	35	0	56
	3 Yr - TOTALS		32	3	42	145	103	7,257	353	1	498
24.	**Blake**	**NO**	**11**	**1**	**13**	**45**	**243**	**2,025**	**115**	**0**	**160**
	1999 (w/CIN)		14	2	16	62	332	2,670	154	2	216
	1998 (w/CIN)		8	0	3	9	103	739	40	0	49
	3 Yr - TOTALS		33	3	32	116	678	5,434	309	2	425
25.	**Green**	**STL**	**8**	**1**	**16**	**54**	**69**	**2,063**	**105**	**0**	**159**
	1999		-	-	-	-	-	-	-	-	-
	1998 (w/WAS)		15	2	23	82	117	3,441	174	1	256
	3 Yr - TOTALS		23	3	39	136	186	5,504	279	1	415
26.	**McNown**	CHI	10	3	8	42	326	1,646	107	0	149
27.	**Chandler**	ATL	14	0	10	30	60	2,236	109	0	139
28.	**Brooks**	NO	8	2	9	39	170	1,514	88	0	127
29.	**Leaf**	SD	11	0	11	33	54	1,883	92	0	125
30.	**Frerotte**	DEN	9	1	9	33	64	1,776	91	0	124
31.	**Flutie**	BUF	11	1	8	30	161	1,700	92	0	122
32.	**Dilfer**	BAL	9	0	12	36	75	1,502	76	0	112
33.	**Banks**	BAL	11	0	8	25	57	1,578	77	1	102
34.	**Aikman**	DAL	11	0	7	22	13	1,632	75	1	97
35.	**Couch**	CLE	7	0	7	21	45	1,483	74	0	95
36.	**Harbaugh**	SD	7	0	8	24	24	1,416	68	0	92
37.	**George**	WAS	6	0	7	21	24	1,389	67	0	88
38.	**Smith**	CIN	11	0	3	9	232	1,253	76	0	85
39.	**Cunningham**	DAL	6	1	6	25	89	849	48	1	73
40.	**Mitchell**	CIN	8	1	3	15	61	966	47	0	62
41.	**Pederson**	CLE	10	0	2	6	68	1,047	52	0	58
42.	**Matthews**	CHI	6	0	3	9	35	964	47	0	56
43.	**Case**	DET	5	1	1	10	117	503	34	1	44
44.	**Graham**	PIT	8	0	1	3	7	899	41	0	44
45.	**B. Huard**	SEA	5	0	3	9	29	540	27	0	36
46.	**Kanell**	ATL	5	0	2	6	0	524	24	0	30

2000 STATISTICAL RESULTS
(QUARTERBACKS — COMBINED BASIC/PERFORMANCE SCORING METHOD)

	NAME	TEAM	GP	RSH TDs	PASS TDs	BASIC PTS	RSH YARDS	PS YARDS	PERF PTS	CONV PTS	FANTASY POINTS
47.	O'Donnell	TEN	6	0	2	6	-2	530	23	0	29
48.	D. Brown	ARI	4	0	2	6	0	467	22	0	28
49.	D. Johnson	ATL	4	0	2	6	11	406	19	0	25
50.	Miller	CHI	3	0	1	3	5	382	18	0	21
51.	Martin	JAC	5	0	2	6	-6	307	13	0	19
52.	D. Huard	MIA	3	0	1	3	0	318	15	0	18
53.	Moon	KC	2	0	1	3	2	208	9	0	12
54.	Moreno	SD	6	0	0	0	20	241	12	0	12
55.	Wright	DAL	4	0	0	0	36	237	11	0	11
56.	Lucas	NYJ	5	0	0	0	42	206	11	0	11
57.	Mirer	SF	1	0	1	4	5	126	6	1	10
58.	Lewis	CAR	5	0	0	0	36	120	8	0	8
59.	Wynn +	CLE	7	0	0	0	15	167	7	0	7
60.	Hasselbeck	GB	4	0	1	3	-7	104	4	0	7
61.	Bishop	NE	7	0	1	3	5	80	3	0	6
62.	Pennington +	NYJ	1	0	1	3	0	67	3	0	6
63.	Greisen	ARI	2	0	1	3	1	65	2	0	5
64.	Stoerner	DAL	1	0	1	3	0	53	2	0	5
65.	Brister	MIN	2	0	0	0	20	82	5	0	5
66.	Van Pelt	BUF	1	0	0	0	0	67	3	0	3
67.	Friesz	NE	1	0	0	0	0	66	3	0	3
68.	Redman	BAL	1	0	0	0	0	19	0	0	0
69.	Craig	CAR	4	0	0	0	4	0	0	0	0
70.	Thompson	CLE	1	0	0	0	0	8	0	0	0
71.	Jackson +	DEN	2	0	0	0	-1	0	0	0	0
72.	Quinn	JAC	1	0	0	0	-2	0	0	0	0
73.	Brady +	NE	1	0	0	0	0	6	0	0	0
74.	Garrett	NYG	2	0	0	0	-4	0	0	0	0
75.	Hoying	OAK	1	0	0	0	-3	0	0	0	0
76.	Detmer	PHI	2	0	0	0	8	0	0	0	0
77.	Rattay +	SF	1	0	0	0	-1	-4	0	0	0
78.	Hamilton +	TB	1	0	0	0	-2	0	0	0	0
79.	Zeier	TB	3	0	0	0	-2	19	0	0	0
80.	Husak +	WAS	1	0	0	0	-1	-2	0	0	0

+ DENOTES COLLEGE DRAFT PICKS

RATING THE PLAYERS FOR 2001
(Quarterbacks—Combined Basic/Performance Point Scoring Method)
GRAB ONE IF YOU CAN

☐ **1. Daunte Culpepper (Minnesota Vikings)**
Head coach Denny Green followed his instincts and went with young Daunte Culpepper in 2000. A full 3,937 passing yards and 33 passing touchdowns, along with 470 rushing yards and seven rushing touchdowns later, Green was proven correct. Looking to 2001, however, Culpepper and the Vikings face the league's toughest schedule.

☐ **2. Kurt Warner (St. Louis Rams)**
A finger injury sidelined Warner for five games in 2000, which contributed to his drop in stats, along with a fall off in offensive production. He may never match his 4,353 passing yards and 41 touchdown passes of 1999, but he'll push his 2000 numbers.

☐ **3. Jeff Garcia (San Francisco 49ers)**
Thrown into the frying pan in 1999 with Steve Young hurt, Garcia struggled. 2000 was different, as Garcia produced 4,278 passing yards, 31 passing touchdowns, 414 rushing yards and four rushing scores. He'll push or near these numbers in 2001 as he quickly continues to develop.

☐ **4. Peyton Manning (Indianapolis Colts)**
Consistently improving, Manning has thrown for 3,739, 4,135 and 4,413 passing yards while throwing for 26, 26 and 33 touchdowns over his three-year career. Despite facing a very difficult schedule in 2001, Mannings, I believe, will continue his progress.

☐ **5. Brett Favre (Green Bay Packers)**
He may not be putting together the numbers he once was, but Favre's 3,812 passing yards and 20 touchdown passes of 2000 are enough to show he still has the potential to be a significant fantasy factor in 2001.

BEST OF THE REST

☐ **6. Rich Gannon (Oakland Raiders)**
Gannon has had impressive numbers since coming to Oakland two years ago. In 1999, Gannon threw for 3,840 yards and 24 touchdowns, while rushing for 298 yards and scoring twice on the ground. In 2000, Gannon threw for 3,430 yards and 28 touchdowns while rushing for 529 yards and four touchdowns. As a dual threat through the air and on the ground, Gannon has more success heading his way again in 2001.

☐ **7. Brian Griese (Denver Broncos)**
Progressing quickly, Griese would have reached the 4,000 yard, 25 touchdown levels in 2000 had he not missed six games with shoulder problems in 2000. He'll look to push these numbers in 2001. Griese did throw for 2,688 yards and 19 touchdowns in 2000, playing in ten games.

☐ **8. Donovan McNabb (Philadelphia Eagles)**
McNabb grabbed the starting role in 2000 and blossomed. He threw for 3,365 yards and 21 touchdowns, while rushing for 629 yards and six touchdowns. As one of the league's newfound double-threat quarterbacks, McNabb will be a highly sought after fantasy pick in 2001.

☐ **9. Mark Brunell (Jacksonville Jaguars)**
Brunell has struggled to stay healthy throughout his career. In finally
doing so in 2000, he recorded 3,640 passing yards and 20 touchdown
passes. With receivers like Jimmy Smith, and Keenan McCardell and
tight end Kyle Brady to throw to again in 2001, success should follow
if he can stay healthy.

☐ **10. Elvis Grbac (Baltimore Ravens)**
He had 4,169 passing yards and 28 touchdown passes when with Kansas
City in 2000. Can he liven up the Ravens' passing game in 2001?

STRONG LONG SHOTS

☐ **11. Kerry Collins (New York Giants)**
Collins has helped dismiss the Giants' boring run-first offensive philosophy. Collin's 3,610 passing yards and 22 touchdown passes of a year
ago are numbers he could surpass in 2001, as the Giants continue to
open things up.

☐ **12. Vinny Testaverde (New York Jets)**
Returning after missing almost the entire 1999 season with a ruptured
achilles, Testaverde had to deal with life without Keyshawn in 2000. In
throwing for 3,732 yards and 21 touchdowns, Testaverde proved he
could still put up decent numbers, but I bet he still misses a guy like
Keyshawn.

☐ **13. Drew Bledsoe (New England Patriots)**
His 3,291 passing yards and 17 touchdown passes in 2000 are not the
numbers he once put together. However, the ten-year, $103 million deal
Bledsoe signed in the offseason may help give his numbers a boost.

☐ **14. Brad Johnson (Tampa Bay Buccaneers)**
How unconservative will Tony Dungy get with Brad Johnson now at
quarterback? Surely receivers Keyshawn Johnson and Jacquez Green
are happy to have Johnson aboard.

☐ **15. Jeff George (Washington Redskins)**
George gets his chance at a starting job again in 2001, as Brad Johnson departs to Tampa Bay. Two things holding Johnson's fantasy stock
back are that the Redskins like to run Stephen Davis often and there's
uncertainty with the Redskins' wide receivers.

HAVE THE POTENTIAL

☐ **16. Trent Green (Kansas City Chiefs)**
Dick Vermeil likes to pass, at least he did in St. Louis, and Trent Green
is certainly no slouch, who should put up good numbers in 2001.

☐ **17. Jeff Blake/Aaron Brooks (New Orleans Saints)**
Blake's broken foot in 2000 led to the emergence of Aaron Brooks,
which sets up a good battle for the starting job in 2001. Regardless, the
Saints are no longer an overly conservative running team.

☐ **18. Steve McNair (Tennessee Titans)**
The ability to run has always helped McNair's fantasy value, though he
failed to score a rushing touchdown in 2000 despite rushing for eight
the year before, playing in just 11 games. His passing numbers aren't
always impressive, but his rushing numbers balance his effectiveness.

☐ **19. Rob Johnson (Buffalo Bills)**
Without Doug Flutie looking over his shoulder, Johnson has the starting job to himself in 2001, which should help his confidence and his numbers.

☐ **20. Chris Chandler (Atlanta Falcons)**
Has struggled since producing 3,154 passing yards and 25 touchdowns in 1998, but, with a fairly easy schedule and a healthier Jamal Anderson to balance the attack, he could rebound his numbers in 2001.

KEEP AN EYE ON

☐ **21. Tony Banks (Dallas Cowboys)**
The Cowboys will have to adjust to life without Troy, and Tony Banks has been known to be inconsistent, though he'll have Rocket Ismail and Joey Galloway as targets.

☐ **22. Kordell Stewart (Pittsburgh Steelers)**
Stewart showed glimpses of restored confidence in 2000 and his 436 rushing yards and seven rushing touchdowns are much more of an allure than his passing numbers.

☐ **23. Jake Plummer (Arizona Cardinals)**
He has the potential and the receivers to put together much better numbers than he has.

☐ **24. Jeff Lewis (Carolina Panthers)**
I don't know how he'll step in and fare for the departed Steve Beuerlein, but I like the potential he has for receivers.

☐ **25. Charlie Batch (Detroit Lions)**
Germane Crowell, Johnnie Morton and tight end David Sloan are nice targets, but the Lions have elected to run more with James Stewart now aboard.

☐ **26. Doug Flutie (San Diego Chargers)**
Flutie gets his chance to start again but for the Chargers.

☐ **27. Matt Hasselbeck (Seattle Seahawks)**
He's a newcomer to the starting ranks.

☐ **28. Jay Fiedler/Ray Lucas (Miami Dolphins)**
The Dolphins receiving crew is always banged up, and Miami seems content to run Lamar Smith often.

☐ **29. Cade McNown/Jim Miller/Shane Matthews (Chicago Bears)**
McNown hasn't set the world on fire his first two seasons and still has Miller and Matthews pushing for work.

☐ **30. Tim Couch (Cleveland Browns)**
The Browns still look woeful on offense.

☐ **31. Jon Kitna/Akili Smith (Cincinnati Bengals)**
Neither impresses me.

ROOKIE PROSPECTS

NAME	TEAM	COMMENT
☐ 1. Michael Vick	ATL	Has bright future but will learn from Chris Chandler for now.
☐ 2. Drew Brees	SD	Will learn from veteran Doug Flutie for now.
☐ 3. Chris Weinke	CNR	At 28 Weinke has maturity to push Jeff Lewis for work.
☐ 4. Quincy Carter	DALL	Future hope for Dallas, it's Tony Banks for now.

Combined Basic/Performance Scoring Method

A LOOK AT THE KICKERS

(A Guide for the Beginner)

Considerations in Choosing a Kicker

The scoring for kickers is identical in both the Basic Scoring Method and the Combined Basic/Performance Scoring Method. (See the section on Kickers for the Basic Scoring Method.)

A 2001 QUICK PICKS—MOCK DRAFT

(My Top "30" Overall Picks for the Combined Basic/Performance Scoring Method)

	NAME	TEAM	POS	COMMENTS
1.	Faulk	STL	RB	Very capable of 2,000 combined yards and 20 TDs.
2.	James	IND	RB	Very capable of 2,000 combined yards and 15 plus TDs.
3.	Culpepper	MINN	QB	Ability to run and pass makes him very valuable.
4.	Warner	STL	QB	Injured finger slowed numbers in 2000; looking to rebound in 2001.
5.	George	TENN	RB	Beginning to push scoring numbers.
6.	Garcia	SF	QB	Over 4,200 yards and 31 TDs in first year as full-time starter in 2001.
7.	Taylor	JAC	RB	Capable of 1,500-2,000 yards and 15-20 TDs.
8.	S. Davis	WASH	RB	Looking to rebound against league's easiest schedule in 2001.
9.	T. Davis	DEN	RB	If healthy in 2001, very capable of big numbers.
10.	Manning	IND	QB	Consistent 4,000-yd QB; pushing TD numbers.
11.	Favre	GB	QB	Looking to rebound to 4,000-yd plateau and push 25 TDs.
12.	Williams	NO	RB	9 TDs and 1,409 combined yards in just 10 games before injury in 2000.
13.	Gannon	OAK	QB	His ability to run and throw, a nice fit for Raiders.
14.	Green	GB	RB	Over 1,700 combined yds and 13 TDs in 2000.
15.	Martin	NYJ	RB	Jets' most-consistent offensive weapon.
16.	Moss	MINN	WR	A receiver always pushing 1,400 yards and 15 TDs.
17.	Griese	DEN	QB	2,688 yds and 19 TDs in just ten games before injury in 2000.
18.	Stewart	DET	RB	Will get a "Lion" share of Detroits offense in 2001.
19.	McNabb	PHIL	QB	Has quickly developed into one of league's best double-threat quarterbacks.
20.	Brunell	JAC	QB	Can run and has the targets to put up good numbers.
21.	Smith	MIA	RB	Surprised many with 1,340 yards and 16 TDs in 2000.
22.	Dillon	CIN	RB	Dillon is the Bengals' offense.
23.	Lewis	BALT	RB	Looking to push his 1,660-yard, six-TD performance as rookie in 2000.
24.	Harrison	IND	WR	Over 3,000 yds and 26 touchdowns over last two seasons.
25.	Grbac	BALT	QB	Will give Ravens' passing attack quick boost.
26.	Bruce	STL	WR	Has rebounded to healthy numbers last two seasons.
27.	Wheatley	OAK	RB	Should score often but Charlie Garner may limit.
28.	Anderson	ATL	RB	Looking to continue to rebound numbers from knee injury.
29.	Owens	SF	WR	With QB Garcia's improvement, so will Owen's numbers improve.
30.	Gonzalez	KC	TE	A tight end who puts up surprising numbers.

This Mock Draft is expanded and updated in *Cliff's Quick Picks: Fantasy Football Draft at a Glance*—a huge 8-panel cheatsheet that examines the top-100 overall picks for the Basic and Combined Basic/Performance methods. Potential fantasy draft picks are also broken down by fantasy position, including the *top-50* running backs and wide receivers, and the *top-25* tight ends, quarterbacks and kickers. *Cliff's Quick Picks* will be available in mid-August and updated weekly, right around your fantasy draft time. Be sure to order! Details and order form, along with a toll-free phone number, and website address appear on the hard insert in the middle of this book.

X
RATING THE PLAYERS:
DISTANCE SCORING METHOD

Let's review how scoring is done using the Distance Scoring Method. As in the Basic Scoring Method, points are awarded for touchdowns scored by players on offense. The difference between this method and the Basic Scoring Method is that in the Distance Scoring Method, the yardage covered on the touchdown play is used to calculate the points awarded—the longer the touchdown, the more points awarded. This scoring method favors exciting touchdowns and rewards players for the yardage they cover on the play.

The Distance Scoring Method presents unique challenges for your draft selection. It's difficult to determine who is going to score the actual touchdowns. In addition, you must predict who is going to score from enough distance to give you the winning edge.

As we did in the preceding methods, we will now look at basic drafting strategies and review the players' 2000 statistics; finally I will rate the players for 2001. No rookies are included in my player ratings. It's too early to size up how they'll fit into each team's scheme. I rate the rookies separately, in Section V of this chapter.

Distance Scoring Method
DRAFTING STRATEGY BY ROUNDS
(A Guide for the Beginner)

1. The draft consists of 12 rounds.

2. Of the 12 players, seven are starters and five are reserves.

3. The starting seven comprise:

1 Quarterback		1 Quarterback
2 Running Backs	OR	2 Running Backs
2 Wide Receivers	FLEX OPTION	3 Receivers
1 Tight End		1 Kicker
1 Kicker		

4. The five reserves can be from any position.

5. Any player from any starting position can be drafted in any round.

ROUND 1: Remember that points are awarded for actual touchdowns scored. Players are awarded two points for every 10 yards on touchdown plays. Our concerns are primarily to get a player who will score often, and secondly to find someone who might score from some distance. In recent years, some prominent wide receivers have begun to score as consistently as the top running backs. These players, along with consistent running backs should be your top picks. In 1998, Viking rookie wide receiver Randy Moss was the leagues' best as he hit 144 points, averaging a whopping 35.6

yards on 17 touchdowns. He was followed by fellow wideouts Antonio Freeman (130 points) and Joey Galloway (106 points) before a running back came in, with Terrell Davis hitting 102 points. A quarterback in this round may also be a consideration but stick to the consistent types like Kurt Warner or Brett Favre.

ROUND 2: Now is probably a good time to pick up a back used as a team's primary ball carrier. He will probably be among the league's elite, if they're not all gone. If you've already grabbed a running back in the first round, take the best wide receiver available.

ROUND 3: In this round, try to grab a good quarterback, one who will throw 25 or more touchdown passes during the year. A consistent quarterback will put points on the scoreboard week after week. Kurt Warner, when he's healthy, and Brett Favre fall into this category unless they are already long gone. Even the next group of signal-callers would be a good consideration here. By the end of the third round, you should have a consistently scoring wide receiver or running back and a solid quarterback.

ROUND 4: In this round, I'd grab either a second running back or a wide receiver, whichever is the best available, to provide a more consistent scoring punch.

ROUND 5: Now it's important to pick up a kicker. Look for a consistent scorer who plays on a team good enough to give him plenty of scoring chances.

ROUNDS 6 through 8: Fill in the starting positions you have left open. If you have followed my suggestions, you lack a tight end and a wide receiver. But if you notice that a player you really like is available at a position you have already partially filled, pick him up, even if you haven't filled all your starting positions. You'll feel better about your lineup, and at the very worst, you'll have either a high-powered reserve or some attractive trade bait.

ROUNDS 9 through 12: These rounds are used to fill in your reserves. It's a good time to take a shot at a rookie. In choosing your reserves, be sure to draft backups for the more injury-prone positions—quarterback, running back, and wide receiver. Even though you're into the less important players by this time, keep alert. Many good picks show up in these late rounds.

Let's now take a look at what to consider when choosing players for each position.

A LOOK AT THE RUNNING BACKS

(A Guide for the Beginner)

Considerations in Choosing a Running Back

1. First, review players' previous performances, especially from last season. Injuries, trades, holdouts, suspensions and the like should be noted. Injuries to Dorsey Levens, Ricky Williams, and Terrell Davis greatly affected their seasons.

2. The first priority in selecting a running back is choosing one who will not only score consistently but who is also capable of long touchdown runs. Our first choice is a fast back who scores regularly. Edgerrin James, Marshall Faulk or Eddie George can score from anywhere.

3. If a quick, consistent scorer is not available on your turn, you should forget about speed and take a reliable, high-scoring big back. Although his touchdown runs may be shorter, he provides you with consistent scoring. In 1992, Rodney Culver of Indianapolis emerged as a short-yardage touchdown specialist. In 1993, Marcus Allen became Kansas City's designated scorer. In 1996, Cincinnati gave that role to Ki-Jana Carter. In 1998, Minnesota's Leroy Hoard pounded in 10 touchdowns.

4. Your next preference should be the back who will probably not score many touchdowns but is likely to get some big yardage when he does score. These are the scatback runners who excel in the open but usually give way to the bigger backs in bruising goal-line situations. This type of player may work out as a good second back in your offense. James Brooks was a popular pick in the past as was Eric Metcalf.

5. Next is a top rookie. Every year there seems to be at least one first-year running back who makes it big. Look at Leonard Russell in 1991. In 1992, Rodney Culver of the Colts produced nine touchdowns. In 1993, rookies Ronald Moore (nine TDs), Natrone Means (eight TDs), Jerome Bettis (seven TDs), and Terry Kirby (six TDs) all provided scoring punch. In 1994, Marshall Faulk made a huge impact with 12 scores. In 1996, Karim Abdul-Jabbar produced 11 scores. In 1997 Antowain Smith scored eight times. In 1998 both Fred Taylor (17 TDs) and Robert Edwards (12 TDs) had big years. In 2000, Michael Anderson sprung for 15 TDs.

6. In most cases, shy away from old or injury-prone running backs. If they have been in the league for many years, they probably won't last a full season without injury and their desire to excel may be dwindling.

7. Finally, beware of players who have injury after nagging injury. They may be good backs, but they can't help you if they're out of the lineup.

In the 2000 statistics that follow, you'll find the players ranked by their fantasy-point totals. Remember that in the Distance Scoring Method, fantasy points are calculated by the length of the touchdown scored—the longer the touchdown play, the more points earned.

NAME	TEAM	GP	RSH	RSH TDs	AVG LGTH	PASS REC	REC TDs	AVG LGTH	TOTAL TDs	AVG LGTH	CONV PTS	FAN-TASY PTS
1. M. Faulk	STL	14	253	18	3.5	81	8	28.4	26	11.1	4	94
1999		16	253	7	9.8	87	5	32.0	12	19.1	2	60
1998		16	324	6	26.5	86	4	35.5	10	30.1	0	70
3 Yr - TOTALS		46	830	31	9.4	254	17	31.1	48	17.1	6	224
2. R. Smith	MIN	16	295	7	29.0	36	3	43.7	10	33.4	0	80
1999		13	221	2	37.0	24	0	0.0	2	37.0	0	18
1998		14	249	6	40.7	28	2	45.5	8	41.9	0	74
3 Yr - TOTALS		43	765	15	34.7	88	5	44.4	20	37.2	0	172
3. James	IND	16	387	13	7.4	63	5	22.2	18	11.6	2	70
1999		16	369	13	9.1	62	4	21.5	17	12.0	0	68
1998		-	-	-	-	-	-	-	-	-	-	-
3 Yr - TOTALS		32	756	26	8.3	125	9	21.9	35	11.8	2	138
4. M. Anderson +	DEN	14	297	15	13.2	23	0	0.0	15	13.2	2	62
1999		-	-	-	-	-	-	-	-	-	-	-
1998		-	-	-	-	-	-	-	-	-	-	-
3 Yr - TOTALS		14	297	15	13.2	23	0	0.0	15	13.2	2	62
5. Br. Mitchell *	PHI	14	25	2	45.5	13	1	13.0	5	53.0	0	58
1999 (w/WAS)		16	40	1	6.0	31	0	0.0	1	6.0	0	2
1998 (w/WAS)		16	39	2	3.5	44	0	0.0	3	35.3	0	24
3 Yr - TOTALS		46	104	5	20.8	88	1	13.0	9	44.9	0	84
6. Dillon	CIN	16	315	7	30.3	18	0	0.0	7	30.3	0	54
1999		15	263	5	5.2	31	1	12.0	6	6.4	0	18
1998		15	262	4	9.0	28	1	17.0	5	10.6	0	16
3 Yr - TOTALS		46	840	16	17.1	77	2	14.5	18	16.9	0	88
7. L. Smith	MIA	15	309	14	12.7	31	2	7.0	16	11.9	0	54
1999 (w/NO)		13	60	0	0.0	20	1	4.0	1	4.0	0	2
1998 (w/NO)		14	138	1	5.0	24	2	21.0	3	15.7	0	15
3 Yr - TOTALS		42	507	15	12.2	75	5	12.0	20	12.1	0	71
8. Dunn	TB	16	248	8	21.9	44	1	23.0	9	22.0	0	52
1999		15	195	0	0.0	64	2	12.0	2	12.0	0	6
1998		16	245	2	26.5	44	0	0.0	2	26.5	0	14
3 Yr - TOTALS		47	688	10	22.8	152	3	15.7	13	21.2	0	72
9. Taylor	JAC	13	292	12	10.4	36	2	13.0	14	10.7	0	50
1999		10	159	6	15.9	10	0	0.0	6	15.9	0	28
1998		15	264	14	17.0	44	3	30.3	17	19.4	0	90
3 Yr - TOTALS		38	715	32	14.3	90	5	23.4	37	15.5	0	168
10. Barber	NYG	16	213	8	20.5	70	1	13.0	9	19.7	0	48
1999		15	62	0	0.0	66	2	17.5	3	40.0	0	28
1998		16	52	0	0	42	3	38.7	3	38.7	0	26
3 Yr - TOTALS		47	327	8	20.5	178	6	27.4	15	27.6	0	102
11. George	TEN	16	403	14	8.7	50	2	5.0	16	8.2	0	46
1999		16	320	9	9.8	47	4	24.0	13	14.2	0	50
1998		16	348	5	11.6	37	1	22.0	6	13.3	2	26
3 Yr - TOTALS		48	1,071	28	9.6	134	7	18.3	35	11.3	2	122
12. S. Davis	WAS	15	332	11	11.4	33	0	0.0	11	11.4	0	42
1999		14	290	17	10.8	23	0	0.0	17	10.8	2	62
1998		13	34	0	0.0	21	2	15.5	2	15.5	0	8
3 Yr - TOTALS		42	656	28	11.0	77	2	15.5	30	11.3	2	112
13. A. Green	GB	16	263	10	10.4	73	3	4.7	13	9.2	0	38
1999 (w/SEA)		8	26	0	0.0	0	0	0.0	0	0.0	0	0
1998 (w/SEA)		9	35	1	6.0	3	0	0.0	1	6.0	0	2
3 Yr - TOTALS		33	324	11	10.0	76	3	4.7	14	9.0	0	40
14. Wheatley	OAK	14	232	9	10.6	20	1	7.0	10	10.3	0	36
1999		16	242	8	11.7	21	3	18.7	11	13.5	0	42
1998 (w/NYG)	4	14	0	0.0		0	0.0		0	0.0	0	
3 Yr - TOTALS		34	488	17	11.1	41	4	15.8	21	12.0	0	78
15. Garner	SF	16	258	7	1.9	68	3	21.7	10	7.8	0	30
1999		16	241	4	7.2	56	2	19.0	6	11.2	0	20
1998 (w/PHI)		10	96	4	5.3	19	0	0.0	4	5.3	0	10
3 Yr - TOTALS		42	595	15	4.2	143	5	20.6	20	8.3	0	60

NAME	TEAM	GP	RSH	RSH TDs	AVG LGTH	PASS REC	REC TDs	AVG LGTH	TOTAL TDs	AVG LGTH	CONV PTS	FAN-TASY PTS
16. Stewart	DET	16	339	10	2.0	32	1	13.0	11	3.0	6	30
1999 (w/JAC)		14	249	13	5.4	21	0	0.0	13	5.4	0	34
1998 (w/JAC)		3	53	2	4.0	6	1	3.0	3	3.7	0	6
3 Yr - TOTALS		33	641	25	3.9	59	2	8.0	27	4.2	6	70
17. Warren **	PHI	12	74	2	21.0	32	1	76.0	3	39.3	0	28
1999 (w/DAL)		15	99	2	4.0	34	0	0.0	2	4.0	0	4
1998 (w/DAL)		9	59	4	4.0	13	1	6.0	5	4.4	0	10
3 Yr - TOTALS		36	232	8	8.3	79	2	41.0	10	14.8	0	42
18. R. Williams	NO	10	248	8	5.8	44	1	13.0	9	6.5	0	26
1999		12	253	2	10.0	28	0	0.0	2	10.0	0	6
1998		-	-	-	-	-	-	-	-	-	-	-
3 Yr - TOTALS		22	501	10	6.6	72	1	13.0	11	7.1	0	32
19. K. Faulk	NE	15	164	4	6.3	51	1	52.0	5	15.4	2	24
1999		11	67	1	15.0	12	1	13.0	2	14.0	0	8
1998		-	-	-	-	-	-	-	-	-	-	-
3 Yr - TOTALS		26	231	5	8.0	63	2	32.5	7	15.0	2	32
20. Cu. Martin	NYJ	16	317	9	3.1	70	2	4.5	11	3.4	0	24
1999		16	367	5	8.6	45	0	0.0	5	8.6	0	16
1998		15	369	8	14.5	43	1	8.0	9	13.8	0	36
3 Yr - TOTALS		47	1,053	22	8.5	158	3	5.7	25	8.2	0	76
21. Ja. Lewis +	BAL	16	309	6	8.7	27	0	0.0	6	8.7	2	22
1999		-	-	-	-	-	-	-	-	-	-	-
1998		-	-	-	-	-	-	-	-	-	-	-
3 Yr - TOTALS		16	309	6	8.7	27	0	0.0	6	8.7	2	22
22. J. Anderson	ATL	16	282	6	9.0	42	0	0.0	6	9.0	2	20
1999		2	19	0	0.0	2	0	0.0	0	0.0	0	0
1998		16	410	14	11.5	27	2	8.5	16	11.1	2	60
3 Yr - TOTALS		34	711	20	10.8	71	2	8.5	22	10.5	4	80
23. Mi. Bates *	CAR	5	5	0	0.0	5	0	0.0	1	92.0	0	20
1999		3	3	0	0.0	1	0	0.0	2	97.0	0	40
1998 (w/ARI)		9	60	6	1.5	1	0	0.0	6	1.5	0	12
3 Yr - TOTALS		17	68	6	1.5	7	0	0.0	9	32.8	0	72
24. Bettis	PIT	16	355	8	5.7	14	0	0.0	8	5.7	0	20
1999		16	299	7	5.5	21	0	0.0	7	5.5	0	21
1998		15	316	3	6.0	16	0	0.0	3	6.0	0	8
3 Yr - TOTALS		47	970	18	5.7	51	0	0.0	18	5.7	0	49
25. Jenkins *	SD	5	8	0	0.0	1	0	0.0	1	93.0	0	20
1999		-	-	-	-	-	-	-	-	-	-	-
1998		-	-	-	-	-	-	-	-	-	-	-
3 Yr - TOTALS		5	8	0	0.0	1	0	0.0	1	93.0	0	20
26. Jordan	OAK	13	46	3	18.7	27	1	21.0	4	19.3	0	20
1999		6	9	2	1.0	8	0	0.0	2	1.0	0	4
1998		3	47	1	10.0	3	0	0.0	1	10.0	0	4
3 Yr - TOTALS		22	102	6	11.4	38	1	21.0	7	12.7	0	28
27. Morris +	BUF	12	93	5	7.6	37	1	18.0	6	9.3	0	20
1999		-	-	-	-	-	-	-	-	-	-	-
1998		-	-	-	-	-	-	-	-	-	-	-
3 Yr - TOTALS		12	93	5	7.6	37	1	18.0	6	9.3	0	20
28. Pittman	ARI	16	184	4	2.5	73	2	23.0	6	9.3	0	20
1999		10	64	2	31.0	16	0	0.0	2	31.0	0	14
1998		6	29	0	0.0	0	0	0.0	0	0.0	0	0
3 Yr - TOTALS		32	277	6	12.0	89	2	23.0	8	14.7	0	34
29. Richardson	KC	16	147	3	10.0	58	3	9.0	6	9.5	0	20
1999		16	84	1	1.0	24	0	0.0	1	1.0	0	2
1998		10	20	2	1.5	2	0	0.0	2	1.5	0	4
3 Yr - TOTALS		42	251	6	5.7	84	3	9.0	9	6.8	0	26
30. Watters	SEA	16	278	7	2.8	63	2	9.0	9	4.2	0	20
1999		16	325	5	7.0	40	2	15.0	7	9.3	0	20
1998		16	319	9	10.4	52	0	0.0	9	10.4	2	35
3 Yr - TOTALS		48	922	21	7.1	155	4	12.0	25	7.9	2	75
31. Prentice +	CLE	15	173	7	4.3	37	1	3.0	8	4.2	0	18

NAME	TEAM	GP	RSH	RSH TDs	AVG LGTH	PASS REC	REC TDs	AVG LGTH	TOTAL TDs	AVG LGTH	CONV PTS	FAN-TASY PTS
32. Rogers *	SEA	0	0	0	0.0	0	0	0.0	1	81.0	0	18
33. E. Smith	DAL	16	294	9	3.3	11	0	0.0	9	3.3	0	18
34. Beasley	SF	15	50	3	1.3	31	3	12.3	6	6.8	0	16
35. Alstott	TB	13	131	5	6.8	13	0	0.0	5	6.8	0	14
36. B. Bennett	CIN	15	90	3	21.0	19	0	0.0	3	21.0	0	14
37. Crockett	OAK	11	43	7	3.6	10	0	0.0	7	3.6	0	14
38. Huntley	PIT	12	46	3	12.3	10	0	0.0	3	12.3	2	14
39. R. Anderson	NYJ	16	27	0	0.0	88	2	25.0	2	25.0	0	12
40. Autry	PHI	10	112	3	1.7	24	1	23.0	4	7.0	0	12
41. Fletcher	SD	15	116	3	4.7	48	1	25.0	4	9.8	0	12
42. Bryson	BUF	16	161	0	0.0	32	2	11.0	2	11.0	2	10
43. Dayne +	NYG	16	228	5	2.8	3	0	0.0	5	2.8	0	10
44. Holcombe	STL	13	21	3	1.0	8	1	12.0	4	3.8	0	10
45. Redmond +	NE	11	125	1	1.0	20	2	15.5	3	10.7	0	10
46. Watson	STL	9	54	4	5.8	10	0	0.0	4	5.8	0	10
47. J. Allen	CHI	16	290	2	11.0	39	1	6.0	3	9.3	0	8
48. Biakabutuka	CAR	12	173	2	1.0	34	2	5.0	4	3.0	0	8
49. Edwards	CLE	12	2	0	0.0	16	2	13.0	2	13.0	0	8
50. Jackson	SF	7	5	1	1.0	5	1	11.0	2	6.0	2	8
51. Moreau +	KC	10	67	4	1.5	0	0	0.0	4	1.5	0	8
52. A. Smith	BUF	10	101	4	4.0	3	0	0.0	4	4.0	0	8
53. T. Allen	NO	4	46	2	1.5	1	0	0.0	2	1.5	2	6
54. Centers	WAS	15	20	0	0.0	80	3	4.7	3	4.7	0	6
55. Coleman	DEN	7	54	1	24.0	1	0	0.0	1	24.0	0	6
56. Hetherington	CAR	10	23	2	1.0	14	1	3.0	3	1.7	0	6
57. Jones +	ARI	14	112	2	7.0	32	0	0.0	2	7.0	0	6
58. Levens	GB	5	77	3	3.0	16	0	0.0	3	3.0	0	6
59. Parmalee	NYJ	4	27	2	12.5	9	0	0.0	2	12.5	0	6
60. Alexander +	SEA	16	64	2	5.5	5	0	0.0	2	5.5	0	4
61. Anders	KC	10	76	2	5.0	15	0	0.0	2	5.0	0	4
62. Ayanbadejo	BAL	8	15	1	1.0	23	1	5.0	2	3.0	0	4
63. Ma. Bates	DET	12	31	2	5.0	15	0	0.0	2	5.0	0	4
64. Carter	NE	15	37	2	1.0	9	0	0.0	2	1.0	0	4
65. Chancey	SD	3	42	2	3.0	1	0	0.0	2	3.0	0	4
66. Cloud	KC	6	30	1	15.0	2	0	0.0	1	15.0	0	4
67. T. Davis	DEN	5	78	2	4.5	2	0	0.0	2	4.5	0	4
68. Enis	CHI	10	36	1	11.0	8	0	0.0	1	11.0	0	4
69. Fazande	SD	11	119	2	2.0	16	0	0.0	2	2.0	0	4
70. W. Floyd	CAR	10	16	1	1.0	17	1	5.0	2	3.0	0	4
71. Griffith	DEN	12	5	0	0.0	16	2	3.5	2	3.5	0	4
72. Holmes	BAL	16	137	2	4.0	32	0	0.0	2	4.0	0	4
73. McCrary	SD	13	7	0	0.0	18	2	5.5	2	5.5	0	4
74. Neal	TEN	7	1	0	0.0	9	2	2.5	2	2.5	0	4
75. Sellers	WAS	7	1	0	0.0	8	2	6.0	2	6.0	0	4
76. Strong	SEA	13	3	0	0.0	22	1	13.0	1	13.0	0	4
77. Rb. Thomas	DAL	12	15	0	0.0	23	2	1.5	2	1.5	0	4
78. Wiley +	DAL	8	24	0	0.0	14	1	15.0	1	15.0	0	4
79. D. Bennett	KC	6	27	1	1.0	2	0	0.0	1	1.0	0	2
80. Finn	IND	5	1	0	0.0	4	1	5.0	1	5.0	0	2
81. Fuamatu-Ma'afala	PIT	6	21	1	5.0	11	0	0.0	1	5.0	0	2
82. Gash	BAL	5	2	0	0.0	6	1	2.0	1	2.0	0	2
83. Henderson	GB	14	2	0	0.0	35	1	7.0	1	7.0	0	2
84. Hicks	WAS	6	29	1	3.0	5	0	0.0	1	3.0	0	2
85. Hoover	CAR	11	89	1	1.0	15	0	0.0	1	1.0	0	2
86. Howard	JAC	2	21	1	9.0	3	0	0.0	1	9.0	0	2
87. A. Johnson	JAC	10	28	1	2.0	12	0	0.0	1	2.0	0	2
88. J. Johnson	MIA	8	50	1	3.0	10	0	0.0	1	3.0	0	2
89. Kaufman	OAK	14	93	0	0.0	13	1	4.0	1	4.0	0	2
90. Linton	BUF	6	38	0	0.0	3	1	4.0	1	4.0	0	2
91. Mack	JAC	3	54	1	3.0	0	0	0.0	1	3.0	0	2
92. Milne	NO	3	2	0	0.0	5	1	4.0	1	4.0	0	2

2000 STATISTICAL RESULTS
(RUNNING BACKS — DISTANCE SCORING METHOD)

NAME	TEAM	GP	RSH	RSH TDs	AVG LGTH	PASS REC	REC TDs	AVG LGTH	TOTAL TDs	AVG LGTH	CONV PTS	FAN-TASY PTS
93. Montgomery	NYG	1	1	1	4.0	0	0	0.0	1	4.0	0	2
94. Moore	NO	5	37	1	3.0	0	0	0.0	1	3.0	0	2
95. Pritchett	PHI	13	58	1	1.0	25	0	0.0	1	1.0	0	2
96. D. Smith	DEN	1	0	0	0.0	1	1	1.0	1	1.0	0	2
97. Staley	PHI	5	79	1	1.0	25	0	0.0	1	1.0	0	2
98. Stith +	JAC	7	20	1	3.0	0	0	0.0	1	3.0	0	2
99. Rd. Thomas	TEN	12	61	0	0.0	8	1	9.0	1	9.0	0	2
100. T. Thomas	MIA	9	28	0	0.0	16	1	2.0	1	2.0	0	2
101. M. Williams	MIN	11	23	0	0.0	4	0	0.0	0	0.0	2	2
102. Abdul-Jabbar	IND	1	1	0	0.0	0	0	0.0	0	0.0	0	0
103. Abdullah	TB	4	16	0	0.0	2	0	0.0	0	0.0	0	0
104. Barnes	CHI	6	15	0	0.0	1	0	0.0	0	0.0	0	0
105. Brown	SEA	2	3	0	0.0	2	0	0.0	0	0.0	0	0
106. Bynum	SD	2	7	0	0.0	2	0	0.0	0	0.0	0	0
107. Canidate +	STL	2	3	0	0.0	1	0	0.0	0	0.0	0	0
108. Christian	ATL	16	9	0	0.0	44	0	0.0	0	0.0	0	0
109. Comella	NYG	15	10	0	0.0	36	0	0.0	0	0.0	0	0
110. Denson	MIA	9	31	0	0.0	14	0	0.0	0	0.0	0	0
111. Dukes	JAC	1	2	0	0.0	0	0	0.0	0	0.0	0	0
112. Dyer +	MIA	1	0	0	0.0	2	0	0.0	0	0.0	0	0
113. C. Floyd	NE	2	2	0	0.0	1	0	0.0	0	0.0	0	0
114. Gary	DEN	1	13	0	0.0	3	0	0.0	0	0.0	0	0
115. Goodman	GB	3	3	0	0.0	1	0	0.0	0	0.0	0	0
116. Gordon	IND	2	4	0	0.0	0	0	0.0	0	0.0	0	0
117. Groce	CIN	6	4	0	0.0	11	0	0.0	0	0.0	0	0
118. Hambrick	DAL	1	6	0	0.0	0	0	0.0	0	0.0	0	0
119. Harris **	NE	3	13	0	0.0	4	0	0.0	0	0.0	0	0
120. Hodgins	STL	3	1	0	0.0	2	0	0.0	0	0.0	0	0
121. Irvin	DET	5	9	0	0.0	8	0	0.0	0	0.0	0	0
122. Jervey	SF	1	1	0	0.0	0	0	0.0	0	0.0	0	0
123. Keaton +	CIN	3	6	0	0.0	0	0	0.0	0	0.0	0	0
124. Kirby	OAK	1	11	0	0.0	3	0	0.0	0	0.0	0	0
125. Kleinsasser	MIN	11	12	0	0.0	10	0	0.0	0	0.0	0	0
126. Konrad	MIA	9	15	0	0.0	14	0	0.0	0	0.0	0	0
127. Kreider	PIT	5	2	0	0.0	5	0	0.0	0	0.0	0	0
128. Lee	PHI	2	1	0	0.0	1	0	0.0	0	0.0	0	0
129. Jo. Lewis	SF	1	1	0	0.0	0	0	0.0	0	0.0	0	0
130. Makovicka	ARI	6	3	0	0.0	6	0	0.0	0	0.0	0	0
131. Ce. Martin	PHI	14	13	0	0.0	31	0	0.0	0	0.0	0	0
132. McAfee	NO	2	2	0	0.0	0	0	0.0	0	0.0	0	0
133. McKinley	ARI	2	0	0	0.0	2	0	0.0	0	0.0	0	0
134. Ba. Mitchell	GB	1	2	0	0.0	0	0	0.0	0	0.0	0	0
135. Morrow	MIN	1	0	0	0.0	1	0	0.0	0	0.0	0	0
136. Morton +	NO	14	36	0	0.0	30	0	0.0	0	0.0	0	0
137. Murrell	WAS	9	20	0	0.0	16	0	0.0	0	0.0	0	0
138. Olivo	DET	3	0	0	0.0	3	0	0.0	0	0.0	0	0
139. Palmer	MIN	1	0	0	0.0	1	0	0.0	0	0.0	0	0
140. Parker	GB	8	18	0	0.0	9	0	0.0	0	0.0	0	0
141. Pass +	NE	4	18	0	0.0	4	0	0.0	0	0.0	0	0
142. Rhett	CLE	5	71	0	0.0	14	0	0.0	0	0.0	0	0
143. Ritchie	OAK	11	0	0	0.0	26	0	0.0	0	0.0	0	0
144. Rivers	ATL	2	8	0	0.0	0	0	0.0	0	0.0	0	0
145. Roan	TEN	1	0	0	0.0	3	0	0.0	0	0.0	0	0
146. Saleh	CLE	1	0	0	0.0	1	0	0.0	0	0.0	0	0
147. Schlesinger	DET	11	1	0	0.0	12	0	0.0	0	0.0	0	0
148. Shaw	NE	4	9	0	0.0	2	0	0.0	0	0.0	0	0
149. Shelton	JAC	6	2	0	0.0	4	0	0.0	0	0.0	0	0
150. M. Smith	ATL	5	19	0	0.0	1	0	0.0	0	0.0	0	0
151. P. Smith +	SF	8	18	0	0.0	2	0	0.0	0	0.0	0	0
152. T. Smith +	NO	12	29	0	0.0	12	0	0.0	0	0.0	0	0
153. Snider	GB	0	0	0	0.0	0	0	0.0	0	0.0	0	0

2000 STATISTICAL RESULTS
(RUNNING BACKS — DISTANCE SCORING METHOD)

NAME	TEAM	GP	RSH	RSH TDs	AVG LGTH	PASS REC	REC TDs	AVG LGTH	TOTAL TDs	AVG LGTH	CONV PTS	FAN-TASY PTS
154. Sowell	NYJ	6	2	0	0.0	6	0	0.0	0	0.0	0	0
155. Stecker	TB	5	12	0	0.0	1	0	0.0	0	0.0	0	0
156. White	CLE	10	47	0	0.0	13	0	0.0	0	0.0	0	0
157. J. Williams	JAC	1	2	0	0.0	0	0	0.0	0	0.0	0	0
158. N. Williams	CIN	9	10	0	0.0	7	0	0.0	0	0.0	0	0
159. Witman	PIT	3	3	0	0.0	5	0	0.0	0	0.0	0	0
160. Zereoue	PIT	2	6	0	0.0	0	0	0.0	0	0.0	0	0

+	DENOTES COLLETE DRAFT PICKS		
*	Br. Mitchell	(PHI)	Scored TD's on a 89 yard kickoff return and a 72 yard punt return.
*	Mi. Bates	(CAR)	Scored TD on a 92 yard kickoff return.
*	Jenkins	(SD)	Scored TD on a 93 yard kickoff return.
*	Rogers	(SEA)	Scored TD on a 81 yard kickoff return.
**	Warren	(PHI)	Played in 11 games with Dallas.
**	Harris	(NE)	Played in 2 games with Denver.

RATING THE PLAYERS FOR 2001
(Running Backs—Distance Scoring Method)
GRAB ONE IF YOU CAN

☐ **1. Marshall Faulk (St. Louis Rams)**
Faulk's 26 touchdowns in just 14 games in 2000 were an NFL record. His ability to score via the pass as well as the run makes him that much more of an attractive fantasy pick again in 2001 in this scoring method.

☐ **2. Edgerrin James (Indianapolis Colts)**
James, like Marshall Faulk, has increased fantasy value because of his ability to score both via the pass and run. In the two years James has been in the league, James scored 13 touchdowns on the ground both seasons and has caught four and five touchdown passes respectively.

☐ **3. Fred Taylor (Jacksonville Jaguars)**
Taylor has been slowed by injury the last two seasons, though he still managed to score 14 times in 2000, despite missing three games. With the ability to pop through a hole for a long score at any time, Taylor, when healthy, is a huge fantasy factor.

☐ **4. Stephen Davis (Washington Redskins)**
Davis and the entire Redskins team slid back from their stellar 1999 effort in 2000. Davis dropped from 17 touchdowns to 11 but I see a rebound to 12-15 scores in 2001.

☐ **5. Eddie George (Tennessee Titans)**
George continues to carry the work load for the Titans, and he's finally become more of a scorer the last two seasons recording 13 and 16 touchdowns respectively.

BEST OF THE REST

☐ **6. Warrick Dunn (Tampa Bay Buccaneers)**
Dunn shouldered more of the load for the Buccaneers in 2000 and will again in 2001. His 22.0 yard average on nine touchdowns a year ago has me excited.

☐ **7. Corey Dillon (Cincinnati Bengals)**
If the Bengals could give Dillon more opportunity to score, Dillon's fantasy stock in this scoring method would really take off. A 30.3 yard average on his seven touchdowns in 2000 is unbelievable.

☐ **8. Terrell Davis (Denver Broncos)**
The Broncos always have a running back score a lot of touchdowns. Last year, with Davis and Olandis Gary, hurt it was rookie Mike Anderson scoring 15 times. If Davis returns healthy he'll return to his scoring role in 2001.

☐ **9. Tiki Barber (New York Giants)**
Barber stole the show from rookie first-round pick Ron Dayne in 2000. His lofty 19.7 average on nine touchdowns in 2000 makes him an attractive fantasy pick in 2001.

☐ **10. Lamar Smith (Miami Dolphins)**
The Dolphins have seemed to have finally found an answer at running back with Lamar Smith. Smith, who scored 16 times in 2000 in his first year with Miami, looks to again be a scoring force in 2001.

STRONG LONG SHOTS

☐ **11. Ahman Green (Green Bay Packers)**
Green scored 13 times, stepping in for the injured Dorsey Levens in 2000. The question now is: will Levens be able to regain his starting job or has Green found a permanent job?

☐ **12. Ricky Williams (New Orleans Saints)**
Williams struggled as a rookie in 1999 but was on his way to a big year in 2000, until a broken ankle sidelined him the last six games of the year. To that point, Williams had already scored nine times in ten games. If healthy all year, big touchdown numbers should be in store, though the drafting of Deuce McAllister raises some questions.

☐ **13. James Stewart (Detroit Lions)**
After scoring 13 times with Jacksonville in 1999, Stewart came to Detroit in 2000 and produced 11 scores. As the feature back again for the Lions in 2001 and with his ability to occasionally pop for long scores, he'll again be a fantasy factor to watch.

☐ **14. Tyrone Wheatley (Oakland Raiders)**
Wheatley has become a very productive scoring force since coming to the Raiders. After scoring 11 times in 1999, Wheatley scored ten times in 2000 despite missing two games to injury. He remains a huge part of the Raiders' scoring plans in 2001.

☐ **15. Jamal Anderson (Atlanta Falcons)**
Anderson made his way back from a knee injury that sidelined him most of 1999 to record six touchdowns. Looking back two years earlier, when he scored 16 times when healthy, we get a better feel for his potential. I expect Anderson to hit the double-digit scoring mark in 2001 but most will likely be from short distances.

☐ **16. Jamal Lewis (Baltimore Ravens)**
As a rookie in 2000, Lewis battled to win the starting job, which resulted in an impressive 1,660 rushing-receiving yards but only six touchdowns. As he continues in the role in 2000, his scoring numbers will climb.

☐ **17. Curtis Martin (New York Jets)**
Hasn't scored consistently the last few seasons, though he did rebound to score 11 times in 2000. Surely as the Jets' most consistent offensive weapon, he has to be given fantasy consideration for 2001.

☐ **18. Emmitt Smith (Dallas Cowboys)**
Though his touchdown production has steadily declined the last three seasons (13, 11 and 9), he's still someone with too much scoring potential to overlook in 2001, though most of his scores in recent years are short range.

☐ **19. Ricky Watters (Seattle Seahawks)**
There's question over Watters's role in 2001 or if he'll be with the Seahawks. Watters scored nine times in 2000, holding off the challenge of rookie first-round pick Shawn Alexander.

☐ **20. Jerome Bettis (Pittsburgh Steelers)**
He has scored 7 and 8 times respectively the last two seasons and mostly from short range, making him a tough fantasy pick in this scoring method though we know he'll get plenty of scoring changes in 2001.

HAVE THE POTENTIAL

☐ **21. Michael Pittman (Arizona Cardinals)**
As long as Pittman holds off the challenge of last year's first-round draft pick, Thomas Jones, Pittman has the potential to score 6-10 times.

☐ **22. J. R. Redmond (New England Patriots)**
A disappointment as a rookie in 2000 but the Patriots believe Redmond has future potential that we may see blossom in 2001.

☐ **23. Priest Holmes (Kansas City Chiefs)**
New head coach Dick Vermeil brings Holmes aboard to push for every-down role.

☐ **24. Duce Staley (Philadelphia Eagles)**
The Eagle's feature back missed most of the 2000 season with a foot injury. There's still some concern over his healthy return. If he is OK to go, he'll be a major force for Philadelphia's offense again in 2001.

☐ **25. Errict Rhett (Cleveland Browns)**
Brought over from Baltimore in 2000 to be the expected starter, Rhett missed over half the season with a foot injury. Returning healthy in 2001, he now faces the challenge of Travis Prentise, who stepped in and did an admirable job with Rhett out in 2000.

SOLID SLEEPERS

☐ **26. James Allen (Chicago Bears)**
Allen continues to build on his role, which should lead to bigger scoring numbers in 2001, though rookie second-round pick Anthony Thomas may push him for work.

☐ **27. Charlie Garner (Oakland Raiders)**
As the 49ers' feature back, Garner went from six touchdowns in '99 to ten touchdowns in '00. As a free agent this offseason, Garner took his services to Oakland where he'll push Tyrone Wheatley for work.

☐ **28. Tim Biakabatuka (Carolina Panthers)**
Injuries always seem to stand in the way of a big, productive year for Biakabatuka.

☐ **29. Sammy Morris (Buffalo Bills)**
Battling the likes of Antowain Smith, Shawn Bryson and Jonathan Linton, Morris won enough playing time to score six times in 2000. Morris is looking to expand his role and numbers in 2001.

☐ **30. Travis Prentise (Cleveland Browns)**
The Browns' third-round draft pick of a year ago scored eight times as a rookie in 2000 but a healthy return of Errict Rhett raises questions.

KEEP AN EYE ON

☐ **31. Mike Alstott (Tampa Bay Buccaneers)**
Usually good for a number of short-yardage scores, Alstott is losing more and more production to Warrick Dunn.

☐ **32. Shawn Alexander (Seattle Seahawks)**
If Watters departs, which is likely, Alexander's fantasy stock takes a quick climb.

☐ **33. Antowain Smith (Buffalo Bills)**
His 147-yard, three-touchdown performance in 2000 season finale

throws Smith back into the Bills' running back picture.

☐ **34. Dorsey Levens (Green Bay Packers)**
Ankle and knee injuries caused him to miss 11 games in 2000, giving Ahman Green his chance to flourish. Has Levens lost his starting job for good?

☐ **35. Garrison Hearst (San Francisco 49ers)**
Off for two years following a serious leg injury, Hearst may return in 2001. If healthy, Hearst may see his fantasy stock take a big leap, especially with Charlie Garner departed to Oakland.

☐ **36. Olandis Gary (Denver Broncos)**
Expected to recover from his knee injury suffered in 2000, Gary has scoring potential, but it will depend on his role and the health of Terrell Davis.

☐ **37. Ron Dayne (New York Giants)**
He scored only five times as a rookie in 2000, as Tiki Barber stole the show. Will he step up in 2001?

☐ **38. Mike Anderson (Denver Broncos)**
Anderson surprised the fantasy world, scoring 15 times as a rookie in 2000 filling in for the injured Terrell Davis and Olandis Gary. With both returning healthy in 2001, his role and production are a huge question.

☐ **39. Kevin Faulk (New England Patriots)**
The Patriots continue to look for an every-down back, and Faulk, though he doesn't fit the mold, was given plenty of opportunity in 2000. His 15.4 yard average on five touchdowns is impressive but will he continue in as prominent role in 2001? J. R. Redmond is the likely starter.

☐ **40. Terrell Fletcher (San Diego Chargers)**
With rookie La Dainian Tomlinson now in San Diego, Fletcher likely returns to his third-down role.

PRIME PROSPECTS

☐ **41. Thomas Jones (Arizona Cardinals)**
Jones, the Cardinals' first-round draft pick of 2000, was a bust as a rookie, being outperformed by Michael Pittman. Will he unseat Pittman as the starter in 2001?

☐ **42. Richard Huntley (Pittsburgh Steelers)**
He scored eight times in 1999 but dropped to three touchdowns a year ago. His 2001 scoring potential likely depends on the play and health of Jerome Bettis.

☐ **43. Paul Davis (San Francisco 49ers)**
Davis will push for more work in 2001.

☐ **44. Tony Richardson (Kansas City Chiefs)**
He had six touchdowns a year ago but will battle Priest Holmes for work in 2001.

☐ **45. Shawn Bryson (Buffalo Bills)**
Another back in the Bill's mix that could step up to more playing time, resulting in more scoring in 2001.

☐ **46. Chris Warren (Philadelphia Eagles)**
Role, production depends on health of Duce Staley.

☐ **47. Fred Beasley (San Francisco 49ers)**
The 49ers' fullback scored six times in 2000.

☐ **48. Frank Moreau (Kansas City Chiefs)**
Another back to whom new head coach Dick Vermeil may give a shot.

☐ **49. Jonathan Linton (Buffalo Bills)**
Another of the Bills' running back candidates.

☐ **50. Zack Crockett (Oakland Raiders)**
He had seven touchdowns in 2000, but Tyrone Wheatley is still the Raiders first choice to score.

DON'T BE SURPRISED

51. Autry (PHIL)
52. Hoover (CAR)
53. Fuamatu-Ma'afala (PITT)
54. Cloud (KC)
55. Canidate (STL)
56. M. Williams (MINN)
57. R. Anderson (NYJ)
58. Edwards (NE)
59. Montgomery (NYG)
60. Hambrich (DALL)

YOU NEVER KNOW

61. J. J. Johnson (MIA)
62. Henderson (GB)
63. Pritchett (PHIL)
64. Murrell (WASH)
65. Denson (MIA)
66. Br. Bennett (CIN)
67. Wiley (DALL)
68. Hicks (WASH)
69. Watson (STL)
70. Edwards (NE)

WORTH MENTIONING

71. Chapman (MINN)
72. Strong (SEAT)
73. Irvin (DET)
74. Parker (GB)
75. Christian (ATL)

ROOKIE PROSPECTS

NAME	TEAM	COMMENT
☐ 1. Michael Bennett	MINN	Answer to Robert Smith's departure.
☐ 2. La Dainian Tomlinson	SD	The Chargers have found themselves talented back to carry the load.
☐ 3. Anthony Thomas	CHI	Will be pushing James Allen.
☐ 4. Kevan Barlow	SF	Nice, all-round back to push for 49ers starting job.
☐ 5. Travis Henry	BUF	Too many players battling for job.
☐ 6. Deuce McAllister	NO	What is Ricky Williams—chopped liver?
☐ 7. Lamont Jordan	NYJ	Future for Jets behind Curtis Martin.
☐ 8. Heath Evans	SEAT	Strong, fullback type.
☐ 9. James Jackson	CLE	Will battle for work with Browns.
☐10. Correll Buckhalter	PHIL	If Duce Staley isn't ready, has a shot.

A LOOK AT THE WIDE RECEIVERS

(A Guide for the Beginner)

Considerations in Choosing a Wide Receiver

This method is like the Basic Scoring Method in that the player must score a touchdown to be awarded points. The difference is that a deep-threat receiver will be more valuable, since more points are awarded for the long touchdown play.

1. First, look at players' previous performances. Injuries, player moves, holdouts, suspensions and the like should be noted. In 2000 the likes of Marcus Robinson, Qadry Ismail and Joey Galloway all had their year-end productivity affected by injuries.

2. The first priority is a receiver from a passing team, preferably a speedy, deep-threat receiver. Newcomer Randy Moss has quickly become an impact player. Antonio Freeman is a consistent pick as well as Terrell Owens of the 49ers, who also rates high.

3. Look for wide receivers who work well with their current quarterbacks. Such is certainly the case for Antonio Freeman and Brett Favre. With Jerry Rice getting beyond his prime, Terrell Owens is becoming a favorite of Jeff Garcia.

4. Look for rookie receivers who have a chance to start, especially if they're fast. Defenses pay little attention to rookies until they become established receivers. This certainly was the case for Keyshawn Johnson and Marvin Harrison in 1997 when both scored eight times. In 1998, rookie Randy Moss set the league on fire with 17 touchdowns.

5. Opposing defenses try to clamp down on wide receivers who have just had a great year or consecutive good years, though "great" receivers keep making great plays.

6. Be leery of a receiver on a team going through a quarterback change. If a wide receiver has had a few good years, much of the credit belongs to his timing with his quarterback. A new quarterback will require a period of adjustment, and during that time the wide receiver's productivity may fall off. Such was the case for Issac Bruce in 1996. His touchdown totals dropped from 13 to 7. And with Stan Humphries out much of 1997 Tony Martin saw his numbers drop off significantly. James Jett saw his production drop in 1998 with Jeff George ailing.

In the 2000 statistics that follow, you'll find the players ranked by their fantasy-point totals. Remember that in the Distance Scoring Method, fantasy points are calculated by the length of the touchdown scored—the longer the touchdown play, the more points earned.

2000 STATISTICAL RESULTS
(WIDE RECEIVERS — DISTANCE SCORING METHOD)

NAME	TEAM	GP	RSH	RSH TDs	AVG LGTH	REC	REC TDs	AVG LGTH	TOTAL TDs	AVG LGTH	CONV PTS	FAN-TASY PTS
1. **Moss**	**MIN**	**16**	**3**	**0**	**0.0**	**77**	**15**	**31.7**	**15**	**31.7**	**2**	**112**
1999		16	4	0	0.0	80	11	32.4	12	35.0	0	101
1998		16	1	0	0.0	69	17	35.6	17	35.6	4	144
3 Yr - TOTALS		48	8	0	0.0	226	43	33.4	44	34.1	6	357
2. **Harrison**	**IND**	**16**	**0**	**0**	**0.0**	**102**	**14**	**27.4**	**14**	**27.4**	**0**	**90**
1999		16	1	0	0.0	115	12	27.6	12	27.6	2	82
1998		12	0	0	0.0	59	7	24.3	7	24.3	2	44
3 Yr - TOTALS		44	1	0	0.0	276	33	26.8	33	26.8	4	216
3. **Alexander**	**KC**	**16**	**3**	**0**	**0.0**	**78**	**10**	**35.3**	**10**	**35.3**	**0**	**82**
1999		15	2	1	82.0	54	2	83.5	3	83.0	0	54
1998		14	0	0	0.0	54	4	22.0	4	22.0	0	22
3 Yr - TOTALS		45	5	1	82.0	186	16	38.0	17	40.6	0	158
4. **Owens**	**SF**	**14**	**3**	**0**	**0.0**	**97**	**13**	**23.7**	**13**	**23.7**	**2**	**78**
1999		14	0	0	0.0	60	4	8.7	4	8.7	0	12
1998		16	4	1	21.0	67	14	22.4	15	22.2	2	84
3 Yr - TOTALS		44	7	1	21.0	224	31	21.2	32	21.1	4	174
5. **Holt**	**STL**	**16**	**2**	**0**	**0.0**	**82**	**6**	**44.5**	**6**	**44.5**	**0**	**60**
1999		15	3	0	0.0	52	6	30.0	6	30.0	0	42
1998		-	-	-	-	-	-	-	-	-	-	-
3 Yr - TOTALS		31	5	0	0.0	134	12	37.3	12	37.3	0	102
6. **R. Smith**	**DEN**	**16**	**6**	**1**	**50.0**	**100**	**8**	**24.8**	**9**	**27.6**	**0**	**60**
1999		14	0	0	0.0	79	4	16.8	4	16.8	0	18
1998		16	6	1	1.0	86	6	27.2	7	23.4	0	42
3 Yr - TOTALS		46	12	2	25.5	265	18	23.8	20	24.0	0	120
7. **Boston**	**ARI**	**16**	**3**	**0**	**0.0**	**71**	**7**	**36.7**	**7**	**36.7**	**0**	**58**
1999		14	5	0	0.0	40	2	7.5	2	7.5	0	6
1998		-	-	-	-	-	-	-	-	-	-	-
3 Yr - TOTALS		30	8	0	0.0	111	9	30.2	9	30.2	0	64
8. **Bruce**	**STL**	**16**	**1**	**0**	**0.0**	**87**	**9**	**27.0**	**9**	**27.0**	**0**	**58**
1999		15	5	0	0.0	77	12	16.3	12	16.3	2	56
1998		4	1	0	0.0	32	1	80.0	1	80.0	0	18
3 Yr - TOTALS		35	7	0	0.0	196	22	23.6	22	23.6	2	132
9. **Graham**	**SD**	**13**	**0**	**0**	**0.0**	**55**	**4**	**62.8**	**4**	**62.8**	**0**	**56**
1999		14	0	0	0.0	57	2	19.5	2	19.5	0	10
1998 (w/PHI)		15	0	0	0.0	47	2	10.0	2	10.0	0	6
3 Yr - TOTALS		42	0	0	0.0	159	8	38.8	8	38.8	0	72
10. **Hakim ***	**STL**	**15**	**5**	**0**	**0.0**	**53**	**4**	**39.7**	**5**	**49.0**	**0**	**56**
1999		14	4	0	0.0	36	8	39.8	9	44.7	0	88
1998		7	2	1	34.0	20	1	9.0	2	21.5	0	10
3 Yr - TOTALS		36	11	1	34.0	109	13	37.4	16	43.1	0	154
11. **Robinson**	**CHI**	**11**	**1**	**0**	**0.0**	**55**	**5**	**52.6**	**5**	**52.6**	**0**	**56**
1999		16	0	0	0.0	84	9	39.9	9	39.9	0	84
1998		3	0	0	0.0	4	1	20.0	1	20.0	0	6
3 Yr - TOTALS		30	1	0	0.0	143	15	42.8	15	42.8	0	146
12. **J. Smith**	**JAC**	**14**	**0**	**0**	**0.0**	**91**	**8**	**29.2**	**8**	**29.2**	**0**	**56**
1999		16	0	0	0.0	116	6	23.2	6	23.2	2	36
1998		16	0	0	0.0	78	8	26.7	8	26.7	0	52
3 Yr - TOTALS		46	0	0	0.0	285	22	26.7	22	26.7	2	144
13. **Ti. Brown**	**OAK**	**16**	**3**	**0**	**0.0**	**76**	**11**	**17.2**	**11**	**17.2**	**0**	**50**
1999		16	1	0	0.0	90	6	18.3	6	18.3	0	30
1998		16	1	0	0.0	81	9	15.0	9	15.0	0	38
3 Yr - TOTALS		48	5	0	0.0	247	26	16.7	26	16.7	0	118
14. **Toomer**	**NYG**	**16**	**5**	**1**	**19.0**	**78**	**7**	**27.2**	**8**	**26.1**	**0**	**50**
1999		16	1	0	0.0	79	6	37.3	6	37.3	0	52
1998		13	0	0	0.0	27	5	25.0	5	25.0	0	30
3 Yr - TOTALS		45	6	1	19.0	184	18	30.0	19	29.3	0	132
15. **Horn**	**NO**	**16**	**6**	**0**	**0.0**	**94**	**8**	**25.2**	**8**	**25.2**	**0**	**48**
1999 (w/KC)		15	2	0	0.0	35	6	34.3	6	34.3	0	48
1998 (w/KC)		10	1	0	0.0	14	1	26.0	1	26.0	0	6
3 Yr - TOTALS		41	9	0	0.0	143	15	28.9	15	28.9	0	102

NAME	TEAM	GP	RSH	RSH TDs	AVG LGTH	REC	REC TDs	AVG LGTH	TOTAL TDs	AVG LGTH	CONV PTS	FAN-TASY PTS
16. Warrick + *	CIN	16	16	2	40.5	51	4	11.0	7	29.6	0	48
1999		-	-	-	-	-	-	-	-	-	-	-
1998		-	-	-	-	-	-	-	-	-	-	-
3 Yr - TOTALS		16	16	2	40.5	51	4	11.0	7	29.6	0	48
17. Freeman	GB	15	2	0	0.0	62	9	21.6	9	21.6	0	46
1999		15	1	0	0.0	74	6	17.0	6	17.0	0	26
1998		15	3	0	0.0	84	14	40.4	14	40.4	2	130
3 Yr - TOTALS		45	6	0	0.0	220	29	29.7	29	29.7	2	202
18. C. Johnson	PHI	15	5	0	0.0	56	7	25.0	7	25.0	0	44
1999		9	0	0	0.0	34	1	28.0	1	28.0	0	6
1998 (w/PIT)		16	1	0	0.0	65	7	19.4	7	19.4	4	38
3 Yr - TOTALS		40	6	0	0.0	155	15	22.6	15	22.6	4	88
19. Conway	SD	14	3	0	0.0	53	5	35.0	5	35.0	0	42
1999 (w/CHI)		9	1	0	0.0	44	4	17.3	4	17.3	0	20
1998 (w/CHI)		14	5	0	0.0	54	3	13.7	3	13.7	0	12
3 Yr - TOTALS		37	9	0	0.0	151	12	23.8	12	23.8	0	74
20. Hilliard	NYG	14	3	0	0.0	55	8	21.6	8	21.6	0	42
1999		16	3	0	0.0	72	3	7.7	3	7.7	0	6
1998		16	1	0	0.0	51	2	10.5	2	10.5	0	8
3 Yr - TOTALS		46	7	0	0.0	178	13	16.7	13	16.7	0	56
21. H. Ward	PIT	16	4	0	0.0	48	4	48.2	4	48.2	0	42
1999		16	2	0	0.0	61	7	15.0	7	15.0	2	32
1998		11	1	0	0.0	15	0	0.0	0	0.0	0	0
3 Yr - TOTALS		43	7	0	0.0	124	11	27.1	11	27.1	2	74
22. Dwight *	ATL	11	5	0	0.0	26	3	34.3	4	43.2	0	40
1999		10	5	1	8.0	32	7	30.6	9	32.5	0	68
1998		7	8	0	0.0	4	1	44.0	2	68.5	0	30
3 Yr - TOTALS		28	18	1	8.0	62	11	32.8	15	40.2	0	138
23. Q. Ismail	BAL	13	0	0	0.0	49	5	34.8	5	34.8	0	40
1999		16	1	0	0.0	68	6	47.2	6	47.2	0	60
1998		-	-	-	-	-	-	-	-	-	-	-
3 Yr - TOTALS		29	1	0	0.0	117	11	41.6	11	41.6	0	100
24. Mason *	TEN	14	1	0	0.0	63	5	19.4	6	27.7	0	38
1999		5	1	0	0.0	8	0	0.0	1	65.0	0	14
1998		14	0	0	0.0	25	3	13.7	3	13.7	0	12
3 Yr - TOTALS		33	1	0	0.0	96	8	17.3	10	27.2	0	64
25. Tr. Brown *	NE	16	6	0	0.0	83	4	19.8	5	29.0	0	34
1999		12	0	0	0.0	36	1	31.0	1	31.0	0	8
1998		7	0	0	0.0	23	1	24.0	1	24.0	0	6
3 Yr - TOTALS		35	6	0	0.0	142	6	22.4	7	28.6	0	48
26. W. Jackson	NO	14	0	0	0.0	37	6	24.0	6	24.0	0	34
1999		-	-	-	-	-	-	-	-	-	-	-
1998		-	-	-	-	-	-	-	-	-	-	-
3 Yr - TOTALS		14	0	0	0.0	37	6	24.0	6	24.0	0	34
27. Lewis *	BAL	8	3	0	0.0	19	1	12.0	3	51.7	0	34
1999		11	5	0	0.0	25	2	22.5	2	22.5	0	10
1998		13	5	0	0.0	41	6	50.5	8	57.4	0	98
3 Yr - TOTALS		32	13	0	0.0	85	9	40.0	13	50.7	0	142
28. McCaffrey	DEN	16	0	0	0.0	101	9	11.2	9	11.2	2	34
1999		15	0	0	0.0	71	7	28.4	7	28.4	0	50
1998		15	0	0	0.0	64	10	18.3	10	18.3	2	50
3 Yr - TOTALS		46	0	0	0.0	236	26	18.6	26	18.6	4	134
29. McCardell	JAC	16	0	0	0.0	94	5	27.6	5	27.6	0	34
1999		16	0	0	0.0	78	5	11.6	5	11.6	2	20
1998		14	0	0	0.0	64	6	27.3	6	27.3	2	40
3 Yr - TOTALS		46	0	0	0.0	236	16	22.5	16	22.5	4	94
30. Chrebet	NYJ	16	3	0	0.0	69	8	13.5	8	13.5	0	32
1999		11	0	0	0.0	48	3	21.7	3	21.7	0	18
1998		16	0	0	0.0	75	8	20.6	8	20.6	0	42
3 Yr - TOTALS		43	3	0	0.0	192	19	17.8	19	17.8	0	92

2000 STATISTICAL RESULTS
(WIDE RECEIVERS — DISTANCE SCORING METHOD)

NAME	TEAM	GP	RSH	RSH TDs	AVG LGTH	REC	REC TDs	AVG LGTH	TOTAL TDs	AVG LGTH	CONV PTS	FAN-TASY PTS
31. McGarity *	DAL	11	6	1	22.0	25	0	0.0	3	48.3	0	32
1999		3	0	0	0.0	7	0	0.0	0	0.0	0	0
1998		-	-	-	-	-	-	-	-	-	-	-
3 Yr - TOTALS		14	6	1	22.0	32	0	0.0	3	48.3	0	32
32. F. Sanders	ARI	16	0	0	0.0	54	6	22.0	6	22.0	0	32
1999		15	0	0	0.0	79	1	6.0	1	6.0	0	2
1998		16	4	0	0.0	89	3	10.3	3	10.3	0	10
3 Yr - TOTALS		47	4	0	0.0	222	10	16.9	10	16.9	0	44
33. Mathis	ATL	15	1	0	0.0	57	5	25.6	5	25.6	0	30
34. Shepherd	MIA	12	4	0	0.0	35	4	30.5	4	30.5	0	30
35. Carter	MIN	16	0	0	0.0	96	9	9.7	9	9.7	0	30
36. D. Jackson +	SEA	16	1	0	0.0	53	6	22.3	6	22.3	0	30
37. Rice	SF	16	1	0	0.0	75	7	16.0	7	16.0	0	30
38. Connell	WAS	13	0	0	0.0	39	3	45.7	3	45.7	0	30
39. Small	PHI	14	1	0	0.0	40	3	34.0	3	34.0	2	26
40. Horne *	STL	4	2	0	0.0	4	2	10.5	3	40.0	0	26
41. Ks. Johnson	TB	16	2	0	0.0	71	8	13.0	8	13.0	0	26
42. Fryar	WAS	14	2	0	0.0	41	5	20.2	5	20.2	0	26
43. Moulds	BUF	16	2	0	0.0	94	5	19.2	5	19.2	0	24
44. Morton	DET	16	4	0	0.0	61	3	29.0	3	29.0	2	24
45. Jett	OAK	11	0	0	0.0	20	2	53.5	2	53.5	0	24
46. Rison	OAK	14	0	0	0.0	41	6	13.5	6	13.5	0	24
47. Crowell	DET	9	1	0	0.0	34	3	31.7	3	31.7	0	22
48. Schroeder	GB	15	2	0	0.0	65	4	23.0	4	23.0	0	22
49. Gadsden	MIA	16	0	0	0.0	56	6	13.7	6	13.7	0	22
50. Glenn	NE	16	4	0	0.0	79	6	14.7	6	14.7	0	22
51. Jenkins *	ARI	13	1	0	0.0	17	0	0.0	1	98.0	0	20
52. D. Hayes	CAR	15	0	0	0.0	66	3	26.7	3	26.7	0	20
53. Howard *	DET	3	0	0	0.0	2	0	0.0	1	95.0	0	20
54. Wilkins	IND	12	3	0	0.0	43	3	26.7	3	26.7	0	20
55. Blackwell *	PIT	1	0	0	0.0	2	0	0.0	1	98.0	0	20
56. Shaw	PIT	14	0	0	0.0	40	4	19.8	4	19.8	0	20
57. Anthony	TB	10	0	0	0.0	15	4	22.2	4	22.2	0	20
58. McDaniel	BUF	16	0	0	0.0	43	2	40.0	2	40.0	0	18
59. Muhammad	CAR	16	2	0	0.0	102	6	17.4	6	17.4	0	18
60. McKnight	DAL	15	0	0	0.0	52	2	41.0	2	41.0	0	18
61. Ogden *	MIA	3	0	0	0.0	2	0	0.0	1	81.0	0	18
62. Dunn *	OAK	4	0	0	0.0	4	0	0.0	1	88.0	0	18
63. Dawkins	SEA	15	0	0	0.0	63	5	11.8	5	11.8	0	18
64. Morris +	KC	15	0	0	0.0	48	3	21.7	3	21.7	0	16
65. D. Ward	NYJ	16	4	0	0.0	54	3	22.0	3	22.0	0	16
66. K. Williams *	TB	3	0	0	0.0	2	0	0.0	1	73.0	0	16
67. Gaylor +	SD	6	0	0	0.0	13	1	62.0	1	62.0	0	14
68. Hatchette	MIN	11	0	0	0.0	16	2	31.5	2	31.5	0	14
69. Jefferson	ATL	14	1	0	0.0	60	2	32.5	2	32.5	0	14
70. Price	BUF	16	2	0	0.0	52	3	20.7	3	20.7	0	14
71. Stokes	SF	14	1	0	0.0	30	3	16.0	3	16.0	2	14
72. Thigpen	TEN	9	0	0	0.0	15	2	32.0	2	32.0	0	14
73. Uwaezuoke *	CAR	4	0	0	0.0	4	0	0.0	1	64.0	0	14
74. Whitted	JAC	6	0	0	0.0	13	3	17.3	3	17.3	0	14
75. Emanuel	MIA	16	3	0	0.0	7	1	53.0	1	53.0	0	12
76. J. Green	TB	15	5	0	0.0	51	1	58.0	1	58.0	0	12
77. P. Johnson	BAL	6	2	0	0.0	12	2	24.0	2	24.0	0	12
78. Lockett	KC	13	0	0	0.0	33	2	26.5	2	26.5	0	12
79. Moore	DET	14	0	0	0.0	40	3	14.0	3	14.0	0	12
80. Pathon	IND	15	1	0	0.0	50	3	15.3	3	15.3	0	12
81. Proehl	STL	12	0	0	0.0	31	4	12.3	4	12.3	0	12
82. Taylor +	BAL	9	3	0	0.0	28	3	15.0	3	15.0	0	12
83. Thrash	WAS	14	10	0	0.0	50	2	27.5	2	27.5	0	12
84. Byrd	CAR	8	0	0	0.0	22	2	18.5	2	18.5	0	10
85. Coles +	NYJ	8	2	0	0.0	22	1	30.0	1	30.0	2	10

2000 STATISTICAL RESULTS
(WIDE RECEIVERS — DISTANCE SCORING METHOD)

	NAME	TEAM	GP	RSH	RSH TDs	AVG LGTH	REC	REC TDs	AVG LGTH	TOTAL TDs	AVG LGTH	CONV PTS	FAN-TASY PTS
86.	Driver	GB	12	1	0	0.0	21	1	32.0	1	32.0	2	10
87.	Foster	DET	7	2	0	0.0	17	1	40.0	1	40.0	0	10
88.	McGriff	DEN	2	0	0	0.0	2	1	43.0	1	43.0	0	10
89.	Poole	NO	10	0	0	0.0	21	1	49.0	1	49.0	0	10
90.	Simmons	NE	10	0	0	0.0	14	1	44.0	1	44.0	0	10
91.	Stokley	BAL	6	1	0	0.0	11	2	18.0	2	18.0	0	10
92.	Booker	CHI	14	2	0	0.0	47	2	16.5	2	16.5	0	8
93.	Dixon +	NYG	7	2	0	0.0	6	1	34.0	1	34.0	0	8
94.	Dyson	TEN	1	0	0	0.0	6	1	30.0	1	30.0	0	8
95.	E. G. Green	IND	5	0	0	0.0	18	1	34.0	1	34.0	0	8
96.	R. Ismail	DAL	8	8	0	0.0	25	1	24.0	1	24.0	2	8
97.	Soward +	JAC	9	3	0	0.0	14	1	33.0	1	33.0	0	8
98.	A. Reed	WAS	6	0	0	0.0	10	1	21.0	1	21.0	0	6
99.	White +	CHI	7	0	0	0.0	10	1	25.0	1	25.0	0	6
100.	Chiaverini	CLE	3	0	0	0.0	8	1	15.0	1	15.0	0	4
101.	Dawson +	CLE	2	0	0	0.0	9	1	13.0	1	13.0	0	4
102.	Jurevicius	NYG	10	0	0	0.0	25	1	13.0	1	13.0	0	4
103.	Kennison	CHI	16	3	0	0.0	55	2	5.5	2	5.5	0	4
104.	Tucker	DAL	10	4	1	17.0	15	0	0.0	1	17.0	0	4
105.	Bailey	SEA	4	0	0	0.0	6	1	6.0	1	6.0	0	2
106.	N. Brown	PHI	9	0	0	0.0	9	1	8.0	1	8.0	0	2
107.	Dugans +	CIN	7	0	0	0.0	14	1	4.0	1	4.0	0	2
108.	Galloway	DAL	1	0	0	0.0	4	1	4.0	1	4.0	0	2
109.	Hawkins	PIT	8	0	0	0.0	19	1	5.0	1	5.0	0	2
110.	Mayes	SEA	11	0	0	0.0	29	1	8.0	1	8.0	0	2
111.	Patten	CLE	11	0	0	0.0	38	1	9.0	1	9.0	0	2
112.	Barlow	JAC	1	0	0	0.0	1	0	0.0	0	0.0	0	0
113.	Bates	CHI	4	1	0	0.0	4	0	0.0	0	0.0	0	0
114.	Brazzell	DAL	2	0	0	0.0	2	0	0.0	0	0.0	0	0
115.	Brisby	NYJ	3	0	0	0.0	4	0	0.0	0	0.0	0	0
116.	M. Brooks	CHI	11	0	0	0.0	26	0	0.0	0	0.0	0	0
117.	R. Brooks	DEN	2	0	0	0.0	3	0	0.0	0	0.0	0	0
118.	B. Brown	CLE	2	0	0	0.0	2	0	0.0	0	0.0	0	0
119.	Burress +	PIT	10	0	0	0.0	22	0	0.0	0	0.0	0	0
120.	Calloway	NE	5	0	0	0.0	5	0	0.0	0	0.0	0	0
121.	Cavil	BUF	3	0	0	0.0	4	0	0.0	0	0.0	0	0
122.	Cody	ARI	10	0	0	0.0	17	0	0.0	0	0.0	0	0
123.	B. Davis	BAL	2	0	0	0.0	3	0	0.0	0	0.0	0	0
124.	S. Davis	NE	1	0	0	0.0	2	0	0.0	0	0.0	0	0
125.	T. Davis	NYG	2	0	0	0.0	2	0	0.0	0	0.0	0	0
126.	Douglas	PHI	1	0	0	0.0	1	0	0.0	0	0.0	0	0
127.	Edwards	PIT	10	3	0	0.0	18	0	0.0	0	0.0	0	0
128.	Engram	CHI	3	1	0	0.0	16	0	0.0	0	0.0	0	0
129.	Farmer	CIN	7	0	0	0.0	19	0	0.0	0	0.0	0	0
130.	Finneran	ATL	4	0	0	0.0	7	0	0.0	0	0.0	0	0
131.	German	ATL	1	0	0	0.0	1	0	0.0	0	0.0	0	0
132.	Griffin	CIN	2	0	0	0.0	2	0	0.0	0	0.0	0	0
133.	Hankton	CAR	3	0	0	0.0	4	0	0.0	0	0.0	0	0
134.	W. Hayes +	NYJ	4	1	0	0.0	6	0	0.0	0	0.0	0	0
135.	Hodge	DAL	2	0	0	0.0	4	0	0.0	0	0.0	0	0
136.	C. Jackson	NE	2	0	0	0.0	5	0	0.0	0	0.0	0	0
137.	L. Jackson	CLE	1	0	0	0.0	1	0	0.0	0	0.0	0	0
138.	Jacquet	SD	1	0	0	0.0	1	0	0.0	0	0.0	0	0
139.	Kv. Johnson	CLE	16	0	0	0.0	57	0	0.0	0	0.0	0	0
140.	Jones	SD	6	0	0	0.0	17	0	0.0	0	0.0	0	0
141.	Lee +	GB	6	0	0	0.0	10	0	0.0	0	0.0	0	0
142.	Martin	MIA	9	0	0	0.0	26	0	0.0	0	0.0	0	0
143.	McDuffie	MIA	6	1	0	0.0	14	0	0.0	0	0.0	0	0
144.	Milburn	CHI	2	1	0	0.0	1	0	0.0	0	0.0	0	0
145.	Miller	DEN	1	0	0	0.0	1	0	0.0	0	0.0	0	0
146.	Mitchell	ARI	3	0	0	0.0	5	0	0.0	0	0.0	0	0

2000 STATISTICAL RESULTS
(WIDE RECEIVERS — DISTANCE SCORING METHOD)

NAME	TEAM	GP	RSH	RSH TDs	AVG LGTH	REC	REC TDs	AVG LGTH	TOTAL TDs	AVG LGTH	CONV PTS	FAN-TASY PTS
147. Montgomery	DEN	1	0	0	0.0	1	0	0.0	0	0.0	0	0
148. Northcutt +	CLE	14	9	0	0.0	39	0	0.0	0	0.0	0	0
149. Parker	KC	3	1	0	0.0	3	0	0.0	0	0.0	0	0
150. Pickens	TEN	5	0	0	0.0	10	0	0.0	0	0.0	0	0
151. Pinkston +	PHI	7	0	0	0.0	10	0	0.0	0	0.0	0	0
152. Porter +	OAK	1	0	0	0.0	1	0	0.0	0	0.0	0	0
153. J. Reed	NO	5	0	0	0.0	16	0	0.0	0	0.0	0	0
154. Ricks	SD	2	0	0	0.0	3	0	0.0	0	0.0	0	0
155. C. Sanders	TEN	15	0	0	0.0	33	0	0.0	0	0.0	0	0
156. Stablein	DET	7	0	0	0.0	8	0	0.0	0	0.0	0	0
157. Stone	NYJ	3	3	0	0.0	0	0	0.0	0	0.0	0	0
158. Streets	SF	11	1	0	0.0	19	0	0.0	0	0.0	0	0
159. Van Dyke	PHI	1	0	0	0.0	1	0	0.0	0	0.0	0	0
160. Walsh	MIN	11	0	0	0.0	18	0	0.0	0	0.0	0	0
161. Walters +	MIN	2	1	0	0.0	1	0	0.0	0	0.0	0	0
162. Westbrook	WAS	2	0	0	0.0	9	0	0.0	0	0.0	0	0
163. C. Williams	ARI	1	0	0	0.0	1	0	0.0	0	0.0	0	0
164. J. Williams +	SEA	5	1	0	0.0	8	0	0.0	0	0.0	0	0
165. Wilson	NO	4	0	0	0.0	11	0	0.0	0	0.0	0	0
166. Yeast	CIN	12	1	0	0.0	24	0	0.0	0	0.0	0	0

+   DENOTES COLLEGE DRAFT PICKS
*   Warrick   (CIN)   Scored TD on a 82 yard punt return.
*   Mason   (TEN)   Scored TD on a 69 yard punt return.
*   Tr. Brown   (NE)   Scored TD on a 66 yard punt return.
*   Hakim   (STL)   Scored TD on a 86 yard punt return.
*   Dwight   (ATL)   Scored TD on a 70 yard punt return.
*   Lewis   (BAL)   Scored TD's on 89 and 54 yard punt returns.
*   McGarity   (DAL)   Scored TD's on 64 and 59 yard punt returns.
*   Horne   (STL)   Scored TD on a 103 yard kickoff return.
*   Jenkins   (ARI)   Scored TD on a 98 yard kickoff return.
*   Uwaezucke   (CAR)   Scored TD on a 64 yard punt return.
*   Howard   (DET)   Scored TD on a 95 yard punt return.
*   Ogden   (MIA)   Scored TD on a 81 yard punt return.
*   Dunn   (OAK)   Scored TD on a 88 yard kickoff return.
*   Blackwell   (PIT)   Scored TD on a 98 yard kickoff return.
*   Ka. Williams (TB)   Scored TD on a 73 yard punt return.

RATING THE PLAYERS FOR 2001
(Wide Receivers—Distance Scoring Method)
GRAB ONE IF YOU CAN

☐ **1. Randy Moss (Minnesota Vikings)**
Moss has scored 17, 12 and 15 touchdowns respectively his first three seasons and averaged 34.1 yards on each. As one of the league's best deep threats, Moss should have continued success in 2001.

☐ **2. Marvin Harrison (Indianapolis Colts)**
After averaging 27.6 yards on his 12 touchdown catches in 1999, Harrison averaged 27.4 yards on his 14 touchdowns in 2000. As the favorite go-to receiver of Peyton Manning, Harrison has more success ahead in 2001.

☐ **3. Marcus Robinson (Chicago Bears)**
Robinson averaged a lofty 39.9 yards on nine touchdown receptions in 1999. Sidelined five games in 2000, Robinson scored only five times but averaged a staggering 52.6 yards on each. As one of the league's best deep threats, Robinson will put up good numbers again in 2001, if he can stay healthy.

☐ **4. Terrell Owens (San Francisco 49ers)**
As quarterback, Jeff Garcia improved and became more confident in 2000, so did Terrell Owens's numbers. Owens scored 13 times in 2000, averaging 23.7 yards on each, playing in just 14 games. He'll push to improve these numbers over a full 16 games in 2001.

☐ **5. Isaac Bruce (St. Louis Rams)**
Having stayed healthy the last two seasons, Bruce recorded 13 touchdowns in 1999 and averaged 27.0 yards on nine touchdowns in 2000. If he can continue to avoid the injuries that cost him back in 1997 and 1998, Bruce will again be a huge fantasy factor in 2001.

BEST OF THE REST

☐ **6. Rod Smith (Denver Broncos)**
Jumping from 79 receptions in 1999 to 100 in 2000, Smith also jumped his touchdown totals from four to nine, averaging 27.6 yards on each. With young Brian Griese improving quickly, so have the numbers of Griese's receivers.

☐ **7. Torry Holt (St. Louis Rams)**
Holt has scored only six times in each of his first two seasons, but his 82 receptions in 2000 show he's getting the ball more often. His 44.5 average on six scores of 2000 show how quickly he's become one of the league's most feared deep threats. I expect he'll expand his scoring numbers in 2001 as his reception level grows.

☐ **8. Antonio Freeman (Green Bay Packers)**
Freeman's lofty 40.4 yard average on 14 touchdowns back in 1998 show, his potential. His numbers have dropped since then, as have his quarterback's, Brett Favre. Freeman's 21.6 yard average on nine touchdowns in 2000 was a bit of a rebound. I see a climb back to the 10-12 touchdown range in 2001.

☐ **9. Eric Moulds (Buffalo Bills)**
Back in 1998, Moulds had a breakout year, averaging a whopping 48.9 yards on nine touchdowns. His touchdowns have dropped off since but in 2000, Moulds climbed to 94 receptions. With quarterback Doug Flutie gone and strong-armed Rob Johnson at the helm, I look for Mould's long touchdown numbers to rebound in 2001.

☐ **10. Derrick Alexander (Kansas City Chiefs)**
With the Chiefs expanding their passing game in 2000, Alexander jumped to 78 receptions and averaged a solid 35.3 yards on ten touchdowns. With excellent downfield ability, Alexander shouldn't have a big dropoff with Dick Vermeil now running the show in Kansas City, though Elvis Grbac's departure may have some effect.

STRONG LONG SHOTS

☐ **11. Jimmy Smith (Jacksonville Jaguars)**
We've been waiting for years for Smith's touchdown levels to climb. Despite 116 receptions in 1999, Smith scored only six times. Smith dropped off to a still impressive 91 receptions in 2000, and averaged 29.2 yards on eight scores. Smith continues to be a double-digit touchdown threat seeing the ball that often.

☐ **12. Keyshawn Johnson (Tampa Bay Buccaneers)**
Johnson scored only eight times on 71 receptions in his first year with the Buccaneers in 2000, but with Brad Johnson now aboard as quarterback I look for his scoring numbers to climb in 2001.

☐ **13. Joe Horn (New Orleans Saints)**
Coming to New Orleans in 2000, Horn perhaps surpassed all expectations, recording 94 receptions and averaging 25.2 yards on eight touchdowns in his first year with the Saints. He'll push these scoring numbers in 2001.

☐ **14. Amani Toomer (New York Giants)**
Toomer has quickly grown his reception and touchdown numbers. In 1999, Toomer tallied 79 receptions, and averaged 37.3 yards on six touchdowns. In 2000, he averaged 26.1 yards on eight scores. I believe he's headed to double-digit scoring in 2001.

☐ **15. Qadry Ismail (Baltimore Ravens)**
Ismail recorded 68 receptions, with six going for touchdowns and a 47.2 average on each, in a breakout season in 1999. Missing three games to injury in 2000 and the Ravens getting more conservative on offense, Ismail dropped to 49 receptions in 2000, scoring five times with a 34.8 average. Bringing in Elvis Grbac should help reboost Ismail's numbers in 2001 if he can stay healthy.

☐ **16. Az-Zahir Hakim (St. Louis Rams)**
On just 36 receptions, Hakim averaged 44.7 yards on nine touchdowns in 1999 and last year jumped to 53 receptions but scored only five times, averaging a staggering 49.0 yards. As another of the talented Ram wideouts, he'll be a huge fantasy factor in this scoring method if he can rebound his touchdown numbers in 2001.

☐ **17. Joey Galloway (Dallas Cowboys)**
Back in 1997 and 1998, Galloway scored 12 times when with the Seahawks, averaging 39.2 yards on his dozen scores in '98. His numbers dropped in 1999, as a long holdout put him out of favor in Seattle and

he was traded to Dallas heading into 2000. A knee injury suffered in the season opener in 2000 forced Galloway to miss the remainder of the 2000 season. The Cowboys hope to have him back putting up healthy numbers in 2001.

☐ **18. David Boston (Arizona Cardinals)**
From 40 receptions and two touchdowns as a rookie in 1999 to averaging 36.7 yards on seven touchdowns and 71 receptions in 2000. Boston has quickly become a solid fantasy consideration.

☐ **19. Cris Carter (Minnesota Vikings)**
Carter doesn't score on many long touchdowns but he does score consistently, posting 13, 12, 13 and 9 touchdowns the last four seasons respectively.

☐ **20. Troy Brown (New England Patriots)**
Last season was a breakout year for Troy Brown, who averaged 29.0 yards on five touchdowns, while grabbing a surprising 83 receptions. As Drew Bledsoe continues to look his way, his numbers should grow in 2001.

HAVE THE POTENTIAL

☐ **21. Derrick Mason (Tennessee Titans)**
Mason out-performed high-priced free agent acquisitions Carl Pickens and Yancey Thigpen in 2000, to the tune of 63 receptions, five of which went for touchdowns in 2000. Mason added another score on a punt return for a 27.7 yard average and looks to build on those numbers with Pickens and Thigpen gone in 2001.

☐ **22. Kevin Johnson (Cleveland Browns)**
After averaging an impressive 31.9 yards on eight touchdowns, while recording 66 receptions as a rookie in 1999, Johnson saw his numbers drop in 2000. With quarterback Tim Couch out much of the year injured, Johnson dropped to 57 receptions and failed to score in 2000. Having Tim Couch healthy in 2001 should again make Johnson a scoring factor.

☐ **23. Muhsin Muhammad (Carolina Panthers)**
Despite recording an impressive 96 and 100 receptions the last two seasons, Muhammad did not put up impressive scoring numbers. Muhammad averaged 17.4 yards on six touchdowns in 1999 and averaged 16.8 yards on eight scores a year ago. Anybody seeing the ball that often, however, is hard to overlook as a fantasy choice.

☐ **24. Michael Westbrook (Washington Redskins)**
Struggling with injuries most of his career, Westbrook finally stayed healthy in 1999 to record 65 receptions and averaged 29.8 yards on nine touchdowns. In 2000, he returned to his injury-prone ways, missing 14 games with a knee injury. The hope is that Westbrook can return to health and healthy numbers in 2001.

☐ **25. Ed McCaffrey (Denver Broncos)**
McCaffrey may not score on many long touchdown plays, but his consistency of scoring, 10, 7 and 9 touchdowns the last three years gives him decent fantasy value in this scoring method for 2001.

SOLID SLEEPERS

☐ **26. Rocket Ismail (Dallas Cowboys)**
In his first year with the Cowboys in 1999, Ismail recorded an impressive 80 receptions and scored seven times with a lofty 40.7 yard average. In 2000, a knee injury sidelined him half the season and Cowboys' quarterbacking woes had only helped him to one touchdown in eight games anyway. The potential and speed are something you can't overlook for 2001.

☐ **27. Darnay Scott (Cincinnati Bengals)**
Before missing the entire 2000 season with a broken leg, Scott had averaged 36.8 yards on seven touchdowns and recorded 68 receptions in 1999. He averaged 38.9 yards on seven scores in 1998. Presumed to be the Bengal's #1 receiver with Carl Pickens gone in 2000, Scott looks to return healthy and assume that role, playing alongside Peter Warrick in 2001.

☐ **28. Patrick Jeffers (Carolina Panthers)**
Jeffers led all receivers in this scoring method when averaging 38.8 yards on 12 touchdowns in 1999 but missed 2000 with a torn ACL. Returning healthy in 2000 should push up his fantasy stock.

☐ **29. Terry Glenn (New England Patriots)**
Troy Brown stole some of Glenn's thunder in 2000 but Glenn still grabbed 79 receptions and averaged 14.7 yards on six scores. A year earlier, despite missing three games to injury, Glenn averaged 46.0 yards on four touchdowns while grabbing 69 receptions. As Drew Bledsoe's favorite target, Glenn always has the potential for scores.

☐ **30. Darren Jackson (Seattle Seahawks)**
As a rookie in 2000, Jackson grabbed 53 receptions and scored six times, averaging 22.3 yards on each, pushing veteran Derrick Mayes out of the #1 receiving role. Jackson should continue to improve in 2000 as should his scoring numbers.

KEEP AN EYE ON

☐ **31. Keenan McCardell (Jacksonville Jaguars)**
He always has good reception and yardage numbers but has trouble scoring with frequency.

☐ **32. J. J. Stokes (San Francisco 49ers)**
With Jerry Rice out of the picture, Stokes could be a fantasy dark horse in 2001.

☐ **33. Terrance Mathis (Atlanta Falcons)**
He had only five touchdowns and a 25.6 yard average in 2000 as the Falcons' passing game struggled. He's very capable of turning those numbers around if he gets help at quarterback.

☐ **34. Peter Warrick (Cincinnati Bengals)**
He averaged 29.6 yards on seven touchdowns as a rookie in 2000, but he needs the Bengals' quarterback job to improve.

☐ **35. Ike Hilliard (New York Giants)**
Despite missing two games to a bruised sternum in 2000, he averaged 21.6 yards on eight touchdowns, as the Giants continue to throw more with Kerry Collins at the helm.

☐ **36. Curtis Conway (San Diego Chargers)**
He averaged 35.0 yards on five touchdowns in his first year with the Chargers in 1999, despite missing two games to a hamstring injury.

☐ **37. James Thrash (Philadelphia Eagles)**
Thrash likely battles rookie Freddie Mitchell for Eagles' #1 receiver job with Charles Johnson and Torrence Small released.

☐ **38. Wayne Chrebet (New York Jets)**
Despite becoming the Jet's #1 receiver following Keyshawn's exit in 2000, Chrebet only scored eight times with an unimpressive 13.5 yard average.

☐ **39. Rob Moore (Arizona Cardinals)**
Moore missed the entire 2000 season with a knee injury but is expected back healthy in 2001.

☐ **40. Shawn Jefferson (Atlanta Falcons)**
He came to Atlanta to help open up their offense in 2000. Jefferson recorded 60 receptions but scored only twice, though the 32.5 yard average gives you an idea of his potential if he scores more.

PRIME PROSPECTS

☐ **41. Albert Connell (New Orleans Saints)**
Connell takes his services to New Orleans to help support Joe Horn. Connell averaged a lofty 44.1 yards on seven touchdowns in 1999 but dropped to only three scores in 2000 though each averaged 45.7 yards.

☐ **42. Johnnie Morton (Detroit Lions)**
The Lions are electing to run more with James Stewart now aboard. Morton scored only three times in 2000 on 61 receptions.

☐ **43. Oronde Gadsden (Miami Dolphins)**
He has scored a half of dozen touchdowns in each of the last two seasons for Miami.

☐ **44. Jeff Graham (San Diego Chargers)**
Graham's 62.8 yard average on four touchdowns in 2000 is impressive but is unlikely to continue in 2001, at least scoring on long touchdowns.

☐ **45. Kevin Dyson (Tennessee Titans)**
Dyson, who missed most of the 2000 season with a knee injury, should get plenty of opportunity in 2001 if healthy, with Carl Pickens and Yancey Thigpen gone.

☐ **46. Plaxico Burress (Pittsburgh Steelers)**
The Steelers are hoping for much more out of their first-round pick of a year ago, who missed a good portion of his rookie year with a wrist injury.

☐ **47. Sylvester Morris (Kansas City Chiefs)**
He showed good potential as a rookie in 2000, recording 48 receptions but scored only three times with a 21.7 yard average.

☐ **48. Bobby Engram (Chicago Bears)**
He had 88 receptions but only four touchdowns in 1999. Last year he missed the entire season with a knee injury. Hoping to return healthy in 2001, he should see the ball often, though he'll face a challenge from rookie first-round pick David Terrell.

☐ **49. Bill Schroeder (Green Bay Packers)**
He had five touchdowns on 74 receptions in 1999 and four touchdowns on 65 receptions in 2000. The potential to score more is there.

☐ **50. O. J. McDuffie (Miami Dolphins)**
McDuffie led the NFL with 90 receptions in 1998 but has struggled with injuries ever since. If he can stay healthy, McDuffie could again be a force for the Dolphins.

DON'T BE SURPRISED

51. J. Green (TB)
52. H. Ward (PITT)
53. Dyson (TENN)
54. Price (BUF)
55. Dawson (CLE)
56. Dwight (SD)
57. Rison (OAK)
58. Sanders (ARIZ)
59. Connell (NO)
60. Bradford (GB)

YOU NEVER KNOW

61. Jett (OAK)
62. Kennison (DEN)
63. McKnight (MIA)
64. Taylor (BALT)
65. Lockett (WASH)
66. Pathon (IND)
67. Emanuel (NE)
68. Hayes (CAR)
69. Wilkins (IND)
70. Patten (NE)

DON'T COUNT THEM OUT

71. Porter (OAK)
72. Chiaverini (CLE)
73. Shaw (PITT)
74. Anthony (TB)
75. Moore (DET)

76. Pickens (DALL)
77. Simmons (NE)
78. Jackson (NO)
79. Hatchette (NYJ)
80. J. Reed (MINN)

WORTH MENTIONING

81. Soward (JAC)
82. Proehl (STL)
83. N. Brown (PHIL)
84. Thigpen (???)
85. Rice (????)

86. D. Ward (MIA)
87. Thompson (WASH)
88. McDaniel (BUF)
89. Booker (CHI)
90. Jurevicius (NYG)

ROOKIE PROSPECTS

NAME	TEAM	COMMENT
☐ 1. Rod Gardner	WASH	Redskins have found another big target for strong-armed George.
☐ 2. David Terrell	CHI	Talented receiver to tandem with Marcus Robinson.
☐ 3. Koren Robinson	SEAT	His success will rest on arm of un-proven Hasslebeck.
☐ 4. Freddie Mitchell	PHIL	Could become Eagles' #1 receiver with Charles Johnson released.
☐ 5. Santana Moss	NYJ	Could help answer some of Jets' receiving problems.

☐ 6. Robert Ferguson	GB	Favre needs help at wide receiver.
☐ 7. Reggie Wayne	IND	Is he the #2 answer opposite Marvin Harrison?
☐ 8. Chris Chambers	MIA	Could help Dolphins in red zone.
☐ 9. Quincy Morgan	CLE	How good is the Brown passing game?
☐10. Chad Johnson	CIN	Did the Bengals need another wide receiver?

Distance Scoring Method

A LOOK AT THE TIGHT ENDS

(A Guide for the Beginner)

Considerations in Choosing a Tight End

1. First, look at players' previous performances. Injuries, player moves, holdouts and suspensions should be noted. The season of Cam Cleeland was marred by injury in 2000.

2. Consistency is common among tight ends. The rankings of the top tight ends seem to change little, with an occasional new name creeping onto the list. It's the Tony Gonzalez, Wesley Walls and Shannon Sharpe's who generally seem to top the list.

3. Your second priority should be to pick up a good tight end from a passing team, like the 49ers, where whomever steps in seems to fare well statistically.

4. When choosing a tight end, first check who his fellow receivers are. A tight end between two good wide receivers will often be left open while opponents double-cover the wide receivers.

5. Any tight end who has the speed to sneak behind the defense for a long touchdown play will reward you with a lot of points. Rickey Dudley, of the Raiders, comes to mind, along with Shannon Sharpe.

6. As with wide receivers, look for a quarterback change to have an adverse effect on a tight end. In a quarterback–tight end combination that has clicked well for many years, the departure of the quarterback is likely to reduce the tight end's productivity.

In the 2000 statistics that follow, you'll find the players ranked by their fantasy-point totals. Remember that in the Distance Scoring Method, fantasy points are calculated by the length of the touchdown scored—the longer the touchdown play, the more points earned.

NAME	TEAM	GP	RSH	RSH TDs	AVG LGTH	PS REC	REC TDs	AVG LGTH	TOTAL TDs	AVG LGTH	CONV PTS	FAN-TASY PTS
1. Gonzalez	KC	15	0	0	0.0	93	9	11.8	9	11.8	0	30
1999		15	0	0	0.0	76	11	17.2	11	17.2	0	52
1998		16	0	0	0.0	59	2	12.0	2	12.0	0	8
3 Yr - TOTALS		46	0	0	0.0	228	22	14.5	22	14.5	0	90
2. Sharpe	BAL	15	0	0	0.0	67	5	25.2	5	25.2	0	28
1999 (w/DEN)		4	0	0	0.0	23	0	0.0	0	0.0	0	0
1998 (w/DEN)		16	0	0	0.0	64	10	16.8	10	16.8	0	42
3 Yr - TOTALS		35	0	0	0.0	154	15	19.6	15	19.6	0	70
3. Pollard	IND	13	0	0	0.0	30	3	31.3	3	31.3	2	26
1999		14	0	0	0.0	34	4	12.0	4	12.0	0	14
1998		10	0	0	0.0	24	4	18.5	4	18.5	4	24
3 Yr - TOTALS		37	0	0	0.0	88	11	19.6	11	19.6	6	64
4. F. Jones	SD	15	0	0	0.0	71	5	16.4	5	16.4	0	22
1999		16	0	0	0.0	56	2	9.0	2	9.0	0	6
1998		16	0	0	0.0	57	3	20.7	3	20.7	2	18
3 Yr - TOTALS		47	0	0	0.0	184	10	16.2	10	16.2	2	46
5. Harris	DAL	16	0	0	0.0	39	5	11.4	5	11.4	2	20
1999 (w/TEN)		8	0	0	0.0	26	1	62.0	1	62.0	2	16
1998 (w/TEN)		14	0	0	0.0	43	2	11.0	2	11.0	0	6
3 Yr - TOTALS		38	0	0	0.0	108	8	17.6	8	17.6	4	42
6. Carswell	DEN	15	0	0	0.0	49	3	20.7	3	20.7	0	16
1999		11	0	0	0.0	24	2	4.5	2	4.5	0	4
1998		4	0	0	0.0	4	0	0.0	0	0.0	0	0
3 Yr - TOTALS		30	0	0	0.0	77	5	14.2	5	14.2	0	20
7. D. Clark	DEN	12	0	0	0.0	27	3	20.0	3	20.0	0	16
1999		1	0	0	0.0	1	0	0.0	0	0.0	0	0
1998		-	-	-	-	-	-	-	-	-	-	-
3 Yr - TOTALS		13	0	0	0.0	28	3	20.0	3	20.0	0	16
8. Dudley	OAK	14	1	0	0.0	29	4	11.0	4	11.0	0	16
1999		13	0	0	0.0	39	9	7.8	9	7.8	0	26
1998		15	1	0	0.0	36	5	18.0	5	18.0	2	24
3 Yr - TOTALS		42	2	0	0.0	104	18	11.3	18	11.3	2	66
9. Glover	NO	10	0	0	0.0	21	4	16.0	4	16.0	0	16
1999 (w/MIN)		14	0	0	0.0	28	1	12.0	1	12.0	0	4
1998 (w/MIN)		15	0	0	0.0	35	5	12.2	5	12.2	0	18
3 Yr - TOTALS		39	0	0	0.0	84	10	13.7	10	13.7	0	38
10. Wycheck	TEN	16	0	0	0.0	70	4	9.8	4	9.8	0	16
1999		16	0	0	0.0	69	2	17.5	2	17.5	0	15
1998		16	0	0	0.0	70	2	8.5	2	8.5	0	6
3 Yr - TOTALS		48	0	0	0.0	209	8	11.4	8	11.4	0	37
11. Bruener	PIT	13	0	0	0.0	17	3	15.7	3	15.7	0	14
1999		10	0	0	0.0	18	0	0.0	0	0.0	0	0
1998		9	0	0	0.0	19	2	9.5	2	9.5	0	6
3 Yr - TOTALS		32	0	0	0.0	54	5	13.2	5	13.2	0	20
12. McWilliams	MIN	8	0	0	0.0	22	3	15.0	3	15.0	0	14
1999 (w/ARI)		9	0	0	0.0	11	1	9.0	1	9.0	0	2
1998 (w/ARI)		13	0	0	0.0	26	4	7.3	4	7.3	0	10
3 Yr - TOTALS		30	0	0	0.0	59	8	10.4	8	10.4	0	26
13. Riemersma	BUF	11	0	0	0.0	31	5	10.6	5	10.6	0	14
1999		13	0	0	0.0	37	4	7.0	4	7.0	0	10
1998		13	0	0	0.0	25	6	10.5	6	10.5	0	20
3 Yr - TOTALS		37	0	0	0.0	93	15	9.6	15	9.6	0	44
14. Williams	STL	8	0	0	0.0	11	3	12.0	3	12.0	2	14
1999		13	0	0	0.0	25	6	7.2	6	7.2	0	16
1998		8	0	0	0.0	15	1	1.0	1	1.0	0	2
3 Yr - TOTALS		29	0	0	0.0	51	10	8.0	10	8.0	2	32
15. Kelly	ATL	12	0	0	0.0	31	2	28.0	2	28.0	0	12
1999		5	0	0	0.0	8	0	0.0	0	0.0	0	0
1998		-	-	-	-	-	-	-	-	-	-	-
3 Yr - TOTALS		17	0	0	0.0	39	2	28.0	2	28.0	0	12

2000 STATISTICAL RESULTS
(TIGHT ENDS — DISTANCE SCORING METHOD)

	NAME	TEAM	GP	RSH	RSH TDs	AVG LGTH	PS REC	REC TDs	AVG LGTH	TOTAL TDs	AVG LGTH	CONV PTS	FAN-TASY PTS
16.	Dilger	IND	15	0	0	0.0	47	3	11.0	3	11.0	0	10
	1999		14	0	0	0.0	40	2	5.5	2	5.5	0	6
	1998		13	0	0	0.0	31	1	9.0	1	9.0	2	4
	3 Yr - TOTALS		42	0	0	0.0	118	6	8.8	6	8.8	2	20
17.	Moore	TB	13	0	0	0.0	29	3	8.0	3	8.0	0	10
	1999		13	0	0	0.0	23	5	13.8	5	13.8	0	20
	1998		13	0	0	0.0	24	4	15.5	4	15.5	0	16
	3 Yr - TOTALS		39	0	0	0.0	76	12	12.9	12	12.9	0	46
18.	Thomason	PHI	7	0	0	0.0	10	5	2.0	5	2.0	0	10
	1999		7	0	0	0.0	14	2	5.0	2	5.0	0	4
	1998 (w/GB)		6	0	0	0.0	9	0	0.0	0	0.0	0	0
	3 Yr - TOTALS		20	0	0	0.0	33	7	2.9	7	2.9	0	14
19.	Brady	JAC	16	0	0	0.0	64	3	5.3	3	5.3	2	8
	1999		13	0	0	0.0	32	1	7.0	1	7.0	2	4
	1998 (w/NYJ)		12	0	0	0.0	30	5	5.4	5	5.4	0	14
	3 Yr - TOTALS		41	0	0	0.0	126	9	5.5	9	5.5	4	26
20.	Lewis	PHI	15	0	0	0.0	69	3	10.7	3	10.7	0	8
	1999		6	0	0	0.0	8	3	7.3	3	7.3	0	8
	1998		-	-	-	-	-	-	-	-	-	-	-
	3 Yr - TOTALS		21	0	0	0.0	77	6	9.0	6	9.0	0	16
21.	Walls	CAR	8	0	0	0.0	31	2	14.5	2	14.5	0	8
	1999		16	0	0	0.0	63	12	12.6	12	12.6	0	44
	1998		14	0	0	0.0	49	5	9.2	5	9.2	0	16
	3 Yr - TOTALS		38	0	0	0.0	143	19	11.9	19	11.9	0	68
22.	Alexander	WAS	16	0	0	0.0	47	2	12.0	2	12.0	0	6
23.	Baxter	NYJ	3	0	0	0.0	4	2	8.0	2	8.0	0	6
24.	Campbell	NYG	8	0	0	0.0	8	3	2.7	3	2.7	0	6
25.	J. Davis	MIN	9	0	0	0.0	17	1	26.0	1	26.0	0	6
26.	T. Davis	GB	9	0	0	0.0	19	2	2.5	2	2.5	2	6
27.	Fauria	SEA	13	0	0	0.0	28	2	6.0	2	6.0	0	6
28.	Franks	GB	14	0	0	0.0	34	1	27.0	1	27.0	0	6
29.	Mili	SEA	12	0	0	0.0	28	3	3.0	3	3.0	0	6
30.	Allred	CHI	5	0	0	0.0	9	1	18.0	1	18.0	0	4
31.	Becht +	NYJ	9	0	0	0.0	16	2	1.5	2	1.5	0	4
32.	Bjornson	NE	8	0	0	0.0	20	2	4.0	2	4.0	0	4
33.	Brigham	OAK	9	0	0	0.0	13	2	3.0	2	3.0	0	4
34.	Chamberlain	DEN	9	0	0	0.0	22	1	11.0	1	11.0	0	4
35.	G. Clark	SF	14	0	0	0.0	38	2	2.5	2	2.5	0	4
36.	Crawford	CAR	4	0	0	0.0	4	1	16.0	1	16.0	0	4
37.	Drayton	KC	7	0	0	0.0	8	2	5.0	2	5.0	0	4
38.	Kinney +	TEN	10	0	0	0.0	19	1	18.0	1	18.0	0	4
39.	Kozlowski	ATL	10	0	0	0.0	15	2	5.0	2	5.0	0	4
40.	Mangum	CAR	11	0	0	0.0	19	1	15.0	1	15.0	0	4
41.	Shea +	CLE	13	0	0	0.0	30	2	5.5	2	5.5	0	4
42.	Sloan	DET	13	0	0	0.0	32	2	5.0	2	5.0	0	4
43.	Wiggins **	NE	6	0	0	0.0	18	2	1.0	2	1.0	0	4
44.	M. Campbell	CLE	7	0	0	0.0	12	1	5.0	1	5.0	0	2
45.	Coates	BAL	7	0	0	0.0	9	0	0.0	0	0.0	2	2
46.	Goodwin	MIA	4	0	0	0.0	6	1	9.0	1	9.0	0	2
47.	Hall	NO	4	0	0	0.0	5	1	1.0	1	1.0	0	2
48.	Hardy	ARI	14	0	0	0.0	27	1	3.0	1	3.0	0	2
49.	Heiden	SD	5	0	0	0.0	6	1	4.0	1	4.0	0	2
50.	Jackson	BUF	4	0	0	0.0	5	1	1.0	1	1.0	0	2
51.	LaFleur	DAL	7	0	0	0.0	12	1	6.0	1	6.0	0	2
52.	McGee	CIN	12	0	0	0.0	26	1	2.0	1	2.0	0	2
53.	Mitchell	NYG	12	0	0	0.0	25	1	1.0	1	1.0	0	2
54.	Rasby	DET	7	0	0	0.0	10	1	5.0	1	5.0	0	2
55.	Rutledge	NE	6	0	0	0.0	15	1	2.0	1	2.0	0	2
56.	Battaglia	CIN	10	0	0	0.0	13	0	0.0	0	0.0	0	0
57.	Broughton	PHI	7	0	0	0.0	12	0	0.0	0	0.0	0	0
58.	Bush	CIN	2	0	0	0.0	3	0	0.0	0	0.0	0	0

2000 STATISTICAL RESULTS
(TIGHT ENDS — DISTANCE SCORING METHOD)

	NAME	TEAM	GP	RSH	RSH TDs	AVG LGTH	PS REC	REC TDs	AVG LGTH	TOTAL TDs	AVG LGTH	CONV PTS	FAN-TASY PTS
59.	Collins	BUF	4	0	0	0.0	6	0	0.0	0	0.0	0	0
60.	Conwell	STL	6	2	0	0.0	5	0	0.0	0	0.0	0	0
61.	Cross	NYG	4	0	0	0.0	4	0	0.0	0	0.0	0	0
62.	Cushing	PIT	3	0	0	0.0	4	0	0.0	0	0.0	0	0
63.	R. Davis	SD	1	0	0	0.0	1	0	0.0	0	0.0	0	0
64.	Dragos	CHI	3	0	0	0.0	4	0	0.0	0	0.0	0	0
65.	Dunn	KC	2	0	0	0.0	2	0	0.0	0	0.0	0	0
66.	Flemister	WAS	1	0	0	0.0	1	0	0.0	0	0.0	0	0
67.	Geason	PIT	3	0	0	0.0	3	0	0.0	0	0.0	0	0
68.	Gedney	ARI	8	0	0	0.0	10	0	0.0	0	0.0	0	0
69.	Hape	TB	5	0	0	0.0	6	0	0.0	0	0.0	0	0
70.	D. Jones	JAC	1	0	0	0.0	1	0	0.0	0	0.0	0	0
71.	Jordan	MIN	5	0	0	0.0	8	0	0.0	0	0.0	0	0
72.	Kinchen	CAR	1	0	0	0.0	1	0	0.0	0	0.0	0	0
73.	Lyman +	CHI	1	0	0	0.0	1	0	0.0	0	0.0	0	0
74.	Mayes	CHI	3	0	0	0.0	4	0	0.0	0	0.0	0	0
75.	Pupunu	DET	2	0	0	0.0	3	0	0.0	0	0.0	0	0
76.	Robinson	STL	4	0	0	0.0	5	0	0.0	0	0.0	0	0
77.	Sinceno	CHI	10	0	0	0.0	23	0	0.0	0	0.0	0	0
78.	Swift	SF	1	0	0	0.0	1	0	0.0	0	0.0	0	0
79.	Tant +	ARI	1	0	0	0.0	1	0	0.0	0	0.0	0	0
80.	Weaver	MIA	6	0	0	0.0	10	0	0.0	0	0.0	0	0
81.	Wetnight	GB	3	0	0	0.0	3	0	0.0	0	0.0	0	0
82.	Yoder	TB	1	0	0	0.0	1	0	0.0	0	0.0	0	0

+   DENOTES COLLEGE DRAFT PICKS
**   Wiggins   (NE)   Played in 2 games with the New York Jets.

RATING THE PLAYERS FOR 2001
(Tight Ends—Distance Scoring Method)
GRAB ONE IF YOU CAN

☐ **1. Tony Gonzalez (Kansas City Chiefs)**
Gonzalez is the top tight end in this league for two straight seasons. He averaged 17.2 yards on 11 touchdowns in 1999 and 11.8 yards on nine touchdowns in 2000, while recording 76 and a whopping 93 receptions. No other tight end came close.

☐ **2. Shannon Sharpe (Baltimore Ravens)**
Sharpe scored ten touchdowns in 1998 but then missed most of the 1999 seasons with a broken collarbone. He returned in 2000 to jump from the Denver Broncos to the Baltimore Ravens. His 67 receptions and 25.2 average on five touchdowns show he can get it done regardless of where he plays.

☐ **3. Fred Jones (San Diego Chargers)**
Jones numbers continue to climb as he becomes more and more involved in the Chargers' offense. Jones grabbed 71 receptions in 2000 and averaged 16.4 yards on five touchdowns. As the Chargers' most consistent offensive weapon, Jones should have more scoring chances in 2001.

☐ **4. Wesley Walls (Carolina Panthers)**
After scoring 12 times in 1999 on 63 receptions, Walls fell victim to a knee injury in 2000, missed eight games and finished with only 31 receptions and two touchdowns. I look for a healthy return in 2001 but not to his 1999 levels, as the Panthers turn to a new quarterback, which raises uncertainty.

☐ **5. Jay Riemersma (Buffalo Bills)**
Riemersma, becoming more involved in the Bills' offense, recorded six and four touchdowns in 1998 and 1999. On his way to pushing those numbers in 2000, Riemersma scored five times but missed five games to a knee injury. I believe 6-8 scores in 2001 is very possible.

BEST OF THE REST

☐ **6. Frank Wycheck (Tennessee Titans)**
Wycheck has recorded a consistent 63, 70, 69 and 70 receptions over the past four seasons but during that stretch produced only 4, 2, 2 and 4 touchdowns. Anybody seeing the ball that often is hard to disregard in fantasy value.

☐ **7. Dwayne Carswell (Denver Broncos)**
With Shannon Sharpe out of the picture in 2000, Carswell pushed numbers to 49 receptions and three touchdowns with a 20.7 average, showing he's also got downfield ability. With Byron Chamberlain also now departed (Minnesota), I look for Carswell to continue to expand his numbers in 2001.

☐ **8. Cam Cleeland (New Orleans Saints)**
Cleeland scored six times on 54 receptions as a rookie in 1998 but has been slowed by injury since, including in 2000 when a ruptured achilles sidelined him all year. If he can return healthy in 2001 and stay that way, I believe he'll score fairly often as the Saints are attacking through the air with more confidence.

☐ **9. Jackie Harris (Dallas Cowboys)**
Harris, coming to Dallas in 2000 became more of a factor than many thought he'd be, as he recorded 39 receptions and five touchdowns. He's been a very consistent performer throughout his career, but the Cowboys' quarterbacking situation raises questions.

☐ **10. Chad Lewis (Philadelphia Eagles)**
Lewis had a breakout year in 2000, as he surprised everyone with 69 receptions but scored only three times. I look for his scoring numbers to improve in 2001 as his young quarterback Donovan McNabb improves.

STRONG LONG SHOTS

☐ **11. Marcus Pollard (Indianapolis Colts)**
Despite competing with a good number of talented Colt offensive players for scoring glory, Pollard has scored 4, 4 and 3 touchdowns the last three seasons respectively. His 31.3 yard average on his three touchdowns of 2000 also shows he can get downfield.

☐ **12. David Sloan (Detroit Lions)**
After averaging a lofty 27.0 yards on four touchdowns and recording 47 receptions in 1999, Sloan scored only twice in 2000 on 32 receptions as the Lion's elected to run more. The Lions may continue to run in 2001, but don't dismiss Sloan as a consistent scoring threat.

☐ **13. Kyle Brady (Jacksonville Jaguars)**
After scoring only once on 32 receptions in his first year with the Jaguars in 1999, Brady ballooned to 64 receptions and scored three times in 2000. Seeing the ball that often should continue to push his scoring numbers in 2001.

☐ **14. Ricky Dudley (Cleveland Browns)**
There's plenty or scoring potential here, reflected in his 5, 9 and 4 touchdowns scored over the last three seasons respectively. However, Dudley won't return to Oakland in 2001, he's joined the less potent Cleveland Browns.

☐ **15. Stephen Alexander (Washington Redskins)**
Though Alexander jumped from 29 receptions in 1999, when he scored three times, to 47 receptions in 2000, Alexander scored only twice. The talent is there to become a scoring force and with strong-armed Jeff George at quarterback, I look for Alexander to be a scoring threat more often in 2001.

HAVE THE POTENTIAL

☐ **16. Greg Clark (San Francisco 49ers)**
Clark scored only twice on 38 receptions in 2000. But as quarterback, Jeff Garcia continues to improve, I think we'll see Clark's scoring numbers climb.

☐ **17. Ken Dilger (Indianapolis Colts)**
Dilger has grown his scoring the last three seasons, scoring 1, 2 and 3 touchdowns, while doing the same with receptions, recording 31, 40 and 47 over the same period. He, however, will continue to battle with many other Colt offensive players for scoring glory again in 2001.

☐ **18. Byron Chamberlain (Minnesota Vikings)**
Chamberlain scored three times on 49 receptions with Denver in 2000.

He's looking to expand these numbers with Minnesota in 2001.

☐ **19. Bubba Franks (Green Bay Packers)**
The Packers were hoping their first-round pick on 2000 could step right in and make a huge impact. He didn't, but there's hope he can build on his 34 receptions and one touchdown of a year ago.

☐ **20. Dave Moore (Tampa Bay Buccaneers)**
He may not score on many long touchdowns, but his consistency makes him an attractive pick, scoring 3, 4, 4, 5 and 3 touchdowns over the last five seasons.

DON'T BE SURPRISED

21. Mitchell (DET)
22. Becht (NYJ)
23. Fauria (SEAT)
24. T. Davis (GB)
25. McGee (CIN)
26. Bruener (PITT)
27. D. Clark (DEN)
28. Shea (CLE)
29. Mili (SEAT)
30. Wiggins (NE)

YOU NEVER KNOW

31. Hardy (ARIZ)
32. Bjornson (OAK)
33. Kelly (ATL)
34. LaFluer (DALL)
35. Williams (OAK)
36. McWilliams (MINN)
37. Sinceno (CHI)
38. Brigham (OAK)
39. Glover (NO)
40. D. Campbell (NYG)

WORTH MENTIONING

41. Allred (CHI)
42. M. Campbell (CLE)
43. D. Jones (JAC)
44. Conwell (STL)
45. Thomason (PHIL)

ROOKIE PROSPECTS

NAME	TEAM	COMMENT
☐ 1. Todd Heap	BALT	Talented but will play behind Shannon Sharpe for now.
☐ 2. Alge Crumpler	ATL	Will push Reggie Kelly for work.

A LOOK AT THE QUARTERBACKS

(A Guide for the Beginner)

Considerations in Choosing a Quarterback

1. First, look at players' previous performances. Injuries, trades, holdouts and suspensions should be noted. In 2000, the seasons of Kurt Warner, Brian Griese and Jeff Blake were hurt by their injuries.

2. Consider quarterbacks who aren't afraid to run the ball in for a touchdown. This opens up an area of scoring possibilities not available to the gimpy-legged quarterback who stays in the pocket. Duante Culpepper of Minnesota and Donovan McNabb of Philadelphia come quickly to mind.

3. Next, does the quarterback's team like to put the ball in the air? The more a team throws the ball, the greater the chance that the quarterback will have a high-scoring year. The Packers' Brett Favre is an obvious early pick.

4. Look for a quarterback who likes to throw deep for those long touchdown passes. Remember, the longer the touchdown, the more points awarded. A quarterback who has a proven deep-threat receiver among his targets is an asset to your team.

5. If you start a quarterback who gets yanked after the first quarter or half of a game, your fantasy team will suffer. Stay away from teams that are struggling to find their weekly signal caller.

In the 2000 statistics that follow, you'll find the players ranked by their fantasy-point totals. Remember that in the Distance Scoring Method, fantasy points are calculated by the length of the touchdown scored—the longer the touchdown play, the more points earned.

2000 STATISTICAL RESULTS
(QUARTERBACKS — DISTANCE SCORING METHOD)

	NAME	TEAM	GP	RSH TDs	TD PS	AVG TD LGTH	COMP	YARDS	YDS PER COMP	CONV PTS	FANTASY POINTS
1.	**Culpepper**	**MIN**	**16**	**7**	**33**	**25.1**	**297**	**3,937**	**13.3**	**2**	**122**
	1999		1	0	0	0.0	0	0	0.0	0	0
	1998		-	-	-	-	-	-	-	-	-
	3 Yr - TOTALS		17	7	33	25.1	297	3,937	13.3	2	122
2.	**Manning**	**IND**	**16**	**1**	**33**	**23.9**	**357**	**4,413**	**12.4**	**1**	**101**
	1999		16	2	26	23.4	331	4,135	12.5	1	84
	1998		16	0	26	19.8	326	3,739	11.5	3	69
	3 Yr - TOTALS		48	3	85	22.5	1014	12,287	12.1	5	254
3.	**Warner**	**STL**	**11**	**0**	**21**	**34.3**	**235**	**3,429**	**14.6**	**1**	**85**
	1999		16	1	41	21.5	325	4,353	13.4	1	113
	1998		1	0	0	0.0	4	39	9.8	0	0
	3 Yr - TOTALS		28	1	62	25.8	564	7,821	13.9	2	198
4.	**Garcia**	**SF**	**16**	**4**	**31**	**18.5**	**355**	**4,278**	**12.1**	**1**	**83**
	1999		13	2	11	22.2	225	2,544	11.3	1	36
	1998		-	-	-	-	-	-	-	-	-
	3 Yr - TOTALS		29	6	42	19.5	580	6,822	11.8	2	119
5.	**Grbac**	**KC**	**15**	**1**	**28**	**21.6**	**326**	**4,169**	**12.8**	**0**	**78**
	1999		16	0	22	28.3	294	3,389	11.5	0	75
	1998		8	0	5	12.8	98	1,142	11.7	0	10
	3 Yr - TOTALS		39	1	55	23.5	718	8,700	12.1	0	163
6.	**Gannon**	**OAK**	**16**	**4**	**28**	**16.5**	**284**	**3,430**	**12.1**	**2**	**76**
	1999		16	2	24	13.6	304	3,840	12.6	1	53
	1998 (w/KC)		12	3	10	27.2	206	2,305	11.2	0	40
	3 Yr - TOTALS		44	9	62	17.1	794	9,575	12.1	3	169
7.	**McNabb**	**PHI**	**16**	**6**	**21**	**17.3**	**330**	**3,365**	**10.2**	**1**	**68**
	1999		11	0	8	18.3	106	948	8.9	3	22
	1998		-	-	-	-	-	-	-	-	-
	3 Yr - TOTALS		27	6	29	17.6	436	4,313	9.9	4	90
8.	**Brunell**	**JAC**	**16**	**2**	**20**	**21.1**	**311**	**3,640**	**11.7**	**1**	**59**
	1999		15	1	14	14.0	259	3,060	11.8	4	33
	1998		13	0	20	21.3	208	2,601	12.5	1	55
	3 Yr - TOTALS		44	3	54	19.3	778	9,301	12.0	6	147
9.	**Collins**	**NYG**	**16**	**1**	**22**	**19.7**	**311**	**3,610**	**11.6**	**0**	**58**
	1999		10	2	8	26.7	191	2,316	12.1	2	32
	1998 (w/NO)		11	1	12	26.3	170	2,213	13.0	2	42
	3 Yr - TOTALS		37	4	42	22.9	672	8,139	12.1	4	132
10.	**Stewart**	**PIT**	**15**	**7**	**11**	**22.5**	**151**	**1,860**	**12.3**	**0**	**57**
	1999		14	2	6	12.5	160	1,464	9.2	0	19
	1998		16	2	11	16.5	252	2,560	10.2	1	29
	3 Yr - TOTALS		45	11	28	18.0	563	5,884	10.5	1	105
11.	**King**	**TB**	**16**	**5**	**18**	**16.7**	**233**	**2,769**	**11.9**	**2**	**52**
	1999		6	0	7	10.1	89	875	9.8	0	11
	1998		-	-	-	-	-	-	-	-	-
	3 Yr - TOTALS		22	5	25	14.9	322	3,644	11.3	2	63
12.	**Griese**	**DEN**	**10**	**1**	**19**	**16.9**	**216**	**2,688**	**12.4**	**1**	**47**
	1999		14	2	14	22.3	261	3,032	11.6	0	44
	1998		1	0	0	0.0	1	2	2.0	0	0
	3 Yr - TOTALS		25	3	33	19.2	478	5,722	12.0	1	91
13.	**Testaverde**	**NYJ**	**16**	**0**	**21**	**14.6**	**328**	**3,732**	**11.4**	**2**	**47**
	1999		1	0	1	27.0	10	96	9.6	0	3
	1998		14	1	29	20.2	259	3,256	12.6	0	80
	3 Yr - TOTALS		31	1	51	18.0	597	7,084	11.9	2	130
14.	**Favre**	**GB**	**16**	**0**	**20**	**17.2**	**338**	**3,812**	**11.3**	**2**	**46**
	1999		16	0	22	15.8	341	4,091	12.0	1	48
	1998		16	1	31	27.1	347	4,212	12.1	1	107
	3 Yr - TOTALS		48	1	73	21.0	1026	12,115	11.8	4	201
15.	**Leaf**	**SD**	**11**	**0**	**11**	**33.5**	**161**	**1,883**	**11.7**	**0**	**43**
	1999		-	-	-	-	-	-	-	-	-
	1998		10	0	2	5.5	111	1,289	11.6	0	2
	3 Yr - TOTALS		21	0	13	29.2	272	3,172	11.7	0	45

2000 STATISTICAL RESULTS
(QUARTERBACKS — DISTANCE SCORING METHOD)

	NAME	TEAM	GP	RSH TDs	TD PS	AVG TD LGTH	COMP	YARDS	YDS PER COMP	CONV PTS	FANTASY POINTS
16.	Bledsoe	NE	16	2	17	15.4	312	3,291	10.5	0	41
	1999		16	0	19	28.2	305	3,985	13.1	0	64
	1998		14	0	20	19.0	263	3,633	13.8	0	51
	3 Yr - TOTALS		46	2	56	21.0	880	10,909	12.4	0	156
17.	Green	STL	8	1	16	18.4	145	2,063	14.2	0	41
	1999		-	-	-	-	-	-	-	-	-
	1998 (w/WAS)		15	2	23	22.3	278	3,441	12.4	1	69
	3 Yr - TOTALS		23	3	39	20.7	423	5,504	13.0	1	110
18.	McNown	CHI	10	3	8	37.6	154	1,646	10.7	0	41
	1999		15	0	8	31.0	127	1,465	11.5	2	33
	1998		-	-	-	-	-	-	-	-	-
	3 Yr - TOTALS		25	3	16	34.3	281	3,111	11.1	2	74
19.	Beuerlein	CAR	16	1	19	12.9	324	3,730	11.5	2	40
	1999		16	2	36	24.1	343	4,436	12.9	0	112
	1998		12	0	17	19.3	216	2,613	12.1	1	44
	3 Yr - TOTALS		44	3	72	20.0	883	10,779	12.2	3	196
20.	Plummer	ARI	14	0	13	25.4	270	2,946	10.9	0	40
	1999		12	2	9	9.9	201	2,111	10.5	0	18
	1998		16	4	17	11.4	324	3,737	11.5	0	39
	3 Yr - TOTALS		42	6	39	15.7	795	8,794	11.1	0	97
21.	Batch	DET	15	2	13	19.4	221	2,489	11.3	0	39
	1999		11	2	13	23.4	151	1,957	13.0	1	46
	1998		12	1	11	28.1	173	2,178	12.6	0	40
	3 Yr - TOTALS		38	5	37	23.4	545	6,624	12.2	1	125
22.	Blake	NO	11	1	13	21.3	184	2,025	11.0	0	38
	1999 (w/CIN)		14	2	16	26.4	215	2,670	12.4	2	58
	1998 (w/CIN)		8	0	3	44.7	51	739	14.5	0	15
	3 Yr - TOTALS		33	3	32	26.0	450	5,434	12.1	2	111
23.	Dilfer	BAL	9	0	12	25.2	134	1,502	11.2	0	36
	1999 (w/TB)		10	0	11	24.1	146	1,619	11.1	0	33
	1998 (w/TB)		16	2	21	28.6	225	2,729	12.1	3	79
	3 Yr - TOTALS		35	2	44	26.5	505	5,850	11.6	3	148
24.	Fiedler	MIA	14	1	14	18.9	204	2,402	11.8	0	36
	1999 (w/JAC)		7	0	2	16.0	61	656	10.8	1	5
	1998 (w/MIN)		5	0	0	0.0	3	41	13.7	0	0
	3 Yr - TOTALS		26	1	16	18.5	268	3,099	11.6	1	41
25.	Kitna	SEA	15	1	18	13.2	259	2,658	10.3	0	36
	1999		15	0	23	17.6	270	3,346	12.4	0	56
	1998		6	1	7	30.3	98	1,177	12.0	0	26
	3 Yr - TOTALS		36	2	48	17.8	627	7,181	11.5	0	118
26.	Chandler	ATL	14	0	10	30.4	192	2,236	11.6	0	35
27.	R. Johnson	BUF	12	1	12	18.3	175	2,125	12.1	0	32
28.	Harbaugh	SD	7	0	8	30.2	123	1,416	11.5	0	30
29.	McNair	TEN	16	0	15	15.6	248	2,847	11.5	0	30
30.	B. Johnson	WAS	12	1	11	19.6	227	2,505	11.0	0	29
31.	Brooks	NO	8	2	9	22.2	113	1,514	13.4	0	28
32.	Frerotte	DEN	9	1	9	18.2	138	1,776	12.9	0	26
33.	Cunningham	DAL	6	1	6	26.5	74	849	11.5	1	22
34.	Banks	BAL	11	0	8	18.1	150	1,578	10.5	1	20
35.	George	WAS	6	0	7	21.1	113	1,389	12.3	0	18
36.	Flutie	BUF	11	1	8	14.6	132	1,700	12.9	0	17
37.	Aikman	DAL	11	0	7	13.1	156	1,632	10.5	1	15
38.	Couch	CLE	7	0	7	9.2	137	1,483	10.8	0	11
39.	Case	DET	5	1	1	40.0	56	503	9.0	1	10
40.	D. Brown	ARI	4	0	2	40.0	40	467	11.7	0	9
41.	Martin	JAC	5	0	2	38.0	22	307	14.0	0	9
42.	Mitchell	CIN	8	1	3	10.7	89	966	10.9	0	9
43.	Graham	PIT	8	0	1	77.0	68	899	13.2	0	8
44.	Bishop	NE	7	0	1	44.0	3	80	26.7	0	5
45.	Kanell	ATL	5	0	2	17.5	57	524	9.2	0	4
46.	Miller	CHI	3	0	1	34.0	47	382	8.1	0	4

	NAME	TEAM	GP	RSH TDs	TD PS	AVG TD LGTH	COMP	YARDS	YDS PER COMP	CONV PTS	FANTASY POINTS
47.	Greisen	ARI	2	0	1	26.0	6	65	10.8	0	3
48.	Hasselbeck	GB	4	0	1	27.0	10	104	10.4	0	3
49.	B. Huard	SEA	5	0	3	7.0	49	540	11.0	0	3
50.	D. Johnson	ATL	4	0	2	11.5	36	406	11.3	0	3
51.	Matthews	CHI	6	0	3	7.0	102	964	9.5	0	3
52.	Mirer	SF	1	0	1	17.0	10	126	12.6	1	3
53.	Smith	CIN	11	0	3	6.0	118	1,253	10.6	0	3
54.	D. Huard	MIA	3	0	1	17.0	39	318	8.2	0	2
55.	O'Donnell	TEN	6	0	2	4.5	36	530	14.7	0	2
56.	Pederson	CLE	10	0	2	9.0	117	1,047	8.9	0	2
57.	Stoerner	DAL	1	0	1	16.0	4	53	13.3	0	2
58.	Moon	KC	2	0	1	8.0	15	208	13.9	0	1
59.	Pennington +	NYJ	1	0	1	5.0	2	67	33.5	0	1
60.	Brady +	NE	1	0	0	0.0	1	6	6.0	0	0
61.	Brister	MIN	2	0	0	0.0	10	82	8.2	0	0
62.	Friesz	NE	1	0	0	0.0	11	66	6.0	0	0
63.	Husak +	WAS	1	0	0	0.0	2	-2	-1.0	0	0
64.	Lewis	CAR	5	0	0	0.0	16	120	7.5	0	0
65.	Lucas	NYJ	5	0	0	0.0	21	206	9.8	0	0
66.	Moreno	SD	6	0	0	0.0	27	241	8.9	0	0
67.	Rattay +	SF	1	0	0	0.0	1	-4	-4.0	0	0
68.	Redman	BAL	1	0	0	0.0	2	19	9.5	0	0
69.	Thompson	CLE	1	0	0	0.0	1	8	8.0	0	0
70.	Van Pelt	BUF	1	0	0	0.0	4	67	16.8	0	0
71.	Wright	DAL	4	0	0	0.0	22	237	10.8	0	0
72.	Wynn +	CLE	7	0	0	0.0	22	167	7.6	0	0
73.	Zeier	TB	3	0	0	0.0	3	19	6.3	0	0

+   DENOTES COLLEGE DRAFT PICKS

RATING THE PLAYERS FOR 2001
(Quarterbacks — Distance Scoring Method)
GRAB ONE IF YOU CAN

☐ **1. Kurt Warner (St. Louis Rams)**
Warner has a track team for a receiving crew and, despite missing five games in 2000 to a finger injury, averaged 34.3 yards on 21 touchdown passes. I look for a rebound to 30 plus touchdowns in 2001.

☐ **2. Daunte Culpepper (Minnesota Vikings)**
Having a receiver like Randy Moss sure helps, especially as a first year starter. Culpepper's 25.1 average on 33 touchdowns and seven rushing touchdowns in 2000 are just an example of what's to come in 2001.

☐ **3. Jeff Garcia (San Francisco 49ers)**
From struggling in 1999, subbing for the injured Steve Young, to 31 touchdown passes and four rushing touchdowns in 2000, Garcia has quickly become a coveted fantasy factor.

☐ **4. Peyton Manning (Indianapolis Colts)**
From throwing 26 touchdowns in each of his first two seasons to averaging 23.9 yards on 33 touchdown passes, Manning continues to improve in every way.

☐ **5. Brian Griese (Denver Broncos)**
The likes of Rod Smith when he and Ed McCaffrey helped Griese to 19 touchdown passes in 2000, when he played in just ten games as he struggled with shoulder problems. Healthy in 2001, I expect Griese to push the 25-30 touchdown range.

BEST OF THE REST

☐ **6. Brett Favre (Green Bay Packers)**
For five straight seasons, Favre threw for over 30 touchdowns, but he dropped off to 22 and 20 touchdowns the last two seasons. I still wouldn't rule out the return to at least 25-plus touchdowns in 2001.

☐ **7. Rich Gannon (Oakland Raiders)**
Gannon has thrown for 24 and 28 touchdowns respectively and has rushed for two and four scores in the two years since joining the Raiders. These are surely numbers to keep in mind looking to 2001.

☐ **8. Donovan McNabb (Philadelphia Eagles)**
It's his ability to run as well as pass for scores that make McNabb an attractive fantasy pick. Becoming the fulltime starter in 2000, McNabb threw for 21 touchdowns and ran for six more. In 2001, facing the league's fourth-easiest schedule, more success is on the way.

☐ **9. Mark Brunell (Jacksonville Jaguars)**
Finally staying healthy an entire season in 2000, Brunell threw for 20 touchdowns, averaging 21.1 yards on each. Having receivers like Jimmy Smith, and Keenan McCardell and tight end Kyle Brady should bring continued success in 2001.

☐ **10. Kerry Collins (New York Giants)**
Targets like Ike Hilliard and Amani Toomer will again help Collins to strong touchdown numbers. In 2000, Collins threw for 22 touchdowns in his first full year as the Giants' starter.

STRONG LONG SHOTS

☐ **11. Elvis Grbac (Baltimore Ravens)**
In 1999, Grbac averaged 28.3 yards per his 24 touchdowns and then 21.6 yards on 28 touchdowns last year, both seasons with Kansas City. Looking to 2001, now in Baltimore, Grbac is aboard to open up the Ravens' passing game. Qadry Ismail and the Ravens' receiving crew are smiling.

☐ **12. Brad Johnson (Tampa Bay Buccaneers)**
With Brad Johnson now aboard, the Buccaneers will open up their passing game, which should benefit Johnson's numbers and receivers Keyshawn Johnson and Jacquez Green.

☐ **13. Jeff Black/Aaron Brooks (New Orleans Saints)**
A broken foot to Jeff Blake opened the door for Aaron Brooks in 2000. Together they combined for 22 touchdown passes, but they'll battle for the starting job in 2001. The winner has the potential to fare well, as the Saints are no longer a boring run-only team

☐ **14. Jeff George (Washington Redskins)**
The strong-armed George takes over, with Brad Johnson departing in the offseason for Tampa Bay. The big question for 2001 is his receivers, with James Thrash (Philadelphia) and Albert Connell (New Orleans) already departed.

☐ **15. Trent Green (Kansas City Chiefs)**
With Elvis Grbac at the helm, the Chiefs threw for 28 touchdowns in 2000. Elvis is gone, however, though new head coach Dick Vermeil likes to throw, as does new offseason acquisition Trent Green. Targets like Derrick Alexander, Sylvester Morris and Tony Gonzalez should help.

HAVE THE POTENTIAL

☐ **16. Vinny Testaverde (New York Jets)**
Recovered from a ruptured achilles suffered in 1999, Testaverde returned to record 21 touchdown passes in 2000 but averaged only 14.6 yards on each, with Keyshawn Johnson departed to Tampa Bay. Though he'll find ways to continue to throw for touchdowns, he'll unlikely be throwing for many long scores with Keyshawn no longer around.

☐ **17. Rob Johnson (Buffalo Bills)**
Doug Flutie has moved on to San Diego, leaving Rob Johnson the starting job by himself. Johnson should be able to show off his arm with more confidence and having a receiver like Eric Moulds will help in boosting his numbers.

☐ **18. Drew Bledsoe (New England Patriots)**
Terry Glenn and Troy Brown, who had a bust out year in 2000, are two nice targets for Bledsoe, but his touchdown numbers have slipped in recent years. Looking to 2001, however, Bledsoe has new incentive to produce, signing a 10-year, $103 million deal in the offseason.

☐ **19. Tony Banks (Dallas Cowboys)**
Targets like Joey Galloway and Rocket Ismail are perfect for this scoring method, however, Banks's inconsistencies are a worry.

☐ **20. Kordell Stewart (Pittsburgh Steelers)**
Stewart gave us reason to hope again in 2000, averaging 22.5 yards on

11 touchdowns but more noticeably scoring seven times on the ground. He'll try to push these numbers in 2001, if he holds the starting job.

KEEP AN EYE ON

☐ **21. Chris Chandler (Atlanta Falcons)**
In the last two seasons, Chandler hasn't neared the 25 touchdowns he produced in 1998, as he's struggled with injury and has just struggled. The likes of Shawn Jefferson, Terrence Mathis and Tim Dwight are still in place if he can get it going again in 2001.

☐ **22. Jeff Lewis (Carolina Panthers)**
There's plenty of uncertainty here with a new starting quarterback, though receivers like Muhsin Muhammad, Patrick Jeffers, and Donald Hayes and tight end Wesley Walls make me optimistic.

☐ **23. Steve McNair (Tennessee Titans)**
He doesn't throw for many touchdowns but he is known to run for scores though he didn't run for a single touchdown in 2000. A year before he ran for eight.

☐ **24. Jake Plummer (Arizona Cardinals)**
He has the targets but he has to stay healthy and confident.

☐ **25. Charlie Batch (Detroit Lions)**
There are nice targets in Germane Crowell and Johnny Morton, but are the Lions content to run more with James Stewart now aboard?

☐ **26. Doug Flutie (San Diego Chargers)**
Can anybody make this team go?

☐ **27. Jon Kitna/Akili Smith (Cincinnati Bengals)**
I like the receivers in Darnay Scott and Peter Warrick but neither quarterback impresses me.

☐ **28. Matt Hasselbeck (Seattle Seahawks)**
Favre's former backup has to prove himself first.

☐ **29. Tim Couch (Cleveland Browns)**
Returning from a fractured right thumb, Couch may not be ready to turn this team around.

☐ **30. Cade McNown/Jim Miller/Shane Matthews (Chicago Bears)**
With a nice set of receivers bouncing in and out of the lineup due to injuries, McNown has thrown for only eight touchdowns in each of his first two years.

☐ **31. Jay Fiedler/Ray Lucas (Miami Dolphins)**
The Dolphins will elect to run Lamar Smith often.

ROOKIE PROSPECTS

NAME	TEAM	COMMENT
☐ 1. Michael Vick	ATL	Has bright future but will learn from Chris Chandler for now.
☐ 2. Drew Brees	SD	Will learn from veteran Doug Flutie for now.
☐ 3. Quincy Carter	DALL	Future hope for Dallas, it's Tony Banks for now.

A LOOK AT THE KICKERS

(A Guide for the Beginner)

Considerations in Choosing a Kicker

1. First, look at players' previous performances. Injuries, player moves, suspensions and holdouts should be noted.

2. A kicker needs scoring opportunities, and one of our main concerns is the team he's playing for. Get a kicker who plays for a team that consistently moves the ball deep into enemy territory, a good offensive or defensive team.

3. Go for a kicker who has played on the same team for a few years. Kickers are treated as if they were a dime a dozen. If they have been with a team a few years, it's a sign of confidence in their consistency.

4. Look at the schedule to gauge the strength of the opposition a kicker will face in 2001. A soft schedule could mean a lot of points. (See Section VI for a ranking of the 2001 schedules.)

5. A consideration that is unique to this method is the length of the field goal. If it comes to choosing between two nearly equal kickers, go with the one who is more consistent from long distances.

In the 2000 statistics that follow, you'll find the players ranked by their fantasy-point totals. Remember that in the Distance Scoring Method for kickers, fantasy points are calculated by the length of the field goal (see the following table), and one point is awarded for each successful extra point.

FIELD GOALS

0– 9 yards...1 point	40–49 yards...5 points
10–19 yards...2 points	50–59 yards...6 points
20–29 yards...3 points	60–69 yards...7 points
30–39 yards...4 points	70 & over....10 points

2000 STATISTICAL RESULTS
(KICKERS – DISTANCE SCORING METHOD)

	NAME	TEAM	GP	EXTRA PTS	EXTRA PT ATT	ACC RATE	10-19	20-29	30-39	40-49	50-59	60 & OVER	FG	FG ATT	ACC RATE	FAN-TASY PTS
1.	**Longwell**	**GB**	**16**	**32**	**32**	**1.000**	**NA**	**7/8**	**10/10**	**13/15**	**3/5**	**NA**	**33**	**38**	**.868**	**176**
	1999		16	38	38	1.000	NA	8/9	8/9	8/10	1/2	NA	25	30	.833	140
	1998		16	41	43	.953	1/1	6/6	13/15	9/10	0/1	NA	29	33	.879	158
	3-Yr TOTALS		48	111	113	.982	1/1	21/23	31/34	30/35	4/8	0/0	87	101	.861	474
2.	**Stover**	**BAL**	**16**	**30**	**30**	**1.000**	**2/2**	**9/9**	**12/13**	**10/12**	**2/3**	**NA**	**35**	**39**	**.897**	**171**
	1999		16	32	32	1.000	4/4	9/9	6/8	7/7	2/5	NA	28	33	.848	138
	1998		16	24	24	1.000	NA	6/6	5/5	10/17	NA	NA	21	28	.750	112
	3-Yr TOTALS		48	86	86	1.000	6/6	24/24	23/26	27/36	4/8	NA	84	100	.840	421
3.	**Gramatica**	**TB**	**16**	**42**	**42**	**1.000**	**NA**	**8/8**	**8/10**	**7/9**	**5/7**	**NA**	**28**	**34**	**.824**	**163**
	1999		15	25	25	1.000	NA	8/8	9/11	7/9	3/4	NA	27	32	.844	138
	1998		-	-	-	-	-	-	-	-	-	-	-	-	-	-
	3-Yr TOTALS		31	67	67		0/0	16/16	17/21	14/18	8/11	0/0	55	66	.833	301
4.	**Nedney ****	**CAR**	**15**	**24**	**24**	**1.000**	**1/1**	**16/16**	**7/8**	**8/10**	**2/3**	**NA**	**34**	**38**	**.895**	**154**
	1999 (w/OAK)		3	13	13	1.000	NA	2/2	2/2	0/1	1/2	NA	5	7	.714	33
	1998 (w/ARI)		12	30	30	1.000	1/1	6/6	1/1	5/8	1/4	NA	13	19	.684	83
	3-Yr TOTALS		30	67	67	1.000	1/1	24/24	10/11	13/19	4/9	0/0	52	64	.813	270
5.	**Akers**	**PHI**	**16**	**34**	**36**	**.944**	**1/1**	**6/6**	**14/15**	**7/10**	**1/1**	**NA**	**29**	**33**	**.879**	**151**
	1999		5	2	2	1.000	NA	NA	NA	2/2	1/3	NA	3	5	.600	18
	1998 (w/WAS)		1	2	2	1.000	NA	NA	NA	0/2	NA	NA	0	2	.000	2
	3-Yr TOTALS		22	38	40	.950	1/1	6/6	14/15	9/14	2/4	0/0	32	40	.800	171
6.	**Mare**	**MIA**	**16**	**33**	**34**	**.971**	**NA**	**7/8**	**9/10**	**12/13**	**NA**	**NA**	**28**	**31**	**.903**	**150**
	1999		16	27	27	1.000	1/1	9/9	17/17	9/14	3/5	NA	39	46	.848	187
	1998		16	33	34	.971	1/1	12/13	5/5	5/7	0/2	NA	22	27	.815	114
	3-Yr TOTALS		48	93	95	.979	1/1	28/30	31/32	26/34	3/7	0/0	89	104	.856	451
7.	**Vanderjagt**	**IND**	**16**	**46**	**46**	**1.000**	**1/1**	**6/6**	**13/13**	**5/6**	**0/1**	**NA**	**25**	**27**	**.926**	**143**
	1999		16	43	43	1.000	2/2	10/10	11/13	10/11	1/2	NA	34	38	.895	177
	1998		14	23	23	1.000	NA	8/8	4/4	9/10	5/7	NA	27	31	.871	140
	3-Yr TOTALS		46	112	112	1.000	4/4	24/24	28/30	24/27	6/10	0/1	86	96	.896	460
8.	**Del Greco**	**TEN**	**16**	**37**	**38**	**.974**	**NA**	**12/14**	**8/9**	**6/9**	**1/1**	**NA**	**27**	**33**	**.818**	**141**
	1999		16	43	43	1.000	1/1	8/8	7/9	4/6	1/1	NA	21	25	.840	123
	1998		16	28	28	1.000	1/1	8/8	15/15	12/15	NA	NA	36	39	.923	174
	3-Yr TOTALS		48	108	109	.991	2/2	28/30	30/33	22/30	2/2	0/0	84	97	.866	438

2000 STATISTICAL RESULTS
(KICKERS — DISTANCE SCORING METHOD)

NAME	TEAM	GP	EXTRA PTS	EXTRA PT ATT	ACC RATE	10-19	20-29	30-39	40-49	50-59	60 & OVER	FG	FG ATT	ACC RATE	FAN-TASY PTS
9. Hollis	JAC	12	33	33	1.000	NA	6/7	8/8	7/8	3/3	NA	24	26	.923	136
1999		16	37	37	1.000	NA	12/13	8/9	10/15	1/1	NA	31	38	.816	161
1998		16	45	45	1.000	1/1	8/10	8/9	4/5	0/1	NA	21	26	.808	123
3-Yr TOTALS		44	115	115	1.000	1/1	26/30	24/26	21/28	4/5	0/0	76	90	.844	420
10. Janikowski +	OAK	14	46	46	1.000	1/1	6/6	6/7	8/14	1/4	NA	22	32	.688	136
1999															
1998															
3-Yr TOTALS		14	46	46	1.000	1/1	6/6	6/7	8/14	1/4	0/0	22	32	.688	136
11. G. Anderson	MIN	16	45	45	1.000	NA	6/6	9/9	7/7	0/1	NA	22	23	.957	133
1999		16	46	46	1.000	NA	6/8	9/11	4/9	0/2	NA	19	30	.633	120
1998		16	59	59	1.000	1/1	11/11	9/9	12/12	2/2	NA	35	35	1.000	202
3-Yr TOTALS		48	150	150	1.000	1/1	23/25	27/29	23/28	2/5	0/0	76	88	.864	455
12. Brien	NO	16	37	37	1.000	2/2	5/5	4/5	12/15	0/2	NA	23	29	.793	133
1999		15	20	21	.952	1/1	8/10	6/7	7/9	2/2	NA	24	29	.828	118
1998		15	31	31	1.000	NA	7/7	3/3	6/6	4/6	NA	20	22	.909	118
3-Yr TOTALS		46	88	89	.989	3/3	20/22	13/15	25/30	6/10	0/0	67	80	.838	369
13. M. Andersen	ATL	16	23	23	1.000	NA	6/6	6/7	11/15	2/3	NA	25	31	.806	132
1999		16	34	34	1.000	NA	6/6	5/8	4/6	0/1	NA	15	21	.714	92
1998		16	51	52	.981	0/1	8/9	7/7	6/9	2/2	NA	23	28	.821	145
3-Yr TOTALS		48	108	109	.991	0/1	20/21	18/22	21/30	4/6	0/0	63	80	.788	369
14. Vinatieri	NE	16	25	25	1.000	0/1	11/13	8/9	7/8	1/2	NA	27	33	.818	131
1999		16	29	30	.967	1/1	14/14	5/7	5/9	1/2	NA	26	33	.788	124
1998		16	32	32	1.000	3/3	8/8	9/14	9/12	2/2	NA	31	39	.795	157
3-Yr TOTALS		48	86	87	.989	4/5	33/35	22/30	21/29	4/6	0/0	84	105	.800	412
15. Brown	PIT	16	32	33	.970	1/1	8/8	9/10	6/9	1/2	NA	25	30	.833	130
1999		16	30	31	.968	2/2	5/5	9/10	8/11	1/1	NA	25	29	.862	131
1998															
3-Yr TOTALS		32	62	64	.969	3/3	13/13	18/20	14/20	2/3	0/0	50	59	.847	261
16. Christie	BUF	16	31	31	1.000	2/2	11/13	4/6	9/13	0/1	NA	26	35	.743	129
1999		16	33	33	1.000	2/2	10/10	7/10	3/9	3/3	NA	25	34	.735	128
1998		16	41	41	1.000	1/1	10/12	12/14	9/11	1/3	NA	33	41	.805	172
3-Yr TOTALS		48	105	105	1.000	5/5	31/35	23/30	21/33	4/7	0/0	84	110	.764	429

2000 STATISTICAL RESULTS
(KICKERS – DISTANCE SCORING METHOD)

	NAME	TEAM	GP	EXTRA PTS	EXTRA PT ATT	ACC RATE	10-19	20-29	30-39	40-49	50-59	60 & OVER	FG	FG ATT	ACC RATE	FAN-TASY PTS
17.	**Seder ***	**DAL**	**15**	**27**	**27**	**1.000**	**2/2**	**5/6**	**9/11**	**9/13**	**0/1**	**NA**	**25**	**33**	**.758**	**129**
	1999		—	—	—	—	—	—	—	—	—	—	—	—	—	—
	1998		—	—	—	—	—	—	—	—	—	—	—	—	—	—
	3-Yr TOTALS		**15**	**27**	**27**	**1.000**	**2/2**	**5/6**	**9/11**	**9/13**	**0/1**	**NA**	**25**	**33**	**.758**	**129**
18.	**Hanson**	**DET**	**15**	**27**	**27**	**1.000**	**2/2**	**6/7**	**10/12**	**4/7**	**2/2**	**0/0**	**24**	**30**	**.800**	**123**
	1999		15	29	29	1.000	NA	8/8	4/4	10/12	4/8	NA	26	32	.813	142
	1998		16	28	29	.966	NA	8/8	7/7	13/15	1/3	NA	29	33	.879	150
	3-Yr TOTALS		**47**	**84**	**85**	**.988**	**2/2**	**22/23**	**21/23**	**27/34**	**7/13**	**0/0**	**79**	**95**	**.832**	**415**
19.	**Elam**	**DEN**	**13**	**49**	**49**	**1.000**	**NA**	**7/7**	**6/7**	**4/9**	**1/1**	**NA**	**18**	**24**	**.750**	**120**
	1999		16	29	29	1.000	1/1	8/8	7/8	8/11	5/7	0/1	29	36	.806	153
	1998		16	58	58	1.000	NA	3/3	13/14	4/6	2/3	1/1	23	27	.852	158
	3-Yr TOTALS		**45**	**136**	**136**	**1.000**	**1/1**	**18/18**	**26/29**	**16/26**	**8/11**	**1/2**	**70**	**87**	**.805**	**431**
20.	**Hall**	**NYJ**	**15**	**30**	**30**	**1.000**	**NA**	**8/9**	**6/8**	**6/12**	**1/3**	**NA**	**21**	**32**	**.656**	**114**
	1999		16	27	29	.931	NA	3/4	17/17	7/12	NA	NA	27	33	.818	139
	1998		16	45	46	.978	NA	9/9	9/13	6/10	1/2	0/1	25	35	.714	144
	3-Yr TOTALS		**47**	**102**	**105**	**.971**	**NA**	**20/22**	**32/38**	**19/34**	**2/5**	**0/1**	**73**	**100**	**.730**	**397**
21.	**Edinger +**	**CHI**	**15**	**21**	**21**	**1.000**	**1/1**	**5/5**	**7/9**	**6/10**	**2/2**	**NA**	**21**	**27**	**.778**	**108**
	1999		—	—	—	—	—	—	—	—	—	—	—	—	—	—
	1998		—	—	—	—	—	—	—	—	—	—	—	—	—	—
	3-Yr TOTALS		**15**	**21**	**21**	**1.000**	**1/1**	**5/5**	**7/9**	**6/10**	**2/2**	**NA**	**21**	**27**	**.778**	**108**
22.	**Carney**	**SD**	**15**	**21**	**21**	**1.000**	**1/1**	**3/3**	**5/7**	**7/10**	**2/4**	**0/0**	**18**	**25**	**.720**	**105**
	1999		15	27	27	1.000	2/2	13/13	6/8	9/12	1/1	NA	31	36	.861	140
	1998		15	22	23	.957	2/2	11/12	5/5	6/8	2/3	NA	26	30	.867	124
	3-Yr TOTALS		**45**	**70**	**71**	**.986**	**5/5**	**27/28**	**16/20**	**22/30**	**5/8**	**0/0**	**75**	**91**	**.824**	**369**
23.	**Wilkins**	**STL**	**11**	**38**	**38**	**1.000**	**2/2**	**5/5**	**6/6**	**3/3**	**1/1**	**NA**	**17**	**17**	**1.000**	**102**
	1999		16	64	64	1.000	1/1	5/5	6/7	7/11	1/4	NA	20	28	.714	146
	1998		15	25	26	.962	NA	4/5	8/8	5/8	3/5	NA	20	26	.769	112
	3-Yr TOTALS		**42**	**127**	**128**	**.992**	**3/3**	**14/15**	**20/21**	**15/22**	**5/10**	**NA**	**57**	**71**	**.803**	**360**
24.	**Richey**	**SF**	**16**	**43**	**45**	**.956**	**NA**	**6/7**	**6/8**	**3/6**	**0/1**	**NA**	**15**	**22**	**.682**	**100**
	1999		16	30	31	.968	1/1	7/7	7/8	5/6	1/1	NA	21	23	.913	112
	1998		16	49	51	.961	NA	9/10	3/4	6/13	NA	NA	18	27	.667	118
	3-Yr TOTALS		**48**	**122**	**127**	**.961**	**1/1**	**22/24**	**16/20**	**14/25**	**1/2**	**NA**	**54**	**72**	**.750**	**330**

2000 STATISTICAL RESULTS
(KICKERS – DISTANCE SCORING METHOD)

	NAME	TEAM	GP	EXTRA PTS	EXTRA PT ATT	ACC RATE	10–19	20–29	30–39	40–49	50–59	60 & OVER	FG	FG ATT	ACC RATE	FAN-TASY PTS
25.	Daluiso	NYG	13	34	34	1.000	NA	8/8	5/8	4/7	NA	NA	17	23	.739	98
	1999		6	9	9	1.000	NA	4/4	3/3	0/2	NA	NA	7	9	.778	33
	1998		16	32	32	1.000	2/2	5/5	6/8	7/11	1/1	NA	21	27	.778	116
	3-Yr TOTALS		35	75	75	1.000	2/2	17/17	14/19	11/20	1/1	0/0	45	59	.763	247
26.	Lindell	SEA	12	25	25	1.000	NA	4/5	1/1	7/8	3/3	NA	15	17	.882	94
27.	Blanchard	ARI	16	18	19	.947	1/1	2/2	9/11	2/5	2/4	NA	16	23	.696	84
28.	Peterson	KC	11	25	25	1.000	1/1	5/5	7/9	2/5	NA	NA	15	20	.750	80
29.	Dawson	CLE	13	17	17	1.000	2/2	4/4	6/6	2/5	NA	NA	14	17	.824	67
30.	Rackers +	CIN	15	21	21	1.000	1/1	5/5	5/9	2/7	NA	NA	12	21	.571	66
31.	Heppner **	WAS	8	17	17	1.000	1/1	4/4	3/6	2/2	0/2	NA	10	15	.667	53
32.	Stoyanovich	STL	8	26	26	.875	NA	2/2	0/2	3/3	0/1	NA	5	8	.625	47
33.	Murray	WAS	6	7	8	1.000	NA	2/2	3/4	3/6	NA	NA	8	12	.667	40
34.	Cunningham	CAR	4	9	9	1.000	NA	2/4	3/3	NA	NA	NA	5	7	.714	27
35.	Hall	STL	3	9	9	1.000	NA	1/1	1/1	1/2	1/1	NA	4	5	.800	27
36.	Conway **	NYJ	4	8	8	1.000	2/2	3/3	NA	1/1	1/1	NA	6	6	1.000	26
37.	Lindsey	JAC	4	5	5	1.000	2/2	NA	1/3	2/2	NA	NA	5	7	.714	23
38.	Husted	WAS	4	8	9	.889	NA	4/4	0/3	0/1	NA	NA	4	8	.500	20
39.	Holmes	NYG	2	3	3	1.000	NA	1/1	1/1	NA	NA	NA	2	2	1.000	10
40.	Lechler	OAK	1	7	7	1.000	NA	NA	0/1	NA	NA	NA	0	1	.000	7
41.	Bentley	WAS	1	0	0	.000	NA	NA	NA	NA	1/1	NA	1	1	1.000	6

+ DENOTES COLLEGE DRAFT PICKS
*   Seder   (DAL) -Scored TD on a 1 yard run.
**   Nedney   (CAR) -Played in 3 games with Denver and 2 games with Oakland.
**   Heppner   (WAS) -Played in 4 games with Seattle.
**   Conway   (NYJ) -Played in 1 game with Oakland and 2 games with Washington.

RATING THE PLAYERS FOR 2001
(Kickers—Distance Scoring Method)
GRAB ONE IF YOU CAN

☐ **1. Martin Gramatica (Tampa Bay Buccaneers)**
Gramatica hit 28 of 34 (.824) field goals in 2000, including 5 of 7 from beyond 50 yards. A strong leg on an improved team with Brad Johnson now at quarterback should bring success in 2001.

☐ **2. Jeff Wilkins (St. Louis Rams)**
A pulled quad muscle cost Wilkins five games in 2000 but his 17 of 17 (1.000) on field goals, including hitting his only attempt over 50 yards, shows he should again be a scoring force in 2001 as long as he stays healthy.

☐ **3. Ryan Longwell (Green Bay Packers)**
The Packers aren't afraid to use Longwell going for long kicks. He hit 3 of 5 attempts beyond 50 yards in 2000, on his way to 33 of 38 (.868) on the year, and leads the league in this scoring method. A consistent 80 percent kicker, Longwell should have more success in 2001.

☐ **4. Matt Stover (Baltimore Ravens)**
A very solid 35 of 39 (.897) field goal accuracy in 2000, as Stover was the Ravens' most consistent offensive weapon. My question for 2001 is: will he will see as many field goal tries with Elvis Grbac now at quarterback?

☐ **5. Joe Nedney (Tennessee Titans)**
Nedney's 34 of 38 (.895) field goal accuracy, including 2 of 3 beyond 50 yards, filling in for Jason Elam in Denver and John Kasay in Carolina in 2000, has the Titans and fantasy fans excited for 2001.

BEST OF THE REST

☐ **6. David Akers (Philadelphia Eagles)**
Akers rewarded Philadelphia with a 29 of 33 (.879) field goal performance in 2000. With the Eagles facing the third-easiest schedule in 2001, Akers should continue to get plenty scoring chances in 2001.

☐ **7. Mike Vanderjadt (Indianapolis Colts)**
Vanderjadt's numbers are very impressive and actually improving. Vanderjadt has hit 27 of 31 (.871), 34 of 38 (.895) and 25 of 27 (.926) field goal attempts over the last three seasons. He'll continue to put up good numbers in 2001, with his accuracy and kicking for the young and talented Colts.

☐ **8. Jason Elam (Denver Broncos)**
Usually among the league's highest-scoring kickers, Elam's numbers dropped in 2000, as he missed three games with a back injury. With the ability to hit the long kick, exampled by his 5 of 7 from beyond 50 yards in 1999, he'll return to prominence in 2001.

☐ **9. Mike Hollis (Jacksonville Jaguars)**
Don't overlook Hollis, who hit 24 of 26 (.923) field goal attempts in 2000, including 3 of 3 beyond 50 yards. The Jaguars just need him to get more scoring chances.

☐ **10. Olindo Mare (Miami Dolphins)**
Mare's numbers continue to improve. In 2000, he hit 28 of 31 (.903) field goal tries but none from beyond 50 yards, though he was 12 of 13 between 40 and 49 yards. He's too consistent of a weapon for Miami not to provide him continued chances in 2001.

STRONG LONG SHOTS

☐ **11. Sebastian Janikoski (Oakland Raiders)**
Janikowski struggled as a rookie in 2000, hitting a disappointing 22 of 32 (.688) field goal attempts. I look for Raider's first-round pick of 2000 and strong-legged kicker to get on track in 2001.

☐ **12. John Kasay (Carolina Panthers)**
Kasay, one of the league's most consistent kickers, missed the last three games of the 1999 season and all of 2000 with a knee injury. Expecting he'll be 100 percent, Kasay should again find himself among the league's top kickers.

☐ **13. Gary Anderson (Minnesota Vikings)**
Anderson recovered from his woeful 19 of 30 (.633) field goal performance in 1999, to hit 22 of 23 (.957) in 2000, with his only miss was from beyond 50 yards. The fact that the Vikings face the league's toughest schedule in 2001 scares me a bit.

☐ **14. Jason Hanson (Detroit Lions)**
He's always it seems in the 80 percent accuracy range, Hanson hit 24 of 30 (.800) field goal attempts in 2000, including 2 of 2 beyond 50 yards. Facing a fairly easy schedule in 2001, Hanson should put up solid numbers in 2001.

☐ **15. Brett Conway (Washington Redskins)**
Brett Conway should realize good results on a team with Jeff George at quarterback and facing the league's easiest schedule.

HAVE THE POTENTIAL

☐ **16. Adam Vinatieri/Owen Pochman (New England Patriots)**
Vinatieri improved to hitting a very solid 27 of 33 (.818) field goal attempts in 2000, including 1 of 2 beyond 50 yards. The Patriots have provided Vinatieri with over 30 field goal tries the last three seasons which helps. In 2001, however, Vinatieri faces the challenge of rookie Owen Pochman.

☐ **17. Tim Seder (Dallas Cowboys)**
Aikman may no longer be aboard, but the Cowboys still have enough offensive weaponry to provide plenty scoring chances.

☐ **18. ????? (New Orleans Saints)**
Doug Brien's replacement should have a chance to fare well with the improved Saints.

☐ **19. Kris Brown (Pittsburgh Steelers)**
When your offense is struggling in the red zone you have to depend on your kicker, and Kris Brown has provided dependability for the Steelers the last two seasons. Brown hit 25 of 29 (.862) field goal tries as a rookie in 1999 and 25 of 30 (.833) in 2000, including 2 of 3 beyond 50 yards along the way.

☐ **20. Steve Christie (Buffalo Bills)**
Two straight seasons of disappointing numbers, as Christie hit 25 of 34 (.735) field goal attempts in 1999 and 26 of 35 (.743) attempts in 2000, missing his sole attempt from beyond 50 yards. The Bills do, however, face a fairly easy schedule in 2001.

KEEP AN EYE ON

☐ **21. Morten Andersen/Jake Arians (Atlanta Falcons)**
For a long time, Andersen has been among the league's best, but is it time to look for a younger replacement?

☐ **22. ???? (San Francisco 49ers)**
Wade Richey struggled in 2000, but the 49ers are improving offensively behind Jeff Garcia, which should improve the scoring chances of the 49ers' new kickers in 2001. Richey signed with San Diego in the off-season. At press time, the 49ers had signed only free agent Jamie Rheem.

☐ **23. Todd Peterson (Kansas City Chiefs)**
Dick Vermeil is in the house, but Elvis Grbac no longer is.

☐ **24. Brad Daluiso/Jon Markam (New York Giants)**
Daluiso had only 17 of 23 (.739) overall in 2000, including 4 of 7 between 40 and 49 yards and no attempts over 50 yards. In 2001 he faces the challenge of rookie Jon Markam.

☐ **25. Cary Blanchard/Bill Gramatica (Arizona Cardinals)**
Is this team ever going to do anything?

☐ **26. Jeff Hall/Brett Conway (New York Jets)**
Despite a two-year deal signed last year, Hall was benched late in 2000 for Brett Conway, after hitting a woeful 21 of 32 (.656) field goal tries.

☐ **27. Wade Richey (San Diego Chargers)**
This team still has to prove itself.

☐ **28. Rian Lindell (Seattle Seahawks)**
Is Matt Hasselbeck the answer at quarterback?

☐ **29. Phil Dawson (Cleveland Browns)**
Does anybody have a good feeling about the Browns?

☐ **30. Paul Edinger (Chicago Bears)**
Where is this team headed?

☐ **31. Neil Rackers/Ritchie Cunningham (Cincinnati Bengals)**
If Rackers 12 of 21 (.571) on field goal attempts in 2000 isn't bad enough, this team has no leadership. Ritchie Cunningham has been brought in to challenge for the job.

A 2001 QUICK PICKS—MOCK DRAFT

(My Top "30" Overall Picks for the Distance Scoring Method)

NAME	TEAM	POS	COMMENTS
1. Warner	STL	QB	Finger injury in 2000 slowed numbers but targets Bruce, Holt and Hakim should help rebound.
2. Faulk	STL	RB	NFL record 26 TDs, playing in 14 games in 2000.
3. James	IND	RB	35 TDs in just two NFL seasons.
4. Culpepper	MINN	QB	Can run or throw and having Randy Moss helps.
5. Moss	MINN	WR	Has averaged 33.4 yards on the 43 TDs he's scored.
6. Taylor	JAC	RB	Very capable of big touchdown numbers if healthy.
7. S. Davis	WASH	RB	Faces league's easiest schedule in 2001.
8. Garcia	SF	QB	Quickly improved numbers as full-time starter in 2000.
9. Manning	IND	QB	Tied for NFL lead with 33 TD passes in 2000.
10. George	TENN	RB	Has finally become consistent scorer.
11. Harrison	IND	WR	Manning's favorite go-to, plenty more TDs in store.
12. Dunn	TB	RB	Can pop the "long one" and will get more work in 2001.
13. Robinson	CHI	WR	Scored nine times on 84 receptions in 1999.
14. Owens	SF	WR	TD numbers will improve as QB Jeff Garcia does.
15. Bruce	STL	WR	One of league's best deep threats when healthy.
16. Griese	DEN	QB	19 TDs in just ten games before shoulder trouble.
17. Favre	GB	QB	Looking to rebound TD numbers after two-year slump.
18. Dillon	CIN	RB	Capable of breaking for long scores.
19. R. Smith	DEN	WR	A big deep threat for Broncos and Brian Griese.
20. T. Davis	DEN	RB	Looking to rebound scoring numbers in 2001.
21. Gannon	OAK	QB	Gannon can run and throw for scores.
22. Barber	NYG	RB	Jumped TD numbers in 2000 and will provide the occasional long score.
23. McNabb	PHIL	QB	Young, improving QB who can hurt you on ground and through air.
24. Smith	MIA	RB	Surprised many with 16 TDs in 2000.
25. Holt	STL	WR	Speedster provides potent Rams another deep threat.
26. Green	GB	RB	Big year in 2000 has earned him more work.
27. Williams	NO	RB	Scored nine times in just ten games before injury in 2000.
28. Freeman	GB	WR	Freeman-Favre looking to rebound scoring numbers.
29. Stewart	DET	RB	Has become Lions' main ground weapon, which will continue to push scoring chances.
30. Moulds	BUF	WR	Struggled scoring in 2000 but averaged 48.9 yards on nine TDs in 1999.

This Mock Draft is expanded and updated in *Cliff's Quick Picks: Fantasy Football Draft at a Glance*—a huge 8-panel cheatsheet that examines the top-100 overall picks for the Basic and Combined Basic/Performance methods. Potential fantasy draft picks are also broken down by fantasy position, including the *top-50* running backs and wide receivers, and the *top-25* tight ends, quarterbacks and kickers. *Cliff's Quick Picks* will be available in mid-August and updated weekly, right around your fantasy draft time. Be sure to order! Details and order form, along with a toll-free phone number, and website address appear on the hard insert in the middle of this book.

XI
RATING OPPOSING NFL DEFENSES
HELPING YOU CHOOSE WHICH PLAYERS
TO START FROM WEEK TO WEEK

Now that you've selected your fantasy team, how do you choose whom to start from week to week? Defensive statistics for the teams your players are up against will prove useful in determining which players to start for a given game. (There are now a good number of fantasy leagues that also draft team defenses. The following section, "Drafting a Team Defense," deals specifically with this, although the present section can also be of help, depending on what defensive statistics your league uses.)

You may be fortunate enough to have three good running backs, but you can only play two. Each week you're faced with a tough decision: Which two should you start? This decision can be made easier by examining the defenses the players are up against. If one of the three will face a defense very tough against the run, the choice is simple: Bench him and play the other two. The same holds true for selecting a quarterback. Look for the defense that is weaker against the pass or has allowed more passing touchdowns.

From year to year, especially since the recent explosion of free-agent movement, team defensive statistics have changed quite a bit. As players move, the defensive performances of their teams are affected, obviously, and this makes predicting how a team defense will play during the upcoming year a little more difficult than it used to be. Still, most defenses manage to stay mostly intact, and many teams simply have a history of playing tough defense, despite gains and losses in personnel.

So keep an eye on the last few years' statistics as a base of comparison; but then follow team defensive performances as the 2001 season progresses, to help you get a better feel for how some of these newly thrown-together squads will fare. This is just one of the precautions a good fantasy owner takes to ensure success during the season. Every once in a while you're going to pick up a few extra points this way—choosing one player over another, based on the defenses they're facing that week—and those little advantages often make the difference between a consistent winner and consistent mediocrity.

As I've said, the statistics in this section are based on how teams did defensively last season, so you may find them useful for only the first few games of 2001. A defense that performed well last year will not necessarily continue to excel this year. To help account for the possibility of a one-year irregularity, however, I have included each team's defensive statistics from both last year and the previous year. This should help you determine whether a defense is improving or on a downward slide; and it should give you an idea of a team defense's consistency against the run or pass.

To evaluate current NFL defenses during the season, you will need to know how they're doing from week to week. I suggest reading a publication that documents current defensive standings. This should definitely help in selecting your weekly fantasy lineup.

In the following charts, I list the defensive rankings according to touch-downs allowed via the pass or rush, and according to yardage allowed via the pass or rush. The defensive touchdown statistics will show fantasy owners who use the Basic, Distance, or Combined Basic/Performance Scoring Methods which teams are toughest to score against via the pass or run. The defensive yardage statistics will help fantasy teams using the Performance Point or Combined Basic/Performance Scoring Method to judge which teams are harder to move the ball against via passing or rush-ing. The better defenses—the teams tough to score on or pick up yardage against—are at the top of the chart, and the weaker defenses are toward the bottom. Obviously, the higher a defense rates, the less eager you will be to start a player against it.

These statistics show us which defenses were hardest to score in both 2000 and a year earlier in 1999. Therefore if your league uses the Basic, Dis-tance or Combined Basic/Performance Scoring Method and you have to choose between a quarterback who is facing the Tampa Bay Buccaneers or one playing the Cincinnati Bengals, you surely would choose the one facing the Bengals. The Bengals ranked 27th in 2000, allowing 26 touch-down passes, and ranked 29th a year earlier surrendering 28 touchdown passing. The Buccaneers, who led the league by allowing only 11 touch-down passes in 1999, dropped to 7th in 2000, but allowed only 15 touch-down passes all year.

How about making a choice between two running backs, one playing the Cleveland Browns or one facing the Baltimore Ravens/ The choice should be simple. The Ravens have ranked 1st in each of the last two sea-sons in allowing the fewest rushing touchdowns. Baltimore surrendered only five touchdowns on the ground in 2000 and six the year before in 1999. The Browns, on the other hand, ranked 30th in 2000, giving up 26 rushing touchdowns and ranked 31st a year earlier, giving up 29 rushing scores. Obviously, you would choose the back facing the more porous Cleveland red zone rushing defense.

If your league uses the Performance Point or Combined Basic/Perfor-mance Scoring Method, though your are now more concerned with yards, you decision making process should be the same. Choosing a quarter-back facing the San Francisco 49ers or one facing the Miami Dolphins should be easy. The 49ers have been atrocius against the pass the last three season. In 1998, the 49ers allowed a lofty 249.5 yards per game through the air, a year later in 1999, the 49ers allowed an average of 269.1 yards per game through the air and last season ranked 30th in the league allowing 260.4 yards per game through the air. Meanwhile, the Dolphins placed 4th against the pass in 1999 allowing 198.0 yards per game through the air and last season ranked 5th, allowing 197.4 yards per game through the air. Choose the quarterback facing the 49ers.

If you're deciding between two running backs, one facing the Seattle Sea-hawks on one facing the San Diego Chargers, the choice should again be easy. The Chargers ranked 3rd in 1999, allowing only 82.6 yards per game on the ground and ranked 4th in 2000 allowing only 82.6 yards per game on the ground. On the flip side the Seahawks ranked 25th in 1999, al-lowing 121.2 yards per game on the ground and were even worse in 2000, ranking 28th allowing a whopping 153.4 rushing yards per game. Certainly you'd choose the player facing the Seahawks.

Although statistics can be useful as guidelines, choosing a starting lineup is rarely a cut-and-dried situation. If you have a franchise or extremely hot player, like a Randy Moss or a Marshall Faulk in 2000, you will probably want to start him no matter which team he is up against. Or, if one of your players is especially hot, you may want to continue to start him until he cools off. This all requires a feel for the game, and with time and experience you'll get better at it.

2000 NFL DEFENSES
RUSHING TOUCHDOWNS ALLOWED

(For Leagues Using the Basic, Distance, or
Combined Basic/Performance Scoring Method)

TEAM	2000 RSH TDs	1999 RSH TDs	1999 LEAGUE RANK
1. Baltimore	5	6	1st (Tie)
2. Green Bay	7	16	25th (Tie)
3. N.Y. Giants	7	13	21st (Tie)
4. Tennessee	7	8	7th (Tie)
5. Oakland	8	10	13th (Tie)
6. Miami	9	6	1st (Tie)
7. N.Y. Jets	9	16	25th (Tie)
8. Pittsburgh	9	10	13h (Tie)
9. Washington	9	16	25th (Tie)
10. Philadelphia	10	12	18th (Tie)
11. San Diego	10	8	7th
12. Carolina	12	13	21st (Tie)
13. Cincinnati	12	22	30th (Tie)
14. New England	12	6	1st (Tie)
15. Tampa Bay	12	8	7th (Tie)
16. Buffalo	13	9	10th (Tie)
17. Denver	13	15	23rd (Tie)
18. Indianapolis	13	12	18th (Tie)
19. Kansas City	13	10	13th (Tie)
20. Detroit	14	12	18th (Tie)
21. Jacksonville	14	6	1st (Tie)
22. New Orleans	14	15	23rd (Tie)
23. Chicago	15	11	16th (Tie)
24. Atlanta	16	16	25th (Tie)
25. Dallas	17	6	1st (Tie)
26. Minnesota	17	9	10th (Tie)
27. St. Louis	18	6	1st (Tie)
28. Seattle	20	9	10th (Tie)

	22	11	16th (Tie)
29. San Francisco	22	11	16th (Tie)
30. Cleveland	26	29	31st
31. Arizona	29	17	29th

2000 NFL DEFENSES
PASSING TOUCHDOWNS ALLOWED

(For Leagues Using the Basic, Distance, or
Combined Basic/Performance Scoring Method)

TEAM	2000 PASS TDs ALLOWED	1999 PASS TDs ALLOWED	1999 LEAGUE RANK
1. Tennessee	10	26	27th (Tie)
2. Baltimore	11	20	12th (Tie)
3. Philadelphia	11	22	19th (Tie)
4. Miami	12	19	8th (Tie)
5. Washington	12	23	22nd (Tie)
6. Pittsburgh	13	20	12th (Tie)
7. Tampa Bay	15	11	1st
8. Detroit	16	21	17th (Tie)
9. New Orleans	17	34	31st
10. N.Y. Jets	17	16	3rd
11. Buffalo	18	12	2nd
12. Cleveland	18	17	4th (Tie)
13. Arizona	19	25	26th
14. Carolina	19	26	27th (Tie)
15. Dallas	20	19	8th (Tie)
16. Indianapolis	22	21	17th (Tie)
17. Atlanta	23	18	6th (Tie)
18. Jacksonville	23	18	6th (Tie)
19. Minnesota	23	20	12th (Tie)
20. New England	23	23	22nd (Tie)
21. N.Y. Giants	23	20	12th (Tie)
22. Seattle	23	19	8th (Tie)
23. Chicago	25	23	22nd (Tie)
24. Kansas City	25	24	24th (Tie)
25. Oakland	25	22	19th (Tie)
26. San Francisco	25	33	30th
27. Cincinnati	26	28	29th
28. Denver	26	17	4th (Tie)
29. Green Bay	28	20	12th (Tie)
30. St. Louis	32	19	8th (Tie)
31. San Diego	33	24	24th (Tie)

2000 NFL DEFENSES
RUSHING YARDAGE ALLOWED

(For Leagues Using the Performance or
Combined Basic/Performance Point Scoring Methods)

	TEAM	**2000**		**1999**		
		RSH YDs ALLOWED	AVG YDs PER GAME	1999 RSH YDs ALLOWED	AVG YDs PER GAME	1999 LEAGUE RANK
1.	Baltimore	970	60.6	1,226	76.6	2nd
2.	N.Y. Giants	1,156	72.3	1,559	97.4	12th
3.	Tennessee	1,390	86.9	1,550	96.9	10th
4.	San Diego	1,422	88.8	1,321	82.6	3rd
5.	Oakland	1,553	97.1	1,564	97.8	13th
6.	Buffalo	1,559	97.4	1,371	85.7	4th
7.	Denver	1,598	99.9	1,737	108.6	19th
8.	Green Bay	1,618	101.1	1,804	112.8	22nd
9.	Tampa Bay	1,648	103.0	1,406	87.9	5th
10.	New Orleans	1,672	104.5	1,774	110.9	20th
11.	Jacksonville	1,683	105.2	1,432	89.5	6th
12.	Pittsburgh	1,693	105.8	1,960	112.5	26th
13.	St. Louis	1,697	106.1	1,187	74.2	1st
14.	Miami	1,736	108.5	1,476	92.3	8th
15.	Minnesota	1,804	112.8	1,625	101.6	15th
16.	San Francisco	1,808	113.0	1,609	100.6	14th
17.	Philadelphia	1,820	113.8	2,000	125.0	28th
18.	Detroit	1,823	113.9	1,531	95.7	9th
19.	Kansas City	1,824	114.0	1,557	97.3	11th
20.	Chicago	1,828	114.3	1,882	117.6	23rd
21.	New England	1,831	114.4	1,795	112.2	21st
22.	Washington	1,847	115.4	1,973	123.3	27th
23.	N.Y. Jets	1,888	118.0	1,691	105.7	16th
24.	Cincinnati	1,925	120.3	1,699	106.2	17th
25.	Indianapolis	1,941	121.3	1,719	107.4	18th
26.	Carolina	1,949	121.8	1,898	118.6	24th
27.	Atlanta	1,983	123.9	2,062	128.9	29th
28.	Seattle	2,454	153.4	1,939	121.2	25th
29.	Cleveland	2,487	155.4	2,736	171.0	31st
30.	Arizona	2,609	163.1	2,265	141.6	30th
31.	Dallas	2,637	164.8	1,444	90.3	7th

2000 NFL DEFENSES
PASSING YARDAGE ALLOWED

(For Leagues Using the Performance or
Combined Basic/Performance Scoring Method)

	TEAM	2000 PASSING YDs ALLOWED	AVG YDs PER GAME	1999 PASSING YDs ALLOWED	1999 AVG YDs PER GAME	1999 LEAGUE RANK
1.	Tennessee	2,761	172.6	3,999	249.9	26th
2.	Dallas	2,882	180.1	3,610	225.6	13th
3.	Washington	2,904	181.5	3,953	247.1	25th
4.	Minnesota	3,127	195.4	4,252	265.8	30th
5.	Miami	3,159	197.4	3,168	198.0	4th
6.	N.Y. Jets	3,166	197.9	3,864	241.5	23rd
7.	Baltimore	3,175	198.4	3,278	204.9	7th
8.	Buffalo	3,175	198.4	2,889	180.6	1st
9.	Pittsburgh	3,249	203.1	3,167	197.9	3rd
10.	Arizona	3,263	203.9	3,386	211.6	9th
11.	Philadelphia	3,286	205.4	3,733	233.3	16th
12.	Detroit	3,372	210.8	4,100	256.3	29th
13.	Jacksonville	3,407	212.9	3,263	203.9	5th
14.	Cleveland	3,447	215.4	3,460	216.3	11th
15.	New Orleans	3,449	215.6	3,821	238.8	20th
16.	Tampa Bay	3,484	217.8	3,164	197.8	2nd
17.	Chicago	3,635	227.2	4,079	254.9	28th
18.	N.Y. Giants	3,669	229.3	3,593	224.6	12th
19.	Indianapolis	3,674	229.6	3,775	235.9	19th
20.	New England	3,694	230.9	3,277	204.8	6th
21.	Green Bay	3,695	230.9	3,690	230.6	15th
22.	Cincinnati	3,730	233.1	4,032	252.0	27th
23.	Kansas City	3,737	223.6	3,768	235.5	18th
24.	Atlanta	3,766	235.4	3,419	213.7	10th
25.	San Diego	3,786	236.6	3,847	240.4	22nd
26.	Carolina	3,838	239.9	3,833	240.0	21st
27.	Oakland	3,976	248.5	3,630	226.9	14th
28.	St. Louis	4,085	255.3	3,867	241.7	24th
29.	Seattle	4,089	255.6	3,746	234.1	17th
30.	San Francisco	4,167	260.4	4,305	269.1	31st
31.	Denver	4,197	262.3	3,299	206.2	8th

XII

DRAFTING A TEAM DEFENSE

A variation of Fantasy Football that has become very popular is drafting a team defense. This variation uses an entire NFL team's defense as an eighth scorer. Points are awarded for every touchdown scored by interception (six points) or fumble recovery (six points), and for every safety (two points). When selecting a defense, look for opportunistic teams that score by taking advantage of their opponents' mistakes. To aid you in selecting a team defense, I'll do two things. First, I'll list last year's defensive fantasy-point totals. Then, because many fantasy leagues also award points for interceptions, fumble recoveries, and sacks. I will lay out how last year's defenses did in those respective categories. Also, to assist you a bit further, I will include each team's totals from the previous year (1999) in these particular categories. The 2000 totals appear in bold face, and the 1999 results appear beside them in parentheses. This comparison may help you determine whether certain defenses have stayed consistent from year to year.

TEAM DEFENSIVE SCORING FOR 2000

TEAM	INTS FOR TDs (1999)	INTS FOR TDs 2000	FUMBLES RETURNED FOR TDs (1999)	FUMBLES RETURNED FOR TDs 2000	SAFETIES (1999)	SAFETIES 2000	FANTASY POINTS (1999)	FANTASY POINTS 2000
1. Denver	(0)	5	(2)	2	(2)	1	(16)	44
2. Oakland	(1)	4	(1)	1	(0)	2	(12)	34
3. Seattle	(2)	3	(0)	2	(0)	1	(12)	32
4. Tampa Bay	(1)	4	(1)	1	(0)	1	(12)	32
5. New Orleans	(1)	4	(1)	1	(0)	0	(12)	30
6. Tennessee	(1)	4	(2)	1	(4)	0	(26)	30
7. San Diego	(0)	4	(2)	0	(1)	1	(14)	26
8. Chicago	(1)	4	(1)	0	(0)	0	(12)	24
9. Indianapolis	(1)	2	(2)	1	(0)	2	(18)	22
10. Buffalo	(0)	1	(1)	2	(0)	0	(6)	18
11. Detroit	(1)	2	(3)	1	(1)	0	(26)	18
12. Miami	(1)	0	(1)	2	(1)	1	(14)	14
13. Pittsburgh	(0)	0	(2)	2	(0)	1	(12)	14
14. Carolina	(0)	2	(0)	0	(0)	0	(0)	12
15. Kansas City	(5)	2	(4)	0	(0)	0	(54)	12
16. Philadelphia	(5)	2	(0)	0	(2)	0	(34)	12
17. San Francisco	(2)	2	(3)	0	(1)	0	(32)	12
18. St. Louis	(7)	0	(1)	2	(1)	0	(50)	12
19. Atlanta	(1)	1	(0)	0	(1)	1	(8)	8
20. Baltimore	(4)	1	(0)	0	(1)	1	(26)	8
21. Cincinnati	(1)	1	(0)	0	(0)	1	(6)	8
22. Green Bay	(2)	1	(1)	0	(1)	1	(20)	8
23. Arizona	(3)	0	(0)	1	(0)	0	(18)	6
24. Cleveland	(0)	1	(0)	0	(0)	0	(0)	6
25. N.Y. Jets	(3)	1	(1)	0	(1)	0	(26)	6
26. Dallas	(4)	0	(1)	0	(1)	1	(32)	2
27. Washington	(3)	0	(1)	0	(0)	1	(24)	2
28. Jacksonville	(3)	0	(1)	0	(3)	0	(30)	0
29. Minnesota	(1)	0	(0)	0	(1)	0	(8)	0
30. New England	(2)	0	(2)	0	(0)	0	(24)	0
31. N.Y. Giants	(2)	0	(1)	0	(0)	0	(18)	0

TEAM DEFENSIVE STATISTICS FOR 2000
(Interceptions)

TEAM	INTERCEPTIONS (1999)	2000	TEAM	INTERCEPTIONS (1999)	2000
1. Miami	(18)	28	16. Seattle	(30)	17
2. Denver	(15)	27	17. Tennessee	(16)	17
3. Detroit	(16)	25	18. Washington	(24)	17
4. Tampa Bay	(21)	25	19. Buffalo	(12)	16
5. Baltimore	(21)	23	20. San Diego	(15)	16
6. Green Bay	(27)	21	21. Atlanta	(12)	15
7. N.Y. Jets	(24)	21	22. Kansas City	(25)	15
8. Oakland	(20)	21	23. Indianapolis	(10)	14
9. New Orleans	(19)	20	24. San Francisco	(13)	13
10. N.Y. Giants	(17)	20	25. Jacksonville	(19)	12
11. Philadelphia	(28)	19	26. Chicago	(14)	11
12. St. Louis	(30)	19	27. Cleveland	(8)	11
13. Carolina	(15)	17	28. Arizona	(17)	10
14. Dallas	(24)	17	29. New England	(16)	10
15. Pittsburgh	(14)	17	30. Cincinnati	(12)	9
			31. Minnesota	(12)	8

TEAM DEFENSIVE STATISTICS FOR 2000
(Fumble Recoveries)

TEAM	FUMBLE RECOVERIES (1999)	2000	TEAM	RUMBLE RECOVERIES (1999)	2000
1. Baltimore	(10)	26	16. New England	(15)	13
2. Carolina	(14)	21	17. Tennessee	(26)	13
3. Jacksonville	(11)	18	18. Cincinnati	(15)	12
4. Pittsburgh	(14)	18	19. Philadelphia	(18)	12
5. Denver	(11)	17	20. Seattle	(6)	12
6. Detroit	(16)	17	21. N.Y. Giants	(7)	11
7. Tampa Bay	(10)	17	22. Arizona	(10)	10
8. Oakland	(13)	16	23. Atlanta	(6)	10
9. Washington	(14)	16	24. Minnesota	(17)	10
10. New Orleans	(15)	15	25. Chicago	(20)	9
11. Cleveland	(12)	14	26. Dallas	(9)	9
12. Kansas City	(20)	14	27. Indianapolis	(11)	8
13. N.Y. Jets	(11)	14	28. San Francisco	(7)	8
14. Buffalo	(9)	13	29. Green Bay	(14)	7
15. Miami	(10)	13	30. San Diego	(12)	6
			31. St. Louis	(5)	6

TEAM DEFENSIVE STATISTICS FOR 2000
(Sacks)

TEAM	SACKS (1999)	2000	TEAM	SACKS (1999)	2000
1. New Orleans	(45)	66	16. N.Y. Jets	(26)	40
2. Tampa Bay	(42)	55	17. Pittsburgh	(41)	39
3. Tennessee	(55)	55	18. San Diego	(41)	39
4. Kansas City	(40)	51	19. Green Bay	(29)	38
5. St. Louis	(54)	51	20. San Francisco	(32)	38
6. Philadelphia	(37)	50	21. Chicago	(36)	36
7. Miami	(39)	48	22. Baltimore	(51)	34
8. N.Y. Giants	(31)	45	23. Minnesota	(46)	33
9. Washington	(40)	45	24. Atlanta	(39)	30
10. Denver	(50)	44	25. New England	(42)	29
11. Oakland	(45)	44	26. Carolina	(36)	28
12. Cleveland	(26)	43	27. Detroit	(50)	28
13. Indianapolis	(41)	43	28. Seattle	(39)	27
14. Buffalo	(38)	42	29. Cincinnati	(35)	26
15. Jacksonville	(57)	40	30. Dallas	(36)	26
			31. Arizona	(32)	23

FANTASY FOOTBALL BASICS

Forming a League

Options to Tackle the NFL's 17-Week Season (with Bye Weeks)

League Scheduling for 4 to 16 Franchises

Playing the Game

Rule Changes or Additions for 2001

THE FUNDAMENTAL CONCEPT

- From 4 to 16 football fans get together to form a fantasy league. Each member of the group is awarded a franchise for the team he or she will put together.

- The newly founded league selects a commissioner and decides on an amount for a franchise entry fee.

- A predetermined schedule is set up or selected so the teams can meet in head-to-head competition.

- The commissioner organizes a fantasy draft where each franchise owner selects scoring players: quarterbacks, running backs, wide receivers, tight ends, and placekickers. These player selections are made from actual NFL player rosters.

- Trading and picking up players is allowed after the draft; all such transactions are subject to the trade guidelines and deadlines of the league.

- Each franchise submits its weekly starting lineup before the franchises meet in head-to-head competition.

- Following the scoring method selected by the league, the weekly results of scores and standings are determined and posted or mailed out to each franchise by the commissioner.

- The season culminates with playoffs and a Fantasy Bowl, using a predetermined playoff structure as a guideline.

I
FORMING A FANTASY LEAGUE

1. NUMBER OF FRANCHISES:
   Any number of franchises from 4 to 16 can be used in forming a fantasy league. Staying with an even number of franchises, however, makes scheduling for your league easier.

2. ENTRY FEES:
   Another item to consider when forming your league is whether to have an entry fee. It is totally up to the league franchises whether to set up some kind of wager system. There are many leagues that do have some sort of payoff system for the season's winners; there also are many leagues, especially those involving young members, that play the game just for fun.

II
THE LEAGUE COMMISSIONER

1. RESPONSIBILITIES:
   A. Coordinating draft day
   B. Keeping league standings and statistics
   C. Logging trade transactions
   D. Logging weekly team lineups
   E. Serving as league treasurer

2. TERM OF OFFICE:
   The length of time served by the commissioner should be determined by a vote of all the franchise owners, with the majority ruling. NOTE: In many leagues the commissioner serves until he or she no longer wants the job.

3. FEES:
   As an added incentive for taking and keeping the job, the commissioner is usually paid a fee by the league. NOTE: One good form of compensation for a commissioner's services is for that person to be exempt from paying the initial franchise fees.

4. OPTIONS:
   If the opportunity presents itself, the ideal situation would be to have someone who is not a franchise owner serve as your commissioner. Finding someone to agree to this won't be easy, but it would prevent many hassles.

III
LEAGUE SCHEDULING

1. NUMBER OF TEAMS IN YOUR LEAGUE:

   Obviously, your league scheduling will depend upon the number of franchises (teams) you wish to have in your league. There are a few things to consider in selecting the number of teams you will allow in your league. The first thing is how much time your commissioner wishes to spend on league involvement. Don't overload that person so badly that he or she personally won't enjoy the game. I have 16 teams in the league for which I serve as commissioner, and I often wish I could cut back to 12 or even 10. In the leagues I'm familiar with, the most common number of teams is either 8 or 10.

   Another consideration is the availability of quarterbacks. Each team usually drafts two NFL starting quarterbacks, one as the starter and the other as a reserve in case of injury. There are only 31 NFL teams, so if you have more than 15 Fantasy Football league franchises, some of your franchises may be without an NFL starting quarterback as a reserve.

   Finally, I would like to emphasize that it would be much better to go with an even number of teams. This provides far easier scheduling and no byes. Most Fantasy Football players are too addicted to the game to survive a bye.

2. SCHEDULING FOR LEAGUES OF VARIOUS SIZES:

   Your first consideration in devising a schedule is that there are 16 games in the regular NFL season. If you decide to have playoffs in your league, you will have to shorten your regular season to, let's say, 12 or 14 games and then use the remaining weeks for your playoffs. You will be drafting players from all 31 NFL teams. Once the 16-game NFL regular season is complete, only members of the NFL playoff teams will continue playing. This means that if you want all the players from your NFL teams to participate in your playoffs, these playoffs must take place before the end of the 16-game NFL regular season. Again, your playoffs will occur sometime during the last four weeks, depending on how many of your teams are involved in them.

   In the event you decide not to have playoffs and a yearly Fantasy Bowl, you can just play the full 16-game schedule and declare that the winner is the Fantasy Franchise with the best record.

   Another major consideration is the NFL schedule, which is played over 17 weeks. See the next section for options on tackling the NFL's 17-week season with bye weeks.

   The following pages demonstrate various scheduling options for leagues with various numbers of teams, along with options for the 17-week NFL season with bye weeks.

TACKLING THE NEW NFL SCHEDULE

(WHICH HAS AT LEAST ONE TEAM OFF EVERY WEEK, ALL SEASON LONG)
IT MAY AFFECT YOUR FANTASY DRAFT STRATEGY AS WELL

Going into the 2001 season, the NFL and fantasy football fans again face a weekly schedule for 31 NFL teams. The odd number of teams obviously means at least one team is off each and every week.

Many smaller fantasy leagues already require their fantasy franchise owners to draft so that if an NFL player's team is off on a given week, he or she can just choose another player from their roster to play for that week. Larger leagues, like the 16-team league I play in, use the Player Carryover Rule. Because there are really not enough players for each of our franchises to have backups at each position, we use the following.

OPTION 1
(For Larger Fantasy Leagues)

If a player and his NFL team are going to be off on week 3, you may still choose to use him on week 3 by carrying over his week 2 performance to use on both week 2 and week 3. (For a more detailed explanation, see League Scheduling, Options to Tackle the NFL's 17-week season.)

In 2000, however, scheduling or submitting lineups for your fantasy league may continue to be difficult. Because there are 31 teams, there obviously is a team off every week and this would then include the season opener on week 1 and week 17, the last week of the year. This presents problems. The Cincinnati Bengals are off week 1. What do you do if you have a Bengal player and you want to start him week 1? Our suggestion is to go ahead and start him on your fantasy team for week 1. However, that means that your game wouldn't end until week 2 when he plays his first game. This is sort of the carryover rule in reverse. Rather than taking a player's results for two weeks—the current week and the following carryover week when he's off—this particular instance would take a player's results from week 2 and use them for week 1. This will only involve players from Arizona in 2001 because they are the only team that is off week 1.

Week 1 would be the only week where this happens. In the following weeks the regular carryover rules would apply. So, if you have a player off on week 2, you would have to choose whether to start him on week 1.

There will be one more instance when this will be a problem and that is if you use the NFL regular season for your playoffs. Again, one team is off every week. That means if you have a player from the (watch to see 2001 schedule) and they are off week 16, you have no way to play him. And if you have a player from New England and they are off on week 17 you won't be able to play him.

If your playoffs start, as ours do, on week 13, realize that the New York Giants are off that week. So anybody who is playoff-bound or has the potential to make the playoffs must decide on week 12 whether to carryover that player's performance to the first playoff game on week 13.

On week 13, those teams continuing their playoff quest or that have the potential to go on in the playoffs, must submit to the commissioner any player from the New York Giants if they choose to carryover his performance to week 14 when the Baltimore Ravens are off.

On week 14, fantasy teams must submit carryover options for any player on the Baltimore Ravens for week 15 when the Carolina Panthers are off.

On week 15, fantasy teams must submit carryover options for any player on the Carolina Panthers for week 16 when the Denver Broncos are off.

On week 16, fantasy teams must submit carryover options for any player on the Denver Broncos for week 17 when the New England Patriots are off.

This means all fantasy teams that are playoff bound or possibly playoff bound, must submit what they want to do with their following week (bye-week players) on the week before the playoffs begin. This is certainly a headache for the commissioner but it's still very manageable. Again, just make sure all playoff-bound teams submit where they want the players who are off the following week in their following week's lineup, as starters or reserves. If a player is not started, he is a reserve.

This is obviously a pain for commissioners and fantasy owners, but until the NFL adds the next expansion team to even up the number of teams, we have to contend with this.

OPTION 2

The other solution is to just pick from your remaining players, of the players not participating in the bye week. This is great for smaller leagues but tough for larger leagues already using the "Carryover Rules." You could enforce this rule in the larger leagues and everybody would just have to deal with having various players off or not eligible to play on weeks their NFL teams are off. I wouldn't recommend this for the playoffs, however, because I'm certain every fantasy team would want to have all its players and its options for all of the playoffs weeks.

OPTION 3

This suggestion, too, is likely to work better for smaller leagues (12 teams or less) because of a lack of players. Following the fantasy league transactions for the week, any fantasy team not able to field a position because of bye weeks, could pick up a player from the unclaimed player pool for just that week. Example: if two of your three wide receivers are both facing a bye week and you must field a second one, you could do a temporary pickup for just that week to fill out your starting lineup. When the game for that week was over, the temporary pickup goes back into the unclaimed player pool.

DRAFTING STRATEGY

How your fantasy league elects to handle this new bye week problem may affect your fantasy draft strategy. If your league elects to go with the option of covering for a bye-week player by picking up another player, you may want to know who is off which weeks, especially during the playoff weeks, late in the year. To assist you with this, we are going to do two things. First, right here we are going to list the 17 weeks of the upcoming NFL season and who is off (which NFL teams have byes) each week. Then, to make it very easy to determine when a player's bye week is, we will show it right with his rating on our Quick Pick - Cheetsheat: EXAMPLE:

RUNNING BACKS

BYE WEEK				
12	1.	James	IND	Likely to score one or two TD's weekly.
10	2.	Faulk	STL	Can score often, both on the ground and through the air.
7	3.	Taylor	JAC	Exploded for 17 TD's as rookie in '98.

This should help you if you need to determine what players you will have at any particular time of the season, especially late in the year during fantasy playoffs.

Here is the list of NFL weeks and the "Bye" teams.

Week

1. Arizona
2. San Diego
3. New Orleans, Pittsburgh, Tampa Bay
4. Chicago, Detroit, Tennessee
5. Dallas, Indianapolis, Oakland
6. Buffalo, Jacksonville, Philadelphia
7. Miami, San Francisco, Seattle
8. Atlanta, Cleveland, Green Bay
9. Cincinatti, Minnesota, St. Louis
10. Washington
11. Kansas City
12. New York Jets
13. New York Giants
14. Baltimore
15. Carolina
16. Denver
17. New England

Regardless of which option you and your fantasy league chooses to use, be sure to decide upfront so that everyone is fully in tune as to how this bye-week fiasco is being handled. Make sure your league rules and the consequences for not abiding by or knowing the proper rule are spelled out well enough for everyone to understand.

OPTIONS TO TACKLE THE NFL'S 17-WEEK SEASON WITH BYE WEEKS

The NFL continues to play its 16-game season over 17 weeks. This gives each NFL team one bye week during the season and will again result in some confusion for Fantasy Football leagues. In several sections of this chapter, I provide suggestions for overcoming problems caused by this schedule. As always, I welcome your ideas and suggestions for dealing with the new NFL schedule.

PLAYING OPTION #1 (for leagues of 10 or fewer teams)

With smaller leagues, you have more options because you have more NFL players to choose from.

1. ROSTER
Expand your original roster from 15 to 20 players.

2. WEEKLY LINEUP SIZE
Maintain the seven-player starting lineup.

3. WEEKLY GAMES
Fantasy teams are allowed to field NFL players only from teams that are playing that week (which is why I don't like this method). For instance, in week #4 you would field from your 15-member fantasy roster a 7-member team of players who are playing that week. If you have Terrell Owens, and the San Francisco 49ers are not playing that week, Owens can't be used. You have to choose from your roster another wide receiver who does play that week.

Leagues using this method should be limited to 10 or fewer teams, because each team has to have at least two starting quarterbacks and two placekickers. Each franchise should be sure not to draft both of its quarterbacks or both of its kickers from the same division. Because the NFL has scheduled its byes somewhat divisionally, a fantasy team that concentrates its players in a single division might not be able to field a certain position if both of its players are off at the same time.

Option #1's Good Points:
This option maintains the immediacy that we fantasy participants have become accustomed to.

Option #1's Drawbacks:
The prime reason I don't care for this option is that there will be one or two weeks when you won't be able to field your top player(s). Worse yet, depending on the NFL schedule, you may be without a quarterback or another player because it just happens that none of your players from that position play that week. *Tackling the 17-Week NFL Schedule*

PLAYING OPTION #2 (for leagues of any size)

This option provides both immediate results and much of the playing tradition that our fantasy leagues are used to. It is the option my league will use because it's the least confusing and easiest to use. After using this method for five entire seasons, I am pleased with its results and recommend it for larger leagues.

1. ROSTER
No changes are necessary.

2. WEEKLY LINEUP SIZE
Maintain the seven-player weekly lineup.

3. WEEKLY GAMES
For your fantasy games, weekly scores are tabulated as usual, but if a fan-

tasy player doesn't play on a given week he can be put in the lineup before the previous week's game — with that previous week's performance counting for both weeks. For instance, after all 31 NFL teams have played a couple of weeks into a season, teams begin to get byes. If one of your prime players is scheduled for a bye on week #5 because his team is off that week, you can insert him for week #5 before the start of that player's game in the previous week (which is week #4). His week #4 performance is used for both week #4 and week #5. For this player, week #5 becomes a carryover week — a week in which he does not play but rather carries his performance stats over from the previous week. How many fantasy points does this player score for you during the carryover week? Exactly as many as he scored for you during the previous week. Please note that commissioners should be prepared in week #4 to begin taking lineups for both week #4 and week #5.

This requires you to think ahead and adjust your roster for byes. Any fantasy team not calling in a lineup on a given week is forced to carry the same positions for its players in the lineup as used the previous week. This means it has forfeited its opportunity to make adjustments for the bye week. If a player is injured and a team forgot to call in and replace him in the lineup, his performance — or non-performance — would be locked in for two weeks if that player was involved in a bye week. The benefit for fantasy leagues is immediate weekly results. All fantasy games end on the same weekend. (For further clarification, please see Section VII, point 4b of this chapter, titled "Riding the Same Lineup During Carryover Weeks.")

4. SUDDEN-DEATH TIEBREAKERS
Commissioners, please note: For players not playing in a given week, the previous week's performances are used when you must dip into the list of reserve players to break a tie. (For the basics of tiebreakers, see Section IX.) This means that all players on NFL teams that bye in a given week **MUST** be inserted the previous week. This ensures that all players are given a spot on the following week's lineup card. Commissioners should insist on getting a positive comment from every Fantasy Franchise as to where in the following week's lineup — on the active list, in the reserves, on the bench — it wants to put players who have byes the following week. **Any team not heard from will have its bye-week players listed exactly as they were listed in the previous week.**

5. LINEUP CHANGES
Lineup changes in this option are twofold. First, concerning the week at hand, only one lineup change is allowed after the weekly lineup is submitted. Second, regarding carryover players — who are submitted one week early to account for a bye the next week — one further lineup change is also allowed. This means that two lineup changes can be allowed per week, but only one change may be used for the current week's lineup. The other may be used only to move players for a forthcoming carryover week. Remember, this change must be made before the carryover player's previous-week game has started.

EXAMPLE: A player is submitted to a starting fantasy lineup for both the current week (week #4) and the following week (week #5) because of an upcoming bye. If he is removed from the starting lineup for the current week (week #4), this is considered the team's lineup change. If you decide to gamble by using his current week's (week #4's) results for only the current fantasy week (week #4) and to remove him from the following week's (week #5) starting lineup, this does not count as week #5's lineup change. If you remove this player from both the current (week #4) and the bye (week #5) starting lineups, it is considered the team's lineup change for the current week but not for the bye week. NOTE: Any player removed from a bye week's starting lineup is automatically placed at the bottom of the bye week's reserve list.

To further clarify:
If a fantasy team elects to change a bye player for the carryover week and does so prior to game time of the current week, this **DOES NOT** count as the current week's lineup change.

6. TRADE NIGHT (Watch Out for Carryover-Player Confusion)
A weekly trade night is allowed, but with one extra guideline for dealing with carryover players. (A carryover player, again, is one whom you keep active, even though his NFL team has a bye, by carrying over his performance from the previous week.)

Your fantasy team can trade or release a carryover player, but the trade or release does not take effect until all of the players involved in this transaction have shed their carryover status. Because a carryover player has already been submitted for your fantasy team's lineup, he will remain officially part of your fantasy team until the carryover week's game—with him in your lineup—has ended. The player you picked up for him may not be used until both the player you traded away and the player you picked up are clear of carryover status.

7. SCHEDULING
See the appropriate scheduling formats in Section III of this chapter.

8. PLAYOFFS
See the appropriate playoff formats in Section III of this chapter.

Option #2's Good Points:
This procedure provides both immediate weekly results and much of the playing tradition that our fantasy leagues are used to.

Option #2's Drawbacks:
This option's only drawback is that a player's performance may count for two games, even if he plays poorly.

NOTE

I highly recommend that commissioners review the consequences of the bye week scheduling format. Address all of your rules issues, including lineups, lineup changes, weekly games, roster transactions, scheduling, and playoff format. And again, please feel free to send me your suggestions. I will certainly look them over for ideas to share with other Fantasy Football participants.

FOUR-TEAM LEAGUE

REGULAR SEASON:
Play a 15-game regular season. Teams play each other five times. (Two teams have seven home games, and the other two have eight.)

PLAYOFFS:
The top two teams after 15 games advance to the Fantasy Bowl. This may be played on either week #16 or week #17. If you're undecided about whether to play your Fantasy Bowl on week #16 or #17, you might want to consider this: Many NFL teams, if they have already secured a playoff spot, may elect to sit their star players on week #17 in order to keep those players healthy for the postseason. Because of this, your league might want to hold its Fantasy Bowl on week #16, so that no star players are eliminated from helping their fantasy teams in the big game.

Key: 1. Read down for week #.
2. Read across top for team # and then down for opponents.
3. The asterisk (*) indicates a home game for the team heading the column.

FOUR-TEAM LEAGUE

Team #	1	2	3	4
Week #				
1	2	1*	4*	3
2	3*	4	1	2*
3	4*	3	2*	1
4	2	1*	4	3*
5	3	4*	1*	2
6	4	3*	2	1*
7	2*	1	4	3*
8	3*	4*	1	2
9	4*	3	2*	1
10	2	1*	4*	3
11	3	4	1*	2*
12	4	3*	2	1*
13	2*	1	4	3*
14	3*	4*	1	2
15	4	3	2*	1*
16	Bye or Fantasy Bowl			
17	Fantasy Bowl			

SIX-TEAM LEAGUE

REGULAR SEASON:

Play a 15-game regular season. Teams play each other three times each. (Three teams have seven home games, and the other three have eight.)

PLAYOFFS: OPTION #1

The top two teams after 15 games advance to the Fantasy Bowl. This may be played on either week #16 or week #17. If you're undecided about whether to play your Fantasy Bowl on week #16 or #17, you might want to consider this: Many NFL teams, if they have already secured a playoff spot, may elect to sit their star players on week #17 in order to keep those players healthy for the postseason. Because of this, your league might want to hold its Fantasy Bowl on week #16, so that no star players are eliminated from helping their fantasy teams in the big game. (For determining who should advance based on record, see Section IV, Playoffs.)

PLAYOFFS: OPTION #2

The top four teams after 15 games advance to the playoffs. On week #16, the four playoff teams are seeded 1 through 4 based on record, with seed #1 playing seed #4 and seed #2 playing seed #3. The winners then advance to the Fantasy Bowl on week #17.

Key: 1. Read down for week #.
2. Read across top for team # and then down for opponents.
3. The asterisk (*) indicates a home game for the team heading the column.

SIX-TEAM LEAGUE

Team #	1	2	3	4	5	6
Week #						
1	2*	1	4*	3	6*	5
2	3*	6*	1	5*	4	2
3	4	5	6	1*	2*	3*
4	5	3*	2	6	1*	4*
5	6*	4	5*	2*	3	1
6	2	1*	4	3*	6	5*
7	3	6	1*	5	4*	2*
8	4*	5*	6*	1	2	3
9	5*	3	2*	6*	1	4
10	6	4*	5	2	3*	1*
11	2*	1	4*	3	6*	5
12	3*	6*	1	5*	4	2
13	4	5	6	1*	2*	3*
14	5	3*	2	6	1*	4*
15	6*	4	5*	2*	3	1
	(Playoffs: Option #1)			(Playoffs: Option #2)		
16	Bye or Fantasy Bowl			Playoffs		
17	Fantasy Bowl			Fantasy Bowl		

EIGHT-TEAM LEAGUE
(OPTION #1)

REGULAR SEASON:
Play a 14-game regular season. Teams play each other twice. (Each team has seven home games.)

PLAYOFFS:
At the end of the 14-game regular season, the top four teams are seeded 1 through 4, as determined by their records. The first round of the playoffs begins on week #15. In the first round, seed #1 plays seed #4 and seed #2 plays seed #3. The winners of round one advance to the Fantasy Bowl during week #16 or week #17. If you're undecided about whether to play your Fantasy Bowl on week #16 or #17, you might want to consider this: Many NFL teams, if they have already secured a playoff spot, may elect to sit their star players on week #17 in order to keep those players healthy for the postseason. Because of this, your league might want to hold its Fantasy Bowl on week #16, so that no star players are eliminated from helping their fantasy teams in the big game. (For determining who should advance based on record, see Section IV, Playoffs.)

Key: 1. Read down for week #.
2. Read across top for team # and then down for opponents.
3. The asterisk (*) indicates a home game for the team heading the column.

EIGHT-TEAM LEAGUE
(OPTION #1)

Team #	1	2	3	4	5	6	7	8
Week #								
1	2*	1	4*	3	6*	5	8*	7
2	3*	4*	1	2	8	7*	6	5*
3	4	8*	6*	1*	7	3	5*	2
4	5	6	8	7*	1*	2*	4	3*
5	6*	5*	7*	8	2	1	3	4*
6	7	3	2*	5	4*	8*	1*	6
7	8*	7	5	6*	3*	4	2*	1
8	2	1*	4	3*	6	5*	8	7*
9	3	4	1*	2*	8*	7	6*	5
10	4*	8	6	1	7*	3*	5	2*
11	5*	6*	8*	7	1	2	4*	3
12	6	5	7	8*	2*	1*	3*	4
13	7*	3*	2	5*	4	8	1	6*
14	8	7*	5*	6	3	4*	2	1*
15				Playoffs				
16			Bye or Fantasy Bowl					
17				Fantasy Bowl				

EIGHT-TEAM LEAGUE
(OPTION #2)

DIVISIONS:
Split league into two divisions of four teams each.

REGULAR SEASON:
Play a 17-game regular season. Each team plays each of the other three teams within its division three times, for nine games. Then each team plays each of the teams in the other division twice, for eight more games. This adds up to a total of 17 regular-season games. (Four teams will have nine home games and four teams will have eight.)

PLAYOFFS:
There aren't any! The team with the best regular-season record becomes the league champion.

Key: 1. Read down for week #.
2. Read across top for team # and then down for opponents.
3. The asterisk (*) indicates a home game for the team heading the column.

EIGHT-TEAM LEAGUE
(OPTION #2)

Team#	SPADE DIVISION				CLUB DIVISION			
	1	2	3	4	5	6	7	8
Week #								
1	2*	1	4*	3	6*	5	8*	7
2	3	4*	1*	2	7	8*	5*	6
3	4	3*	2	1*	8	7*	6	5*
4	5*	6	7*	8	1*	2	3*	4
5	6*	7	8	5*	4	1	2*	3*
6	7*	8*	5	6	3*	4*	1	2
7	8	5*	6*	7*	2	3	4	1*
8	2	1*	4	3*	6	5*	8	7*
9	3*	4	1	2*	7*	8	5	6*
10	4*	3	2*	1	8*	7	6*	5
11	5	6*	7	8*	1	2*	3	4*
12	6	7*	8*	5	4*	1*	2	3
13	7	8	5*	6*	3	4	1*	2*
14	8*	5	6	7	2*	3*	4*	1
15	2*	1	4*	3	6*	5	8*	7
16	3	4*	1*	2	7	8*	5*	6
17	4	3*	2	1*	8	7*	6	5*

TEN-TEAM LEAGUE
(Can be used with either Playing Option #1 or #2)

DIVISIONS:
Split league into two divisions of five teams each.

REGULAR SEASON:
Play a 13-game regular season. Each team plays each of the four other teams within the division twice, for eight games. (During the two meetings of any two teams, each should be the home team once.) Then each team plays each of the teams in the other division once, for five more games. (Five teams will have six home games, and the other five will have seven.)

PLAYOFFS:
The top three of the five teams in each division advance to the playoffs. In the first round, the first-place team in each division is awarded a bye. The second- and third-place teams play each other. This takes place on week #14. Winners from week #14 then advance to play the first-place team in their division on week #15. Winners advance to the Fantasy Bowl, to be held either on week #16 or #17. If you're undecided about whether to play your Fantasy Bowl on week #16 or #17, you might want to consider this: Many NFL teams, if they have already secured a playoff spot, may elect to sit their star players on week #17 in order to keep those players healthy for the post-season. Because of this, your league might want to hold its Fantasy Bowl on week #16, so that no star players are eliminated from helping their fantasy teams in the big game. (For determining who should advance based on record, see Section IV, Playoffs.)

Key: 1. Read down for week #.
2. Read across top for team # and then down for opponents.
3. The asterisk (*) indicates a home game for the team heading the column.

TEN-TEAM LEAGUE

Team #	SPADE DIVISION					CLUB DIVISION				
	1	2	3	4	5	6	7	8	9	10
Week #										
1	2*	1	4*	3	6*	5	8*	7	10*	9
2	3*	5*	1	7*	2	10*	4	9*	8	6
3	4	8*	5*	1*	3	9	10	2	6*	7*
4	5	4	9	2*	1*	7	6*	10*	3*	8
5	10	3	2*	5	4*	8*	9*	6	7	1*
6	2	1*	5	6*	3*	4	10*	9	8*	7
7	3	5	1*	9	2*	7*	6	10	4*	8*
8	5*	7*	4	3*	1	8	2	6*	10	9*
9	4*	3*	2	1	10*	9*	8	7*	6	5
10	8	9	7	5*	4	10	3*	1*	2*	6*
11	6	4*	10*	2	8	1*	9	5*	7*	3
12	9*	10	6*	8*	7	3	5*	4	1	2*
13	7*	6	8	10	9	2*	1	3*	5	4*
14					Playoffs					
15					Playoffs					
16					Bye or Fantasy Bowl					
17					Fantasy Bowl					

TWELVE-TEAM LEAGUE
(OPTION #1)

DIVISIONS:
   Split league into three divisions of four teams each.

REGULAR SEASON:
   Play a 14-game regular season. Each of the four teams in a division plays the other three twice, for a total of six games. Each team also plays all the other eight teams once, for a total of eight games. This makes up the 14-game, regular-season schedule.

PLAYOFFS: OPTION #1 (Four-Team Playoff)
   The top team in each division advances to the playoffs, along with one wild-card team (whichever second-place team has the best record). The four teams are seeded 1 through 4. Seed #1 plays seed #4 and seed #2 plays seed #3. The first-round game is played on week #15 with the winners advancing to the Fantasy Bowl on week #16 or #17. If you're undecided about whether to play your Fantasy Bowl on week #16 or #17, you might want to consider this: Many NFL teams, if they have already secured a playoff spot, may elect to sit their star players on week #17 in order to keep those players healthy for the postseason. Because of this, your league might want to hold its Fantasy Bowl on week #16, so that no star players are eliminated from helping their fantasy teams in the big game. (For determining who should advance based on record, see Section IV, Playoffs.)

PLAYOFFS: OPTION #2 (Eight-Team Playoff)
   (The benefit of this option is that it keeps more teams in the playoff hunt longer.) The top team in each division advances to the playoffs, along with five wild-card teams. The wild-card teams are the five best teams based on record, not including divisional champions. The eight teams are seeded 1 through 8 based on record. In the first round, seed #1 plays seed #8, seed #2 plays seed #7, seed #3 plays seed #6, and seed #4 plays seed #5. These first-round games take place on week #15. The winners of the first round are then reseeded for the semifinal round played on week #16. Of the remaining four teams seed #1 (based on record) plays seed #4 and seed #2 plays seed #3. The winners then advance to play in the Fantasy Bowl on week #17.

Key: 1. Read down for week #.
   2. Read across top for team # and then down for opponents.
   3. The asterisk (*) indicates a home game for the team heading the column.

TWELVE-TEAM LEAGUE
(OPTION #1)

Team #	Spade Division				Club Division				Heart Division			
	1	2	3	4	5	6	7	8	9	10	11	12
Week #												
1	2*	1	4*	3	6	5*	8	7*	10	9*	12	11*
2	3*	4*	1	2	7*	8*	5	6	11*	12*	9	10
3	4	3	2*	1*	8	7	6*	5*	12	11	10*	9*
4	5	6*	11	12*	1*	2	9*	10	7	8*	3*	4
5	6	7*	9	10*	11*	1*	2	12*	3*	4	5	8
6	12*	11	8*	6	9	4*	10*	3	5*	7	2*	1
7	11*	10	6*	5	4*	3	12	9*	8	2*	1	7*
8	7	8*	12	9*	10	11	1*	2	4	5*	6*	3*
9	8*	9	7*	11*	12*	10*	3	1	2*	6	4	5
10	10*	12	5*	7	3	9*	4*	11*	6	1	8	2*
11	9	5*	10	8	2	12	11	4*	1*	3*	7*	6*
12	2	1*	4	3*	6*	5	8*	7	10*	9	12*	11
13	3	4	1*	2*	7	8	5*	6*	11	12	9*	10*
14	4*	3*	2	1	8*	7*	6	5	12*	11*	10	9
	(Playoffs: Option #1)								(Playoffs: Option #2)			
15	Playoffs								Playoffs			
16	Bye or Fantasy Bowl								Playoffs			
17	Fantasy Bowl								Fantasy Bowl			

TWELVE-TEAM LEAGUE
(OPTION #2)

DIVISIONS:
Split league into two divisions of six teams each.

REGULAR SEASON:
Play a 16-game regular season. Each of the six teams in a division plays each of the other five teams twice, for a total of 10 games. Each team also plays all the teams from the other division once each, for another six games. This makes a total of 16 games. (Each team has eight home games and eight away games.)

PLAYOFFS:
The top team from each division advances to the Fantasy Bowl on week #17.

Key: 1. Read down for week #.
2. Read across top for team # and then down for opponents.
3. The asterisk (*) indicates a home game for the team heading the column.

TWELVE-TEAM LEAGUE
(OPTION #2)

	SPADE DIVISION						CLUB DIVISION					
Team #	1	2	3	4	5	6	7	8	9	10	11	12
Week#												
1	2*	1	4*	3	6*	5	8*	7	10*	9	12*	11
2	3*	6*	1	5*	4	2	9	12*	7*	11*	10	8
3	4	5*	6	1*	2	3*	10*	11	12	7	8*	9*
4	5	3	2*	6	1*	4*	11	9*	8	12*	7*	10
5	6*	4*	5	2	3*	1	12	10*	11*	8	9	7*
6	7	8*	9*	10*	11	12*	1*	2	3	4	5*	6
7	8*	9	10	11	12*	7	6*	1	2*	3*	4*	5
8	9*	10*	11*	12	7*	8	5	6*	1	2	3	4*
9	10	11	12	7*	8	9*	4	5*	6	1*	2*	3*
10	11*	12*	7*	8*	9	10	3	4	5*	6*	1	2
11	12	7	8	9	10*	11*	2*	3*	4*	5	6	1*
12	2	1*	4	3*	6	5*	8	7*	10	9*	12	11*
13	3	6	1*	5	4*	2*	9*	12	7	11	10*	8*
14	4*	5	6*	1	2*	3	10	11*	12*	7*	8	9
15	5*	3*	2	6*	1	4	11*	9	8*	12	7	10*
16	6	4	5*	2*	3	1*	12*	10	11	8*	9*	7
17						Fantasy Bowl						

FOURTEEN-TEAM LEAGUE

DIVISIONS:
Split league into two divisions of seven teams each.

REGULAR SEASON:
Play a 14-game regular season. Each of the seven teams within a division plays every other team twice, for a total of 12 games. Each team also plays two teams at random from the other division, thus making up the 14-game schedule.

PLAYOFFS: OPTION #1 (Four-Team Playoff)
At the end of the regular season, the top two teams in each division are awarded playoff spots. The four playoff teams are then seeded 1 through 4, as determined by record. Seed #1 plays seed #4 and seed #2 plays seed #3. The first-round game is played on week #15 with the winners advancing to the Fantasy Bowl on week #16 or #17. If you're undecided about whether to play your Fantasy Bowl on week #16 or #17, you might want to consider this: Many NFL teams, if they have already secured a playoff spot, may elect to sit their star players on week #17 in order to keep those players healthy for the postseason. Because of this, your league might want to hold its Fantasy Bowl on week #16, so that no star players are eliminated from helping their fantasy teams in the big game. (For determining who should advance based on record, see Section IV, Playoffs.)

PLAYOFFS: OPTION #2 (Six-Team Playoff)
The top team in each division automatically advances to the playoffs. The second- and third-place teams in each division are also awarded playoff spots as wild-card teams. (Another choice within this option would be to take, as wild-card teams, the next four teams in the standings based on record, regardless of division. Either way, you have four wild-card teams.)

In the first round of the playoffs, the divisional winners are awarded byes. The four wild-card teams meet to see who will advance to play the divisional winners. These first-round games will take place on week #15. If you use the second- and third-place teams in each division as wild cards, the winner advances to meet its divisional champ on week #16. On the other hand, if you use the four next-best teams, regardless of division, as your wild-card teams, the winners advance to meet the divisional champs using the following matchups: The divisional champ with the better regular-season record plays the wild-card survivor with the inferior record; and the divisional champ with the inferior record plays the wild-card survivor with the better record.

The winners of these games then meet in the Fantasy Bowl on week #17.

Key: 1. Read down for week #.
2. Read across top for team # and then down for opponents.
3. The asterisk (*) indicates a home game for the team heading the column.

FOURTEEN-TEAM LEAGUE

Team #	SPADE DIVISION							CLUB DIVISION						
	1	**2**	**3**	**4**	**5**	**6**	**7**	**8**	**9**	**10**	**11**	**12**	**13**	**14**
Week #														
1	2*	1	4*	3	6*	5	14	9	8*	11	10*	13	12*	7*
2	3	7*	1*	5*	4	13	2	10*	14	8	12	11*	6*	9*
3	4*	6	7	1	12	2*	3*	11	13*	14*	8*	5*	9	10
4	5	3*	2*	11	1*	7*	6	12*	10	9*	4*	8	14	13*
5	6*	4	10	2*	7	1	5*	13	11*	3*	9	14*	8*	12
6	7	9	5*	6*	3	4	1*	14*	2*	12	13*	10*	11	8
7	8	5*	6	7	2	3*	4*	1*	12	13*	14	9*	10	11*
8	5*	4*	11*	2	1	7	6*	14	13	12*	3	10	9*	8*
9	2	1*	7*	6	8*	4*	3	5	14*	13	12*	11	10*	9
10	3*	12*	1	7*	6	5*	4	9*	8	14	13	2	11*	10*
11	4	3	2*	1*	7*	9*	5	10	6	8*	14*	13*	12	11
12	13*	7	6*	5	4*	3	2*	11*	10*	9	8	14	1	12*
13	6	5	4	3*	2*	1*	10*	12	11	7	9*	8*	14*	13
14	7*	6*	5	14*	3*	2	1	13*	12*	11*	10	9	8	4
	(Playoffs: Option #1)							(Playoffs: Option #2)						
15	Playoffs							Playoffs						
16	Bye or Fantasy Bowl							Playoffs						
17	Fantasy Bowl							Fantasy Bowl						

SIXTEEN-TEAM LEAGUE
(OPTION #1: 12-game regular season,
with 12 teams in playoffs)

DIVISIONS:

Split league into four divisions of four teams each.

REGULAR SEASON:

Play a 12-game regular season. Each of the four teams within a division plays the other three twice, for a total of six games. Each team also plays two teams from each of the other three divisions once, for a total of 6 more games, to round out the 12-game schedule.

12-TEAM PLAYOFFS: OPTION #1

The top team in each division automatically advances to the playoffs. The second- and third-place teams in each division are also awarded playoff spots. This excludes only the last-place team in each division, leaving 12 playoff teams and keeping a large number of teams in the race as long as possible.

In the first round of the playoffs, the first-place teams are awarded byes. The teams that finished second and third in their divisions meet in the divisional wild-card games on week #13.

The winners advance to meet the divisional champs on week #14. The divisional wild-card winners meet their respective divisional champions to determine who will represent the division in the semifinals.

Week #14's winners advance to the semifinals on week #15. The teams representing the Spade and Club divisions meet, as do the teams representing the Diamond and Heart divisions.

The winners become the Black and Red conference champions, respectively, and meet in the Fantasy Bowl on week #16. (For determining who should advance based on record, see Section IV, Playoffs.)

12-TEAM PLAYOFFS: OPTION #2

The top team in each division automatically advances to the playoffs. Then the eight best remaining teams—based on record and regardless of division—are awarded wild-card playoff spots.

In the first round of the playoffs, the four divisional winners are awarded byes. The eight wild-card teams are seeded 1 through 8, based on record. Seed #1 plays seed #8, seed #2 plays seed #7, seed #3 plays seed #6, and seed #4 plays seed #5. This takes place on week #13.

The winners advance to meet the division champs on week #14. In this round, the division champs are seeded 1 through 4 and the wild-card winners are seeded 5 through 8. Again it will be seed #1 vs. seed #8, seed #2 vs. seed #7, seed #3 vs. seed #6, and seed #4 vs. seed #5. The winners advance to the semifinals on week #15, this time seeded 1 through 4, again based on record. Seed #1 meets seed #4 and seed #2 meets seed #3, with the winners advancing to the Fantasy Bowl on week #16 or #17. If you're undecided about whether to play your Fantasy Bowl on week #16 or #17, you might want to consider this: Many NFL teams, if they have already secured a playoff spot, may elect to sit their star players on week #17 in order to keep those players healthy for the postseason. Because of this, your league might want to hold its Fantasy Bowl on week #16, so that no star players are eliminated from helping their fantasy teams in the big game. (For determining who should advance based on record, see Section IV, Playoffs.)

Key: 1. Read down for week #.
2. Read across top for team # and then down for opponents.
3. The asterisk (*) indicates a home game for the team heading the column.

SIXTEEN-TEAM LEAGUE
(OPTION #1)

| | BLACK CONFERENCE | | | | | | | RED CONFERENCE | | | | | | | |
| | SPADE | | | CLUB | | | | DIAMOND | | | | HEART | | | |
Team #	1	2	3	4	5	6	7	8	9	10	11	12	13	14	15	16
Week #																
1	2*	1	4*	3	6*	5	8*	7	10*	9	12*	11	14*	13	16*	15
2	3	4*	1*	2	7	8*	5*	6	11	12*	9*	10	15	16*	13*	14
3	4*	3*	2	1	8	7*	6	5*	12	11*	10	9*	16	15*	14	13*
4	5	6*	8	7*	1*	2	4	3*	14*	16	13	15*	11*	9	12	10*
5	9*	10	11*	12	13*	14	15*	16	1	2*	3	4*	5	6*	7	8*
6	13	16*	15	14*	9	10*	11	12*	5*	6	7*	8	1*	4	3*	2
7	8*	7	6*	5	4*	3	2*	1	16*	15	14*	13	12*	11	10*	9
8	10	9*	12	11*	16	15*	14	13*	2	1*	4	3*	8	7*	6	5*
9	16*	14	13*	15	10	9*	12*	11	6	5*	8*	7	3	2*	4*	1
10	2	1*	4	3*	6	5*	8	7*	10	9*	12	11*	14	13*	16	15*
11	3*	4	1	2*	7*	8	5	6*	11*	12	9	10*	15*	16	13	14*
12	4	3	2*	1*	8*	7	6*	5	12*	11	10*	9	16*	15	14*	13

	(12-Team Playoff)
13	Playoffs (Round 1)
14	Playoffs (Round 2)
15	Playoffs (Semifinals)
16	Bye or Fantasy Bowl
17	Fantasy Bowl

SIXTEEN-TEAM LEAGUE
(OPTION #2: 14-game regular season, 8 teams in playoffs)

DIVISIONS:
Split league into four divisions of four teams each.

REGULAR SEASON:
Play a 14-game regular season. Each of the four teams within a division plays the other three twice, for a total of six games. In addition, each team plays two teams from the other conference's two divisions once—for four more games—and also plays each of the teams from the other division of its own conference once each—for a total of four

more games. This makes a grand total of 14 regular-season games.

PLAYOFFS:

The top team in each division automatically advances to the playoffs. Of the teams that did not win their divisions, the four teams with the best records are awarded playoff spots as wild-card teams. These four teams advance, regardless of division. (Example: If the second- and third-place teams from the Spade Division both have better records than the second-place team from the Heart Division, both Spade teams advance, not the Heart team with the poorer record.)

For the first round of the playoffs, the division champs are seeded 1 through 4 and the four wild-card teams are seeded 5 through 8. Seed #1 plays seed #8, seed #2 plays seed #7, seed #3 plays seed #6, and seed #4 plays seed #5. This first round takes place during week #15. The winners then advance to the semifinals on week #16. Again the teams are seeded, this time 1 through 4, based on record. Seed #1 plays seed #4 and seed #2 plays seed #3. The winners of these semifinal games advance to the Fantasy Bowl on week #17. (For determining who should advance based on record, see Section IV, Playoffs.)

Key: 1. Read down for week #.
2. Read across top for team # and then down for opponents.
3. The asterisk (*) indicates a home game for the team heading the column.

SIXTEEN-TEAM LEAGUE
(OPTION #2)

| | BLACK CONFERENCE | | | | | | | | RED CONFERENCE | | | | | | | |
| | SPADE | | | | CLUB | | | | DIAMOND | | | | HEART | | | |
Team #	1	2	3	4	5	6	7	8	9	10	11	12	13	14	15	16
Week #																
1	2*	1	4*	3	6*	5	8*	7	10*	9	12*	11	14*	13	16*	15
2	3	4*	1*	2	7	8*	5*	6	11	12*	9*	10	15	16*	13*	14
3	4*	3*	2	1	8	7*	6	5*	12	11*	10	9*	16	15*	14	13*
4	5	6*	8	7*	1*	2	4	3*	14*	16	13	15*	11*	9	12	10*
5	9*	10	11*	12	13*	14	15*	16	1	2*	3	4*	5	6*	7	8*
6	13	16*	15	14*	9	10*	11	12*	5*	6	7*	8	1*	4	3*	2
7	8*	7	6*	5	4*	3	2*	1	16*	15	14*	13	12*	11	10*	9
8	10	9*	12	11*	16	15*	14	13*	2	1*	4	3*	8	7*	6	5*
9	16*	14	13*	15	10	9*	12*	11	6	5*	8*	7	3	2*	4*	1
10	7*	8*	5*	6*	3	4	1	2	15*	13*	16*	14*	10	12	9	11
11	6	5	7	8	2*	1*	3*	4*	13	14	15	16	9*	10*	11*	12*
12	2	1*	4	3*	6	5*	8	7*	10	9*	12	11*	14	13*	16	15*
13	3*	4	1	2*	7*	8	5	6*	11*	12	9	10*	15*	16	13	14*
14	4	3	2*	1*	8*	7	6*	5	12*	11	10*	9	16*	15	14*	13
15	Playoffs (Round 1)															
16	Playoffs (Semifinals)															
17	Fantasy Bowl															

IV
PLAYOFFS & PAYOFFS

Many fantasy leagues will choose the before mentioned playoff structures or may choose to play out the entire regular season and have their Fantasy playoff teams redraft going into the actual NFL playoffs. For a further explanation of this option—see Chapter IX—option 3 in this guide.

Now for further playoff recommendations, see the following.

1. PLAYOFFS: WHO SHOULD ADVANCE
   For each of the various preceding schedules, I included a suggested playoff structure. You may choose to follow these regular-season schedules and playoff structures, or you may decide to set up your own. Whether you use the structure I suggest or one you have devised yourself, you are also going to need a tiebreaker system in case some teams have identical win-loss records. Here is the tiebreaker system that I like:

   1. Best win-loss record
   2. Most points scored during the regular season
      (There is a reason for putting most points scored as a tiebreaker before head-to-head competition. I feel any fantasy team could get lucky during the season and have a good game against a good team. The true test of a good fantasy team is how it fares throughout the entire season. This is better reflected by a comparison of the point totals scored during the entire season.)
   3. Head-to-head competition (most points vs. team tied with)
   4. Best conference record
   5. Most points allowed
      (The team that allowed more points wins the tiebreaker. This is an indication of which team played a tougher schedule.)
   6. Coin flip

2. PLAYOFFS: DETERMINING THE HOME TEAM
   In the event your league uses a sudden-death tiebreaker, you will need a system to determine which will be the home team. Since the team with the better record should always be the home team, the same system used for determining who should advance to the playoffs would also apply nicely here. Remember the importance of the home team when using the sudden-death tiebreaker. The team that is determined to be the home team will have the first shot at breaking the tie. Again, the system used to determine the home team in the playoffs is the same one used for determining who should advance as listed above.

3. LEAGUE PAYOFFS:
   Our league has a small entry fee that is paid at the beginning of the year by each franchise. The purse that is collected is divided up by first paying the commissioner. (We let our commissioner play for free, which serves as payment for duties and services. Therefore we don't actually take money out of the purse to pay the commissioner, but the purse is smaller because that person has not contributed.) The remainder of the money is divided up to provide payment for the following:

   1. First place—Fantasy Bowl winner
   2. Second place—Fantasy Bowl runner-up

3. Third place—winner, third-place playoff
4. Fourth place—loser, third-place playoff
5. Trophies for top four teams
6. Stamps, photocopying, & miscellaneous (used by commissioner for issuing weekly results to franchise owners)

V
THE DRAFT

Draft day may become the sports event of the year for most of you, but it can turn into a real headache for your commissioner if he or she is not properly prepared. The following is a layout of how our draft is set up and run. Everything is set up for a 16-team league, but the process can easily be adapted to the number of teams you have in your league.

1. SETTING UP A DRAFT DAY:
   One of the toughest jobs a commissioner faces is selecting a draft day. It is essential to find a day when all the franchises can be represented. In a small league (8 teams or fewer), it shouldn't be very difficult to find a time convenient for all team owners. In leagues of 10 or more, such as the one I'm involved with, select a date that is within two weeks of the National Football League regular-season opener. Then send out a notice more than a month in advance to inform all the teams of the draft date.

2. TEAM REPRESENTATION:
   With each team having a month's advance notice, there shouldn't be any reason that a team can't have a representative there to draft for the franchise, even if the owner can't be present.

   NOTE: After a year or two of having one of your Fantasy Franchise owners draft for both his team and another team that couldn't make it to the draft, you will begin to get many objections from the other franchise owners. Their beef is legitimate: How can an owner from one team put his heart into drafting for another team? It ruins the whole concept of the draft. So in our league, we follow these rules:

   A. No team is allowed to draft for another.
   B. Any team not represented at the draft must make its selections from the players remaining after the draft. (This has never happened.)

3. DRAFT ASSISTANT:
   If a commissioner owns a franchise himself, he may want to seek an assistant for draft day, someone who can take care of logging picks as they are called off, and so on. This leaves the commissioner free to concentrate on his draft. I have done this for the last four years, and it has worked out tremendously for both me and my assistant. In fact, my assistants have thanked me for such a good time.

4. DETERMINING TEAM NUMBERS AND DIVISIONS:
   Once each team is present, the draft can begin. The process for determining each franchise's team number for the purpose of scheduling and naming divisions is as follows:

   A. From a deck of cards select the Ace, Two, Three, and Four of each of the four suits, giving you 16 cards, one for each franchise.
   B. The 16 cards are shuffled and cut; each team takes one card to determine both its team number and the division it will be competing in.
   C. The 16 cards are interpreted as follows:

Black Conference			Red Conference		
Spade	Ace of Spades	— Team #1	**Diamond**	Ace of Diamonds	— Team # 9
Division	Two of Spades	— Team #2	**Division**	Two of Diamonds	— Team #10
	Three of Spades	— Team #3		Three of Diamonds	— Team #11
	Four of Spades	— Team #4		Four of Diamonds	— Team #12
Club	Ace of Clubs	— Team #5	**Heart**	Ace of Hearts	— Team #13
Division	Two of Clubs	— Team #6	**Division**	Two of Hearts	— Team #14
	Three of Clubs	— Team #7		Three of Hearts	— Team #15
	Four of Clubs	— Team #8		Four of Hearts	— Team #16

5. 12 ROUNDS / 7 STARTERS:

After determining team number and division, we move on to the actual draft. In our league, we draft players in 12 rounds. In selecting these 12 players, we must remember that 7 of them will be used in our starting lineup, which consists of two running backs, two wide receivers, one tight end, one quarterback, and one kicker. The remaining five picks will be reserves and can be from any of the above-mentioned positions.

6. DRAFTING ORDER:

We've found that we can best provide a fair draft and parity throughout the league by flopping the drafting order every other round. When determining the order of the draft, we first draw cards for the first round and then reverse that order for the second round.

This works out well, since the franchise that is lucky enough to get the #1 overall pick in the first round won't pick again until the 16th pick in the second round. Another way to look at this is that if you have the misfortune of picking 16th in the first round, you will automatically be given the #1 pick in the second round—two picks in a row. This process has worked out well and keeps the draft balanced pretty evenly. It also prevents someone who is lucky at picking cards from getting all the early picks in each of the rounds.

To determine the order of the draft, 16 cards are preselected from a whole deck. The cards used are the Ace through the Eight of Spades and the Ace through the Eight of Hearts. The 16 cards are shuffled, cut, and passed out. The order of the draft will be as follows:

Ace of Spades	— 1st Pick	Ace of Hearts	— 9th Pick
Two of Spades	— 2nd Pick	Two of Hearts	— 10th Pick
Three of Spades	— 3rd Pick	Three of Hearts	— 11th Pick
Four of Spades	— 4th Pick	Four of Hearts	— 12th Pick
Five of Spades	— 5th Pick	Five of Hearts	— 13th Pick
Six of Spades	— 6th Pick	Six of Hearts	— 14th Pick
Seven of Spades	— 7th Pick	Seven of Hearts	— 15th Pick
Eight of Spades	— 8th Pick	Eight of Hearts	— 16th Pick

Remember, each even-numbered round is in the reverse order of the previous odd-numbered round. So, if you grabbed the Four of Spades for your first-round pick, you would automatically draft 13th in the second round. This procedure is repeated for rounds 3 and 4 and so on, with a new draw of cards every odd round until the 12 rounds are complete.

7. SPEEDING UP YOUR DRAFT:

When drafting 192 players, as we do in our league, the process can sometimes become too long and drawn out. What we have developed is a quicker process for determining the order for all the rounds. Instead of drawing the cards every two rounds, we take six decks of cards which consist of the 16 predetermined cards (Ace through Eight of Spades and Hearts) and label the decks A through F. That means each group of 16 cards is labeled with a letter.

Each of the six decks of cards is shuffled, cut, and spread out, face down, on the table. Each franchise approaches the table and selects one card from each letter group. The following table shows the determination of drafting order for all of the rounds:

Deck marked with letter		
	"A" — — Rounds 1 and 2	
	"B" — — Rounds 3 and 4	
	"C" — — Rounds 5 and 6	
	"D" — — Rounds 7 and 8	
	"E" — — Rounds 9 and 10	
	"F" — — Rounds 11 and 12	

Samples:

Deck "A"

Ace of Spades	— —	Draft 1st, 1st Round	— —	16th, 2nd Round
Two of Spades	— —	Draft 2nd, 1st Round	— —	15th, 2nd Round
Ace of Hearts	— —	Draft 9th, 1st Round	— —	8th, 2nd Round

Deck "D"

Ace of Spades	— —	Draft 1st, 7th Round	— —	16th, 8th Round
Two of Spades	— —	Draft 2nd, 7th Round	— —	15th, 8th Round
Two of Spades	— —	Draft 2nd, 7th Round	— —	15th, 8th Round
Ace of Hearts	— —	Draft 9th, 7th Round	— —	8th, 8th Round

This process also allows some time for forming last-minute drafting strategies. After determining the drafting order for all the rounds, we take a 10-minute break to allow the teams to set up their picks, now that they know in what order they will draft.

8. TIME LIMIT:

In many cases, such as in our league's draft of 192 players, the draft can last many, many hours. To prevent the draft from dragging on too long, we have established a limit on the time a team has to make each pick.

In the early rounds, this should be no problem, since most of the better, more well-known players are being drafted. However, in the later rounds, selecting a player becomes more involved and may take longer.

The rules on the time limit for drafting players are as follows:

A. Two minutes are allowed per pick.
B. If the time limit has been exceeded, the next team in line will then be able to pick. Following that choice, go back to the team that was skipped.

C. Four minutes are allowed if a team has two consecutive picks (such as when an owner has the last pick of an odd round and automatically has the first pick of the second round).

D. If a team exceeds the four-minute limit for its consecutive picks, it must wait until after the next two teams are allowed picks before being allowed to make its selection(s).

E. A stopwatch should be used, and a warning should be given to the team that is selecting when there are 30 seconds left.

NOTE: Below is a sample of the boards we use at our draft. They are about 2 feet by 3 feet in actual size, making it easy for everyone in the room to see. The draft assistant logs the draft picks as they are called off, making our draft run smoothly and giving it a more professional appearance.

2001
FANTASY FOOTBALL DRAFT
(ROUND #1)

Fantasy Team #	Player Drafted	Pro Team	Pos
1			
2			
3			
4			
5			
6			
7			
8			
9			
10			
11			
12			
13			
14			
15			
16			

VI
ROSTER CHANGES/TRANSACTIONS

Because the 17-week NFL season may affect some transaction procedures, please refer to the suggestions for handling this schedule, found at the beginning of this chapter under "Trade Night."

After the draft has been completed, you may find that you're not happy with all of the players you chose, or, during the course of the season, one of your players may be sidelined with an injury or for some other reason. In either of these events, you may choose to make a trade or pick up another player.

1. PICKUPS AND TRADES:
   During the course of the season, you may elect to pick up or trade for another player. This can be done, provided that your roster never exceeds 12 players. For every player added to your roster, another must be dropped.

   A. Once a player is dropped by an FFL team, he becomes a free agent and is eligible to be picked up by any other franchise. He is, in effect, put on waivers.
   B. There are two types of roster changes that can be made. The first is actually labeled a *pickup*. This occurs when a team decides to pick up a player from the pool of players left unclaimed following the draft. Remember, for every additional player you pick up, you must also drop a player from your current roster to keep it at 12.
   C. Although there will be a limit of only one or two trades between teams, there is no limit to how many players can be picked up from the unclaimed pool.
   D. The other type of transaction is the *trade*. It's a move by one team in the league to trade a player to another team in the league. A limit of one or two of these exchanges or trades should be allowed per year. This prevents any two franchise owners who are close friends from trading between themselves exclusively in an attempt to build one super team between the two of them. In the event of a two-for-one trade, where one team offers two players in exchange for one better player, each team's roster must still end up with 12. This means that the team receiving the two players must drop an additional player besides the one it traded. The team giving up the two players and receiving only one must pick up another player from the unclaimed pool.
   E. Limit the number of transactions per franchise per trade night to three. For leagues using a phone-in method for transactions, this means that one transaction may be made in the first hour allotted, and two may be made in the second hour.

2. COMMISSIONER RESPONSIBILITIES:

   A. To ease the commissioner's load, I suggest having your trade night the same night as you take lineups. This will then tie up only one night in league transactions.
   B. Set a time limit of two hours.
   C. Keep good records to avoid the possibility of two teams picking up

the same player.
D. I suggest the commissioner charge a small fee for each trade, for his or her time and the paperwork involved.

3. LEAGUE HANDLING OF PICKUPS AND TRADES (COMMISSIONER):
There are a number of ways to handle pickups and trades, based on how your league is handled by its commissioner. The first thing to determine is whether league transactions are going to be handled in person or by telephone. Here are some options:

A. Phone-In Leagues

OPTION #1: The Worst Goes First
This method allows the team with the worst record each week to have first chance at making its transactions. (My league tried this the last couple of years and it worked well. I'm sure we'll continue to use it in the future.)
a. In the weeks preceding the season, when transactions are allowed after the league's fantasy draft, the team with the worst record from the previous season will go first, then the team with the next worst record, and so on.

NOTE: OPTION #1
In the event new teams have been added to the league, cards should be drawn at the draft to determine the order of the new teams' transactions. The transaction slots for new teams should be inserted right into the rest of the league's transaction order.

NOTE: OPTION #2
If your league has brought in a number of new teams, you may choose to use the reverse order of the first round of your draft for the weeks prior to the season.

b. On a given transaction night the commissioner calls each franchise, starting with the one with the worst record. For teams with identical records, the following tiebreakers will be used:
1. Worst record
2. Fewest points scored
3. Most points allowed (tougher schedule)
4. Coin flip
c. Each franchise is responsible for giving the commissioner a telephone number where someone can be reached for transactions during the season. If no one will be at the number on a given night, the franchise is responsible for informing the commissioner prior to the transaction day and time, and for leaving a new number where someone can be reached.
d. When a commissioner cannot reach a fantasy team:
1. If a commissioner receives no answer at the given franchise number, he or she will assume that the franchise desires no transactions that evening and, after allowing 10 rings, the commissioner may go on to the next team. If the team involved calls later in the hour to make transactions, this team will go to the end of the list.

2. If a commissioner gets a busy signal, he or she must continue to call that team for three minutes. If the commissioner still cannot get through on the line, he or she goes on to the next team. If the skipped team calls in and wants to make transactions, it must go to the end of the list for first-hour transactions.
3. If a commissioner reaches a telephone recorder, he or she should leave a message noting the time of the call. If the team calls back and wants to make transactions, it must go to the end of the list.

NOTE: Some owners have called the commissioner back several times a night, in order to stay at the end of the list. The point of this is to find out which players have been dropped by other teams. This is a big nuisance. To prevent this from going on all night, we follow this rule: No team can pick up a player dropped after its original position within that hour. For example, if a franchise owner who is fourth on the list for picking up a player bypasses his moves and wants to drop to the bottom of the list, he may not pick up any player dropped in the fifth position or later. He must wait for his second hour's transaction position to try to obtain one of those dropped players. And a team would have no advantage in moving to the end of the list in the second hour, because it cannot pick up any player dropped after its original transaction position until the following week.

NOTE: If an owner leaves a message on the commissioner's recorder detailing whom the owner wants to pick up, this message should be disregarded by the commissioner. Only transactions made person-to-person over the phone should be considered. The commissioner who receives such a message should ignore it and attempt to contact the owner according to the rules detailed above.

e. Three transactions per night:
(One the first hour, up to two the second hour, for a total of three.)
NOTE: A 2-for-1 trade is considered only one transaction for either team.

If any team was bypassed in the first hour's transactions because of no answer or a busy signal and also failed to contact the commissioner, that team forfeits one of its allowed transactions for the evening. With a maximum of three transactions per transaction night, the first hour's selection would be forfeited. The reason for allowing only one transaction the first hour is to provide each team a shot at obtaining at least one significant player. If the commissioner allowed two transactions in the first hour, very few desirable players would be left by the time the owners choosing later got their chance.

f. Second-hour transactions:
1. The only teams that will be called back by the commissioner

are those that expressed an interest in making second-hour transactions when called during the first hour. They should be called back in the same sequence as during the first hour.

2. If any team did not talk to the commissioner during the first hour but wants to make a trade during the second hour, that team goes to the end of the list—behind those that did express, during the first hour, an interest in making second-hour transactions. If more than one team calls in, they will be called back in the sequence they called in.

g. Transaction-position trading:

Two teams may desire to trade their weekly transaction-position numbers. This may come as part of a trade condition. The two teams can be allowed to trade their transaction positions on the condition that both teams must make a first-hour transaction. This will hopefully prevent any two teams in cahoots from just passing their favorable positions to each other. So both teams have to make this first-hour transaction. The commissioner must be assured that this condition has been met before the transaction-position trading is allowed. (This position trading should only be allowed prior to the trade deadline and should not be allowed in the roster-expansion draft or the playoff player-additon draft. The team trading a favorable early position has nothing to gain, since another player or draft pick cannot be included. So such a trade is probably not on the up-and-up, and as a commissioner I would not, and did not, allow such a trade.)

OPTION #2: First Come, First Served

Efficient handling of the weekly phone call-in:

Trades should be handled on a first-come, first-served basis. There may be many trade nights when the teams in your league are looking to pick up the same player. To prevent any hassles or showing of favoritism, state a time you will start taking calls. Take the phone off the hook five minutes before your declared starting time. Then at precisely, say, 6:00 P.M., put the phone back on the hook and begin taking calls.

a. Each franchise may have only one caller trying to place the transaction order. (Some teams have only one owner while others have many.) If more than one owner from a franchise calls within the same hour, the franchise goes to the bottom of the callback list, unless the transactions by the penalized team have already been accepted by the commissioner.

b. Set a limit of one transaction in the first hour and two in the second hour, for a total of three. This will keep you from being on the phone for a long time. This will also give the other teams a chance at the more highly desired players.

c. Offer no advice to teams calling in as to whom you think they should pick up. If a team calls in looking for a player to fill a particular position, let the caller suggest whom he or she wants and offer no help.

d. In the event that you, as commissioner, are looking for a player and want to be fair to both your league and yourself, you could handle it the way I do: If a player goes unclaimed for 10 minutes after the trading hour has started, the commissioner is allowed to pick up the player. Again, the commissioner, like the rest of the owners, can pick up no more than two players at a time. He or she cannot pick up a second or third player until after 10 minutes into the second hour. In the event your league meets on transaction night, the commissioner will draw a card like anyone else to determine the order of pickups.

B. Weekly Get-Together Leagues

OPTION #1: The Worst Goes First
For those leagues that meet weekly, an easy and fair way to handle transactions is the worst-goes-first option, as defined in Option #1 for phone-in leagues. The team with the worst record gets to make its selections first, and so on. If two teams have identical records, the following tiebreakers will be used:
1. Worst record
2. Least points scored
3. Most points allowed (tougher schedule)
4. Coin flip

OPTION #2: Cut the Cards
Use a deck of cards to determine who goes first, and then second, and so on.

OPTION #3: Player Bidding
Another option used in many fantasy leagues for player transactions is *player bidding.* Fantasy teams pick up players from the unclaimed-player pool by bidding for them.
a. Fantasy teams use the trade night to bid on players. If only one team bids on a player, then obviously it acquires the player. If more than one team bids on a player, then the player goes to the team with the highest bid.
Example: Let's say a player goes undrafted but gets hot, so a number of fantasy teams in the league are interested in him. Team A bids $3.00. Team B bids $2.00. Team C bids $5.00. Team C, the highest bidder, gets the player.
b. In the event of two or more teams making the same highest bid, the commissioner will advise each team of this at the end of the evening and let each make another bid, with the highest bidder in this new round of bids getting the player. Or, the league may choose to allow the team with the poorer record at the time to get the player that both teams made identical bids on. (NOTE: If three teams bid on a player but only two have identical high bids, only the two high bidders are allowed to re-bid at the end of the evening.)
c. Because it is not known until the end of the evening which teams get which players, the Fantasy Franchise acquiring the player may not use him as part of its team that week. However, that franchise must announce which player from its team is being released, so the rest of the league is notified of who is going back in the player pool.

d. Do not allow the commissioner, if he or she is also a franchise owner, the advantage of knowing what the other teams are bidding. The commissioner must give his or her bid to another league member at the outset of the evening. In the event the commissioner wants to bid on a player also wanted by the franchise owner whom he normally calls with his bid, he would just place his bid with a different owner that week.

OPTION #4: No-Trade Leagues
For leagues in which the commissioner elects not to get involved in handling trades, you may decide to increase the number of rounds for your league draft. Instead of drafting 12 rounds, you could increase your draft to 15 rounds. This would give each team a chance to stock enough players at each position to survive the year, thus eliminating the need for trades.

NOTE: If a no-trade league is your choice, I'd advise you to hold an "Expansion Draft" midway through the season. By that time, a number of franchises in your league are likely to have multiple injuries and may not be able to field players at various positions.

4. TRANSACTION DEADLINE:
A transaction deadline day that will fall during the season should be established before the season starts. One suggestion would be to have the deadline one week after the halfway point of the season. From that day on, the 12 players who make up a franchise roster must finish the season with that team.

There are a number of ways to help a fantasy team that suffers player injuries after the trade deadline and therefore cannot field a full team. Your league has two options. One deals with a player on injured reserve, and the other simply allows every franchise to obtain more players after the trade deadline, to avoid not having each position covered in the event of an injury. (I prefer the second option. Your league may also elect to use both options, which would allow your franchises to expand rosters after the trade deadline and replace a player who is out for a minimum of four weeks.)

OPTION #1: Injured-Reserve and Cut-Player Options:
a. Injured-Reserve Option:
1. The only exception to the transaction deadline would be the case of a player being injured after this date. In many instances, this would leave a team without a player at a particular position.
2. Any FFL team that suffers an injury after the transaction deadline has an option. If the injured player goes on the NFL injured-reserve list (which puts him out for the season), that franchise may replace him with another player from the unclaimed-player pool. The new player must play the same position as the player released. The injured player, once released from his permanent team after the deadline, is out for the year. He may not be picked up by any other team. Proof that a player is on injured reserve should be obtained from a current, reliable source of sports information, such as *USA Today, The Sporting News, Pro Football Weekly,* or your local newspaper.

3. Another option would be to replace a player who has missed more than four consecutive weeks and whose NFL team elected not to put him on injured reserve. This player would have to miss four consecutive weeks following the trade deadline. However, this may be difficult to prove in some situations, such as those involving receivers, who may appear in a game without actually catching a pass. This is why this rule should be closely examined and voted on prior to the season by the fantasy league.

NOTE: Unless your league specifically votes otherwise, this rule applies only to players who go on injured reserve. Fantasy players lost because of trades, waivers, or cuts do not fall under this rule. Example: If a fantasy player is cut by an NFL team, his fantasy team is still stuck with him unless your league adopts the cut-player option described later in this section.

NOTE: If you have a good player and you elect to replace him using injured-reserve option #3 above, he is lost to you for the season. However, this may be a necessary loss. You really don't have the luxury of an injured reserve in your fantasy league. You can take an injured player out of the *starting* lineup, but even then he takes up bench space that could be occupied by a healthy player. You just have to decide for yourself whether your good-but-injured player is so valuable that you can afford to have him sit, useless, on your bench, while you wait to find out whether he'll be back or not.

NOTE: Commissioners should require that any FFL team using this rule to pick up a player on injured reserve send in a copy of some statement verifying that this player is out. This is proof in case any questions or protests from other teams arise later.

4. A final option should be considered. The NFL's injured-reserve clause now requires a player on injured reserve to remain there for the rest of the season, as opposed to the previous four-week rule. Because of this, NFL teams may refrain from putting injured players on injured reserve, since that would mean losing the players for the entire season. So some players may be sidelined for weeks without ever being placed on injured reserve. Under previous Fantasy Football rules, this could cause a fantasy team some problems, since the owner of such a player could do nothing with him until he was placed on injured reserve, or until he had missed four consecutive weeks. This is a long time to be without a player, so here is a suggestion for how to deal with this rule:
   a. A fantasy team can now replace an injured player who has not been placed on injured reserve, if that player's prognosis indicates he'll be out for four weeks or longer.
   b. The fantasy team wishing to take advantage of this option must present verification of the player's prognosis to the commissioner. This is done via an authoritative publication (*USA Today, TSN, Pro Football Weekly,* local newspaper) agreed

upon by the league prior to the beginning of the season.

   c. The injured player can only be replaced by another player at the same position.

   d. The released player cannot be picked up by any other team. He is unavailable for the remainder of the season in your fantasy league.

b. Cut-Player Option:

Because some franchise owners have been frustrated by being stuck with players cut from NFL teams after the trade deadline, I have included the following option, on which your league can vote.

If a fantasy team possesses a player who has been cut, waived, or released after your league's trade deadline, that player may be replaced under the following provisions:

1. The player being released by the fantasy team must be replaced by a player from the same position.

2. The player being released by the fantasy team, like a player released because he is on injured reserve, cannot be picked up by any other team and is released from the player pool.

3. The fantasy team releasing the player must do so the same week as the player is released from his NFL team. Here are some rules for this release:

   a. If your trade night is Thursday night and the NFL player has been released during the seven days including or preceding your trade day, he must be transacted that night. However, the player's release by his NFL team and the date of that release must be proved on trade night. A clipping from a reliable daily publication is sufficient proof.

   b. If the NFL transaction cannot be proved on trade night—if someone has heard that it occurred earlier that day, for example, but cannot yet offer proof—the fantasy team holding that player must conduct its transaction on the next trade night, the following week.

   c. If the transaction by the fantasy team isn't done in the proper week, that fantasy team is stuck with the player.

4. This rule does *not* apply to NFL players *traded* to another NFL team after your trade deadline. However, it does apply to players cut, waived, or released by an NFL team even if they are picked up by another NFL team that same week.

OPTION #2: Roster-Expansion Draft:

Another alternative for your league is to allow roster expansion after the trade deadline. You could do this instead of, or in addition to, Option #1. Because players suffer minor injuries that don't necessitate their going on injured reserve, many fantasy teams find themselves short a player or two in any given week. To help eliminate this problem, the 12-player limit should be expanded to 14 following the trade deadline, allowing each franchise two more spots on its roster. This will keep all positions filled despite weekly injuries that may occur. The rules for expanding to 14 players after the trade deadline are as follows:

a. Player Eligibility:
   1. Players drafted for the roster-expansion draft may come only from the unclaimed-player pool.
   2. Any player dropped by a franchise after the trade deadline does not go into the unclaimed-player pool for another team to pick up and may not be used in the playoff player-addition draft. (This may only happen if your league uses both the roster-expansion draft and the Injured-Reserve/Cut-Player Options.)
b. Transaction Procedures:
   1. *Leagues that meet, in person, to make roster-expansion selections:* In leagues where all the franchise owners are able to get together for the roster expansion, the selecting should start with the team with the worst record and work its way through to the team with the best record. The team with the worst record selects one player, and the rest of the teams continue until each franchise has selected its 13th player. Then, starting over again, the team with the worst record selects its 14th player and so on until each franchise has 14 members. The 14-player roster is now permanent. (If two teams have identical records, then the team that has scored the fewest points is designated the "worst" and should select first. If two teams have identical records and identical points, then a coin toss should determine their draft order.)

   NOTE: If a team does not have a representative at the roster expansion draft, it must select its two additional players after all of the other teams are done.

   2. *Leagues that use the phone for expansion selections:* I suggest using a method similar to that used during the year by your league. The drafting should be done in two one-hour periods. The first hour should be to select player #13 on the roster (designated as the first round of the Player Addition Draft), and the second hour should be for player #14 (second round).

NOTE:
   1. If a fantasy team chooses, when called, not to pick up a player but calls back within the first hour of the roster-expansion draft, it may pick up a first-round player but must go to the bottom of the list.
   2. If a fantasy team is not reached by the commissioner and fails to call in at all to take a player during the first round of the roster-expansion draft, that team forfeits its right for the remainder of the year to one of the two players it could have chosen during the roster-expansion draft. That team may, however, select one player during any of the remaining regular-season weeks to add to its roster.
   3. A fantasy team electing to draft one player during the first round of the expansion draft and electing not to pick a second player during the draft's second round is also eligible to pick up a second selection during any of the remaining regular-season weeks. A fantasy team that does not participate in the first hour of the expansion draft forfeits its right to expand its roster by two players. Such a team may expand by only one and would

end up with a maximum of 13 players rather than 14.

4. The order of selecting roster-expansion players following the roster-expansion draft date will follow the transaction procedures used by your league during the season.

OPTION #3: Playoff Player-Addition Draft:
To further ensure Fantasy Franchises against finding themselves short a player at playoff time, I suggest incorporating a playoff player-addition draft. This would expand each playoff team's roster by one player, giving it a possible total of 15.

a. The player can be from any position.

b. The player must be selected from the unclaimed-player pool as it stood prior to the player-transaction deadline. No player dropped by one Fantasy Franchise after the player-transaction deadline may be selected in this draft.

c. The playoff player-addition draft will take place on the trade night prior to the fantasy playoffs.

d. A team not participating in the player-addition draft on that evening forfeits, for the remainder of the playoffs, its right to add a player to its roster.

e. Selections in the playoff player-addition draft will follow the transaction procedures used by your league during the season.

NOTE: Transactions made in the roster-expansion draft and the playoff player-addition draft should carry the normal transaction fees to be paid to the commissioner.

OPTION #4: Injured-Reserve or Cut-Player Option Combined With the Roster-Expansion Draft and the Playoff Player-Addition Draft:
The roster-expansion draft and the playoff player-addition draft were incorporated to try to protect fantasy teams from having to field an incomplete team following the trade deadline. Though these two draft expansions help, they are not fail-safe methods. Injuries to NFL players have become so common in recent years that allowing the injured-reserve and the cut-player options in addition to these drafts may be desirable in many leagues. If a league uses this option, the following rules should be applied.

a. A fantasy team using the injured-reserve or cut-player option to pick up a player must do it in the same transaction order as previously described. So a fantasy team that has an injured-reserve option because one of its players has gone on injured reserve will elect to use either this or the player-addition option when its turn comes that week. If that fantasy team uses its injured-reserve option the first time through transactions on a given night, and wants to make a second move using a player-addition option, the owner must advise the commissioner following the first transaction. That team will then be called back the second time through for the second move.

b. A fantasy team owner who wants to take advantage of the injured-reserve rule must contact the commissioner prior to the transaction night so that the commissioner can insert him in the transaction order.

c.   A fantasy team using the injured-reserve option must do so within the transaction week the player is placed on injured reserve. This is enforced so that a fantasy team cannot ride a player's injury until a move will be most advantageous. (If one of your players is placed on injured reserve on Friday, for instance, and your league's transaction night is Thursday, you would have to make your move the following Thursday. If you do not make the move within that transaction week, the player is stuck on your team.)

d.   A player picked up using the injured-reserve rule must play the same position as the player released.

OPTION #5: Drafting Team Quarterbacks and/or Team Kickers: Many leagues have opted to draft a team quarterback or kicker, rather than to draft specific quarterbacks or kickers. This is largely due to the high injury rate among quarterbacks and the high turnover at the kicking position. Drafting the Chicago Bears' quarterbacks rather than specifically naming Cade McNown or Jim Miller will prevent many transactions and questions. (My league has never used this option and has made the drafting of backup quarterbacks quite a strategy. So it makes it interesting either way.)

VII
LINEUPS

Because the 17-week NFL season may affect some of the handling procedures for transactions, please refer to the suggestions at the beginning of this chapter to see how to handle this change.

The commissioner should set up a night and a period of time (for example, 6:00 to 8:00 p.m.) when he or she is free and can take everyone's lineup. To make it easier on the commissioner, lineup submissions can be scheduled for the same night as trades are taken. The commissioner would then be involved only one night. The following can be used as a commissoner's guide for taking lineups:

1. COMMISSIONER FAVORITISM:
Commissioners, make sure to have your franchise owners prepared when they call you. Each one should be able to call you, read off the lineup, and get off the phone. Don't let them call you and ask your opinion on whom they should start or which NFL teams play which. I've run into this on plenty of occasions and it's really frustrating, especially if it's a good friend doing it to me. Besides taking up a lot of my time, it puts me in an awkward position. I don't feel it is ethical for a league commissioner to show any favoritism and guide a team's choice of whom to start. The easiest way to remedy this kind of problem is to make sure, at the draft, that each team understands: No lineup will be logged in the books unless the team calling it in is ready to give the full lineup without guidance from the commissioner.

2. LINEUP NIGHT:
The day selected for taking lineups should be later in the week, allowing every team in the league a chance to check on its players, via the newspaper or television, for injuries or other late-breaking news that would change its strategy for the game.

NOTE: On the *first* lineup night, there could be a problem if a team forgets to call in its lineup. Since there is no previous week's lineup to carry over, I would suggest handling it this way: Simply insert the team's starting lineup according to the draft order in which the players were taken. In other words, the first players drafted from each starting position are inserted as that team's starters. The first two running backs drafted are the team's starting running backs, the first two wide receivers drafted are the starting wideouts, and so on. Once the starters have been determined, the reserves are listed, also in the order they were drafted, regardless of position. The first player drafted who did not fit into a starting position is the first reserve, the second non-starter drafted is the second reserve, and so on.

3. FANTASY WEEKS THAT START EARLY:
If you elect to take lineups on Thursday nights, for instance, and there is a National Football League game scheduled for that day, your lineup and trade night should automatically be changed to Wednesday. This prevents anybody's calling in his lineup after the Thursday game has started. It's important that all lineups be given prior to the first game played that week. Even your FFL teams that don't have any players participating in these

games still must have their lineups in on the same night as the teams that do have players involved. This gives every team the same amount of time to check the media for injury or other pertinent news. Once the kickoff from the first NFL game of the week occurs, all FFL games for that week have officially begun.

4a. RIDING THE SAME LINEUP:

If a team fails to call the commissioner and submit a lineup, its previous week's lineup will automatically be used. This means that in leagues using carryover-player scores for bye weeks, teams will also be locking in their bye-week players for both weeks if they fail to call in to the commissioner.

4b. RIDING THE SAME LINEUP DURING CARRYOVER WEEKS:

Because of the bye-week player lock-ins from the previous week, your league may run into another problem. The problem comes up when a fantasy team puts in a weekly lineup and changes the position of a carryover player from starter one week to reserve the next. In other words, the team elects to start a carryover player in the current week's game but decides not to use him as a starter the next week. If, the following week, the fantasy team fails to call in its lineup, it is forced to ride the previous week's lineup. But that becomes a problem for the carryover player who was scheduled to move from a starting position the previous week to a reserve position in the carryover week. In this event, the commissioner will automatically use the first player of the same position from the fantasy team's reserve list and insert that player as a starter to fill the carryover player's vacancy.

All the reserves move up a notch until all reserve positions are filled in. There is also a reverse of this. A fantasy team may have a carryover player it elects to use as a reserve the current week and as a starter for the following week's carryover game. If the fantasy team fails to call in its weekly lineup the following week, this again presents a problem. Let's say this player is a running back, for instance. Now you have one starting running back (the carryover player) and two other running backs riding from the previous week's lineup. Which ones are inserted? I recommend, for the sake of consistency, that the first running back listed from the previous week be the other starter alongside the carryover player. The second running back listed should go on the reserves in the spot that the carryover player occupied. Commissioners, take a close look at this, and recommend to your franchises that they carefully choose the order of the players in the lineups they give you. Or suggest that they call in every week to assure themselves they have their lineups just as they desire them. (This situation will come up!)

5. OPTIONS:

A. One Lineup Change: Here is an option I use in our league. After its original starting lineup is called in, each FFL team is allowed one lineup change. This must be done prior to the first National Football League game that week. If your original lineup is called in on Thursday and the first National Football League game for that week is played on Sunday, your commissioner can set up a period of time (between 11:00 a.m. and 12 noon on Sunday, for example) when each team has a chance to call in its one lineup change. This allows every team a chance to check Sunday morning's paper for any late-breaking news. By Sunday morning, a player's playing status should be pretty well determined. The opponent should then be notified of the lineup change prior to the game. The following restrictions apply to any such lineup changes:

1. The lineup change is legitimate if the commissioner is contacted in person prior to the start of the first NFL game.
2. If, for some reason, an owner cannot reach the commissioner to confirm a lineup change, that owner should contact two other franchise owners, notifying them of the intended change.
3. Leaving a lineup change on an answering machine is unacceptable, because the time of the call usually cannot be confirmed. (Recording a message can be acceptable if the answering system automatically records the time of the call, as many now do. This should be voted on by the league prior to the season.)
4. Contacting just your opponent to confirm a lineup change is not acceptable, unless your opponent is also the commissioner. If you cannot reach the commissioner, your opponent can—and should—be one of the two teams you contact (see rule #2 above), but a second team must be notified as well.
5. Both the commissioner and the opposing team should be notified as soon as possible after the decision has been made.

In the event that you replace one of your starters by using this one lineup change, the replaced player then automatically takes the spot of the reserve in your lineup.

NOTE: Because of the new carryover setup, lineup changes involving the following week's carryover players will be handled differently. For rules on trading or releasing a carryover player, consult the section titled "Trade Night," under Playing Option #2 (part of Options to Tackle the 17-Week Season). Also refer to the page preceding this one for rules relating to carryover player lock-ins, when an owner does not call in a lineup.

B. Sudden-Death Tiebreaker: Commissioners, don't forget to write in every team's reserve players for use in the sudden-death tiebreaker. (See Section IX, "Variations on Fantasy Football: Sudden-Death Tiebreaker," for details.)

VIII
SELECTING A SCORING METHOD

After finding the right person to head your league as commissioner, your next step is to establish which method of scoring your league will use. In the following pages, I describe the four methods of scoring that are most commonly used. I have also included a few variations used by different leagues. You may want to expand on the rules a little yourself. After reading through the following rules for the different methods, select the one you feel will give your league the most enjoyment. Before we consider the four methods individually, let's look at the general rules that apply to all of them.

NOTE: Before your regular season begins, you should establish which particular sports-reporting source you are going to use for your game results. This should be done because of possible discrepancies in scoring or possible missing stats. Among your options, of course, are your local newspaper, *USA Today, The Sporting News* (which will be received a week later), and *Pro Football Weekly*. Select one for your league's official results, but in case of a discrepancy, have two backups for help in deciding the correct scoring.

NUMBER OF PLAYERS:
A. At the fantasy draft, each franchise will draft 12 players.
B. Of the 12 NFL players selected on draft day, seven will be used in your starting lineup and the other five will be reserves.
C. Of the starting seven players, the following positions will make up the starting lineup:

*STANDARD OPTION (used by most leagues):
1 Quarterback   2 Wide Receivers   1 Kicker
2 Running Backs   1 Tight End

*FLEX OPTION: Because of the many varieties of formations being used today, like the two-tight-end offense or the H-back (see below), many leagues use the Flex Option in an attempt to simplify the decision of whether a player is qualified as a wide receiver, tight end, or H-back. We suggest that leagues go to three receivers, with no limitations on how many are wide receivers, tight ends, or H-backs.

Here is the FLEX OPTION:
1 Quarterback   3 Receivers   1 Kicker
2 Running Backs

(The position of H-back, a recent phenomenon in the NFL, is used to designate what most would consider a blocking tight end. Usually this player lines up in the backfield and goes in motion either to block or run a pass pattern. If you do not use this Flex Option, H-backs would most likely fall into the tight-end category.)

D. On some occasions, you may find players who are able to play a few positions or who change positions during the course of the year. You may need to set up some sort of rule to clarify at what position that player must be used. An example is Jim Jensen, who played for the

Miami Dolphins in the 1980s. Jensen could have been listed at a variety of positions, including quarterback, wide receiver, and tight end. A number of years ago, the San Diego Chargers converted Rod Bernstine from tight end to running back in the preseason. At our draft, our league elected to vote him in as a running back for the season. Many other leagues left him as a tight end because of preseason publications showing him at that position. It should be determined prior to the season at which position your league will accept these players.

The rule we have established for clarification of position is as follows:

1. Choose one respected sports magazine to use as your league's book. The position listed in this book is the position the player must be drafted for.

2. Your league may choose, in certain instances, to take a vote right at the league's draft to designate a player's position. Such was the case for the Chargers' Rod Bernstine in 1990. We voted Bernstine to be designated a running back based on how our league felt he would most often be used during the season. And last year, Eric Metcalf, used as a running back part of his career and as a wide receiver at other times, was voted to be a wide receiver after being dealt to San Diego.

3. If during the course of the year the player switches positions, a team may change his position with the following provisions:

   a. The fantasy owner must provide evidence to the commissioner that his player has been playing that position for at least two consecutive weeks. The fantasy owner cannot sit on the move. In other words, he or she must make the move when the player is currently playing that new position for his NFL team (with proof that he has been at that position for at least the previous two weeks). The owner may not wait until a player has switched back to his original position, and then choose which of the two positions he or she would prefer that player to play. For example, if Eric Metcalf, starts the year as a wide receiver in your fantasy league, he will remain a wide receiver unless he is switched to running back for at least two weeks. At that point, the fantasy franchise that owns Metcalf can decide to switch him to running back. But if Metcalf is switched back to wide receiver before the fantasy owner elects to move him to running back, then that owner must play him as a wide receiver. He or she no longer has the option of using Metcalf as a running back, unless he is switched again later in the season and the process is repeated.

   b. If that fantasy team owner is the commissioner, two other team owners of the league must approve the switch.

   c. One publication you could use for this rule is *Pro Football Weekly,* which lists the players by position each week.

4. If a team has a protest against an opponent with a player in this situation, the protest must be lodged prior to the start of their game. Once the game has started, no protest may be made. All commissioner decisions should be fair and are final.

THE BASIC SCORING METHOD

The Basic Scoring Method is the most commonly used scoring method. It is the tabulation of actual scoring done in NFL games by various NFL players. Let's take a look at how this is done.

1. SCORING TABULATION BY POSITION:
   The following are the seven starting positions, broken down by the number of points tallied for each score.

   A. Quarterbacks
      1. Three points are awarded for each touchdown pass thrown.
      2. Six points are awarded for each touchdown scored rushing.
      3. Six points are awarded for each touchdown scored receiving a pass (in the event that a quarterback becomes a pass receiver in a play).

   B. Running Backs, Wide Receivers, Tight Ends
      1. Six points are awarded for each touchdown scored, either by running or catching a pass.
      2. Three points are awarded for each touchdown pass thrown (such as in a halfback option).

   C. Kickers
      1. Three points are awarded for each field goal.
      2. One point is awarded for each extra point.

   D. All Fantasy-Positioned Players (Two-point conversions)
      1. If a player (quarterback, running back, wide receiver, tight end) runs in the two-point conversion, he is awarded the two points.
      2. If the two-point conversion involves a pass, the player who catches the pass is awarded two points, and the player who throws the pass is awarded one point. (This is similar to a touchdown pass, where the receiver is awarded six points and the quarterback is awarded three points.)

2. ADDITIONAL SCORING POSSIBILITIES:
   A. If a running back or wide receiver doubles as a punt or kickoff returner and scores a touchdown on a runback, the six points awarded for a touchdown apply.
   B. If any player recovers a fumble in the end zone for a touchdown, the six points for a touchdown are awarded.

3. SAMPLE SCORING FOR A FANTASY FOOTBALL GAME:
   To better explain the scoring process of the Basic Scoring Method, let's look at two fictitious fantasy teams. You will be team #1 and I will be team #2.

   First, let's put together a scorecard listing our starting lineups. (See Detail A.)

Detail A

TEAM # 1			TEAM # 2		
QB	Favre (GB)		QB	Aikman (DALL)	
RB	J. Anderson (ATL)		RB	Faulk (St L)	
RB	A. Smith (BUF)		RB	Thomas (DALL)	
WR	Johnson (PHIL)		WR	Robinson (CHI)	
WR	Freeman (GB)		WR	Ismail (DALL)	
TE	Conwell (St L)		TE	Wetnight (CHI)	
K	Andersen (ATL)	_____	K	Seder (DALL)	_____

As commissioner of a league, I have found the easiest way to tally scores is to use the following key:

A. Quarterbacks, Running Backs, Wide Receivers, and Tight Ends

    1. For each rushing or pass-receiving touchdown, a T is marked to the right of the player's team initials on the scorecard. (Remember, six points are tallied for each.)

    2. For each touchdown pass thrown, a P is marked in the same area. (Remember, three points are tallied for each.)

B. Kickers

    1. For each field goal, an F is marked, again next to a player's team initials. (Remember, three points are tallied for each.)

    2. For each extra point, an X is marked in the same area. (Remember, one point is awarded for each.)

Taking some sample box scores, let's fill in our scorecard.

Looking first at your team (team #1), we will start with your quarterback, Brett Favre of the Green Bay Packers. Using the following box score from the Packers-Bears game (see Detail B), we find that Favre threw two touchdown passes, one to Freeman and one to Franks. The box score shows him rushing for one touchdown. In our scorecard we would put one T for the rushing touchdown and two Ps for the two touchdown passes.

Detail B

BEARS 23, PACKERS 21

```
Green Bay        7  7  0  7  —  21
Chicago          7  0  7  9  —  23
```
Chi-Robinson 35 pass from McNown (Edinger kick)
GB-Favre 1 run (Longwell kick)
GB-Freeman 31 pass from Favre (Longwell kick)
Chi-Engram 22 pass from McNown (Edinger kick)
Chi-McNown 6 run (kick failed)
GB-Franks 5 pass from Favre (Longwell kick)
Chi-FG Edinger 22
A-35,908

His score would then add up to 12 points—6 points for the one rushing touchdown and 6 points for the two touchdown passes thrown (3 points each). Now our scorecard would look like this. (See Detail C.)

Detail C

	TEAM # 1			TEAM # 2	
QB	Favre (GB) TPP	12	QB	Aikman (DALL)	
RB	J. Anderson (ATL)		RB	Faulk (St L)	
RB	A. Smith (BUF)		RB	Thomas (DALL)	
WR	Johnson (PHIL)		WR	Robinson (CHI)	
WR	Freeman (GB)		WR	Ismail (DALL)	
TE	Conwell (St L)		TE	Wetnight (CHI)	
K	Andersen (ATL)	___	K	Seder (DALL)	___

Using the following box scores, (Detail D), let's fill in the rest of our scorecard to determine a winner.

CARDINALS 31, EAGLES 7

Philadelphia	0	0	0 7	—	7
Arizona	7	7	10 7	—	31

Ariz-Pittman 12 run (Blanchard kick)
Ariz-Rb Moore 10 pass from Plummer (Blanchard kick)
Ariz-FG Blanchard
Ariz-Jones 1 run (Blanchard kick)
Ariz-Hardy 29 pass from Plummer (Blanchard kick)
Phil-Small 20 pass from McNabb (Akers kick)

RAMS 24, COWBOYS 17

St. Louis	7	0	7 10	—	24
Dallas	0	7	3 7	—	17

St L-Conwell 13 pass from Warner (Wilkins kick), 3:26
Dal-McKnight 14 pass from Aikman (Seder kick), 14:43
Dal-FG Seder 41, 3:00
St L-Bruce 16 pass from Warner (Wilkins kick), 7:37
St L-Holt 8 pass from Warner (Wilkins kick), 1:06
St L-FG Wilkins 20, 8:00
Dal-LaFleur 2 pass from Aikman (Cunningham kick), 12:57

FALCONS 31, BILLS 14

Buffalo	0	7	0 7	—	14
Atlanta	3	14	7 7	—	31

Atl-FG Andersen 40
Atl-Mathis 7 pass from Chandler (Andersen kick)
Atl-J. Anderson 10 run (Andersen kick)
Buf-Price 13 pass from Flutie (Christie kick)
Atl-J. Anderson 1 run (Andersen kick)
Atl-J. Anderson 6 pass from Chandler (Andersen kick)
Buf-Moulds 28 pass from Flutie (Christie kick)

BEARS 23, PACKERS 21

Green Bay	7	7	0 7	—	21
Chicago	7	0	7 9	—	23

Chi-Robinson 35 pass from McNown (Edinger kick)
GB-Favre 1 run (Longwell kick)
GB-Freeman 31 pass from Favre (Longwell kick)
Chi-Engram 22 pass from McNown (Edinger kick)
Chi-McNown 6 run (kick failed)
GB-Franks 5 pass from Favre (Longwell kick)
Chi-FG Edinger 22

Continuing with team #1, next we evaluate Jamal Anderson of the Atlanta Falcons. Looking at the Atlanta–Buffalo game, we find that Anderson ran for two touchdowns and caught a touchdown pass. In his slot on the scorecard, we would mark three Ts and give him 18 points.

Next is the other running back, Antowain Smith of the Buffalo Bills. Again, we look at the Atlanta–Buffalo box score, and this time we find that Smith failed to score. So this one is easy; just a put a big zero in his results column.

Move on now to your first wide receiver, Charles Johnson of the Philadelphia Eagles. Looking at the Philadelphia–Phoenix game, we find that Johnson also failed to score, so again we mark a zero in the results column.

Your other wide receiver is Antonio Freeman of the Green Bay Packers. This time your luck prevails, as we see Freeman scored on a touchdown pass from your quarterback, Brett Favre. Mark a T and give him six points.

Now check out Ernie Conwell, the tight end of the St. Louis Rams. Conwell scored on a touchdown pass from Kurt Warner, so give him a T and six points.

Last would be Morton Andersen, kicker for the Atlanta Falcons. Andersen was successful on one field-goal attempt and four extra-point tries. Give him one F and four Xs, resulting in seven points.

Now let's take a look at my team, team #2, starting with my quarterback, Troy Aikman of the Dallas Cowboys. Looking at the Rams–Cowboys game, we can see that Aikman threw one touchdown to James McKnight and one to David LaFleur. Give him two Ps and six points.

Next is Marshall Faulk of the St. Louis Rams. Looking again at the Rams–Cowboys game, we find Faulk did not score. Mark a zero in his slot.

In the Dallas–Los Angeles box score, we find that my other running back, Robert Thomas, also failed to score, so mark zero in his slot.

Marcus Robinson of the Chicago Bears scored once on a touchdown reception against Green Bay. Give him a T and six points.

Rocket Ismail of the Dallas Cowboys failed to score in their game with the Rams. Give Ismail a big zero in his slot.

Tight end, Ryan Wetnight of the Chicago Bears was another one of my players who failed to score. Mark a zero in his space in the scorecard.

Lastly, my kicker, Tim Seder of the Cowboys, booted one field goal and had two extra points. Give him one F for the field goal and two Xs for the two extra points, totaling five points.

Now our final scorecard should look something like this. (See Detail E.)

Detail E

	TEAM # 1			TEAM # 2	
QB	Favre (GB) TPP	12	QB	Aikman (DALL) PP	6
RB	J. Anderson (ATL) TTT	18	RB	Faulk (St L)	0
RB	A. Smith (BUF)	0	RB	Thomas (DALL)	0
WR	Johnson (PHIL)	0	WR	Robinson (CHI) T	6
WR	Freeman (GB) T	6	WR	Ismail (DALL)	0
TE	Conwell (St L) T	6	TE	Wetnight (CHI)	0
K	Andersen (ATL) FXXXX	7	K	Seder (DALL) FXX	5
		49			17

Congratulations on your first Fantasy Football victory!

What follows are samples of how one league's weekly score sheets may look after the conclusion of its fantasy games.

Basic Scoring Method Samples

FFL Box Scores

	Tm# 3 The Overachievers		Pts		Tm# 1 The Crashdummies		Pts
QB	(Ariz.) Plummer	PP	6	QB	(Seat.) Kitna	PP	6
RB	(G.B.) Levens	T	6	RB	(Buf.) A. Smith	T	6
RB	(Ind.) James		0	RB	(Wash.) Murrell		0
WR	(Dall.) R. Ismail		0	WR	(S.F.) Rice	TT	12
WR	(Buf.) Price		0	WR	(Seat.) Mayes	T	6
TE	(K.C.) Gonzalez		0	TE	(Tenn.) Wycheck		0
K	(N.E.) Vinatieri	FXX	5	K	(Minn.) Anderson	FFXX	8
Reserves				**Reserves**			
1	(Balt.) Johnson			1	(N.O.) R. Williams		
2	(Den.) McCaffrey			2	(N.O.) Horn		
3	(Ariz.) Rb. Moore			3	(N.E.) Glenn		
4	(Mia.) Drayton			4	(N.Y.G.) Hilliard		
5	(Ariz.) F. Sanders			5	(Jac.) McCardell		
			17				**38**

VS.

	Tm# 2 Lodi's Big Daddys		Pts		Tm# 4 East Side Gladiators		Pts
QB	(S.D.) Harbaugh	P	3	QB	(K.C.) Grbac		0
RB	(Seat.) Watters	TT	12	RB	(Mia.) L. Smith		0
RB	(Den.) Davis	T	6	RB	(S.D.) Chancey	T	6
WR	(Oak.) T. Brown	T	6	WR	(Mia.) Martin		0
WR	(N.Y.G.) Toomer		0	WR	(Minn.) C. Carter		0
TE	(T.B.) Harris		0	TE	(Seat.) Fauria		0
K	(Det.) Hanson	XX	2	K	(Atl.) Andersen	FXX	5
Reserves				**Reserves**			
1	(Det.) Stewart			1	(T.B.) Alstott		
2	(T.B.) K. Johnson			2	(Wash.) Westbrook		
3	(Balt.) Holmes			3	(Dall.) Galloway		
4	(Car.) Biakabatuka			4	(N.E.) Bjornson		
5	(OAK) Rison			5	(S.D.) Leaf		
			29				**11**

VS.

	Tm# 7 Mediterranean Meatballs		Pts		Tm# 5 Treanor's Electric Co		Pts
QB	(Oak.) Gannon	P	3	QB	(N.Y.J.) Testaverde	P	3
RB	(Wash.) Davis		0	RB	(Atl.) J. Anderson	TT	12
RB	(Minn.) R. Smith		0	RB	(S.F.) Garner		0
WR	(G.B.) Freeman		0	WR	(Phil.) C. Johnson		0
WR	(Tenn.) C. Sanders		0	WR	(Jac.) Smith	T	6
TE	(Minn.) McWilliams	T	6	TE	(N.Y.G.) Mitchell	T	6
K	(Balt.) Stover	XXXX	4	K	(S.D.) Carney	XX	2
Reserves				**Reserves**			
1	(N.Y.G.) K. Collins			1	(Phil.) McNabb		
2	(Det.) Morton			2	(T.B.) Anthony		
3	(Phil.) Small			3	(N.O.) L. Smith		
4	(N.Y.G.) Barber			4	(Car.) Floyd		
5	(Clev.) Prentice			5	(Atl.) Mathis		
			13				**29**

VS.

	Tm# 6 F-Troop		Pts		Tm# 8 J.M.D. Warriors		Pts
QB	(S.F.) Garcia	PP	6	QB	(Buf.) Flutie	PP	6
RB	(T.B.) Dunn		0	RB	(N.Y.G.) Barber		0
RB	(Dall.) E. Smith		0	RB	(Oak.) Kaufman		0
WR	(Ind.) Harrison		0	WR	(S.D.) Graham		0
WR	(Oak.) Jett	T	6	WR	(Chi.) Engram	T	6
TE	(N.O.) Cleeland		0	TE	(G.B.) Franks	T	6
K	(S.F.) Richey	FXX	5	K	(St.L.) Wilkins	FFXXXXX	11
Reserves				**Reserves**			
1	(Den.) Griese			1	(G.B.) Freeman		
2	(Car.) Muhammad			2	(S.F.) Stokes		
3	(Cin.) A. Smith			3	(N.E.) K. Faulk		
4	(Wash.) Centers			4	(Chi.) McNown		
5	(N.Y.J.) Chrebet			5	(Tenn.) Pickens		
			17				**29**

FFL STANDINGS

(Black Conference)

Spade Division	Team #	Won	Lost	Tie	Points	Points Agst
The Crashdummies	1	7	4	0	314	234
Lodi's Big Daddys	2	6	5	0	241	227
The Overachievers	3	5	6	0	237	283
East Side Gladiators	4	2	9	0	205	317

Club Division	Team #	Won	Lost	Tie	Points	Points Agst
Mediterranean Meatballs	7	8	3	0	283	244
Treanor's Elec. Co.	5	7	4	0	274	247
Armchair Sleepers	6	5	6	0	231	245
J.M.D.Warriors	8	3	8	0	248	287

(Red Conference)

Diamond Division	Team #	Won	Lost	Tie	Points	Points Agst
Costra Nostra	10	8	3	0	220	187
D.C. Express	11	7	4	0	285	236
F-Troop	12	5	6	0	186	224
Boyer's Spoilers	9	4	7	0	197	294

Heart Division	Team #	Won	Lost	Tie	Points	Points Agst
French Connection	13	10	1	0	329	164
The Medics	16	4	7	0	237	242
The Bogarts	14	4	7	0	204	250
The Jayhawks	15	3	8	0	286	296

THIS WEEK'S SCORES

Team # 3 (17)	Team # 2 (29)
Team # 1 (38)	Team # 4 (11)
Team # 5 (29)	Team # 8 (23)
Team # 7 (13)	Team # 6 (17)
Team # 11 (30)	Team # 10 (18)
Team # 9 (9)	Team # 12 (5)
Team # 13 (28)	Team # 14 (16)
Team # 15 (14)	Team # 16 (8)

THIS WEEK'S TRANSACTIONS

Tm#		Dropped/Tm-Pos	Acquired/Tm-Pos
1	5	Dunn TB RB	Bettis Pitt RB
2	7	Carter Minn WR	Moulds Buf WR
3	16	Morton Det WR	McCaffrey Den WR
4	12	Drayton Mia TE	Sharpe Balt TE
5	13	Johnson Phil WR	Schroeder GB WR
6		_____	_____
7		_____	_____
8		_____	_____
9		_____	_____
10		_____	_____

THE PERFORMANCE POINT METHOD

The Performance Point Method is a tabulation of scoring based on a player's yardage performance, not his touchdowns. It differs from the Basic Scoring Method in that less luck is involved. In the Basic Scoring Method, a player may rush for 120 yards in a game, but never score a touchdown, leaving his fantasy franchise unrewarded for his performance. The Performance Point Method, however, looks only at a player's yardage performance and, although the final scores are not typical football scores as in the Basic Method, it is an interesting way to play the game. Let's take a look at this method of scoring.

1. SCORING TABULATION BY POSITION:
   The following is the scoring breakdown by each position:

   A. Quarterbacks, Running Backs, Wide Receivers, Tight Ends
      1. These players are awarded one point for every 20 yards passing.
      2. They are awarded one point for every 10 yards rushing.
      3. They are awarded one point for every 10 yards pass receiving.
      4. No players will have points deducted for having negative yardage in a game. That is, if a player has two rushes that account for minus 12 yards, he is not penalized one point.
      5. You must tabulate the passing, rushing, and pass-receiving scores separately. For instance, if a quarterback passes for 300 yards and rushes for 29 yards, you cannot add the yardage together. You would just award him 15 points for his passing yardage and then 2 more points for his rushing yardage, giving him 17 total points. This also applies to the rushing and pass-receiving yardage of a running back or wide receiver. If, for example, a running back rushes for 97 yards and catches passes for 24 yards, you can't add the yardages together. Again, you just take his 97 rushing yards and award him nine points and then take his 24 pass-receiving yards and award him two more points. This would give him a total of 11 points.

Passing Yardage	Rushing Yardage	Pass-Receiving Yardage
0 — 19 yds: 0 pts	0 — 9 yds: 0 pts	0 — 9 yds: 0 pts
20 — 39 yds: 1 pt	10 — 19 yds: 1 pt	10 — 19 yds: 1 pt
40 — 59 yds: 2 pts	20 — 29 yds: 2 pts	20 — 29 yds: 2 pts
60 — 79 yds: 3 pts	30 — 39 yds: 3 pts	30 — 39 yds: 3 pts
80 — 99 yds: 4 pts	40 — 49 yds: 4 pts	40 — 49 yds: 4 pts
100 — 119 yds: 5 pts	50 — 59 yds: 5 pts	50 — 59 yds: 5 pts
120 — 139 yds: 6 pts	60 — 69 yds: 6 pts	60 — 69 yds: 6 pts
140 — 159 yds: 7 pts	70 — 79 yds: 7 pts	70 — 79 yds: 7 pts
160 — 179 yds: 8 pts	80 — 89 yds: 8 pts	80 — 89 yds: 8 pts
180 — 199 yds: 9 pts	90 — 99 yds: 9 pts	90 — 99 yds: 9 pts
200 — 219 yds:10 pts	100 — 109 yds:10 pts	100 — 109 yds:10 pts

And so on   And so on   And so on

B. Kickers
   Points awarded are the same as in the Basic Scoring Method, except when a kicker for some reason would carry the ball and pick up yardage.
   1. Three points are awarded for each field goal.
   2. One point is awarded for each extra point.
   3. If a kicker rushes for yardage on a blocked kick, for example, he is awarded rushing points for the amount of yardage gained. Or if he completes a pass, he again is awarded the passing points for the yardage gained.

2. SAMPLE SCORING FOR A FANTASY FOOTBALL GAME:
   The following key will help you in logging each player's scoring results:
   A. Quarterbacks, Running Backs, Wide Receivers, Tight Ends
      1. For passing yardage, mark a P followed by a comma and then the number of points associated with that player's passing results. Then put parentheses around that group. For example, (P,14) would show that a player threw for between 280 and 299 yards. He receives 1 point for every 20 yards, giving him 14 passing points.
      2. For rushing yardage, mark an R, again followed by a comma and then the number of points associated with that player's rushing results. Then put parentheses around that group. For example, (R,9) would show that the player rushed for between 90 and 99 yards. He receives one point for every 10 yards, giving him nine rushing points.
      3. For pass-receiving yardage, mark a P with a small r, followed by a comma and the number of points associated with that player's pass-receiving results. Then put parentheses around that group. The notation (Pr,6) would show that the player caught passes resulting in between 60 and 69 yards. He receives one point for every 10 yards, giving him six pass-receiving points.
      4. Also, quarterbacks, running backs, wide receivers, and tight ends may be involved in a two-point conversion. If a player, regardless of his position, successfully passes for a two-point conversion, he is awarded one point. If a player, again regardless of his position, rushes or receives for a two-point conversion, he is awarded two points.
   B. Kickers
      1. For each field goal, mark an F (three points for each).
      2. For each extra point, mark an X (one point for each).
      3. If a kicker is involved in any play where he may have passed for more than 20 yards or rushed or caught a pass amounting to more than 20 yards, the appropriate number of points previously explained applies.

      To explain better and demonstrate the scoring process of the Performance Point Method, we will again set up two fictitious fantasy teams. Use the following lineups in Detail F and the box scores shown in Detail G to figure out the score between team #5 and team #6.

Detail F

TEAM # 5

QB	Gannon (OAK)
RB	Stewart (DET)
RB	Bettis (PITT)
WR	T. Brown (OAK)
WR	Mayes (SEAT)
TE	Bjornson (NE)
K	Janikowski (OAK) _____

TEAM # 6

QB	Kitna (SEAT)
RB	Fletcher (SD)
RB	Kaufman (OAK)
WR	Glenn (NE)
WR	H. Moore (DET)
TE	Sharpe (BALT)
K	Hanson (DET) _____

Detail G

LIONS 23, BUCS 20

Tampa Bay   7 6 0 7 — 20
Detroit   810 310 — 23
    TB-Moore 4 pass from
King (Gramatica kick)
    Det-Stewart 3 run (Hanson kick)
    Det-FG Hanson 34
    TB-Anthony 29 pass from
King (kick failed)
    Det-FG Hanson 36
    Det-FG Hanson 38
    Det-H. Moore 6 pass from
Batch (Hanson kick)
    TB-K. Williams 29 pass from
King (Gramatica kick)
    A-54,133
    INDIVIDUAL STATISTICS
    RUSHING—Tampa Bay,
Dunn 23-44, Alstott 11-63.
Detroit, Stewart 15-56,
Batch 2-20.
    PASSING—Tampa Bay,
King 28-42-1-373.
Detroit, Batch 19-25-0-180.
    RECEIVING—Tampa Bay,
Anthony 8-136, J. Greene 8-67,
K. Williams 5-82, Moore 3-49, Alstott
4-39. Detroit, Stewart 5-81,
Morton 2-21, H. Moore 4-46.
    MISSED FIELD GOALS—
Tampa Bay, Gramatica 29.
Detroit, Hanson 55.

RAIDERS 30, CHARGERS 14

San Diego   7 0 7 0 — 14
Oakland   7 6 314 — 30
    SD-Conway 40 pass from
Harbaugh (Carney kick)
    OAK-Kaufman 8 run (Janikowski
kick)
    OAK-FG Janikowski 21
    OAK-FG Janikowski 32
    OAK-FG Janikowski 28
    SD-Fletcher 2 run (Carney kick)
    OAK-T. Brown 4 pass from
Gannon (Janikowski kick)
    OAK-Kaufman 5 run (Janikowski
kick)
    A-57,325
    INDIVIDUAL STATISTICS
    RUSHING—San Diego, Fletcher
18-78, Chancey 3-5.
Oakland, Kaufman 16-72,
    PASSING—San Diego, Harbaugh
20-36-1-236.
Oakland, Gannon 21-30-1-332.
    RECEIVING—San Diego,
Fletcher 5-43, Chancey 5-40, Graham
3-41, Conway 7-112.
Oakland, Jett 8-134,
T. Brown 6-93, Kaufman 5-49,
Dudley 3-54.
    MISSED FIELD GOALS—None.

RAVENS 30, STEELERS 17

Pittsburgh	3	7	0	7 —	17
Baltimore	9	14	7	0 —	30

Pit-FG N. Johnson 34
Balt-Q. Ismail 64 pass from
Banks (kick failed)
Balt-FG Stover 30
Balt-J. Lewis 3 pass from
Banks (Stover kick)
Pit-Stewart 3 run (Brown kick)
Balt-Sharpe 4 pass from Banks
(Stover kick)
Balt-J. Lewis 1 pass from
Banks (Stover kick)
Pit-Bettis 2 pass from Stewart
(N. Johnson kick)
A-72,313
INDIVIDUAL STATISTICS
RUSHING—Pittsburgh, Bettis
6-40, Stewart 4-29.
Baltimore, Holmes 12-66, Ja. Lewis
15-43, Banks 2-(minus 2).
PASSING—Pittsburgh, Stewart
14-33-2-202.
Baltimore, Banks 14-22-0-199.
RECEIVING—Pittsburgh, Edwards
5-66, Bettis 1-9, Bruener 4-96.
Baltimore, Sharpe 4-30, Holmes
3-45, Q. Ismail 1-64, J. Lewis
2-4, Ja. Lewis 1-33, Evans 2-16.

SEAHAWKS 24, PATRIOTS 6

New England	0	6	0	0 —	6
Seattle	3	7	7	7 —	24

Sea-FG Peterson 29
Sea-Mayes 46 pass from Kitna
(Lindell kick)
NE-Bjornson 33 pass from
Bledsoe
(kick failed)
Sea-Watters 16 pass from Kitna
(Lindell kick)
Sea-Kitna 2 run (Lindell kick)
A-59,688
INDIVIDUAL STATISTICS
RUSHING—New England,
K. Faulk 12-48, Bledsoe 2-4.
Seattle, Watters 26-116, Kitna
2-11.
PASSING—New England,
Bledsoe10-22-1-104,
Seattle, Kitna 13-21-0-230.
RECEIVING—New England,
Glenn 4-37, Tr. Brown 4-36,
Bjornson 3-52, Simmons 2-14.
Seattle, Mayes 7-133, Jackson
2-62, Watters 3-26.
MISSED FIELD GOALS—Seattle,
Lindell 25.

Starting with team #5, let's take a look at quarterback Rich Gannon of the Oakland Raiders. First, in looking at his passing stats, we find he completed 21 of 30 passes for 332 yards. In our scorecard, we would mark a P followed by a comma and then a 16, representing one point for every 20 yards he gained passing. Then we would look at both the rushing and pass-receiving stats to see if he had any additional points. As we can see, he didn't. Let's take a look at our scorecard with Gannon's stats logged in. (See Detail H.)

Detail H

TEAM # 5			TEAM # 6	
QB	Gannon (OAK) (P,16)		QB	Kitna (SEAT)
RB	Stewart (DET)		RB	Fletcher (SD)
RB	Bettis (PITT)		RB	Kaufman (OAK)
WR	T. Brown (OAK)		WR	Glenn (NE)
WR	Mayes (SEAT)		WR	H. Moore (DET)
TE	Bjornson (NE)		TE	Sharpe (BALT)
K	Janikowski (OAK)	____	K	Hanson (DET) ____

Continuing with team #5, we look at James Stewart, running back of the Detroit Lions. Of course, with a running back, we first look at the rushing and pass-receiving stats for his point total, but don't forget to look at the passing stats in the event he may have thrown an option pass. We find Stewart had 15 carries for 56 yards and five receptions for 81 yards. In his slot on the scorecard we would mark (R,5) for his rushing stats and (Pr,8) for his pass-receiving stats, totaling 13 points.

Then move on to Jerome Bettis of the Pittsburgh Steelers. We find Bettis rushing six times for 40 yards and catching one pass for nine yards. In his slot we would mark only (R,4), representing his rushing yardage, because his nine yards of pass-receiving yardage is not enough to qualify him for any pass-receiving points. His total points, therefore, would be only four.

Tim Brown of the Oakland Raiders is next. Looking at the pass-receiving stats first, we find he caught six passes for 93 yards, shown as (Pr,9), but he also carried the ball once for 20 yards, shown as (R,2). This would give him 11 points for his performance.

Now let's look at Derrick Mayes of the Seattle Seahawks. Mayes appears only in the pass-receiving stats, where we see he caught seven passes for 133 yards, shown as (Pr,13), totaling 13 points.

On to Eric Bjornson, tight end of the New England Patriots. Again, Bjornson appears only in the pass-receiving stats, where we find he caught three passes for 52 yards, shown as (Pr,5), totaling five points.

Team #5's kicker is Sebastian Janikowski of the Oakland Raiders. Just to make sure, we check the passing, rushing, and pass-receiving stats and find he gained no yardage. Now, looking at the scoring stats, we find he kicked three field goals and three extra points, shown as FFFXXX, totaling 12 points.

Now let's go on to team #6. First we will look at the quarterback, Jon Kitna of the Seattle Seahawks. Looking first at his passing stats, we find he was 13 of 21 for 230 yards, shown as (P,11). We also find under the rushing stats that he had two rushes for 11 yards, shown as (R,1). Combining the two, we would give him 12 total points.

Move on to Terrell Fletcher of the San Diego Chargers. In the rushing stats, we find he had 18 rushes for 78 yards, shown as (R,7). In the pass-receiving stats, we find he had five catches for 43 yards, shown as (Pr,4). Again, combining the two, we would total 11 points.

Next comes Napolean Kaufman of the Oakland Raiders. Looking at the rushing stats, we find he rushed 16 times for 72 yards, shown as (R,7), and under the receiving stats, we find he caught five passes for 49 yards, shown as (Pr,4), giving him a total of 11 points.

On to Terry Glenn wide receiver for the New England Patriots. Glenn has only pass-receiving yardage—four catches for 37 yards, shown as (Pr,3), totaling three points.

Herman Moore of the Detroit Lions is next. Moore also has only pass-receiving yardage, with four receptions for 46 yards, shown as (Pr,4), totaling four points.

Now we will look at the tight end, Shannon Sharpe of the Baltimore Ravens. Again, we find Sharpe has only pass-receiving yardage, with four catches for 30 yards, shown as (Pr,3), totaling three points.

Lastly, the kicker is Jason Hanson of the Detroit Lions. Hanson has no yardage stats, so we just have to tally his three field goals and two extra points, shown as FFFXX, totaling 11 points.

Let's check to see how our final scorecard will look. (See Detail I.)

Detail I

TEAM # 5			TEAM # 6		
QB	Gannon (OAK) (P,16)	16	QB	Kitna (SEAT) (P,11) (R,1)	12
RB	Stewart (DET) (R,5) (Pr,8)	13	RB	Fletcher (SD) (R,7) (Pr,4)	11
RB	Bettis (PITT) (R,5)	4	RB	Kaufman (OAK) (R,7) (Pr,4)	11
WR	T. Brown (OAK) (Pr,9) (R,2)	11	WR	Glenn (NE) (Pr,3)	3
WR	Mayes (SEAT) (Pr,13)	13	WR	H. Moore (DET) (Pr,4)	4
TE	Bjornson (NE) (Pr,5)	5	TE	Sharpe (BALT) (Pr,3)	3
K	Janikowski (OAK) FFFXXX	12	K	Hanson (DET) FFFXX	11
		74			55

We can see by this final score that typical football scores are rare, but the Performance Point Method can be a very interesting way to play the game.

What follows are samples of how one league's weekly score sheets may look after the completion of its fantasy games.

FFL Box Scores

Tm# 3 — The Overachievers VS. Tm# 1 — The Crashdummies

Pos	The Overachievers		Pts		Pos	The Crashdummies		Pts
QB	(Ariz.) Plummer	P,19	19		QB	(Seat.) Kitna	P,7	7
RB	(G.B.) Levens	R,9	9		RB	(Buf.) A. Smith	T	0
RB	(Ind.) James	R,1	1		RB	(Wash.) Murrell		0
WR	(Dall.) R. Ismail	Pr,3	3		WR	(S.F.) Rice	Pr,10	10
WR	(Buf.) Price	Pr,1	1		WR	(Seat.) Mayes	Pr,6	6
TE	(K.C.) Gonzalez		0		TE	(Tenn.) Wycheck	Pr,5	5
K	(N.E.) Vinatieri	FXX	5		K	(Minn.) Anderson	FFXX	8
Reserves					**Reserves**			
1	(Balt.) Johnson				1	(N.O.) R. Williams		
2	(Den.) McCaffrey				2	(N.O.) Horn		
3	(Ariz.) Rb. Moore				3	(N.E.) Glenn		
4	(Mia.) Drayton				4	(N.Y.G.) Hilliard		
5	(Ariz.) F. Sanders				5	(Jac.) McCardell		
			38					**36**

Tm# 2 — Lodi's Big Daddys VS. Tm# 4 — East Side Gladiators

Pos	Lodi's Big Daddys		Pts		Pos	East Side Gladiators		Pts
QB	(S.D.) Harbaugh	P,11	11		QB	(K.C.) Grbac		0
RB	(Seat.) Watters	R,4 Pr,4	8		RB	(Mia.) L. Smith		0
RB	(Den.) Davis	R,3 Pr,1	4		RB	(S.D.) Chancey	R,2 Pr,2	4
WR	(Oak.) T. Brown	Pr,11	11		WR	(Mia.) Martin		0
WR	(N.Y.G.) Toomer	Pr,5	5		WR	(Minn.) C. Carter	Pr,4	4
TE	(T.B.) Harris	Pr,3	3		TE	(Seat.) Fauria	Pr,2	2
K	(Det.) Hanson	XX	2		K	(Atl.) Andersen	FXX	5
Reserves					**Reserves**			
1	(Det.) Stewart				1	(T.B.) Alstott		
2	(T.B.) K. Johnson				2	(Wash.) Westbrook		
3	(Balt.) Holmes				3	(Dall.) Galloway		
4	(Car.) Biakabatuka				4	(N.E.) Bjornson		
5	(OAK) Rison				5	(S.D.) Leaf		
			44					**15**

Tm# 7 — Mediterranean Meatballs VS. Tm# 5 — Treanor's Electric Co

Pos	Mediterranean Meatballs		Pts		Pos	Treanor's Electric Co		Pts
QB	(Oak.) Gannon	P,8	8		QB	(N.Y.J.) Testaverde	P,8	8
RB	(Wash.) Davis		0		RB	(Atl.) J. Anderson	R,14	14
RB	(Minn.) R. Smith		0		RB	(S.F.) Garner		0
WR	(G.B.) Freeman	Pr,1	1		WR	(Phil.) C. Johnson	Pr,2	2
WR	(Tenn.) C. Sanders	Pr,2	2		WR	(Jac.) Smith	Pr,2	2
TE	(Minn.) McWilliams	Pr,1	1		TE	(N.Y.G.) Mitchell	Pr,4	4
K	(Balt.) Stover	XXXX	4		K	(S.D.) Carney	XX	2
Reserves					**Reserves**			
1	(N.Y.G.) K. Collins				1	(Phil.) McNabb		
2	(Det.) Morton				2	(T.B.) Anthony		
3	(Phil.) Small				3	(N.O.) L. Smith		
4	(N.Y.G.) Barber				4	(Car.) Floyd		
5	(Clev.) Prentice				5	(Atl.) Mathis		
			16					**32**

Tm# 6 — F-Troop VS. Tm# 8 — J.M.D. Warriors

Pos	F-Troop		Pts		Pos	J.M.D. Warriors		Pts
QB	(S.F.) Garcia	P,13	13		QB	(Buf.) Flutie	P,9	9
RB	(T.B.) Dunn		0		RB	(N.Y.G.) Barber	R,4	4
RB	(Dall.) E. Smith	R,14	14		RB	(Oak.) Kaufman	R,6	6
WR	(Ind.) Harrison	Pr,1	1		WR	(S.D.) Graham	Pr,3	3
WR	(Oak.) Jett	Pr,7	7		WR	(Chi.) Engram	Pr,1	1
TE	(N.O.) Cleeland	Pr,5	5		TE	(G.B.) Franks	Pr,4	4
K	(S.F.) Richey	FXX	5		K	(St.L.) Wilkins	FFXXXXX	11
Reserves					**Reserves**			
1	(Den.) Griese				1	(G.B.) Freeman		
2	(Car.) Muhammad				2	(S.F.) Stokes		
3	(N.E.) A. Smith				3	(N.E.) K. Faulk		
4	(Wash.) Centers				4	(Chi.) McNown		
5	(N.Y.J.) Chrebet				5	(Tenn.) Pickens		
			45					**38**

FFL STANDINGS

(Black Conference) Spade Division	Team #	Won	Lost	Tie	Points	Points Agst
The Crashdummies	1	7	4	0	432	381
Lodi's Big Daddys	2	6	5	0	421	394
The Overachievers	3	5	6	0	373	391
East Side Gladiators	4	2	9	0	307	455

Club Division	Team #	Won	Lost	Tie	Points	Points Agst
Mediterranean Meatballs	7	8	3	0	402	356
Treanor's Elec. Co.	5	7	4	0	388	344
Armchair Sleepers	6	5	6	0	351	365
J.M.D.Warriors	8	3	8	0	310	372

(Red Conference) Diamond Division	Team #	Won	Lost	Tie	Points	Points Agst
Costra Nostra	10	8	3	0	397	336
D.C. Express	11	7	4	0	346	302
F-Troop	12	5	6	0	323	316
Boyer's Spoilers	9	4	7	0	297	345

Heart Division	Team #	Won	Lost	Tie	Points	Points Agst
French Connection	13	10	1	0	469	317
The Medics	16	4	7	0	398	403
The Bogarts	14	4	7	0	367	367
The Jayhawks	15	3	8	0	343	377

THIS WEEK'S SCORES

Team # 3 (38)	Team # 2 (44)		
Team # 1 (36)	Team # 4 (15)		
Team # 7 (16)	Team # 6 (45)		
Team # 5 (32)	Team # 8 (38)		
Team # 11 (45)	Team # 10 (37)		
Team # 9 (44)	Team # 12 (30)		
Team # 15 (48)	Team # 14 (42)		
Team # 13 (52)	Team # 16 (29)		

THIS WEEK'S TRANSACTIONS

Tm#		Dropped/Tm-Pos	Acquired/Tm-Pos
1	5	Dunn TB RB	Bettis Pitt RB
2	7	Carter Minn WR	Moulds Buf WR
3	16	Morton Det WR	McCaffrey Den WR
4	12	Drayton Mia TE	Sharpe Balt TE
5	13	Johnson Phil WR	Schroeder GB WR
6			
7			
8			
9			
10			

THE COMBINED BASIC/PERFORMANCE SCORING METHOD

Many leagues have decided to add interest to their fantasy games by using a combination of both the Basic Scoring Method and the Performance Point Method. This provides the best of both worlds, since a player is rewarded for the big yardage numbers he earns as well as for the times he crosses the goal line. Using this method, a fantasy team won't be so frustrated when a player rushes or receives for 150 yards but doesn't score any Basic Scoring Method points. On the other hand, if a player rushes three times for six yards but scores twice, he is rewarded more by this method than by the Performance Point Method alone. This Combined Scoring Method is becoming quite popular, especially among established leagues.

Because this Combined Basic/Performance Scoring Method is simply the combination of the previously described Basic Scoring and Performance Point Methods, there is no need for a separate new rules section. A player's total points are tabulated by adding his fantasy points from the Basic Scoring Method (touchdowns and touchdown passes) to his points from the Performance Point Method (yardage). Guidelines for both of these scoring methods are laid out in the previous two sections.

*There is a section in Chapter I (Section X) that concentrates on this new scoring method, giving last year's statistics and giving player ratings for the upcoming 2001 season.

THE DISTANCE SCORING METHOD

The Distance Scoring Method is a tabulation of scoring that uses the yardage covered in a touchdown-scoring play to determine the number of points awarded to the player who scored. This method rewards the "big play" players, those who score on long, exciting plays, as compared to the big fullback who scores on one-yard plunges. Let's take a look at our fourth method of scoring.

1. SCORING TABULATION BY POSITION
   A. Quarterbacks, Running Backs, Wide Receivers, Tight Ends
      1. The following points are awarded
         for touchdowns scored by either
         rushing or passing receiving:

Distance of TD scored	Points Awarded	TD Pass Thrown	Awarded
1 — 9 yards	2 points	1 — 9 yards	1 point
10 — 19 yards	4 points	1 — 19 yards	2 points
20 — 29 yards	6 points	20 — 29 yards	3 points
30 — 39 yards	8 points	30 — 39 yards	4 points
40 — 49 yards	10 points	40 — 49 yards	5 points
50 — 59 yards	12 points	50 — 59 yards	6 points
60 — 69 yards	14 points	60 — 69 yards	7 points
70 — 79 yards	16 points	70 — 79 yards	8 points
80 — 89 yards	18 points	80 — 89 yards	9 points
90 — 99 yards	20 points	90 — 99 yards	10 points

   B. Kickers
      1. The following points are awarded for each field goal:

Distance of Field Goal	Points Awarded
1 — 9 yards	1 point
10 — 19 yards	2 points
20 — 29 yards	3 points
30 — 39 yards	4 points
40 — 49 yards	5 points
50 — 59 yards	6 points
60 — 69 yards	7 points
70 yards & over	10 points

      2. A kicker is awarded one point for each extra point.

TWO-POINT CONVERSIONS

Two-point conversions are scored just like touchdowns. If a player runs in a two-point conversion, he is awarded two points. If the conversion involves a pass, the receiver is awarded two points and the passer is awarded one.

2. SAMPLE SCORING FOR A FANTASY FOOTBALL GAME

The following key will help in logging each player's scoring results. In the area on the scorecard following the player's team name, use the following guidelines:

A. Include with All Players
1. For a touchdown scored by means of rushing or pass receiving, mark a T followed by a comma, then the associated number of points for the distance of the touchdown scored, and lastly surround the group with parentheses. For example, (T,8) would indicate a touchdown scored from between 30 and 39 yards out.
2. For a touchdown pass thrown, mark a P followed by a comma, then the appropriate number of points for the distance of the touchdown pass thrown, and lastly surround the group with parentheses. For example, (P,5) would indicate a touchdown pass thrown from between 40 and 49 yards out.

B. Kickers
1. For field goals, mark an F followed by a comma, then the associated number of points for the distance of the field goal, and lastly surround the group with parentheses. For example, (F,4) would indicate a field goal from between 30 and 39 yards out.
2. For each successful extra point, mark an X (one point for each). As we did with both the Basic Scoring Method and the Performance Point Method, we will again set up two fictitious fantasy teams to demonstrate further the Distance Scoring Method. We will use the lineups shown in Detail J and the box scores shown in Detail K.

Detail J

	TEAM # 7			TEAM # 8	
QB	Garcia (SF)		QB	McNown (CHI)	
RB	Garner (SF)		RB	Pittman (ARIZ)	
RB	Staley (PHIL)		RB	Enis (CHI)	
WR	R. Ismail (DALL)		WR	Anthony (TB)	
WR	Freeman (GB)		WR	F. Sanders (ARIZ)	
TE	Hardy (ARIZ)		TE	Clark (SF)	
K	Richey (SF)	_____	K	Akers (PHIL)	_____

Detail K

BEARS 23, PACKERS 21

Green Bay	7	7	0	7	—	21
Chicago	7	0	7	9	—	23

Chi-Robinson 35 pass from McNown (Boniol kick)
GB-Favre 1 run (Longwell kick)
GB-Freeman 31 pass from Favre (Longwell kick)
Chi-Engram 22 pass from McNown (Boniol kick)
Chi-McNown 6 run (kick failed)
GB-Franks 5 pass from Favre (Longwell kick)
Chi-FG Boniol 22
A-35,908

CARDINALS 31, EAGLES 7

Philadelphia	0	0	0	7	—	7
Arizona	7	7	10	7	—	31

Ariz-Pittman 12 run (Blanchard kick)
Ariz-F. Sanders 10 pass from Plummer (Blanchard kick)
Ariz-FG Blanchard
Ariz-Jones 1 run (Blanchard kick)
Ariz-Hardy 29 pass from Plummer (Blanchard kick)
Phil-Small 20 pass from McNabb (Akers kick)
A-21,902

LIONS 23, BUCS 20

Tampa Bay	7	6	0	7	—	20
Detroit	8	10	3	10	—	23

TB-Moore 4 pass from King (Gramatica kick)
Det-Stewart 3 run (Hanson kick)
Det-FG Hanson 34
TB-K. Williams 29 pass from King (kick failed)
Det-FG Hanson 36
Det-FG Hanson 38
Det-H. Moore 6 pass from Batch (Hanson kick)
TB-Anthony 29 pass from King (Gramatica kick)
A-54,133

RAIDERS 30, CHARGERS 14

San Diego	7	0	7	0	—	14
Oakland	7	6	3	14	—	30

SD-Conway 40 pass from Harbaugh (Carney kick)
OAK-Kaufman 8 run (Janikowski kick)
OAK-FG Janikowski 21
OAK-FG Janikowski 32
OAK-FG Janikowski 28
SD-Fletcher 2 run (Carney kick)
OAK-T. Brown 4 pass from Gannon (Janikowski kick)
OAK-Kaufman 5 run (Janikowski kick)
A-57,325

49ERS 42, COWBOYS 17

Dallas	3	7	0	7	—	17
San Francisco	21	0	7	14	—	42

SF-Garner 6 pass from Garcia (Richey kick)
SF-Levy, 56 punt return (Richey kick)
Dal-FG Seder 47
SF-Rice 77 pass from Garcia (Richey kick)
Dal-Aikman 1 run (Seder kick)
SF-Clark 18 pass from Garcia (Richey kick)
Dal-R. Ismail 13 pass from Aikman (Seder kick)
SF-Hanks 48 interception return (Richey kick)
SF-Garner 16 pass from Young (Richey kick)
A-59,002

Beginning with team #7, we will start with the quarterback, Jeff Garcia of the San Francisco 49ers. Looking at the box scores from Detail K, we find that in the 49ers–Cowboys game, Garcia threw four touchdown passes. The first, from six yards, is shown as (P,1). The next, from 77 yards, is shown as (P,8). The third, from 18 yards, is shown as (P,2). The last, from 16 yards, is shown as (P,2). Combining all four gives him 13 total points. Let's check how this would look in our scorecard. (See Detail L.)

Detail L

	TEAM # 7				TEAM # 8	
QB	Garcia (SF) (P,1)	13		QB	McNown (CHI)	
	(P,8) (P,2) (P,2)			RB	Pittman (ARIZ)	
RB	Garner (SF)			RB	Enis (CHI)	
RB	Staley (PHIL)			WR	Anthony (TB)	
WR	R. Ismail (DALL)			WR	F. Sanders (ARIZ)	
WR	Freeman (GB)			TE	Clark (SF)	
TE	Hardy (ARIZ)			K	Akers (PHIL)	
K	Richey (SF)	___				___

Now let's fill in the rest of the scorecard, following the previously mentioned key.

Next for team #7 is Charlie Garner, running back for the San Francisco 49ers. Looking at the box scores, we find Garner caught two touchdown passes; the first, from six yards, is shown as (T,2), and the other, from 16 yards, is shown as (T,4). This totals six points.

Let's move on to Duce Staley of the Philadelphia Eagles. Taking a good look at the Philadelphia–Arizona game, we find that Staley failed to score, giving him zero points.

Okay, how about Rocket Ismail of the Dallas Cowboys? Ismail did catch a Troy Aikman touchdown pass from 13 yards out, shown as (T,4), totaling four points.

Antonio Freeman of the Green Bay Packers is the other wide receiver. Looking at the Green Bay–Chicago game, we find that Freeman failed to score, so mark his slot with a big zero.

The tight end is Terry Hardy of the Arizona Cardinals. In the Arizona–Philadelphia box score, we can see Hardy scored on a 29-yard pass reception, shown as (T,6), totaling six points.

Team #7's kicker is Wade Richey of the San Francisco 49ers. In the 49ers–Cowboys box score, we find Richey was successful on all six extra-point attempts, shown as XXXXXX, totaling six points.

Now let's look at team #8, starting with the quarterback, Cade McNown of the Chicago Bears. In the Chicago–Green Bay box score, we find McNown first threw a touchdown pass to Curtis Conway from 35 yards out, shown as (P,4), then threw another touchdown pass to Bobby Engram from 22 yards out, shown as (P,3), and finally ran in a touchdown from six yards out, shown as (T,2). These all combine to make a total of nine points.

Next is Michael Pittman of the Arizona Cardinals. Glancing at the Arizona– Philadelphia box score, we find Pittman running in a 12-yard touchdown run, shown as (T,4), totaling four points.

The other running back for team #8 is Curtis Enis of the Chicago Bears. Enis failed to score in the Chicago–Green Bay game and thus ends up with a zero in his point-results column.

Let's move on to Reidel Anthony of the Tampa Bay Buccaneers. Anthony a wide receiver, scored on a 29-yard touchdown pass, shown as (T,6), to total six points.

Checking the other wide receiver, Frank Sanders of the Arizona Cardinals, we find Sanders caught a 10-yard touchdown pass in the Philadelphia–Arizona game, shown as (T,4), giving him four points.

Team #8's tight end is Greg Clark of the San Francisco 49ers. In studying the 49ers–Cowboys game, we find Clark was the recipient of one of the four touchdown passes thrown by Steve Young. The 18-yard touchdown reception by Clark is shown as (T,4), giving him four points.

Last we evaluate the kicker, David Akers of the Philadelphia Eagles. Looking at the Philadelphia–Arizona game, we find Akers was only able to account for one extra point and had no field goals. This is shown as an X, totaling one point.

Let's take a look at how our final scorecard would appear. (See Detail M.)

Detail M

	TEAM # 7				TEAM # 8	
QB	Garcia (SF) (P,1) (P,8) (P,2) (P,2)	13		QB	McNown (CHI) (P,4) (P,3) (T,2)	9
RB	Garner (SF) (T,2) (T,4)	6		RB	Pittman (ARIZ) (T,4)	4
RB	Staley (PHIL)	0		RB	Enis (CHI)	0
WR	R. Ismail (DALL) (T,4)	4		WR	Anthony (TB) (T,6)	6
WR	Freeman (GB)	0		WR	F. Sanders (ARIZ) (T,4)	4
TE	Hardy (ARIZ) (T,6)	6		TE	Clark (SF) (T,4)	4
K	Richey (SF) XXXXXX	6		K	Akers (PHIL) X	1
		35				28

What follows are samples of how one league's weekly score sheets may look after the completion of its fantasy games.

Distance Scoring Method Samples

FFL Box Scores

Tm# 3 — The Overachievers VS. Tm# 1 — The Crashdummies

Pos	The Overachievers		Pts		Pos	The Crashdummies		Pts
QB	(Ariz.) Plummer	P,1 P,2	3		QB	(Seat.) Kitna	P,1 P,3	4
RB	(G.B.) Levens	T,2	2		RB	(Buf.) A. Smith	T,2	2
RB	(Ind.) James		0		RB	(Wash.) Murrell		0
WR	(Dall.) R. Ismail		0		WR	(S.F.) Rice	T,14 T,2	16
WR	(Buf.) Price		0		WR	(Seat.) Mayes	T,6	6
TE	(K.C.) Gonzalez		0		TE	(Tenn.) Wycheck		0
K	(N.E.) Vinatieri	FXX,5	7		K	(Minn.) Anderson	XXF,3 F,3	8
Reserves					**Reserves**			
1	(Balt.) Johnson				1	(N.O.) R. Williams		
2	(Den.) McCaffrey				2	(N.O.) Horn		
3	(Ariz.) Rb. Moore				3	(N.E.) Glenn		
4	(Mia.) Drayton				4	(N.Y.G.) Hilliard		
5	(Ariz.) F. Sanders				5	(Jac.) McCardell		
			12					36

Tm# 2 — Lodi's Big Daddys VS. Tm# 4 — East Side Gladiators

Pos	Lodi's Big Daddys		Pts		Pos	East Side Gladiators		Pts
QB	(S.D.) Harbaugh	P,2	2		QB	(K.C.) Grbac		0
RB	(Seat.) Watters		0		RB	(Mia.) L. Smith		0
RB	(Den.) Davis	T,2	2		RB	(S.D.) Chancey	T,6	6
WR	(Oak.) T. Brown	T,14	14		WR	(Mia.) Martin		0
WR	(N.Y.G.) Toomer		0		WR	(Minn.) C. Carter		0
TE	(T.B.) Harris		0		TE	(Seat.) Fauria		0
K	(Det.) Hanson	XX	2		K	(Atl.) Andersen	XXF,3	5
Reserves					**Reserves**			
1	(Det.) Stewart				1	(T.B.) Alstott		
2	(T.B.) K. Johnson				2	(Wash.) Westbrook		
3	(Balt.) Holmes				3	(Dall.) Galloway		
4	(Car.) Biakabatuka				4	(N.E.) Bjornson		
5	(Oak.) Rison				5	(S.D.) Leaf		
			20					11

Tm# 7 — Mediterranean Meatballs VS. Tm# 5 — Treanor's Electric Co

Pos	Mediterranean Meatballs		Pts		Pos	Treanor's Electric Co		Pts
QB	(Oak.) Gannon	P,8	1		QB	(N.Y.J.) Testaverde	P,7	7
RB	(Wash.) Davis		0		RB	(Atl.) J. Anderson		4
RB	(Minn.) R. Smith		0		RB	(S.F.) Garner		0
WR	(G.B.) Freeman		0		WR	(Phil.) C. Johnson		0
WR	(Tenn.) C. Sanders		0		WR	(Jac.) Smith	T,4	4
TE	(Minn.) McWilliams	T,4	4		TE	(N.Y.G.) Mitchell	T,6	6
K	(Balt.) Stover	XXXX	4		K	(S.D.) Carney	XX	2
Reserves					**Reserves**			
1	(N.Y.G.) K. Collins				1	(Phil.) McNabb		
2	(Det.) Morton				2	(T.B.) Anthony		
3	(Phil.) Small				3	(N.O.) L. Smith		
4	(N.Y.G.) Barber				4	(Car.) Floyd		
5	(Clev.) Prentise				5	(Atl.) Mathis		
			9					23

Tm# 6 — F-Troop VS. Tm# 8 — J.M.D. Warriors

Pos	F-Troop		Pts		Pos	J.M.D. Warriors		Pts
QB	(S.F.) Garcia	P,1 P,7	8		QB	(Buf.) Flutie	P,3 P,2	5
RB	(T.B.) Dunn		0		RB	(N.Y.G.) Barber		0
RB	(Dall.) E. Smith		0		RB	(Oak.) Kaufman		0
WR	(Ind.) Harrison		0		WR	(S.D.) Graham		0
WR	(Oak.) Jett	T,2	2		WR	(Chi.) Engram		0
TE	(N.O.) Cleeland		0		TE	(G.B.) Franks	T,2	2
K	(S.F.) Richey	XXF,4	6		K	(St.L.) Wilkins	XXXXXF,3 F,4	13
Reserves					**Reserves**			
1	(Den.) Griese				1	(G.B.) Freeman		
2	(Car.) Muhammad				2	(S.F.) Stokes		
3	(Cin.) A. Smith				3	(N.E.) R. Faulk		
4	(Wash.) Centers				4	(Chi.) McNown		
5	(N.Y.J.) Chrebet				5	(Tenn.) Pickens		
			16					20

FFL STANDINGS

(Black Conference) Spade Division	Team #	Won	Lost	Tie	Points	Points Agst
The Crashdummies	1	7	4	0	444	357
Lodi's Big Daddys	2	6	5	0	404	398
The Overachievers	3	5	6	0	377	374
East Side Gladiators	4	2	9	0	302	419

Club Division	Team #	Won	Lost	Tie	Points	Points Agst
Mediterranean Meatballs	7	8	3	0	396	342
Treanor's Elec. Co.	5	7	4	0	382	322
Armchair Sleepers	6	5	6	0	368	358
J.M.D.Warriors	8	3	8	0	333	372

(Red Conference) Diamond Division	Team #	Won	Lost	Tie	Points	Points Agst
Costra Nostra	10	8	3	0	387	309
D.C. Express	11	7	4	0	316	287
F-Troop	12	5	6	0	366	322
Boyer's Spoilers	9	4	7	0	342	353

Heart Division	Team #	Won	Lost	Tie	Points	Points Agst
French Connection	13	10	1	0	453	329
The Medics	16	4	7	0	427	404
The Bogarts	14	4	7	0	339	345
The Jayhawks	15	3	8	0	326	356

THIS WEEK'S SCORES

Team # 3 (12)	Team # 2 (20)
Team # 1 (36)	Team # 4 (11)
Team # 7 (9)	Team # 8 (20)
Team # 5 (23)	Team # 6 (16)
Team # 11 (40)	Team # 10 (12)
Team # 9 (12)	Team # 12 (7)
Team # 15 (22)	Team # 14 (16)
Team # 13 (23	Team # 16 (8)

THIS WEEK'S TRANSACTIONS

Tm#	Dropped/Tm-Pos	Acquired/Tm-Pos
1	5 Dunn TB RB	Bettis Pitt RB
2	7 Carter Minn WR	Moulds Buf WR
3	16 Morton Det WR	McCaffrey Den WR
4	12 Drayton Mia TE	Sharpe Balt TE
5	13 Johnson Phil WR	Schroeder GB WR
6		
7		
8		
9		
10		

IX
VARIATIONS ON FANTASY FOOTBALL

Up to this point, I have explained the scoring for the three most commonly used methods. Now I want to show you a few variations that some leagues use.

1. DRAFT AN NFL DEFENSE OR SPECIALTY TEAM
In another league, team defense is used an an eighth player. That is, every franchise in the fantasy league would draft a team defense. If any member of the defensive team scores a touchdown, either by way of interception or fumble recovery, six points are awarded. If a team scores by means of a safety, two points are awarded.

Let's say you drafted the San Francisco 49ers to be your team defense. Looking at the box score in Detail O for the 49ers-Cowboys game, we find that Merton Hanks of the 49ers intercepted a pass for a touchdown. This would give your team six additional points.

You will notice that Eric Davis ran back a punt for a touchdown. Although he is a member of the defensive team, the touchdown would not count because it was scored while he was playing on a specialty team. Only a defensive touchdown scored by a member of a defensive team by means of an interception or fumble recovery will be counted.

Detail O

49ERS 42, COWBOYS 17

Dallas   3 7 0 7 — 17
San Francisco   21 0 7 14 — 42
   SF-Garner 6 pass from Garcia (Richey kick), 2:30
   SF-Davis, 56 punt return (Richey kick), 6:37
   Dal-FG Seder 47, 10:58
   SF-Rice 77 pass from Garcia (Richey kick), 11:23
   Dal-Aikman 1 run (Seder kick), 6:49
   SF-Clark 18 pass from Garcia (Richey kick), 4:40
   Dal-R. Ismail 13 pass from Aikman (Seder kick), :17
   SF-Hanks 48 interception return (Richey kick), 4:32
   SF-Garner 16 pass from Garcia (Richey kick), 8:31
   A-59,002

Again, let's take a look at our scorecard. (See Detail P.)

Detail P

TEAM # 1		
QB	Favre (GB) TPP	12
RB	J. Anderson (ATL) TTT	18
RB	A. Smith (BUF)	0
WR	C. Johnson (PHIL)	0
WR	Freeman (GB) T	6
TE	Conwell (St L) T	6
K	Andersen (ATL) FXXX	6
TD	49ers T	6
		54

2. TIEBREAKERS

Because the 17-week NFL season may affect some handling procedures for transactions, please refer to the suggestions in the beginning of this chapter to see how to handle this change.

OPTION #1: Sudden-Death Tiebreaker (for leagues using the Basic Scoring Method or the Distance Scoring Method)

Here is where your reserves come in. In our league we have seven starters and five reserves. When it is time to call in lineups, not only do we list our seven starters, but we also list our five reserves. This listing of our reserves is used in the event of a tie after regulation play. If there is a tie, we go through the reserves to break the tie. The first team scoring any additional points is the winner.

The home team (as predetermined on the league schedule) is granted the first opportunity to break the tie. If the home team's first reserve scores, the game is over; whatever number of points he scored determines the final score. If he failed to score, we go to the vistors first reserve to see if he scored. If he did, his team wins the game. If both of the teams first reserves failed to score, we continue on to the second overtime period. Again, we go to the home team's player first. If he scores, the game is over. If not, we go to the visitors second player. This continues until the tie is finally broken or until all the reserves are used. If none of the reserves from either team can break the deadlock, then the game is declared a tie.

To show how this tiebreaker works, let's take a look at a game between team #3 and team #4 (see Detail Q). First we are going to assume that the score, after tallying each of the teams starters, ended up knotted at 17-17. To break the tie, we would first go to team #3, which was the predetermined home team, to see if its first reserve scored. Team #3's first reserve player is Torrance Small of the Philadelphia Eagles. Looking at the box score for the Arizona-Philadelphia game (see Detail R), we find that Small failed to score.

Next we jump to team #4's first reserve, who is Jake Plummer of the

Arizona Cardinals. In checking the game box score, we find that Plummer threw two touchdown passes. Plummer is credited with three points, for throwing a touchdown to break the tie. The second touchdown pass is not needed or used in the tabulation for the final score. Only his first score can be tabulated into the final fantasy game score. (See below, point #1 under "Additional Rules for Tie Breakers.") Now the final score would read team #4, 20, and team #3, 17. There is no need to continue with the rest of the reserves once the tie is broken. Let's take a look at our final scorecard. (See Detail Q.)

Detail Q

TEAM # 5			TEAM # 6		
QB	_____	6	QB	_____	3
RB	_____	0	RB	_____	6
RB	_____	0	RB	_____	0
WR	_____	6	WR	_____	0
WR	_____	0	WR	_____	6
TE	_____	0	TE	_____	0
K	_____	5	K	_____	2
		17			17

	Reserves			Reserves	
1	Small (PHIL)	0	1	Plummer (ARIZ) P	3
2	Davis (WASH)		2	C. Johnson (PHIL)	
3	K. Johnson (TB)		3	T. Brown (OAK)	
4	Pittman (ARIZ)		4	J. Anderson (ATL)	
5	Stokes (SF)		5	Enis (CHI)	
		17			20

Detail R

CARDINALS 31, EAGLES 7

Philadelphia	0	0	0	7 —	7
Arizona	7	7	10	7 —	31

Ariz-Pittman 12 run (Blanchard kick)
Ariz-F. Sanders 10 pass from Plummer (Blanchard kick)
Ariz-FG Blanchard
Ariz-Jones 1 run (Jacke kick)
Ariz-Hardy 29 pass from Plummer (Blanchard kick)
Phil-C. Johnson 20 pass from McNabb (Akers kick)
A-21,902

Formerly, a tie could be broken by any player scoring at least one point. So most fantasy teams carried an additional kicker; this made it very easy to score, because most kickers score at least one extra point. Since a kicker in the NFL cannot kick an extra point to break a tie, why should it be allowed in Fantasy Football? Now a tie can be broken by any scoring player—except a kicker, unless he kicks a field goal. If he kicks seven extra points and no field goals, the tie is not broken. So a tie can be broken in sudden death by:

1) Any player scoring a touchdown
2) Any player (usually a quarterback) throwing a touchdown pass
3) A kicker kicking a field goal (extra points cannot break a tie)
4) A team defense scoring a safety or a touchdown

ADDITIONAL RULES FOR TIEBREAKERS:
1) Only the first score will be used. If a quarterback throws three touchdowns only one will be shown in the final fantasy game score. If a kicker hits three field goals, again only one will be tabulated into the game's final score.
2) In the event that a player who is used as a reserve tie breaker both runs and passes for a score, the score of more value will count. In this case, the touchdown run will be counted for the tie breaker and six points will be awarded in the final score.
3) The points scored to break a tie will be used in the final score and will be used in league standings.

OPTION #2: Reserves Tiebreaker (for leagues using the Perfor-mance Point Scoring Method)

Because in the Performance Point Scoring Method almost every player is assured of scoring some points, a tie-breaking method other than sudden death should be used. An effective and fair method for breaking a tie in this case is the Reserves Tie-Breaking Method. Here the team whose reserves score the most total points wins. This keeps any home team with a kicker as first reserve from getting an automatic win. If the score remains tied after adding all the reserve players' points from each team, then revert to sudden death to break the tie, making the home team's first reserve first, and so on. If the score still remains tied, the game is declared a tie. Because so many points are usually added up using this method, the total points from this tie breaker do not count for either team in the Points Scored column of the league standings. (See Detail S.)

Detail S

TEAM # 3			TEAM # 4		
QB	_____	6	QB	_____	3
RB	_____	0	RB	_____	6
RB	_____	0	RB	_____	0
WR	_____	6	WR	_____	0
WR	_____	0	WR	_____	6
TE	_____	0	TE	_____	0
K	_____	5	K	_____	2
		17			17

	Reserves			Reserves	
1	Small (PHIL)	0	1	Plummer (ARIZ)	6
2	Davis (WASH)	6	2	C. Johnson (PHIL)	6
3	K. Johnson (TB)	0	3	T. Brown (OAK)	0
4	Pittman (ARIZ)	12	4	J. Anderson (ATL)	6
5	Stokes (SF)	6	5	Enis (CHI)	0
		24			18

Because team #3's reserves accounted for 24 points, compared to 18 points for team #4, team #3 is the victor. The final score remains 17-17, and team #3 gets the win. Each team receives 17 points in the standings. Remember, the additional points accumulated by the reserves are not added to the game's final score or the teams yearly point totals. Reserves can accumulate a lot of points, and final scores can wind up in the 70s or 80s as a tie breaker. It would be unfair to use those large totals in the league standings. This is especially true if your league's #1 tie breaker in the win-loss column is most points scored.

3. PLAYOFF REDRAFT

Another twist used by some people is to redraft for their league's playoffs. The teams that make the fantasy league's playoffs will draft from the NFL playoff teams the week immediately following the end of the NFL regular season. (Four fantasy teams is a good number to have for playoff teams, keeping in mind that only 10 NFL teams advance to the playoffs, which greatly decreases the number of players from which to choose.) This twist obviously carries with it many strategies. First, the four teams that advance do not meet in head-to-head competition; rather, the winner is determined by the most points accumulated by the fantasy team through the entire round of the NFL playoffs. With this variation, not only do you want the better players, but you also must keep in mind that valuable players are those from teams you feel will make it beyond the first round, so that they will play in more games and have more chances to score points for you.

Here is a more detailed description of how this is done:

A. Redraft:

16 Players
2 quarterbacks
4 running backs
4 wide receivers
2 tight ends
2 kickers
2 team defenses

B. Player Protection: Any fantasy team can protect up to three of its regular-season players for the playoffs.

C. Drafting order: After the protected players are determined by each fantasyteam,a group of four player cards can be used to determine drafting order, with every round being in the reverse order of the previous round.

D. Scoring:

Quarterbacks:	3 points (TD pass thrown) 6 points (TD rushing)
Running Backs, Wide Receivers, & Tight Ends:	3 points (TD pass thrown on a halfback option) 6 points (TD rushing or receiving)
Kickers:	3 points (field goal) 1 point (extra point)
Team Defense:	6 points (interception or fumble-recovery score) 2 points (safety) 1 point (interception) 1 point (fumble recovery)
Any Player:	2 points (conversion, rushing or throwing) 1 point (conversion thrown)

All NFL players' performances are counted until their teams are eliminated from the playoffs. The fantasy team amassing the most points through the NFL playoffs, including the Super Bowl, is declared the league's winner.

4. LIFE-LONG FRANCHISES

We have found many fantasy leagues in which the teams from the previous season draft only incoming rookies. This method of playing has many positive and negative sides. On the positive side, it provides ownership like the real thing; you must build on your team each year. If you have a good young team, you may enjoy success for a number of years.

On the other hand, if you have a poor team you may not enjoy waiting for years until your rookies pan out and your franchise finally realizes success. Also, being a little biased, I don't think your fantasy draft would be as enjoyable. In our league the draft is the social event of the year. Being able to start fresh and have a shot at picking a Fantasy Bowl team is truly exciting.

5. PLAYER AUCTIONING

Another option that is used is to hold a player "auction" rather than a player draft. This is done by each franchise's buying into the league for a set number of dollars. These dollars are then used to buy or payroll teams.

Let's take this by steps:

A. An order for choosing which player is to be auctioned is determined. This can be done by a draw of cards or by letting the team with the worst record from the previous year select the first player, and so on.

B. Once a player is up for auction, the bidding begins and goes around the room. For the sake of discussion, we'll establish that this league's entry fee is $100.00 per franchise. The bidding for the player on the auction block begins at $1.00. The bidding goes around the room in clockwise order, with each team having a chance to increase the bid or pass completely.

C. There is no ceiling on the player bids.

D. The bidding for players continues until each team has acquired 12 players.

E. The total cost of the 12 players must not exceed $100.00, or whatever the entry fee is.

SAMPLE OF AUCTION DRAFTING:

ROUND #1

	Player Auctioned			Team#	Price
1	James	IND	RB	6	$27
2	Taylor	JAC	RB	1	$31
3	Faulk	STL	RB	14	$24
4	Favre	GB	QB	2	$22
5	Watters	SEAT	RB	11	$20
6	J. Anderson	ATL	RB	13	$21
7	Warner	STL	QB	5	$22
8	Moss	MINN	WR	7	$24
9	Davis	WASH	RB	3	$22
10	Freeman	GB	WR	16	$25
11	E. Smith	DALL	RB	4	$26
12	Carter	MINN	WR	9	$21
13	Garner	SF	RB	8	$22
14	Martin	NYJ	RB	10	$18
15	George	TENN	RB	15	$19
16	K. Johnson	TB	WR	12	$22

Player Auctioned			Team#	Price
1 Bettis	PITT	RB	10	$17
2 Levens	GB	RB	8	$14
3 Wheatley	OAK	RB	7	$18
4 Stewart	DET	RB	2	$15
5 Tm. Brown	OAK	WR	15	$18
6 Pickens	TENN	WR	4	$20
7 Chandler	ATL	QB	12	$17
8 R. Smith	MINN	RB	4	$14
9 Brunell	JAC	QB	3	$16
10 Mathis	ATL	WR	13	$12
11 Galloway	DALL	WR	16	$13
12 Ja. Lewis	BALT	RB	1	$14
13 Dillon	CIN	RB	6	$13
14 Gonzalez	KC	TE	11	$15
15 Freeman	GB	WR	9	$18
16 Davis	DEN	RB	5	$19

6. DRAFT AN NFL COACH

Some leagues draft an NFL coach who serves as an eighth man in their lineup. If the coach of the NFL team wins his game, the fantasy team is awarded three points. Let's say you had drafted Steve Mariucci of the San Francisco 49ers and the 49ers beat the Cowboys. Three points would have been awarded and your scorecard would have looked like this, with a W marked after Mariucci's team initials to signify the win. (See Detail N.)

Detail N

TEAM # 1

QB	Favre (GB) TPP	12
RB	J. Anderson (ATL) TTT	18
RB	A. Smith (BUF)	0
WR	C. Johnson (PHIL)	0
WR	Freeman (GB) T	6
TE	Conwell (St L) T	6
K	Andersen (ATL) FXXX	7
C	Mariucci (SF) W	3
		51

---

7. WEEKLY OFFICE POOLS

Some week your office may find it fun to throw in a couple of bucks and draft a fantasy team. My research found this to be very popular. Get 4 or even 10 or more football followers each to draft a team for a given weekend's slate of games. To keep it simple and fun, we suggest the following as a guide:

A. Each team selects 7 players
>   1 Quarterback
>   2 Running Backs
>   3 Receivers (can be wide receivers or tight ends)
>   1 Kicker

B. Use our Basic Scoring Method for scoring points awarded:

Quarterbacks:	3 points (TD pass thrown)
	6 points (TD rushing)
Running Backs and Receivers:	3 points (TD pass thrown on a halfback option)
	6 points (TD rushing or receiving)
Kickers:	3 points (field goal)
	1 point (extra point)

C. Payoffs
>   Up to 6 teams
>   1st Place - 75% of pot
>   2nd Place - 25% of pot
>   6 teams and up
>   1st Place - 50% of pot
>   2nd Place - 25% of pot
>   3rd Place - 15% of pot
>   Commissioner - 10% of pot

Winners are determined by the total number of points amassed by the seven players selected by the fantasy team.

X
2001 NFL SCHEDULE
(ALL TIMES ARE CENTRAL STANDARD TIME)

WEEK 1
Sunday, Sept. 9
(Open date: Arizona)
Carolina at Minnesota, 12:00 p.m.
Chicago at Baltimore, 12:00 p.m.
Detroit at Green Bay, 12:00 p.m.
Indianapolis at N.Y. Jets, 12:00 p.m.
New England at Cincinnati, 12:00 p.m.
New Orleans at Buffalo, 12:00 p.m.
Oakland at Kansas City, 12:00 p.m.
Pittsburgh at Jacksonville, 12:00 p.m.
Seattle at Cleveland, 12:00 p.m.
Tampa Bay at Dallas, 12:00p.m
Atlanta at San Francisco, 3:15 p.m.
St. Louis at Philadelphia, 3:15 p.m.
Washington at San Diego, 3:15 p.m.
Miami at Tennessee, 7:30 p.m.

Monday, Sept. 10
N.Y. Giants at Denver, 8:00 p.m.

WEEK 2
Sunday, Sept. 16
(Open date: San Diego)
Arizona at Washington, 12:00 p.m.
Buffalo at Miami, 12:00 p.m.
Cincinnati at Tennessee, 12:00 p.m.
Dallas at Detroit, 12:00 p.m.
Denver at Indianapolis, 12:00 p.m.
Green Bay at N.Y. Giants, 12:00 p.m.
New England at Carolina, 12:00 p.m.
Philadelphia at Tampa Bay, 12:00 p.m.
San Francisco at New Orleans, 12:00 p.m.
Atlanta at St. Louis, 3:05 p.m.
Jacksonville at Chicago, 3:15 p.m.
Kansas City at Seattle, 3:15 p.m.
N.Y. Jets at Oakland, 3:15 p.m.
Cleveland at Pittsburgh, 7:30 p.m.

Monday, Sept.17
Minnesota at Baltimore, 8:00 p.m.

WEEK 3
Sunday, Sept. 23
(Open dates: New Orleans, Pittsburgh, Tampa Bay)
Baltimore at Cincinnati, 12:00 p.m.
Buffalo at Indianapolis, 12:00 p.m.
Carolina at Atlanta, 12:00 p.m.
Detroit at Cleveland, 12:00 p.m.
Minnesota at Chicago, 12:00 p.m.
N.Y. Giants at Kansas City, 12:00 p.m.
Oakland at Miami, 12:00 p.m.
San Diego at Dallas, 12:00 p.m.
Tennessee at Jacksonville, 12:00 p.m.
N.Y. Jets at New England, 3:05 p.m.
Philadelphia at Seattle, 3:15 p.m.
St. Louis at San Francisco, 3:15 p.m.
Denver at Arizona, 7:35 p.m.

Monday, Sept.24
Washington at Green Bay, 8 p.m.

WEEK 4
Sunday, Sept. 30
(Open dates: Chicago, Detroit, Tennessee)
Green Bay at Carolina, 12:00 p.m.
Indianapolis at New England, 12:00 p.m.
Kansas City at Washington, 12:00 p.m.
Miami at St. Louis, 12:00 p.m.
New Orleans at N.Y. Giants, 12:00 p.m.
Pittsburgh at Buffalo, 12:00 p.m.
Tampa Bay at Minnesota, 12:00 p.m.
Baltimore at Denver, 3:15 p.m.
Cincinnati at San Diego, 3:15 p.m.
Cleveland at Jacksonville, 3:15 p.m.
Seattle at Oakland, 3:15 p.m.
Atlanta at Arizona, 4:05 p.m.
Dallas at Philadelphia, 7:30 p.m.

Monday, Oct. 1
San Francisco at N.Y. Jets, 8:00 p.m.